Microsoft® Word 2000

Made Easy

By
Katie Layman
Gavilan College, Gilroy, California
and
LaVaughn Hart
Chabot-Las Positas Community College District
Pleasanton, California

Prentice Hall
Upper Saddle River, NJ 07458

Library of Congress Cataloging-in-Publication Data

Layman, Katie.
    Microsoft Word 2000 made easy / Katie Layman and LaVaughn Hart.
        p.   cm.
    Includes index.
    ISBN 0-13-012951-8
    1. Microsoft Word.   2. Word processing.   I. Hart, LaVaughn.   II. Title.
    Z52.5.M52L396 2000
    652.5'5369--dc21
                                                                        99-16574
                                                                        CIP

Acquisitions Editor: *Elizabeth Sugg*
Developmental Editor: *Judy Casillo*
Production Editor: *Eileen O'Sullivan*
Director of Production and Manufacturing: *Bruce Johnson*
Managing Editor: *Mary Carnis*
Manufacturing Manager: *Ed O'Dougherty*
Cover Art: *Marjorie Dressler*
Cover Design: *Maureen Eide*
Marketing Manager: *Shannon Simonsen*
Printer/Binder: *RR Donnelley, Willard*

© 2000 by Prentice-Hall, Inc.
Upper Saddle River, New Jersey 07458

Printed in the United States of America

10 9 8 7 6 5 4 3 2 1

ISBN: 0-13-012951-8

Prentice-Hall International (UK) Limited, *London*
Prentice-Hall of Australia Pty. Limited, *Sydney*
Prentice-Hall Canada, Inc. *Toronto*
Prentice-Hall Hispanoamericana, S.A., *Mexico*
Prentice-Hall of India Private Limited, *New Delhi*
Prentice-Hall of Japan, Inc., *Tokyo*
Prentice-Hall (Singapore), Pte. Ltd.
Editora Prentice-Hall do Brasil, Ltda., *Rio de Janeiro*

Contents at a Glance

CONTENTS

Finish-Up

PREFACE

The Layman/Hart Approach

The Layman/Hart instructional approach is to provide students with simple step-by-step instructions to quickly master the Microsoft® Word 2000 program. Numerous hands-on activities and easy-to-follow instruction lists within the chapters allow students to learn by doing. All of these carefully guided walk-throughs are accompanied by thorough, but brief, explanations of each Word function being introduced, making the Layman/Hart *Microsoft Word® 2000* textbook appropriate for use in individualized instruction programs as well as for use in traditional lecture/lab classrooms.

Task-Oriented

By focusing on the tasks students need to perform, the Layman/Hart *Microsoft® Word 2000* textbook aids instructors in their efforts to assist students in acquiring the work-ready skills needed to succeed in today's job market.

Real-World Documents

As students work through the text's activities, they are introduced to the proper format for various business documents (e.g., memorandums, letters, e-mail messages, reports—some incorporating Internet information, résumés, and newsletters). All of the text's activities are based on authentic real-world documents. Proper formatting of business documents is integrated with learning program features.

Language Arts Skills

Students receive training and reinforcement of their basic English and grammar skills with the assistance of the Enriching Language Arts Skills section provided at the end of each chapter. One end-of-chapter activity even includes spelling and grammatical errors that can be corrected by the student. "The Gregg Reference Manual" authored by William A. Sabin is used as a guide to create the grammer and punctuation rules.

Authentic Assessment

The *Next Step* and *Checking Your Step* activities reinforce students' reading, writing, thinking, and decision-making skills.

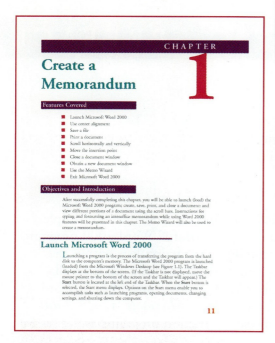

Chapter Openings

preview the chapter features and objectives.

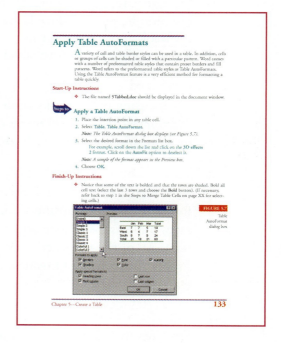

Start-Up and Finish-Up Instructions

provide easy entry and exit points.

Step-by-Step Instructions

are clear, thorough, and concise.

Self-Check Quizzes

enable students to check their understanding of chapter concepts and procedures.

Enriching Language Arts Skills

promote vocabulary building and grammar reinforcement.

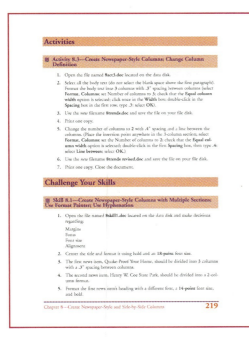

Hands-on Guided Activities
provide practice of new features while creating real-world business documents.

Challenge Your Skills Activities
promote decision-making skills.

Checking Your Step Production Projects
allow students to develop their critical-thinking skills.

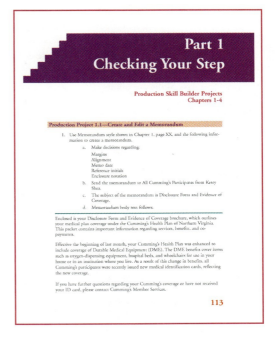

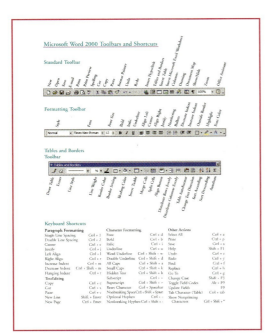

Microsoft Word 2000 Toolbars and Shortcuts Guide
are included at the back of the textbook for quick reference.

Skills Table

Skills, Competencies, Authentic Assessment	How Met in *Microsoft Word 2000 Made Easy*	Where to Look
Basic Skills		
Reading—Locates, understands, and interprets written information in prose	Start-Up and Finish-up Instructions	Every chapter—e.g., Chapter 3, page 59.
	Step-by-step instructions for functions	Every chapter—e.g., Chapter 4, pages 88–89
	Guided end-of-chapter activities	Every chapter—e.g., Chapter 6, pages 167–171
	Challenge Your Skills activities	Every chapter—e.g., Chapter 6, pages 171–173
Writing—communicates thoughts, ideas, information, and messages in writing	Self-Check questions including true/false, multiple choice, and short answer questions	Every chapter—e.g., Chapter 9, pages 248–249
	Create e-mail messages	Various chapters—e.g., Chapter 9, pages 253–256
Language Arts Skills—spelling, punctuation, and basic grammar rules	Enriching Language Arts Skills	Every chapter—Chapter 12, pages 325–326
Arithmetic/Mathematics—performs basic computations and approaches practical problems	Create table formulas	Chapter 6, page 156 and Production Skill Building Project 2.1, page 221
Thinking Skills		
Decision Making—specifies goals and evaluates and chooses best alternative	Challenge Your Skills activities	Every chapter—e.g, Chapter 13, pages 365–366
	Production Skill Building Projects	All parts—e.g., Part 2, pages 221–225
Creative Thinking—generates new ideas	Challenge Your Skills activities	Every chapter—e.g., Chapter 13, page 365
	Production Skill Building Projects	All parts—e.g., Part 3, pages 327–332
Problem Solving—Recognizes a problem; devises and implements a plan of action	Challenge Your Skills activities	Every chapter—e.g., Chapter 10, pages 284–287
	Production Skill Building Projects	All parts—e.g., Part 4, pages 431–433
Authentic Assessment		
Reinforcement activities	Challenge Your Skills activities	Every chapter—e.g., Chapter 11, pages 309–312
	Production Skill Building Projects	All parts—e.g., Part 3, page 327
Language Arts Skills	Correct misspelled words, punctuation and/or grammar errors	All chapters—e.g., Chapter 4, Skill 4.3 page 110
		Every part—e.g., Part 1, Production Project 1.4, pages 116–118

Instructor Support Materials

A comprehensive Instructor's Resource Manual is available which contains a chapter overview, student objectives, lecture notes, teaching suggestions, and one or more additional activities for each chapter. Also provided are solutions for the end-of-chapter short-answer questions.

Included with the Instructor's Resource Manual is a set of instructor disks. The instructor's disks contain formatted files for the practice activities, end-of-chapter activities, challenge activities, and production and theory tests.

To the Student

Every chapter is divided into several sections with each section explaining a different Word function. An overview of each function is provided followed by Start-Up Instructions which present information or actions to be taken in order to prepare you for a hands-on practice activity. Perform the Start-Up Instructions before beginning the step-by-step instructions. The numbered step-by-step instructions guide you through each action necessary to perform the feature being learned.

Step-by-step instructions are identified by the [Steps to] icon. Finish-Up Instructions follow each set of step-by-step instructions and indicate what should be performed in order to complete the practice activity.

The text for many chapter activities is provided on the accompanying data disk. When you see the ▪ icon in the text, it indicates that the text (data) is available on disk. This saved text is necessary in order to perform the activity identified by the disk icon.

Answer the Self-Check Quiz questions and check your answers with the answer key provided at the back of the book. Study the vocabulary words, punctuation, capitalization, or typing rule provided in the Enriching Language Arts Skills section. Many of these vocabulary words and punctuation rules are used in one of the activities in the Challenge Your Skills section at the end of each chapter and in the final Production Skill Builder project provided in each part.

Acknowledgements

A hearty thank you to our editor, Elizabeth Sugg, for her avid support and interest in our projects. Your willingness to work with us during scheduled and unscheduled business hours is very much appreciated. We prize your ideas, energy, and enthusiasm and look forward to working with you on our future projects.

A huge thank you to Judy Casillo, Developmental Editor, who coordinated all aspects of this project. Thank you especially for providing pertinent information and for your prompt responses to our questions and concerns. Your attention to every detail made our work more enjoyable! We find it difficult to express in words our appreciation for your superior support. Thank you, thank you!

Audrey Ching, Chabot-Las Positas Community College District, thank you is too small of a word to express how much we appreciate your keystroke testing skills. You provided us with questions and suggestions that assisted in creating accurate instructions, activities, and function explanations. And a huge thank you for your quick turn-around time.

Deborah Leighton at Maine Proofreading Services, once again you are the best! We appreciate your superb copyediting skills and your quick turn-around time. Your queries and comments assisted us in making important improvements to our manuscript.

Willie Caldwell, your unlimited enthusiasm for the Layman/Hart books is greatly enjoyed! We look forward to your hosting a workshop at Houston Community College, Stafford Campus' new facilities. We applaud your leadership and organizational skills.

Paul Wiren, you are amazing! You went beyond the call of duty to handle all the details for desktop publishing this manuscript. Your energy, spitit and perserverence is truly appreciated. Your positive attitude, enthusiam, and good judgement were welcomed attributes. Thank you so very much.

KL
LH

Microsoft Office User Specialist (MOUS)—Microsoft Word 2000

Standardized Coding Number	Activity	Where To Look
W2000.1	**Working with text**	
W2000.1.1	Use the Undo, Redo, and Repeat command	Pages 44, 159
W2000.1.2	Apply font formats (Bold, Italic and Underline)	Pages 61-62
W2000.1.3	Use the SPELLING feature	Page 67
W2000.1.4	Use the THESAURUS feature	Page 238
W2000.1.5	Use the GRAMMAR feature	Page 240
W2000.1.6	Insert page breaks	Pages 260, 270
W2000.1.7	Highlight text in document	Pages 39-41
W2000.1.8	Insert and move text	Pages 41, 87-89
W2000.1.9	Cut, Copy, Paste, and Paste Special using the Office Clipboard	Pages 87-91, 247, I-44
W2000.1.10	Copy formats using the Format Painter	Page 213
W2000.1.11	Select and change font and font size	Pages 65-67
W2000.1.12	Find and replace text	Pages 91-94
W2000.1.13	Apply character effects (superscript, subscript, strikethrough, small caps and outline)	Page 375
W2000.1.14	Insert date and time	Page 58
W2000.1.15	Insert symbols	Page 176
W2000.1.16	Create and apply frequently used text with AutoCorrect	Pages 7-8, 371
W2000.2	**Working with paragraphs**	
W2000.2.1	Align text in paragraphs (Center, Left, Right and Justified)	Pages 14-15, 59-60
W2000.2.2	Add bullets and numbering	Pages 96-100
W2000.2.3	Set character, line, and paragraph spacing options	Pages 367-370
W2000.2.4	Apply borders and shading to paragraphs	Pages 440, 351-352
W2000.2.5	Use indentation options (Left, Right, First Line and Hanging Indent)	Pages 96, 234-235, 183
W2000.2.6	Use TABS command (Center, Decimal, Left and Right)	Pages 185-187
W2000.2.7	Create an outline style numbered list	Pages 523-527
W2000.2.8	Set tabs with leaders	Pages 187-188
W2000.3	**Working with documents**	
W2000.3.1	Print a document	Page 18
W2000.3.2	Use print preview	Page 70
W2000.3.3	Use Web Page Preview	Page B–8
W2000.3.4	Navigate through a document	Pages 19-22
W2000.3.5	Insert page numbers	Pages 267-269
W2000.3.6	Set page orientation	Page 439
W2000.3.7	Set margins	Page 180
W2000.3.8	Use GoTo to locate specific elements in a document	Page 21
W2000.3.9	Create and modify page numbers	Pages 267-269
W2000.3.10	Create and modify headers and footers	Pages 262-266
W2000.3.11	Align text vertically	Page 131
W2000.3.12	Create and use newspaper columns	Pages 204-208
W2000.3.13	Revise column structure	Pages 207-208, 460
W2000.3.14	Prepare and print envelopes and labels	Pages 314-319
W2000.3.15	Apply styles	Pages 389-395
W2000.3.16	Create sections with formatting that differs from other sections	Pages 204, 530-583
W2000.3.17	Use click & type	Pages 145-146
W2000.4	**Managing files**	
W2000.4.1	Use save	Page 16
W2000.4.2	Locate and open an existing document	Page 38
W2000.4.3	Use Save As (different name, location or format)	Page 43
W2000.4.4	Create a folder	Page 418
W2000.4.5	Create a new document using a Wizard	Pages 23, 72
W2000.4.6	Save as Web Page	Pages B-5
W2000.4.7	Use templates to create a new document	Pages 395-398
W2000.4.8	Create Hyperlinks	Pages B-6–B-8
W2000.4.9	Use the Office Assistant	Pages 5, 36-37
W2000.4.10	Send a Word document via e-mail	Pages 284, 286, 327, 365
W2000.5	**Using tables**	
W2000.5.1	Create and format tables	Pages 121-130
W2000.5.2	Add borders and shading to tables	Pages 160-162
W2000.5.3	Revise tables (insert & delete rows and columns, change cell formats)	Pages 124-126, 128-130, 152
W2000.5.4	Modify table structure (merge cells, change height and width)	Pages 128-129
W2000.5.5	Rotate text in a table	Pages 445-446
W2000.6	**Working with pictures and charts**	
W2000.6.1	Use the drawing toolbar	Pages B-8
W2000.6.2	Insert graphics into a document (WordArt, ClipArt, Images)	Pages 343, 346, 353, 448

Microsoft Office User Specialist (MOUS)—Microsoft Word 2000 Expert

Standardized Coding Number	Activity	Where To Look
W2000E.1	**Working with paragraphs**	
W2000E.1.1	Apply paragraph and section shading	Pages 351, 440, 447, 458-459, 527-573
W2000E.1.2	Use text flow options (Windows/Orphans options and keeping lines together)	Pages 269-271
W2000E.1.3	Sort lists, paragraphs, tables	Pages 320, 385-387
W2000E.2	**Working with documents**	
W2000E.2.1	Create and modify page borders	Pages 346, 349
W2000E.2.2	Format first page differently than subsequent pages	Pages 262-263, 530, 532-533
W2000E.2.3	Use bookmarks	Pages 515, 560-561, 600
W2000E.2.4	Create and edit styles	Pages 389-395
W2000E.2.5	Create watermarks	Pages 356-358
W2000E.2.6	Use find and replace with formats, special characters and non-printing elements	Pages 91-95
W2000E.2.7	Balance column length (using column breaks appropriately)	Pages 209-210
W2000E.2.8	Create or revise footnotes and endnotes	Pages 271-277
W2000E.2.9	Work with master documents and subdocuments	Pages 557-561
W2000E.2.10	Create and modify a table of contents	Pages 530-532
W2000E.2.11	Create cross-reference	Pages 560-561
W2000E.2.12	Create and modify an index	Pages 533-536
W2000E.3	**Using tables**	
W2000E.3.1	Embed worksheets in a table	Pages 577-579
W2000E.3.2	Perform calculations in a table	Pages 155, 567-570
W2000E.3.3	Link Excel data as a table	Pages 577, I-13–I-15
W2000E.3.4	Modify worksheets in a table	Pages 577-578, I-14–I-15
W2000E.4	**Working with pictures and charts**	
W2000E.4.1	Add bitmapped graphics	Pages 441, B-9
W2000E.4.2	Delete and position graphics	Page 352
W2000E.4.3	Create and modify charts	Pages 573-576
W2000E.4.4	Import data into charts	Pages 574-576
W2000E.5	**Using mail merge**	
W2000E.5.1	Create main document	Pages 293-294
W2000E.5.2	Create data source	Pages 289-293
W2000E.5.3	Sort records to be merged	Pages 320-323
W2000E.5.4	Merge main document and data source	Pages 295-296
W2000E.5.5	Generate labels	Pages 316-319
W2000E.5.6	Merge a document using alternate data sources	Pages 595-597
W2000E.6	Using advanced features	
W2000E.6.1	Insert a field	Pages 58, 294, 600
W2000E.6.2	Create, apply and edit macros	Pages 398-400
W2000E.6.3	Copy, rename, and delete macros	Pages 398-400
W2000E.6.4	Create and modify form	Pages 475-482
W2000E.6.5	Create and modify a form control (e.g., add an item to a drop-down list)	Pages 477-485
W2000E.6.6	Use advanced text alignment features with graphics	Pages 344-345, 442
W2000E.6.7	Customize toolbars	Pages 4-5
W2000E.7	**Collaborating with workgroups**	
W2000E.7.1	Insert comments	Pages 512-515
W2000E.7.2	Protect documents	Pages 424-425
W2000E.7.3	Create multiple versions of a document	Pages B-9–B-10
W2000E.7.4	Track changes to a document	Pages 505-508
W2000E.7.5	Set default file location for workgroup templates	Page 396
W2000E.7.6	Round Trip documents from HTML	Pages B-1–B-3

Start-Up

Before You Begin . . .

What Is Word 2000?

Microsoft Word is one of the most popular word processing programs in the world. Microsoft Word 2000 is the latest version of Word for the Windows environment. The Word program is one component of the Microsoft Office 2000 package. The Microsoft Office Standard Edition package includes the following programs: Word (word processing), PowerPoint (presentations), Excel (electronic spreadsheet), and Outlook (personal information manager). These Microsoft programs can be purchased as part of the Microsoft Office package or individually.

System Recommendations for Microsoft Word 2000

Recommended System Requirements
75-MHz Pentium Processor with a CD-ROM and a 14,400 baud (or faster) modem
32 MB RAM
189–195 MB hard disk space available
Windows 95/98, Window NT Version 4.0, or Windows 2000
SVGA graphics adapter and monitor
Mouse or other pointer device

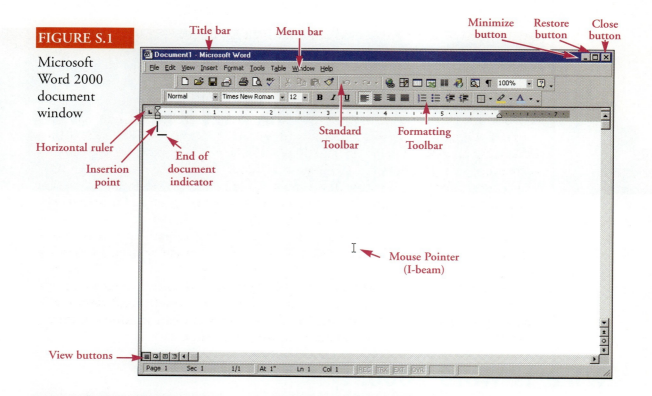

Microsoft
Word 2000
document
window

Title bar

Menu bar

Minimize
button

Restore
button

Close
button

Horizontal ruler

Insertion
point

End of
document
indicator

Standard
Toolbar

Formatting
Toolbar

Mouse Pointer
(I-beam)

View buttons

The Word Document Window

The Word document window displays after the program is launched (loaded).
The window is displayed in full size (maximized). (See Chapter 16 for changing
the window size.) A Word 2000 document window is shown in Figure S.1.

The *Title bar* displays at the top of the window and contains the application
name and document title. The **Close** button displays on the right side of the
Title bar and when selected closes the Word program. The **Minimize** and
Restore buttons are displayed on the right side of the Title bar and are used to
change the size of the application window. When the **Minimize** button is selected, the application is reduced to a button on the Taskbar, and the Desktop or
another application window is displayed. To return the program to the screen,
click on the **Microsoft Word** button in the Taskbar. (See Chapter 16 for additional information on managing document windows.)

The *Menu bar* displays directly below the Title bar. Each menu in the Menu
bar contains commands that are used to instruct Word to perform specific functions. To drop down the menu and view the menu commands, move the mouse
pointer to the desired menu and click once. When two down arrows display on
the bottom of the menu list, this indicates that the menu can be expanded to
display additional options. Pause for a moment or click on the two down arrows
to expand the menu. To select a command, move the mouse pointer onto the
command and click once. If a triangle displays to the right of a menu command,
additional commands are available. Point to the command to display the additional commands.

Each *drop-down menu* has a list of menu commands that are accessed easily
by pointing and clicking the mouse or by pressing a designated letter from the
keyboard. An underline displays beneath one letter in each menu command that

can be typed to select the desired option. Listed beside some of the commands are keystrokes that can be used to activate a command. For example, in the **File** menu, **Ctrl+S** displays next to the Save command, and **Ctrl+P** displays next to the Print command. Some menu commands are followed by three periods (e.g., Save As...) to indicate that, if selected, a dialog box will display.

The *dropdown menus and toolbars* will display with different options or buttons depending on the most recently used option or button. For example, if the **Edit** menu is dropped down and the **Replace** option is selected from the expanded menu, the next time the **Edit** menu is displayed, the **Replace** option will display. (In other words, the drop-down menu will not need to be expanded to view the Replace command.) Similarly, the most recently used **Toolbar** buttons will display on the **Standard** and **Formatting** Toolbars.

Toolbars can be displayed and used to quickly activate frequently used Word functions. The Standard Toolbar and Formatting Toolbar are defaulted (preset) to display on the screen.

A *horizontal ruler* displays below the toolbars and contains a measurement scale that shows the placement of tabs, column margins, and left and right margins. A vertical ruler displays on the left side of the document window (in Print Layout View only) and also contains a measurement scale.

The Mouse (Pointer Device)

There are various types of pointer devices. The mouse pointer device and the trackball are presently the most popular. The mouse is a handheld device used to move an arrow or rectangular symbol (pointer symbol) on the screen. The mouse pointer is moved over the screen area until the pointer symbol touches the item or items to be selected. The left button on the mouse device is pressed to initiate the desired action, such as selecting options, sizing windows, formatting text, or creating objects.

Generally, the mouse is held between the thumb and little or ring finger. The index finger or middle finger is used to press the mouse buttons. To maintain consistent control of the mouse, hold the mouse motionless when pressing the mouse buttons.

When the mouse is moved over a flat surface, the pointer symbol moves in the same direction on the screen. When the mouse reaches the edge of the flat surface, hold the mouse firmly, lift, and relocate. Also, alternating between a short rubbing stroke and lifting the mouse slightly using wrist movement can be very helpful when the mouse reaches the edge of the flat surface.

The pointer symbol changes shape depending on the location on the screen where the pointer is positioned. For example, when the mouse pointer touches a Toolbar button, a left-pointing arrow displays. However, when the mouse pointer touches text in the document window, an I-beam displays.

The trackball pointer device is stationary; the ball is moved by a finger or the palm of the hand. The trackball can be built into the keyboard, or it can be connected to the computer via a cable.

Different techniques are used to initiate an action with the pointer device. The following list shows the basic actions:

Click   Press the left button once and release.

Double-click	Press the left button twice rapidly.
Drag	Press and hold down the left mouse button while moving the mouse or trackball.
Point	Move the mouse pointer to a specific position on the screen.

The Insertion Point

The insertion point indicates the location where the next action is to take place and displays as a bold, blinking vertical line. The insertion point will move to characters and lines that have been typed; however, the insertion point will not move into blank space unless the **Enter** key or **Spacebar** is pressed. As the **Enter** key or **Spacebar** is pressed or text is typed, the insertion point moves. See also Steps to Move the Insertion Point Quickly in Chapter 1, on page 21.

The mouse device can be used to move the insertion point by placing the pointer symbol at the desired location and pressing (clicking) the left mouse button once. Also, when Num Lock is turned off, the direction (arrow) keys on the 10-key numeric keypad can be used to move the insertion point up, down, left, or right one character or line at a time. On many keyboards, a duplicate set of arrow keys is provided.

The Toolbars

Word provides an easy way to access frequently used commands via the toolbars (see Figure S.2). The Standard Toolbar and the Formatting Toolbar are two rows of buttons that display below the Menu bar. A mouse must be used to select a button on a toolbar. When the mouse pointer is placed on a button in a toolbar, a *ToolTip* showing the name of the button appears under the button.

The Standard Toolbar and the Formatting Toolbar are the preset (default) Toolbars because they contain options for working quickly with commonly used Word features. The Standard Toolbar contains a variety of buttons that are used for document creation (including creating tables and columns) and for saving, printing, and opening documents. The Standard Toolbar also contains buttons for rearranging text (i.e., **Cut**, **Copy**, and **Paste**), obtaining Help, and changing the viewing size of the text.

The Formatting Toolbar contains buttons that are used to quickly format text such as fonts, point sizes, indents, and alignment. The Formatting Toolbar also contains buttons that are used to create bullets, numbering, and borders. Other Toolbars can be accessed by moving the mouse pointer to either the Formatting or Standard Toolbar and clicking the *right* mouse button once to display a list of available Toolbars.

If Toolbars are not displayed on the screen, select **View**, **Toolbars**, then select the Toolbar(s) to be displayed by moving the mouse pointer to the name and clicking the left mouse button once. A check mark appears in the box in front of each Toolbar name that will display in the document window. When each desired Toolbar has been selected, choose **OK** or press the **Enter** key.

Standard Toolbar

Formatting Toolbar

Toolbars can be created and customized by adding and removing buttons. Also, some specialized Toolbars, such as the Header and Footer Toolbar, will automatically appear when you use certain features.

At the right side of the **Standard and Formatting Toolbars**, a small down arrow displays. Click on the down arrow to display the **Add or Remove Buttons** option. Choose the button(s) desired or deselect any buttons that you do not want displayed on the Toolbar.

The Office Assistant

The Office Assistant is new in Office 2000 and is the main link to Help. When the Office Assistant button 🔲 is selected, a list of options displays. Select one of the options, or type specific words or a question to locate the desired information. For example, type the words **Office Assistant** or **What Is the Office Assistant?** and choose the **Search** button. A list of specific options relating to the Office Assistant display. Select the option desired.

The Office Assistant is defaulted to display when the Word program is loaded. The defaulted Office Assistant displays as a paper clip with two large eyes and is named "Clippit." Other Assistants, such as "Scribble the cat," can be selected in the Office Assistant Gallery. Select the **Options** button in the Office Assistant message window to display the Office Assistant dialog box.

To show the Office Assistant, select the **Office Assistant** button 🔲. To hide the Office Assistant, select the **Close** button on the Office Assistant box.

The Rulers

The horizontal ruler is a bar that displays above the document window and contains a measurement scale showing the placement of tabs, column margins, and left and right margins. It is used to change tabs and margin settings without accessing a menu. Also, a vertical ruler displays at the left of the document window when Print Layout View or Print Preview is active. The horizontal ruler is preset to display after the Word program is launched. If the horizontal ruler does not appear on the screen, select **View**, **Ruler** to display the ruler. The rulers can be removed from the screen by selecting **View**, **Ruler**. (See Steps to Display or Remove the Ruler(s) in Chapter 7.)

The Nonprinting Characters

In Word for Windows, nonprinting characters, such as the end of paragraph markers, tabs, and spaces, normally do not appear on the screen. However, when editing, it may be useful to see the location of nonprinting characters on the screen. If the nonprinting characters are not displaying on the screen, select the **Show/Hide** button ¶ on the Standard Toolbar. Select the **Show/Hide** button ¶ again to turn the nonprinting characters off. A button that is used to turn a feature on and off is referred to as a *toggle* button. *Toggling* is the term used when a feature is turned off and on by selecting the same button.

If the **Show/Hide** button is clicked on and the symbols do not display, click on the **Tools** menu and select **Options**. On the **View** tab, click on **All** in the **Formatting marks** area.

The View Modes

Word for Windows has several ways of presenting a document on the screen. When creating and editing documents, two view modes may be used. In the Normal View mode, a simplified screen is displayed. This reduces the amount of memory needed so the program works faster and therefore is the best mode to use for keying text. The Print Layout View mode is a WYSIWYG (wizz-ee-wig or What You See Is What You Get) display. All the elements on the page are shown in proper relation to one another.

The Print Layout View mode is useful when formatting text and to check the page arrangement before printing, but it uses a lot of memory, so scrolling through the document or editing may be slower. To check that the Normal View mode is selected, choose **View** in the Menu bar. The miniature page beside the Normal option displays with an "indented" light-gray border that contains a darker gray line at the top and right of the miniature page. If necessary, move the mouse pointer to **Normal** and click. To select a different view from the **View** menu, move the mouse pointer to the desired view and click the left mouse button once.

 Change Views

1. Move the mouse pointer to the **View** menu and click once.

   Note: A list of options displays. An indented light-gray border displays beside the currently selected view option.

2. Select the desired view, i.e., **Normal** or **Print Layout**.

   For example, check that the **Normal** option is selected. (If necessary, move the mouse pointer to the **Normal** option and click once.)

Shortcut:

1. Move the mouse button to the **Normal View** 🗏 or **Print Layout View** 🗐 button located at the bottom left of the document window and click once.

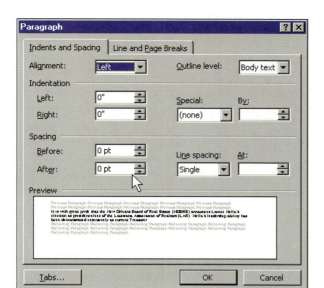

The Dialog Boxes

Dialog boxes provide additional Word commands. Often dialog boxes display after menu commands are selected. For example, when the **Format**, **Paragraph** command is selected, the Paragraph dialog box displays (see Figure S.3).

In a dialog box, instructions are given to the program by selecting from a list of options and/or by typing information. Often a dialog box contains commands followed by three periods (...). When these commands are selected, a second dialog box with additional options displays. The second dialog box allows the user to provide more specific information on how the chosen command is to be accomplished.

In many dialog boxes, two or more tabs display. For example, in the Paragraph dialog box shown in Figure S.3, two tabs display, i.e., Indents and Spacing and Line and Page Breaks. When a tab is selected, a card with options displays. For example, in the Paragraph dialog box shown in Figure S.3, the Indents and Spacing card is displayed and contains indentation and spacing options. The Line and Page Breaks options are displayed by moving the mouse pointer to the Line and Page Breaks tab and clicking once.

Information about the options in a dialog box can be obtained by selecting the Help button ? and clicking on an option. A Help box displays containing a description of the option.

The Automatic-As-You-Type Features

Word has three features, *AutoCorrect, AutoFormat,* and *AutoComplete,* that automatically change or insert text and graphics while you type. These automatic features are defaulted on but can be easily turned off.

The *AutoCorrect* feature automatically corrects common typing and spelling errors. When a commonly misspelled word is typed incorrectly followed by pressing the **Spacebar**, **Tab**, or **Enter** key, the correct word is immediately displayed in the document window. For example, if the characters "teh" are typed followed by a space, Word will automatically display the correct word, "the." Also, if two uppercase letters are typed followed by other lowercase letters and a space, Word will change the second uppercase letter to a lowercase letter. Many commonly misspelled words are identified and the correct spellings automatically inserted by the AutoCorrect feature. These words can be deleted and/or additional words can be included in the list of commonly misspelled words. Select **Tools**, **AutoCorrect**, and choose the **AutoCorrect** tab to see a list of options.

To create your own AutoCorrect word(s), type the abbreviation or misspelled word in the **Replace** box. Press the **Tab** key and type the correct word(s) in the **With** box. Select **Add** and **OK**. For example, type the misspelled word, *doucment* in the **Replace** box and type the correct word, *document* in the **With** box.

The *AutoFormat As You Type* feature automatically formats headings, bulleted and numbered lists, borders, etc., as you type. For example, after an asterisk is typed followed by a space or tab, the following lines of text typed become a bulleted list. Press **Enter** twice to discontinue the bulleted list. Another example of the AutoFormat feature is that word(s) display in italics after typing an underline before and after the word(s). To change the AutoFormat options, select **Tools**, **AutoCorrect**, and choose the **AutoFormat** tab.

The *AutoComplete* feature recognizes the first several characters typed and displays a ScreenTip that suggests a complete word(s) or date. For example, if you type the characters, *Janu*, the ScreenTip displays *January*. If this is the correct word, press the **Enter** key to display the entire word in the document. If you are typing quickly and the Screen Tip displays, continue to type and the ScreenTip will be removed automatically from the screen.

To turn the AutoComplete feature on or off, select **Tools**, **AutoCorrect** and select the **AutoText** tab. The **Show AutoComplete tip for AutoText and dates** option displays at the top of the AutoText card.

The Automatic Spell and Grammar Checking Features

The Automatic Spell Checking feature looks for misspelled words as you type. If a misspelled word is identified, a red wavy line displays below the word. The red wavy line does not print. Correctly spelled words, such as proper names, may also be marked with red wavy lines because the words are not included in Word's dictionary file(s). (For additional information concerning the spelling feature and Word's dictionary files, see Chapter 3.) To turn off Spelling as you type, select **Tools**, **Options**, **Spelling & Grammar** tab, and deselect the **Check spelling as you type** option.

The Automatic Grammar Checking feature looks for grammatically incorrect phrases, sentences, and/or punctuation as you type. If incorrect text is identified, a green wavy line displays below the word(s). The green wavy line does not print. (For additional information concerning the grammar checking feature, see Chapter 9.)

Part 1
The Beginning Step

Create and Edit Business Documents

Chapters 1–4

- Launch Microsoft Word 2000
- Use center alignment
- Save a file
- Print a document
- Scroll horizontally and vertically
- Move the insertion point
- Close a document
- Obtain a new document window
- Use the Memo Wizard
- Exit Word 2000
- Use the Help feature
- Open a document
- Select text
- Delete and insert text
- Save and rename a file
- Use the Undo and Redo features
- Use the automatic date feature
- Change alignment
- Use bold, underline, and italic
- Change margins
- Change fonts
- Check spelling
- Display documents using Print Preview and Zoom view
- Use the Letter Wizard
- Move and copy text
- Find and replace text
- Indent text
- Create numbered and bulleted lists
- Print selected text

CHAPTER

1

Create a Memorandum

Features Covered

- Launch Microsoft Word 2000
- Use center alignment
- Save a file
- Print a document
- Scroll horizontally and vertically
- Move the insertion point
- Close a document window
- Obtain a new document window
- Use the Memo Wizard
- Exit Microsoft Word 2000

Objectives and Introduction

After successfully completing this chapter, you will be able to launch (load) the Microsoft Word 2000 program; create, save, print, and close a document; and view different portions of a document using the scroll bars. Instructions for typing and formatting an interoffice memorandum while using Word 2000 features will be presented in this chapter. The Memo Wizard will also be used to create a memorandum.

Launch Microsoft Word 2000

Launching a program is the process of transferring the program from the hard disk to the computer's memory. The Microsoft Word 2000 program is launched (loaded) from the Microsoft Windows Desktop (see Figure 1.1). The Taskbar displays at the bottom of the screen. (If the Taskbar is not displayed, move the mouse pointer to the bottom of the screen and the Taskbar will appear.) The **Start** button is located at the left end of the Taskbar. When the **Start** button is selected, the Start menu displays. Options on the Start menu enable you to accomplish tasks such as launching programs, opening documents, changing settings, and shutting down the computer.

11

FIGURE 1.1

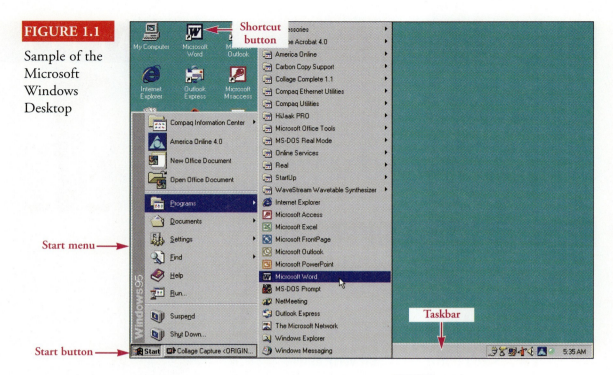

Sample of the
Microsoft
Windows
Desktop

To launch a program, select the **Start** button , move the mouse pointer to the **Programs** option, and click on the desired program.

Shortcut buttons (pictures) display in the Windows Desktop screen (see Figure 1.1). Each shortcut represents a program or application. A program can be launched by double-clicking on the desired shortcut.

The Microsoft Office Shortcut Bar may also display at the top or side of the Windows Desktop. The buttons on the Microsoft Office Shortcut Bar provide access to the Microsoft Office programs.

When the Microsoft Word program is launched, the Word document window displays with a Title bar, a Menu bar, a Standard Toolbar, a Formatting Toolbar, and a Ruler at the top of the screen and a Status bar and usually a Drawing Toolbar at the bottom of the screen (see Figure 1.2).

Start-Up Instructions

❖ The computer and monitor should be turned on and the Windows Desktop displayed on the screen. If necessary, see your instructor and write down on the following lines the steps needed to display the Windows Desktop on your screen.

_____

_____

❖ Place a formatted file disk in drive A or B.

Steps to ## Launch (Load) the Microsoft Word 2000 Program

1. Click once on the Start button.
2. Move the mouse pointer to the Programs option.

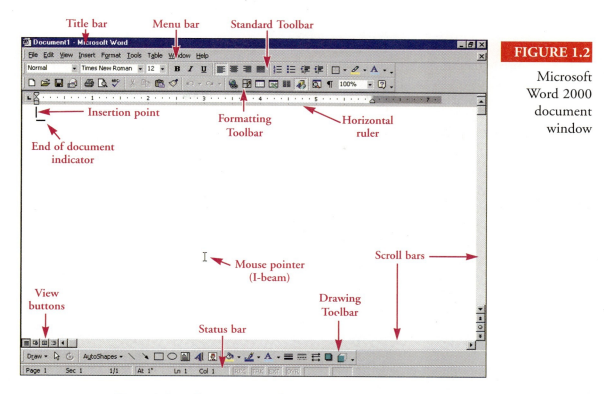

FIGURE 1.2

Microsoft
Word 2000
document
window

Note: A list of programs and program groups displays.

3. Move the mouse pointer to **Microsoft Word** and click once.

Note: The Microsoft Word 2000 copyright screen displays briefly, then the Microsoft Word document window displays (see Figure 1.2).

If a different method is used to launch Microsoft Word on your computer, see your instructor or instructional assistant and write the steps needed on the following lines.

_____

_____

Formatting

Formatting is the process of determining the placement and arrangement of a document when it is printed on a page. The arrangement of a document includes the amount of blank space in the left, right, top, and bottom margins. Formatting also includes alignment, underline/bold text, capitalization, and the number of vertical and horizontal spaces used between words and lines.

The purpose of formatting is to arrange text in a manner that is attractive and easy to read. This textbook includes information on formatting memorandums, letters, tables, reports, mailing labels, newsletters, reports, etc.

In this chapter, formatting using different justification options will be introduced to create memorandum styles. The **Center** and **Left** alignment options will be discussed as well as the format for the paragraphs of a memorandum. Alignment options and text format options will be used to create many documents in this book.

To help you quickly create common business documents, Word provides predefined formats called *templates* (see Appendix C). In addition, Word provides Wizards to assist you in creating both the standard text and format (see Use the Memo Wizard later in this chapter).

Word Wrap

One automatic formatting feature of word processing programs is word wrap. As you type text, the **Enter** key is pressed only at the end of a paragraph or short line. When text reaches the right margin, the insertion point automatically returns to the beginning of the next line. This automatic return feature is called *word wrap*.

Word wrap automatically formats the paragraph to adjust to the left and right margins; if words are inserted or deleted from the paragraph, text automatically readjusts to the margins.

Create a Memorandum

A memorandum is informal correspondence usually sent between individuals within the same company. There are many acceptable formats for memorandums. In a traditional memorandum, a heading such as *Memorandum*, *Memo*, or *Interoffice Correspondence* is typed or preprinted at the top of the page. The memorandum heading is followed by the recipient's name, author's name, date, and subject. The words *To:*, *From:*, *Date:*, and *Subject:* or *Re:* usually precede the recipient's name, author's name, the date and subject and are called "lead words." Lead words can be typed in the memorandum or preprinted.

The lead word To: may be followed by the recipient's name, a name that identifies a group of individuals (e.g., sales representatives or district managers), or by the word Distribution. When the memorandum is to be sent to a group, a distribution list can be typed after the reference initials identifying the individuals who are part of the group. If copies of the memo are to be sent to other individuals, the notation "c:" is typed below the distribution list followed by the name(s) of the person(s) to whom copies are to be sent.

As you type the main text of the memorandum (body text), word wrap automatically begins new lines. The **Enter** key is pressed twice after each paragraph. Each paragraph begins at the left margin. After the final paragraph, the **Enter** key is pressed twice. Then the initials of the person writing, a forward slash (/), and the initials of the person typing the memorandum are typed.

Start-Up Instructions

❖ Use the following information to begin creating the memorandum shown in Figure 1.3.

Use Center Alignment (Horizontal Centering)

1. The insertion point should be located on the left side of the screen.
2. Type the word(s) to be centered.

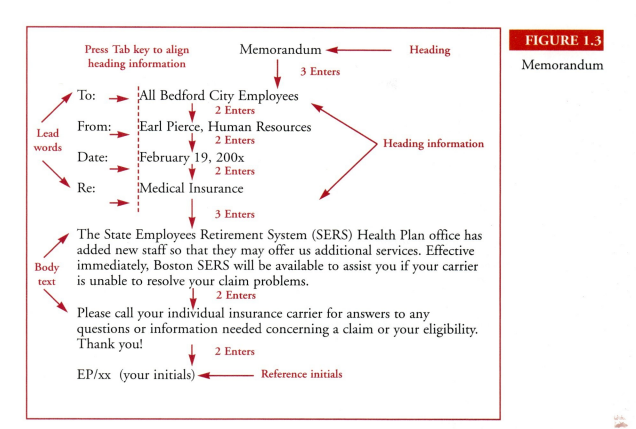

Press Tab key to align heading information

Memorandum ← Heading

3 Enters

To: → All Bedford City Employees

2 Enters

Lead words

From: → Earl Pierce, Human Resources

2 Enters

Heading information

Date: → February 19, 200x

2 Enters

Re: → Medical Insurance

3 Enters

Body text

The State Employees Retirement System (SERS) Health Plan office has added new staff so that they may offer us additional services. Effective immediately, Boston SERS will be available to assist you if your carrier is unable to resolve your claim problems.

2 Enters

Please call your individual insurance carrier for answers to any questions or information needed concerning a claim or your eligibility. Thank you!

2 Enters

EP/xx (your initials) ← Reference initials

For example, type **Memorandum**. (Do not type the period.)

3. Select the **Center** button 📑 on the Formatting Toolbar.

   Note: The word Memorandum is horizontally centered in the document window.

4. Press **Enter** once.

5. Select the **Align Left** button 📑 on the Formatting Toolbar to return the insertion point to the left side of the screen.

   Note: The word Memorandum is now horizontally centered on the screen, and the insertion point is located at the left margin, one line below the heading.

Start-Up Instructions

❖ Press the **Enter** key two more times to create two blank lines after the heading.

❖ Continue with the Steps to Create a Memorandum. Backspace to correct errors made while typing. Remember that a red wavy line below a word indicates a word not recognized by Word, and a green wavy line below a word(s) indicates a grammar question. For now, ignore any errors noticed *after* the memorandum is typed.

❖ After typing the characters **Febr** in the word February, an AutoComplete tip displays the completed word, February. Press **Enter** to accept the word, or continue to type the entire word as usual.

Create a Memorandum

1. Type the lead word followed by a colon; press the **Tab** key. Type the heading information and press **Enter** twice.

    For example, type **To:**. Press the **Tab** key. Type **All Bedford City Employees** and press **Enter** twice. Continue to type the lead words and heading information shown in Figure 1.3.

    *Note: The **Tab** key is pressed once or twice after the lead words in order to align the heading information and to provide space after the lead words and before the information that follows. Visually check that the heading information following the lead words is aligned. Always replace the "x's" in the year with the current year.*

2. Press the **Enter** key one additional time after the reference line (Re:).

    For example, after typing **Medical Insurance**, press the **Enter** key three times.

    *Note: There will be three **Enters** after the reference (Re:) line heading information.*

3. With the insertion point at the left margin, begin typing the text of the first body text paragraph shown in Figure 1.3. When the insertion point reaches the right margin, continue typing. Word wrap will automatically return the insertion point to the left margin. Press the **Enter** key twice at the end of each paragraph.

    Note: The paragraph lines may not end with the same words as shown in Figure 1.3 because of styles and sizes of fonts.

4. Press **Enter** twice after the last paragraph; type **EP** in uppercase letters followed by a forward slash (/) and type your initials in lowercase letters, e.g., EP/kl. (See reference initials in Chapter 3, page 56.)

Finish-Up Instructions

❖ Continue with the Steps to Save a New File.

❖ **Remember:** Word 2000 displays a red wavy line below any word(s) or characters that are not recognized. That's OK; you will learn to make corrections in Chapter 2.

Save a File

After a document is created, it must be saved to the computer's hard disk or to a floppy disk. Saving is the process of transferring the document from the computer's temporary memory to permanent memory on a hard disk or floppy disk. A saved document is referred to as a *file* or *data file*.

When a document is saved, a filename is assigned. A filename can be 1 to 255 characters in length and can include spaces. If desired, a period and a one- to three-letter filename extension can be added (see What Is a Filename? in Appendix A). If a filename extension is not typed, Word automatically adds the extension .doc to the filename when a document is saved.

Before a named document is saved, the location of the disk where the file is to be saved must be selected. For example, if a file is to be saved to a disk that is located in the A drive, Word must be instructed to access the A drive.

Files can also be saved to different folders on the computer's hard disk or to floppy disks. For example, a memo file could be saved to a folder named **c:\memos** (see What Are Folders and Paths? in Appendix A).

Once a document has been saved, the filename and location display in the Title bar. If a previously saved document is changed (edited), selecting the **Save** button on the Standard Toolbar or choosing **File**, **Save** will save the edited file immediately using the filename displayed in the Title bar. To save the edited file with a new filename, see Steps to Use Save As to Rename a File in Chapter 2, page 43.

Start-Up Instructions

❖ A file disk should be placed in the A or B drive.

❖ The memorandum typed from Figure 1.3 should be displayed in the document window.

Save a New File

1. Select the **Save** button 🖫 on the Standard Toolbar.

   Note: The Save As dialog box displays because the file has not been previously saved (see Figure 1.4). A suggested filename is highlighted in the File name box.

2. If desired, type a different filename in the File name box. (When the first character of the new filename is typed, the highlighted filename will be erased.)

   For example, type **1insurance**. (Do not type the period.)

   Note: Check the accuracy of the filename before continuing. If necessary, use the Backspace key to erase any incorrect characters; type the correct characters.

To Select a Different Disk Drive

3. Move the mouse pointer to the **Save in** box and click the left mouse button once.

   Note: A list of available drives and folders displays.

4. Move the mouse pointer to the desired disk drive option and click once. The disk drive options are identified by the drive size and letter, e.g., 3½ Floppy (A:).

   For example, move the mouse pointer to the disk drive option that identifies the drive where your file disk is located and click once.

   *Note: The newly selected drive displays in the **Save in** box, e.g., 3½ Floppy (A:) (Shown in figure 1.4 on page 18).*

To Complete the Save Process

5. Select the **Save** button.

FIGURE 1.4

Save As dialog
box

Note: In a moment, the document is saved on the file disk that is located in the selected disk drive, and the document name is displayed in the Title bar of the document window, e.g., **1insurance.doc**. *The three-letter extension* **.doc** *is added automatically to the filename when the file is saved.*

Select a Different Folder

Note: The following steps are for your information.

1. Select **File, Save As**. Move the mouse pointer to the down triangle at the right of the **Save in** box and click on the desired drive option.

   Note: A list of available folders (directories) and/or disk drives displays below the Save in box.

2. Move the mouse pointer to the desired folder (directory) name and double-click.

   Note: A list of available subfolders may display. The **Up One Level** *button* 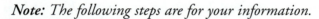*, located to the right of the Save in box, can be used to display the previous folder (directory).*

Print a Document

A document can be printed using two methods. When the **Print** button on the Standard Toolbar is selected, the entire file prints immediately, using the default (preset) settings in the Print dialog box. Selecting the **File, Print** command or using the shortcut keystrokes **Ctrl** and **p** displays the Print dialog box and printing starts after **OK** is selected. Other options can be selected in the Print dialog box, such as printing individual pages or a section of a document. Additional information concerning printing is discussed in Chapters 4 and 10.

While memos are commonly printed and distributed to the recipients, memos and other documents can be sent via e-mail (electronic mail) to other computers connected to a network. A memo or other document is linked as an attachment to an e-mail message. In Word, the **File, Send To, Mail Recipient** command is used to access an e-mail application such as Microsoft Exchange or Outlook.

Start-Up Instructions

❖ The printer should be turned on. If you are sharing a printer, check that the switch box or local area network (LAN) printer is selected for your printer.

❖ The document to be printed (e.g., **1insurance.doc**) should be displayed in the document window.

Print a Document Using the Print Button

1. Select the Print button 🖨 on the Standard Toolbar.

   *Note: If there is more than one printer available to the computer, use the **File, Print** command to initiate printing to ensure that the correct printer is selected.*

Finish-Up Instructions

❖ Continue with the Steps to Use the Mouse for Vertical or Horizontal Scrolling on pages 20.

Print a Document Using the File, Print Command

Note: The following steps are for your information.

1. Select **File, Print**.

2. Check that the desired options are selected and that the correct printer is selected. If necessary, see your instructor or instructional aide for assistance.

3. Select **OK** to start printing.

Scroll Horizontally and Vertically

Scrolling is the process of moving text quickly up, down, left, or right in order to view parts of the document not displayed in the document window. A vertical scroll bar displays at the right of the screen, and a horizontal scroll bar displays at the bottom of the screen. Each scroll bar contains a scroll box and scroll arrows (controlled by the mouse) that can be used to view various parts of a document (see Figure 1.5). The **Previous Page** ⬆ and **Next Page** ⬇ buttons located at the bottom of the vertical scroll bar can be used to scroll quickly from page to page in a multi-page document.

Start-Up Instructions

❖ The file named **1insurance.doc** that was typed from Figure 1.3 should be displayed in the document window. Use the following steps to practice vertical and horizontal scrolling.

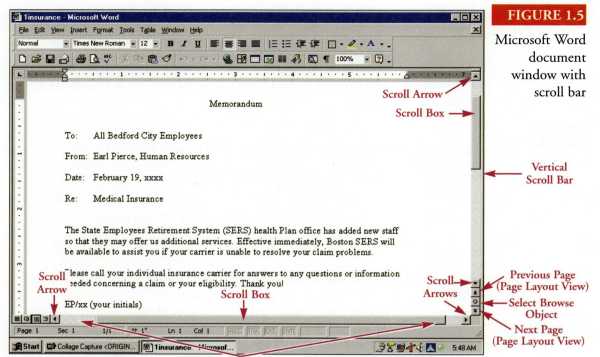

FIGURE 1.5

Microsoft Word document window with scroll bar

 Steps to ## Use the Mouse for Vertical or Horizontal Scrolling

1. Place the mouse pointer on the scroll box in the vertical scroll bar on the right side of the document window; press and hold the left mouse button, then drag the scroll box up or down to scroll. Release the mouse button.

   For example, move the mouse pointer to the vertical scroll box; press and hold the left mouse button while dragging the box down approximately 1"; release the mouse button.

   Note: The text on the screen scrolls. If text is not displayed, use the scroll box to scroll up. When the scroll box is moved, the insertion point does not change location in the text. To change the location of the insertion point, see the Steps to Move the Insertion Point Quickly on page 21.

2. Place the mouse pointer on the up scroll arrow located at the top of the vertical scroll bar or the down scroll arrow located at the bottom of the vertical scroll bar and click the left mouse button once to scroll the text down or up one line at a time.

   For example, place the mouse pointer on the down scroll arrow located at the bottom of the scroll bar and click once or twice.

   Note: Holding down the left mouse button while pointing on the up or down scroll arrows will cause the text to move continuously up or down.

3. Place the mouse pointer on the scroll box in the horizontal scroll bar at the bottom of the document window; press and hold the left mouse button and drag the scroll box to the left or right. Release the mouse button.

For example, move the mouse pointer to the scroll box in the horizontal scroll bar; press and hold the left mouse button while dragging the box to the right approximately 1". Release the mouse button.

Finish-Up Instructions

❖ Move the scroll box in the horizontal scroll bar to the left or right until the document looks centered on the screen. If desired, move the scroll box in the vertical scroll bar to the top of the scroll bar.

Move the Insertion Point

To relocate the insertion point to various parts of the document, use the arrow keys, or move the mouse pointer and click on the desired location. For example, the mouse can be used to relocate the insertion point to any position in the document by pointing on the desired position and clicking once. The up, down, left, and right arrow keys as well as the **Page Up**, **Page Down**, **Home**, and **End** keys can also be used to relocate the insertion point.

Start-Up Instructions

❖ The file named **1insurance.doc** that was typed from Figure 1.3 should be displayed in the document window. Use the following steps to practice moving the insertion point.

 ## Move the Insertion Point Quickly

Using the Mouse

1. Move the mouse pointer to any location in the document and click. The insertion point moves to that location.

   Note: If the desired location is not visible in the document window, scroll the text to display the desired location. (See Steps to Use the Mouse for Vertical or Horizontal Scrolling on page 20.)

2. To move the insertion point to a different page, choose the **Select Browse Object** button ⊙ at the bottom of the vertical scroll bar. Select the **Go To** option button →. Check that the **Page** option is highlighted in the Go to what box. Type the page number desired in the Enter page number box of the Go To tab. Select the **Go To** button. When the selected page appears, select **Close** to exit the dialog box.

Using the Keyboard

1. To move the insertion point to the beginning of the current line, press the **Home** key.

2. To move the insertion point to the end of the current line, press the **End** key.

3. To move the insertion point to the beginning of the document, press and hold the **Ctrl** key and tap the **Home** key once (**Ctrl** and **Home**).

4. To move the insertion point to the last character in the document, press and hold the **Ctrl** key and tap the **End** key once (**Ctrl** and **End**).

5. To move the insertion point one word to the left, press the **Ctrl** and **left arrow** keys.

6. To move the insertion point one word to the right, press the **Ctrl** and **right arrow** keys.

7. To move the insertion point to the top of the previous screen, press the **Page Up** key.

8. To move the insertion point to the top of the next screen, press the **Page Down** key.

9. To move the insertion point to the top of the screen, hold down the **Alt** and **Ctrl** keys while pressing the **Page Up** key once.

10. To move the insertion point to the bottom of the screen, hold down the **Alt** and **Ctrl** keys while pressing the **Page Down** key once.

11. To move the insertion point to a different page, press **F5** or **Ctrl** and **g** to display the Go To option. Type the page number desired, then press **Enter**. When the selected page appears, press **Esc** to remove the Find and Replace dialog box from the screen.

Close a Document Window

Once a document has been typed, saved, and printed, the document is usually cleared from the document window before a new document is begun. However, more than one document window can be displayed on the screen at one time. (See Chapter 16, The Windows in Word.) Closing a document is often referred to as *clearing a document* from the screen. After a document is closed, a blank document window can be displayed and a new document typed, or an existing document can be opened. If more than one document has been opened, you may need to close another document window or select **File**, **New** to obtain a clear document window.

Start-Up Instructions

❖ The file named **1insurance.doc** should be displayed in the document window.

 Close a Document

1. Select **File, Close** or select the **Close Window** button ☒ located at the right edge of the Menu bar (the bottom ☒). The document will be removed from the document window.

   *Note: If the message, "Do you want to save the changes you made to [filename]?" displays, select **No** to close without saving changes. Repeat step 1 if more than one window is open. When there are no more documents in the document window, the Menu bar displays in black letters. The Toolbars are no longer displayed in black letters and are "dimmed" on the screen.*

Finish-Up Instructions

❖ Continue with the Steps to Use the Memo Wizard.

Obtain a New Document Window

An empty document window displays each time the Word program is launched. After a document has been created in the first document window, a new, empty document window must be obtained to create another document. An empty document window can be obtained by selecting the **New Blank document** button on the Standard Toolbar.

Steps to **Obtain a New Document Window**

> *Note: The following step is for your information.*

1. Select the **New Blank Document** button on the Standard Toolbar.

Use the Memo Wizard

Word provides Wizards to help you create documents such as memos, letters, faxes, and awards. Wizards contain predefined formats. Each Wizard provides questions that guide you step by step through the process of creating the chosen document type. By answering questions, you specify how the document is to appear. For example, if the Memo Wizard is selected, the first question to answer is, "Do you want to include a heading?" Other questions provide Word with specific information to display in the document. Using a Wizard is one of the easiest methods to create documents.

Once the Wizard questions are answered, the document format, including the typed responses, displays in the document window. Placeholders display between brackets (e.g., [Click here and type names]) to indicate where additional information should be typed. When you click on a placeholder, the placeholder is highlighted. When a character is typed, the placeholder is erased and replaced with the newly typed character(s). As text is typed, the **Enter** key is pressed only once between paragraphs. Additional space between paragraphs will automatically be inserted.

Steps to **Use the Memo Wizard**

1. Select **File, New**.

   Note: The New dialog box displays (see Figure 1.6 on page 24).

2. Move the mouse pointer to the tab labeled **Memos** and click once.

3. Double-click on the **Memo Wizard** icon.

   Note: In a few moments, the Memo Wizard dialog box displays.

4. Select the desired Memo Wizard option.

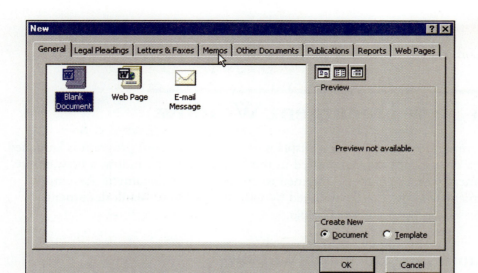

FIGURE 1.6

New dialog box

For example, check that the **Start** option is selected. If necessary, select the **Start** option.

5. Select the **Next** button.

6. Select the desired style.

   For example, check that **Contemporary** is selected. If necessary, select **Contemporary**.

7. Select the **Next** button.

8. Select or type the title for the memo.

   For example, check that the option **Yes. Use this text** is chosen and that **Interoffice Memo** displays.

9. Choose **Next**.

10. Select the header items desired.

    For example, a check mark should be displaying beside the following options:

    Date:
    From:
    Subject:

    Note: Text can be deleted by selecting the text to be replaced and typing the new text (see Steps to Select Text, Chapter 2).

11. If necessary, delete the name displayed in the From box by moving the mouse pointer to the right of the last character in the box and clicking. Press the **Backspace** key to delete the existing text. Type the name of the person sending the memo.

    For example, delete any name displaying in the From box and type the first and last name of a friend.

12. Click in the **Subject** box and type the desired subject for the memo.

    For example, if the desired subject displays, continue to step 13. If the desired subject does not display, click in the **Subject** box and type **PC Policies Review**.

13. Choose **Next**.

14. Select the desired To and/or Cc option and type the information desired.

   For example, if necessary click in the **To** box and type **See Distribution List Below**; check that Cc is *not* selected.

15. Choose the desired distribution list location option.

   For example, check that the option to place your distribution list on a separate page is **No**.

16. Select the **Next** button.

17. Select the closing items to be included in the memorandum.

   For example, if necessary, choose the **Writer's initials** and **Typist's initials** options. Delete the initials displayed in the **Writer's initials** box by pointing to the initials displayed and double-clicking and then typing in uppercase letters the first and last initials of your friend. For example, RB.

   Double-click in the **Typist's initials** box. Type your initials in lowercase letters. For example, mt. Check that Enclosures and Attachments are not selected. (No check mark should display beside the Enclosures and Attachments options.)

   Note: Characters and/or words in an option box are highlighted by double-clicking or selecting the characters/words. Once a key is pressed on the keyboard, the highlighted characters/words are immediately deleted and the new character displays.

18. Select the **Next** button.

19. If the memorandum will contain more than one page, select the desired items to be placed in the header/footer.

   For example, because this memo will be only one page, check that no options are selected. (If necessary, deselect all options.)

20. Select the **Next** button.

   Note: The Memo Wizard Finish dialog box displays.

21. Select the **Finish** button.

   Note: In a few moments, the top portion of a memorandum displays in the document window. The Office Assistant also displays.

22. Select the **Cancel** button in the Office Assistant box.

   Note: Click on the down arrow in the vertical scroll bar to view the memo. The lead words Date:, To:, From:, RE:, and the current date display. The information that was chosen or typed earlier is displayed including the writer's and typist's initials.

   When the document created using the Memo Wizard Contemporary style displays in the document window, several very light-gray graphics will have been inserted (see Figure 1.7). Placeholders have been inserted at the locations where additional information is needed to complete the memo (e.g., [Click here and type your memo text.]). Also, the words "Document# - Memo, month/day/year" display in the Title bar.

FIGURE 1.7

Memorandum
created using
the Memo
Wizard
Contemporary
style

interoffice memo

Date: 4/5/99

To: See Distribution List Below

From: (Type your friend's name here.)

RE: PC Policies Review

The latest draft of the PC Policies manual is ready for final review. Everyone will have one last
opportunity to comment on this document before it is published. (*Press Enter once.*)

Please provide your comments in writing to me no later than Friday of next week. Also, plan to attend
our next PC Standards Review Committee meeting scheduled for two weeks from today. (*Do not
press Enter.*)

XX/xx (Type your friend's initials in uppercase/type your initials in lowercase letters.)

Distribution:

Frank Carpenter

Betty Smith

Jim Victor

Finish-Up Instructions

❖ Move the mouse pointer to the placeholder below the horizontal line that contains the statement "Click here and type your memo text" and click once. Type
the memo body text as shown in Figure 1.7. Backspace to correct errors made
while typing. Remember, use word wrap and press the **Enter** key at the end of a
paragraph. Since some of the blank lines have been included in the Memo
Wizard, it is only necessary to press the **Enter** key once after the first paragraph.

Note: The lines may not end exactly as shown in Figure 1.7.

❖ Press the **right** and **down arrow** keys to locate the insertion point to the right
of your initials and press **Enter** once. Type the distribution list as shown in
Figure 1.7.

❖ Save the memorandum on your file disk; use the filename **1memowiz.doc**.
(Select the **Save** button on the Standard Toolbar; type the filename in the
File name box; if necessary, click on the down triangle beside the **Save in** box
and click on the drive letter where your file disk is located; select **Save**.) The
filename does not display in the Title bar; however, the memo is saved with
the new filename, **1memowiz**.

❖ Print one copy (select **File**, **Print**; choose **OK**).

*Note: When the memo prints, notice the graphic lines and image that were
inserted by the Memo Wizard Contemporary style (see Figure 1.7).*

Exit Microsoft Word 2000

After completing your work, the Microsoft Word 2000 program is exited and the Windows Desktop displays. Remember to always save your files before exiting the Word 2000 program.

 Steps to **Exit Word 2000**

Note: If necessary, save your file before exiting the Word 2000 program using the *Steps to Save a New File on page 17.*

1. Select **File, Exit**.

Note: If a message displays, "Do you want to save changes to . . . ?", select **Yes** to save changes, **No** to abandon changes, or **Cancel** to return to the document window.

The Next Step

Chapter Review and Activities

Self-Check Quiz

(T) F 1. Launching is the process of transferring the Word 2000 program from a hard disk to the computer's memory.

(T) F 2. Formatting is the process of determining the placement and arrangement of a document when it is printed on a page.

(T) F 3. To center a line of text, type the text, then select the **Center** button [image] on the Formatting Toolbar.

T (F) 4. To print all the text in a file, select **File, Print,** ~~Close~~. OK

T (F) 5. A document can only be saved to a floppy disk.

T (F) 6. When the scroll box is moved in the scroll bar, the insertion point moves in the document to the location where the scroll bar is moved.

7. The lead word To: in a memorandum is followed by _____.
   a. one recipient's name
   b. a name that identifies a group of individuals
   c. the word Distribution
   (d.) All of these answers are correct.

8. Press the **Enter** key to _____.
   a. begin a new paragraph
   b. end a short line
   c. Both a and b are correct.

9. In two sentences, briefly describe the purpose of the Memo Wizard.
   To creat memo's more auto

10. Briefly state two ways to return the insertion point to the top of a document.
    cntrl Hold — scroll Then click —

Enriching Language Arts Skills

Each chapter contains spelling/vocabulary words and basic rules for punctuation, capitalization, or grammar. The last *Challenge Your Skills* activity in each chapter is identified by the ➤ symbol and contains mistakes in spelling, punctuation, capitalization, and/or grammar that are to be corrected. These activities should be corrected and proofread. The only errors to be corrected on the Challenge Your Skills Activities are taken from the punctuation and Grammar rules covered in the current or prior chapters of this textbook.

Spelling/Vocabulary Words

confirmation—the act of verifying, proving, or validating.
guarantee—a promise as to the quality or durability of a product or service; warranty.
itinerary—a schedule for a trip or journey; travel plans.

Introductory Adverbs and Phrases

A comma often follows an introductory adverb or phrase, because the word or phrase provides a transition from the previous sentence. Some common introductory adverbs/phrases are: however, for example, also, consequently, and in other words.

Examples:

A decision was made yesterday to postpone the approval of the budget. Consequently, the purchase order for the new desks will be delayed.

The post office requested that we use the new extended zip code. In other words, use the current 5-digit zip code followed by the new 4-digit extension.

Activities

Activity 1.1—Create a Memorandum

1. If necessary, launch (load) the Word 2000 program (see page 12), or choose the **New Blank Document** button on the Standard Toolbar.

2. If errors are made while typing and/or a red or green wavy line displays below a word(s), use the **Backspace** key to delete the incorrect characters then type the correct word. For this chapter, ignore any errors noticed after the memo is typed.

3. Type the following memorandum using the spacing shown.

Memorandum

x 3

To: All Homeowners

x 2

From: L. T. Starkweather

x 2

Date: (Use current date)

x 2

Re: Architectural Rules and Guidelines

x 3

The revised Architectural Control Committee Rules and Guidelines booklet is available and can be picked up in the Executive office, Building E, Room 5.

x 2

Also, you will find a weed abatement policy that the Board of Directors recently adopted. Reducing fire hazards and eliminating unattractive weeds and debris are the primary purposes of the policy.

x 2

Keep both policies pertaining to the Shoreline Homes Association in your files.

x 2

LTS/xx (your initials)

---

4. Save the file on your file disk; use the filename **1guidelines.doc**. (Select the **Save** button on the Standard Toolbar; type the filename; if necessary, click in the **Save in** box and click on the drive letter where your file disk is located; select **Save**.)

5. Print one copy (select **File**, **Print**; choose **OK**). Close the document to clear the document window (select **File**, **Close** or click the **Close Window** button located on the right side of the Menu bar (the bottom x)).

Activity 1.2—Create a Memorandum Using the Memo Wizard

1. If necessary, launch (load) the Word 2000 program (see page 12).

2. Select **File**, **New**.

3. Select the **Memos** tab and double-click on **Memo Wizard**.

4. With the **Start** option selected, choose the **Next** button.

5. Use the following information to answer the Memo Wizard questions.

   a.   Check that the **Contemporary** style is selected. Choose **Next**.

    b.   Check that **Yes. Use this text** is selected and that **Interoffice Memo** displays. Select **Next**.

    c.   Check that **Date**, **From**, and **Subject** are selected. In the From box, delete any existing name and type the name of a friend.

    d.   In the Subject box, delete any existing text. Type **Faculty Evaluation** and select **Next**.

    e.   In the To box delete any existing text, and type **Selected Part-time Faculty**. Check that the Cc option is *not* selected.

    f.   Check that the option to place your distribution list on a separate page is **No**. Select **Next**.

    g.   Check that the Writer's initials and Typist's initials options are selected. Change the Writer's initials to your friend's initials (uppercase letters). Your initials should display in the Typist's initials box (lowercase letters). Select **Next**.

    h.   Check that none of the header and footer options are selected. Select **Next**.

    i.   Select the **Finish** button. Select **Help, Hide the Office Assistant**.

6. Click in the placeholder below the horizontal line and type the memo body text as follows. If errors are made while typing and/or a red or green wavy line displays below a word, use the **Backspace** key to delete the incorrect characters and type the correct word. For this chapter, ignore any errors noticed after the memo is typed.

In keeping with the policies of East Valley Junior College, each new part-time faculty member will be evaluated by the third month of the semester.

Prior to an in-class observation, a member of the administration will contact you to set up a meeting in order to review your course outline, instructional strategies, and methods. A follow-up session will take place to review the observation and discuss any recommendations.

If you have questions, please call me at extension 5388.

XX/xx (your friend's initials in uppercase/your initials in lowercase)

Distribution:

Jan Bunker

Henry Irish

Becky Pang

---

7. Save the file on your file disk; use the filename **1faculty eval.doc**. (Select the **Save** button on the Standard Toolbar; type the filename; if necessary, click in the **Save in** box and click on the drive letter where your file disk is located; select **Save**.)

8. Print one copy (select **File**, **Print**; choose **OK**). Close the document to clear the document window (select **File**, **Close**).

Activity 1.3—Create a Memorandum Using the Memo Wizard

1. If necessary, launch (load) the Word 2000 program (see page 12).

2. Select **File**, **New**.

3. Select the **Memos** tab and double-click on **Memo Wizard**.

4. With the Start option selected, choose the **Next** button.

5. Use the following information to answer the Memo Wizard questions.

    a. Check that the **Professional** style is selected. Choose **Next**.

    b. Check that **Yes. Use this text** is selected and that **Interoffice Memo** displays. Select **Next**.

    c. Check that **Date**, **From**, and **Subject** are selected. In the From box, delete any existing text and type **KTMB Transmitter Campaign Group**.

    d. In the Subject box, delete any existing text. Type **Tax Deductible Donation** and select **Next**.

    e. In the To box, delete any existing text and type **Bruce Simon**. Check that the Cc option is not selected.

    f. Check that the option to place your distribution list on a separate page is **No**. Select **Next**.

    g. Check that the **Writer's initials** and **Typist's initials** options are selected. Change the Writer's initials to **TCG** (uppercase letters). Your initials should display in the Typist's initials box (lowercase letters). Select **Next**.

    h. Check that none of the header and footer options are selected. Select **Next**.

    i. Select the **Finish** button. Select **Help**, **Hide the Office Assistant**.

6. Click in the placeholder below the horizontal line and type the memo body text as follows. In the second paragraph, type two hyphens (--) to make a dash (—). If errors are made while typing and/or a red or green wavy line displays below a word, use the **Backspace** key to delete the incorrect characters and type the correct word. For this chapter, ignore any errors noticed after the memo is typed.

Your assistance in helping KTMB lay a foundation for the future so it can continue to serve the Bay Area communities is very much needed.

A donation of $50, $100, or $200 could be made in two installments—one now and the other by March 1, 200x.

Please make checks payable to KTMB Transmitter Campaign.

7. Save the file on your file disk; use the filename **1KTMB Campaign.doc**. (Select the **Save** button on the Standard Toolbar; type the filename; if necessary, click in the **Save in** box and click on the drive letter where your file disk is located; select **Save**.)

8. Print one copy (select **File**, **Print**; choose **OK**).

9. Close the document to clear the document window (select **File**, **Close**).

Challenge Your Skills

The *Challenge Your Skills* section at the end of each chapter contains a group of activities that will reinforce your understanding of the chapter's concepts. The activities require decision-making and critical-thinking skills. The *Challenge Your Skills* activities should be completed only after completing appropriate chapter drills and activities.

Skill 1.1—Create a Memorandum

1. If necessary, launch the Word 2000 program, or select the **New** button.

2. If errors are made while typing and/or a red or green wavy line displays below a word, use the **Backspace** key to delete the incorrect characters and type the correct word. For this chapter, ignore any errors noticed after the memo is typed.

3. Send the memorandum to Renee Price from Nathan Pascal. The subject of the memorandum is Repairs at 315 Carolyn Avenue, #2. Use the current date; include writer's and typist's reference initials.

Thank you for calling Otto Newland Construction to make repairs to your rental unit. A 48 x 48 double-strength clear window was replaced in the second bedroom. Several kitchen cabinet door hinges were repaired.

The louvered window cover at the stairway was fixed by connecting each wooden slat with the main shutter spine. Also, the coaxial cable was replaced in the living room.

If you have any questions concerning the described work, please call me at 1-800-555-9292.

NP/xx

---

4. Save the file on your file disk; use the filename **1repairs.doc**.

5. Print one copy and close the document to clear the document window.

Skill 1.2—Create a Memorandum Using the Memo Wizard

1. If necessary, launch the Word 2000 program.

2. Select **File**, **New**. Select the **Memos** tab and double-click on **Memo Wizard**.

3. Select the memo style of your choice.

4. The memorandum is from Dale Guy, Bookstore Manager. Insert the appropriate initials in the Writer's initials and Typist's initials boxes.

5. Send the memorandum to All Staff. The subject of the memorandum is Adoption Forms. In the Cc box, type **Director of Academic Services**.

6. If errors are made while typing and/or a red or green wavy line displays below a word, use the **Backspace** key to delete the incorrect characters and type the correct word. For this chapter, ignore any typing errors noticed after the memo is typed.

For your convenience, we have supplied information that was submitted for your Art History course last quarter.

Please check the book title(s) and ISBN numbers for any changes you may want to make to ensure the proper textbook is ordered.

Returning your book order early will assist us in promptly processing your adoption selection.

7. Save the file on your file disk; use the filename **1adoption.doc**.

8. Print one copy and close the document to clear the document window.

●◆ Skill 1.3—Create a Memorandum Using the Memo Wizard; Language Arts

1. If necessary, launch the Word 2000 program.

2. Select **File, New**. Select the **Memos** tab and double-click on **Memo Wizard**.

3. Select a memorandum style of your choice.

4. The memorandum is from Alicia Warren. Insert the appropriate initials in the Writer's initials and Typist's initials boxes.

5. Send the memorandum to Kyle Hoffman. The subject of the memo is Itinerary.

6. While typing the following document, correct three spelling errors and one punctuation error. If errors are made while typing and/or a red or green wavy line displays below a word, use the **Backspace** key to delete the incorrect characters and type the correct word. For this chapter, ignore any typing errors noticed after the memo is typed.

Kyle, you will be staying at the Riverside Hotel when you arrive in Fort Lauderdale. The address is 735 E. Las Olas Blvd. The phone number is (305) 555-3388. The room is held on a credit card to gaurantee late arrival. The reservation confirnation number is #86522.

Our tentative Tuesday itinirary is as follows:

8:30 a.m.	Meet at hotel
9:00 a.m.	Pick up the LCD panel at rental store
9:30 a.m.	Depart for Browning Corporation
10:00 a.m.	Make presentation
11:30 a.m.	Pick up food for the working lunch
12:00 noon	Arrive at Artist's Supplies
12:30 p.m.	Working lunch with three managers
3:30 p.m.	Return rented LCD panel
4:00 p.m.	Review presentations and follow-up
5:00 p.m.	Return to hotel

Before you arrive I'll call you to confirm our tentative schedule. I look forward to working with you again!

7. Save the file on your file disk; use the filename **1itinerary**.

8. Print one copy and close the document to clear the document window.

→ Skill 1.4—Integrating Microsoft Office—Use the Memo Wizard

1. Launch the Word 2000 program by selecting the **Start** button and choosing **New Office Document**.

2. In the New Office Document dialog box, select the **Memos** tab. Double-click on the **Memo Wizard**.

3. Select a memorandum style of your choice. The memo is from Mary Ann Harris. Insert the appropriate initials in the Writer's initials and Typist's initials boxes.

4. Send the memorandum to GIS Agents. The subject of the memorandum is Purchase of Portfolios.

5. The memo is to be distributed to the following: Wayne Cleaver, Sherry Kahn, Denny Kawaski, Elizabeth Tam, and Juan Walker.

6. If errors are made while typing and/or a red or green wavy line displays below a word, use the **Backspace** key to delete the incorrect characters and type the correct word. For this chapter, ignore any errors noticed after the memo is typed.

Global Investment Services (GIS) will soon acquire the investment portfolios of Rancano Financial Consultants (RFC). RFC is a small mutual fund investment consulting firm that has experienced financial difficulty and is being liquidated.

As part of the liquidation process, GIS has agreed to purchase RFC's client investment portfolios. This will ensure that the investment programs continue without loss to the investors.

We think that the acquisition of RFC's portfolios will help us control our unit expenses, which is certainly in everyone's best interest. If you have any questions on the acquisition, please contact my assistant, Mona Waltz.

7. Save the file on your file disk; use the filename **1RFC portfolios**.

8. Print one copy and close the document to clear the document window.

Edit a Memorandum

2

- Use the Help feature
- Open a document
- Select text
- Delete text
- Insert text
- Replace text using the Overtype mode
- Save and rename a file
- Use the Undo and Redo features

Objectives and Introduction

After successfully completing this chapter, you will be able to open a previously created document; select, delete, insert, and replace text; and save a document with a new filename. You will also be able to use the Undo, Redo, and Help features.

Use the Help Feature

Word has a Help feature which provides detailed information about program topics and specific instructions for performing commands. The Help feature can be accessed at any time from the **Help** menu or from any dialog box.

The Help feature is accessed easily from the **Help** menu. When the Microsoft Word 2000 **Help** option is chosen, the Office Assistant displays. (See Figure 2.1.)

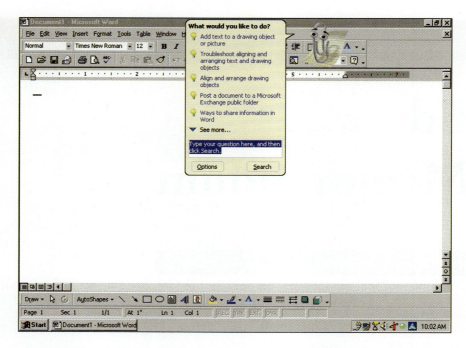

FIGURE 2.1

Microsoft Word Help Office Assistant

The Office Assistant allows you to type a question and then displays Help topics related to your question. The Office Assistant can also be accessed by selecting the **Help** menu and then choosing the **Office Assistant** option.

Help can also be accessed in a dialog box by selecting the **Help** button ?, then clicking on one of the dialog box options. Help information displays for the selected option.

To display Help information about buttons on a Toolbar or other areas of the document window, access the context-sensitive Help by selecting the **What's This?** option in the Help menu or by pressing the **Shift** and **F1** keys, then moving the mouse pointer to the item and clicking the mouse button once.

Start-Up Instructions

❖ While performing the following Steps to Access Help Using the Office Assistant instructions, a clear document screen or a document can be displaying in the document window.

Access Help Using the Office Assistant

1. Select the **Microsoft Word Help** button ? on the Standard Toolbar or click on the Help menu and choose **Show the Office Assistant.**

   Note: The Office Assistant pop-up menu displays with an area to type in your question.

2. Type your question.

   For example, type **How do I center text?**

3. Select **Search**.

   Note: A list of topics related to your question displays.

4. Select the desired option.

For example, click once on **Center text.** If necessary, click once in the Help window to display the entire Help window.

Note: The information on the selected topic displays beside the Microsoft document window.

Note: Continue with Steps to Print a Help Topic.

 ## Print a Help Topic

1. The desired Help topic should be Center text.

For example, the **Select text and graphics by using the mouse** Help topic should be displaying in the Microsoft Word Help window.

2. Select the **Print** button located in the Microsoft Word **Help** window.

Note: The Print dialog box displays.

3. Select **OK**.

 ## Hide the Office Assistant

1. Select **Help**.
2. Click on **Hide the Office Assistant**.

 ## Exit the Help Feature

1. Select the **Close** button ☒ in the Title bar of the Microsoft Word Help window.

Start-Up Instructions

❖ While performing the following Steps to . . . instructions, a clear document screen or a document can be displaying in the document window.

Note: Continue with the Steps to Access the Help Feature from a dialog box.

 ## Access the Help Feature from a Dialog Box

1. Display the desired dialog box.

For example, select the **Open** button 🖼 on the Standard Toolbar to display the Open dialog box.

2. Click on the **Help** button ? in the Title bar of the dialog box.

Note: The mouse pointer displays with a question mark.

3. Move the mouse pointer to the item where information is desired and click once.

For example, move the mouse pointer to the **Look in** box and click once.

Note: A Help box displays with information about the selected item.

4. To remove the Help box, move the mouse pointer away from the Help box and click once.

Note: The Open dialog box displays again on the screen.

Finish-Up Instructions

❖ If desired, complete any actions necessary using the options in the dialog box or select **Cancel** to return to the document window.

Start-Up Instructions

❖ While performing the following Steps to Access the Contex-Sensitive Help Feature instructions, a clear document screen or a document can be displaying in the document window.

Access the Context-Sensitive Help Feature

1. Select **Help, What's This?** or press the **Shift** and **F1** keys.

Note: A question mark is added to the mouse pointer.

2. Move the mouse pointer to the item where information is desired and click once.

For example, move the mouse pointer to the **Save** button 🖫 on the Standard Toolbar and click once.

Note: A Help box displays containing information on the Save feature.

3. To close the Help box, move the mouse pointer away from the Help box and click once.

Open a Document

Before a file can be edited, the saved document must be opened and displayed in the document window. Opening a document is the process of transferring a document file from a disk to the computer's memory. When a file is opened, the document displays in a new document window. Several files can be opened (in memory) at the same time (see Chapters 9 and 16).

The last nine files previously opened are listed at the bottom of the **File** menu. To open one of the listed files, move the mouse pointer to the filename and click once. If Word cannot locate the selected file, a message displays, "Word cannot open [path/filename]."

The contents of a file can be viewed using the Preview option in the Open dialog box. The Preview option enables you to view the contents of a file before the file is opened into a document window. The document cannot be edited in Preview, only viewed. The Preview option is accessed by selecting a filename in the **Open** dialog box and selecting the **View** button 🖳. The contents of the document display at the right in the dialog box (Figure 2.2).

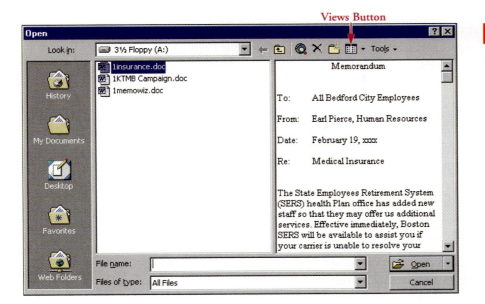

Views Button

FIGURE 2.2

Open dialog box

 Open a Document

1. Select the **Open** button 📂 on the Standard Toolbar.

   Note: The Open dialog box displays (see Figure 2.2).

2. To display the files stored on a different disk drive or folder, move the mouse pointer to the **Look in** box and click once. Move the mouse pointer to the desired disk drive or folder (directory) option and click twice.

3. Move the mouse pointer to the desired filename and click once to select the filename.

   For example, click once on the file named **1insurance.doc**.

   *Note: If the Preview option is active, the contents of the selected file displays at the right in the dialog box. If the Preview option is not active, select the **Views** button 🔲 and choose Preview. You can double-click on the filename to open the file without previewing the file's contents.*

4. Select **Open**.

   Note: The selected file displays in the document window.

Select, Delete, and Insert Text

Text can be deleted by using the **Backspace** key or the **Delete** key. When the **Backspace** key is pressed, the character or space to the *left* of the insertion point is erased. When the **Delete** key is pressed, the character or space to the *right* of the insertion point is erased. Text deleted using the **Backspace** or **Delete** keys can be returned to the screen by using the **Edit, Undo** command or the **Undo** button 🔙 on the Standard Toolbar (see Use the Undo and Redo Features, page 44).

Selected text can be erased and replaced without using either the **Delete** or **Backspace** key. Select the text to be deleted. When the first character of the new text is typed, the selected text is automatically deleted.

Text can also be selected and then deleted. Select a character, word, sentence, line, paragraph, or entire document and delete by pressing the **Delete** or **Backspace** key.

Text is inserted by placing the insertion point at the location where the new characters are to be typed and then typing the characters. As the inserted text is typed, the characters to the right of the insertion point move over and provide space for the new text. Changing text by deleting and inserting is often referred to as *editing text*.

Select Text

Using the Drag Method

➤ *To select any quantity of text,* move the mouse pointer (I-beam) to the beginning of the text to be selected; press and hold the left mouse button while dragging the mouse to highlight the desired text. Release the mouse button.

Using the Extend Selection Method

➤ *To select any quantity of text,* move the mouse pointer (I-beam) to the left of the first character to be selected and click the left mouse button once. Move the mouse pointer to the light-gray **EXT** flag in the Status bar at the bottom of the document window and double-click the left mouse button. Move the mouse pointer (I-beam) to the right of the last character to be selected and click the left mouse button once. To turn off the extend selection mode, double-click on the **EXT** flag or press the **Esc** (escape) key.

Uning the Shift and Click Method

➤ *To select any quantity of text,* move the mouse pointer (I-beam) to the left of the first character to be selected and click the left mouse button once. Move the mouse pointer (I-beam) to the right of the last character to be selected. Press and hold the **Shift** key and click the left mouse button once. Release the **Shift** key.

➤ *To select a word,* move the mouse pointer to any character in the desired word and double-click.

➤ *To select a line,* move the mouse pointer into the left margin beside the desired line until a right arrow displays; click the left mouse button once.

➤ *To select a sentence,* move the mouse pointer anywhere in the sentence, hold down the **Ctrl** key, and click once.

➤ *To select a paragraph,* move the mouse pointer to any location within the paragraph and click three times, or move the mouse pointer into the left margin beside the desired paragraph until a right arrow displays and double-click.

➤ *To select the entire document,* select **Edit, Select All,** or move the mouse pointer into the left margin until the right arrow displays and triple-click.

Using Keystrokes

➤ *To select the entire document,* press **Ctrl** and **a**.

➤ *To select any quantity of text,* place the insertion point to the left of the character at the beginning of the text to be selected. Press **F8** or hold down the **Shift** key, then use any of the following keystrokes:

➤ *To select one character to the right or left,* press the **right arrow** or **left arrow** key.

➤ *To select one line up or down,* press the **up** or **down arrow** key.

➤ *To select to the end of the line,* press the **End** key.

➤ *To select to the beginning of the line,* press the **Home** key.

➤ *To select to the beginning of the document,* press the **Ctrl** and **Home** keys.

➤ *To select to the end of the document,* press the **Ctrl** and **End** keys.

➤ *To select to the top of the previous screen,* press **Page Up**.

➤ *To select to the top of the next screen,* press **Page Down**.

➤ *To select one word to the left or right,* press **Ctrl** and the **left** or **right arrow** key.

➤ *To select one paragraph up or down,* press **Ctrl** and the **up** or **down arrow** key.

➤ *To select to the end of the sentence,* place the insertion point at the beginning of the desired text; press **F8**, then press the key corresponding to the punctuation mark at the end of the sentence.

➤ *To select to the next instance of any specific letter or number,* place the insertion point at the beginning of the desired text; press **F8**, then press the key corresponding to that letter or number (e.g., press "g" to select all characters through the next occurrence of the letter "g").

Note: *To turn off the extend selection mode, press the **Esc** key or double-click on the **EXT** flag in the Status bar.*

Turn Off Select

1. To turn off select and remove the highlight from the text, click once.

Delete Text

1. Once the desired text has been selected, press the **Delete** key.

Shortcut:

1. To delete an entire word, position the insertion point to the right of the final character in the word to be deleted and press **Ctrl** and **Backspace**.

Insert Text or Spaces

1. Place the insertion point to the left of the character or space that will follow the inserted text or space.

2. Type the text or space to be inserted.

Replace Text Using the Overtype Mode

When text is replaced using the Overtype mode, the original character(s) is deleted and new characters are substituted. For example, if the insertion point is located to the left of the character *b* in the word *band* and the character *s* is typed, the *b* is deleted and the character *s* displays on the screen, changing the word to *sand*. Replacing text using the Overtype mode is accomplished by double-clicking on the **OVR** flag in the Status bar then typing the new character(s). When the Overtype mode is turned on, the OVR flag in the Status bar darkens. The Overtype mode is turned off by double-clicking on the OVR flag again. When the Overtype mode is off, the OVR flag dims (becomes light gray) in the Status bar. Overtype is also referred to as *typeover*.

Steps to **Replace Text**

1. Place the insertion point to the left of the first character of the text to be replaced.
2. Double-click on the **OVR** flag in the Status bar.

   Note: The OVR flag in the Status bar darkens.

FIGURE 2.3

Edited memorandum

Memorandum

To: All Bedford City Employees

From: Earl Pierce, Human Resources   ——Assistant Director,

Date: February 19, 200x

Re: Medical Insurance

The State Employees Retirement System (SERS) Health Plan office has

added new staff so that they may offer us additional services. Effective

~~immediately,~~ next week Boston SERS will be available to assist you if your carrier

is unable to resolve your claim problems.

The Human Resources office staff will be available to assist you with general questions about our Health Plan System.

Please call your individual insurance carrier for answers to any questions

or information needed concerning a claim or your eligibility and for claims and eligibility questions related to your eligible dependents.

Thank you!

EP/xx (your initials)

---

3. Type the new character(s).

4. When you have finished replacing the text, double-click on the **OVR** flag again to turn (toggle) the Overtype mode off.

    Note: To restore the replaced text, see the Steps to Use the Undo and Redo Features.

Start-Up Instructions

❖ The file named **1insurance.doc** typed in Chapter 1 (Figure 1.3) should be opened and displayed in the document window. (If necessary, select the **Open** button on the Standard Toolbar; click in the **Look in** box and click on the drive letter where the file disk is located; double-click on the desired file-name.)

❖ Review the steps to select and/or delete text and the steps to replace text using the Overtype mode. Make the changes shown in Figure 2.3. (Do not change the line spacing for the memorandum body text.)

❖ Continue with the Steps to Use Save As to Rename a File.

Save and Rename a File

Once a document (file) has been edited, the changed file can be saved using a new filename. By using a different filename, the original file is not changed and the edited file is saved under a new filename. If the edited file is saved with the original filename, the original file is erased and replaced by the changed file.

Start-Up Instructions

❖ The file named **1insurance.doc** should be displayed in the document window.

Use Save As to Rename a File

1. With the document displayed in the document window, select **File, Save As**.

2. Type the new filename. (If necessary, select the drive where the file disk is located by clicking in the **Save in** box and selecting the desired disk drive option, or type the drive letter followed by a colon and the filename.)

    For example, type **2insurance revised** in the File name box. If necessary, click in the **Save in** box and select the drive where your file disk is located.

3. Select **Save**.

Finish-Up Instructions

❖ Print one copy (select **File**, **Print**; choose **OK**).

❖ If additional changes are made to the document, select the **Save** button on the Standard Toolbar to save the document and not rename it. If no changes are made to the document after printing, clear the screen (select **File**, **Close**).

Use the Undo and Redo Features

Text that has been selected and deleted with the **Delete** or **Backspace** keys can be recalled (or put back) into the document. When text is recalled, the deleted text is retrieved to the screen. Recalling text into a document on the screen is referred to as *undo*.

In addition to recalling text, the **Undo** command can reverse many editing actions. Word will undo remembered actions one at a time working from the most recent to the earliest action each time the **Edit**, **Undo** command or the **Undo** button is selected. When the arrow next to the **Undo** button is selected, a list of remembered actions displays. Selecting any one item on the list will reverse all changes back to the selected action. For example, three sentences are deleted one after the other. The Undo list is displayed and the third item is selected; all three deleted sentences will return to the document screen.

Text that has been recalled using **Undo** can be deleted again by selecting the **Edit**, **Redo** command or the **Redo** button. If the **Edit** menu is selected, the exact wording of the **Undo** and **Redo** commands will vary depending on the last action taken. For example, if text has been deleted, the **Undo** command will read **Undo Clear**. When deleted text has been restored, the **Redo** command will read **Redo Clear**.

Start-Up Instructions

❖ Select the **New** button on the Standard Toolbar. Type the paragraph shown in Figure 2.4.

❖ Select and delete the first sentence.

❖ Select and delete the last sentence.

Steps to Undo Deleted Text

1. After the text has been selected and deleted, select the **Undo** button on the Standard Toolbar.

    For example, select the left side of the **Undo** button to redisplay the last sentence in the paragraph.

    Note: The last sentence deleted returns to the screen and displays highlighted in its original location.

2. Select the **Undo** button again to reverse the next to the last action.

    For example, select the left side of the **Undo** button again to redisplay the first sentence in the paragraph.

Start-Up Instructions

❖ Click once to deselect the highlighted sentence.

❖ The paragraph previously typed from Figure 2.4 should be displayed in the document window.

FIGURE 2.4

Practice
paragraph to use
Undo and **Redo**
commands

The Association rules have been updated. The updated rules will be placed in your mailbox over the weekend. The revised rules are easy to read and comprehend.

 Steps to **Redo Deleted Text**

1. After the deleted text is reinserted, select the **Redo** button  to delete it again.

   For example, select the left side of the **Redo** button to delete the first sentence in the paragraph again.

2. Select the **Redo** button again to reverse the next previous undo action.

   For example, select the left side of the **Redo** button to delete the last sentence in the paragraph again.

Finish-Up Instructions

❖ Close but do not save the document (select **Close Window** button, **No**).

The Next Step
Chapter Review and Activities

Self-Check Quiz

T F 1. Once text has been selected and deleted from a docuent, the text cannot be recalled.

T F 2. A file can be opened by selecting the **Open** button on the Standard Toolbar, clicking in the **Look in** box and selecting the drive letter where the file disk is located, and then double-clicking on the desired filename.

T F 3. Use the **Delete** key to delete characters to the right of the insertion point.

T F 4. The **Backspace** key is used to delete characters to the left of the insertion point.

T F 5. When text is replaced, the original characters are deleted and new characters are substituted.

6. Overtype is turned on and off by _____.
   a. double-clicking on the **OVR** flag in the Status bar
   b. pressing the **up arrow** key
   c. pressing the **down arrow** key
   d. either b or c

7. To select the entire document, _____.
   a. press **Ctrl** and **a**
   b. select **View, Document**
   c. select **Edit, Document**
   d. select **Tools, Select All**

8. The Help feature can be accessed by _____.
   a. selecting **Help, Microsoft Word Help**
   b. pressing **Shift** and **F1**
   c. selecting the **Microsoft Word Help** button
   d. all of the above

9. Briefly state two ways to select a paragraph.

10. List the three steps to save and rename a file.

Enriching Language Arts Skills

Spelling/Vocabulary Words

novel—different; unusual; original.
potential—capable of being developed; not yet actual or real.
significant—having or expressing meaning; important.

Introductory (Dependent) Clauses

A comma should follow a dependent clause. (A dependent clause has both a subject and a verb, but cannot stand alone as a sentence.) An introductory dependent clause often begins with *if, in, when, since,* or *as.*

Example:

As you prepare your expense report, remember to use the updated gasoline rate schedule.

Activities

Activity 2.1—Open a File and Edit a Memorandum

1. If necessary, launch the Word program.

2. Open the file named **1guidelines.doc** that was typed in Chapter 1, page 29. (Select the **Open** button on the Standard Toolbar; if necessary, click in the **Look in** box and click on the drive letter where the file disk is located; click on the desired filename and select **Open**.) If necessary, type Activity 1.1 on page 29.

3. Make the revisions shown. (Do not change the line spacing of the body text.)

Memorandum

To: All Homeowners

From: L. T. Starkweather, Board President

Date: (current date)

Re: Architectural Rules and Guidelines

The revised Architectural Control Committee Rules and Guidelines booklet is available and can be picked up in the Executive office, Building C, Room 6A.

at the last Board meeting

Also, you will find a weed abatement policy that the Board of Directors recently adopted.

Reducing fire hazards and eliminating unattractive weeds and debris are the primary

purposes of the policy.   This policy provides a means to ensure that vacant lots are maintained in a reasonable and timely fashion.

Keep both policies pertaining to the Shoreline Homes Association in your files.

LTS/xx

---

4. Proofread and correct any errors.

5. Use the *new* filename **2guidelines rev** and save the revised file. (Select **File**, **Save As**; type the new filename; if necessary, click in the **Save in** box and click on the drive letter where your file disk is located; select **Save**.)

6. Print one copy (select **File**, **Print**; choose **OK**). Close the document to clear the document window (select **File**, **Close**).

Activity 2.2—View and Open a File; Edit a Memorandum

1. If necessary, launch the Word program.

2. Open the file named **1faculty eval.doc** that was typed in Chapter 1, page 30. (Select the **Open** button on the Standard Toolbar; if necessary, click in the Look

in box and click on the drive letter where your file disk is located; click on the desired filename and select **Open**.) If necessary, create the memo in Activity 1.2 on page 30.

3. Make the revisions shown. (Do not change the line spacing of the body text.)

Interoffice Memorandum

Date: (current date)

To: Selected Part-time Faculty

From: (type a friend's name)

RE: Faculty Evaluations

                        accordance
In ~~keeping~~ with the policies of East Valley Junior College, each new part-time faculty

member will be evaluated by the third month of the semester. *We also evaluate returning part-time faculty on a rotational basis.*

Prior to an in-class observation, a member of the administration will contact you to set up
                                                                    materials,
a meeting in order to review your course outline, instructional strategies, and methods. A

follow-up session will take place to review the observation and discuss any

recommendations.

                        regarding the evaluation process
If you have questions, please call me at extension 5388.

XX/xx (your friend's initials in uppercase/your initials in lowercase)

Distribution:

Jan Bunker

Henry Irish

Becky Pang

---

4. Proofread and correct any errors.

5. Use the *new* filename **2faculty eval rev** and save the revised file. (Select **File**, **Save As**; type the new filename; if necessary, click in the **Save in** box and click on the drive letter where your file disk is located; select **Save**.)

6. Print one copy (select **File**, **Print**; choose **OK**). Close the document to clear the document window (select **File**, **Close**).

Activity 2.3—Create and Edit a Memorandum

1. If necessary, launch the Word program or select the **New** button.

2. Type the following memorandum.

Interoffice Memorandum

To: See Distribution Below

From: Bonnie Parker

Date: (Use current date)

Re: Hours for Building Lock-up

Although the alarm system is now in place, our security program will not function well unless all employees cooperate.

The lobby doors and south employee door will be unlocked Monday through Friday from 8:30 a.m. to 5:30 p.m. These doors must remain locked at all other times.

Since the front desk will close at 5:30 p.m. every day, we request that everyone in the facility log out in the after-hours logbook.

BP/xx (your initials)

Distribution:
Kay F. King
Samuel Richardson
Tom Sweet

3. Save the file on your file disk; use the filename **2Lock-up.doc**. (Select the **Save** button on the Standard Toolbar; type the filename; if necessary, click in the **Save in** box and click on the drive letter where the file disk is located; select **Save**.)

4. Print one copy (select **File**, **Print**, **OK**).

5. Make the revisions shown. (Do not change the line spacing for the body text.)

Interoffice Memorandum

To: See Distribution Below

From: Bonnie Parker, Facilities Supervisor

Date: (Use current date)

Re: Hours for Building Lock-up

Although the alarm system is now in place, our security program will not function well unless all employees cooperate.

The lobby doors and south employee door will be unlocked Monday through Friday from 8:300 a.m. to 5:30 p.m. These doors must remain locked at all other times. If an employee exits or enters a locked door, it is their responsibility to relock the door.

Since the front desk will close at 5:30 p.m. every day, we request that everyone in the facility log out in the after-hours logbook after closing time located on the front reception desk

BP/xx (your initials)

Distribution:

Kay F. King

Samuel Richardson

Thomas Sweet

---

6. Proofread and correct any errors.

7. Use the *new* filename **2Lock-up revised** and save the revised file. (Select **File**, **Save As**; type the new filename; if necessary, click in the **Save in** box and click on the drive letter where your file disk is located; select **Save**.)

8. Print one copy (select **File**, **Print**, choose **OK**). Close the document to clear the document window (select **File**, **Close**).

Challenge Your Skills

Skill 2.1—Create and Edit a Memorandum

1. If necessary, launch the Word program or select the **New** button.

2. Create a memorandum using the following information:

    a. Send the memorandum to Robert T. Fox from Helen Loop. The subject of the memorandum is Naming the Public Facilities Building.

    b. Use the current date; include the writer's and your reference initials.

The purpose of this memorandum is to transmit a copy of the nomination form which has been received by my office. The proposed name for the downtown shelter building is Loretta K. Martinez.

Council policy #8, Naming of City-Owned Land and Facilities, requests that a nomination form be submitted to the City Clerk who then forwards the information to the appropriate commission for review.

Please contact me if you have any questions.

---

3. Save the file; use the filename **2naming.doc**.

4. Use the following information to edit the memorandum:

    a. Place a comma after Robert T. Fox's name and type his title, **Youth Commission Chair**.

    b. Place a comma after Helen Loop's name and type her title, **City Clerk**.

    c. Delete the first body text paragraph and insert the following paragraph:

        The nomination form to use the name Loretta K. Martinez for the downtown shelter building has been received in my office.

    d. Add the following sentence at the end of the second body text paragraph:

        The policy also calls for a public hearing to be held to solicit public comment on the proposal.

5. Proofread and correct any errors.

6. Use the *new* filename **2naming revised** and save the file.

7. Print one copy of the memo. Close the document.

Skill 2.2—Create and Edit a Memorandum Using the Memo Wizard

1. If necessary, launch the Word program.

2. Use the Memo Wizard and the following information to create the memorandum:

   a. The professional memorandum style should be selected.

   b. Make decisions regarding the memo heading and items to be included in the memo (e.g., Date, To, From, and Subject).

   c. The memo is from Sidney Reith. The subject of the memo is Computer Reporting System. The writer's initials and typist's initials should be included (you are the typist).

   d. The memo is to All Marketing Managers. A copy should be sent to Blanca L. Perlman, Regional Manager.

   e. No header or footer information is needed.

   f. Use the following body text.

Now that we are online and gaining proficiency with the computer reporting system, I'd like to focus on one specific aspect of the program.

Contained in the Property Status Report is a Marketing Source analysis. We need to check the information provided in the Marketing Source to ensure that this information is up to date.

If you need instructions on inputting the marketing source data, contact me.

---

   g. Use the following names and create a distribution list:

   Paul Anderson
   Bernard S. Franz
   Marielle Rockwood

3. Save the file; use the filename **2reporting.doc**.

4. Use the following information to edit the memorandum:

   a. Place a comma after Sidney Reith's name and type his title, **Marketing Manager**.

   b. In the first sentence of the second body text paragraph after the words Marketing Source, add the following words: **and Leasing Agent**.

   c. After the second body text paragraph, add a new paragraph as follows:

   Personally, I believe we should drop the lead sheets that are currently being used to track leasing sources. However, we should keep a record of this information in some form before dropping the current lead sheet method.

   d. After the words contact me in the last body text paragraph, insert the following words: **as soon as possible**.

5. Proofread and correct any errors.

6. Use the *new* filename **2reporting revised** and save the file.

7. Print one copy of the memo.

8. Optional: Fax the memo to your instructor via a local fax, or write an e-mail message to your instructor that you are sending this assignment. Attach this file to your e-mail message.

9. Close the document.

➥ Skill 2.3—Create and Edit a Memorandum; Language Arts

1. If necessary, launch the Word program or select the **New** button.

2. Use the following information to create a memorandum:

   a. Send the memorandum to Javier Silver from Scott Haslam. The subject of the memorandum is CampusLink Advertising Program.

   b. Use the current date; include your reference initials.

   c. Correct three spelling words and two punctuation errors. Remember to check for the spelling words and grammar rules discussed in both Chapters 1 and 2.

I've reviewed Fresno State's CampusLink advertising program. It looks like a novvel way to advertise. However I don't believe that it is likely to reach a signifecant number of potintial clients.

What is the total cost of the program? Does the initial cost include the artwork and setup fees?

Since our housing availability is at an all-time low now is probably not a good time to spend more money on advertising. I suggest you find out the particulars on the program costs. Perhaps when our traffic slows down, we can look at giving this program a trial run.

---

3. Save the file; use the filename **2CampusLink.doc**.

4. Use the following information to edit the memorandum:

   a. Place a comma after Scott Haslam's name and type his title, **Advertising Manager.**

   b. In the second body text paragraph after the second question, add the following:

      Is the $1,200 a one-time fee? How long does the ad run?

   c. Replace the last two sentences in the third body text paragraph with the following sentence:

      Let's get more information regarding the costs and make a decision later next month when our traffic slows down.

5. Proofread and correct any errors.

6. Use the *new* filename **2CampusLink revised** and save the file.

---

7. Print one copy.

8. Optional: Fax the memo to your instructor via a local fax, or write an e-mail message to your instructor that you are sending this assignment. Attach this file to your e-mail message.

9. Close the document.

→ Skill 2.4—Integrating Microsoft Office—Create a Memorandum

1. Select the **Start** button and choose **New Office Document**.

2. In the New Office Document dialog box, select the **Memos** tab. Double-click on the **Memo Wizard**.

3. Select a memorandum style of your choice. The memo is from Manuel Cornejo. Insert the appropriate writer's initials and typist's initials.

4. Send the memorandum to All Housing Managers. The subject of the memorandum is New Pest Control Service.

5. The memo is to be distributed to the following (alphabetize by last name): Melvin Sanchez, Sr., Kathy T. Kemp, Harvey Atkins, and Mary Ann Leong.

We have replaced Cooper Pest Control with a new company called Nevada American Exterminator. Cooper was given a 30-day notice last Friday.

The new company, Nevada American Exterminator, will begin service starting the beginning of next month. I gave our representative, Donna Valdez, your names and phone numbers, so she will probably be calling you up sometime soon.

If you have any questions, please call me.

---

6. Save the file; use the filename **2Pest.doc**.

7. Use the following information to edit the memorandum.

   a. In the first body text paragraph, delete the second sentence.

   b. In the second body text paragraph, delete the last sentence and add the following sentences:

      The company representative is Donna Valdez. I sent her a copy of your names and telephone numbers, so she will probably be calling you sometime soon in order to get better acquainted and to talk about scheduling.

   c. At the end of the third body text paragraph, add the following sentence:

      Your patience is very much appreciated!

8. Use the *new* filename **2Pest revised** and save the file.

9. Print one copy and close the document.

Create Business Letters

3

Features Covered

- Use the automatic date feature
- Change alignment
- Use bold, underline, and italic text attributes
- Change margins
- Change fonts
- Check spelling
- Display documents and text using Print Preview and Zoom
- Use the Letter Wizard

Objectives and Introduction

After successfully completing this chapter, you will be able to use the automatic date feature, change alignment, use text attributes such as bold, italic, and underline, and change margins and fonts to create attractive business letters. In addition, this chapter covers convenient features such as Spelling, Print Preview, Zoom, and the Letter Wizard, which makes preparing documents easier.

Business Letters

A letter is formal written communication used to convey information from one business to another or from one individual to another. Business letters are one of the most important types of written communication.

Traditionally, letters have followed one of two styles: a modified block or block style. With the development of word processing equipment and programs, the block style has become the most frequently used letter style. With the block style, all lines of the letter begin at the left margin (see Figure 3.1).

Another style of letter that is now being used is the AMS (Administrative Management Society) simplified letter style. The AMS simplified style omits the salutation and complimentary closing. A subject line and the typewritten signature

FIGURE 3.1

Traditional
block style letter

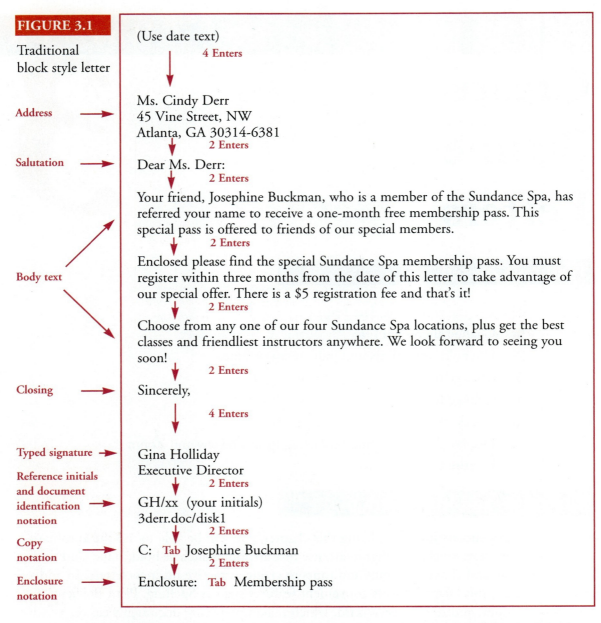

are typed in uppercase letters. Like the traditional block style, all lines of the letter begin at the left margin (blocked). See Figure 3.2.

At the bottom of a letter, the following information may be included:

➤ Reference initials identifying the author and typist. The author's initials are typed in capital letters and the typist's initials in lowercase letters, e.g., LG/xx. (The x's indicate where you type your initials.) If desired, the author's initials can be omitted and only the typist's initials used. If the author and typist are the same person, reference initials are optional.

➤ A document identification notation showing the filename and location of the document, e.g., 3derr.doc/disk1.

➤ If a photocopy of the letter is to be sent to another person(s), a copy notation is typed. A photocopy is indicated by either an uppercase or

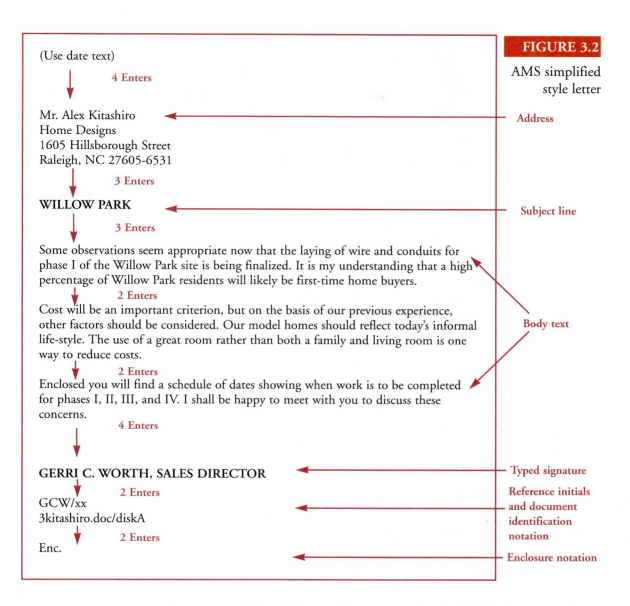

FIGURE 3.2

AMS simplified
style letter

(Use date text)

4 Enters

Mr. Alex Kitashiro — Address
Home Designs
1605 Hillsborough Street
Raleigh, NC 27605-6531

3 Enters

WILLOW PARK — Subject line

3 Enters

Some observations seem appropriate now that the laying of wire and conduits for phase I of the Willow Park site is being finalized. It is my understanding that a high percentage of Willow Park residents will likely be first-time home buyers.

2 Enters

Cost will be an important criterion, but on the basis of our previous experience, other factors should be considered. Our model homes should reflect today's informal life-style. The use of a great room rather than both a family and living room is one way to reduce costs. — Body text

2 Enters

Enclosed you will find a schedule of dates showing when work is to be completed for phases I, II, III, and IV. I shall be happy to meet with you to discuss these concerns.

4 Enters

GERRI C. WORTH, SALES DIRECTOR — Typed signature

2 Enters

GCW/xx — Reference initials and document identification notation
3kitashiro.doc/diskA

2 Enters

Enc. — Enclosure notation

lowercase c followed by a colon, e.g., c:. Press the **Tab** key once and type the name; press **Enter**. Sometimes two C's are used, e.g., Cc:.

*Note: Always press the **Tab** key before each listed name; otherwise the names may not align when fonts are changed.*

➤ If the letter contains a statement that an item(s) is being enclosed, type an enclosure notation two **Enters** below the document identification notation or two **Enters** below a copy notation, e.g., Enc., or Enclosure: Membership pass; Enclosures 2; or Enc. (2).

➤ After a business letter has been typed, formatted, reviewed, and proofread, a final copy is printed. A final letter is customarily printed on letterhead stationery. The letterhead information usually includes the company name, address, phone number, and fax number. Typically, the letterhead information is preprinted on company stationery. Today, however, many individuals who use word processing and desktop publishing programs create their own letterheads. In Chapter 13,

FIGURE 3.3

Traditional
block style
letter printed
on letterhead
stationery with
text attributes

SUNDANCE SPA

380 TWO PEACHTREE WAY
(404) 555-4822

ATLANTA, GA 30308
(404) 555-4302 (FAX)

(Use date text)

Ms. Cindy Derr
45 Vine Street, NW
Atlanta, GA 30314-6381

Dear Ms. Derr:

Your friend Josephine Buckman, who is a member of the **Sundance Spa**, has referred your name to receive a <u>one-month free</u> membership pass. This *special pass* is offered to friends of our special members.

Enclosed please find the special **Sundance Spa** membership pass. You must register within three months from the date of this letter to take advantage of our special offer. There is a $5 registration fee and that's it!

Choose from any of our four **Sundance Spa** locations, plus get the best classes and friendliest instructors anywhere. *We look forward to seeing you soon!*

Sincerely,

Gina Holliday
Executive Director

GH/xx
3derr.doc/disk1

c: Josephine Buckman

Enclosure: Membership pass

a letterhead will be created. A letter printed on company letterhead in final form will look similar to the one shown in Figure 3.3.

Use the Automatic Date Feature

Word provides two methods for automatically inserting the date into a document: the date will always remain the same or the date will be updated. In order for the current date to be inserted by Word, the date must be stored in the computer's memory. After selecting the date format in the Data and Time dialog box, the current date is placed automatically in the document by Word. If the document is opened on a different date, the date will not change unless edited manually.

If the date is to be updated, select the **Update automatically** option in the Date and Time dialog box. Then, if the document is opened and printed at a later date, the date is automatically changed to the current date.

In the Date and Time dialog box, various formats are listed for the date. For example, the day can be displayed followed by the month and year (14 July 2000).

Start-Up Instructions

❖ An empty document window should be displayed on the screen. If necessary, select the **New** button on the Standard Toolbar.

Steps to ▶ **Insert the Date as Text**

1. Select **Insert, Date and Time**.

   Note: The Date and Time dialog box displays.

2. Click once on the desired date format.

   For example, click once on the third format, which displays the month, day, and year (September 30, 2000).

3. Check that the Update automatically option is *not* selected (i.e., no check mark should display in the option box). If necessary, click on the **Update automatically** option to deselect.

4. Select **OK**.

   Note: The current date is inserted at the location of the insertion point. If necessary, the date can be changed.

Finish-Up Instructions

❖ Type the traditional block style letter shown in Figure 3.1 on page 56 using the spacing shown. If the Office Assistant displays, you may ignore it or select the **Cancel** option to remove it from the screen.

   Note: The paragraph lines may not end with the same words as shown in Figure 3.1.

❖ After typing the letter, use the filename **3derr** and save the file on your file disk. (Select the **Save** button on the Standard Toolbar; type the filename; if necessary, click in the **Save in** box and click on the drive letter where your file disk is located; select **Save**.)

❖ Print one copy (select the **Print** button).

Change Alignment

The term alignment is used to describe the relationship of text to the left and right margins. Four different types of alignment are available as buttons on the Formatting Toolbar: **Align Left**, **Center**, **Align Right**, and **Justify** (see Figure 3.4). With left alignment, text is aligned at the left margin but is not aligned at the

FIGURE 3.4

The four types of alignment

Align Left Button

This is an example of left alignment (Align Left). The text is aligned at the left margin.

Align Right Button

This is an example of right alignment (Align Right). The text is aligned at the right margin.

Align Justify Button

This is an example of justified alignment (Justify). Text begins and ends exactly at the left and right margins, except for the last line of the paragraph.

Align Center Button

This is an example of center alignment (Center). An equal amount of blank space displays to the left and right of the centered text.

right margin (ragged right). Left alignment is the default (preset) setting for Word. Right alignment is the opposite of left alignment, i.e., text is aligned at the right margin, not at the left margin (ragged left). Center alignment positions text so that an equal amount of blank space displays to the left and right of the text. Justify alignment adjusts lines to begin and end at the left and right margins.

With justify alignment, additional spaces are placed between words to align the text at both the left and right margins. The extra spaces between words may make the text difficult to read and visually unattractive. Therefore, left alignment is used for most business correspondence, and justify alignment is used primarily in narrow columns and formal documents.

Start-Up Instructions

❖ The file named **3derr.doc** should be displayed in the document window.

Steps to **Change Alignment**

1. Select the text for which alignment is to be changed. (If necessary, see Chapter 2, page 40, for information on selecting text.)

   For example, select all the paragraphs in the body text of the letter (**Ctrl** and **a**).

2. Move the mouse pointer to the Justify alignment button 📄 on the Formatting Toolbar and click once.

   Note: The lines of the body text paragraph end at the same horizontal space, i.e., the text is aligned at the right and left.

Finish-Up Instructions

❖ Click once to deselect the letter paragraphs.

❖ Use the *new* filename **3justified.doc** and save the file on your file disk (select **File**, **Save As**; type the new filename; if necessary, click in the **Save in** box and click on the drive letter where your file disk is located; select **Save**).

❖ Print one copy (select the **Print** button).

Use Text Attributes

Emphasis can be added to words by using font styles and effects such as bold, underline, and italic. Some font styles and effects can be chosen by selecting the desired font style or effect in the Font dialog box. More frequently, font styles/effects are set by using the **Bold**, **Underline**, and **Italic** buttons on the Formatting Toolbar or by using the corresponding keystrokes. More than one font style/effect can be applied to the same text characters, e.g., <u>**bold and underline**</u>. Traditionally, font styles are referred to as text attributes. (See Figure 3.3).

The bold font style prints words darker on the page as compared to other printed words. Text to be printed in bold will display darker on the screen than the other characters.

Words are underlined in printed text to show emphasis. Once the text to be printed underlined is selected and the underline feature is used, the text displays underlined in the document window. The trend, however, is to replace underlining with italic or bold to add emphasis.

The italic font style prints text somewhat slanted to the right. However, there are some dot matrix printers that do not print italicized text. Once the text to be italicized is selected and the italic attribute is applied, the text displays slightly slanted on the screen.

Other effects can also be applied to text from the Font dialog box, Select **Format**, **Font** and choose the desired effect, such as double-underline, super-script, subscript, or small capitals.

Start-Up Instructions

❖ The file named **3justified.doc** should be displayed in the document window.

Bold Text After Typing

1. Select the text to be printed in bold. (If necessary, see Chapter 2, page 40, for information on selecting text.)

   For example, select the words **Sundance Spa** in the first sentence in the first paragraph.

2. Select the **Bold** button ☐ on the Formatting Toolbar.

Bold Text While Typing

Note: The following step is for your information.

1. As you are typing, type an **asterisk** before and after the text to be bolded.

Underline Text

1. Select the text to be underlined. (If necessary, see Chapter 2, page 40, for information on selecting text.)

For example, select the words **one-month free** in the first sentence of the first paragraph.

2. Select the **Underline** button on the Formatting Toolbar.

Italicize Text

1. Select the text to be italicized. (If necessary, see Chapter 2, page 40, for information on selecting text.)

    For example, select the words **special pass** in the second sentence of the first paragraph.

2. Select the **Italic** button on the Formatting Toolbar.

Finish-Up Instructions

❖ Select the words **Sundance Spa** in the first sentence of the second paragraph and bold the text.

❖ Select the words **Sundance Spa** in the first sentence of the third paragraph and bold the text.

❖ Select the final sentence in the third paragraph and bold and italicize the text.

❖ Use the *new* filename **3bold.doc** and save the file on your file disk (select **File, Save As**; type the new filename; if necessary, click in the **Save in** box and click on the drive letter where your file disk is located; select **Save**).

❖ Continue with the Steps to Change Margins

Remove Bold, Underline, or Italic Text Attributes

Note: The following steps are for your information.

1. Select the desired text.

2. Select the **Bold, Underline,** or **Italic** buttons on the Formatting Toolbar.

Change Margins

Generally, Word's default (preset) margins are used to print a letter. If a letter is unusually short or long, however, it may be desirable to change the document's margins. Margins can be changed in the Page Setup dialog box or by using the Ruler (see Chapter 7, page 181). In this chapter, the Page Setup dialog box will be used to set margins.

The top and bottom margins are preset to 1 inch. When using a standard size 8½ x 11-inch paper and a combined top and bottom margin of 2 inches, 9 inches remain for typed lines on a page. Depending on the information preprinted in a letterhead, the top margin can vary between 2 and 3 inches. The bottom margin on an average length letter generally remains unchanged. The left and right document margins are preset for 1.25 inches. With these settings, 6 inches are available across the page.

When margins are changed using Page Setup and no text is selected, the changes affect the entire document. If text is selected before margins are changed, the changes affect only the selected text. Word identifies the text with different margins as a section (see Chapter 8).

The margins can be changed in the document at any time, i.e., before or after the document is typed. Changing the margins is best accomplished after the document is completed, because a decision can more easily be made whether margins should be changed depending on the length of the document. A letter should be printed on the page with the space around the edges of the letter evenly balanced. After a letter is typed, estimate the desired placement of the document on the page.

The number of words in the letter body text and the depth of the letterhead are used to make decisions regarding margin changes. The following are some suggested margin settings for letters:

	Top Margin	Left and Right Margins
Short letter (under 100 words*)	2.5"	2.0"
Average letter (100–200 words)	2.0"	1.25"–1.5" (Word's default margin: 1.25")
Long letter (over 200 words)	1.75"	1.0"

*See Word Count, Chapter 9, page 236.

Before printing the final letter, preview the entire document on the screen by selecting the **Print Preview** button on the Standard Toolbar (see Print Preview later in this chapter).

Start-Up Instructions

❖ The file named **3bold.doc** should be displayed in the document window.

❖ The insertion point can be located at any position in the document.

 ## Change Margins

1. Select **File, Page Setup**.

   Note: The Page Setup dialog box appears (see Figure 3.5). The Page Setup dialog box contains separate sections for changing margins, paper size, paper source, and layout. These sections are designed to look like index cards, with tabs at the top of the card. Only the options on the top card (the active card) can be accessed. To activate a card, move the mouse pointer to the desired tab and click once.

2. Choose the desired tab.

   For example, check that the **Margins** tab is selected. If necessary, move the mouse pointer to the **Margins** tab and click once.

FIGURE 3.5

Page Setup
dialog box with
Margins tab
activated

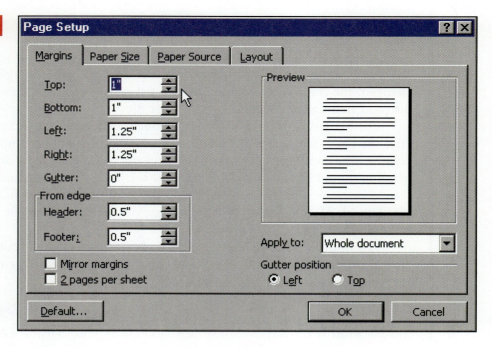

3. *To change the top margin,* if necessary, triple-click in the **Top** box to highlight the figure and type the desired margin in inches.

    For example, type **1.5**. (Do not type the last period.)

    Note: With the current margin figure highlighted in a margin box, the new amount is typed, automatically replacing the existing figure(s). If the insertion point displays in the margin box and the amount is not highlighted, delete the original amount and type the new amount. Typing a final zero or the quotation mark is unnecessary.

    To change the bottom margin, triple-click in the **Bottom** box to highlight the figure and type the desired margin in inches.

    For example, check that 1" displays.

    To change the left margin, triple-click in the **Left** box to highlight the figure and type the desired margin in inches.

    For example, type **1.5**. (Do not type the last period.)

    To change the right margin, triple-click in the Right box to highlight the figure and type the desired margin in inches.

    For example, type **1.5**. (Do not type the last period.)

4. Select **OK**.

Finish-Up Instructions

❖ Use the *new* filename **3margins.doc** and save the file on your file disk (select **File, Save As**; type the new filename; if necessary, click in the **Save in** box and click on the drive letter where your file disk is located; select **Save**).

❖ Print one copy (select the **Print** button).

Change Fonts

By using a variety of typefaces (fonts) and sizes, the appearance of letters, reports, résumés, or other business documents can be enhanced. A typeface is a specific design (shape) of type, such as Arial or Times New Roman. A font includes all the letters, numbers, symbols, and punctuation marks for a given typeface in one size and style. For example, Arial 14-point bold is one font, and Times New Roman 10-point italic is another font.

Each printer has one or more built-in fonts. Many built-in fonts, such as Courier, are monospaced and fixed-pitch (i.e., each character is allocated the same amount of horizontal space).

TrueType fonts are the most common fonts used with the Word program. These fonts are proportional and scalable (i.e., the horizontal space allocated for each character varies based on the width of the character, and the characters can be printed in almost any size).

Scalable/proportional fonts are measured in points. There are approximately 72 points in an inch. A 24-point character is approximately one-third inch tall. Generally, a 10- to 12-point font is used for the text of business letters, memorandums, and reports.

Traditionally, when using a typewriter with monospaced fonts, the Spacebar was pressed twice after a final punctuation mark. When using proportionally spaced fonts, the **Spacebar** is pressed only once after a final punctuation mark because a single space is sufficient to visually separate sentences. Also, when initials are used for both the first and middle names, such as E.R. Gilbert, the space may be omitted between the two initials. Additional information on letter and word spacing is available in Chapter 14.

Font characteristics, such as font name, font size, and appearance (bold, underline, italics), can be changed by selecting the **Font** option on the Format menu. In addition, the font name can be changed by selecting the down arrow beside the **Font** button `Times New Roman` on the Formatting Toolbar; the font size can be changed by selecting the down arrow beside the **Font Size** button `12` on the Formatting Toolbar; and the appearance of text can be changed by selecting the **Bold**, **Underline**, or **Italic** buttons on the Formatting Toolbar. When the down arrow beside the **Font** button is selected, the latest fonts used are displayed at the top of the alphabetized Font list.

Font changes take effect at the insertion point, so any text typed from that point forward in the document will reflect the different font characteristics. However, existing text before or after the insertion point will not pick up the new formatting. To apply the font changes to specific text, select the text before choosing the desired font options.

Start-Up Instructions

❖ The file named **3margins.doc** should be displayed in the document window.

 Steps to ## Change Font, Size, and/or Appearance

1. Select the text to which the new font is to be applied.

For example, select the entire document by pressing **Ctrl** and **a**.

2. Move the mouse pointer to the down arrow located beside the **Font** button `Times New Roman` on the Formatting Toolbar and click once.

   Note: A list of available fonts displays.

3. Move the mouse pointer to the desired font name and click once.

   For example, scroll down and select **Garamond** or make a decision of your own.

   Note: The text is changed to the new font.

4. With the text selected, move the mouse pointer to the down arrow beside the **Font Size** button `12` on the Formatting Toolbar and click once.

   Note: A list of available sizes displays.

5. Move the mouse pointer to the desired size and click once.

   For example, select **11**.

   Note: The text is changed to 11 point.

To Make Multiple Font Changes at One Time

6. Select the desired text.

   For example, select the enclosure notation (**Enclosure: Membership pass**).

7. Select **Format, Font**.

   Note: The Font dialog box displays containing three tabs: Font, Character Spacing, and Text Effects.

8. If necessary, select the **Font** tab.

   Note: The Font options, such as font names, font style and size, and other font effects are displayed.

9. Move the mouse pointer to the desired font size and click once.

   For example, select **10** in the Size box or make a decision of your own.

10. Move the mouse pointer to the desired text attribute in the Font style box and click once.

    For example, select **Bold Italic**.

    Note: Word displays a sample of the chosen font name, size, and appearance in the Preview box located in the lower portion of the dialog box. The displayed sample is only an approximate size and style.

11. Select **OK**.

    Note: If the nonprinting characters are turned on, a small square box displays to the left of the bolded and italicized text. This symbol indicates that a built-in heading style containing text flow format instructions has been applied. (For more information, see Chapter 10 for text flow information; see Chapter 15 for built-in styles.)

To Change Font Size Only

12. Select the desired text.

    For example, select the document identification notation (**3derr.doc/disk1**).

13. Move the mouse pointer to the down arrow located beside the **Font Size** button [11 ▾] on the Formatting Toolbar and click once.

14. Move the mouse pointer to the desired size and click once.

    For example, select **9**.

Finish-Up Instructions

❖ A letter printed on letterhead is shown in Figure 3.3. If desired, practice changing fonts, font sizes, text attributes, margins, and alignment.

❖ Use the *new* filename **3fonts.doc** and save the file on your file disk (select **File**, **Save As**; type the new filename; if necessary, click in the **Save in** box and click on the drive letter where your file disk is located; select **Save**).

❖ Print one copy (select the **Print** button). Close the document (select **File**, **Close**).

Check Spelling

When the Automatic Spell Check feature is turned on, Word checks the spelling of each word and identifies duplicate words and irregular capitalization as the document is typed. When a word is found that is not in one of Word's dictionaries, a red wavy line displays below the word. A list of words similar to the unrecognized words can be displayed by moving the mouse pointer to the marked word and clicking the *right* mouse button. One of the suggested words can be selected, or the marked word can be selected in the document window and then typed correctly. If desired, unrecognized words can be added to the dictionaries.

Word has two types of dictionaries: a main dictionary and custom dictionaries. The main dictionary is used to check the spelling of words for all documents. Custom dictionaries are created by individual users and contain terms that an individual uses frequently. For example, you might create a custom dictionary that contains terms such as Gavilan, Hollister, or Buckman. An unlimited number of custom dictionaries can be created.

The custom dictionaries are accessed by selecting the **Dictionaries** option in the Spelling & Grammar tab of the Options dialog box. To display the contents of the preset Custom Dictionary, choose the **Edit** button. The **CUSTOM.DIC** file displays. Words can be added or deleted in this file. Close and save the **CUSTOM.DIC** file.

If the same word is typed twice, the duplicated word will be marked with a red wavy line. The duplicated word can be removed by selecting **Delete Repeated Word**. To leave both occurrences of the duplicated word, **Ignore** is selected. Words that contain irregular capitalization, such as tHe or RighT, will also be marked by the Automatic Spell Check feature.

To turn the Automatic Spell Check feature on or off, select **Tools**, **Options**, choose the **Spelling & Grammar** tab, and select (or deselect) the **Check spelling as you type** option. Other options on the Spelling & Grammar tab also enable you to specify whether or not suggestions should be made when incorrectly spelled words are identified, and whether or not words typed in all uppercase letters or that begin with numbers should be checked.

If the Check spelling as you type option is not used, the document can be spell-checked by selecting the **Spelling** button on the Standard Toolbar. The Spelling dialog box displays, containing the first unrecognized word and a list of suggested words. The **Ignore**, **Ignore All**, **Add**, **Change**, and **Change All** options can be used to make corrections as needed.

Not all errors in a document are discovered when using the Automatic Spell Check feature or when the Spelling button is selected. For example, words easily misspelled or mistyped, such as there/their, form/from, she/he, are not identified as incorrect words. Therefore, once the document is checked for spelling, it should also be carefully proofread for accurate meaning.

Start-Up Instructions

Note: The icon *indicates that the data (text) is available on disk. The data disk is provided with your book.*

❖ Open the file named **3smith.doc** located on the data disk (select the **Open** button on the Standard Toolbar; if necessary, click in the **Look in** box and click on the drive letter where the data disk is located; double-click on the filename).

*Note: The Automatic Spell Check feature must be turned on to complete the following steps. If necessary, select **Tools**, **Options**, choose the **Spelling & Grammar** tab, select the **Check spelling as you type** option, and select **OK**.*

❖ Use the following steps and spell-check the file named **3smith.doc**. After spell-checking the document, be sure to proofread the document carefully for the meanings of words and sentences.

 ## Spell Check a Document

1. Move the mouse pointer to the first word marked with a red wavy line.

   For example, move the mouse pointer to the word **beeing** in the first sentence.

2. Click the *right* mouse button to display a list of suggested words (see Figure 3.6).

3. Select the correctly spelled word.

   For example, select **being**.

   Note: The green underline is also removed. (See chapter 9 for using the Grammar Check.)

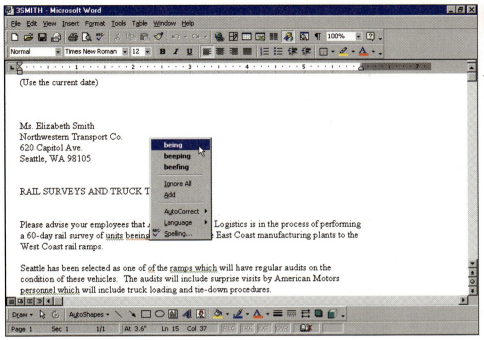

4. Continue to review the document for words marked with a red wavy line. To make corrections, move the mouse pointer to the marked word, click the *right* mouse button, and select the desired option.

   For example, move the mouse pointer to the word "of" marked with a red wavy line in the second paragraph. Click the *right* mouse button and select the **Delete Repeated Word** option.

5. If the correct spelling of a word is not on the list, other options can be selected.

   a. Select **Ignore All** to ignore the current instance of the word.

   b. Select **Add** to add the word to a custom dictionary. (The word will automatically be added to the default custom dictionary.) To choose a different custom dictionary, select **Tools**, **Options**, choose the **Spelling & Grammar** tab, select the **Custom dictionary** option, and click on the desired dictionary.

   c. To correct a word that is not found in any of Word's dictionaries, select the word in the document window and type the correctly spelled word.

      For example, select the **xx** in the reference initials and type your initials.

Finish-Up Instructions

❖ Use the *new* filename **3spell check.doc** and save the file on your file disk (select **File**, **Save As**; type the new filename; if necessary, click in the **Save in** box and click on the drive letter where your file disk is located; select **Save**).

❖ Optional: Print one copy (select the **Print** button).

Display Documents and Text Using Print Preview and Zoom

A full document page can be displayed by selecting either the **Print Preview** button on the Standard Toolbar, or by selecting **View, Full Screen**. If the Print Layout View mode is selected, a full page can also be displayed by selecting the down triangle beside the **Zoom** button and choosing the **Whole Page** option. Displaying a document page assists in making decisions on the alignment of text and the amount of blank space in the margins.

When the **Print Preview** button is selected, the Preview window displays. The Standard and Formatting Toolbars are removed from the screen and the Print Preview Toolbar displays. The Print Preview Toolbar buttons are used to change how the document is displayed and to print the document (see Figure 3.7) for a description of the Print Preview Toolbar buttons). A horizontal ruler and a vertical ruler can be displayed at the top and left of the Preview window. (If necessary, select the **View Ruler** button to display the rulers.) The horizontal and vertical rulers can be used to change the top, bottom, left, and right margins and to set paragraph indents. (For additional information, see Chapter 7, Use the Rulers to Change Margins and to Set Indents.)

When the mouse pointer is moved into the page area of the Preview window, the pointer resembles a magnifying glass. To enlarge a portion of the page so that the text can be read and edited if desired, move the mouse pointer to the desired area and click once. To return the display to a full page, click the mouse button again.

The Zoom feature has the capability of magnifying or reducing the displayed text. The percentage of magnification or reduction can be selected or

FIGURE 3.7			
		Print	Print the displayed document.
Description of Print Preview Toolbar buttons		Magnifier	Magnify a portion of the page displayed in the Print Preview window. To edit a document in the Preview window, deselect the **Magnifier** button.
		One Page	Display a single page of a multi-page document.
		Multiple Pages	Display several pages of a multi-page document.
	42%	Zoom	Enlarge or reduce the display size.
		View Ruler	Show (or hide) the horizontal and vertical rulers.
		Shrink to Fit	Reduce the font size of text so that the text will fit on fewer pages.
		Full Screen	Hide the Title bar, Menu bar, ruler bars, scroll bars, and Status bar and enlarge the page area. To return the Menu bar to the screen and reduce the page area, select the **Full Screen** button again or choose the **Close Full Screen** option in the Full Screen window
	Close	Close	Exit the Preview window.
		Help	Obtain context-sensitive help.

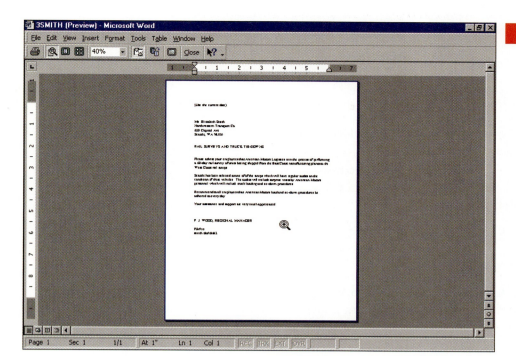

FIGURE 3.8

Print Preview
window

specified in the Zoom dialog box. The Zoom dialog box contains Zoom To options and a Preview box. Preset percentages can be selected, or specified percentages between 10% and 500% can be typed. The preset Zoom options are also available by selecting the down triangle beside the **Zoom** button on the Standard Toolbar or the Print Preview Toolbar. Also, a specific magnification or reduction percentage between 10% and 500% can be typed in the **Zoom** box.

Start-Up Instructions

❖ The file named **3spell check.doc** should be displayed in the document window.

 ## Use Print Preview

1. Select the **Print Preview** button ⬚ on the Standard Toolbar.

   Note: An entire document page containing the letter displays on the screen (see Figure 3.8).

2. To exit Preview window, select the **Close** button on the Print Preview Toolbar.

 ## Use Zoom View

1. Select **View, Zoom**.

   Note: The Zoom dialog box displays.

2. Select the desired viewing percentage from the **Zoom To** area, or double-click in the Percent box and type the desired percentage (between 10% and 500%).

   For example, point to the number in the Percent box, double-click, and type **125**.

3. Select **OK**.

Shortcut:

1. Select the down arrow beside the **Zoom** button `100%` on the Standard Toolbar or Print Preview Toolbar.

2. Select the desired percentage, or type the desired percentage in the **Zoom** box and press **Enter**.

    For example, if desired, select **75%**.

Finish-Up Instructions

❖ Close the document (select **File**, **Close**).

Start-Up Instructions

❖ Optional: Type the AMS simplified style letter shown in Figure 3.2 (select the **New** button to obtain a new document window).

❖ Review the document and check each word that is marked with a red wavy line. If a word is misspelled, make the necessary correction (move the mouse pointer to the word, click the *right* mouse button, and choose the correct spelling). Also, be sure to proofread the document. For now, ignore any word(s) marked with a green wavy line.

❖ Use the filename **3kitashiro** and save the file on your file disk (select the **Save** button; type the new filename; if necessary, click in the **Save in** box and click on the drive letter where your file disk is located; select **Save**).

❖ Print one copy (select **File**, **Print**; choose **OK**). Close the document (select **File**, **Close**).

Use the Letter Wizard

Word provides a Letter Wizard to assist in the creation of common business letters. The Letter Wizard asks questions regarding letter style, recipient's name and address, return address, type of paper the letter will be printed on, and whether an envelope or label should be created to accompany the letter.

Once the Letter Wizard's questions are answered, the Office Assistant box displays and you are given the opportunity to create an envelope or label to accompany the letter. The top portion of the letter is displayed in the document window based on the information you have provided. Placeholders are inserted at locations in the document where information is needed, for example, a company name.

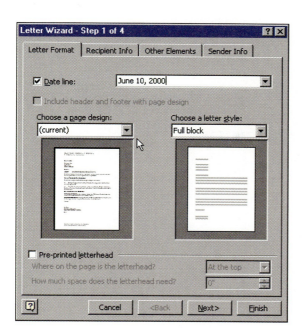

FIGURE 3.9

Letter Wizard -
Step 1 of 4
dialog box

Steps to **Use the Letter Wizard**

1. Select **File, New**.

2. If necessary, select the **Letters & Faxes** tab.

3. Double-click on **Letter Wizard**.

   Note: In a moment a sample letter and the Office Assistant display.

4. Select the **Send one letter** option in the Office Assistant box.

   Note: The Letter Wizard - Step 1 of 4 dialog box displays (see Figure 3.9).

5. Choose the desired tab.

   For example, check that the **Letter Format** tab is displayed.

6. Check and/or select the letter format options desired.

   For example,

   a. Check that the **Date line** option is selected and that the date displays in the Month, day, year format (e.g., June 10, 2000). If necessary, click on the down arrow beside the **Date line** box and select the appropriate date format.

   b. Select **Choose a page design** and select **Contemporary Letter**.

   c. Check that **Full block** displays in the **Choose a letter style** option. If necessary, select the **Choose a letter style** option and select **Full block**.

   d. Check that Pre-printed letterhead is *not* selected.

7. Select **Next**.

   Note: The Recipient Info tab information displays.

8. Enter the name, address, and salutation for the person the letter is being sent to.

For example,

    a. Click in the **Recipient's name** box and type **Ms. Leslie Huskey**. (Do not type the period.)

    b. Click in the **Delivery address** box and type the recipient's address:

       101 East Avenue
       Tucson, AZ 85716-4134

    c. Select the **Business salutation** option. Check that Dear Ms. Huskey: displays in the Salutation example box. If necessary, click in the example box and type **Dear Ms. Huskey:**.

9. Select **Next**.

    Note: The Other Elements tab information displays.

10. Choose any desired option and type the information needed.

    For example, no additional information is necessary.

11. Select **Next**.

    Note: The Sender Info tab information displays.

12. Enter the desired sender information and complimentary close.

    For example,

    a. Click in the **Sender's name** box, delete any existing name, and type your name.

    b. Click in the **Return address** box and type

       Sentinel Peak Industries
       434 Appleton Road
       Blacksburg, VA 20460-2604

    c. Check that **Sincerely,** displays in the Complimentary closing option. If necessary, choose the **Complimentary closing** option and select **Sincerely,**.

    d. In the Writer's/typist's initials box, type your initials in lowercase letters.

13. Select **Finish**.

    Note: The Office Assistant box displays.

14. To make an envelope to accompany the letter, select **Make an envelope** in the Do more with the letter? options.

    *Note: The Envelope and Labels dialog box displays containing incorrect recipient and return address information. The Envelopes tab should be selected. If necessary, click on the **Envelopes** tab. Select the **Delivery address** shown and type Leslie Huskey's name and address (see step 8a-b). In the Return address box, select the text and type the return address information shown in step 12b. The Return address omit option should be deselected*

15. Select the **Add to Document** option.

    *Note: Select **No** to not save the new return address as the default address. (For additional information on creating envelopes and labels, see Chapter 11.) The envelope displays in the document window.*

16. Select the **Next Page** button ▼ on the bottom right of the vertical scroll bar.

    Note: The top portion of the letter displays.

17. Create and modify the document as desired.

    Note: If necessary, scroll down to view the document text.

    For example:

    a. Check the delivery address and salutation. If necessary, make corrections.

    b. Select the letter paragraph and type the following body text:

       We appreciate your inquiry about our company's products and services. (Press Enter once.)

       We believe that our products and customer service reflect our goal to put the customer first. Tomorrow I will be sending you some material regarding our products and services. (Press Enter once.)

       I will contact you next week to see if you have any questions or need any additional information. (Do not press Enter.)

Finish-Up Instructions

❖ Change the top margin to 3 inches (with the insertion pointer located anywhere on the page containing the letter, select **File**, **Page Setup**, **Margins** tab, type **3** in the Top margin box and choose **OK**).

❖ Change the font size for the entire document (press **Ctrl** and **a**, choose the **Font Size** button, select **12**).

❖ Save the file using the filename **3letter wizard** (select the **Save** button; type the new filename; if necessary, click in the **Save in** box and click on the drive letter where your file disk is located; select **Save**).

❖ Print one copy (select **File**, **Print**; choose **OK**).

    Note: To print the envelope, you may need to manually insert paper into the printer. If necessary, see your instructor or instructional assistant.

❖ Close the document (select **File**, **Close**).

The Next Step

Chapter Review and Activities

Self-Check Quiz

T F 1. When a font change is made for selected text, the changed font affects only the selected text.

T F 2. When Word does not recognize the spelling of a word, a red wavy line displays below the unrecognized word.

T **F** 3. The document identification notation is typed ~~above~~ the reference initials. *Below*

T **F** 4. In the traditional letter style, the **Enter** key is pressed four times after typing the last body text paragraph. *2 times then the closing*

5. The _____ button is selected to view an entire page in the document window.
   a. **Open**
   b. **Print Preview**
   c. **Print**

6. Word's default (preset) margins are _____.
   a. 1" top and bottom, 1.25" left and right
   b. 1" left and right, 1.25" top and bottom
   c. 1" left, right, top, and bottom

7. To bold a paragraph, first select the paragraph, then select _____.
   a. **View, Bold, OK**
   b. **Insert, Bold**
   c. the **Bold** button on the Formatting Toolbar

8. List the top, left, and right margins that are suggested for an average letter (100–200 words).

9. List the four different types of alignment.
   Left   Justified
   Center

10. State one reason for using Print Preview to view a document before printing.
    To see If It is centered write

Enriching Language Arts Skills

Spelling/Vocabulary Words

deducted—to take out; subtract.
promotion—advancement; furtherance; an act or material provided on behalf of a product.
standard—anything accepted as a basis for comparison.

Appositives

Appositives are words that immediately follow a noun and further identify the noun but usually are not necessary to the meaning of the sentence. Appositives are set off by commas.

Example:

Ester Tam, a copyeditor for eight years, will be our new senior editor.

Activities

Activity 3.1—Create a Traditional Block Style Letter and Use the Bold Text Attribute

1. Launch Word or select the **New** button.

2. Type the following letter using the traditional block style letter (see Figure 3.1 on page 56).

(Use date text)

4X

Maria Ng, Director
City Services
1390 Webster Street, Suite 12
Oakland, CA 94612-8123

2X

Dear Ms. Ng:

2X

Empire is excited to send you this special preview of our Meeting and Presentation Solutions catalog. Inside you will find a wide selection of top-notch presentation products and user-friendly solutions for delivering dynamic visual and written presentations.

2X

We hope you will make Empire your main presentation products resource. We promise you low prices, same-day shipping, and armchair convenience.

We at Empire look forward to hearing from you. Order our full-line Meeting and Presentation Solutions catalog toll free by phone: 1-800-555-9292 or fax: 1-800-555-7062.

Cordially,

Efren D. Stein
Market Development Coordinator

EDS/xx
3ng.doc/d2

Enc.

---

3. Bold each occurrence of the word Empire (select the text; select the **Bold** button on the Formatting Toolbar).

4. Save the file on your file disk; use the filename **3ng.doc**. (Select the **Save** button on the Standard Toolbar; type the filename; if necessary, click in the **Save in** box and click on the drive letter where your file disk is located; select **Save**.)

5. Print one copy (select the **Print** button). Close the document (select **File**, **Close**).

Activity 3.2—Create a Traditional Block Style Letter; Use Justified Alignment; Change Margins and Font

1. Launch Word or select the **New** button.

2. Type the following letter using the traditional block style letter (see Figure 3.1 on page 56).

(Use date text)

Dr. Carol Luers, DDS
802 Old Trenton Road, Suite 4
Trenton, NJ 08690-2123

Dear Dr. Luers:

Enclosed is the letter you requested from our attorney concerning the insurance request for Jeffrey's dental work.

I have also enclosed a check for $100 to be applied to our account. We would like to resume our dental care and pay cash for all future dental work. If you need any further assistance in submitting the invoice to the previous insurance company, please call me at 555-6952.

We appreciate your patience while we get back on our feet after Edward's surgery.

Sincerely,

E. J. Pepper

EJP/xx
3luers.doc/d2

C: Farris Denny, Attorney

Enclosures: Letter from attorney
               Check for $100

3. Change the left, right, and top margins to **1.5"** (place the insertion point at any location in the document; select **File**, **Page Setup**, **Margins** tab; triple-click in the margin boxes and type the desired margins; select **OK**).

4. Change to **Justify** alignment (select all body text paragraphs, click on the **Justify** alignment button on the Formatting Toolbar).

5. Change the font to Garamond or make a choice of your own (select all the text; select the down arrow beside the **Font** button on the Formatting Toolbar; select the desired font).

6. Save the file on your file disk; use the filename **3luers.doc**. (Select the **Save** button on the Standard Toolbar; type the filename; if necessary, click in the **Save in** box and click on the drive letter where your file disk is located; select **OK**.)

7. Print one copy (select the **Print** button). Close the document (select **File**, **Close**).

Activity 3.3—Create an AMS Simplified Style Letter, Use Bold and Italic; Change Margins, and Check Spelling; Use Print Preview

1. Launch Word or select the **New** button.

2. Type the following letter using the AMS simplified style letter (see Figure 3.2 on page 57). Use the bold and italic text attributes as shown.

(Use date text)

4X

Thomas and Yolanda Roper
8432 Cedar View Drive
Jeffersonville, IN 47130-7805

3X

POST-ADOPTION REQUEST

3X

This is in response to your recent request for post-adoption services. We were unable to locate an adoption record using the information you provided.

2X

We can ask the Office of the State Registrar to research their files to determine if an adoption occurred in Indiana and use that information to continue our research. The fee for their services is $9.

2X

We can take no action on any request submitted without the fee. If you want us to continue our research, please return this letter, your original request, and the $9 fee.

4X

ARTIE FUENTES, ADOPTION SERVICES CHIEF

2X

AF/xx
3roper.doc/disk4

3. Change the left and right margins to **2"** and the top margin to **1.75"** (place the insertion point anywhere in the document; select **File**, **Page Setup**, **Margins** tab; triple-click in the margin boxes and type the desired margins; select **OK**).

4. Review the document and check each word that is marked with a red wavy line. If a word is misspelled, make the necessary correction (move the mouse pointer to the word, click the *right* mouse button, and choose the correct spelling).

5. Use the Print Preview feature to display the entire document in the document window (select the **Print Preview** button on the Standard Toolbar; select **Close**).

6. Save the file on your file disk; use the filename **3roper.doc**. (Select the **Save** button on the Standard Toolbar; type the filename; if necessary, click in the **Save in** box and click on the drive letter where your file disk is located; select **Save**.)

7. Print one copy (select the **Print** button). Close the document (select **File**, **Close**).

1. If necessary, launch Word.

2. Select **File**, **New**. On the **Letters & Faxes** tab, double-click on **Letter Wizard**. Select the **Send one letter** option in the Letter Wizard Assistant's box.

   *Note: If the Assistant's box continues to display, select the Assistant's **Close** button.*

3. On the Letter Format tab, check and/or select the following format options: **Date line**, **Contemporary Letter** page design, **Full block** style. Check that Pre-printed letterhead is *not* selected. Select **Next**.

4. On the Recipient Info tab, enter the name and address for the following person:

   Mr. Henry LoVerde (Recipient's name)
   739 Georgia Avenue SW (Delivery address)
   Knoxville, TN 37919-4483

5. Select the **Business salutation** option. Select **Next**.

6. The Other Elements tab information displays. No options should be chosen. Select **Next**.

7. On the Sender Info tab, type your name in the **Sender's name** box. Click in the **Return address** box and type:

   Brenning Software
   324 W. Natanes Road
   Stamford, CT 06904-3432

8. Check that **Sincerely,** displays in the Complimentary closing option.

9. Type your initials in lowercase letters in the Writer's/typist's initials box. Select **Finish**.

10. In the Office Assistant's box, select **Make an envelope**. Select the **Delivery address** shown and type Mr. LoVerde's name and address (see step 4). In the Return address box, select the text and type the return address information (see step 7).

11. Select the **Add to Document** option. Select **No** to not save the new return address as the default address.

12. Modify and create the document as follows:

    a. Scroll down and check the delivery address and salutation. Make any necessary corrections.

    b. Select the letter paragraph and replace it with the following text:

       Thank you for your order number 3005 for our U.S. Road Maps software package. (Press **Enter** once.)

       Your shipment has been delayed because the program is currently being updated. We will ship the updated program by the end of next week. (Press **Enter** once.)

If you wish to change your order, please let us know. We apologize for the delay and any inconvenience this may cause you. (Do not press **Enter.**)

13. Change the top margin to **3"** (with the insertion point located anywhere in the letter, select **File**, **Page Setup**, **Margins** tab; type **3** in the top margin box; select **OK**).

14. Change the font size (press **Ctrl** and **a**, choose **Font Size** button, select **11**).

15. Save the file on your file disk; use the filename **3LoVerde.doc**. (Select the **Save** button on the Standard Toolbar; type the filename; if necessary, click in the **Save in** box and click on the drive letter where your file disk is located; select **Save**.)

16. Print one copy (select the **Print** button).

17. Optional: Fax the letter to your instructor via a local fax, or write an e-mail message to your instructor that you are sending this assignment. Attach this file to your e-mail message.

18. Close the document (select **File**, **Close**).

Challenge Your Skills

Skill 3.1—Create and Edit a Traditional Block Style Letter

1. Use the traditional block style letter and the following information:

   a. Use the current date.

   b. Send the letter to Leona and Duade Navarro, PO Box 1075, Lake City, FL 32056-1075

   c. Use Dear Leona and Duade for the salutation.

   d. Make decisions regarding:

   Alignment
   Margins
   Fonts
   Use of bold, italic, and underline text attributes

   e. The letter body text follows:

   Last month a letter describing the Lions Gate project was mailed to you. It is my pleasure to update you on the recently revised plan for our project.

   Over the past two years we have worked together with the county and the environmental community to solve their concerns. As you may recall, our plan includes fifty homes, a daily fee golf course, and a 75-room overnight facility.

Please take a few moments to read over the enclosed project description. Our goal is to inform the community of this new and revised plan and to seek the support of people like yourself.

Please feel free to contact me directly at (904) 555-3878 with any questions, comments, or suggestions. We will be hosting a number of presentations for community members over the next few months.

    f.   Use an appropriate complimentary closing.

    g.   The letter is from Kristopher P. Boney, Vice President.

    h.   Include your reference initials, document identification notation, and enclosure notation.

2.   Save the file on your file disk; use the filename **3navarro** and print one copy.

3.   Use the following information to change the letter:

    a.   Add the following sentence to the end of the third body text paragraph:

        We hope that you approve of the substantial revisions that we have made, and we look forward to having your support for the project.

    b.   Delete the last sentence in the fourth paragraph beginning "We will be hosting . . ."

4.   Remember to proofread the document and check the spelling of words that are marked with a red wavy line.

5.   Use the *new* filename **3navarro revised** and save the file on your file disk.

6.   Print one copy and close the document.

Skill 3.2—Create and Edit an AMS Simplified Style Letter

1.   Use the AMS simplified style letter and the following information:

    a.   Use the current date.

    b.   Send the letter to Benjamin T. Fine, 375 Auburn Street, Howard Beach, NY 11414-3489.

    c.   The subject of the letter is PROFIT SHARING.

    d.   Make decisions regarding:

        Alignment
        Margins
        Fonts
        Use of bold, italic, and underline text attributes

    e.   The letter body text follows:

        It is a pleasure to announce that PGR Logic has once again achieved a level of financial success that will result in the payment of profit sharing for the tenth consecutive quarter. The bonus plan has been designed to pay a profit-sharing bonus based on reaching certain financial goals.

In light of the operating income achieved in our last quarter, a 6.5 percent profit-sharing bonus will be paid based on a regular employee's base salary earned during the quarter.

Additionally, the company's financial success has resulted in PGR Logic making a contribution to the 401(k) plan which will be paid in the third quarter of the year to accounts of employees who participate.

    f.   The letter is from PAULA NEWSOME, FINANCIAL DIRECTOR.

    g.   Include your reference initials and document identification notation.

2.   Use the filename **3fine** and save the file on your file disk.

3.   Use the following information to change the letter:

    a.   Insert the following paragraph above the last paragraph:

    Profit-sharing checks will be mailed to your home on the second Monday of next month. Thank you for your efforts in meeting our company goals!

4.   Remember to proofread the document and check the spelling of words that are marked with a red wavy line.

5.   Use the *new* filename **3fine revised** and save the file on your file disk.

6.   Print one copy.

7.   Optional: Fax the letter to your instructor via a local fax, or write an e-mail message to your instructor that you are sending this assignment. Attach this file to your e-mail message.

8.   Close the document.

➹ Skill 3.3—Create and Edit a Traditional Block Style Letter; Language Arts

1.   Use the traditional block style letter and the following information:

    a.   Use the current date.

    b.   Send the letter to Roslyn E. Balbino, 3112 West 21st Place, Chicago, IL 60623-7083.

    c.   Make decisions regarding:

    Appropriate salutation
    Alignment
    Margins
    Fonts
    Use of bold, italic, and underline text attributes
    Appropriate complimentary closing

    d.   Correct three spelling and two punctuation errors.

    e.   The letter body text follows:

    We hope you are enjoying your United Bank checking account.

Because you have been the recipient of our special prommotion you received six months of free checking. Now that the promotion is over, we will begin charging your account our standerd fee. There is no action required on your part; the service charge will be dedukted automatically from your basic business checking account.

For your information, the enclosed brochures contain information detailing each of our checking accounts. If you decide one of our other checking accounts would better serve your needs, please call Robert at (312) 555-6063. Robert Bradley our accounts officer, will handle all details for you.

Thank you for banking with United Bank.

  f.   Use an appropriate complimentary closing.

  g.   The letter is from Frederick Baldwin, Senior Branch Manager.

  h.   Include your reference initials, document identification notation, and enclosure notation.

2. Remember to proofread the document and check the spelling of words that are marked with a red wavy line.

3. Save the file on your file disk; use the filename **3balbino**.

4. Print one copy and close the document.

Edit and Enhance Documents

Features Covered

- Move text
- Copy text
- Find text
- Replace text automatically
- Enhance text using the Bullets, Numbering, and Indent features
- Print selected text

Objectives and Introduction

After successfully completing this chapter, you will be able to rearrange text using the Move and Copy features, search for specified text, and replace text automatically. You will also be able to create enumerated and bulleted lists using the Bullets and Numbering feature, indent paragraphs from the left margin, and print selected text.

Move Text

Moving text is the process of relocating text. For example, a paragraph in the middle of a letter can be moved to the end of the letter. Paragraphs, sentences, or lines can be moved. Generally, once text has been typed, retyping should be unnecessary.

The text to be moved must first be selected. Once the text is selected, Word provides several methods for moving the text. Two methods for moving text are described in the following Steps to Move Text Using the Cut and Paste Commands and Steps to Move Text Using the Drag and Drop Text Feature.

Start-Up Instructions

❖ ■ Open the file named **4Able.doc** located on the data disk (select the **Open** button on the Standard Toolbar; if necessary, click in the **Look in** box and click on the drive letter where the data disk is located; double-click on the filename).

❖ To display the current date at the top of the letter, click once on the existing date and press the **F9** key.

Move Text Using the Cut and Paste Commands

1. Select the desired text.

   For example, move the mouse pointer to the left of the first character in the second paragraph, press and hold the mouse button, and drag downward to select the paragraph and the following blank line.

2. Select the **Cut** button ✂ on the Standard Toolbar.

   Note: The text is deleted (cut) from the original location and placed in the Clipboard. The Clipboard is temporary memory that holds deleted or copied text.

3. Place the insertion point to the left of the first character or space that will follow the moved text.

   For example, move the insertion point to the left of the first character in the first paragraph.

4. Select the **Paste** button 📋 on the Standard Toolbar to insert the text at the new location.

   Note: The second paragraph is now the first paragraph. A copy of the moved text remains in the Clipboard (temporary memory) until replaced by other cut, deleted, or copied text or the computer is shut down.

Finish-Up Instructions

❖ Use the *new* filename **4cut and paste.doc** and save the file on your file disk (select **File, Save As**; type the filename; if necessary, click in the **Save in** box and click on the drive letter where your file disk is located; select **Save**).

❖ Print one copy (select the **Print** button). Close the document (select **File, Close**).

Start-Up Instructions

❖ 💾 Open the file named **4Able.doc** located on the data disk (select the **Open** button on the Standard Toolbar; if necessary, click in the **Look in** box and click on the drive letter where the data disk is located; double-click on the filename).

❖ To display the current date at the top of the letter, click once on the existing date and press the **F9** key.

Move Text Using the Drag and Drop Text Feature

1. Select the desired text.

For example, move the mouse pointer to the left of the first character in the second paragraph, press and hold the mouse button, and drag downward to select the paragraph and the following blank line.

2. Move the mouse pointer into the selected (highlighted) text.

3. Press and hold the left mouse button while dragging the mouse pointer and insertion point to the new location.

For example, while holding the mouse button, drag the mouse pointer and insertion point to the left of the first character in the first paragraph.

Note: An outline of a square displays at the bottom of the mouse pointer, and the insertion point is a dotted vertical line.

4. Release the mouse button.

*Note: The paragraph is moved to the new location. If the paragraph does not display at the desired location, select the **Undo** button and repeat steps 3 and 4.*

Finish-Up Instructions

❖ If desired, click the left mouse button once to deselect the text.

❖ Use the *new* filename **4move.doc** and save the file on your file disk (select **File**, **Save As**; type the filename; if necessary, click in the **Save in** box and click on the drive letter where your file disk is located; select **Save**).

❖ Print one copy (select the **Print** button). Close the document (select **File**, **Close**).

Copy Text

Copying text is the process of duplicating text. For example, a document, sentence, name, or paragraph may need to appear again on the page, in another part of the current document, or in a different document. Text can be copied from the original location and repeated in a second location. The text to be copied must first be selected. Once the text has been selected, Word provides several methods for copying text. Two methods for copying text are described in the following Steps to Copy Text Using the Copy and Paste Commands and Steps to Copy Text Using the Drag and Drop Text Feature.

Start-Up Instructions

❖ Open the file named **1insurance.doc** typed in Chapter 1, page 15 (select the **Open** button on the Standard Toolbar; if necessary, click in the **Look in** box and click on the drive letter where the file disk is located; double-click on the filename).

❖ The following steps will be used to make a copy of all the memorandum text in the file named **1insurance.doc**. Both copies will appear on the same page.

Copy Text Using the Copy and Paste Commands

1. Select the text to be copied.

   For example, select the existing text by choosing **Edit, Select All**.

2. Select the **Copy** button on the Standard Toolbar.

   Note: A copy of the selected text is placed in the Clipboard. The Clipboard is temporary memory that holds deleted or copied text.

3. Place the insertion point to the left of the first character or space that will follow the copied text.

   For example, move the insertion point to the right of your initials and press the **Enter** key three times.

4. Select the **Paste** button on the Standard Toolbar to insert the copied text into the document.

   Note: When the copied text is inserted, the insertion point is located at the end of the copied text. Use the up arrow key to move up through the document to see the original text. The text that was copied remains in the original location and a duplicate is displayed in the new location. A copy of the copied (or deleted) text also remains in the Clipboard (temporary memory) until replaced by other copied (or deleted) text or the computer is shut down.

Finish-Up Instructions

❖ Use the *new* filename **4copy and paste.doc** and save the file on your file disk (select **File, Save As**; type the filename; if necessary, click in the **Save in** box and click on the drive letter where your file disk is located; select **Save**).

❖ Print one copy (select the **Print** button). Close the document (select **File, Close**).

Start-Up Instructions

❖ Open the file named **1insurance.doc** typed in Chapter 1, page 15 (select the **Open** button on the Standard Toolbar; if necessary, click in the **Look in** box and click on the drive letter where the file disk is located; double-click on the filename).

❖ Move the insertion point to the bottom of the document (**Ctrl** and **End**) and press **Enter** three times.

❖ The following steps will be used to make a copy of all the memorandum text. Both copies will appear on the same page.

Copy Text Using the Drag and Drop Text Feature

1. Select the desired text.

For example, select the existing text by choosing **Edit, Select All**.

2. Move the mouse pointer to any location in the selected (highlighted) text.

3. Press and hold the left mouse button while dragging the mouse pointer and insertion point to the new location. Do not release the mouse button yet.

   For example, while holding the mouse button, drag the mouse pointer and insertion point to the third blank line below your initials. Do not release the mouse button yet.

   Note: An outline of a square displays at the bottom of the mouse pointer, and the insertion point is a dotted vertical line.

4. To copy text, press and hold the **Ctrl** key.

   Note: A plus (+) symbol displays in a small square below the mouse pointer. The text is no longer highlighted.

5. Release the mouse button and then release the **Ctrl** key.

   Note: The memo displays in the original location, and a duplicate displays in the new location. Use the up and down arrow keys to view the copied memo and the original memo.

Finish-Up Instructions

❖ If necessary, click the left mouse button once to deselect the text.

❖ Use the *new* filename **4copy.doc** and save the file on your file disk (select **File, Save As**; type the filename; if necessary, click in the **Save in** box and click on the drive letter where the file disk is located; select **Save**).

❖ Print one copy (select the **Print** button). Close the document (select **File, Close**).

Find Text

The Find command is used to locate a word or group of words in a document. The Find command can also be used to locate codes such as margins and justification. When the Find command is accessed, the Find and Replace dialog box displays with the Find tab selected (see Figure 4.1). Options on the Find tab are used to give Word more information on how to perform the Find operation. See Figure 4.2 for information on each Find option. Find is also referred to as search.

Start-Up Instructions

❖ ▪ Open the file named **4drill3.doc** located on the data disk (select the **Open** button on the Standard Toolbar; if necessary, click in the **Look in** box and click on the drive letter where the data disk is located; double-click on the filename).

FIGURE 4.1

Find and
Replace dialog
box with Find
tab selected

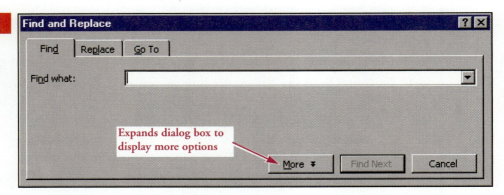

 Find Text

1. Select **Edit, Find**.

   Note: The Find and Replace dialog box displays with the Find tab selected. The insertion point is located in the Find what box (see Figure 4.1).

2. Type the word or words to be found in the Find what box.

   For example, type **SCWD** in the Find what box.

FIGURE 4.2

Options on the
Find and
Replace tabs in
the Find and
Replace dialog
box

Match case	Locates words that exactly match the case of the text typed in the Find what box. When selected on the Replace tab, text is replaced with capitalization matching that in the Replace with box rather than that of the original text.
Find whole words only	Locates the next occurrence of matching text that is a word by itself.
Use wildcards	Allows searches using wildcard characters for some letters or numbers. This is useful when words may not be spelled in exactly the same way; for example, the pattern sa?e would find sale, same, sane, and sake.
Sounds like	Allows searches for words that sound like the text in the Find what box; for example if night is typed in the Find what box and the Sound like option is selected, knight or nite would be found as matches.
Find all word forms	Finds all forms of a word, such as sit, sitting, and sat.
Search	
All	The All setting will search through all text for a match. It is the default setting whenever there is no block of text selected before the Find or Replace command is selected.
Down	Text is searched from the position of the insertion point to the end of the document.
Up	Text is searched from the position of the insertion point to the beginning of the document.
Format	A drop-down list of formatting options will appear when this button is selected. The formatting options can be used to find or replace text that has been bolded or italicized.
Special	A drop-down list of special characters will appear. Select one of these characters to add it to the text in the Find what box or the Replace with box.

3. Select the More button to expand the dialog box to display options for instructing Word on how to perform the Find operation. (See Figure 4.2 for an explanation of these options.)

   Note: If the dialog box is already expanded, a Less button displays.

4. Select the desired options below the Find what box. A check mark displays in the box next to the selected option to indicate that the option is turned on. To turn an option on or off, click once on the box next to the option.

   For example, select Find whole words only.

5. Select the desired search direction by clicking on the arrow next to the Search box and clicking once on the desired direction.

   For example, to search the entire document, check that All displays in the Search box.

6. Select the Find Next button.

   Note: The first occurrence of the specified text is highlighted in the document window. If you cannot see the highlighted text, move the mouse pointer into the Title bar of the Find and Replace dialog box, press and hold the mouse button and drag down to move the dialog box. Release the mouse button.

7. The text can be edited by moving the mouse pointer to the location in the document where editing is to occur and clicking once to activate the document window.

   a. Edit by deleting, inserting, or replacing.

      For example, move the mouse pointer to the highlighted text in the document window and click once. Type Summer County Water District.

   b. To continue to search for the next occurrence of the same text, select the Find Next button in the Find dialog box.

      For example, continue the Find process and change all occurrences of SCWD to Summer County Water District.

   Note: When Word cannot find any additional occurrences of the specified text, the message displays "Word has finished searching the document."

8. Select OK.

9. Select Cancel to remove the Find and Replace dialog box.

Finish-Up Instructions

❖ When the entire text has been searched, use the *new* filename 4Find and save the file on your file disk (select File, Save As; type the filename; if necessary, click in the Save in box and click on the drive letter where your file disk is located; select Save).

❖ Print one copy (select the Print button). Close the document (select File, Close).

Replace Text Automatically

Replacing text automatically is the process of locating and deleting specific text or codes and inserting new text or codes. The document is searched for a specific word/code or group of words/codes. Each occurrence of the specified text can be replaced automatically with new text.

When the Replace command is selected, the Find and Replace dialog box displays with the Replace tab selected (see Figure 4.3). Options on the Replace tab are used to give Word more information about the text to be replaced. The options available are the same as those in the Find dialog box, but there are slight differences in their functions. For example, if the Match case option is selected, Word replaces the text with capitalization matching the capitalization of the word(s) in the Replace with box rather than matching the capitalization of the text being replaced. See Figure 4.2 for an explanation of the options on the Replace tab.

Undo Replaced Text

Because Word replaces all occurrences of specified text rapidly, it may be necessary to undo the replaced text if words are found that should not have been changed. Select the **Cancel** button in the Find and Replace dialog box to exit and to return the insertion point to the document window. Select the **Undo** button one or more times until the desired words display in the document.

Start-Up Instructions

❖ Open the file named **4drill3.doc** located on the data disk (select the **Open** button on the Standard Toolbar; if necessary, click in the **Look in** box and click on the drive letter where the data disk is located; double-click on the filename).

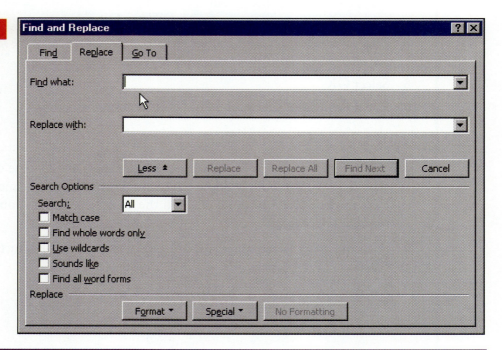

FIGURE 4.3

Expanded Find and Replace dialog box with the Replace tab selected

Replace Text Automatically

1. Select **Edit, Replace**.

   Note: The Find and Replace dialog box displays with the Replace tab selected. The insertion point is located in the Find what box (see Figure 4.3).

2. In the Find what box, type the text to be replaced.

   For example, type **SCWD** in the Find what box.

3. Click in the **Replace with** box.

4. Type the new text in the Replace with box.

   For example, type **Sam Clark Water Department**. (Do not type the period.)

5. Select the **More** button to expand the dialog box and display options for instructing Word on how to perform the Replace operation.

   *Note: If the dialog box is already expanded, a **Less** button displays.*

6. Select the desired options below the Replace with box. A check mark will display in the box next to the selected option to indicate that the option is turned on. To turn the option on or off, click once on the box next to the option.

   For example, select or check that **Find whole words only** is chosen. Select the **Match case** option. (If necessary, select the Use wildcards option to turn it off.)

7. Select the desired search direction by clicking on the arrow next to the **Search** box and clicking once on the desired direction.

   For example, make sure **All** appears in the Search box to search the entire document.

8. Select the **Replace All** button.

   Note: Word quickly replaces the specified text. The message "Word has completed its search of the document and has made [#] replacements" displays.

9. Select **OK** and **Close** to return to the document window.

Finish-Up Instructions

❖ Use the *new* filename **4replace.doc** and save the file on your file disk (select **File**, **Save As**; type the filename; if necessary, click in the **Save in** box and click on the drive letter where your file disk is located; select **Save**).

❖ Print one copy (select the **Print** button). Close the document (select **File**, **Close**).

Enhance Text Using the Bullets, Numbering, and Indent Features

Text can be indented to improve readability and to enhance the document's appearance. If the Indent feature is used, all lines of a paragraph are indented from the left margin. The first time the **Increase Indent** button is selected, the insertion point or text moves to the first preset tab and all text is indented at that position. If the **Increase Indent** button is selected a second time, the insertion point or text moves to the second preset tab. Select the **Decrease Indent** button to reduce the amount of space text is indented from the left margin.

Numbers, letters, or bullets (special characters placed to the left of a paragraph) can be inserted into a document to provide extra emphasis or to improve readability. The desired number, letter, or bullet style is chosen from a list of available styles displayed in the Bullets and Numbering dialog box. Various number styles are available, such as 1., 2., 3. or I., II., III. Uppercase and lowercase letter styles are also available, such as A., B., C. or a), b), c). Some of the bullet styles available are small or large circles (● or ●) or a diamond (♦).

Numbers, letters, or bullets can be inserted as text is typed or after the text has been typed. To insert numbers, letters, or bullet characters automatically as text is typed, the Automatic Bulleted List option must be turned on (select **Tools, AutoCorrect, AutoFormat** tab). When the **Automatic bulleted list** option is turned on, a list can be created by typing 1., A., or * (an asterisk indicating a bulleted list is to be created), pressing the **Spacebar** or **Tab** key, typing the desired text, and pressing the **Enter** key once. When the **Enter** key is pressed, Word automatically converts the text to a numbered, lettered, or bulleted list and the next number, letter, or bullet displays at the left margin. If the **Enter** key is pressed twice, the numbering, lettering, or bulleting feature is turned off.

Start-Up Instructions

❖ Open the file named **4drill4.doc** located on the data disk (select the **Open** button on the Standard Toolbar; if necessary, click in the **Look in** box and click on the drive letter where the data disk is located; double-click on the filename).

 Create Paragraphs Using the Indent Feature

1. With the paragraph(s) to be indented displayed in the document window, place the insertion point to the left of the first character of the paragraph to be indented or select the paragraphs to be indented.

   For example, select paragraphs 2–5 (beginning with The payment of . . . and ending with When replacing . . .).

2. Select the **Increase Indent** button on the Formatting Toolbar.

   Note: All lines of the selected paragraphs are indented.

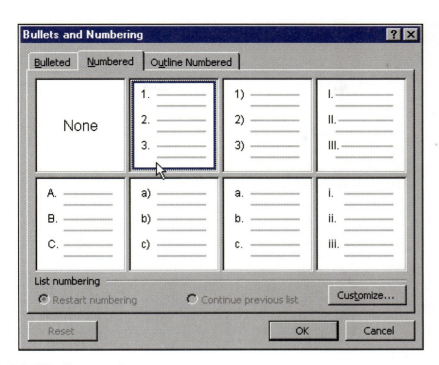

FIGURE 4.4

Bullets and
Numbering
dialog box with
the Numbered
tab selected

Finish-Up Instructions

❖ Use the *new* filename **4indented.doc** and save the file on your file disk (select **File**, **Save As**; type the filename; if necessary, click in the **Save in** box and click on the drive letter where your file disk is located; select **Save**).

❖ Print one copy (select the **Print** button). Close the document (select **File**, **Close**).

Start-Up Instructions

❖ Open the file named **4drill4.doc** located on the data disk (select the **Open** button on the Standard Toolbar; if necessary, click in the **Look in** box and click on the drive letter where the data disk is located; double-click on the filename).

Steps to **Create a Numbered or Bulleted List**

1. Select the paragraphs to be numbered or bulleted.

   For example, select paragraphs 2–5 (beginning with The payment of . . . and ending with When replacing . . .).

2. Select **Format, Bullets and Numbering**.

   Note: The Bullets and Numbering dialog box displays. A tab must be active before numbering or bullet options can be selected. The top tab is active (see Figure 4.4). The options for each bullet or numbering type are on a card designed to look like an index card in a file.

3. To activate the desired tab, move the mouse pointer to its tab and click once.

   For example, if necessary, select the **Numbered** tab.

FIGURE 4.5

Paragraphs
Numbered
Automatically

Southern Home Repair
Terms and Conditions

I have read and agree to the following terms and conditions:

1. The payment of contract will be 40% in advance and the balance due upon completion of work.

2. Operator will exercise precautions, but shall not be held responsible for any damage to plant life, roof coverings, or for damage to stucco, plaster, or other finished work adjacent to areas where work is being completed.

3. Any alteration from this contract requiring extra labor or materials shall be performed upon additional authorization and extra cost to cover the costs incurred.

4. When replacing only portions of floor covering, tile, or Sheetrock, the operator will try to match existing styles and textures where practical. However, no guarantee can be given because of fading, change in materials sizes and dye lots, or similar problems.

5. Owner agrees to carry the expense of fire and allied perils insurance for the premises where work is being performed.

_____   _____
Owner   Date

Note: The Numbered tab displays in front of the other tabs and is now the active tab. Sample cards of the various numbering formats are displayed.

4. Select the desired bullets or numbering option by moving the mouse pointer to the sample and clicking the left mouse button once.

   For example, select the numbering option to the right of None (e.g., 1., 2., 3.)

5. Select **OK**.

   Note: The selected paragraphs are numbered and remain highlighted. Your document should look similar to Figure 4.5. If items in a numbered list are moved, the items are automatically renumbered.

Finish-Up Instructions

❖ If desired, click once to deselect the numbered list.

❖ Use the *new* filename **4numbered.doc** and save the file on your file disk (select **File**, **Save As**; type the filename; if necessary, click in the **Save in** box and click on the drive letter where your file disk is located; select **Save**).

❖ Print one copy (select the **Print** button).

Shortcut:

Note: The following steps are for your information.

1. Select the text to be numbered or bulleted.

2. Select the **Bullets** button or the **Numbering** button ▦ on the Formatting Toolbar.

Note: The text will be formatted immediately with the options that were selected the last time the Bullets and Numbering dialog box was accessed.

Steps to ▶ Remove Bullets or Numbering

Note: The following steps are for your information.

1. Select the paragraph(s) from which bullets or numbers are to be removed.

2. Select the **Bullets** ▦ or **Numbering** ▦ button.

Start-Up Instructions

❖ The file named **4numbered.doc** should be displayed in the document window.

Steps to ▶ Create a Bulleted List and Customize the Bullet Character

1. Select the paragraphs to be bulleted.

   For example, select the paragraphs that are currently numbered.

   Note: When the numbered or bulleted list is selected, the number or bullet character will not be highlighted. That's OK.

2. Select **Format, Bullets and Numbering**.

3. Check that the **Bulleted** tab is selected. (If necessary, move the mouse pointer to the **Bulleted** tab and click once.)

4. Select the **Customize** button.

   Note: The Customize Bulleted List dialog box displays.

5. Select the **Bullet** button.

   Note: The Symbol dialog box displays.

6. Click on the down triangle located to the right of the **Font** box.

   Note: A list of fonts displays.

7. Click on the desired font name.

   For example, scroll down the list of fonts until **Wingdings** displays. Click on **Wingdings**.

8. Click on the desired symbol.

   For example, click on any symbol. Notice that when you click on a symbol, the symbol is enlarged. Continue to click on symbols until you find a symbol that you like.

9. Select **OK** to exit the Symbols dialog box.

10. Select **OK** to exit the Customize Bulleted List dialog box and return to the document window.

Finish-Up Instructions

❖ If desired, click once to deselect the bulleted list.

❖ Use the *new* filename **4bulleted list.doc** and save the file on your file disk (select **File, Save As**; type the filename; if necessary, click in the **Save in** box and click on the drive letter where your file disk is located; select **Save**).

❖ Print one copy (select the **Print** button). Close the document (select **File, Close**).

Start-Up Instructions

❖ Select the **New** button to display an empty document window.

❖ Type the following: **A List of My Favorite Things** and press the **Enter** key twice.

Create a Numbered or Bulleted List As Text Is Typed

1. Type the number or letter followed by a period, or type an asterisk to indicate that a bulleted list is to be created.

   For example, type * (an asterisk).

2. Press the **Tab** key once and type the first item in the list.

   For example, press the **Tab** key and type the name of one of your favorite things.

3. Press the **Enter** key once.

   Note: When the Enter key is pressed, the asterisk is converted to a bullet character, and the text following the bullet character is indented.

4. Continue to type the items that should be numbered, lettered, or bulleted. Press the **Enter** key once between each item.

   For example, create a list of your five favorite things.

5. To end the numbered, lettered, or bulleted list, press the **Enter** key twice.

Finish-Up Instructions

❖ Use the filename **4favorites.doc** and save the file on your file disk (select the **Save** button; if necessary, click in the **Save in** box and click on the drive letter where your file disk is located; select **Save**).

❖ Print one copy (select the **Print** button).

❖ Close the document (select **File, Close**).

Print Selected Text

Once a document has been typed, only part of the text can be printed if desired. For example, a single paragraph from a document containing several paragraphs can be printed. First, the portion of text to be printed is selected. Then the **File**, **Print** command is selected and the **Selection** option is chosen. The selected text prints beginning at the top of the sheet of paper.

Start-Up Instructions

❖ Open the file named **4numbered.doc** located on your file disk (select the **Open** button on the Standard Toolbar; if necessary, click in the **Look in** box and click on the drive letter where your file disk is located; double-click on the filename).

 Print Selected Text

1. Select the text to be printed.

   For example, select all the numbered paragraphs.

2. Select **File**, **Print**.

3. Choose the **Selection** option in the Print range area.

   Note: A black dot displays beside the Selection option.

4. Select **OK** to print the selected text.

Finish-Up Instructions

❖ Close the document (select **File**, **Close**).

The Next Step

Chapter Review and Activities

Self-Check Quiz

(T) **F** 1. The Find command is used to locate a word or group of words in a document.

T (F) 2. Moving text is the process of duplicating text.

(T) **F** 3. Before text can be copied or moved, the text is selected.

T F 4. To begin the Replace function, select **Edit**, **Replace**.

T F 5. A single paragraph from a document containing multiple paragraphs cannot be selected and printed.

6. Bullet characters can be inserted to the left of selected paragraphs by choosing _____.
   a. **Format, Bullets and Numbering**
   b. **Tools, Bullets**
   c. **Edit, Bullets and Numbering**

7. When using the drag and drop method to move text, _____.
   a. the text must be selected
   b. a mouse must be used
   c. keystrokes can be used
   d. both a and b

8. When the **Increase Indent** button is selected, _____.
   a. the text is indented from both the left and right margins
   b. a bullet character is inserted at the left of the selected paragraphs
   c. all text is indented from the left margin

9. Which option in the Replace dialog box should be selected in order to instruct Word to find only the whole word(s) typed in the Find what box?

10. What is the difference between selecting **Format**, **Bullets and Numbering** and selecting the **Bullets** button on the Formatting Toolbar?

Enriching Language Arts Skills

Spelling/Vocabulary Words

atrium—an open central area; a courtyard.
obstacle—something that stands in the way or holds up progress toward a goal.
punctuality—acting or arriving at a specified time; prompt.
stressful—something that is subject to pressure or strain; a mentally or emotionally disruptive effect.

Compound Adjectives and Coordinating Conjunctions

Hyphenate two words that precede and describe a noun and function as a single adjective.

Example:

Senior management will be in a high-level conference all day Thursday.

A comma is placed before a coordinating conjunction (e.g., and, or, but) that joins two independent clauses (i.e., clauses that are complete sentences). No comma is placed before a coordinating conjunction if one or both clauses are dependent.

Examples:

We will respond promptly to the questionnaire, but we cannot complete the information within the five working days allowed. (Two independent clauses.)

We mailed a final request Friday and await a response. (One independent and one dependent clause.)

Activities

Activity 4.1—Create a Numbered List and Move Text

1. Launch Word or select the **New** button.

2. Type the following paragraphs using the spacing shown.

   Note: *Type two hyphens (--) to make a dash (—).*

Microsoft Word 2000 Features

Shortcut Menus—provide instant access to many features. Shortcut menus appear when you click the *right* mouse button on text, an object, or screen element such as a Toolbar.

Automatic Spell Checking—Word checks your spelling as you type. A red wavy line displays below words that are not recognized by Word's dictionaries.

DrawingToolbar—contains buttons that allow you to create graphics right in Word.

Wizards—with Wizards, you answer a few questions and Word sets up the basic format and layout of common documents. Some Wizards, such as the Letter Wizard, also provide prewritten text for documents.

Automatic Grammar Checking—as you type, Word automatically checks your document for grammatical errors. A green wavy line displays below possible grammar errors. An explanation of the possible error and suggestions on correcting the error can be obtained by clicking the *right* mouse button and choosing the Grammar option.

---

3. Number all paragraphs except the title using standard numbers (1., 2., 3., etc.) (select all paragraphs to be numbered, select **Format, Bullets and Numbering**, select the **Numbered** tab, select the **1., 2., 3.,** numbering style sample, select **OK**).

4. Remember to proofread the document and check the spelling of words that are marked with a red wavy line.

5. Save the file on your file disk; use the filename **4Word Features.doc** (select the **Save** button; type the filename; if necessary, click in the **Save in** box and click on the drive letter where your file disk is located; select **Save**).

---

6. Print one copy (select the **Print** button).

7. Move the items as shown.

   *Note: To remove unwanted bullets or numbers, place the insertion point to the right of the bullet character or number and select the **Bullets** or **Numbering** button.*

Microsoft Word 2000 Features

1. Shortcut Menus—provide instant access to many features. Shortcut menus appear when you click the *right* mouse button on text, an object, or screen element such as a Toolbar.

2. Automatic Spell Checking—Word checks your spelling as you type. A red wavy line displays below words that are not recognized by Word's dictionaries.

3. DrawingToolbar—contains buttons that allow you to create graphics right in Word.

4. Wizards—with Wizards, you answer a few questions and Word sets up the basic format and layout of common documents. Some Wizards, such as the Letter Wizard, also provide prewritten text for documents.

5. Automatic Grammar Checking—as you type, Word automatically checks your document for grammatical errors. A green wavy line displays below possible grammar errors. An explanation of the possible error and suggestions on correcting the error can be obtained by clicking the *right* mouse button and choosing the Grammar option.

---

8. Use the *new* filename **4Word Features rev.doc** and save the file on your file disk (select **File**, **Save As**; type the filename; if necessary, click in the **Save in** box and click on the drive letter where your file disk is located; select **Save**).

9. Print one copy (select the **Print** button).

10. Close the document (select **File**, **Close**).

Activity 4.2—Create a Bulleted List and Replace Text Automatically

1. Launch Word or select the **New** button.

2. Type the following memorandum.

Interoffice Memorandum

X 3

To: Branch Managers
        x2

From: Elliott Austin
        x0

Date: (Use current date)

                    × 2

Re: Floor Management Standards

                         × 3

Floor managing means the swift acknowledgment of all clients who enter a branch. No customer should feel ignored, neglected, or slighted. There should always be a designated Floor Manager for every day and hour of business.

                    × 2

The standards for the FM are:

                    × 2

The FM is the person designated to be in charge of quickly moving our clients to a point of service.

                    × 2

The FM is noted on the branch schedule. The designated FM does not wait in the lobby for customer traffic, but is responsible for responding to lobby traffic.

                    × 2

The lobby must be managed by the FM. The FM completes customer paperwork, answers questions, troubleshoots, and directs clients while keeping an eye on the lobby.

                    × 2

Our clients will never wait longer than five minutes to be acknowledged.

                    × 2

Please post these FM standards in the employee's work area so that our goals and standards will be a part of your everyday bank operations.

                    × 2

EA/xx
4Austin memo/disk4

---

3. Select the first four paragraphs below the paragraph that begins, "**The standards for . . .**" and create a bulleted list (select **Format, Bullets and Numbering**; select the **Bulleted** tab; select the **Star** style or make a choice of your own; select **OK**). Click once to deselect the list.

4. Remember to proofread the document and check the spelling of words that are marked with a red wavy line.

5. Save the file on your file disk; use the filename **4Austin memo.doc** (select the **Save** button; type the filename; if necessary, click in the **Save in** box and click on the drive letter where the file disk is located; select **Save**).

6. Print one copy (select the **Print** button).

7. Replace all occurrences of **FM** with **Floor Manager** (place the insertion point at the top of the document; select **Edit, Replace**; type **FM** in the Find what box; type **Floor Manager** in the Replace with box; if necessary, select the **More** button to expand the dialog box; if necessary, select **Find whole words only** and **Match case**; select **Replace All**).

8. Use the *new* filename **4Austin memo rev.doc** and save the file on your file disk (select **File**, **Save As**; type the filename; if necessary, click in the **Save in** box and click on the drive letter where your file disk is located; select **Save**).

9. Print one copy (select the **Print** button).

10. Close the document (select **File**, **Close**).

Activity 4.3—Copy, Edit, and Print Selected Text

1. Open the file named **4numbered.doc**, or type the document shown on page 98 (Figure 4.5).

2. Change the numbered list to a bulleted list (select the numbered items, select **Format**, **Bullets and Numbering**, select the **Bulleted** tab, select the **Diamond** style bullet or make a choice of your own; select **OK**). Click once to deselect the list.

3. Add three **Enters** at the bottom of the document.

4. Select the entire document (press **Ctrl** and **a**).

5. Copy the entire document by selecting the **Copy** button.

6. Press **Ctrl** and **End** to place the insertion point in the blank line at the bottom of the document.

7. Select the **Paste** button to insert a copy of the document.

8. Make the following changes to the pasted copy. (Do not change the line spacing.)

Southern Home Repair
Terms and Conditions

I have read and agree to the following terms and conditions:

45%
◆ The payment of contract will be ~~40%~~ in advance and the balance due upon completion of work.

paint, wallpaper,
◆ Operator will exercise precautions, but shall not be held responsible for any damage to plant life, roof coverings, ~~or for damage to~~ stucco, plaster, or other finished work adjacent to areas where work is being completed.

◆ Any alteration from this contract requiring extra labor or materials shall be performed upon additional authorization and extra cost to cover the costs incurred.

If during the course of the work additional damage is discovered, a supplemental bid will be given.

◆ When replacing only portions of floor covering, tile, or Sheetrock, the operator will try to match existing styles and textures where practical. However, no guarantee can be given because of fading, change in materials sizes and dye lots, or similar problems.

◆ Owner agrees to carry the expense of fire and allied perils insurance for the premises where work is being performed.

¶ All materials and labor are guaranteed for one year from the date of completion.

_____   _____
Owner   Date

9. Change the bottom margin to .75". (Select **File**, **Page Setup**. On the **Margins**, tab, triple-click in the Bottom box, type .75, and select **OK**.)

10. Use the *new* filename **4terms.doc** and save the file on your file disk (select **File**, **Save As**; type the filename; if necessary, click in the **Save in** box and click on the drive letter where your file disk is located; select **Save**).

11. Select the edited copy and print one copy (select **File**, **Print**; choose the **Selection** option and select **OK**).

12. Close the document (select **File**, **Close**).

Activity 4.4—Create Paragraphs Using the Indent Feature

1. Launch Word or select the **New** button.

2. Use the traditional block style and type the following letter.

(Use the current date)

Johnnie Wallace
845 Main Street, Apt. 5
Harrisonburg, VA 22807

Dear Johnnie:

You are invited to celebrate a special sales event at your favorite store! Join us at the Hi-Tech Clothing store for our special three-day sale, next Tuesday, Wednesday, and Thursday.

You will save an extra 10% on all men's, women's, and children's apparel, footwear and accessories, and more.

You will receive the lowest monthly payments of any major retailer. Our credit terms make your shopping a pleasure! When you make any purchase of $400 or more, you'll receive our low monthly payment. In addition, you will receive a free set of freshwater pearls.

So come on in and enjoy unbeatable savings, selections, and value. We also have some extra savings certificates to give you when you come to the children's department.

Sincerely,

Geoffrey T. Pears
Credit Department Vice President

GTP/xx
4Wallace letter.doc/diskP

3. Use the **Increase Indent** button to indent the second and third body text paragraphs .5" from the left margin (select the second and third paragraphs; select the **Increase Indent** button).

4. Save the file on your file disk; use the filename **4Wallace letter.doc** (select the **Save** button; type the filename; if necessary, click in the **Save in** box and click on the drive letter where your file disk is located; select **Save**).

5. Remember to proofread the document and check the spelling of words that are marked with a red wavy line.

6. Print one copy (select the **Print** button).

7. Close the document (select **File**, **Close**).

Challenge Your Skills

Skill 4.1—Create a Numbered List; Move and Edit Text

1. Use the following information to create a memorandum:

   a. Send the memo to Sales Associates from Carole Pemberton, Division Manager.

   b. Use the current date.

   c. The subject of the memo is Current Sales Promotion.

   d. Send copies to J. Laucella and G. Hurst.

   e. The unformatted memorandum body text follows:

Enclosed are photographs to assist in building your current sales promotion displays.

Please note the following:

Apricotlites have been discontinued and CherryWiz quantities reduced in order to incorporate Supreme Chocolates and expand on the successful Coconut Minis. CherryWiz should be placed next to snack crackers for a common price point. Supreme Chocolates should be placed in the space previously occupied by CherryWiz.

Order quantities will be communicated through the central ordering office and will be processed automatically. Sales representatives will not key in any orders.

Orders reflect only the quantities necessary to build displays. Make plans early to order refill quantities when necessary.

Stores will require extra service calls during this promotion. Let your stores know when you will be visiting their sites.

Announcement to the stores of this promotion has already been distributed. Orders will now be processed electronically. The new electronic order processing will ensure accurate and timely delivery of products.

Remember—proper point of sale, displays, and shelf!

    f.   Include the author's and typist's reference initials, e.g., CP/xx.

2. Select and number the third, fourth, fifth, and sixth body text paragraphs.

3. Remember to proofread the document and check the spelling of words that are marked with a red wavy line.

4. Use the filename **4Sales Promo.doc** and save the file on your file disk.

5. Move items 3 and 4 above item number 2.

6. Delete the last paragraph and insert the following two paragraphs:

> Advise stores now of their upcoming shipment and make plans to build displays. Stores resisting this promotion should be advised to call Edna Meyer or T. J. Brackbill (department buyers) at 555-8811.
>
> LET'S SELL SOME PRODUCTS!

7. Use the *new* filename **4Sales Promo rev.doc** and save the file on your file disk.

8. Print one copy and close the document.

Skill 4.2—Copy and Edit Text

1. Type the following announcement text.

Join us for the first meeting of the newly created social planning committee

The Fun Ones.

Working together for sharing good times with fabulous people.

All employees are welcome!

January 10, 200x
Red Lobster Restaurant

Please RSVP to Berry Tighe, Ext. 8935

---

2. Make decisions regarding:

   Centering
   Bolding
   Fonts and point sizes
   Hint: Use one font and point sizes between 14 and 18.

3. Remember to proofread the document and check the spelling of words that are marked with a red wavy line.

4. Use the filename **4announcement.doc** and save the file on your file disk.

5. Print one copy.

6. Place approximately 5–7 **Enters** after the last line of text.

7. Select and copy the announcement. Place the insertion point at the bottom of the document (**Ctrl** and **End**) and paste a copy of the announcement.

   Hint: There will be two copies of the announcement on one page.

8. Save the file again using the same filename, **4announcement.doc**.

9. Print one copy and close the document.

◦◦ Skill 4.3—Replace Text Automatically; Language Arts

1. Use the traditional block style letter and the following information:

   a. Change both the left and right margins to 1" and the top margin to 1.5".

   b. Use the current date.

   c. Send the letter to The Honorable Ruth Ann Hesselbein, United States Congresswoman, P.O. Box 6922, Flint, MI 48508-6922.

<ol type="a" start="4">
<li>The letter is from Alexis H. Parshall, Executive Director.</li>
<li>Include appropriate reference initials and document identification.</li>
<li>Correct three spelling errors and three punctuation errors.</li>
</ol>

Dear Congresswoman Hesselbein:

Thank you for accepting the invitation to serve as our special guest speaker for the STC graduation. The ceremony will take place in the atriem of the community services building at 610 Lawrence Road in Montrose.

The STC is graduating a class of 25 participants, all of which are women. Some of them have gone through extremely stressfull life experiences, including family deaths, financial hardships, homelessness, and illness. However they have overcome these and other obstacles. The students have come a long way and I am proud of each of them.

The STC class has been in session for five months, and the students have earned up to 16 college-level credits. The classes met for seven hours a day with homework assigned each night and heavy emphasis on attendance, punctuallity, and professionalism.

Many of the women have verbalized their fears about venturing into the workforce, as well as their excitement about starting a new career. I know they will consider themselves fortunate to have their Congresswoman speak to them.

I appreciate that you are taking time from your busy schedule to speak at the STC graduation ceremony. If you have any questions please feel free to contact me.

Very truly yours,

<ol start="2">
<li>Use the filename **4Hesselbein.doc** and save the file on your file disk.</li>
<li>Automatically replace all occurrences of **STC** with **Skills Training Center**.
*Hint: Remember to select the **Match case** option.*</li>
<li>Save the file again using the same filename, **4Hesselbein.doc**.</li>
<li>Print one copy.</li>
<li>Close the document.</li>
</ol>

→ Skill 4.4—Integrating the Microsoft Office/Use the Letter Wizard

<ol>
<li>Select the **Start** button and choose the **New Office Document** option.</li>
<li>Select the **Letters & Faxes** tab and double-click on **Letter Wizard**.</li>
<li>Use the following information to create the letter.
<ol type="a">
<li>Select the **Send one letter** option.</li>
<li>Click in the **Choose a page design** box and select the **Contemporary Letter** option.</li>
</ol>
</li>
</ol>

---

c. **Full block** should display in the Choose a letter style box.

d. Send the letter to Mr. Vincent Elder, Jr., 4622 S. Maryland Parkway, Las Vegas, NV 89154-3301.

e. Select the **Business salutation** option.

f. The sender's name is Kirsten Fuenes. Omit the return address.

g. Ms. Fuenes's title is Marketing Executive. The company name is United Visa, Ltd.

h. Select an appropriate complimentary closing.

i. Include the writer's initials (KF) and typist's initials (your initials and one enclosure).

4. Select the text in the paragraph following the salutation and type body text as follows:

The road to financial success has many milestones. You have just reached one such milestone.

During this limited-time offer, you have been pre-approved for a United Visa card with free membership for one year.

Congratulations on reaching this very special milestone. Fill out the enclosed, pre-approved form and mail it today! I very much look forward to welcoming you as a card member.

5. Include the document identification, 4Elder offer/diskV.

   Hint: If necessary, delete any extra blank lines at the end of the document.

6. Use the filename **4Elder offer.doc** and save the file on your file disk.

7. Print one copy.

8. Optional: Fax the letter to your instructor via a local fax, or write an e-mail message to your instructor that you are sending this assignment. Attach this file to your e-mail message.

Part 1
Checking Your Step

Production Skill Builder Projects
Chapters 1-4

Production Project 1.1—Create and Edit a Memorandum

1. Use Memorandum style shown in Chapter 1, page 13, and the following information to create a memorandum.

   a. Make decisions regarding:

      Margins
      Alignment
      Memo date
      Reference initials
      Enclosure notation

   b. Send the memorandum to All Cumming's Participants from Kerry Shea.

   c. The subject of the memorandum is Disclosure Form and Evidence of Coverage.

   d. Memorandum body text follows:

Enclosed is your Disclosure Form and Evidence of Coverage brochure, which outlines your medical plan coverage under the Cumming's Health Plan of Northern Virginia. This packet contains important information regarding services, benefits, and co-payments.

Effective the beginning of last month, your Cumming's Health Plan was enhanced to include coverage of Durable Medical Equipment (DME). The DME benefits cover items such as oxygen-dispensing equipment, hospital beds, and wheelchairs for use in your home or in an institution where you live. As a result of this change in benefits, all Cumming's participants were recently issued new medical identification cards, reflecting the new coverage.

If you have further questions regarding your Cumming's coverage or have not received your ID card, please contact Cumming's Member Services.

113

2. Save the file; use the filename **1cummings.doc**.

3. Revise the memorandum as follows:

    a.   In the From line, insert Ms. Shea's title, Employee Services Representative, after her name.

    b.   Delete the last sentence in the second body text paragraph, which begins "As a result . . ."

    c.   After the second body text paragraph, insert the following new paragraph:

        Please review the packet of materials carefully as it will help you to understand and receive the maximum benefits provided by your medical plan.

    d.   Replace the last body text paragraph with the following paragraph:

        If you have questions regarding your Cumming's medical plan coverage, please contact Jonah Romero at 1-800-555-3488.

4. Remember to proofread the document and check the spelling of words that are marked with a red wavy line.

5. Use the *new* filename **1p Employee benefits.doc** and save the file on your file disk.

6. Print one copy and close the document.

Production Project 1.2—Use the Memo Wizard, Create a Numbered List, and Move Text

1. Use the Memo Wizard and the following information to create a memorandum:

    a.   Use the Professional style.

    b.   Use an appropriate memo title.

    c.   Choose the desired header items (the memo is from Oscar Borgest and the subject is Employee Safety).

    d.   The memo is to All Managers with copies to Brenda Cardosa, Charles Westbrook, and Edith Zetz. (***Hint:*** *Type all names on one line.*)

        Note: *There is no distribution list.*

    e.   The body text follows:

Last week a fire alarm was sounded in Building H followed by the arrival of several safety vehicles under full lights and sirens. After inspecting the building, the Fire Captain whose team responded to the alarm found that the building had not been fully vacated as required under state law.

Fortunately, there was no fire. However, there was no way of knowing this until an inspection of the facilities had been completed. If there had been a serious emergency, those who failed to evacuate could have been in serious danger. Furthermore, the individuals who were negligent in failing to evacuate could have placed themselves and others in a serious liability position subject to penalties under the law.

If a fire alarm sounds, or an earthquake, bomb threat, or other potential emergency situation occurs, state law requires the following procedures:

Ensure that all employees in your charge remove themselves to an area away from the building.

Keep streets and walkways clear for emergency vehicles and personnel.

Immediately evacuate all persons from your office area.

Close the door to the vacated room.

Your cooperation in keeping our work environment safe is greatly appreciated. If you have any questions, please call me at Ext. 6733.

---

2. Number the four paragraphs that follow the third body text paragraph.

3. Select a font of your choice with a point size of 12 for all lines except the memorandum title.

4. Remember to proofread the document and check the spelling of words that are marked with a red wavy line.

5. Save the file; use the filename **1p employee safety.doc**.

6. Optional: Print one copy.

7. Move the items numbered 3 and 4 above the items numbered 1 and 2.

8. Save the file again using the same filename, **1p employee safety.doc**.

9. Print one copy.

10. Optional: Fax this memo to your instructor via a local fax, or write an e-mail message to your instructor that you are sending this assignment. Attach this file to your e-mail message.

11. Close the document.

Production Project 1.3—Use the Letter Wizard and Replace Text

1. Use the Letter Wizard and the following information to create a letter:

   a. Select **File**, **New**. Select the **Letters & Faxes** tab. Double-click on **Letter Wizard**.

   b. Send one letter. Select **OK**.

c. Choose the Contemporary Letter page design and the Full block letter style.

d. The recipient's name is Mr. Blake Lassiter, and the delivery address is B.L. Circuits, 305 San Benito Street, Hollister, CA 95023-5001.

e. Choose Business option for the salutation.

f. Send a copy of the letter to Mallory T. Ritter.

g. The letter is written by Rosa Kupper, Buyer.

h. The letter body text follows:

It has come to my attention that materials are being delivered after 5 p.m. Our receiving hours are from 8 a.m. to 5 p.m. Any materials received after these hours will be rejected unless there is prior approval from the buyer.

For quicker paper processing, please make sure all paperwork refers to our purchase order numbers. For those vendors that get a confirming purchase order with "refer to RMS . . .," make sure you have the updated revision of the RMS. If you do not have the updated revision, please contact me.

Also, if our RMS does not comply with yours, please contact me or Mallory Ritter to have the RMS changed.

i. Make decisions regarding document identification and reference notations. The document will be named **1p Receiving Materials.doc**.

2. Remember to proofread the document and check the spelling of words that are marked with a red wavy line.

3. Use the filename **1p Receiving Materials.doc** and save the document on your file disk.

4. Optional: Print one copy.

5. Replace **RMS** with **Received Materials Status**.

6. Save the file again using the same filename.

7. Print one copy.

8. Optional: Fax this letter to your instructor via a local fax, or write an e-mail message to your instructor that you are sending this assignment. Attach this file to your e-mail message.

9. Close the document.

➡ Production Project 1.4—Create and Edit a Letter; Language Arts

1. Use the traditional block style letter and the following information:

a. Send the letter to Albert and Carol Roth, 58 Tanyard Road, Sewell, NJ 08080-6811.

b.   The letter is from Terence H. Copeland, Claims Department Assistant.

c.   Make decisions regarding:

> Margins
> Alignment
> Appropriate salutation
> Font type and size so that the letter will print on one page
> Appropriate complimentary closing
> Reference initials
> Document identification

2.   Correct two spelling errors and three punctuation errors.

3.   The body text follows:

We have completed our investigation as to the cause and origin of your loss. After my stanndard inspection I determined the loss occurred when a hose in the hall bath burst due to wear and tear. We have issued a check for the water damage. Since the wear and tear is not covered in your policy the hose that burst would be your responsibility.

According to Gale Womack, our claims manager the decision to exclude payment for the hose is based on the following language in your insurance policy, i.e., "Perils Insured Against" Items 1 and 9 from Coverage A Dwelling and Coverage B Other Structures.

We guarentee insurance for direct physical loss to property described in Coverages A and B except:

Losses excluded under General Exclusions; and

Wear and tear; marring; deterioration; inactive defect; mechanical breakdown; rust; mold; wet or dry rot; contamination; smog; settling, cracking, or expansion of pavements.

If any of these cause water to escape from a plumbing, heating, or air conditioning system or household appliance, we cover loss caused by the water.

Since the loss to the water hose was not included in this coverage, we deny payment for the repair to the hose.

---

4.   Select the fourth and fifth body text paragraphs and create a bulleted list. You choose an appropriate bullet character.

5.   Italicize the sixth body text paragraph, which begins "If any of these cause . . ."

6.   Replace the final body text paragraph with the following paragraph:

If you have any questions or additional information that you believe would cause me to reevaluate this decision, please feel free to contact me. We are

committed to satisfying all of our claimants during and at the conclusion of the claim handling process.

7. Remember to proofread the document and check the spelling of words that are marked with a red wavy line.

8. Use the filename **1p Roths claim letter.doc** and save the file on your file disk.

9. Print one copy.

10. Optional: Fax this letter to your instructor via a local fax, or write an e-mail message to your instructor that you are sending this assignment. Attach this file to your e-mail message.

11. Close the document.

Part 2
A Step Further

Work with Special Features

Chapters 5–8

- Create a table
- Insert table rows and columns
- Change column widths
- Merge cells
- Change alignment of cell contents
- Center a table horizontally and vertically
- Convert tabbed text to a table
- Apply table AutoFormats
- Sort a table numerically and alphabetically
- Move and delete a row or column
- Copy and delete a table
- Calculate columns/row totals
- Copy a formula
- Customize table borders and shading

- Insert single and double underlines
- Insert special symbols
- Insert automatic borders
- Change the case of text
- Use the rulers to change margins and to set indents
- Set tabs
- Use nonbreaking spaces
- Use the Résumé Wizard
- Create newspaper-style columns
- Create customized columns
- Insert column breaks
- Use hyphenation
- Use the Format Painter feature
- Create side-by-side columns

5

Create a Table

- Create a table
- Insert rows
- Insert columns
- Change column widths
- Display a different Toolbar
- Merge cells
- Change horizontal/vertical alignment of cell contents
- Set row height
- Center a table horizontally and vertically
- Convert tabbed text to a table
- Apply table AutoFormats

Objectives and Introduction

After successfully completing this chapter, you will be able to create a table, increase and decrease column widths, insert columns and rows, and merge table cells. In addition, you will be able to change row height, center a table horizontally and vertically, and create a table using existing text.

Traditionally, a table is created by calculating the location of column tabs so that when the table is printed it will be centered horizontally on the page. Tables in this book will be created using the Tables feature, which will determine the column widths and row heights automatically.

The Tables feature is used to organize information into columns and rows without using tab settings. Figure 5.1 shows a sample table. Table information can include either text or numbers or both.

Create a Table

A table can be easily created using the **Insert Table** button ▦ on the Standard Toolbar or the **Insert, Table** options in the **Table** menu. Also, text typed in

FIGURE 5.1

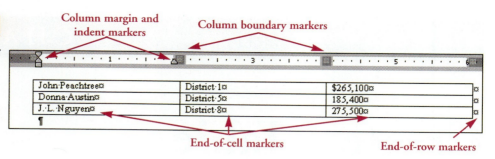

Horizontal ruler with sample table displaying nonprinting symbols

Column margin and indent markers

Column boundary markers

End-of-cell markers

End-of-row markers

columns can be converted to a table by using the **Insert Table** option in the **Table** menu. Once the number of table columns and rows are specified, table border lines display in the document window. Border lines can print or they can be removed if desired (see Chapter 6, page 163).

If the table borders have been turned off, gridlines can be displayed to indicate the rows and columns on the screen. Table gridlines display on the screen but do not print. If the table gridlines do not display, select **Table, Show Gridlines**.

The table lines form columns and rows. The intersection of each column and row is called a *cell*. Cells are generally identified by a cell address, such as A5 or C29. The cell address specifies the column and row in which the insertion point is located. Imagine that the columns are labeled from left to right, A, B, C, etc., and that the rows are numbered down the left side of the table beginning with row 1.

Column boundary markers display on the ruler and indicate the left and right sides of the columns. When the insertion point is located in a column cell, the ruler shows indent markers to indicate the current column (see Figure 5.1). If nonprinting symbols are turned on, end-of-cell markers, end-of row markers, and a select all symbol display.

The **Tab** key, **Shift** and **Tab** keys, or the arrow keys can be used to move the insertion point from cell to cell. After text is typed in one cell, press the **Tab** key or the right arrow key to move the insertion point to the next cell. To return to the previous cell, press the **Shift** and **Tab** keys or the left arrow key.

Text typed in each table cell wraps around in the cell. If the **Enter** key is pressed in a cell, the cell automatically increases in height. If text within a cell is to be indented, press the **Ctrl** and **Tab** keys.

Start-Up Instructions

❖ An empty document window should be displayed. If necessary, select the **New** button.

Create a Table

1. Move the mouse pointer to the **Insert Table** button 🔲 on the Standard Toolbar. Click the mouse button once.

   Note: A miniature grid displays at the location of the Insert Table button (see Figure 5.2).

2. Press and hold the left mouse button while dragging to highlight the desired number of columns and rows. Release the mouse button.

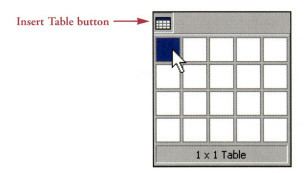

Insert Table button

FIGURE 5.2

Miniature table grid

1 x 1 Table

For example, drag to highlight a 3 x 3 table; release the mouse button.

Note: The table columns and rows display with a ½ point single-line border.

Finish-Up Instructions

❖ To type the unformatted information in each cell, press the **Tab** key or the arrow keys to move from cell to cell and row to row. Type the unformatted information shown in Figure 5.1. Type the dollar sign and commas when entering the numbers in the third column.

*Note: If the **Enter** key is mistakenly pressed while typing information in a table cell, press the **Backspace** key to delete the unwanted return. If the **Tab** key is pressed after the last cell entry, check that the insertion point is located in any cell in the last row and select **Table, Delete, Rows**.*

❖ Use the filename **5Budget.doc** and save the file on your file disk (select the **Save** button; type the filename; if necessary, click in the **Save in** box and click on the drive letter where your file disk is located; select **Save**).

❖ Optional: Print one unformatted copy.

Format and Modify a Table

Formatting a table is the process of completing such tasks as increasing or decreasing the column widths, merging table cells, changing the alignment of cell contents, and centering the table horizontally on the page. The primary goals of formatting a table are to present a pleasing appearance and to make reading easier. To produce a formatted table with an appealing appearance, visually adjust the width and height of cells and the alignment of text within the cells.

Text in a table can be selected as discussed in Chapter 2. In addition, several shortcut methods are available for selecting table rows and columns. *To select a row,* move the mouse pointer into the left margin beside that row until a right-pointing arrow displays, then click once. *To select a column,* move the mouse pointer above that column until a down-pointing arrow displays, then click once. *To select the entire table*, click on the **Select All** symbol located at the top left cell of the table. Also, options in the **Table** menu can be used to select a cell, row, column, or the entire table.

When the insertion point is located in any table cell, the **Insert Table** button changes to an **Insert Rows** button . When a table column is selected, the **Insert Table** button changes to an **Insert Columns** button. If one or more cells are selected, the **Insert Table** button changes to an **Insert Cells** button. Use the **Insert Rows/Columns** button to insert one or more rows above the cell containing the insertion point or to insert one or more columns to the left of the column containing the insertion point.

Modifying a table can also include changing row height. Row height is the amount of space between the top and bottom cell lines. When row height is increased, the cell text will be placed at the top of the cell and the additional space will be added between the text and the bottom cell line. Two row height options are available: **At Least** and **Exactly**. Row height is changed in the Table Properties dialog box on the Row tab.

By default, Word increases or decreases the row height automatically to accommodate any amount and size of text typed in the cells. When the **At least** option is selected, a minimum amount of space is specified for each row. If text is added, the row height will be increased to accommodate the new text; if text is deleted, the row height will not be decreased any less than the minimum amount specified. If the **Exactly** option is selected, a specific row height amount can be set for each row; however, when text is added or deleted, the row height will not adjust automatically. If needed, a new row height amount can be entered.

The contents in a cell(s) can be changed to align horizontally at the top, center, left, right or bottom of the cell by using the **Tables and Borders Toolbar**. Choose the down arrow beside the **Align** button. Also, the cell contents can be changed to align vertically in a cell. Use the **Text Direction** button on the **Tables and Borders Toolbar** or choose the **Format menu** and click on **Text Direction**. To display the Tables and Borders Toolbar, select the **Tables and Borders** button on the Standard Toolbar

Two or more cells in a row can be merged (joined) to provide space for information that relates to more than one cell or column. This is useful for table titles or column heading rows.

Word provides shortcut menus for easy access to options related to a specific feature. The *right* mouse button is pressed to obtain a shortcut menu. For example, if several cells are selected and the right mouse button is pressed, the shortcut menu displays with various options such as **Cut**, **Copy**, **Paste**, **Delete Cells**, **Merge Cells**, and **Borders and Shading**.

Start-Up Instructions

❖ The file named **5Budget.doc** should be displayed in the document window.

❖ The **Print Layout** view should be selected. If necessary, select **View**, **Print Layout**.

❖ Turn on **Nonprinting Symbols**. If necessary, select the **Show/Hide** button ¶ in the Standard Toolbar

Steps to

Insert Table Rows

1. To select the number of rows to be inserted, place the mouse pointer to the left side of the row that will be located below the inserted rows. When the

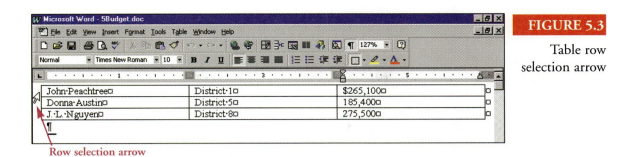

FIGURE 5.3

Table row
selection arrow

Row selection arrow

right-pointing arrow displays, press and hold the left mouse button while dragging the mouse downward to highlight the number of rows to be inserted (see Figure 5.3).

> For example, obtain the right-pointing arrow beside row 1 and drag downward to select rows 1 and 2, making sure that the end-of-row markers are selected.

Note: To insert a single row, place the insertion point in the row below where the new row will be inserted; it is not necessary to highlight the row.

2. Place the mouse pointer on the **Insert Rows** button ⬚ on the Standard Toolbar and click once.

*Note: To insert a row at the end of a table, move the insertion point to the last table cell and press the **Tab** key.*

Shortcut:

1. Point to the highlighted row or the row containing the insertion point and click the *right* mouse button; choose **Insert Rows**.

Finish-Up Instructions

❖ Click once to deselect the new table rows.

❖ Place the insertion point in the first table cell.

❖ Use the **Tab** key or arrow keys to move from cell to cell and type the following text into the new cells as shown.

Yearly Budget		
Supervisor	District	Budget Amount

❖ Use the *new* filename **5Budget R1.doc** and save the file on your file disk (select **File**, **Save As**; type the new filename; if necessary, click in the **Save in** box and click on the drive letter where your file disk is located; select **Save**).

Start-Up Instructions

❖ The file named **5Budget R1.doc** should be displayed in the document window.

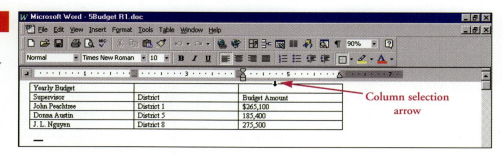

FIGURE 5.4

Table column selection arrow

Column selection arrow

Insert Table Columns

1. *To insert a single column,* select the column to the right of where the new column will be inserted by moving the mouse pointer to the top border of the desired column until a down arrow displays; click once (see Figure 5.4).

   For example, select the third column.

   To insert a column to the right of the last table column, move the mouse pointer to the top of the end-of-row markers until a down arrow displays; click once.

   To insert multiple columns, move the mouse pointer to the top border of the first column until a down arrow displays and drag right to select the number of columns desired.

   *Note: A column can also be selected by placing the insertion point in any cell of the desired column and then choosing **Table, Select, Column**.*

2. Place the mouse pointer on the **Insert Columns** button 🔳 on the Standard Toolbar and click once.

   Note: The new column is highlighted, and the previously selected column is moved to the right.

Shortcut:

1. Point to the highlighted column and click the *right* mouse button; choose **Insert Columns**.

Finish-Up Instructions

❖ Click once to deselect the new table column.

❖ Click in the second row of the new column. Type the following information into the new column. Remember to press the down arrow after typing each word(s).

> **Director**
> **William Howard**
> **Crystal DeLeon**
> **Ian Von Horn**

❖ Use the *new* filename **5Budget C2.doc** and save the file again on your file disk (select **File, Save As**; type the new filename; if necessary, click in the

Save in box and click on the drive letter where your file disk is located; select **Save**).

Start-Up Instructions

❖ The file named **5Budget C2.doc** should be displayed in the document window.

Change Column Widths

1. Move the mouse pointer to a table column border until a double-headed arrow displays.

   For example, point to the table column border between the first and second columns until the horizontal double-headed arrow displays.

2. *To decrease a column width,* press and hold the left mouse button while dragging the mouse to the left.

   To increase a column width, press and hold the left mouse button while dragging the mouse to the right.

   For example, visually estimate and drag the mouse pointer approximately **0.5"** to the left until the column marker on the ruler is located at approximately 1.25 inches.

   Note: The column width changes; the table width does not change.

Finish-Up Instructions

❖ Move the mouse pointer to the column border between the second and third columns until a double-headed arrow displays. Visually estimate and drag the column border to the left until the column marker is approximately at the 2¾ inch mark on the ruler (the width of the second column will be approximately 1¼ inches).

❖ Repeat steps 1 and 2 of the Steps to Change Column Widths to decrease the widths in the third and fourth columns. Drag the column border between the third and fourth columns to the left so that the column marker is located at approximately 4¼ inches.

❖ Drag the column border at the right of the fourth column to the left so that the column marker is located at approximately 5½ inches.

❖ Use the *new* filename **5Budget W3.doc** and save the file on your file disk (select **File, Save As**; type the new filename; if necessary, click in the **Save in** box and click on the drive letter where your file disk is located; select **Save**).

Display the Tables and Borders Toolbar

1. Point to the Standard or Formatting Toolbar and click once with the *right* mouse button.

2. Choose the desired Toolbar.

   For example, choose **Tables and Borders**.

Shortcut:

1. Select the **Tables and Borders** button on the Standard Toolbar

Start-Up Instructions

❖ The Tables and Borders Toolbar should be displayed. (If necessary, select the **Tables and Borders** button on the Standard Toolbar.)

❖ The file named **5Budget W3.doc** should be displayed in the document window.

Merge Table Cells

1. *To select cells to be merged,* move the mouse pointer inside the left cell border until the right-pointing arrow displays. Press and hold the left mouse button while dragging the mouse to select the desired cells.

   To select an entire row to be merged, move the mouse pointer outside the cell border to the left side of the desired row until the right-pointing arrow displays; click once.

   For example, select row 1.

2. Select the **Merge Cells** button on the Tables and Borders Toolbar.

Shortcut:

1. Highlight the desired cells or row; point to the highlighted cells and click the *right* mouse button; choose **Merge Cells**.

Finish-Up Instructions

❖ Use the same filename, **5Budget W3.doc**, and save the file again (select the **Save** button).

❖ Continue with the Steps to Change the Horizontal Alignment of Cell Contents.

Start-Up Instructions

❖ The table named **5Budget W3.doc** should be displayed in the document window.

Change the Horizontal Alignment of Cell Contents

1. Select the cells where justification is to be changed. (If necessary, see step 1 in the Steps to Merge Table Cells above.)

   For example, select rows 1 and 2.

2. Select the desired alignment button on the Formatting Toolbar.

   For example, select the **Center** alignment button on the Formatting Toolbar.

Finish-Up Instructions

❖ Continue with the Steps to Change Table Row Height.

Start-Up Instructions

❖ The file named **5Budget W3.doc** should be displayed in the document window.

 Steps to **Change Table Row Height**

1. Select the row(s) where the row height is to be changed. (If necessary, see step 1 of the Steps to Merge Table Cells on page 128.)

   For example, select rows 1 and 2.

2. Select **Table, Table Properties**.

3. If necessary, select the **Row** tab.

   For example, check that the **Row** tab is selected. (If necessary, select the **Row** tab.)

   Note: The Table Properties dialog box displays with the Row tab forward. (see Figure 5.5).

4. Select the **Specify height** option in the Size area.

5. Change the setting in the **Specify height** box either by clicking on the up/down arrows to increase/decrease the current setting or by triple-clicking on the figure in the **Specify height** box and typing the desired setting.

6. Select the desired **Row height is** option.

   For example, check that the **Row height is** option displays At least. If necessary, select **At least**.

   For example, triple-click on the figure in the **Specify height** box and type **.3**.

7. Select **OK**.

   Note: Rows 1 and 2 are increased in height.

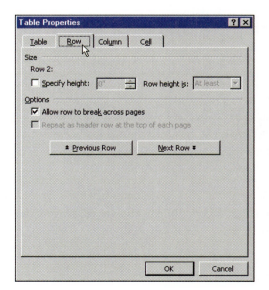

Finish-Up Instructions

❖ Use the same filename, **5Budget W3.doc**, and save the file again (select the **Save** button).

Start-Up Instructions

❖ The file named **5Budget W3.doc** should be displayed on the screen.

❖ The Tables and Borders Toolbar should be displayed. (If necessary, select the **Tables and Borders** button on the Standard Toolbar.)

Change Vertical Alignment of Cell Contents

1. Select the desired cell(s).

   For example, select rows 1 and 2.

2. Select the desired vertical alignment.

   For example, select the **Align... button** 🔲 on the Tables and Borders Toolbar and click on the Align Center button.

Shortcut:

1. Highlight the desired cell(s); point to the highlighted cell(s); *right* mouse click; choose **Cell Alignment**; select the desired alignment button.

Finish-Up Instructions

❖ If necessary, click once to deselect the table cells.

❖ Select the last three cells in the fourth column, which contain the sales amounts; select the **Align Right** button 🔳 on the Formatting Toolbar.

   Note: Your table should look similar to the following table.

Yearly Budget			
Supervisor	District	Director	Budget Amount
John Peachtree	District 1	William Howard	$265,100
Donna Austin	District 5	Crystal DeLeon	185,400
J. L. Nguyen	District 8	Ian Von Horn	275,500

❖ Use the *new* filename **5Budget HV4.doc** and save the file on your file disk (select **File, Save As**; type the new filename; if necessary, click in the **Save in** box and click on the drive letter where your file disk is located; select **Save**).

Start-Up Instructions

❖ The file named **5Budget HV4.doc** should be displayed in the document window.

Center a Table Horizontally

1. Place the insertion point in any cell in the table and click the *right* mouse button.

2. Select **Table Properties**.

3. If necessary, select the **Table** tab.

4. Select the desired option in the Alignment area.

    For example, select the **Center** option.

5. Select **OK**.

    Note: The table displays horizontally centered in the document window.

Finish-Up Instructions

❖ Use the same filename, **5Budget HV4.doc**, and save the file again (select the **Save** button).

❖ Print one copy (select the **Print** button). Close the document (select **File**, **Close**).

Center a Table or Text Vertically

Table rows or lines of text can be centered vertically on a page between the top and bottom margins. On an 8 ½- x 11-inch sheet of paper, approximately 66 lines (6 lines per inch) or approximately 50 table rows (4.5 rows per inch) can be printed. Text that occupies fewer than 54 lines (66 - 12 = 2-inch top/bottom margins) and tables that occupy fewer than 45 rows will usually display more attractively on a page if the lines/rows are centered between the top and bottom margins. The tables typed in this book will be fewer than 20 rows; therefore, vertical centering will be used.

Start-Up Instructions

❖ The file named **5Budget HV4.doc** should be displayed in the document window.

 Center a Table or Text Vertically

1. With the insertion point located in any table cell, select **File, Page Setup**.

    Note: The Page Setup dialog box displays.

2. Select the **Layout** tab.

3. Click in the **Vertical alignment** box.

4. Select the desired alignment option.

    For example, select the **Center** vertical alignment option.

5. Select **OK**.

*Note: Select the **Print Preview** button on the Standard Toolbar to view the table centered vertically on the page. Select **Close** to return to the document window.*

Finish-Up Instructions

❖ Use the *new* filename **5Budget V5.doc** and save the file on your file disk (select **File, Save As**; type the new filename; if necessary, click in the **Save in** box and click on the drive letter where your file disk is located; select **Save**).

❖ Print one copy (select the **Print** button). Close the document (select **File, Close**).

Convert Tabbed Text to a Table

Text that is separated by tabs and hard returns can be easily converted to a table. Once the tabbed text is typed, select the text and select the **Insert Table** button 🔲 on the Standard Toolbar, or choose the **Convert, Text to Table** options in the **Table** menu.

Once text is converted to a table, the information is contained in individual cells and surrounded by table borders. The information in the cells can be formatted (e.g., alignment, bold, italics, underline) by using the buttons on the Formatting Toolbar, and the structure of the table can be modified by selecting the desired options from the **Table** menu.

Start-Up Instructions

❖ Select the **New Blank Document** button 🔲 on the Standard Toolbar to create a new document.

❖ Type the text to be converted to a table. Press the **Tab** key once between each item, and press the **Enter** key at the end of the first three lines. Do *not* press the **Enter** key after typing the last line.

❖ Type the information shown in Figure 5.6. (The columns may not appear aligned on the screen; that's OK.)

Steps to ▶ **Convert Tabbed Text to a Table**

1. Select all lines of the desired tabbed text.

   For example, select all four lines of text.

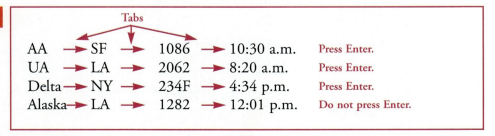

FIGURE 5.6				
Tabbed text to be converted to a table	AA → SF → 1086 → 10:30 a.m.			Press Enter.
	UA → LA → 2062 → 8:20 a.m.			Press Enter.
	Delta → NY → 234F → 4:34 p.m.			Press Enter.
	Alaska → LA → 1282 → 12:01 p.m.			Do not press Enter.

2. Select the Insert Table button 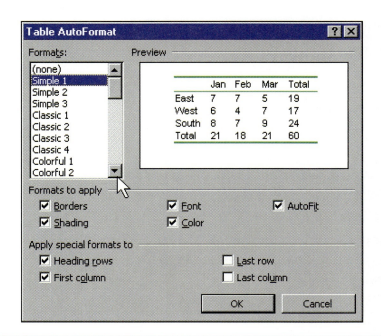 on the Standard Toolbar.

Finish-Up Instructions

❖ Change the widths in each column to approximately 1 inch. (If necessary, see the Steps to Change Column Widths on page 127.)

❖ Center the table horizontally (click anywhere in the table, select **Table**, **Table Properties**, **Table** tab, **Center** alignment, **OK**).

❖ Use the filename **5Tabbed.doc** and save the file on your file disk (select the **Save** button; type the filename; if necessary, click in the **Save in** box and select the drive letter where your file disk is located; select **Save**).

Apply Table AutoFormats

A variety of cell and table border styles can be used in a table. In addition, cells or groups of cells can be shaded or filled with a particular pattern. Word comes with a number of preformatted table styles that contain preset borders and fill patterns. Word refers to the preformatted table styles as Table AutoFormats. Using the Table AutoFormat feature is a very efficient method for formatting a table quickly.

Each Table AutoFormat contains choices for borders, shading, fonts, and colors. If desired, you can choose to apply only specific formats. For example, you might choose to apply only the borders and shading formats contained in a specific AutoFormat. When a Table AutoFormat is selected, the **AutoFit** option will adjust the widths of the columns to accommodate the text. If table cells have been merged or if you have adjusted column widths, deselect the **AutoFit** option before applying a Table AutoFormat.

FIGURE 5.7

Table AutoFormat dialog box

Start-Up Instructions

❖ The file named **5Tabbed.doc** should be displayed in the document window.

Apply a Table AutoFormat

1. Place the insertion point in any table cell.

2. Select **Table, Table AutoFormat**.

   Note: The Table AutoFormat dialog box displays (see Figure 5.7).

3. Select the desired format in the Formats list box.

   For example, scroll down the list and click on the **3D effects 2** format. Click on the **AutoFit** option to deselect it.

   Note: A sample of the format appears in the Preview box.

4. Choose **OK**.

Finish-Up Instructions

❖ Notice that some of the text is bolded and that the rows are shaded. Bold all cell text (select the last 3 rows and choose the **Bold** button). (If necessary, refer back to step 1 in the Steps to Merge Table Cells on page 128 for selecting cells.)

❖ Use the *new* filename **5Autoformat.doc** and save the file on your file disk (select **File, Save As**; type the new filename; if necessary, click in the **Save in** box and click on the drive letter where your file disk is located; select **Save**).

❖ Optional: Print a copy of the file.

Start-Up Instructions

❖ The file named **5Autoformat.doc** should be displayed in the document window.

Edit the Table AutoFormats

1. Place the insertion point anywhere within the table.

2. Select **Table, Table AutoFormat**.

   Note: The Table AutoFormat dialog box displays.

3. Select the desired format in the Formats list box.

   For example, scroll through the list and select the **Classic 3** format.

   Note: A sample of the format appears in the Preview box.

4. Select (or deselect) the desired formats in the Formats to apply box.

   For example, deselect **AutoFit, Heading rows**, and **First column**.

Note: The heading row color and the first column bold style disappear from the sample table in the Preview box.

5. Select **OK**.

Finish-Up Instructions

❖ Use the *new* filename **5Format edit.doc** and save the file on your file disk (select **File**, **Save As**; type the new filename; if necessary, click in the **Save in** box and click on the drive letter where your file disk is located; select **Save**).

❖ Insert a new row above the first row. (If necessary, refer to the Steps to Insert Table Rows on page 124.)

❖ Type the following text in the new row.

Airline	City	Flight No.	Arrival Time

❖ Select the cells in the first row and change the point size to **14 point**. (If necessary, refer to step 1 in the Steps to Merge Table Cells on page 128 for selecting a row.)

❖ Select all rows and adjust the column widths as necessary so that the contents of each cell are on a single line. (If necessary, refer to the Steps to Change Column Widths on page 127.)

❖ Format the table using the **List 4** AutoFormat (select **Table**, **Table AutoFormat**; select **List 4** in the Formats list box and choose **OK**).

❖ Use the same filename, **5Format edit.doc**, and save the file (select the **Save** button).

❖ Print a copy of the table (select the **Print** button). Close the document (select **File**, **Close**).

Remove a Table AutoFormat

Note: The following steps are for your information.

1. Place the insertion point anywhere within the table.

2. Select **Table, Table AutoFormat**.

Note: The Table AutoFormat dialog box displays.

3. Select **(none)** at the top of the Formats list box.

4. Select **OK**.

The Next Step

Chapter Review and Activities

Self-Check Quiz

T F 1. A table can be created by selecting the **Insert Table** button on the Standard Toolbar.

T F 2. The intersection of each column and row is called a cell.

T F 3. The **Enter** key is pressed in the last row cell to insert a new table row.

T F 4. Formatting a table can include increasing or decreasing the table column widths.

T F 5. Text that is separated by tabs and hard returns can be converted to a table.

6. To indent text in a cell, press _____.
   a. **Tab**
   b. **Shift** and **Tab**
   c. **Ctrl** and **Tab**
   d. either a or c

7. A table can be centered horizontally on a page by selecting _____.
   a. **Table, Cell Height and Width**
   b. **Table, Alignment**
   c. **Table, Table AutoFormat**
   d. none of the above

8. To select a table row, move the mouse pointer _____ and click once.
   a. inside the second cell of a row
   b. to the left of the row, outside the cell border
   c. above any column
   d. none of the above

9. State the primary purpose for formatting a table.

10. Give one reason for merging table cells.

Enriching Language Arts Skills

Spelling/Vocabulary Words

development—to make fuller, bigger, better.
preference—to like better.
revision—an improvement, amendment, or update.

Dollar Amount Formats

Use a comma to separate the number digits into groups of thousands. No space is placed between a number and the dollar sign. If even numbers are used in the body of a document or if a column of numbers has even dollar amounts, the zeros are omitted. Even dollar amounts should be right justified; if the numbers include decimal points, the numbers should be right aligned, or a decimal tab should be set to align the numbers properly. When dollar amounts in a column are to be added, dollar signs are placed only in front of the first item in the column and the total.

Example:

$$\begin{array}{r} \$28,655,342 \\ 1,389 \\ \underline{10,843} \\ \$28,667,574 \end{array}$$

Activities

Activity 5.1—Create and Format a Table; Align Numbers; Center a Table Horizontally

1. In a new document window, create a table with 4 rows and 3 columns (select the **Insert Table** button on the Standard Toolbar; press and hold the mouse button and drag to highlight a **4 x 3** table; release the mouse button).

2. Type the unformatted text as shown.

    *Hint: Remember to press the **Tab** key to move from cell to cell.*

Fidelity National Fund	Yearly increase	$1,256.25
BCI Affiliated	Bi-annual increase	245.65
Lincoln Growth Fund	Quarterly increase	152.90
Interworld Ltd. Fund	Yearly increase	1,525.88

3. Use the filename **5funds.doc** and save the file on your file disk (select the **Save** button; type the filename; if necessary, click in the **Save in** box and click on the drive letter where your file disk is located; select **Save**).

4. Use the following information to format the table:

a. Change the alignment of the text in the third column to **Right** (select the third column and select the **Align Right** button on the Formatting Toolbar; click once to deselect the cells).

b. Change the alignment of the text in the second column to **Center** (select the second column and select the **Center** alignment button on the Formatting Toolbar; click once to deselect the cells).

c. Visually estimate and change the width of the third column to approximately 1". (Place the mouse pointer on the column border at the right side of the table until the double-headed arrow displays; press and hold the mouse button while dragging the border to the left until the column marker on the ruler is located at approximately 5 inches. Release the mouse button.)

d. Select all table rows (with the insertion point in any table cell, choose **Table**, **Select Table**). Select the **12-point** font size.

e. Center the table horizontally on the page. (Place the insertion point in any table cell, *right*-mouse click, select **Table Properties**, choose **Center** alignment on the **Table** tab, select **OK**.)

Note: Your table should look similar to the following table:

Fidelity National Fund	Yearly increase	$1,256.25
BCI Affiliated	Bi-annual increase	245.65
Lincoln Growth Fund	Quarterly increase	152.90
Interworld Ltd. Fund	Yearly increase	1,525.88

5. Use the same filename, **5funds.doc**, and save the file again (select the **Save** button).

6. Print one copy (select the **Print** button). Close the document (select **File**, **Close**).

Activity 5.2—Create and Format a Table; Insert Rows; Merge Cells; Change Row Height; Change Column Width; Center a Table Horizontally

1. In a new document window, create a table with 5 rows and 2 columns (select the **Insert Table** button on the Standard Toolbar; press and hold the mouse button while dragging to highlight a 5 x 2 table; release the mouse button).

2. Type the unformatted text as shown.

Total Population	260,967,000
Males	127,367,981
Females	133,599,019
Baby Boomers	77,000,000
Rural Population	66,964,000

3. Use the filename **5US Demographics.doc** and save the file on your file disk (select the **Save** button; type the filename; if necessary, click in the **Save in** box and click on the drive letter where your file disk is located; select **Save**).

4. Change the alignment of the second column to **Right** (select the second column; select the **Align Right** button).

5. Insert three rows above the first row (select the first three rows, then select the **Insert Rows** button on the Standard Toolbar).

6. Merge the cells in the first row (select the first row; point to the highlighted cells and click the *right* mouse button; choose **Merge Cells**).

7. Merge the cells in the second row (select the second row; point to the highlighted cells and click the *right* mouse button; choose **Merge Cells**).

8. Set the center alignment for the text that will be typed in the first two rows. (Select the first two rows; select the **Center** alignment button on the Formatting Toolbar.)

9. Change the row height for the first two rows to **24 points**. (Select the first two rows; select **Table, Table Properties, Row** tab; click on the **Specify height** option; select the down arrow in the **Row height is** box and choose **Exactly**; click on the up arrow in the **Specify height** box until .3 displays; **OK**.)

10. Locate the insertion point in row 1 and type the title **U.S. Demographics**. Notice that the text centers.

11. Locate the insertion point in row 2 and type the subtitle (**Approximately**).

12. In row 3, type the column heading **Category** in the first cell and the heading **Population** in the second cell and center the column headings.

13. Visually estimate and change the width of each column to approximately **2"**. (Place the mouse pointer on the column border between the columns until the double-headed arrow displays; press and hold the mouse button while dragging the border to the left until the column marker on the ruler is located at approximately 2 inches. Release the mouse button. Locate the right column gridline at approximately **3.75"**.)

14. Select the text in row 1 and change the font size to **18 point**. Select the text in row 2 and change the font size to **14 point**. (Select the row; select the down arrow beside the **Font Size** button and choose the desired font size.)

15. Select rows 1 and 2 and change the vertical alignment of the cells (select the **Tables and Borders** button on the Standard Toolbar. Select the down arrow beside the **Align** button and choose **Align Center**).

16. Select and bold the text in rows 1–3 (select rows 1–3; select the **Bold** button).

    Note: Your table should look similar to the following table:

U.S. Demographics	
(Approximately)	
Category	Population
Total Population	260,967,000
Males	127,367,981
Females	133,599,019
Baby Boomers	77,000,000
Rural Population	66,964,000

17. Center the table horizontally on the page (right mouse click in any table cell, choose **Table Properties**, select **Center** alignment on the **Table** tab, **OK**).

18. Use the same filename, **5US Demographics.doc**, and save the file again.

19. Print one copy (select the **Print** button). Close the document (select **File**, **Close**).

Activity 5.3—Create and Format a Table; Insert a Column; Apply AutoFormats; Center a Table Horizontally and Vertically

1. In a new document window, create a table with 5 rows and 3 columns (select the **Insert Table** button on the Standard Toolbar; press and hold the mouse button while dragging to highlight a 5 x 3 table; release the mouse button).

2. Type the unformatted text as shown.

Surge Suppressor Comparisons		
Brand	Cost	Score
Surge Patrol 9504	$50	87
Perma Power RXD-410	60	73
SL Waber Surge Sentry DS4LP	51	75

3. Use the filename **5Surge suppressor comp.doc** and save the file on your file disk (select the **Save** button; type the filename; if necessary, click in the **Save in** box and click on the drive letter where your file disk is located; select **Save**).

4. Use the following information to format the table:

   a. Insert a new column between the last two columns in the table. (Select the third column; select the **Insert Columns** button on the Standard Toolbar.)

   b. Type the following information into the new column cells and press the down arrow to move to the next cell.

Outlets
6
4
4

c. Select the entire table (with the insertion point in any table cell, choose **Table**, **Select**, **Table**). Change the font size to **12 point**.

d. Merge the cells in the first row (select the first row; point to the highlighted cells and click the *right* mouse button; choose **Merge Cells**; click once to deselect the row).

e. Center the title and column headings in the first two rows (select the first two rows; select the **Center** alignment button on the Formatting Toolbar; click once to deselect the rows).

f. Right align the dollar amounts and numbers in the last three columns. (If desired, select the **Zoom** button and choose **75%**; select the cells containing dollar amounts or numbers; select the **Align Right** button.)

g. Visually estimate and change the width of all columns. (Place the mouse pointer on the column border until the double-headed arrow displays; press and hold the mouse button while dragging the border left to the desired position. Release the mouse button. The column markers on the ruler should be located at approximately $2\frac{1}{4}$, $3\frac{1}{4}$, $4\frac{1}{4}$, and $5\frac{1}{4}$ inches.)

h. Apply the **Grid 8** AutoFormat to the table and deselect **AutoFit**. (With the insertion point in any table cell, select **Table**, **Table AutoFormat**; select **Grid 8**; if necessary, deselect **AutoFit**, **OK**.)

    *Note: If a mistake is made and **AutoFit** is not deselected, the width of the first row will change. If necessary, select **Edit**, **Undo AutoFormat** and complete step 4h. again.*

i. Select and bold the text in the second row. (Select the second row; select the **Bold** button on the Formatting Toolbar; click once to deselect the row.)

    Note: Your table should look similar to the following:

Surge Suppressor Comparisons			
Brand	**Cost**	**Outlets**	**Score**
Surge Patrol 9504	$50	6	87
Perma Power RXD-410	60	4	73
SL Waber Surge Sentry DS4LP	51	4	75

5. Center the table horizontally on the page (*right*-mouse click in any table cell, choose **Table Properties**, select **Center** alignment on the **Table** tab, **OK**).

6. Center the table vertically on the page (with the insertion point in any table cell, select **File**, **Page Setup**, **Layout**; click in the **Vertical alignment** box; select **Center**; select **OK**).

7. Use the same filename, **5Surge suppressor comp.doc**, and save the file again.

8. Print one copy (select the **Print** button). Close the document (select **File**, **Close**).

Challenge Your Skills

Skill 5.1—Create and Format a Table; Insert a Column; Change Row Height; and Apply Table AutoFormat

1. Create a table with 12 rows and 3 columns.

2. Type the information shown below in the table.

Packing List		
Item	Building/Room	Box No.
Copier 425	Wilson/256	A4
Printer 231	Bero/513	B6
Personal Computer 915	Wilson/254	C3
Personal Computer 952	Babbitt/108	D8
Chair 54	Wilson/251	D1
Conference Table 105	Wilson/251	D5
Credenza 211	Babbitt/107	E4
Lateral File 58	Babbitt/107	E1
Vertical File 65	Babbitt/107	E5
Executive Chair 23	Wilson/256	D6

3. Use the following information to format the table:

    a. Insert a new column between the second and third columns.

    b. Change the alignment for the new column to **Center**.

    c. Type the text as shown into the new column:

Quantity
1
2
1
3
4
1
2
6
9
2

    d.   Change the alignment for the last column to **Right,** including the column head.

    e.   Change the font for the entire table to **Garamond, 11 point** or make a font choice of your own.

    f.   Adjust the widths of the columns so that the table information is appealing and easy to read.

    g.   Merge the cells in row 1.

    h.   Change the alignment of row 1 to **Center.**

    i.   Change the height of the first row to at least .3".

    j.   Apply a Table AutoFormat of your choice.

    *Hint: Remember to deselect the **AutoFit** option if necessary.*

4. Center the table horizontally and vertically.

5. Use the filename **5Packing List.doc** and save the file.

6. Print one copy and close the document.

Skill 5.2—Create and Format a Table; Insert Rows and a Column

1. Create a table with 8 rows and 2 columns.

2. Type the unformatted text as shown:

Expense Categories	Amount Budgeted
Salaries	$150,000
Benefits	70,000
Long-term land/building expenses	250,000
Short-term land/building expenses	140,000
Office and computer supplies	20,000
Miscellaneous expenses	7,800
Insurance expenses	20,580

3. Use the following information to format the table:

    a. Insert a row above the item Office and computer supplies.

    b. Type the following information into the new row:

       Computer equipment   68,550

    c. Insert a column between the two columns.

    d. Type the following information into the new column cells, beginning in the first row. (Do not type the semicolons.)

       Actual Amount Spent; $148,252.70; 68,425.88; 350,501.75; 285,866.50; 65,856.90; 32,451.89; 5,415.20; 17,895.26

    e. Insert a row at the top of the table. Set the row height for the new row to .5".

    f. Merge the cells in row 1 and type the title **Winton Typesetting and Design** in this row; use **Center** alignment.

    g. Adjust the column widths so that the information appears attractive and easy to read.

    h. Make decisions regarding the alignment of the table information so that the table appears attractive and easy to read.

       Hint: Change alignment of column headings and dollar amounts. Horizontally center the table.

    i. Apply a Table AutoFormat of your choice.

       Hint: Remember to deselect the AutoFit option.

4. Use the filename **5Winton expenses.doc** and save the file.

5. Print one copy and close the document.

●◆ Skill 5.3—Create and Format a Memorandum Containing a Table; Language Arts

1. Use the following information to create a memorandum:

    a. The memo should be sent to Gordon's Fish Bait Franchises. The memo is from Terry Fitzgerald, Vice President, Sales and Marketing.

    b. The subject of the memo is New District Sales Team.

    c. Use the current date; include your reference initials.

    d. Correct three spelling errors, one punctuation error, and one dollar amount format error.

    e. After creating the table, format the cells as desired (e.g., increase or decrease column widths, change the alignment of column headings and dollar amounts, choose an appropriate Table AutoFormat).

    f. The memorandum body text follows:

In keeping with our policy of training each Gordon's Fish Bait franchise in sales and marketing techniques, a new District Sales Team has been created. Mark Slovikian has been promoted to the position of Sales Team Leader, and Terry Aquila will take over Mark's former duties in the Franchise Marketing area.

The development of the new District Sales Team also allows us to revise the three Sales Teams currently in place so that all team members will work in the district closest to their home base.

The following table shows the revishions in the sales teams and the goals that have been assigned to them by the Board of Directors for the upcoming year:

Team Leader	Team Members	Goal
Abby Darnella	Richard Kimbell Barbara Felix Dennis O'Connell	$155,200
Dinu Mohamed	Sing Lu-Yang Melanie Pattelli George Robertson	186,000
Mark Slovikian	Jennifer Martin Pamela DeSalva Thomas Whitten	85,100
Nathan Tannenberg	Melvin Schollenberg May Vu Soledad Carcinola	266500

A schedule of sales team visits for each district will be released shortly. If there are certain weeks that would be more convenient for your franchise please call Natalie Smith at (314) 555-2443 and let her know your perferences so these can be considered during the scheduling process.

2. Use the filename **5New District Sales Team.doc** and save the file on your file disk.

3. Print one copy.

4. Close the document.

Skill 5.4—Use Click and Type

1. Select the **New Blank Document** button on the **Standard Toolbar**.

2. Select a **50%** Zoom View.

3. Move the mouse pointer to the middle of the screen and double-click.

    Note: The insertion point displays in the middle of the page.

4. Type your name, current date, and Skill 5.4 each on separate lines

   Note: The text is automatically centered on the page.

5. Move the mouse pointer to the bottom right of the page and double-click.

6. Type your instructor's name.

   Note: *The name is automatically right aligned.*

7. Save the file using the filename **5 my title page**.

8. Print one copy.

9. Close the document.

Edit a Table

Objectives and Introduction

After successfully completing this chapter, you will be able to rearrange text in tables by sorting table rows or by moving and deleting table rows and columns. You will also be able to copy a table, delete a table, calculate column and row totals, copy a formula to another cell, customize or remove table borders and shading, and use single and double underlines.

Sort a Table Numerically and Alphabetically

After a table has been created, you may want to rearrange the information. If the information needs to be arranged in order, for instance, alphabetically by name or numerically by sales or zip code, Sort provides a quick way to accomplish this. The only requirement is that the information that determines the sort order must be in its own column. For example, to sort alphabetically by name, the names must be in a separate column.

147

If the entire table is to be sorted, place the insertion point in any cell of the selected table and select **Table**, **Sort**. The entire table will automatically be selected for sorting. When only a portion of the table is to be sorted, select the rows to be sorted before selecting **Table**, **Sort**. *(Note: The rows must be next to one another.)*

After the Sort dialog box is displayed, the Sort by criteria must be entered. The sort criteria for a table identifies which column will determine the order, whether the sort type is Text, Number, or Date, and whether the sort order is Ascending or Descending. Ascending order starts with the lowest number and goes to the highest number, or starts with the letter A and goes to the letter Z. Descending order begins with the highest number and goes to the lowest number, or starts with Z and goes to A (reverse alphabetical order).

Title or subtitle rows must be excluded from the sort. If there is only one row to be excluded, select the entire table, then select the **My list has Header row** option in the Sort dialog box to exclude the first row from the sort. If more than one row must be excluded, select only the portion of the table that is to be sorted. After setting the sort criteria, make sure the **My list has No header row** option in the Sort dialog box is selected before beginning the sort.

Start-Up Instructions

❖ 🖫 Open the file named **6ptable1.doc** located on the data disk.

 Steps to **Sort Table Rows Numerically**

1. Select the rows of the table to be sorted.

    For example, select all table cells except the first two rows, which contain the table title and column headings.

2. Select **Table, Sort**.

    Note: The Sort dialog box displays (see Figure 6.1).

3. To change the Sort by option, click on the down arrow located to the right of the **Sort by** box and click on the desired option.

FIGURE 6.1

Sort dialog box

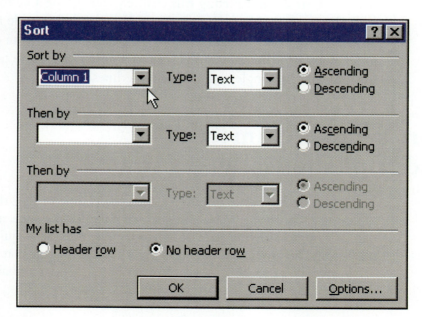

For example, click on the down arrow located to the right of the **Sort by** box and click on **Column 3** to sort the table by the third column.

4. To select a different type of sort, i.e., **Text**, **Number**, or **Date**, click on the down arrow located to the right of the Type box and select the desired type.

   For example, check that **Number** displays. (If necessary, select **Number**.)

5. Select the sort order, i.e., **Ascending** or **Descending**.

   For example, select **Descending**.

6. Select **OK**.

   Note: After a moment, the sorted table displays. The table rows have been sorted using the information in column 3.

Finish-Up Instructions

❖ Use the *new* filename **6numeric sort.doc** and save the file on your file disk.

❖ Print one copy and close the document.

Start-Up Instructions

❖ Open the file named **6ptable2.doc** located on the data disk.

Steps to ▶ Sort Table Rows Alphabetically

1. Select the rows of the table to be sorted.

   For example, select the entire table by placing the insertion point in any table cell and choosing **Table, Select, Table**.

   *Note: In **Print Layout View** the entire table can be selected by clicking on the **Select Table** icon located at the top left corner of the table.*

2. Select **Table, Sort**.

3. To change the Sort by option, click on the down arrow located to the right of the **Sort by** box and click on the desired option.

   For example, click on the down arrow located to the right of the **Sort by** box and click on **Salesperson** to sort the table by the first column.

   *Note: The My list has Header row should be selected. (If necessary, select the **My list has Header** row option.)*

4. To select a different type of sort, i.e., **Text**, **Number**, or **Date**, click on the down arrow located to the right of the Type box and select the desired type.

   For example, check that **Text** displays. (If necessary, select **Text**.)

5. Select the sort order, i.e., **Ascending** or **Descending**.

   For example, select **Ascending**.

6. Select **OK**.

Note: The salespeople's names are listed alphabetically. Notice that first names were used to sort the rows that contained individuals with the same last name.

Finish-Up Instructions

❖ Use the *new* filename **6text sort.doc** and save the file on your file disk.

❖ Print one copy and close the document.

Move a Table Column and Row

A table column or row can be moved to another column or row location within a table. When a column or row is moved, the column or row is deleted from the original location and relocated. When a column or row is copied, the column or row displays in the original location and in the new location.

The column or row to be moved must be selected before the move process can be performed. The selected row or column can then be moved using either the drag and drop or the cut and paste method (see Chapter 4).

Before inserting a cut column, place the insertion point in any cell in the column that will be located to the right of the moved column. Before inserting a cut row, place the insertion point in any cell in the row that will be located below the moved row.

Start-Up Instructions

❖ Open the file named **6ptable3.doc** located on the data disk.

❖ The nonprinting characters should be displayed. If necessary, select the **Show/Hide** button ¶.

❖ Turn on Print Layout view. (If necessary, select the **Print Layout View** button located on the left of the horizontal scroll bar.)

Steps to ▶ **Move a Table Column**

1. Select the column to be moved by moving the mouse pointer to the border line at the top of the column until a down arrow displays. Click once to select and highlight the column.

   For example, move the mouse pointer to the border line at the top of column 3 (i.e., Part No.) and click the mouse button once.

2. Move the mouse pointer into the selected column until the left-pointing arrow displays. Press and hold the mouse button until an outlined box displays at the bottom of the mouse pointer and a dotted insertion point appears (see Figure 6.2). Drag the dotted insertion point to the column that will appear to the right of the moved column. Release the mouse button.

   For example, move the mouse pointer into the selected column (i.e., column 3) until the left-pointing arrow displays; press and hold the mouse button while dragging the dotted insertion point to column 2. Release the mouse button.

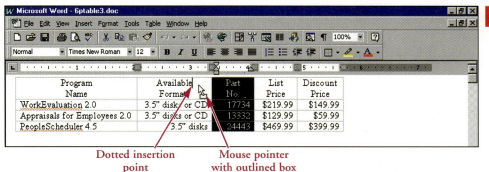

FIGURE 6.2

Move a column using drag and drop

Dotted insertion point   Mouse pointer with outlined box

*Note: Column 3 is moved to the left of column 2. A column can also be moved by using the **Cut** and **Paste** buttons on the Standard Toolbar.*

3. Click once to deselect the column..

Note: The column widths may need to be adjusted after columns are moved.

Finish-Up Instructions

❖ Use the *new* filename **6column move.doc** and save the file on your file disk.

❖ Print one copy.

Start-Up Instructions

❖ The file named **6column move.doc** should be displayed in the document window.

Move a Table Row

1. Select the row to be moved by placing the mouse pointer outside the gridline/border to the left of the desired row until a right-pointing arrow displays and click once.

> For example, move the mouse pointer outside the gridline/border to the left of row 3 until a right-pointing arrow displays. Click once to select the entire row.

2. Move the mouse pointer into the selected row until the left-pointing arrow displays. Press and hold the mouse button until an outlined box displays at the bottom of the mouse pointer and a dotted insertion point appears. Drag the dotted insertion point to the first cell in the row that will be located below the moved row. Release the mouse button.

> For example, move the mouse pointer into the selected row (i.e., row 3) until the left-pointing arrow displays. Press and hold the mouse button while dragging the dotted insertion point to the first cell in row 2. Release the mouse button.

*Note: Row 3 is moved above row 2. A row can also be moved by using the **Cut** and **Paste** buttons on the Standard Toolbar.*

3. Click once to deselect the row.

❖ With the insertion point located in any table cell, select **Table**, **Table AutoFormat** and click on the **Classic 2** format. Select **OK**.

❖ Use the *new* filename **6row move.doc** and save the file on your file disk.

❖ Print one copy.

Note: Your table should look similar to the following:

Program Name	Part No.	Available Formats	List Price	Discount Price
PeopleScheduler 4.5	24443	3.5" disks	$469.99	$399.99
WorkEvaluation 2.0	17734	3.5" disks or CD	$219.99	$149.99
Appraisals for Employees 2.0	13332	3.5" disks or CD	$129.99	$59.99

Delete a Table Column and Row

When editing a table, a column or row can be deleted. A column or row is deleted by first selecting the column or row to be deleted and then selecting the **Delete Columns** or **Delete Rows** option in the **Table** menu. The **Delete** option in the **Table** menu changes depending on the selected cells. If a row is selected, the **Delete** option displays **Delete Rows**; if a column is selected, the **Delete** option displays **Delete Columns**. When a portion of a column or row is selected, the **Delete** option displays **Delete Cells**. A column or row can also be deleted by selecting the row or column and then selecting the **Cut** button on the Standard Toolbar.

If a column or row is deleted by mistake, select **Edit**, **Undo** from the Menu bar (or select the **Undo** button on the Standard Toolbar) to retrieve and display the deleted column or row. If other actions have been performed after the column or row was deleted, select **Edit**, **Undo** (or the **Undo** button) repeatedly until the deleted row or column displays again.

❖ The file named **6row move.doc** should be displayed in the document window.

 Delete a Table Column

1. Select the column to be deleted. (If necessary, refer to step 1 in the Steps to Move a Table Column on page 150.)

   For example, select column 2.

2. Select **Table, Delete, Columns**.

   *Note: The second column is deleted and the columns on the right moved to the left. If a table column is deleted by mistake, select the **Undo** button to retrieve the deleted column.*

Shortcut:

1. Point to the highlighted column, click the *right* mouse button, and choose Delete Columns.

Finish-Up Instructions

❖ Center the table horizontally (with the insertion point in any table cell, select **Table**, **Table Properties**, **Table** tab, choose **Center** in the alignment area, **OK**).

❖ Use the *new* filename **6delete col.doc** and save the file on your file disk.

❖ Print one copy (select the **Print** button).

Start-Up Instructions

❖ The file named **6delete col.doc** should be displayed in the document window.

Delete a Table Row

1. Select the row to be deleted. (If necessary, refer to step 1 in the Steps to Move a Table Row on page 151.)

    For example, select row 2.

2. Select **Table, Delete, Rows**.

    Note: Row 2 is deleted. If a table row is deleted by mistake, select the **Undo** *button to retrieve the deleted row.*

Shortcut:

1. Point to the highlighted row, click the *right* mouse button, and choose Delete Rows.

Finish-Up Instructions

❖ Use the *new* filename **6delete row.doc** and save the file on your file disk.

❖ Continue with the Steps to Copy a Table.

Copy a Table

An entire table can be copied to another window or to another location within the current document window. A table can be copied for many reasons:

➤ to make changes to the copied table without changing the original table.

➤ to save paper by placing two items on a page.

➤ to use the table information in another letter, memorandum, or report.

❖ The file named **6delete row.doc** should be displayed in the document window.

 ## Copy a Table

1. Highlight the entire table by placing the insertion point in any table cell and selecting Table, Select, Table or click on the Select Table icon located at the top left corner of the table.

2. Select the Copy button on the Standard Toolbar.

3. Locate the insertion point at the desired position.

    For example, locate the insertion point below the table (press **Ctrl** and **End**)and press **Enter** twice to insert blank lines.

4. Select the Paste button on the Standard Toolbar.

    Note: A copy of the table is inserted at the location of the insertion point.

Finish-Up Instructions

❖ Use the *new* filename **6table copy.doc** and save the file on your file disk.

❖ Continue with the Steps to Delete a Table, or close the document.

Delete a Table

A table can be deleted by selecting the entire table and choosing the **Delete, Table** options in the **Table** menu. If a table is deleted by mistake, select the **Undo** button on the Standard Toolbar to retrieve and redisplay the deleted table.

Start-Up Instructions

❖ The file named **6table copy.doc** should be displayed in the document window.

 ## Delete a Table

1. Highlight the entire table by placing the insertion point in any table cell. Select Table, Select, Table or click on the Select Table icon located at the top left of the table.

    For example, select the first table on the screen.

2. Select Table, Delete, Table.

Shortcut:

1. With the insertion point in the highlighted table, click the *right* mouse button once; choose Cut.

Finish-Up Instructions

❖ Close the document but do not save the file.

Calculate a Column and Row Total

Table cells containing values are calculated by inserting formulas to add, subtract, multiply, or divide. A value is a number used to obtain a mathematical result. A text number is a number that will not be used to compute a result. Examples of text numbers are social security numbers or product numbers (e.g., P599).

Table formulas are easily created in the Formula dialog box. The insertion point is first placed in the cell that will contain the column or row calculation, and then the **Formula** option is selected from the **Table** menu. The Formula dialog box displays, usually with the SUM formula displayed, which is the default. (Word assumes the cell values are to be added.) If the cells are not to be added, a different formula can be typed, or options can be selected from the Paste functions box to create the desired formula. Normally cell addresses are used in formulas to indicate which values are to be calculated. For example, SUM(B1+B2) tells Word to add the values in cells B1 and B2. Word also provides shortcuts for adding all the values in a column or row. When the formula SUM(ABOVE) is placed in the last cell of a column, the values of all cells in the column are added. Similarly, when the formula SUM(LEFT) is placed in the last cell of a row, the values in the cells located to the left are added.

The results of the formula are inserted into the cell as a field. The field contains special codes that instruct Word to insert information into the table cell. The results of the field display in the table cell and are shaded gray when the I-beam is moved to the result value and the mouse button is clicked. When the formula results display in gray, the field codes can be turned on or off by moving the mouse pointer to the center of the formula result, pressing the *right* mouse button, and selecting the **Toggle Field Codes** option. The field code replaces the gray results, e.g., { =SUM(ABOVE) }.

A formula is deleted by selecting and highlighting the cell that contains the formula and either pressing **Delete,** selecting the **Cut** button on the Standard Toolbar, or selecting the **Cut** option in the **Edit** menu. The cell is selected by moving the mouse pointer into the cell until the right-pointing arrow displays and then clicking the mouse button once.

If values are changed in the table cells, the cells that contain formula results will need to be recalculated (updated). Formula results can be recalculated by selecting the cell that contains the formula (or by selecting the entire table if more than one needs to be recalculated) and pressing **F9**. The formula results can also be recalculated by moving the mouse pointer to the cell that contains the formula, clicking the *right* mouse button, and choosing the **Update Field** option on the Shortcut menu.

Word analyzes the number format of the cell values in the formula to determine an appropriate number format for the formula results. For example, if any of the cells in the formula contain a dollar sign, Word will format the formula results with a dollar sign. If desired, the number format for the formula results can be changed using the **Number format** option in the Formula dialog box.

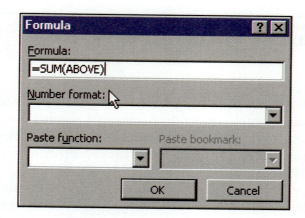

FIGURE 6.3

Formula dialog
box

After a formula has been placed in a cell, the formula can be copied to another cell by moving the insertion point to the desired location and selecting **Edit, Repeat Formula**. However, you must use the **Edit, Repeat Formula** command before any other action is taken. The **Edit, Repeat Formula** command is available only immediately after a formula has been created. If any other action is taken, the **Edit, Repeat Formula** command may not be available.

Start-Up Instructions

❖ Open the file named **6calc.doc** located on the data disk.

❖ The nonprinting characters should be displayed. If necessary, select the **Show/Hide** button.

Steps to **Use a Formula to Calculate the Sum of a Column**

1. Select the cell that will contain the formula results.

   For example, select the last cell of column 2.

2. Select **Table, Formula**.

   Note: The Formula dialog box displays as shown in Figure 6.3.

3. Create the appropriate formula in the Formula box either by typing the formula or by selecting a **Paste function** option and then completing the formula by typing the necessary information in the Formula box.

   For example, check that the formula =SUM(ABOVE) displays in the Formula box. (If necessary, type =SUM(ABOVE) in the Formula box.)

4. In the Number format box, type the desired format, or select the down arrow beside the Number format box and choose a format.

   For example, click on the down arrow beside the Number format box and select the $#,##0.00;($#,##0.00) format.

   Note: If no number format is specified, Word attempts to apply a format by using the same format as the numbers in the cells being totaled.

5. Select **OK**.

   Note: The figure $111,616.41 displays in the last cell of column 2.

Shortcut:

1. Select the desired cell, choose the **AutoSum** button Σ on the **Tables and Borders** Toolbar.

Finish-Up Instructions

❖ Calculate the sum of column 3 (select the last cell of column 3 and repeat steps 2–5 in the Steps to Use a Formula to Calculate the Sum of a Column, or click on the **AutoSum** button).

Note: The figure $235,671.36 displays in the last cell of column 3.

❖ Use the *new* filename **6calc expenses.doc** and save the file on your file disk.

Start-Up Instructions

❖ The file named **6calc expenses.doc** should be displayed in the document window.

❖ Change the figures in the table as edited in Figure 6.4. Then use the Steps to Edit Table Figures and Recalculate to recalculate the column totals.

Edit Table Figures and Recalculate

1. Move the I-beam to the figure in the cell containing a formula.

   For example, move the mouse pointer (I-beam) to the last cell in column 2.

2. Click the *right* mouse button once.

3. Select **Update Field.**

   Note: The original formula results are replaced with the recalculated formula results. The figure $153,598.61 displays in the last cell of column 2.

Shortcut:

1. Click in the cell containing a formula.

2. Press **F9**.

Expense Category	Far East District	Middle East District
Labor	$78,850.26 ~~$44,540.52~~	$98,244.67
Materials	22,982.00	59,893.85 ~~77,243.00~~
Supplies	18,255.88	23,442.36
Utilities	15,922.46 ~~8,250.00~~	12,895.95 ~~10,952.00~~
Insurance	17,588.01	25,789.33
Totals	$111,616.41	$235,671.36

FIGURE 6.4

Edited table

Finish-Up Instructions

❖ Recalculate the formula result in the last cell in column 3 using the Steps to Edit Table Figures and Recalculate.

❖ Use the same filename, **6calc expenses.doc**, and save the file again.

❖ Print one copy.

Start-Up Instructions

❖ The file named **6calc expenses.doc** should be displayed in the document window.

❖ The nonprinting characters should be displayed. If necessary, select the **Show/Hide** button.

❖ Turn on **Print Layout View** (select the **Print Layout** button located on the left of the vertical scroll bar).

❖ Insert one table column after column 3. (Move the mouse pointer to the top of the end-of-row markers until the down arrow displays and click once to highlight the end-of-row markers. Select the **Insert Columns** button on the Standard Toolbar.)

❖ Type the column heading **Total Expenses** in the first cell of column 4.

Total a Row

1. Select the cell where the new total is to be inserted.

   For example, select the second cell in the last column.

2. Select **Table, Formula**.

   Note: The Formula dialog box displays.

3. Create the appropriate formula in the Formula box, either by typing the formula or by selecting a **Paste function** option, and then complete the formula by typing the necessary information in the Formula box.

   For example, check that the formula **=SUM(LEFT)** displays in the Formula box. (If necessary, type **=SUM(LEFT)** in the Formula box.)

4. In the Number format box, type the desired format, or select the down arrow beside the Number format box and choose a format.

   For example, click on the down arrow beside the Number format box and select the **$#,##0.00;($#,##0.00)** format.

5. Select **OK**.

   Note: The figure $177,094.93 displays.

Shortcut:

1. With the insertion point located in the desired cell, select the **AutoSum** button **Σ** on the **Tables and Borders** Toolbar.

   Note: This shortcut only applies to the first row to be calculated in a table.

Finish-Up Instructions

❖ Use the *new* filename **6total row.doc** and save the file on your file disk.

   Note: The remaining row totals will be calculated by continuing with the following instructions.

Start-Up Instructions

❖ The file named **6total row.doc** should be displayed in the document window.

❖ Calculate the total of row 3 by repeating steps 2–5 in the Steps to Total a Row. In step 3, double-click on ABOVE and type LEFT. the formula =SUM(LEFT) should display. In step 4, select the Number format **#,##0.00**.

 Copy a Formula

1. Place the insertion point in the cell where the formula is to be copied.

   For example, place the insertion point in the last cell of row 4.

2. Select **Edit, Repeat Formula**.

   Note: The formula =SUM(LEFT) will be copied into the last cell of row 4, and the results of the formula will appear in the cell using the number format previously selected.

Finish-Up Instructions

❖ Repeat steps 1–2 in the Steps to Copy a Formula to copy the formula to the last cell in rows 5 and 6.

❖ Repeat steps 2–5 in the Steps to Total a Row to calculate row 7. Set the number format to **$#,##0.00;($#,##0.00)**, or select the last column cell and choose **AutoSum**.

❖ Insert a new row above the first row in the table (click to the left of the border in row 1, and select the **Insert Rows** button).

❖ Merge the cells in row 1 (select row 1, point to the selected cells, click the *right* mouse button, and choose **Merge Cells**).

❖ Type the title **District Expenses** in the top row of the table. Check that all headings are centered.

   Note: Your table should look similar to the following table:

District Expenses			
Expense Category	Far East District	Middle East District	Total Expenses
Labor	$78,850.26	$98,244.67	$177,094.93
Materials	22,982.00	59,893.85	82,875.85
Supplies	18,255.88	23,442.36	41,698.24
Utilities	15,922.46	12,895.95	28,818.41
Insurance	17,588.01	25,789.33	43,377.34
Totals	$153,598.61	$220,266.16	$373,864.77

❖ Use the *new* filename **6copy formula.doc** and save the file on your file disk.

❖ Print one copy.

Customize Table Borders and Shading

In Chapter 5, instructions for applying Table AutoFormats were discussed. In this chapter, applying individual borders and shading options is discussed. Rather than choosing from various preformatted combinations of borders and shades for an entire table, individual borders and shades can be applied to a table. For example, borders can be placed around a single cell, a group of cells, or the entire table. Or, only row borders (horizontal lines) or column borders (vertical lines) can be added. The style of the borders can vary from solid lines to double or dashed lines. Also, the thickness of the borders can be changed by clicking on the **Line Weight** button in the Tables and Borders Toolbar and selecting the desired weight.

In addition to adding borders, cells can be shaded (filled) with a variety of shades or fill patterns. Shades (or gradients) generally refer to a certain shaded percentage of a color. For example, a 10% shade appears as a light gray. Customized borders and shades are often used to draw attention to certain parts of a table, such as a row or column total or a grand total.

Borders and shading are applied by using either the Tables and Borders Toolbar or the **Borders and Shading** option in the **Format** menu. After selecting

FIGURE 6.5

Tables and Borders Toolbar

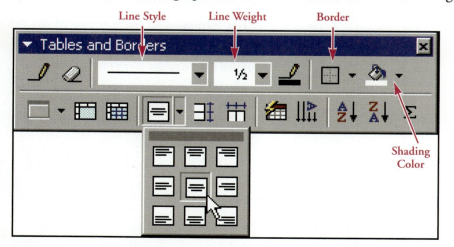

the desired cells, choose the **Tables and Borders** button ⊞ on the Standard Toolbar to display the Tables and Borders Toolbar (see Figure 6.5). The buttons on the Tables and Borders Toolbar are used to specify the width and position of borders and the type of shading to apply. When the mouse pointer is placed on any button in the Tables and Borders Toolbar, a ToolTip (description of the button) displays. To turn off the Tables and Borders Toolbar, select the **Close** button on the Tables and Borders Toolbar.

To remove borders, select the table or cells, display the Tables and Borders Toolbar, choose the down arrow beside the **Border** button ▦, and select **No Border**. *(Note: The name of the Border button changes based on the last selected border.)* To remove shading, select the cells to which the shading has been applied, display the Tables and Borders Toolbar, click on the down arrow next to the **Shading Color** button, then select **No Fill**.

Start-Up Instructions

❖ The file named **6copy formula.doc** should be displayed in the document window.

❖ The Tables and Borders Toolbar should be displayed. (If necessary, select the **Tables and Borders** button on the Standard Toolbar.)

❖ If the insertion point is a pencil, turn off **Draw Table** by clicking once on the **Draw Table** button.

❖ Increase the row height of the first two rows to .3". (Select the first two rows; select **Table**, **Table Properties**, **Row** tab, click on **Specify height**; triple-click on the figure in the **Specify height** box, type **.3**; select **OK**).

❖ Select the remaining rows and increase the row height to .2".

❖ Select the first two rows and click on the down arrow beside the **Align...** button ▤ on the Tables and Borders Toolbar; choose **Align Center**.

❖ Select columns 2, 3, and 4 of rows 3–8, choose the **Align...** button, and then select the **Align Bottom Right** button ▤.

❖ Select column 1, rows 3–8, choose the **Align...** button, and then select the **Align Bottom Left** button ▤.

 ## Modify a Row Border

1. Select the row to be modified.

   For example, select row 2.

2. Click on the down arrow next to the **Line Style** box on the Tables and Borders Toolbar (see Figure 6.5) and select the desired style.

   For example, select the seventh line style (i.e., double lines).

3. Select the **Border** button ▦ on the Tables and Borders Toolbar.

   *Note: A list of border placement options displays (see Figure 6.6). The name of the **Border** button changes based on the last selected border, e.g., Outside Border, Top Border, No Border.*

4. Choose the desired border placement.

For example, select the **Bottom Border** option.

5. Click once in the table to deselect the row.

Note: The line style for the bottom of row 2 displays a double border line.

Finish-Up Instructions

❖ Use the *new* filename **6modified border.doc** and save the file on your file disk.

Start-Up Instructions

❖ The file named **6modified border.doc** should be displayed in the document window.

❖ The Tables and Borders Toolbar should be displayed. If necessary, select the **Tables and Borders** button on the Standard Toolbar.

Apply Shading to Table Cells

1. Select the cell or cells to be shaded.

For example, select all the cells in column 4, which contains the total expense figures, including the column heading.

2. Click the down arrow beside the **Shading Color** button ![icon] on the Tables and Borders Toolbar to display the drop-down list of available fills (see Figure 6.6). Select the desired shade.

For example, select the **Gray - 15%** option (first row, fifth option).

3. Click once in the table to deselect the cells.

Note: A 15% gray shade displays on the screen in column 4.

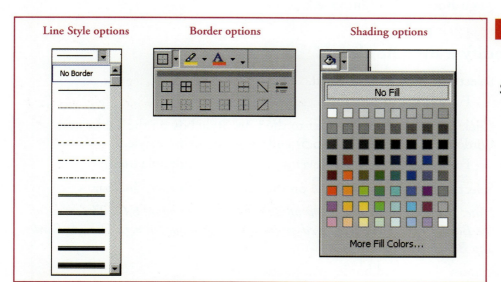

Line Style options   Border options   Shading options

FIGURE 6.6

Line Style, Border, and Shading options on the Tables and Borders Toolbar

Finish-Up Instructions

❖ Select the last table row and apply the **Gray - 15%** shade (repeat steps 2 and 3 of the Steps to Apply Shading to Table Cells).

❖ Select rows 1 and 2, then select the **Bold** button on the Formatting Toolbar.

❖ If necessary, widen the columns so that the column headings display on one line.

❖ Use the same filename, **6modified border.doc**, and save the file again.

Note: Your table should look similar to the following:

District Expenses			
Expense Category	**Far East District**	**Middle East District**	**Total Expenses**
Labor	$78,850.26	$98,244.67	$177,094.93
Materials	22,982.00	59,893.85	82,875.85
Supplies	18,255.88	23,442.36	41,698.24
Utilities	15,922.46	12,895.95	28,818.41
Insurance	17,588.01	25,789.33	43,377.34
Totals	$153,598.61	$220,266.16	$373,864.77

❖ Print one copy. Close the document.

Start-Up Instructions

❖ The file named **6modified border.doc** should be displayed on the screen.

❖ The Tables and Borders Toolbar should be displayed. (If necessary, select the **Tables and Borders** button on the Standard Toolbar.)

Remove All Borders in a Table

1. Highlight the entire table by placing the insertion point in any table cell and selecting Table, Select, Table.

2. Select the down arrow next to the Border button ▢▾ on the Tables and Borders Toolbar.

   Note: The Border placement options display.

3. To remove borders around all cells, select the No Border option.

   *Note: The borders are removed from all table cells. The table gridlines display. If the gridlines do not display, select **Table, Show Gridlines**.*

4. Click once in the table to deselect the table cells.

Finish-Up Instructions

❖ Use the *new* filename **6No border.doc** and save the file on your file disk.

❖ Continue with the Steps to Insert Double Underlines.

Insert Single and Double Underlines

Double underlines are placed under a column total amount to emphasize the total. When double underlines are used, table borders are generally not printed. When a column is totaled, a single underline is used to separate the last column amount from the total amount. The single underline traditionally extends the width of the total amount. Therefore, one or more spaces are placed to the left of the last column number to extend the underline.

Traditionally, the dollar sign ($) in the first figure and the last figure of a column align. Since there is often an additional digit in the total amount, extra space is needed between the dollar sign and the first digit in the first column entry. Placing a space in the **Number format** box (select **Table**, **Formula**) when typing the desired format will provide the extra space to ensure the alignment of the dollar signs. If necessary, the insertion point can be placed between the dollar sign and following figure and the **Spacebar** pressed to add an extra space.

Once the column total has been calculated, the amount is selected and the **Font** option in the **Format** menu is chosen. The underline style is changed to double in the Font dialog box.

Start-Up Instructions

❖ The Tables and Borders Toolbar should be displayed. If necessary, select the **Tables and Borders** button on the Standard Toolbar.

❖ The file named **6No border.doc** should be displayed.

❖ Place the insertion point between the dollar sign and the first digit of the figure in row 3, column 2. Press the **Spacebar** one time. Repeat for the figure in row 3, column 3.

❖ Underline the cells in row 7 that contain figures (select the cells containing the figures; select the **Underline** button).

❖ Extend the underline below the last column amount in each cell of row 7 (place the insertion point to the left of the first digit in the cell and press the **Spacebar** repeatedly until the underline extends the length of the total amount, including the dollar sign).

 Insert Double Underlines

1. Select the desired cells.

   For example, select the cells in row 8, which contains total amounts.

2. Select **Format, Font**.

   Note: The Font dialog box displays.

3. Select the desired tab.

For example, check that the **Font** tab is selected. (If necessary, select the **Font** tab.)

4. Click in the **Underline** style box to display the list of available underline styles.

5. Select the **Double** underline (fourth option).

6. Select **OK**.

7. Click once to deselect the cells.

   *Note: To view the double underlines, select the **Print Preview** button, then move the mouse pointer over the table and click once to magnify the view. Select **Close** to return to the document window.*

Finish-Up Instructions

❖ Use the *new* filename **6double.doc** and save the file on your file disk.

❖ Print one copy. Close the document.

Self-Check Quiz
Language Arts
Activities
Challenge Your Skills

The Next Step

Chapter Review and Activities

Self-Check Quiz

T F 1. A table row or column can be moved.

T F 2. To delete a table column, select the column and press **Delete**.

T F 3. An entire table can be copied to another document window or to another location in the current document window.

T F 4. If values in table cells are changed, the column or row totals can be recalculated by selecting the **Recalculate** option from the **Table** menu.

5. A row can be deleted by selecting the row and choosing the _____ option from the **Table** menu.
   a. **Delete Table**
   b. **Delete Rows**
   c. **Delete Formatting**
   d. none of the above

6. A moved column is deleted from the original location and _____ a new location.
    a. duplicated in
    b. copied to
    c. relocated to
    d. reproduced in

7. The _____ Toolbar is used to apply borders and shading to table cells.
    a. Formatting
    b. Rows and Columns
    c. Tables and Borders
    d. Standard

8. To insert double underlines, the _____ dialog box must be displayed.
    a. Character Format
    b. Paragraph Format
    c. Style
    d. none of the above

9. Write down the formula to sum the contents of cells in a table row.

10. Give one reason for adding borders and/or shading to a table.

Enriching Language Arts Skills

Spelling/Vocabulary Words

anticipated—expected; looked forward to.
budget—a plan for spending money or resources.
per diem—an amount allowed for daily expenses.

Single and Double Underlines for Dollar Amounts

Place a single underline between the last column amount and the total amount. Traditionally, the single underline extends the width of the amount with the most characters, including the dollar sign. Add spaces before the digits in the last column amount to extend the underline. In a table without borders, a total amount is usually emphasized by placing double underlines beneath the total amount.

Example:

$110,550
3,600
_2,820_
$116,970

Activities

Activity 6.1—Calculate the Total of the Columns and Rows; Copy a Formula; Customize Borders

1. In a new document window, create a table with 6 rows and 4 columns.

2. Display the Tables and Borders Toolbar (choose the **Tables and Borders** button on the Standard Toolbar).

3. Type the unformatted information as shown.

   Remember: Text will automatically wrap around in cells.

General Fund Transfers			
Account	August	September	Totals
Personnel	$92,005.29	$92,854.66	
Equipment	50,510.80	86,451.21	
Fulfillment	35,890.22	35,815.91	
Totals			

4. Use the following information to format the table:

   a. Merge the cells in the first row (select row 1; select **Table**, **Merge Cells**).

   b. Center and bold the title and column headings in the first two rows (select the rows; select the **Center** alignment and **Bold** buttons).

   c. Right align the cells containing amounts and the cells that will contain the totals (select the desired cells and choose the **Align Right** button). (It's OK that some of the cells are currently empty.)

   d. Calculate the sum for column 2 (select the last cell of column 2; select **Table**, **Formula**; the Formula box displays =**SUM(ABOVE)**; click on the down arrow beside the Number format box; select the **$#,##0.00;($#,##0.00)** option; select **OK**).

   e. Copy the formula placed in the last cell of column 2 to the last cell in columns 3 and 4 (place the insertion point in the desired cell, select **Edit**, **Repeat Formula**).

   Note: $0.00 displays in the last cell of column 4. That's OK.

   f. Calculate the total for row 3, column 4 (select the desired cell, select **Table**, **Formula**; the Formula box displays =**SUM(LEFT)**; click on the down arrow beside the Number format box and select the **$#,##0.00($#,##0.00)** option; select **OK**).

   g. Follow the instructions in step 4f. and calculate the row total for row 4. Change the formula to read =**SUM(LEFT)**, and the number format should be **#,##0.00**.

h. Copy the formula to row 5 (click in the last cell in row 5; select **Edit**, **Repeat Formula**).

i. Recalculate the total in the last cell of row 6 (place the insertion point in the cell, click the *right* mouse button, and select **Update Field**).

j. Insert one space between the dollar sign and the first digit in row 3, columns 2 and 3, to align the dollar sign with the column totals.

k. Change the font size to **12 point** for the entire table (select **Table**, **Select**, **Table**; click on the down arrow next to the **Font Size** button and select **12**).

l. If necessary, visually estimate and adjust the column widths so that the columns containing figures are approximately the same width.

5. Change the line weight to ¾ **pt** (select the entire table; on the Tables and Borders Toolbar, click on the **Line Weight** button, choose ¾ **pt**; choose the **Border** button, select **All Borders**).

   Note: Your table should look similar to the following table:

General Fund Transfers			
Account	August	September	Totals
Personnel	$ 92,005.29	$ 92,854.66	$184,859.95
Equipment	50,510.80	86,451.21	136,962.01
Fulfillment	35,890.22	35,815.91	71,706.13
Totals	$178,406.31	$215,121.78	$393,528.09

6. Use the filename **6General Fund.doc** and save the file on your file disk.

7. Optional: Fax this table to your instructor via a local fax, or write an e-mail message to your instructor that you are sending this assignment. Attach this file to your e-mail message.

8. Print one copy and close the document.

Activity 6.2—Move Columns and Rows; Copy and Sort a Table; Apply Borders and Shading; Delete a Table

1. In a new document window, create a table with 7 rows and 4 columns.

2. Type the unformatted information as shown:

   Remember: Text will automatically wrap around in cells.

El Gato Equipment			
Advertising Costs			
Item	1998	1999	2000
Four-color brochures	100,950	150,800	200,850
Sales meetings	10,900	12,600	13,900
Television ads	560,200	750,000	800,200
Premiums	25,900	35,600	34,000

3. Move the columns and rows as described in the following instructions:

    a. Move the column containing the 2000 information between columns 1 and 2 (select column 4; move the mouse pointer into the selected column until a left-pointing arrow displays; press and hold the mouse button while dragging the dotted insertion point to column 2; release the mouse button).

    b. Move the column containing the 1999 information between columns 2 and 3 (see step 3a, if necessary).

    c. Move row 6 (i.e., Television ads) above row 5 (i.e, Sales meetings) (select row 6; move the mouse pointer into the selected row until a left-pointing arrow displays; press and hold the mouse button while dragging the dotted insertion point to row 5; release the mouse button).

4. Use the following instructions to format the table:

    a. Merge the cells in row 1 (select row 1, select **Table**, **Merge Cells**). Repeat to merge the cells in row 2.

    b. If necessary, increase the width of the first column so that the text displays on one line. Visually estimate and adjust the widths of the remaining columns so that those columns are approximately 1" wide.

    c. Right align the cells containing the years and dollar amounts (select the cells containing the years and the dollar amounts; select the **Align Right** button).

    d. Center and bold the title and subtitle in rows 1 and 2, and center the cell contents vertically (select rows 1 and 2; select the **Center** alignment and the **Bold** buttons, then select the **Align** button on the Tables and Borders Toolbar and choose **Align Center**).

    e. Bold the row containing the column headings (select row 3; select the **Bold** button).

    f. Select the entire table and change the row height to **.3**". (Choose **Table**, **Select**, **Table**; select **Table**, **Table Properties**, **Row** tab, click on **Specify Height**; double-click on the figure in the **Specify Height** box, type **.3**", **OK**.)

g. Select cells 3–7 in column 1 and use a **10%** shade (select the cells; on the Tables and Borders Toolbar, select the down arrow beside the **Shading Color** button; select **Gray - 10%**). Repeat but use a **Gray - 15%** shade for rows 1 and 2.

h. Change the inside and outside table borders to ¼ **pt** line weight (select the entire table; click on the **Line Weight** button, choose ¼ **pt**; select the **Border** button, then select the **All Borders** option).

i. Center the table horizontally (place the insertion point in any table cell; select **Table, Table Properties, Table** tab, **Center** alignment, **OK**).

j. Change the bottom border of row 2 to the 1½ **pt** line weight (select row 2; click on the **Line Weight** button, choose 1½ **pt**; select the **Border** button and choose the **Bottom Border** option). Repeat to change the right border of rows 3–7 in column 1 to the 1½ **pt** line weight (select rows 3–7 in column 1; choose the **Right Border** option).

5. Use the filename **6El Gato.doc** and save the file on your file disk.

6. Copy the entire table (select the entire table and select the **Copy** button).

7. Move the insertion point below the table and press **Enter** twice to insert two blank lines. Select the **Paste** button to insert a copy of the table.

8. Sort the second table in descending order based on the column containing the 2000 data. (Select rows 3–7; select **Table, Sort**, select the **Header row** option. In the Sort by box, choose **2000**. In the Type box, choose **Number**; select **Descending; OK**.)

9. Use the *new* filename **6El Gato 2.doc** and save the file on your file disk.

10. Print one copy.

11. Delete the first table (select the entire table and choose **Table, Delete, Table**).

12. Optional: Print the table.

13. Close the document (do not save the modified file).

Activity 6.3—Calculate Column Totals; Delete a Row and Column; Remove Borders and Shading; Insert Double Underlines

1. Open the file named **6ice cream.doc** located on the data disk.

2. Calculate the sum of column 2 (select the last cell of column 2, select **Table, Formula**; check that the formula **=SUM(ABOVE)*100** displays; click in the **Number format** box and choose **0%**; select **OK**). Repeat to calculate the sum of columns 3 and 4.

3. Use the *new* filename **6survey.doc** and save the file on your file disk.

4. Edit the table as follows:

      a.   Delete the row that contains the Stars and Stripes information (select the row; select **Table**, **Delete**, **Rows**).

      b.   Recalculate the total in column 2 (move the I-beam to the last cell in column 2 and click once; click the *right* mouse button and select **Update Field**). Repeat to recalculate the totals in columns 3 and 4.

      c.   Delete column 4 (the Best Ad information). (Select column 4; select **Table**, **Delete**, **Columns**.)

5.   Finalize the table as follows:

      a.   Merge the cells in row 1 (select row 1, point to the selected cells; click the *right* mouse button; choose **Merge Cells**). Repeat to merge the cells in row 2.

      b.   Select columns 2 and 3 in row 8 (Pineapple Squash Surprise). Select the **Underline** button.

      c.   Select columns 2 and 3 in row 9 (Totals). Place a double underline below the total amounts (select **Format**, **Font**, **Font** tab, **Underline** style; click on the **Double** underline, **OK**).

      d.   Center the table horizontally (place the insertion point in any table cell; select **Table**, **Table Properties**, **Table** tab; choose **Center** in the alignment area, **OK**).

      e.   Select the column headings in row 3 and choose the **Italic** button.

      f.   Remove the table borders (select the entire table; select the **Border** button; select the **No Border** option).

      g.   Remove the shading from rows 3 and 9 (select the desired row; select the down arrow beside the **Shading Color** button, and select **None**).

6.   Use the *new* filename **6survey formatted.doc** and save the file on your file disk.

7.   Print one copy and close the document.

Challenge Your Skills

Skill 6.1—Create a Table and a Formula

1.   Create a two-column table using the following information:

      a.   The title of the table is Hutch's Full Service Car Wash.

      b.   The price of the Deluxe Wash is $13.50.

      c.   The price of the Standard Wax is $5.99.

      d.   The price of the Hand Polish is $6.50.

      e.   The price of the Oil Change and Lube is $23.89.

      f.   The charge for Car Pick-up and Delivery is $3.50.

      g.   Sales tax is $4.40.

      h.   Calculate the total amount due.

2. Make decisions regarding:

   > Alignment of table contents
   > Row height
   > Column widths
   > Placement of the table on the page (vertically and horizontally)
   > Borders
   > Shading
   > Number format and dollar sign placement

3. Use the filename **6Hutch.doc** and save the file.

4. Optional: Fax this table to your instructor via a local fax, or write an e-mail message to your instructor that you are sending this assignment. Attach this file to your e-mail message.

5. Print one copy and close the document.

☛ Skill 6.2—Calculate Column Totals; Language Arts Skills

1. Use the traditional block style letter and the following information:

   a. Send the letter to Ms. Jan Istask, Regional Director, Felix Enterprises, 9645 Mission Street, Redwood City, CA 94063.

   b. The letter is from Marla T. Abmed, District Manager.

   c. Make decisions regarding:

      > Margins
      > Alignment
      > Date
      > Salutation
      > Closing
      > Alignment of table contents
      > Formulas and number formats
      > Column widths
      > Table borders and shading
      > Reference initials
      > Document identification

   d. Correct three spelling errors, two punctuation errors, and one dollar amount format error.

   e. Letter body text follows:

      I am sure you are aware that our corporate travel expenses have been rising much faster than anticepated for the current budget year. This is the result of some major increases in airfares by TXA airlines and the loss of our corporate discount rate at the Ramadaon Hotel Chain due to the inappropriate behavior of a few staff members at the last sales meeting.

There is very little we can do about the airfares since TXA's hub is at our closest airport and the staff members who caused the problem have been dismissed (except, of course, for CEO John Richards). Until our next budget year starts, we will be forced to keep all expenses within the current budchet, despite the increases. Therefore the board has made the following changes in the travel allowances and reimbursement policy.

Per Deim Amount		
Items	Current Rate	New Rate
Hotel	$125.00	$65.00
Breakfast	15.00	9.50
Lunch	25.00	$12.50
Dinner	35.00	15.50
Airport parking	5.00	2.50
Car rental	45.00	35.00
Total Per Diem		

I realize these rates will force sales representatives to change hotels, and my assistant, Rick Mathers, is in the process of developing a list of possible hotels in all the major areas we service. If you find that there is no suitable accommodation in a particular area, an exception may be made; however, you will need to write an exception report and attach it to your reimbursement request. As before, breakfast, lunch, and dinner rates are flexible as long as your total for meals does not exceed the total amount shown.

If you have any questions regarding these rate changes please call me.

2. Use the filename **6rate change.doc** and save the file.

3. Print one copy.

4. Optional: Fax this table to your instructor via a local fax, or write an e-mail message to your instructor that you are sending this assignment. Attach this file to your e-mail message.

5. Close the document.

Create a Résumé

Objectives and Introduction

After successfully completing this chapter, you will be able to insert automatic single-line and double-line borders and special characters; change margins using the rulers; and set tabs to format an attractive, easy-to-read résumé. You will also use the Résumé Wizard to create a résumé.

Tab settings can be changed so that paragraphs can be indented in an attractive manner. Emphasis can be added to text by using text attributes such as bold, underline, and italic. Special symbols, such as the accent marks in résumé, can be inserted easily into a document. In addition, emphasis can be added by placing special symbols (bullets or arrows) in front of desired paragraphs (see Figures 7.3 and 7.7).

Create a Résumé

A résumé is a document that summarizes a person's education, work experience, and work skills. A résumé is submitted to a prospective employer when applying for a job. Because a résumé serves as a person's introduction to a prospective employer, it is important that the résumé be attractive and easy to read. A résumé may be formatted using the Tab and Indent features or a table.

As a general rule, it is preferable to keep your résumé to one or two pages. If your résumé is two or more pages, a header containing your name and the page numbers should be placed on the second and following pages. Inserting a header is covered in Chapter 10. In this book, we will limit our résumés to one page.

A Résumé Wizard is available to take you step by step through the creation of a résumé. When the Résumé Wizard is selected, a series of dialog boxes displays requesting information about the style, type of résumé, headings, and text to be included.

In many large companies, résumés are scanned into a computer. The résumé scanning system reviews the résumés and extracts information about the applicants, such as the applicant's name, address, and phone numbers. The system also extracts information about the applicant's work history and skills.

When preparing a résumé that could be scanned, remember the following:

➤ Use good-quality plain white paper or light beige paper.

➤ Use a font that is clear and crisp. Avoid small font sizes, underlining, or italic.

➤ Avoid using lots of graphic images or graphic lines that may confuse the scanning program.

Insert Special Symbols

Special text symbols, such as the é's in résumé, and graphic symbols, such as ❖ and ☆, can be inserted into a document by accessing Word's special symbols. Special symbols, such as mathematical symbols, foreign letters, and graphic symbols, are not on the computer keyboard.

Text symbols, such as é ,©, or ö can be selected from most of the fonts available on your system. If a text symbol is selected using a specific font, that font will not change even if the font in the document window is changed. To change the symbol font when the font in the document window changes, select the (**normal text**) font option in the Symbol dialog box. In other words, if the (**normal text**) font is selected in the Symbol dialog box, the font of the chosen special symbol will automatically be changed when the font of the text in the document window is changed. The Wingdings font provides many graphic symbols, such as ☆, ❖, ✈, and ✂. The Symbols font provides many mathematical and scientific symbols, such as ±, and ÷.

Special characters can also be inserted using the AutoCorrect feature. For example, if ==> (two equal signs followed by the greater than symbol) is typed and the **Tab** or **Spacebar** is pressed, the AutoCorrect feature automatically inserts a character. A list of some of the special characters that can be inserted automatically is shown in Figure 7.1. The ☺, ☺, and ☹ and other special characters are used in informal e-mail messages. To view a complete list of symbols that can be inserted using the AutoCorrect feature, select **Tools**, **AutoCorrect**.

Word also automatically converts characters such as straight quotation marks (") and dashes (--) to their correct typographical symbols, i.e., opening and closing quotation marks (" ") and an em dash (—).

FIGURE 7.1

You Type	AutoCorrect Inserts	You Type	AutoCorrect Inserts
(c)	©	<--	←
(r)	®	<==	⬅
(tm)	™	-->	→
:)	☺	==>	➡
:|	☺	<=>	⬌
:(	☹		

Single- and double-line borders can be quickly inserted into a document. To insert a single-line border, type three hyphens (---) and press the **Enter** key. Word automatically converts the three hyphens to a single-line border that extends from the left margin to the right margin. A double-line border is created by typing three equal signs (===) and pressing **Enter**. If the Office Assistant is displayed, a message appears stating that Word has automatically converted your typing to a solid black border.

Start-Up Instructions

❖ The nonprinting symbols should be displayed. If necessary, select the **Show/Hide** button.

❖ Type an **R** (to begin typing the word RÉSUMÉ).

 Steps to **Insert Special Symbols**

1. Place the insertion point at the location where the special symbol should be inserted.

   For example, the insertion point should be located immediately following the letter R.

2. Select **Insert, Symbol**.

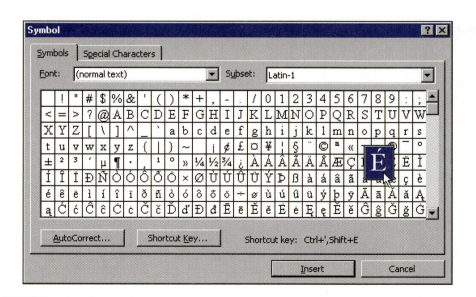

FIGURE 7.2

Symbol dialog box

Note: The Symbol dialog box displays (see Figure 7.2). Check that the Symbols tab is selected.

3. Move the mouse pointer to the down arrow located to the right of the Font box and click once.

4. Select the desired font by clicking on the down arrow beside the Font box, scrolling up or down the list of fonts to display the desired font, and clicking on the font name.

   For example, scroll up the list of fonts until (**normal text**) displays. Move the mouse pointer to (**normal text**) and click once.

5. Move the mouse pointer to the desired symbol. Click once to highlight and enlarge the symbol.

   For example, move the mouse pointer to the **É** symbol (fifth row, fourth button from the right) and click once.

   Note: The symbol is highlighted and enlarged.

6. Select **Insert** to copy the selected symbol into the document at the location of the insertion point.

   Note: The Symbol dialog box remains on the screen. If necessary, move the Symbol dialog box. (Move the mouse pointer to the Symbol dialog box Title bar, press and hold the mouse button, and drag to the right.)

7. Click in the document window at the desired location and type the additional text.

   For example, move the mouse pointer to the right of the **É** character and click once. Type **SUM**. (Do not type the final period.)

8. To insert the selected symbol again, select the **Insert** button in the Symbol dialog box.

   For example, check that the **É** is highlighted in the Symbol dialog box and select **Insert**.

9. When all needed symbols have been inserted into the document, select **Cancel** in the Symbol dialog box.

   For example, select **Cancel** to remove the Symbol dialog box from the screen.

Finish-Up Instructions

❖ Press the **Enter** key once to insert a blank line below the word RÉSUMÉ.

❖ Center the word RÉSUMÉ.

❖ Continue with the Steps to Insert Automatic Borders.

 ## Insert Automatic Borders

1. Place the insertion point at the location where the border is to be inserted.

For example, place the insertion point in the blank line below the word RÉSUMÉ.

2. Press the **hyphen** key three times (---) to create a single-line border.

   Note: To create a double-line border, press the equals key three times (===).

3. Press the **Enter** key.

   Note: The three hyphens are automatically converted to a single-line border below the word RÉSUMÉ.

Finish-Up Instructions

❖ Press the **Enter** key three times to insert three blank lines below the border.

   Note: The name and address will be inserted in the résumé later in this chapter.

❖ Type the heading **Educational Background** and press the **Enter** key twice.

❖ Type **==>** (two equal signs followed by the greater than symbol) and press the **Tab** key.

   Note: The AutoCorrect feature automatically converts the typed characters to an ➜.

❖ Type the following:

   Word Processing and Keyboarding, Adult Education Program, Union High School District

❖ Press the **Enter** key once.

   *Note: Word has inserted a second ➜ and converted the text to a bulleted list. If a second ➜ character is not inserted. press the **Backspace** key once. Then choose **Tools, AutoCorrect**, select the AutoFormat As You Type tab, choose the Automatic bulleted lists option, and select **OK**. Press the **Enter** key.*

❖ Type the following:

   Commerce College, Manila, Philippines. Received diploma in Business

❖ Press the **Enter** key three times.

❖ Use the filename **7Special characters.doc** and save the file on your file disk.

Change the Case of Text

After text has been typed, Word can automatically change the case of the text to all uppercase characters, all lowercase characters, sentence case (capitalizes the first letter of the first word at the beginning of a sentence or the first letter of the first word after a sentence), and title case (capitalizes the first letter of each selected word). In addition, the tOGGLE cASE option changes the case of selected text from uppercase to lowercase and lowercase to uppercase.

When using the Change Case feature, the text to be changed is selected. Choose **Format, Change Case**, and select the desired case option. The case of selected text can also be changed by pressing the **Shift** and **F3** keys until the text displays in the desired case. However, the case of a letter(s) can only be changed to all uppercase, all lowercase, or sentence case when using the **Shift** and **F3** method.

❖ The file named **7Special characters.doc** should be displayed in the document window.

 Change the Case of Characters

1. Select the desired text.

 For example, select the word RÉSUMÉ.

2. Select **Format, Change Case**.

3. Choose the desired option.

 For example, select **Title Case**.

4. Select **OK**.

5. Click once to deselect the text.

Finish-Up Instructions

❖ Use the same filename, **7Special characters.doc**, and save the file again.

Use Rulers to Change Margins and to Set Indents

A horizontal ruler containing margin, paragraph, indent, and tab markers can be displayed below the Formatting Toolbar. Also, in Print Layout View, a vertical ruler displays at the left side of the document window. The rulers show measurements in inches (see Figure 7.3). The left and right margins, paragraph indents, and tab locations can be set by using the mouse to move the appropriate markers on the horizontal ruler. The vertical ruler can be used to set the top and bottom margins of a document and to check the placement of text on the page. The **Print Layout View** or **Print Preview** button must be selected to change margins using the horizontal and vertical rulers.

The margin amounts and line length (in inches) can be displayed by pressing the **Alt** key while moving the left or right margin boundary markers. The top or bottom margin amount can also be viewed by pressing the **Alt** key while moving the top or bottom margin boundary markers.

The horizontal ruler can be used to set four types of paragraph indents: first line indent, hanging indent, left indent, and right indent. To set any of the four indent types, move the mouse pointer to the appropriate indent marker on the horizontal ruler, press and hold the mouse button, and drag the indent marker to the desired location. The indent markers are identified in Figure 7.3. A sample of each indent type is shown in Figure 7.4. Paragraph indents can also be created by selecting **Format, Paragraph, Indents and Spacing** tab, and the **Left**, **Right**, and **Special** (i.e., First Line and Hanging) indent options.

Start-Up Instructions

❖ The file named **7Special characters.doc** should be displayed in the document window.

❖ If necessary, select the Print Layout View (select the **Print Layout View** button at the bottom left of the document window).

Display or Remove the Ruler(s)

1. Select **View, Ruler**.

   *Note: The horizontal ruler displays below the Formatting Toolbar. A vertical ruler displays in Print Preview or Print Layout View. If the ruler(s) is displayed, selecting **View**, **Ruler** will remove the ruler(s) from the screen.*

Change the Left and Right Margins Using the Ruler

1. Select the down arrow beside the **Zoom** button and choose **Page Width** so that the left and right edges of the page display.

2. Move the mouse pointer to the left margin boundary (see Figure 7.3) until a double-headed arrow displays.

   Note: The ToolTip Left Margin displays below the double-headed arrow.

3. Press and hold the **Alt** key. Press and hold the mouse button to display a dotted vertical line. Drag the left margin boundary marker until the desired left margin amount displays at the left side of the ruler. Release the **Alt** key and the mouse button.

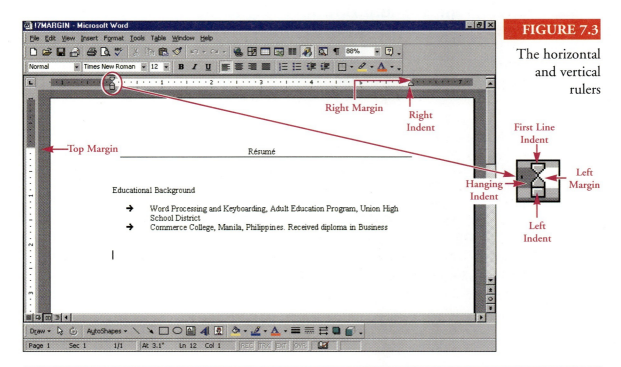

FIGURE 7.3

The horizontal and vertical rulers

For example, drag the left margin boundary marker to the right until **1.75"** displays at the left side of the ruler. Release the **Alt** key and the mouse button.

Note: The text moves to the new left margin.

4. Move the mouse pointer to the right margin boundary marker (see Figure 7.3) until a double-headed arrow displays.

Note: The ToolTip Right Margin displays below the double-headed arrow.

5. Press and hold the **Alt** key. Press and hold the mouse button to display a dotted vertical line. Drag the right margin boundary marker until the desired right margin amount displays at the right side of the ruler. Release the **Alt** key and the mouse button.

For example, drag the right margin boundary marker to the left until approximately **1.75"** displays at the right side of the ruler. Release the **Alt** key and the mouse button.

Finish-Up Instructions

❖ Use the *new* filename **7margins.doc** and save the file on your file disk.

Start-Up Instructions

❖ The file named **7margins.doc** should be displayed in the document window.

❖ If necessary, select the Print Layout View (select the **Print Layout View** button at the bottom left of the document window).

❖ The horizontal and vertical rulers should be displayed on the screen. If necessary, select **View**, **Ruler**.

Change the Top and Bottom Margins Using the Ruler

1. *If changing the top margin,* scroll up the document window so that the top edge of the page is displayed.

For example, if necessary, scroll up the document window so that the top edge of the page is visible.

If changing the bottom margin, scroll down the document window so that the bottom edge of the page is visible.

2. Move the mouse pointer to the top or bottom margin boundary marker until a double-headed arrow displays.

For example, move the mouse pointer to the top margin boundary marker (see Figure 7.3) until the double-headed arrow displays.

Note: The margin boundaries are the thin horizontal lines that separate the dark gray areas of the vertical ruler from the white areas. When the mouse pointer is placed on the top margin boundary, the ToolTip Top Margin displays below the double-headed arrow.

3. Press and hold the **Alt** key. Press and hold the mouse button to display a dotted horizontal line. Drag the top or bottom margin boundary marker until the desired margin amount displays. Release the **Alt** key and mouse button.

For example, drag the top margin boundary marker down until **1.5"** displays at the top of the vertical ruler. Release the **Alt** key and the mouse button.

Finish-Up Instructions

❖ Use the same filename, **7margins.doc**, and save the file again.

❖ Continue with the Steps to Indent Paragraphs Using the Horizontal Ruler.

Start-Up Instructions

❖ The file named **7margins.doc** should be displayed in the document window.

❖ If necessary, select the Print Layout View (select the **Print Layout View** button at the bottom left of the document window).

❖ The horizontal and vertical rulers should be displayed on the screen. If necessary, select **View**, **Ruler**.

❖ Press **Ctrl** and **End** to place the insertion point in the third blank line below the bulleted list.

❖ Type the heading **Employment Experience** and press the **Enter** key twice.

❖ Type the following:

IBM Corporation, Cambridge, MA—2 years
Inspector Operator for quality control of printed circuit boards.
Performed end-of-line quality control for all boards in unit.

Conner Peripherals, Easton, MD—1 year
Assembly Operator. Performed duties such as die plating, putting caps on parts, and die inspection.

National Nutrition Council, Philippines—1 year
Clerk II. Assisted with budget preparation. Prepared vouchers for monetary appropriation and handled staff budget requests.

❖ Press the **Enter** key three times after the last sentence.

Indent Paragraphs Using the Horizontal Ruler

1. Place the insertion point in the desired paragraph, or select the paragraphs to be indented.

For example, place the insertion point anywhere in the sentence that begins **Inspector Operator . . .**

2. Move the mouse pointer to the desired indent marker.

For example, move the mouse pointer to the left indent marker on the ruler (see Figure 7.3).

Note: The ToolTip Left Indent displays below the mouse pointer.

FIGURE 7.4

A first line indent has been set for this paragraph. The first line of the text is indented from the left margin; however, subsequent lines begin at the left margin. First line indents can be created by selecting **Format**, **Paragraph**, double-clicking in the **First Line** option box, and typing the desired indent amount. The ruler can also be used to create first line indents.

This paragraph has been indented from the left margin. All lines of the paragraph will be indented from the left margin. This type of indent can be created by selecting the **Increase Indent** button on the Formatting Toolbar.

This paragraph has been indented from the right margin. All lines of the text are indented from the right margin. This type of paragraph indention is often used in conjunction with a left indent to create paragraphs that are indented from both the left and right margins.

➡ This is a sample of a bulleted hanging indent. The first line of the paragraph begins with the bullet character at the left margin, and the following lines are indented. The **Numbering** and **Bullets** buttons on the Formatting Toolbar are often used to create this type of indented paragraph.

Hanging indents can be used to create bibliographies, glossaries, bulleted lists using symbols, etc. Hanging indents can be created by selecting **Format**, **Paragraph**, choosing **Hanging** in the Special box, and typing the desired indent amount. The ruler can also be used to create hanging indents.

3. Press and hold the mouse button and drag the indent marker to the desired location on the horizontal ruler.

For example, drag the left indent marker to .25" on the horizontal ruler.

Note: If the left indent marker is selected, the left indent marker, hanging indent marker, and the first line indent marker move as one unit. If the first line indent marker is selected, the first line indent marker moves and the left indent marker and hanging indent marker remain at the left margin. When the hanging indent marker is selected, the hanging indent marker and the left indent marker move as one unit, and the first line indent marker remains at the left margin.

4. Release the mouse button.

Finish-Up Instructions

❖ Place the insertion point in the line that begins **Assembly Operator**.

❖ Repeat steps 2–4 to create a left indent for the paragraph at .25".

❖ Place the insertion point in the line that begins **Clerk II**.

❖ Repeat steps 2–4 to create a left indent for the paragraph at .25".

❖ Use the same filename, **7margins.doc**, and save the file again.

❖ Continue with the **Start-Up Instructions** on page 185.

Set Tabs

By default, tabs are set every one-half inch. Small, light-gray marks are placed at each one-half inch mark at the bottom of the ruler. If desired, tabs can be changed to indent information at a position other than the preset tabs. The five basic types of tabs are: left, center, right, decimal, and bar. When a bar tab (|)is set, text aligns at the first tab you set or aligns at the first default tab *after* the bar tab. Leader characters, such as dots, dashes, or underlines that display between tabbed information, can be set for left, right, center, and decimal tabs. All five types of tabs can be set using the Tabs dialog box (see Figure 7.6). The Tabs dialog box is also used to set tabs with leader characters. Tabs can also be set by using the **Tab Alignment** button to choose the tab type and then clicking at the desired location on the horizontal ruler.

When tabs are set using the horizontal ruler, the **Tab Alignment** button, displayed at the left of the ruler (see Figure 7.5), is selected to choose the desired tab type. Each time you click on the **Tab Alignment** button, a different tab alignment symbol displays. The seven tab alignment symbols are shown in Figure 7.5.

When creating a document, type the text and press the **Tab** key once between each section (column) of information. Once all the text is typed, tab settings can be adjusted to create a more readable and attractive presentation. Also, the Table features can be used to type and format each column of information.

When a new tab is set, the default tab(s) to the left of the new tab is automatically cleared. If necessary, all tab settings can be deleted to return to the default tab settings.

Start-Up Instructions

❖ The file named **7margins.doc** should be displayed in the document window.

❖ The horizontal ruler should be displayed on the screen. If necessary, select **View, Ruler**.

❖ Place the insertion point in the blank line below the single-line border at the top of the document.

❖ Type the following:

    a. **Melba C. Aguas** and press the **Tab** key once. Type **386 Foothill Road**. (Do not type the period.)

Note: Don't worry for now about aligning the text. The address information will be aligned at the right margin using the Steps to Set Tabs Using the Horizontal Ruler on page 185.

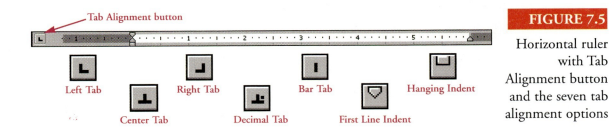

Tab Alignment button

Left Tab   Center Tab   Right Tab   Decimal Tab   Bar Tab   First Line Indent   Hanging Indent

FIGURE 7.5

Horizontal ruler with Tab Alignment button and the seven tab alignment options

b.   Press the **Enter** key once.

c.   Type **410-555-0727** and press the **Tab** key once. Type **Preston, MD 21655-0051**. (Do not type the period.)

Set Tabs Using the Horizontal Ruler

1. Place the insertion point at the location where tabs are to be set, or select the text for which tabs are to be set.

   For example, select the two lines you just typed (name, address, and phone number).

2. Check that the desired tab alignment symbol displays at the left of the horizontal ruler. If necessary, click on the **Tab Alignment** button until the desired tab alignment symbol displays.

   For example, click on the **Tab Alignment** button until the **Right** Tab ⬛ displays.

   Note: The seven tab alignment symbols available for setting tabs using the horizontal ruler are shown in Figure 7.5.

3. Move the mouse pointer to the desired position on the ruler and click to set the tab location.

   For example, move the mouse pointer to approximately 4.75" on the ruler and click.

   Note: A right tab symbol is placed on the ruler at 4.75".

Finish-Up Instructions

❖ Continue with the Steps to Move a Tab.

Move a Tab

1. Place the insertion point at the location where the tabs are to be set, or select the text for which tabs are to be set.

   For example, if necessary, select the two lines you just typed (name, address, and phone number).

2. Move the mouse pointer to the tab symbol to be moved.

   For example, move the mouse pointer to the **right** tab symbol located at 4.75" on the ruler.

3. Press and hold the mouse button and drag the symbol to the desired location on the ruler.

   For example, drag the **right** tab symbol to 5" (the right margin) on the ruler.

4. Release the mouse button.

Finish-Up Instructions

❖ Use the *new* filename **7Tabs.doc** and save the file on your file disk.

❖ Continue with the Steps to Set Tabs Using the Tabs Dialog Box.

Remove a Tab from the Horizontal Ruler

For Your Information

Note: The following steps are for your information.

1. Move the mouse pointer to the desired tab symbol on the ruler.
2. Press and hold the mouse button and drag the tab symbol off the ruler. Release the mouse button.

Set Tabs Using the Tabs Dialog Box

1. Place the insertion point at the location where the tabs are to be set, or select the text for which tabs are to be set.

   For example, select the two bulleted items located below the Educational Background heading.

2. Select **Format, Tabs**.

   Note: The Tabs dialog box displays (see Figure 7.6). Your insertion point is located in the Tab stop position box.

3. To set a tab, type the desired tab location in the Tab stop position box.

   For example, type **5**. (Do not type the period.)

4. To select a different tab alignment, move the mouse pointer to the Alignment box and click on the desired type.

   For example, select **Right**.

Insert Leader Characters

5. In the Leader area, select the desired leader character.

   For example, select number **2** (dot leaders).

6. Select **Set**.

7. When all needed tabs have been set, select **OK**.

   Note: The right tab symbol displays on the ruler at 5". Continue with the following Finish-Up Instructions.

FIGURE 7.6

Tabs dialog box

FIGURE 7.7

Completed
résumé

Résumé

Melba C. Aguas

386 Foothill Road

410-555-0727

Preston, MD 21655-0051

Educational Background

➡ Word Processing and Keyboarding, Adult Education Program, Union
High School District 5/96
➡ Commerce College, Manila, Philippines. Received diploma in
Business 5/93

Employment Experience

IBM Corporation, Cambridge, MA—2 years
  Inspector Operator for quality control of printed circuit boards.
  Performed end-of-line quality control for all boards in unit.

Conner Peripherals, Easton, MD—1 year
  Assembly Operator. Performed duties such as die plating, putting caps
  on parts, and die inspection.

National Nutrition Council, Philippines—1 year
  Clerk II. Assisted with budget preparation. Prepared vouchers for
  monetary appropriation and handled staff budget requests.

References

Available upon request.

Finish-Up Instructions

❖ Place the insertion point to the right of the last character in the word
District. Press the **Tab** key once.

*Note: Dot leader characters display from the end of the word District to the tab
stop at 5".*

❖ Type **5/96**. (Do not type the period.)

❖ Move the insertion point to the right of the last character in the word
Business located in the next line. Press the **Tab** key once and type **5/93**. (Do
not type the period.)

❖ Use the following information to complete the résumé shown in Figure 7.7.

a. Press **Ctrl** and **End** to move the insertion point to the end of the document.

b. Type the heading **References** and press **Enter** twice. Type **Available upon request.**

c. Increase the font size for the name (Melba C. Aguas) to **16 point.**

d. Apply the bold text attribute for all headings as shown in Figure 7.7.

e. Increase the font size for the headings **Educational Background**, **Employment Experience**, and **References** to **14 point.**

❖ Use the *new* filename **7Aguas resume.doc** and save the file on your file disk.

❖ Print one copy. Close the document.

Create Evenly Spaced Tabs

Note: The following steps are for your information.

1. Place the insertion point at the location where the evenly spaced tabs are to be set, or select the text for which evenly spaced tabs are to be set.

2. Select **Format, Tabs**.

3. If other tabs have been set, select **Clear All** to delete the existing tabs.

4. Click on the up or down arrow located beside the **Default tab stops** box until the desired spacing displays, or double-click in the **Default tab stops** box and type the desired spacing.

5. Select **OK**.

Create a Résumé Using a Table

A résumé can also be formatted in two columns. Using the Table features, side-heads, such as Employment Experience, Educational Background, and References used in the résumé shown in figure 7.7 can be typed in the first column and related information can be placed in the second column. The widths of each table column can be adjusted to accommodate headings and text. Some of the advantages of using a table to format a résumé are ease of setup and formatting, ease of reading, and visual attractiveness.

Start-Up Instructions

❖ A new empty document window should be displayed. If necessary, select the **New Blank Document** button.

Create a Résumé Using a Table

❖ Use the following information to create the résumé shown in Figure 7.8.

❖ Change the font to **Garamond** or make a font choice of your own. Use bold and italic text attributes as shown.

- ❖ Use the horizontal ruler and change the left and right margins to **1.5"**. Use the vertical ruler and change the top margin to **1.5"**.

- ❖ Type, center, and bold the heading information.

  Note: The é for the word Résumé is found in the (normal text) font. (See Figure 7.2.)

- ❖ Create a table with 2 columns and 7 rows. Decrease the width of column 1 and increase the width of column 2. (If necessary, see Chapters 5 and 6 for information on changing the width of table columns.)

- ❖ Bold the headings in column 1. Use italic as shown.

- ❖ Select the table and remove the border lines (select the down arrow beside the **Border** button on the Formatting Toolbar and select the **No Border** option).

FIGURE 7.8

Résumé created using a table

Résumé
Tony Holmes
280 Olive Court, #10
San Jose, CA 95136-3505
(408) 555-5123

3 Enters

Employment Experience	*Wells Fargo Bank,* San Jose, California Enter Business Loan Specialist. Responsible for providing quality customer service to the branches as well as to customers with business loans. September 1999 to the present. Enter and Tab twice *Bank of the West,* San Jose, California Enter Express Agent. Responsible for providing quality service to customers for their checking and savings accounts. June 1994 to August 1999. Enter and Tab
Educational Background	San Jose City College, San Jose, California Enter Studied word processing, English, and business math. September 1995 to 1998. Enter and Tab twice Fresno City College, Fresno, California Enter Studied general office courses including microcomputer applications. September 1993 to June 1994. Enter and Tab twice High School Diploma, Clovis High School, Clovis, California. Received 1992. Enter and Tab
Special Skills	Proficient with Microsoft Excel, Microsoft Word for Windows, and PageMaker. Enter and Tab
References	Available upon request.

❖ Use the filename **7Holmes.doc** and save the file on your file disk.

❖ Print one copy and close the document.

Use a Nonbreaking Space

Sometimes two words, such as dates or a person's first and last names, should be printed on the same line. A nonbreaking space can be inserted between the words to instruct Word to always print the words on the same line. For example, the date September 25, 200x, should print on the same line; therefore, a nonbreaking space is placed between September and 25 and between the comma and 200x. A nonbreaking space is also referred to as a *hard space*.

Insert a Nonbreaking Space

Note: The following steps are for your information.

1. Move the insertion point to the location where the nonbreaking space should be inserted.

2. Press the **Delete** key once to delete the space between characters.

3. Press and hold the **Ctrl** and **Shift** keys and then press the **Spacebar** once (**Ctrl** and **Shift** and **Spacebar**) to insert a nonbreaking space.

*Note: The nonbreaking space symbol (°) is inserted to represent the nonbreaking space. (If necessary, click on the **Show/Hide** button ¶ to display the nonprinting symbols, e.g., paragraph, tab, and nonbreaking space symbols.)*

Use the Résumé Wizard

The Résumé Wizard is available to take you through the steps of creating a résumé. When the Résumé Wizard is selected, dialog boxes display, requesting information about the type and style of the résumé, the name and address of the person for whom the résumé is being created, and the headings to be included in the résumé. When the **Finish** button is selected, Word sets up the résumé according to the choices you made. Also, the Office Assistant displays with several topics that can help you complete the résumé, including **Add a Cover Letter** and **Send Resume to Someone**. You can select one of these options or choose **Cancel** to remove the Office Assistant.

The Résumé Wizard has set up the résumé in a table and inserted placeholders at the locations where text is needed. Select the placeholders and insert the desired information. To create additional listings for any category, insert a row, copy placeholder(s) or information from the previous row, and type the desired text.

Use the Résumé Wizard

1. Select **File, New**.

FIGURE 7.9

Résumé Wizard
dialog box

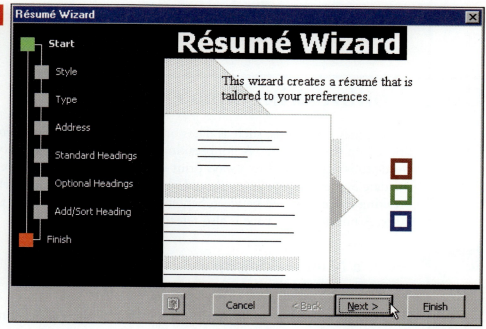

2. Choose the **Other Documents** tab.

3. Double-click on the **Resume Wizard** option.

   Note: The Résumé Wizard dialog box displays (see Figure 7.9).

4. Select the **Next** button to begin the Wizard.

5. Choose a Résumé style.

   For example, select the **Professional** style.

6. Select **Next**.

7. Select the type of résumé to be created.

   For example, select **Entry-level résumé**.

8. Select **Next**.

9. Type the name of the person for whom the résumé is being created.

   For example, type **Wendy Norman**.

10. Click in the **Address** box and type the address that should display in the résumé.

    For example, type:

    8542 Zyle Road
    Austin, TX 78737

11. Click in the **Phone** box and type the phone number to be displayed in the résumé.

    For example, type **512-555-4927**. (Do not type the period.)

12. Click in the **Fax** and/or **Email** box and type the desired information.

    For example, click in the **Fax** box and type **512-555-4433**. (Do not type the period.)

13. Select **Next**.

14. Select the headings to be included in the résumé.

    For example, select the **Education**, **Languages**, **Work experience,** and **References** headings. Deselect the Objective heading .

15. Select **Next**.

16. Select any additional headings desired.

    For example, no additional headings need to be selected.

17. Select **Next**.

18. Type any desired headings and select the **Add** button to create additional headings.

    For example, type **Special Skills** and select the **Add** button.

19. Review the headings and use the **Move Up** or **Move Down** buttons to reorder the headings.

    For example, click on the **Special Skills** heading and click the **Move Up** button to move the Special Skills heading above the References heading.

20. Select **Next**.

21. Select **Finish**.

    Note: The Office Assistant displays with options to add a cover letter, change the résumé style, shrink the résumé to fit on less pages, send the résumé to someone, get help on another topic, or cancel the Office Assistant.

22. Select the desired Office Assistant option.

    For example, select the **Cancel** option to remove the Office Assistant.

23. Complete the résumé by clicking on the placeholder text and typing the desired information.

    For example, complete the résumé shown in Figure 7.10.

Finish-Up Instructions

❖ Select the address and phone number and change the font size to **10 point**.

❖ Select all lines below Wendy Norman's name and change the font size to **12 point**.

❖ Use the filename **7Norman resume** and save the file on your file disk.

❖ Print one copy and close the document.

FIGURE 7.10

Résumé created using the Résumé Wizard

| | | 8542 Zyle Road | Phone 512-555-4927 |
| | | Austin, TX 78737 | Fax 512-555-4433 |

Wendy Norman

| **Education** | 1993 - 1997 | University of Texas | Austin, Texas |

B.A. Education

- Major courses: Computer-Aided Instruction, Word Processing, Spreadsheets, Databases, and Electronic Publishing.

| **Languages** | Fluent in Spanish |

| **Work experience** | 1994 - Present | Wendy's Tutorial Service | Austin, Texas |

Elementary School Math Tutor

- Tutor elementary school students in computer and math skills. Responsibilities included preparing individualized lesson plans for each child, reporting progress to parents, maintaining records, managing business checking account and paying state and federal taxes on income from the business.

| **Special Skills** | Typing: 85 words per minute. Experienced with Microsoft Office 97 including Word, Excel, PowerPoint, and Access. |

| **References** | Available upon request. |

The Next Step

Chapter Review and Activities

Self-Check Quiz

T (F) 1. Tabs are set by default every inch in Word.

(T) F 2. One type of tab is the bar tab.

T (F) 3. A single-line border can be inserted by typing three equal signs (===) and pressing the **Enter** key.

(T) F 4. The special symbols are accessed by selecting **Insert, Symbol.**

5. Word can change the case of letters to _____.
    a. all uppercase
    b. all lowercase
    c. title case
    d. any of the above

6. The horizontal ruler can be used to _____.
    a. set left and right margins
    b. set top and bottom margins
    c. set tabs
    d. both a and c

7. The horizontal and vertical rulers can be displayed in _____.
    a. the Normal View
    b. the Print Layout View
    c. Print Preview
    d. either b or c

8. Special _____ can be inserted into a document.
    a. mathematical symbols
    b. foreign letters
    c. Wingdings graphic symbols
    d. all of the above

9. List two advantages for using a table to create a résumé.

10. Describe and state the purpose of a résumé.

Enriching Language Arts Skills

Spelling/Vocabulary Words

ecology—the interaction between living organisms and their environment; the way plants, animals, and people live together in a specific region.
post-secondary—years of education after high school.
wetlands—a lowland, swampy area.

Commas Used in a Series

Commas separate words and/or ideas listed in a series.
Example:
The mailing list was sent to Karen Smith, Georgia Cain, and Perry Arnston.

Activities

Activity 7.1—Create a Résumé; Set Tabs; and Insert Special Symbols

1. Use the following information to type the heading Résumé.

    a. Type the letter **R**.

    b. Insert the special character é [select **Insert**, **Symbol**; on the Symbols tab, (**normal text**) should be displayed in the Font box; select the é symbol (fifth row, fourth button from the right), select **Insert**].

    c. Click to the right of the é in the document; type **sum**. Insert the é character again. Select the **Close** button in the Symbol dialog box. Press **Enter** once.

2. Center and bold the word **Résumé**.

3. Insert a single-line automatic border (place the insertion point in the blank line below the word Résumé; type three hyphens and press **Enter**).

4. Press the **Enter** key three times.

5. Use the following information and change the right and left margins to **1.7"**.

    a. If necessary, display the ruler (select **View**, **Ruler**).

    b. In the Print Layout View, choose the **Zoom** button and select **Page Width**.

    c. Change the left margin (place the mouse pointer on the left margin boundary marker until a double-headed arrow displays; press and hold the **Alt** key while dragging the margin marker until **1.7"** displays; release the mouse button and the **Alt** key).

    d. Repeat step 5c. using the right margin boundary marker and change the right margin to **1.7"**.

6. Change the top margin to **1.5"** (move the mouse pointer to the top margin boundary marker until a double-headed arrow displays; press and hold the **Alt** key while dragging the top margin boundary marker down until **1.5"** displays; release the mouse button and the **Alt** key).

7. If desired, return to 100% Zoom view (select the **Zoom** button and choose **100%**).

8. Place the insertion point in the first blank line that follows the single-line border at the top of the document. Type the following information and press the **Tab** key once between the first and second columns:

    Tyler Reston   **383 Longview Drive**
    415-555-1395   **San Mateo, CA 94402-3804**

9. Select the two lines containing the name, phone number, and address. Set a tab using the ruler (click on the **Tab Alignment** button until the **Right Tab** symbol displays; move the mouse pointer to 4.75" on the ruler and click once; drag the tab marker to the right margin and release the mouse button).

10. Place the insertion point in the third blank line below the phone number. Type the sidehead **Educational Background** and press **Enter** twice.

11. Type the following paragraphs and use the AutoCorrect feature to create the bullet character ➡ (type two equal signs followed by the greater than symbol, e.g., ==> and press the **Tab** key).*(Remember: Type two hyphens to make a dash.)*

   ➡ **Microcomputer Applications Program, Burlingame ROP (Skills Center), Burlingame, California**

   ➡ **San Francisco City College, San Francisco, California—received diploma in Business Administration**

   ➡ **Milpitas High School, Milpitas, California—received diploma**

   Press **Enter** three times.

12. Create the leader tab that will follow each of the three bulleted items in the Educational Background section (select the three bulleted items, choose **Format**, **Tabs**, type **5.13** in the Tab stop position box, select **Right** alignment, choose the number **2** dot leader character, select **OK**).

13. Use the following information to insert the dates for each of the bulleted items.

   a. Place the insertion point to the right of the last character in the word California in the first bulleted item, press the **Tab** key once, and type **6/96**.

   b. Place the insertion point to the right of the last character in the word Administration in the second bulleted item, press the **Tab** key once, and type **5/95**.

   c. Place the insertion point to the right of the last character in the word diploma in the third bulleted item, press the **Tab** key once, and type **6/92**.

14. Place the insertion point on the third blank line below the bulleted items. Type the sidehead **Employment Experience** and press the **Enter** key twice.

15. Type the following information.

   **San Francisco Newspaper Agency, Menlo Park, California—2 years
   Worked in the following positions: Customer Service Representative, Dispatcher, and Coin Machine Operator.**

   **Goldeneye Trucking, Palo Alto, California—1 year
   Customer Service Representative/Dispatcher. Typed, filed, handled phones, and processed bank deposits and incoming and outgoing mail.**

   **Los Altos Senior Center, Los Altos, California—2 years (Part-time)
   Volunteer: Helped serve supper and assisted in the kitchen.**

   Press **Enter** three times.

16. Indent the paragraphs below each company name. (Place the insertion point anywhere in the paragraph beginning "Worked in the . . ." and move the mouse pointer to the left indent marker on the ruler. Press and hold the **Alt** key and drag until **.25"** displays on the horizontal ruler; release the mouse button and the

Alt key.) Repeat for the remaining two paragraphs that follow the company names.

17. Place the insertion point in the third blank line below the Employment Experience section (**Ctrl** and **End**). Type the following:

    Special Skills (press **Enter** twice)

    Proficient in the following microcomputer applications: Microsoft Word, Microsoft Excel, PageMaker, and Microsoft Works for Windows. Studied English, Business Math, and Office Procedures. (Press **Enter** three times.)

    References (Press **Enter** twice.)

    Available upon request.

18. Select the entire document and change the font to **Garamond**, or make a font choice of your own.

19. Select the name, **Tyler Reston**, select **Bold**, and change the font size to **14 point**. Select each sidehead, bold, and change the font size to **14 point**.

    Note: The résumé should look similar to the following:

Résumé

Tyler Reston   383 Longview Drive
415-555-1395   San Mateo, CA 94402-3804

Educational Background

➜ Microcomputer Applications Program, Burlingame ROP (Skills Center), Burlingame, California 6/96
➜ San Francisco City College, San Francisco, California—received diploma in Business Administration. 5/95
➜ Milpitas High School, Milpitas, California—received diploma 6/92

Employment Experience

San Francisco Newspaper Agency, Menlo Park, California—2 years
    Worked in the following positions: Customer Service Representative, Dispatcher, and Coin Machine Operator.

Goldeneye Trucking, Palo Alto, California—1 year
    Customer Service Representative/Dispatcher. Typed, filed, handled phones, and processed bank deposits and incoming and outgoing mail.

Los Altos Senior Center, Los Altos, California—2 years (Part-time)
    Volunteer: Helped serve supper and assisted in the kitchen.

Special Skills

Proficient in the following microcomputer applications: Microsoft Word, Microsoft Excel, PageMaker, and Microsoft Works for Windows. Studied English, Business Math, and Office Procedures.

References

Available upon request.

---

20. Use the filename **7Reston.doc** and save the file.

21. Print one copy and close the document.

Activity 7.2—Create and Edit a Résumé Using a Table

1. Use a table and the following information to type the résumé shown.

   a. Use bold and italic text attributes as shown. Adjust column widths as necessary.

   b. Select a font of your own choice in a point size of 10 or 12.

   c. Use a special text character for the é's in Résumé. The é is found in the (normal text) symbols font.

   d. Remove the table borders.

Résumé
Barbara T. Albert
508 Dover Drive
Kansas City, MO 64139-8118

Education	Webster University, St. Louis, Missouri B.A. in Business Administration, Minor in Office Administration Studied Behavioral Science in Business, Business Law, Office Administration and Communications, Economics and Management, and Accounting. 5/96
Experience	*Management World Magazine,* Trevose, PA. Full-time editor/reporter. Responsible for covering statewide meetings on management and office technology and developing feature articles. Submit all work electronically. June 1996 to present. Professional Secretaries International, Kansas City, Missouri. Part-time reporter. Responsibilities include reporting on meetings of the Association of Information System Professionals, National Association of Legal

Secretaries, and the Administrative Management Society. Submit all work electronically. 9/92 to present.

Webster University, St. Louis, Missouri. Part-time office assistant in Admissions and Records department. Answered telephones, researched student records, distributed inter-office mail, and ordered supplies. 9/92 to 6/95.

Activities   Recording secretary for the Kentucky state chapter of the National Association of Legal Secretaries, a member of Kentucky Horseback Club, and a volunteer in the newborn nursery at County General Hospital.

References   Available upon request.

2. Use the filename **7Albert resume.doc** and save the file.

3. Print one copy and close the document.

Challenge Your Skills

Skill 7.1—Create Your Own Résumé

1. Create your own résumé using Figure 7.7 or Figure 7.8 as a guide. Make a decision to use the table format or to use tabs and indents to format your résumé. If desired, use the Résumé Wizard.

2. If necessary, change margins to increase or decrease the amount of text that will fit on a page. For example, if your résumé is short, it may be desirable to increase the left, right, and top margins. If your résumé is long, decrease the left, right, top, and bottom margins.

3. Remember to insert special characters for the é's in the word Résumé.

4. Use one or two fonts to enhance the appearance of your résumé. Use bold, italic, or underline text attributes as desired.

5. Proofread carefully.

6. Use the filename **7my resume.doc** and save the file.

7. Print one copy and close the document.

Skill 7.2—Create a Résumé with Special Characters; Language Arts

1. Create a résumé for Delia H. Cortezo using the following information.

    a. Make decisions regarding:

Résumé format
Margins
Tab settings and indentions
Fonts
Hard spaces
Uppercase and lowercase headings
Bold and italic text attributes
Special symbols
References

b. Correct three spelling errors and one punctuation error.

c. Delia lives at 887 Seascape Drive, Mt. Pleasant, SC 29447, (803)555-8312.

d. Delia graduated in 1987 with a B.S. in English from the University of South Carolina, Columbia, South Carolina. She is currently a master's degree candidate in Environmental Journalism at the University of Charleston, Charleston, South Carolina.

e. Delia's work experience is as follows:

Marine Habitat, Pawleys Island, South Carolina
Communications Director
6/90-Present

Job responsibilities include: writing proposals, reports, and articles for publication regarding the marine animals, plants and ekology of South Carolina wetlends.

Piedmont Publications, Columbia, South Carolina
Reviewer
6/87-5/90

Job responsibilities included reviewing manuscripts for publication in the area of secondary and post-seconndary biology education. Specifically, manuscripts were assessed and editing suggestions were made regarding content and reading level.

University of South Carolina, Columbia, South Carolina
Newspaper Editor
9/86-6/87
Job responsibilities included overseeing the publication of a daily newspaper for a campus of 3,000 faculty and students.

f. Delia's references are:

Paul L. Washington, Ph.D., Director, Marine Habitat, 17 Ocean Avenue, Pawleys Island, SC 29477, (803)555-2898

Ellen Hutsell, Senior Editor, Piedmont Publications, 1275 Maple Avenue, Columbia, SC 29301, (803)555-1002

2. Use the filename **7Delia Cortezo.doc** and save the file.

3. Print one copy and close the document.

Create Newspaper-Style and Side-by-Side Columns

8

Features Covered

- Create newspaper-style columns
- Customize columns
- Insert column breaks
- Use hyphenation feature
- Use the Format Painter feature
- Create side-by-side columns using a table

Objectives and Introduction

After successfully completing this chapter, you will be able to use the **Columns** button and the Columns dialog box to format text in newspaper-style columns and to create side-by-side columns (parallel columns) using a table. In addition, you will learn how to control the flow of text in newspaper-style columns using section and column breaks and how to use the hyphenation and Format Painter features to improve the look and readability of columnar text.

Columns of text can be arranged in newspaper or side-by-side styles. Text in newspaper-style columns wraps around from line to line, column to column, and page to page (see Figure 8.2). Paragraphs of related text can be arranged in side-by-side columns so that information can be read from left to right. The hyphenation feature can be used to improve the readability of columnar text by reducing the amount of space at the end of lines and avoiding large gaps of space between words. Sideheads or subheads are often bolded or put in a different font or size for emphasis. Formatting, such as bold and font size, can be quickly applied to multiple items using the Format Painter feature.

Create Newspaper-Style Columns

Newspaper-style columns are created by formatting text as columns, either before or after the text is typed. The simplest method is to first type the text and then create the column format.

When printing newspaper-style columns, the title is often centered on the page with the remainder of the text divided into multiple columns. To create more than a one-column format, the document must be divided into more than one section. Each section can have distinctive document formatting, such as a one- or two-column layout, and different margins. There are four types of section breaks: **Next page**, **Continuous**, **Even page**, and **Odd page**. The **Next page** option begins the next section on a new page. The **Continuous** option begins the next section on the same page. The **Even page** option begins the next section on the following even-numbered page of the document. The **Odd page** option begins the next section on the following odd-numbered page of the document

A quick way to create columns is to select the **Columns** button ▦ on the Standard Toolbar and then choose the desired number of columns. Word automatically places a Continuous section break in a document when text is selected and multiple columns are created using the **Columns** button. Also, equal column widths are automatically calculated based on the page margins, with a default .5" spacing (blank space between columns) inserted between columns.

If different column settings are desired, use the Columns dialog box. The number of columns, space between columns, and column widths also can be specified in the Columns dialog box (see Figure 8.1).

In the Columns dialog box, the *Number of columns* box is used to specify the number of desired columns (the default is 1). Once the number of columns is specified, Word automatically calculates equal widths for each column and determines the left and right margins for each column. The width of each column and the distance between each column displays in the *Width and spacing* boxes. If the number of columns or distance between columns is changed, the column widths are automatically recalculated when the insertion point is moved to another option or when **OK** is selected.

The *Width and spacing* boxes in the Columns dialog box are used to specify the width of each column and the amount of space (in inches) between the columns. The default spacing between columns (.5 inches) is often changed if there are more than two columns on the page.

If the *Equal column width* option is selected (turned on), only the column width and spacing for the first column need to be entered; Word will automatically adjust the rest of the columns to the same width and distance apart. When the *Equal column width* option is turned off, column width and spacing can be entered for each column. The column widths and spacing between columns can also be changed by dragging the column marker on the horizontal ruler.

A line can be placed between columns by selecting the *Line between* option. Other types of lines and borders can be placed around a column using the **Format, Borders and Shading** command or the Tables and Borders Toolbar (see Chapter 6).

The *Apply to* options are used to specify the text to be affected by the settings selected in the Columns dialog box. For example, the **This point forward** option in the *Apply to* box is selected to apply column settings from the location of the insertion point forward in the document.

Depending on the view selected, Word displays the text in different column formats. In Normal View, only one column at a time is displayed. To see the columns across the page, select the **Print Layout View** button or choose **View**, **Print Layout**. The text can be displayed in any size by first selecting the **Zoom** button then selecting the desired zoom option.

Text in newspaper-style columns automatically flows from the bottom of one column to the top of the next column and from the bottom of one page to the top left column of the next page (see Figure 8.2). The term *snaking* is often used to describe text that flows from column to column or page to page.

The text flow of newspaper-style columns can be controlled by inserting a column break to force text to the next column or page. A column break is inserted by selecting **Insert**, **Break**, **Column Break**. A column break moves the insertion point and any text that follows the insertion point to the top of the next column. If the insertion point is located in the final column of the page, the text is forced to the top left column of the next page.

After newspaper-style columns are typed, extra space may display at the end of lines, making the information difficult to read. Hyphenation can be used to avoid extra end-of-line space and to improve the appearance and readability of the text by aligning words more evenly at the margin.

Start-Up Instructions

❖ Open the file named **8drill1.doc** located on the data disk.

❖ Use the Normal View (if necessary, select the **Normal View** button at the bottom left of the document window).

❖ Select **75% Zoom View**. (click on the down arrow to the right of the **Zoom** button and choose 75%).

❖ Display nonprinting symbols (if necessary, select the **Show/Hide** button).

Steps to **Create Newspaper-Style Columns**

1. Select the text to be placed in columns.

    For example, place the I-beam to the left of the first word in the sidehead **Capital . . .** Press and hold the mouse button and drag downward to select all the paragraphs up to the sidehead **Condo Buyers . . .** (including the blank line before the sidehead **Condo Buyers . . .**).

2. Click on the **Columns** button ▦ on the Standard Toolbar.

3. Move the mouse pointer to the desired number of columns and click the mouse button once.

    For example, click on the second column from the left to create a two-column layout.

*Note: The view changes automatically to **Print Layout View**. Below the centered title, a section break displays with a double-dotted line and the words "Section Break (Continuous)." Click anywhere in the area containing the two columns; the words "Sec 2" display on the left side of the Status bar.*

Finish-Up Instructions

❖ Use the *new* filename **8two columns.doc** and save the file on your file disk.

Start-Up Instructions

❖ The file named **8two columns.doc** should be displayed in the document window.

❖ Scroll down the screen and click to the left of the **C** in the sidehead **Condo Buyers . . .** Press **Enter** twice to add two additional blank lines.

Create Customized Columns

1. Select the text where the customized columns are to begin (or anywhere in the document if the customized columns are to affect the entire section).

   For example, select the sidehead **Condo Buyers HMC Requirement** and the paragraphs that follow to the end of the document. Be sure to select the blank line at the end of the document.

2. Select **Format, Columns**.

   Note: The Columns dialog box displays (see Figure 8.1).

3. In the Number of columns box, type the number of columns.

   For example, type **3**.

4. Click once in the **Width** box in the Width and spacing area.

FIGURE 8.1

Columns dialog box

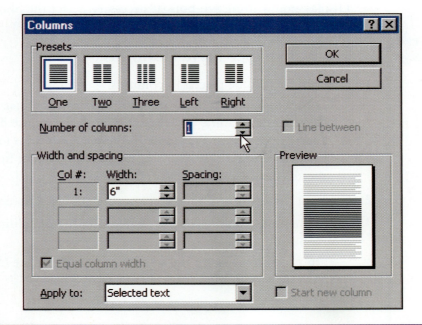

Note: This action requires Word to calculate the column widths based on the new number typed in the Number of columns box; the program will then allow the spacing between columns to be changed.

5. Check that the **Equal column width** option is turned on (i.e., a check mark displays in the option box).

6. Triple-click in the **Spacing** box in the first row and type the amount of spacing to be placed between columns, or click on the up or down triangles located to the right of the **Spacing** box until the desired spacing amount displays.

   For example, triple-click in the **Spacing** box in the Width and spacing area and type **.3**. (Do not type the final period.)

   Note: If the spacing amount is not highlighted, delete the amount before typing the new spacing amount.

7. Select the **Line between** option box to place a line between the columns.

   Note: A check mark should display beside the Line between option. The Preview box displays an example of a 3-column format with vertical lines between the columns.

8. Choose the desired Apply to option.

   For example, check that the **Selected text** option is displayed.

9. Select **OK**.

   Note: Click once to deselect the text. Turn off nonprinting symbols (select the Show/Hide button). Click on the down arrow beside the Zoom button and choose Whole Page to view the entire page; click on the down arrow beside the Zoom button and choose 100% to return to normal size.

Finish-Up Instructions

❖ Use the *new* filename **8multiple columns.doc** and save the file on your file disk.

❖ Print one copy.

Start-Up Instructions

❖ The file named **8multiple columns.doc** should be displayed in the document window.

❖ Display nonprinting symbols (select the **Show/Hide** button on the Standard Toolbar).

 ## Change the Column Definition

1. Place the insertion point at any location in the section to be affected by the column change.

   For example, if necessary, scroll up to display the section of the document that contains two columns. Click in the section

FIGURE 8.2

Text formatted
in multiple
columns

Example of a two-
column format

Example of a three-
column format

Example of a one-
column format

U.S Realtor Association Briefs

Example of a one-
column format

Capital Gains Passage

Passage of a capital gains tax cut took another step forward last week with the introduction of a bipartisan bill, sponsored by Senators More (R-NM) and Kingston (D-MD). The bill resembles the capital gains tax cut bill passed by the House last month and supported by the U.S. Realtor Association.

The U.S. Realtor Association is predicting that passage of compromise capital gains legislation will most likely not be passed until later this year.

Updated information will be provided as soon as possible.

AB 839 Passes First Hurdle

AB 839 would amend the California Government Code to restore MCC funding to pre-1995 levels. As most real estate professionals are aware, MCC funding for San Diego County was reduced by nearly 1,700 certificates this year by the California Debt Limit Committee. AB 839 would prevent MCC funding from becoming the political football it has become this year.

Condo Buyers HMC Requirement

Earlier this year, the Home Mortgage Corporation (HMC), a secondary lender federally mandated to provide mortgage funds for low and moderate income home buyers, issued new condominium lending guidelines affecting California.

The HMC announced that it will not purchase loans on condominium units in California zip codes designated as high and moderate earthquake risks unless the condominium project maintains

earthquake insurance and liquid reserves in the amount of the deductible.

Impact on Available Loans

It is unclear at present what the immediate impact will have on the volume of condominium loans available to Californians since there are no estimates of the dollar volume of past commitments yet outstanding. It is recommended that all Realtors encourage borrowers to make inquiries of lenders as to their earthquake policy

requirements at the first point of contact.

At this point in time, alternative sources of funds, e.g., portfolio lenders, and other public and private investors, are still available, as other investors have not yet followed HMC's policy lead. The California Realtor Association continues to aggressively pursue a legislative solution, both at the state and federal levels, to prevent HMC's policy from having an impact in California.

Call the Public Concerns hotline at 555-3844 for more information.

where the two columns are displayed ("Sec 2" displays in the Status bar).

2. Select **Format, Columns**.

3. Make any desired changes to the number of columns, spacing, or other options.

   For example, click once on the **Line between** option to place a line between the columns.

4. Select **OK**.

Note: A line displays between the columns in the two-column section of the document.

Finish-Up Instructions

❖ Insert a second blank line after the last column entry (press **Ctrl** and **End** to move the insertion point to the end of the document; press **Enter** once).

❖ Select the two blank lines at the end of the document.

❖ With the paragraph symbols highlighted, select the **Columns** button on the Standard Toolbar and click on **1** column.

❖ Click once to deselect the two blank lines.

❖ Click in the second blank line at the end of the document.

❖ Type, center, and bold the following sentence:

Call the Public Concerns hotline at 555-3844 for more information.

*Note: Select the down arrow beside the Zoom button and choose **Whole Page**. Notice that the one-column format is in effect for the last line. The three-columns have been more balanced across the page, with each column having approximately the same number of lines. This balanced effect was created when the final section break was inserted to change the number of columns to one. Your document should look similar to Figure 8.2.*

❖ Use the *new* filename **8final columns.doc** and save the file on your file disk.

❖ Print one copy and close the document.

Start-Up Instructions

❖ Open the file named **8Gloria.doc** located on the data disk.

❖ Select the body text (move the I-beam to the left of the *G* in the word *Gloria* in the first paragraph, press and hold the mouse button, and drag downward to select all paragraphs including the paragraph symbol at the end of the document).

❖ Create two newspaper columns (select the **Columns** button, select the second column).

Note: The text will display in one column at this time. That's OK.

❖ If desired, click once to deselect the text.

❖ If necessary, change to Print Layout View (select the **Print Layout View** button at the bottom left of the document window).

❖ Select the down arrow beside the **Zoom** button and choose **75%**.

Steps to **Insert a Column Break to Control the Flow of Text**

1. Locate the insertion point to the left of the first character of text to be placed in another column.

For example, place the insertion point to the left of the first character in the paragraph that begins "Her hobbies . . ."

2. Select **Insert, Break, Column Break, OK**.

Note: The text following the insertion point is moved to the second column.

Finish-Up Instructions

❖ Center the text vertically on the page (select all text; select **File**, **Page Setup**, **Layout** tab, **Vertical Alignment**, **Center**; click in the **Apply To** box, select **Whole Document**, **OK**).

❖ If desired, select the down arrow beside the **Zoom** button and choose **Whole Page** to display the vertically centered columns. Select the down arrow beside the **Zoom** button and choose **100%** to return to normal size.

❖ Use the *new* filename **8Gloria profile.doc** and save the file on your file disk.

❖ Print one copy and close the document.

Use Hyphenation

Hyphenation is the process of dividing a word at the right margin so that the first part of the word prints at the end of the line and the remainder of the word prints at the beginning of the next line. Hyphenating words is used to make line endings at the right margin look more even (less ragged) or to avoid large gaps of space between words in a line with justified alignment. Word has two hyphenation features that are available through the **Tools**, **Language**, **Hyphenation** command. The **Automatically hyphenate document** option will insert hyphens in a document without asking for approval. The **Manual** hyphenation feature finds locations where a word could be hyphenated, then prompts you to accept, reject, or change the position for each hyphen it proposes.

When text is typed, regular, nonbreaking, and optional hyphens can be inserted. A regular hyphen breaks compound words at the right margin when necessary. For example, the hyphenated word well-defined will divide after the hyphen if the hyphen falls at the right margin.

A nonbreaking hyphen, such as the hyphen in the compound name Jones-Meyer, is inserted between words that should always appear on the same line of text. A nonbreaking hyphen is inserted by pressing and holding the **Ctrl** and **Shift** keys while tapping the **hyphen** (-) key once. The nonbreaking hyphen is also referred to as a required hyphen.

An optional hyphen can be inserted by placing the insertion point to the left of the character that will follow the hyphen and pressing the **Ctrl** and **hyphen** (-) keys. When a word that contains an optional hyphen does not fall at the end of line, the hyphen is hidden. In other words, an optional hyphen will only display in the document window and print if the hyphenated word should fall at the end of the line.

Word provides several options to control the hyphenation process. These options are **Hyphenate words in CAPS**, **Hyphenation zone**, and **Limit consecutive hyphens to**.

When the **Hyphenate words in CAPS** option is selected, Word will review any words typed in all uppercase letters for possible hyphenation. If this option is not selected, words typed in all uppercase letters will not be hyphenated.

Word uses a hyphenation zone to determine if a word needs to be hyphenated. The hyphenation zone is an allowable distance between the right margin and the end of the line. When the zone is small, the right margin will be less ragged, but more words may need to be hyphenated. A larger hyphenation zone will reduce the number of hyphenated words, but will produce a more ragged edge. Generally, the default hyphenation zone produces a visually acceptable hyphenation area.

The **Limit consecutive hyphens to** option is used to specify a maximum number of consecutive lines that can end with hyphens. As a general rule, the maximum number of consecutive lines that can end with hyphens should be limited to two or three.

After a document has been edited, proofread, and prepared for final form, view the document and check if there are gaps of space between words or if there are large spaces at the right margins. If the gaps or spaces are visually unattractive, hyphenation may be desirable.

Start-Up Instructions

❖ Open the file named **8Gloria profile.doc** created earlier in this chapter.

❖ Place the insertion point at the beginning of the document (**Ctrl** and **Home**).

Manually Hyphenate Text

1. Read the following guidelines for correct word division before proceeding to step 2.

   a. Hyphenate only between syllables. Use a dictionary if necessary.

   b. Avoid hyphenating words of five characters or less, e.g., *often*.

   c. Hyphenate a word so that at least three characters remain on the line, e.g., *in-* or *ly.*, but not *i-* or *ly* without the period.

   d. Place a hyphen after a vowel, e.g., *initi-ate*.

   e. Place a hyphen between double consonants, e.g., *accom-modate*.

   f. Do not hyphenate the last word of a paragraph; do not hyphenate the last word on a page.

   g. Avoid hyphenating words at the end of more than two consecutive lines.

   h. Do not hyphenate proper nouns, e.g., Apprenticeship Council.

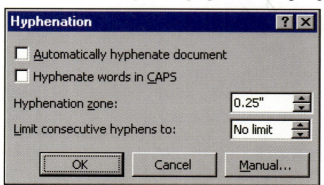

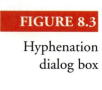

FIGURE 8.3

Hyphenation dialog box

Note: When Word has checked a document for possible words to be hyphenated, there may not be any words hyphenated.

2. Select **Tools, Language, Hyphenation**.

Note: The Hyphenation dialog box displays (see Figure 8.3).

3. Select **Manual**.

Note: The Manual Hyphenation dialog box displays with the first word to be hyphenated in the Hyphenate at box.

4. Use the the guidelines for hyphenation listed in step 1 and select one of the following options for each word:

   ➤ To skip the word, select **No**.

   ➤ To hyphenate the word where Word has placed the blinking cursor, select **Yes**.

   ➤ To hyphenate the word at a different location, move the mouse pointer to the desired location and click once, then select **Yes**.

Note: The selected hyphen shows the maximum number of characters that can fit in the line. Select a hyphenation point to the left of this line.

5. When Word cannot find any more words to hyphenate, the message "Hyphenation is complete." displays. Select **OK** to return to the document window.

Finish-Up Instructions

❖ Scroll down to view the hyphenated text. If necessary, correct any errors in hyphenation. To insert an optional hyphen, press **Ctrl** and **hyphen** (-). Use optional hyphens when manually hyphenating text.

❖ Use the *new* filename **8manual hyphenation.doc** and save the file on your file disk.

❖ Print one copy and close the document.

Start-Up Instructions

❖ Open the file named **8final columns.doc** created earlier in this chapter.

Automatically Hyphenate Text

1. Place the insertion point at the beginning of the document (if necessary, press **Ctrl** and **Home**).

2. Select **Tools, Language, Hyphenation**.

3. Select the desired Hyphenation option.

   For example, select the **Automatically hyphenate document** option.

Note: A check mark should display in the Automatically hyphenate document box. Check that the Hyphenate words in CAPS option is not selected (no check mark displays beside the Hyphenate words in CAPS option). When this option is selected, words in all caps will be hyphenated, including acronyms such as YMCA or UNICEF.

4. To set the maximum number of consecutive lines that can end with hyphens, click on the up or down triangles located to the right of the Limit consecutive hyphens to option.

> For example, click on the up triangle beside the Limit consecutive hyphens to box until 2 displays.

5. Select **OK**.

Note: When the entire document has been reviewed for possible words to be hyphenated, any words that were hyphenated display with a hyphen at the end of the text line(s). Scroll through the document to observe any hyphenated words. Depending on the selected font and point size, the hyphenation zone setting, and the words used in the document, there may not be any words hyphenated. In addition, there may be hyphenated words that do not follow the guidelines on page 211.

Finish-Up Instructions

❖ Use the *new* filename **8auto hyphenation.doc** and save the file on your file disk.

❖ Print one copy and close the document.

Use the Format Painter

Different font styles and font sizes are often used to enhance and emphasize text such as sideheads. A uniform appearance will result if the format for each sidehead is the same. The Format Painter feature can be used to quickly copy the format from one text item to another.

To use the Format Painter feature, select the text containing the desired format. To copy paragraph formatting, such as alignment, indents, and bullet characters, include the paragraph mark when selecting text. Word stores paragraph formatting in the paragraph mark. To copy only text attributes, do not include the paragraph mark when selecting text.

If the format is to be copied to multiple paragraphs, double-click on the **Format Painter** button (located on the Standard Toolbar). If the format is only to be copied to a single paragraph, click once on the **Format Painter** button ⬚. After clicking on the **Format Painter** button ⬚, the paragraph(s) where the format is to be copied is selected. When the mouse button is released, the format is immediately copied to the selected text.

If the **Format Painter** button was selected by clicking once, the **Format Painter** feature is turned off when the mouse button is released. If the **Format Painter** button was selected by double-clicking, the **Format Painter** feature remains in effect until the **Format Painter** button is selected again.

Start-Up Instructions

❖ Open the file named **8final columns.doc** created earlier in this chapter.

Copy Formats Using the Format Painter Button

1. Select and format the text from which the format is to be copied.

   For example, select the first sidehead, **Capitol Gains Passage**. Click on the **Font** button and select the **Arial** font, or make a font choice of your own. Click on the **Font size** button and select **14**.

2. With the formatted text selected, double-click on the **Format Painter** button on the Standard Toolbar.

   Note: The mouse pointer changes to a paintbrush with an I-beam when the pointer is moved into the document window.

3. Select the text where the formatting is to be copied.

   For example, select the sidehead **AB 839 Passes First Hurdle**.

   Note: The copied format will be immediately applied to the selected text.

4. Repeat step 3 to copy the format to the desired paragraphs.

   For example, copy the format to all remaining sideheads in the document.

5. When the format has been copied to all desired paragraphs, click on the **Format Painter** button once to turn off the Format Painter feature.

Finish-Up Instructions

❖ Select the title at the top of the document. Change the font to **Arial**, **14 point**.

❖ Use the *new* filename **8format painter.doc** and save the file on your file disk.

❖ Print one copy and close the document.

Create Side-by-Side Columns Using a Table

Side-by-side columns are blocks of related information that are placed next to each other so that information can be read easily from left to right. Text in side-by-side columns wraps within each column. When using side-by-side columns, the information in the first column and the related information in the second column may vary in length. For example, the information in the first column could include only one or two lines of text while the related information in the second column includes three or more lines of text. Side-by-side columns are also referred to as parallel columns.

Side-by-side columns are created in Word using a table. To create a table with the desired number of columns and rows, see Chapter 5. When typing, text automatically wraps around within each table cell.

FIGURE 8.4

Side-by-side columns created using a table

For Members Only

Professional Legislative Advocacy   *Tab*   What happens in the government arena affects your business. At the Cedar Rapids Real Estate Board, legislative representation is provided to ensure your interests are protected. **Enter** and **Tab**

Whistle Stop Rally   *Tab*   Each year the Cedar Rapids Real Estate Board holds a fund-raiser to support your local political and government activities. **Enter** and **Tab**

Support Local Political and Government Activities   *Tab*   All funds will be used to support your Board's efforts to protect private property rights and interests. **Enter** and **Tab**

Join the Fun!   *Tab*   An evening of auction, dancing, and barbecue will take place on the last weekend this month.

Start-Up Instructions

❖ The text shown in Figure 8.4 will be used to create side-by-side columns using a table.

❖ A new document window should be displayed. (If necessary, select the **New** button.)

❖ Type the title, **For Members Only**, and press **Enter** three times. Select the title. Choose **Center** alignment and **Bold**. Place the insertion point on the third blank line below the title. (If necessary, select **Align Left** to place the insertion point at the left margin.)

Steps to

Create Side-by-Side Columns Using a Table

1. Move the mouse pointer to the Insert Table button on the Standard Toolbar. Highlight the desired number of columns and rows.

   For example, highlight a 4 x 2 table.

2. Type the text for column 1.

   For example, type **Professional Legislative Advocacy** (see Figure 8.4).

3. Press the Tab key to move the insertion point to column 2.

4. Type the text for the first paragraph in column 2.

   For example, type the paragraph beginning **What happens in the . . .** After the last character in the paragraph, press **Enter** once.

Note: The text wraps around within it's own cell.

5. Press the Tab key to move the insertion point back to column 1.

Finish-Up Instructions

❖ Repeat steps 2–5 to type the remaining information in Figure 8.4.

❖ Select the table and remove the border lines (with the table selected, click on the down arrow beside the **Borders** button on the Formatting Toolbar and select the **No Border** button).

❖ Use the filename **8side-by-side.doc** and save the file on your file disk.

❖ Print one copy and close the document.

The Next Step

Chapter Review and Activities

Self-Check Quiz

T F 1. When typing newspaper columns, select **Insert, Break, Column Break, OK** to insert a column break.

T F 2. The **Format Painter** button is a quick method for adding pictures to a document.

T F 3. Newspaper-style columns can be created before or after text is typed.

T F 4. The amount of blank space between newspaper columns cannot be changed.

T F 5. The Table feature is used to create side-by-side columns.

6. A vertical line can be added between columns by selecting the _____ option in the Columns dialog box.
   a. **Spacing**
   b. **Line between**
   c. **Width**
   d. **Vertical line**

7. Which of the following guidelines should be remembered when hyphenating text?
    a. Avoid hyphenating words of fewer than five characters.
    b. Place hyphens between double consonants.
    c. Hyphenate between syllables.
    d. all of the above

8. What are the default settings Word uses when the **Columns** button is selected to create columns?

9. When and why should hyphenation be used?

10. Show the correct hyphenation points for the following words:

    opportunity   seminar   thoroughly

Enriching Language Arts Skills

Spelling/Vocabulary Words

mumbo jumbo—confusing language or activity.
pitfalls—unexpected difficulties or hidden dangers.
typography—the act of printing with type; the arrangement and appearance of printed materials.

Using the Abbreviations *e.g.* and *i.e.*

The abbreviation *e.g.* is used in place of "for example" and is often used when there are many possible examples and only a few are listed. The abbreviation *i.e.* is used in place of "that is" and is used when all potential conditions are listed. A period follows each initial with no space between the period and the initial. A comma follows the final period.

Examples:

There are many word processing programs that include desktop publishing features, e.g., WordPerfect, Microsoft Word, and WordPro.

When the president's name is typed in the signature line, use his first name initial only and include Sr., i.e., J. Thomas-Meyers, Sr.

Activities

Activity 8.1—Create Newspaper-Style Columns; Use Format Painter

1. Open the file named **8act1.doc** on the data disk.

2. Create newspaper columns:

    a. Move the I-beam to the left of the **R** in the first word of the first sidehead, **Report Corporate Changes**. Press and hold the mouse button and drag downward to select all paragraphs.

    b. Select the **Columns** button on the Standard Toolbar. Select **2** columns.

3. Use the **Format Painter** button to format the sideheads:

    a. Format the first sidehead, **Report Corporate Changes**. Choose a different font and make the sidehead bold and larger than the body text.

    b. With the first sidehead selected (highlighted), double-click on the **Format Painter** button on the Standard Toolbar.

    c. Select the second sidehead, **New Wage Reporting** (**Public Works**).

    d. Repeat step 3c. until all the sideheads are formatted.

    e. Click once on the **Format Painter** button to turn off the Format Painter feature.

4. Select the report title and change the font to match the font selected for the sideheads.

5. Use the *new* filename **8Painter.doc** and save the file on your file disk.

6. Print one copy. Close the document.

Activity 8.2—Create Side-by-Side Columns Using a Table

1. Type, center, and bold the title, **Recognition Roster**. Press **Enter** three times.

2. Create and keyboard the following side-by-side columns:

    a. Select the **Insert Table** button on the Standard Toolbar.

    b. Drag the mouse pointer to select a 3 x 2 table.

    c. With the insertion point in the first table cell, type each entry from left to right.

*Hint: Use the **Tab** key to move from cell to cell. Press the **Enter** key once after each paragraph in the second column.*

Recognition Roster

Neal Pence	Equipment Mechanic Assistant Neal Pence received a letter of appreciation from Code Enforcement Inspector Rowena Harty for his kind assistance and timely response to her locked car dilemma.
Cynthia Mello	Carpenter Cynthia Mello received a memo of commendation for her can-do attitude, initiative, enthusiasm, and positive approach during a remodeling project in the Accounting Division.

Shannon Trotter and Claude MacKenzie	Gardener Shannon Trotter and Groundsworker Claude MacKenzie received letters of appreciation from Antonio Chavez for their excellent work and outstanding gardening at the City Hall complex.

3. Select the table and remove the border lines (select the **Borders** button on the Formatting Toolbar, choose the **No Border** button).

4. Use the filename **8recognition roster.doc** and save the file on your file disk.

5. Print one copy. Close the document.

Activity 8.3—Create Newspaper-Style Columns; Change Column Definition

1. Open the file named **8act3.doc** located on the data disk.

2. Select all the body text (do not select the blank space above the first paragraph). Format the body text into **3** columns with **.3"** spacing between columns (select **Format, Columns**; set Number of columns to **3**; check that the **Equal column width** option is selected; click once in the **Width** box; double-click in the **Spacing** box in the first row, type **.3**; select **OK**).

3. Use the *new* filename **8trends.doc** and save the file on your file disk.

4. Print one copy.

5. Change the number of columns to **2** with **.4"** spacing and a line between the columns. (Place the insertion point anywhere in the 3-column section; select **Format, Columns**; set the Number of columns to **2**; check that the **Equal column width** option is selected; double-click in the first **Spacing** box, then type **.4**; select **Line between**; select **OK**.)

6. Use the *new* filename **8trends revised.doc** and save the file on your file disk.

7. Print one copy. Close the document.

Challenge Your Skills

Skill 8.1—Create Newspaper-Style Columns with Multiple Sections; Use Format Painter; Use Hyphenation

1. Open the file named **8skill1.doc** located on the data disk and make decisions regarding:

    Margins
    Fonts
    Font size
    Alignment

2. Center the title and format it using bold and an **18-point** font size.

3. The first news item, Quake-Proof Your Home, should be divided into **3** columns with a **.3"** spacing between columns.

4. The second news item, Henry W. Coe State Park, should be divided into a 2-column format.

5. Format the first news item's heading with a different font, a **14-point** font size, and bold.

6. Use the Format Painter and apply the heading format to the second news item's heading.

7. Format the first sidehead in the first article as desired. Use the Format Painter and apply the sidehead format to the other sideheads in both articles.

8. Hyphenate the entire document.

9. Use the *new* filename **8quake.doc** and save the file on your file disk.

10. Print one copy. Close the document.

Skill 8.2—Create Newspaper-Style Columns; Language Arts

1. Open the file named **8skill2.doc** located on the data disk.

2. Format the document creatively and attractively using multiple columns. Make your own decisions regarding:

   Margins
   Alignment
   Fonts
   Format for title and sideheads
   Use of Format Painter
   Use of text attributes such as bold, italic, and underline
   Number of columns and whether to use a different number of columns for part of the document
   Amount of space between columns
   Line between columns
   Hyphenation

3. Correct three spelling errors and three punctuation errors.

4. Use the *new* filename **8desktop publishing.doc** and save the file on your file disk.

5. Print one copy. Close the document.

Part 2
Checking Your Step

Production Skill Builder Projects
Chapters 5–8

Production Project 2.1—Create Formulas, Insert a Row, and Recalculate

1. Create the table shown. Type the following unformatted information into the table cells.

   Note: The text may wrap around in the cells differently than shown because of the fonts and point sizes selected on your computer.

Overdue Accounts			
Third Quarter			
Customer	Thirty Days	Sixty Days	Ninety Days
Hubbard's Repair	$5,430	$2,120	$1,099
JCP Service	573	400	150
Marina Plumbing	10,145	5,600	2,865
Wilson's Plumbing	908	585	0
Totals			

2. Select and merge the cells in row 1. Also merge the cells in row 2.

3. Make decisions regarding:

   Alignment for title, subtitle, and column heading cells
   Alignment for columns containing dollar amounts
   Table lines
   Shading for cells
   Column widths

4. Create formulas to calculate the column totals.

5. Insert a row between rows 6 and 7. Type the following information into the new row of table cells: **Jeff's Construction**; **9,560**; **4,800**; **3,200**. (Do not type the semicolons.) Recalculate the table column totals.

221

6. Use the filename **2p Project overdue 1.doc** and save the file on your file disk.

7. Print one copy and close the document.

Production Project 2.2—Create a Résumé, Set Tabs, and Insert Special Symbols

1. Use the following information to type the résumé shown on page 223.

   a. Type and format the title, **Résumé**.

   b. Insert an automatic border below the title.

   c. Change the top and bottom margins to .75". Change the left and right margins to **1"**.

   d. Place the insertion point below the border line. Type the name **Lisa Ann Fancher**. Press the **Tab** key once and type the address and press **Enter**. Type the phone number. Press the **Tab** key once and type the city, state, and zip. Press the **Enter** key three times.

   e. Select the two lines containing the name, address, and phone number and set a right tab that will align at the right margin.

   f. Place the insertion point on the third blank line below the phone number. Type the first sidehead, e.g., **Educational Background**, and press **Enter** twice. Do not format the sidehead until the résumé has been completely typed.

   g. Type the three bulleted paragraphs using the AutoCorrect feature to create the bullet character. Do not type the dates or set up the right tab until step h. Press the **Enter** key three times after the final bulleted paragraph. Remember to press the Tab key once after typing the first AutoCorrect arrow.

   h. Select all three bulleted paragraphs and set a right tab with a dot leader character that will align with the right margin.

   i. At the end of each bulleted paragraph, press the **Tab** key and type the dates shown.

   j. Place the insertion point in the third blank line below the bulleted paragraphs. Type the second sidehead, e.g., **Employment Experience**. Do not format the sidehead until the résumé is completely typed.

   k. Type the remaining paragraphs and headings of the résumé. Do not indent the paragraphs until step l.

   l. Indent the paragraph that begins "Assisted teacher in . . ." .25" from the left margin.

   m. Use the Format Painter to copy the indent format to the paragraphs below each job title and company name.

   Hint: To copy the indent format, be sure to select the paragraph symbol at the end of the paragraph that begins "Assisted teacher in . . ."

   n. Select the entire résumé and change the font size to **11 point**.

o. Make decisions on bolding, font sizes, italics, and any other attributes to enhance the appearance of the name and sideheads.

Résumé

Lisa Ann Fancher
408-555-3646

8309 Shore Road, #15
Milpitas, CA 95035-6712

Educational Background

➔ A.A. Degree, Mission College, Santa Clara, California—studied courses in Business Information Systems and Early Childhood Development 5/99
➔ Metropolitan Adult Education, San Jose, California—studied Business and Marketing courses 9/97-8/98
➔ Diploma, Fremont High School, Fremont, California 6/96

Employment Experience

Teacher's Aide, Kim's Children's Center, Milpitas, California—1 year
Assisted teacher in class, watched a class of third graders at recess, organized outdoor games, and greeted parents.

Stock Clerk, Volt Supply Company, San Jose, California—2 years
Used a scale, stocked shelves, used a computer for processing labels, and handled the shipping and receiving of products.

Assistant Copier, Murray Printing, Santa Clara, California—2 years
Printed, collated, and bound personalized calendars; answered phones; boxed calendars for UPS; and prepared information packets.

Cashier, Kmart, Milpitas, California—3 years (Part-time)
Performed all cashiering operations such as opening and closing the register and counting cash. Also, cleaned and straightened aisles. Worked with management and assisted with customer relations.

Special Skills

Type 50 wpm. Experienced with Microsoft Word and PageMaker for Windows, and Microsoft Word and Excel on the Macintosh. Proficient with phone communications and customer service.

References

Available upon request.

---

2. Use the filename **2p Fancher resume.doc** and save the file on your file disk.

3. Print one copy and close the document.

---

1. Create the following document using a table to format side-by-side columns. Make decisions regarding:

   Margins
   Alignment
   Fonts
   Font size
   Width of columns
   Bold/underline/capitalization of title, subtitle, and sideheads
   Hyphenation
   Use of Table AutoFormats and/or Format Painter features

Chapter News
American Medical Assistants

Fairfax Chapter	The Fairfax Chapter is trying to stay active and to grow. By this time next month, we will have had our first joint seminar with the Washington, D.C., chapter. Joanna Turner and Amy Hagenbaugh have been tremendous in helping to put on the seminar.
	We are planning to host the State Convention next year. It will be a very interesting meeting, and we are proud to extend our hospitality to the Virginia Society.
Tidewater Chapter	The Tidewater Chapter has had a variety of good speakers this quarter. Dr. Renee Myer, an audiologist, gave a very interesting presentation on Communication with the Hard of Hearing Patient.
Rockbridge Chapter	The Rockbridge Chapter has been busy adding new members to our group. Please welcome Lydia Sedwick and Bobby Ashworth.
	A brunch was held in honor of our new members. The speaker was Julia Grover, who spoke on Liability in a Medical Office. The attendance was excellent, and we had a very enjoyable brunch.
Southside Chapter	The Southside Chapter is busy preparing for the Annual State Convention! There is much to do in preparation for the convention, and we hope everyone will come and enjoy the educational programs and fellowship.

---

2. Use the filename **2p Chapter news.doc** and save the file on your file disk.

3. Print one copy.

4. Optional: Fax this document to your instructor via a local fax, or write an e-mail message to your instructor that you are sending this assignment. Attach this file to your e-mail message.

5. Close the document.

➽ ▬ Production Project 2.4—Create Newspaper Columns; Language Arts

1. Open the file named **2pact4.doc** located on the data disk.

2. Use newspaper-style columns and the following information to complete the document. Make decisions regarding:

> Margins and font size to fit document on one page
> Number of columns
> Spacing between columns
> Line between columns
> Alignment
> Fonts
> Spacing before and after sideheads
> Bold/italic/capitalization of title and sideheads
> Use of bullets or numbering to emphasize the list after the first
>   paragraph
> Hyphenation

3. Correct one spelling error and seven punctuation errors.

4. Use the filename **2project rice.doc** and save the file.

5. Print the document

6. Optional: Fax this document to your instructor via a local fax, or write an e-mail message to your instructor that you are sending this assignment. Attach this file to your e-mail message.

7. Close the document.

Part 3
A Step Up

Create Reports and Special Documents

Chapters 9–12

- Create additional space between paragraphs
- Change vertical line spacing
- Use Word Count
- Use the Thesaurus
- Use grammar check
- Use the Shrink to Fit feature
- Copy text between windows
- Create headers and footers
- Print page numbers
- Control text flow (widow/orphan)
- Create footnotes and endnotes
- Print specific pages
- Create a data souce file and main document
- Merge a main document with a data source file
- Edit a data source file and main document
- Output merged letters directly to a printer
- Select data records to be merged
- Create envelope addresses
- Create a full page of the same label
- Create mailing labels for different addresses
- Create and sort mailing labels using a new main document and an existing data source file
- Create and print a single label

CHAPTER

Create a One-Page Document

Features Covered

- Create additional space between paragraphs
- Change paragraph formats including vertical line spacing
- Use the Shrink to Fit feature
- Use Word Count
- Use the Thesaurus
- Use grammar check
- Use standard paragraphs to assemble personalized documents
- Copy text between windows

Objectives and Introduction

After successfully completing this chapter, you will be able to use the Paragraph dialog box to change vertical line spacing, spacing between paragraphs, alignment, and paragraph indention. You will learn how to use Word Count, Thesaurus, grammar check and the shrink to fit features to improve a document, and you will learn to assemble personalized documents using standard paragraphs and copy text between document windows.

A one-page document can be a promotional piece, essay, minutes of a meeting, an agenda, report, or any type of document that describes an event or provides information.

Create a One-Page Document

Documents have traditionally been created with either vertical line spacing of one (single-spacing) or vertical line spacing of two (double-spacing). With a typewriter, vertical line spacing of two is accomplished by pressing the Return key twice after each sentence or by moving a lever on the typewriter to set the desired vertical spacing. Vertical line spacing in Word can be set at any interval

229

desired (see Steps to Change Vertical Line Spacing and Paragraph Formats later in this chapter).

Generally when a document is formatted with vertical line spacing of one, paragraphs begin at the left margin with an extra line space between paragraphs (see Figure 9.1). This extra space can be added by pressing the **Enter** key twice between paragraphs, but it can also be added using the Paragraph dialog box. Usually, no extra spacing is placed between paragraphs when vertical line spacing of two is used, but the first line of each paragraph is indented approximately one-half inch from the left margin (see Figure 9.4). If vertical line spacing will be greater than 1.3 lines, the formatting guidelines for line spacing of two should be used (i.e., first line indent and no extra spacing between paragraphs).

Either left alignment or justified alignment can be used in a one-page document, depending on the writer's preference and the appearance of the document. Long quotes or other paragraphs that should be given special attention are often indented from both the left and right margins with a vertical line spacing of one.

Format a Document

A standard 8½ x 11-inch sheet of paper using the default 1 inch top and bottom margins has 9 vertical inches available for printed text. Normally, the default margins will be used when creating a one-page document; however, if desired, the margins can be changed.

The document title is usually centered and often emphasized by using bold, by changing to a different font, or by capitalizing all the letters. If a subtitle is used, one blank line follows the title. A subtitle is usually centered and typed in lowercase letters except the first letter of each main word which is capitalized. Initial caps is the phrase used to indicate words/phrases typed with the first letter of each main word capitalized.

Additional space is added before the first paragraph of a document and before and after each sidehead in the document. This gives the reader visual clues as to where the document begins and where each important idea is discussed. The additional spacing should equal one to two lines of text and should be consistent throughout the document.

Start-Up Instructions

❖ Open the file named **9NOBRE1.doc** located on the data disk.

❖ Place the insertion point to the left of the first character in the body text and press **Enter** twice to add additional space between the subtitle (Leadership Appointments) and the first paragraph. Also, insert a blank line between the title and subtitle.

❖ Center the title and subtitle.

❖ Nonprinting characters, such as tabs and paragraph markers, should be displayed in the document window. If necessary, select the **Show/Hide** button on the Standard Toolbar.

FIGURE 9.1

NOBRE News ◄——— Report title

Leadership Appointments ◄——— Report subtitle

It is with great pride that the New Orleans Board of Real Estate (NOBRE) announces Lonnie Nello's election as president-elect of the Louisiana Association of Realtors (LAR). Nello's leadership ability has been demonstrated extensively as current Treasurer for LAR, service for 15 years as a board member, and eight years as a National Realtor Association participant. He also served one year as the President of NOBRE.

12 points additional space

Who Is Lonnie Nello? ◄——— Sidehead

12 points additional space

Mr. Nello is a high-performance leader with vision, experience, and commitment who is addressing the radical changes in the real estate industry. He is an expert in business who is successfully meeting the fiscal realities of a constantly changing business environment.

12 points additional space

He is a thoughtful and concerned leader who is personally motivated to seeking quality solutions for the future. Nello realizes that technology, consumer demands, and shrinking profits are mandating a dramatic reworking of traditional real estate practices.

12 points additional space

In every buying decision, you ask, "How does this investment increase my profitability?" You must now make a decision whether to invest resources to remain Realtors. Nello is dedicated to enhancing the value of your membership.

12 points additional space

In discussing his immediate plans for the board, Nello comments:

12 points additional space

"My most immediate concern is to strengthen the Louisiana Association of Realtors by updating our use of technology and connecting our computer systems nationwide. In addition, I will be meeting with each member of the board to obtain ideas on ways to improve our service and profitability."

12 points additional space

Lourdes Vargas, Past-President of NOBRE ◄——— Sidehead

12 points additional space

Lourdes Vargas, who was last year's NOBRE President, was nominated to serve as a National Realtor Association (NRA) Director for a three-year term. She was instrumental in making local changes during a time when real estate prices were constantly changing.

12 points additional space

Miguel Soledad, Past-President of LAR ◄——— Sidehead

12 points additional space

Miguel Soledad has been nominated to serve as IMPAC Trustee, subject to approval by the LAR Board of Directors. The appointment will be discussed at next month's meeting. The IMPAC Trustees hold the vital role of determining LAR support or opposition to statewide ballot initiatives and local property rights issues that could have statewide significance.

One-page document showing standard formatting with vertical line spacing of one and left justification

Body text paragraphs

Paragraph indented from left and right margin

Steps to **Create a One-Page Document with Additional Space Between Paragraphs**

1. Select the text to which the paragraph formatting is to be applied.

FIGURE 9.2

Paragraph dialog
box

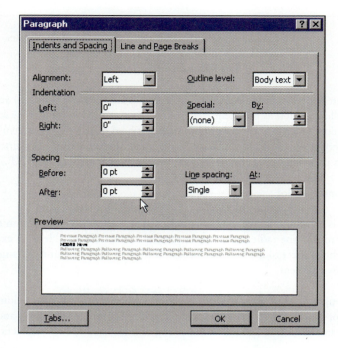

For example, select all the paragraphs and sideheads below the
subtitle. [Click to the left of the first body text paragraph,
double-click on the **EXT** (**Extend**) button in the **Status Bar**,
hold down the **CTRL** key, and press the **End** key.]

2. Select **Format, Paragraph**.

   Note: The Paragraph dialog box displays (see Figure 9.2).

3. The Indents and Spacing tab should be selected. If necessary, select the
   Indents and Spacing tab.

4. Click on the up or down triangle located in the Spacing area to the right of
   the After box until the desired spacing displays, or double-click on the figure
   displayed in the After box and type the new spacing.

   For example, click on the up triangle located to the right of
   the After box until **12 pt** displays.

   *Note: The following abbreviations can be used in the Spacing area: pi = picas, pt
   = points, li = lines, in = inches, cm = centimeters. Inserting a space between the
   number and the measurement is optional.*

5. Select **OK**.

6. Click once to deselect the text.

Finish-Up Instructions

❖ Use the *new* filename **9NOBRE2 spacing after.doc** and save the file on your
   file disk.

❖ Use the following information to indent a paragraph from the left and right
   margins.

   a. For example, place the insertion point in the paragraph, that begins
      "My most immediate . . ."

b. Select **Format, Paragraph**.

c. The Indents and Spacing tab should be selected. If necessary, select the **Indents and Spacing** tab.

d. Double-click on the zero in the Left indentation box. Type **.5**. Double-click on the zero in the Right indentation box and type **.5**.

    *Note: The Indentation area shows the measurement in inches. Press the **Tab** key once to display the new settings in the Preview box.*

e. Select **OK**.

    Note: The paragraph is indented .5" from both the left and right margins.

❖ Use the same filename, **9NOBRE2 spacing after.doc**, and save the file again.

❖ Print one copy.

Change Vertical Line Spacing and Paragraph Formats

Additional space can be created between lines of text by changing the vertical line spacing. The added space can be used, for example, to accommodate handwritten changes to draft letters or reports. Also, a report set for line spacing of two may be easier to read. The line spacing options available in Word are: *Single, 1.5 lines, Double, At least, Exactly,* and *Multiple.* The Line spacing option box is located on the Indents and Spacing tab of the Paragraph dialog box (see Figure 9.2).

On a typewriter, single-spacing traditionally meant that a fixed amount of space (approximately .164") was placed between text lines. Also, the amount of space between text lines did not change if a larger font was used.

When using Word, *Single* line spacing means that the point size of the text plus an amount equal to approximately 20% of the point size is placed between lines of text. For example, if a 12-point font size is selected and single-spacing is chosen, the actual amount of line spacing is approximately 14 points (.194").

This is a sample of 12-point text and single line spacing.

This is a sample of 18-point text and single line spacing.

This is a sample of 24-point text and single line spacing.

FIGURE 9.3

Sample of single line spacing in various point sizes

The actual amount of line spacing changes depending on the point size of the text (see Figure 9.3).

If the *Double* line spacing option is selected, the amount of line spacing is equal to twice the single line spacing amount. For example, if the single line spacing amount is 14 points, 28 points of line spacing will be inserted when the **Double** line spacing option is selected.

The *1.5 lines* option places one and a half times the single line spacing amount between the text lines. For example, if the single line spacing amount is 12 points, 18 points of line spacing will be inserted when the **1.5 lines** option is selected.

To increase or decrease the line spacing by an amount other than Double or 1.5 Lines, the *Multiple* option is selected, and the desired line spacing increment is typed in the At box. For example, to triple the amount of line spacing, select the **Multiple** option and type **3** in the At box; to decrease the amount of line spacing by 25%, select the **Multiple** option and type **.75** in the At box.

The *At least* option sets a minimum amount of line spacing. If necessary, Word will automatically adjust the line spacing to accommodate large fonts or graphic images. When the *Exactly* option is selected, an exact line spacing can be typed in. The line spacing is then fixed at that measurement regardless of changes in font size.

Line spacing can also be changed by selecting the text and pressing the appropriate shortcut key: **Ctrl** and **1** for single line spacing, **Ctrl** and **2** for line spacing of two (double), and **Ctrl** and **5** for line spacing of 1.5.

In addition to setting line spacing, the Paragraph dialog box can be used to specify paragraph formatting such as indents and alignment. For example, the Paragraph dialog box can be used to set left and right paragraph indents and to create hanging and first line indents. A sample of each indention type can be found in Figure 7.4 (Chapter 7, page 184).

The Special box in the Indentation area of the Paragraph dialog box contains three options: First Line, Hanging, and (none). The *First Line* option applies the indentation only to the first line of a paragraph. The *Hanging* option applies the indentation to the second and following lines of a paragraph (the first line of a hanging indent begins at the left margin). The *(none)* option is the default setting.

Start-Up Instructions

❖ The file **9NOBRE2 spacing after.doc** should be displayed in the document window.

❖ If necessary, turn on nonprinting symbols (select the **Show/Hide** button).

Change Vertical Line Spacing and Paragraph Formats

1. Place the insertion point in the desired paragraph, or select the paragraphs to be changed.

    For example, place the insertion point in the first body text paragraph.

2. Select **Format, Paragraph**.

3. Make any formatting changes as desired.

   For example, change all of the following items:

   a. Click in the **Line spacing** box. Select the **1.5 lines** option.

   b. Move the mouse pointer to the down triangle located to the right of the After box and click twice to display **0 pt**.

   c. Click in the **Special** box in the Indentation area. Select the **First line** option.

   Note: The default 0.5" displays in the By box.

   d. Click in the **Alignment** box. Select the **Justified** option.

4. Check that all options are set as desired; select **OK**.

5. Use the **Format Painter** button ⬚ to copy the paragraph formatting to all other desired paragraphs. When all desired paragraphs have been formatted, click once on the **Format Painter** button to turn off the Format Painter feature.

   For example, select the first body text paragraph, including the paragraph symbol at the end of the paragraph, and double-click on the **Format Painter** button ⬚. To continue using **Format Painter**, select the next body text paragraph. Repeat for all body text paragraphs except the indented paragraph. Click once on the **Format Painter** button ⬚ to turn off the Format Painter feature.

   Note: Do not use the Format Painter to format the sideheads. The sideheads will be formatted in a moment. The document will display on two pages. That's OK.

Finish-Up Instructions

❖ Format the first sidehead with 6 points of space before and 12 points of space after (select the first sidehead; select **Format**, **Paragraph**; click on the up or down triangle to display **6 pt** in the Before box and **12 pt** in the After box). Then use the **Format Painter** button ⬚ to copy the format to the other sideheads.

❖ Click in the indented paragraph. Select **Format**, **Paragraph**. Click on the up triangle to display **12 pt** in the Before box (**12 pt** should also be displayed in the After box). Select **Justified** alignment. Select **OK**.

❖ Use the *new* filename **9NOBRE3 Format Painter.doc** and save the file on your file disk.

❖ Continue with the Steps to Use the Shrink to Fit Feature.

Use the Shrink to Fit Feature

With the Shrink to Fit feature, Word automatically reduces the font size of text in an effort to fit a document on fewer pages. For example, after typing and formatting a report, you view the document using Print Preview and notice that only a few lines of text display on page 3 of the report. When the **Shrink to Fit** button ⬚ is selected, Word reduces the font size of the report text so that all the text will display on two pages.

After using the Shrink to Fit feature, check the document to make sure that the font size is readable. If necessary, the **Undo** button can be used to reverse the font size change.

Start-Up Instructions

❖ The file named **9NORBE3 Format Painter.doc** should be displayed in the document window.

 Use the Shrink to Fit Feature

1. Select the **Print Preview** button ⬚.

2. Select the **Multiple Pages** button ⬚ and choose the desired number of pages to be displayed.

   For example, check that two pages display. If necessary, select the **Multiple Pages** button ⬚ and click on the middle button in the first row to display two pages.

3. Select the **Shrink to Fit** button ⬚.

   Note: The document now displays on a single page. The font size of the text has been reduced so that the text will fit on fewer pages.

4. Select the **Close** button to return to the document window.

Finish-Up Instructions

❖ Use the *new* filename **9Shrink to Fit.doc** and save the document on your file disk.

❖ Print one copy.

   Note: Your document should look similar to the one shown in Figure 9.4.

Use Word Count

Word can compile various statistics for either an entire document or for a selected portion of a document. When **Tools**, **Word Count** is selected, the number of pages, words, characters (without spaces and with spaces), paragraphs, and lines are calculated and displayed in the Word Count dialog box.

When only a portion of a document is selected, the statistics displayed in the dialog box relate only to the selected text. A total word, character, or line count is useful when preparing a document that must meet specific guidelines, e.g., a school research paper or an article submitted for publication.

FIGURE 9.4

One-page document showing standard formatting with vertical line spacing of 1.5 lines, justification, and first line indents

NOBRE News

Leadership Appointments

It is with great pride that the New Orleans Board of Real Estate (NOBRE) announces Lonnie Nello's election as president-elect of the Louisiana Association of Realtors (LAR). Nello's leadership ability has been demonstrated extensively as current Treasurer for LAR, service for 15 years as a board member, and eight years as a National Realtor Association participant. He also served one year as the President of NOBRE.

Who Is Lonnie Nello?

Mr. Nello is a high-performance leader with vision, experience, and commitment who is addressing the radical changes in the real estate industry. He is an expert in business who is successfully meeting the fiscal realities of a constantly changing business environment.

He is a thoughtful and concerned leader who is personally motivated to seeking quality solutions for the future. Nello realizes that technology, consumer demands, and shrinking profits are mandating a dramatic reworking of traditional real estate practices.

In every buying decision, you ask, "How does this investment increase my profitability?" You must now make a decision whether to invest resources to remain Realtors. Nello is dedicated to enhancing the value of your membership.

In discussing his immediate plans for the board, Nello comments:

"My most immediate concern is to strengthen the Louisiana Association of Realtors by updating our use of technology and connecting our computer systems nationwide. In addition, I will be meeting with each member of the board to obtain ideas on ways to improve our service and profitability."

Lourdes Vargas, Past-President of NOBRE

Lourdes Vargas, who was last year's NOBRE President, was nominated to serve as a National Realtor Association (NRA) Director for a three-year term. She was instrumental in making local changes during a time when real estate prices were constantly changing.

Miguel Soledad, Past-President of LAR

Miguel Soledad has been nominated to serve as IMPAC Trustee, subject to approval by the LAR Board of Directors. The appointment will be discussed at next month's meeting. The IMPAC Trustees hold the vital role of determining LAR support or opposition to statewide ballot initiatives and local property rights issues that could have statewide significance.

Start-Up Instructions

❖ The file named **9Shrink to Fit.doc** should be displayed in the document window.

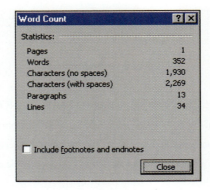

FIGURE 9.5

Word Count
dialog box

Use Word Count

1. Select **Tools, Word Count**.

   Note: The Word Count dialog box, similar to Figure 9.5, displays. Write down the number (amount) of words and paragraphs displayed.

2. Select **Close** to return to the document window.

Finish-Up Instructions

❖ Optional: Print one copy. At the top of the printed document, handwrite the total number of words and paragraphs.

❖ If any changes are made to the document, save the file again using the same filename, **9Shrink to Fit.doc**.

❖ Close the document.

Use the Thesaurus

Word stores a list of words that have the same or similar meaning (synonyms) in the Thesaurus. A writer attempts to use words that will effectively communicate ideas. A thesaurus assists a writer by providing synonyms to convey his/her message more clearly. Word's Thesaurus can be used during the writing process or after a document has been written.

When the **Thesaurus** command is selected, a dialog box displays containing a list of possible meanings for the selected word, designated as nouns, verbs, and/or adjectives. See Figure 9.6. The synonym(s) for the highlighted word in the Meanings box is displayed in the list located to the right of the Meanings box. When a synonym is highlighted, it also appears in the Replace with Synonym box. If the word Antonym displays next to a word on the Replace with Synonym list, the word has an opposite meaning.

In the Thesaurus dialog box, a writer can replace the word with a synonym or antonym, look up another word, or select various meanings of the word to view different lists of synonyms or antonyms. (If the selected word cannot be found, an alphabetical list of words closely resembling the selected word displays.) After Word replaces the selected word with a different word, the word

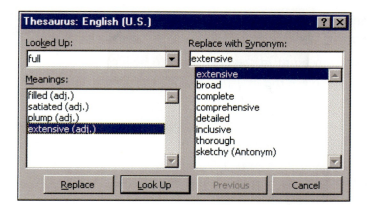

FIGURE 9.6

Thesaurus dialog
box

ending may need to be corrected to match the meaning of the sentence or for verb-subject agreement.

Start-Up Instructions

❖ Open the file named **9annual.doc** located on the data disk.

 ## Select Synonyms from the Thesaurus

1. Place the insertion point in the word to be looked up in the Thesaurus.

   For example, place the insertion point in the word **full** in the second sentence of the body text.

2. Select **Tools, Language, Thesaurus**.

   Note: The Thesaurus dialog box displays (see Figure 9.6).

3. From the words listed under the heading Meanings, select the word closest to the meaning of the word in the sentence.

   For example, click once on the word **extensive**.

   Note: If there are more meanings than can be displayed at one time, the scroll bar on the right side of the Meanings box will be activated. Scroll through the listed meanings until the desired meaning displays.

4. Select the desired replacement word from the Replace with Synonym list.

   For example, click once on the word **complete**.

   Note: The word selected will immediately appear in the Replace with Synonym box at the top of the list.

5. Select **Replace**.

   Note: The word full is automatically replaced with the word complete.

6. Place the insertion point in the next word to be looked up.

   For example, place the insertion point in the word **benefits** in the first sentence of the second body text paragraph.

7. Select **Tools, Language, Thesaurus**.

8. In the Meanings list, the word reimbursement displays. Scan through the synonyms list and determine if there is a suitable replacement. If no suitable replacement word displays, select **Cancel**.

For example, because there is no suitable replacement for the word benefits under any of the meanings shown, select **Cancel**.

9. Place the insertion point in the next word to be looked up.

   For example, place the insertion point in the word **subtracting** in the first sentence of the third body text paragraph.

10. Select **Tools, Language, Thesaurus** and scan the listed words. Select the desired synonym and choose **Replace**.

    For example, double-click on **Related Words** and select the word **deduct**. Select **Replace**. In the document window, add **ing** to the word **deduct**.

Finish-Up Instructions

❖ Place the insertion point in the word donations in the last sentence of the third body text paragraph; select **Tools**, **Language**, **Thesaurus**; select **contributions** in the Replace with Synonym list; select **Replace**.

❖ Use the *new* filename **9thesaurus.doc** and save the file on your file disk.

❖ Print one copy. Close the document.

Use the Grammar Check

Word's grammar checking program reviews a document for grammatical, spelling, and writing-style errors. When the grammar checking program is activated by selecting **Tools, Spelling & Grammar**, the text is checked against a list of grammar rules, such as passive verb usage, subject-verb agreement, double negatives, repetitive expressions, punctuation errors, and capitalization.

The grammar rules used to check text can be viewed or changed by selecting **Tools, Options** and the **Spelling & Grammar** tab or by selecting **Options** in the Spelling and Grammar dialog box. Select a writing style, such as Casual, Standard, or Formal. To customize any of the writing sets, select **Settings.** Then review the grammar style options shown in the Grammar Settings dialog box. If there is a check mark in the box in front of the rule, the rule is selected and will be applied to the document. The Formal Writing style is used in the Steps to Use Grammar Checking.

If the **Show readability statistics** option is activated on the Spelling & Grammar tab, the word, character, paragraph, and sentence counts display along with the average number of sentences in a paragraph, words per sentence, and characters per word. Also listed in the statistics is the Flesch Reading Ease readability number. The number displayed by the Flesch Reading Ease score rates text based on a 100-point scale. The higher the score the easier it is to understand the information. Any Flesch Reading Ease score between 60 and 70 is considered an effective reading level for most individuals.

During the grammar checking process, suggested changes are displayed in green for a grammar item and in red for a spelling item. The suggested grammar change can be accepted or ignored, or the sentence can be rewritten. The grammar suggestions should be used only as a guide, because the grammar informa-

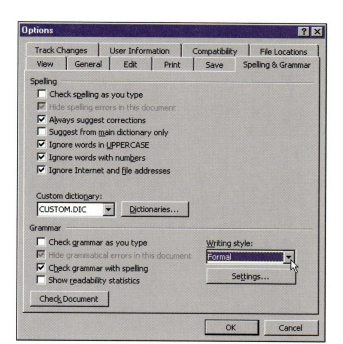

FIGURE 9.7

Spelling &
Grammar
Options tab

tion may or may not be correct according to other grammatical sources or according to the content/context of the sentence(s).

Start-Up Instructions

❖ Open the file named **9saving.doc** located on the data disk.

❖ The insertion point should be located at the beginning of the document. (If necessary, press **Ctrl** and **Home.**)

Steps to → ## Use Grammar Checking

1. The document to be grammar checked must be saved and displayed in the document window.

2. Select **Tools, Options, Spelling & Grammar** tab.

   Note: The Spelling & Grammar tab displays (see Figure 9.7).

3. Select and deselect the options as desired for checking grammar:

   For example,

   a. In the Grammar section, check that the **Check grammar with spelling** option is selected.

   b. The **Show readability statistics** should be deselected.

   c. The Writing style should be Formal. (If necessary, click in the **Writing style** box and choose **Formal.**)

   d. Select **OK**.

4. Select **Tools, Spelling and Grammar.**

   Note: The Spelling and Grammar dialog box displays. The first potential problem is highlighted in the document window and displays in the Subject-Verb Agreement area of the Spelling and Grammar dialog box. The specific item in

Spelling and
Grammar dialog
box

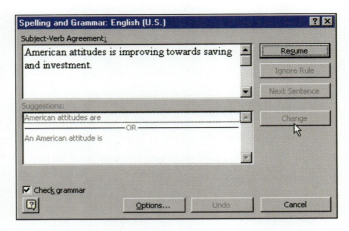

question displays in green. For example, the first sentence in the first paragraph displays with the words "American attitudes is" in green. The Suggestions box displays two possible solutions: "American attitudes are" or "An American attitude is" (see Figure 9.8).

5. Select the **Change** button to make the first change suggested.

   Note: In a moment, the next potential problem displays in green: "In addition, Americans increased their wealth dramatically and are recognizing the need to save and invest wisely."

6. Since the sentence is grammatically correct, select the **Next Sentence** button.

   Note: If necessary, move the Spelling and Grammar dialog box. Move the mouse pointer to the dialog box Title bar. Press and hold the mouse button. Drag the box down and to the right.

7. Edit the next phrase displayed in green, "are selected."

   For example, in the document window, delete the word "are"
   and type the word **were**. Select **Change**.

   Note: The words "were selected" are highlighted. "Were selected" is a correct phrase.

8. Select the **Ignore** button.

   Note: The next item to be checked is ". . .for many of their savings needs and turned to brokerage firms for investments." The words are correct.

9. Choose the **Ignore** button.

   Note: The next item to be checked is "industry have." The first suggestion, "industry has," is correct.

10. Select the **Change** button.

    Note: When the grammar check is finished, the message displays, "The spelling and grammar check is complete."

11. Select **OK**.

    Note: If the Readability Statistics box displays, select OK.

Finish-Up Instructions

❖ Use the *new* filename **9grammar.doc** and save the file.

❖ Print one copy. Close the document.

Use Standard Paragraphs to Assemble Personalized Documents

Text that is used repeatedly can be saved and opened when needed. For example, a will created by a lawyer contains many standard paragraphs that are common to all wills. The standard paragraphs are saved in a separate document, and the desired paragraphs are retrieved to assemble a document created for a specific individual.

The first part of the process to assemble documents using standard paragraphs is to create and save a document that contains the standard paragraphs. The second part of the process is to open a new document and type the information that is specific to the personalized document, e.g., date, name, address, and nonstandard paragraphs.

The final process to assemble documents using standard paragraphs is to copy text from the standard paragraphs document to the personalized document. Each document is placed in a separate document window. For example, the standard paragraphs document and the personalized document are both open and each is in a separate window.

The windows containing each document can be displayed with one window at the top and one window at the bottom of the screen (see Figure 9.10) or side by side (see Figure 9.12). The drag and drop method of copying text can be used to copy information from the document window containing the standard paragraphs into the document window containing the personalized document. (For information on using the drag and drop method to copy text, see Chapter 4, page 90.)

Start-Up Instructions

❖ A new document should be displayed on the screen. If necessary, click on the **New** button on the Standard Toolbar to create a new document.

❖ Type the current date, inside address, salutation and first two paragraphs of the letter shown in Figure 9.9. Press the **Enter** key three times after the second paragraph.

❖ If the Office Assistant displays, click on the **Cancel** button.

❖ If necessary, turn on nonprinting symbols (select the **Show/Hide** button).

❖ Use the filename **9Kern letter.doc** and save the personalized letter on your file disk.

   Note: The remainder of the letter will be typed later.

❖ Open the file named **9Standard.doc** located on the data disk. This file contains the standard paragraphs that will be copied into the personalized letter.

Steps to ▶ Arrange Document Windows Side By Side

1. Select **Window, Arrange All** to display a document window for each open document.

FIGURE 9.9

Personalized
document using
standard
paragraphs
(**9Kern letter.doc**)

(Use current date)

Ms. Leanna Kern
GM Telecom
6803 NE Broadway Street
Portland, OR 97212-0301

Dear Ms. Kern:

Your registration has been received to attend the upcoming Computers and Communications Conference.

The date, location, and description of your selected sessions are as follows:

Copy the following standard paragraphs from the list of seminar information in the file named **9Standard.doc**:

February 12-13 conference date and location information

Improving Computer Performance—

Real Uses for Business Multimedia—

If you need additional information about the seminar or hotel accommodations, please call 1-800-555-8202.

Sincerely,

Hazel Walters
Seminar Coordinator

HW/xx
9Kern letter.doc/disk1

*Note: The screen is divided into two document windows (see Figure 9.10). One document window contains the file named **9Standard.doc**, and the other document window contains the file named **9Kern letter.doc**.*

2. Move the mouse pointer to the right edge of the top document window until the left-pointing arrow of a double-headed arrow displays.

   For example, move the mouse pointer to the right edge of the top document window until the left-pointing arrow of the double-headed arrow displays.

3. Press and hold the mouse button and drag to the left until the document window is the desired width. Release the mouse button.

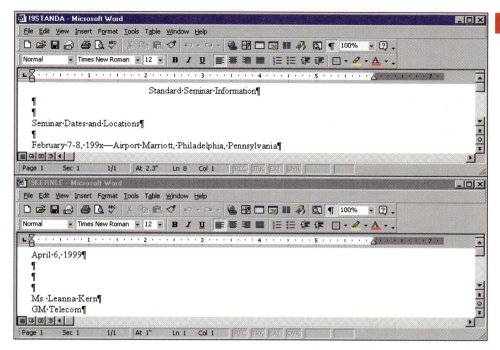

FIGURE 9.10

Screen with two document windows open

For example, press and hold the mouse button and drag to the left until the document window is approximately half the screen width (see Figure 9.11). Release the mouse button.

4. Move the mouse pointer to the left edge of the lower document window until the right-pointing arrow of a double-headed arrow displays.

   For example, move the mouse pointer to the left edge of the lower document window until the right-pointing arrow of the double-headed arrow displays.

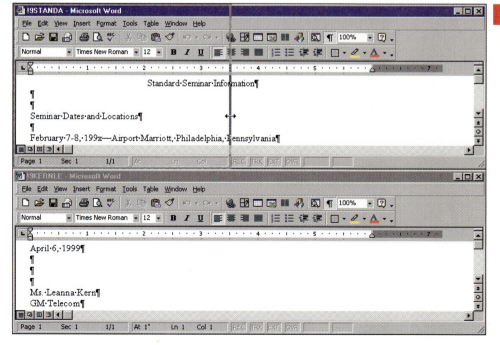

FIGURE 9.11

Screen with the width of one document window being changed

FIGURE 9.12

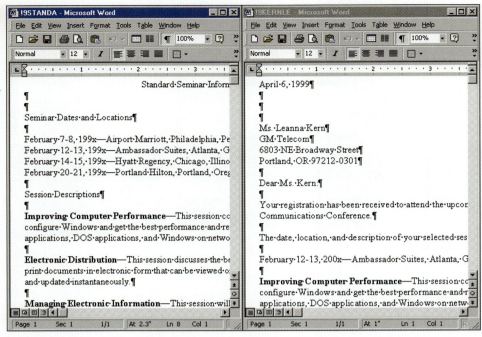

5. Press and hold the mouse button and drag to the right until the document window is the desired width. Release the mouse button.

    For example, press and hold the mouse button and drag to the right until the document window is approximately half the screen width.

6. Continue to adjust the width and depth of the document windows as needed.

    For example,

    a. Move the mouse pointer to the top edge of the lower document window until a double-headed arrow displays.

    b. Press and hold the mouse button and drag up until the top of the document window is at the top of the screen. Release the mouse button.

    c. Move the mouse pointer to the bottom edge of the document window at the left of the screen until a double-headed arrow displays.

    d. Press and hold the mouse button and drag down until the bottom of that document window is just above the Status bar. Release the mouse button.

    Note: The document windows are now displayed side by side on the screen (see Figure 9.12).

Finish-Up Instructions

❖ Continue with the Steps to Use Drag and Drop to Copy Text Between Windows.

❖ If necessary, scroll to view the last paragraph of the **9Kern letter.doc**.

Use Drag and Drop to Copy Text Between Windows

1. In the document window containing the standard paragraphs, select the desired text to be copied to the personalized document.

   For example, if necessary, click in the window containing the **9standard.doc** document. Select **February 12-13, 200x—Ambassador Suites, Atlanta, Georgia.**

2. Move the mouse pointer into the selected (highlighted) text.

3. Press and hold the mouse button while dragging the mouse pointer and insertion point to the desired location in another document window. Do not release the mouse button.

   For example, while holding the mouse button, drag the mouse pointer and the insertion point to the second blank line below the second body text paragraph in the document named **9Kern letter.doc**. Do *not* release the mouse button.

4. Press and hold the **Ctrl** key.

   Note: A plus symbol displays in a small rectangle below the mouse pointer.

5. With the insertion point at the desired location in the personalized document, release the mouse button and then release the **Ctrl** key.

   For example, with the insertion point located at the second blank line below the second body text paragraph, release the mouse button and then release the **Ctrl** key.

   Note: The copied text displays in the personalized document window.

6. Click once to deselect the text in the personalized letter.

Finish-Up Instructions

❖ Use the following information to complete the personalized letter.

   a. Repeat steps 1–6 to copy the paragraph that begins **Improving Computer Performance**, including the blank line that follows the paragraph, into the personalized document. The copied paragraph should be placed on the second blank line below the conference date (i.e., February 12-13, 200x).

   b. Repeat steps 1–6 to copy the paragraph that begins **Real Uses for Business Multimedia**, including the blank line that follows the paragraph, into the personalized document. The copied paragraph should be placed on the second blank line below the paragraph that begins **Improving Computer Performance**.

   c. Maximize the window containing **9Kern letter.doc**. Type the final paragraph, complimentary closing, typed signature, title, reference initials, and document identification as shown in Figure 9.9.

❖ Save the personalized document file using the same filename, **9Kern letter.doc**.

❖ Print one copy of the personalized document. Close both documents.

Self-Check Quiz
Language Arts
Activities
Challenge Your Skills

The Next Step

Chapter Review and Activities

Self-Check Quiz

T **F** 1. The first line of a paragraph in a document with vertical line spacing of one is always indented.

T F 2. A thesaurus contains synonyms, which assist a writer in communicating clearly.

T **F** 3. A document typed with vertical line spacing of two is always printed with justified alignment.

T **F** 4. The changes suggested by the grammar checking program should always be used to correct the grammar in a document.

5. The standard paragraphs file must be _____ before copying text to personalize a document.
   a. open in a document window
   b. created
   c. closed
   d. both a and b

6. If a document is formatted with vertical line spacing of two, _____.
   a. the first line of each paragraph should be indented
   b. extra space should be added before each paragraph
   c. the body text should be right aligned.
   d. none of these

7. A document title is often centered and printed in _____.
   a. a different font
   b. italic
   c. lowercase letters
   d. none of these

8. With the Shrink to Fit feature, Word reduces the _____ of text.
   a. font size
   b. line spacing
   c. margins
   d. indents

9. List the names of the menu and submenu selected in order to display the Word Count dialog box.

   Tools, Word Count.

10. State one purpose for using standard paragraphs to assemble personalized documents.

Enriching Language Arts Skills

Spelling/Vocabulary Words

assessing—estimating or judging the value of something; appraising; evaluating.
certified—to declare via a formal document that a thing is true or accurate.
comprehensive—wide in scope; complete; inclusive.
forum—an assembly or program for the discussion of public matters.
independent—self-governing; not connected with others.
productivity—fertile; marked by abundant production.
technical—having special and practical knowledge especially of a mechanical or scientific subject.

Spelling Hint

The Spell Checking feature approves words that are correctly spelled; however, a correctly spelled word can be incorrectly used in a sentence. After using the Spell Checking feature, proofread the document for words used incorrectly.

Examples:

of, off	*you, your, you're*	*is, it, in, if*	*to, too, two*	*its, it's*
no, not	*for, from, form*	*a, as, an*	*there, their*	*used, sued*
so, sow	*who, whom*	*pair, pare*	*piece, peace*	*here, hear*

Activities

Activity 9.1—Change the Paragraph Format; Use Shrink to Fit and Word Count

1. Open the file named **9act1.doc** located on the data disk.

2. Select the title. Use **14 point**, **bold**, and center the title. Place the insertion point after the title and press **Enter** twice.

3. Use the Paragraph dialog box to insert a space equal to one blank line (12 points) after each paragraph (select all paragraphs except the title; select **Format**, **Paragraph**; click twice on the up triangle located to the right of the After box in the Spacing area to display **12 pt**; select **OK**).

4. Select the first sidehead, **Who to Call**. Use **bold** and **12 point**.

5. Use the Format Painter button to copy the formatting of the first sidehead to the other sideheads. (With the first sidehead highlighted, double-click on the **Format Painter** button, then select each of the other sideheads. Click once on the **Format Painter** button to turn off the Format Painter.)

6. Use the Shrink to Fit feature to reduce the font size of the report text so that the text displays on one page (select the **Print Preview** button; select the **Shrink to Fit** button; select the **Close** button to return to the document window).

7. Use the *new* filename **9telephone activity1.doc** and save the file on your file disk.

8. Print one copy.

9. Select **Tools**, **Word Count** to determine the total number of words in the document. Handwrite the number of words and number of paragraphs at the top of your printed copy. Select **Close**.

10. Close the document.

■ Activity 9.2—Create Personalized Letters Using Standard Paragraphs

1. Open the file named **9Standard.doc** located on the data disk.

2. Create a new file and type the current date, the inside address, salutation, and first paragraph of the personalized letter that follows. Press the **Enter** key three times after the first body text paragraph.

   Note: Wait until step 4 before copying the standard paragraphs.

(Use current date)

Mr. Dale J. Stahl, Jr.
972 Bonnie View Road
Cincinnati, OH 45230-6004

Dear Mr. Stahl:

Thank you for your interest in attending our Computers and Communications Conferences. Below is a listing of the upcoming conference dates and a description of the two seminars in which you have expressed an interest.

> Copy the following standard paragraphs from the list of seminar information in the file named **9Standard.doc**:
>
> Copy all four seminar locations and dates.
>
> Copy the paragraph that begins "Real Uses for Business Multimedia."
>
> Copy the paragraph that begins "Managing Electronic Information."

If you need additional information about the seminars or hotel accommodations, please call 1-800-555-8686.

Sincerely,

Jerry Alvardo
Director

JA/xx
9Stahl letter.doc/disk3

---

3. Use the filename **9Stahl letter.doc** and save the file on your file disk.

4. Display the standard paragraphs document and the personalized document side by side on the screen using the following information:

    a. Select **Window**, **Arrange All**.

    b. Move the mouse pointer to the right edge of the top document window until the left-pointing arrow of the double-headed arrow displays. Press and hold the mouse button and drag to the left until the document window is approximately half the screen width. Release the mouse button.

    c. Move the mouse pointer to the left edge of the bottom document window until the right-pointing arrow of the double-headed arrow displays. Press and hold the mouse button and drag to the right until the document window is approximately half the screen width. Release the mouse button.

    d. Move the mouse pointer to the top edge of the lower document window until a double-headed arrow displays. Press and hold the mouse button and drag up until the top of the document window is just below the Toolbars. Release the mouse button.

    e. Move the mouse pointer to the bottom edge of the document window located at the left of the screen until a double-headed arrow displays. Press and hold the mouse button and drag down until the document window is at the bottom of the screen. Release the mouse button.

5. Use drag and drop to copy the standard paragraphs from the file named **9Standard.doc** as indicated. (Select the desired paragraphs; move the mouse pointer into the selected text, press and hold the mouse button while dragging the mouse pointer and insertion point to the desired location in the personalized document; press and hold the **Ctrl** key; release the mouse button and then release the **Ctrl** key.)

6. Type the final paragraph, complimentary closing, typed signature, title, reference initials, and document identification.

7. Save the personalized document using the same filename, **9Stahl letter.doc**.

---

8. Print one copy of the file named **9Stahl letter.doc**. Close the file named **9Stahl letter.doc**.

9. Create a new file and type the current date, inside address, salutation, and first paragraph of the following personalized letter. Press the **Enter** key three times after the first body text paragraph.

(Use current date)

Ms. Vera Arbor
Center for Research and Development
6019 Monterey Avenue, Suite 12
Gilroy, CA 95020-3505

Dear Ms. Arbor:

We appreciate your request for information regarding our upcoming West Coast seminar. Currently, the following seminar is scheduled for the western region:

Copy the location and date information for the Portland, Oregon, seminar from the list of standard seminar information in the file named **9Standard.doc**.

With regard to your interest in increasing office productivity, the following seminar is recommended:

Copy the paragraph that begins "Electronic Distribution" from the list of standard seminar information in the file named **9Standard.doc**.

I hope to see you at our western region seminar.

Sincerely,

Hazel Walters
Seminar Coordinator

HW/xx
9Arbor letter.doc/disk2

---

10. Use the filename **9Arbor letter.doc** and save the file on your file disk.

11. Repeat steps 4a. to 4e. to display the document window containing **9Standard.doc** and the document window containing the file named **9Arbor letter.doc** side by side on the screen.

12. Use drag and drop to copy the paragraphs indicated from the file named **9Standard.doc**.

13. Type the final paragraph, complimentary closing, typed signature, title, reference initials, and document identification.

14. Save the personalized document using the same filename, **9Arbor letter.doc**.

15. Print one copy of the file named **9Arbor letter.doc** and close all document windows.

Activity 9.3—Change Paragraph Formats and Use the Thesaurus

1. Open the file named **9act3.doc** located on the data disk.

2. Select the entire document except the title and subtitle and use the following information to format the paragraphs:

   a. Add space after each paragraph equal to one blank line (12 points). (Select **Format**, **Paragraph**, click on the up triangle located to the right of the After box until **12 pt** displays.)

   b. Set the line spacing to **At least 1.5 pt** (click in the **Line spacing** box, click on **At least**; click on the up triangle located to the right of the At box until **1.5 pt** displays).

   c. Select **OK**.

3. Select the title and subtitle. Change the font size to **14 point** and select **Bold**.

4. Select the sidehead **Condition**. Change the font size to **14 point** and select **Bold**.

5. Use the Thesaurus to find synonyms for the underlined words (place the insertion point in an underlined word; select **Tools**, **Language**, **Thesaurus**). Bold the replaced synonyms and remove the underlining.

   Note: There may not be appropriate synonyms for all underlined words. Also, remember to check word endings after words are replaced.

6. Use the *new* filename **9synonyms 3.doc** and save the file on your file disk.

7. Print one copy.

8. Optional: Fax this document to your instructor via a local fax, or write an e-mail message to your instructor that you are sending this assignment. Attach this file to your e-mail message.

9. Close the document.

Activity 9.4—Use Grammar Checking and Paragraph Formatting

1. Open the file named **9act4.doc** located on the data disk.

2. Format the entire document to have vertical spacing of **1.5 lines**, a first line indent of **.3"**, and justified alignment. (Select the entire document; select **Format, Paragraph**, click in the **Line spacing** box, and select **1.5 lines**. Click in the **Special** box and select **First line**. Click on the down triangle located to the right of the By box until **0.3"** displays. Click in the **Alignment** box and select **Justified** alignment. Select **OK**.)

3. Use the *new* filename **9grammar check 4.doc** and save the file on your file disk.

4. Use the grammar checking feature to check the document using the following information:

   a. Select **Tools, Options, Spelling & Grammar** tab.

   b. Check that the **Check grammar with spelling** option in the **Grammar** area is chosen.

   c. Choose the **Formal** option in the Writing style box; select **OK**.

   d. With the insertion point at the top of the document, choose **Tools, Spelling and Grammar**.

   e. The phrase "is overlooked" is grammatically correct; select the **Ignore** button.

   f. The phrase "are being added" is grammatically correct; select the **Ignore** button.

   g. A fragmented sentence displays, "A second solution to...". Click to the left of the "t" in "to" and type the word "is" followed by a space. Select the **Change** button.

   h. Select **OK**.

5. Use the *new* filename **9computers grammar check.doc** and save the corrected file on your file disk.

6. Print one copy.

7. Optional: Fax this document to your instructor via a local fax, or write an e-mail message to your instructor that you are sending this assignment. Attach this file to your e-mail message.

8. Close the document.

Challenge Your Skills

Skill 9.1—Change the Paragraph Format; Use Shrink to Fit and Word Count

1. Open the file named **9skill1.doc** located on the data disk.

2. Use the Paragraph dialog box to add **12 points** of space between the body text paragraphs and to choose an appropriate alignment.

3. Edit the document as follows:

a. Add the sideheads:

Employer/Employee Relationship above body text paragraph 2.
Technical Training Program above body text paragraph 3.
Management Trainee Program above body text paragraph 4.
Employee Assistance Program above body text paragraph 6.

b. Make decisions regarding font, spacing, and bolding for the first sidehead. Use **Format Painter** to copy the formatting to each sidehead.

4. Make decisions regarding the format of the title, e.g., alignment, spacing after, font, size, and bolding.

5. If necessary, use Shrink to Fit to reduce the font size so that the text displays on one page.

6. Use the *new* filename **9personnel.doc** and save the file.

7. Print one copy

8. Use Word Count to determine the total number of words in the document. Handwrite the number of words at the top of your printed copy.

9. Optional: Fax this document to your instructor via a local fax, or write an e-mail message to your instructor that you are sending this assignment. Attach this file to your e-mail message.

10. Close the document.

■ Skill 9.2—Change the Paragraph Format and Use the Thesaurus

1. Open the file named **9skill2.doc** located on the data disk.

2. Change the paragraph format to vertical line spacing of **1.5 lines**.

3. Change the format for the items under the sidehead Cautions to a bulleted or numbered list, single-spaced.

4. Make decisions regarding:

   Margins
   Alignment
   Title alignment and capitalization
   Bold
   Sidehead font size and capitalization
   Indents and spacing after paragraphs

   Hint: If First line indents are to be set for the body text, select the first body text paragraph including the paragraph symbol. Set the First line indent desired. Set spacing after paragraphs as desired then use the Format Painter to apply the formatting to other body text paragraphs.

5. If necessary, use Shrink to Fit to place all the document text on one page.

6. Use the Thesaurus to make decisions for replacing (or *not* replacing) the bolded words. Italicize the substituted words.

7. Use the *new* filename **9drip irrigation.doc** and save the file on your file disk.

8. Print one copy

9. Optional: Fax this document to your instructor via a local fax, or write an e-mail message to your instructor that you are sending this assignment. Attach this file to your e-mail message.

10. Close the document.

☞ Skill 9.3—Create Standard Paragraphs and Assemble Personalized Documents; Language Arts

Part I

1. Type the following standard list of available support services as shown.

2. Correct three spelling errors, five misused words, and two punctuation errors.

Standard List of Available Support Services

Productivity Enhancement

Dupont Plus is a program offering a increased level of software information, access, service and support to increase knowledge and enhance productivity for the serious software user.

Developer Assistance

Dupont Developer it the best source for development-related technecal, strategic, and resource information.

Online Dupont

Online Dupont provides access too the Dupont Knowledge Database, Software Programs Library, and User and Developer forums. Call 800-555-2424 for information on access to Online Dupont.

Hard Copy

Dupont Press offers a variety of books and technical references for computer users and programmers at all levels, including comprehensive reference and how-to information.

Point of View

Express your point of view by joining Dupont's registered customer list and by sending in your ideas, comments, or tips. Make suggestions on future Dupont software programs. If your suggestion is used, a cash bonus of $50-$500 will be yours.

Independent Supporters

Independant Supporters are companies not owned or financed by Dupont that provide consulting, development, technical support, and other services for Dupont products. Call for information or for a Dupont Independent Supporter near your.

Certified Professional Program

The Dupont Certified Professional Program is a comprehensive certification program for assesing and maintaining software-related skills. It can be used as part of an ongoing employee training program or it can be used independently by persons motivated to improve their skills and marketability.

Consulting Services

Dupont Consulting Services help both end-user organizations and third-party software developers worldwide to design and build information technology solutions suing Dupont programs.

3. Use the filename **9standard list of services.doc** and save the standard list on your file disk.

4. Print one copy.

Part II

1. If necessary, open the file named **9standard list of services.doc**.

2. The standard list of available support services will be used to construct two 1-page documents to be posted on bulletin boards to provide employees with information.

3. For each document, make decisions regarding:

> Line spacing (one or two)
> Alignment
> Margins
> Bold
> Fonts

4. Create a new file and type the following personalized document shown on page 258.

WORD PROCESSORS, ASSISTANTS, AND CLERKS
Available Dupont Services

Copy the following paragraphs in the order listed from the standard list of available support services (**9standard list of services.doc**).

Productivity Enhancement
Developer Assistance
Point of View
Certified Professional Program
Consulting Services

5. Use the filename **9word processors.doc** and save the personalized document on your file disk. Print one copy. Close the document.

6. Create a new file and type the following personalized document:

PROGRAMMERS AND SYSTEM DESIGNERS
Available Dupont Services

Copy the following paragraphs in the order listed from the standard list of available support services (**9standard list of services.doc**).

Productivity Enhancement
Online Dupont
Hard Copy
Point of View
Certified Professional Program

7. Use the filename **9programmers.doc** and save the personalized document on your file disk.

8. Print one copy.

9. Close all the document windows.

Create a Multi-Page Document

10

Features Covered

- Create headers and footers
- Print page numbers
- Control text flow
- Create footnotes and endnotes
- Print specific pages

Objectives and Introduction

After successfully completing this chapter, you will be able to create a multi-page document, print page numbers on each page, and use the Text Flow feature to control text. You will also be able to create and edit headers, footers, footnotes, and endnotes, as well as print a specific page(s).

A multi-page document consists of two or more pages that describe an event or provide information. Examples of multi-page business documents include term papers, brochures, and legal documents.

Create a Multi-Page Document

Like a one-page document, a multi-page document can be created with vertical line spacing of one (single-spacing) or two (double-spacing). Pages of a multi-page document are formatted in the same way as a one-page document, with default margins set at 1 inch top and bottom and 1.25 inches left and right (see Chapter 9, Figures 9.1 and 9.4.)

Each page of a multi-page document is separated by either an automatic or manual page break. An automatic page break is inserted by Word when the number of available vertical lines on the page is filled. When text is edited, automatic page breaks, known as soft page breaks, are automatically adjusted so that the maximum number of lines fits on each page.

FIGURE 10.1

Hard page break
in Normal View

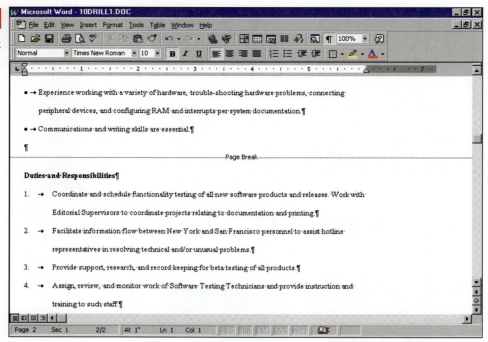

If a new page is desired before the available lines on the page are filled, a manual page break, also referred to as a hard page break, is inserted by pressing the **Ctrl** and **Enter** keys or by selecting **Insert**, **Break**, **Page Break** (Figure 10.1). Because a manual page break will always remain at the location where it was inserted, each manual page break should be checked when a document is edited and deleted if necessary. To delete a manual page break, select the page break and press the **Delete** key.

Pages of a multi-page document can be viewed on the screen to see the placement of the lines, sideheads, page numbers, headers, and footers. The current page is viewed either by using the Print Layout View then selecting **View**, **Zoom**, **Whole Page** or by selecting the **Print Preview** button. In either view, additional pages can be displayed by pressing the **Page Up** and **Page Down** keys or by selecting the **Previous Page** ▲ and **Next Page** ▼ buttons, which are located at the bottom of the vertical scroll bar (see Figure 10.3). In the Print Preview mode, 2 to 21 pages can be displayed on the screen at one time by selecting the **Multiple Pages** button and clicking on the desired number of pages.

Create Headers and Footers

Generally, a multi-page document includes headers and/or footers. A header is a title or information that prints in the top margin of the second and following pages (see Figures 10.2 and 10.4). A footer is a title or information that prints in the bottom margin of each page (see Figure 10.4). Headers and footers can consist of more than one line of text. Once created, headers and footers can be edited or deleted.

When headers are used, the header information is not normally printed on the first page of a document but prints at the top of the second and following pages. When footers are used, the title information along with the page number

FIGURE 10.2

Samples of
header styles

Right Moves Presentation
Page 2
March 25, 199x

Three-line header for multiple-page
memorandum or report

This process will not fail if made a part of the presentation format discipline. In addition, remember that no more than three recommended changes should be presented at one time.

One-line header for a multiple-page letter

Ms. Holly Pierce   Page 2   March 25, 199x

Costs included in this invoice are from final preparation by a Senior Engineer, review by a Principal, geotechnical drafting and typing, and reproduction of the Distress Investigation report. Expenses are for film purchase, developing, and printing.

(optional) prints at the bottom of every page. The default position for headers is .5" from the top of the page, and the default position for footers is .5" from the bottom of the page.

A header or footer is created by selecting **View**, **Header and Footer**. The screen will display a header area with the insertion point in the first space. If the Print Layout View is not active, the view mode will automatically switch to Print Layout View. The document text will be dimmed as a reminder that it cannot be edited until the Header and Footer area is closed. (The **Show/Hide Document Text** button can be selected on the Header and Footer Toolbar to remove the text from the screen temporarily.)

The Header and Footer Toolbar will display above the header area. To create a footer, select the **Switch Between Header and Footer** button 🔲 on the Header and Footer Toolbar. After the text for the header or footer is typed and formatted, select the **Close** button on the Header and Footer Toolbar to return to the document window.

A header or footer can be viewed by selecting **View**, **Print Layout** or by choosing the **Print Preview** button. To edit a header or footer, double-click on the header or footer text in the document window or select **View**, **Header and Footer**. If necessary, select the **Switch Between Header and Footer button** 🔲, then select the **Show Next** 🔲 or **Show Previous** 🔲 button on the Header and Footer Toolbar until the desired header or footer appears.

Three different headers or footers can be created: one for even pages, one for odd pages, and one for the first page. The footers in this textbook are examples of different even- and odd-page footers. Also, the footer on the first page of each chapter in this textbook is an example of a different first page footer, i.e., only the page number is shown with no accompanying text. Because a header is not usually printed on the first page of a document, a different first page header is used to create a blank, or empty, header for page 1.

If the format of a document is changed, the format for the header or footer can be changed to match the new document format. For example, if the fonts are changed for the entire document, the fonts for the header and/or footer can also be changed.

To make it easier to align header/footer text in the center of the page and at the right margin, the header and footer areas have default tab settings: one center tab in the center of the document and one right tab at the default right margin. If the left and/or right margins are changed for the text in the document, the position of the center and right tabs must be changed. (For information on moving a tab, see Chapter 7, page 186.)

Start-Up Instructions

❖ Open the file named **10drill1.doc** located on the data disk.

❖ Check that the Print Layout View is turned on. (If necessary, select **View, Print Layout**.)

Steps to   ## Create a Blank First Page Header

1. With the insertion point located at any position on page 1, select View, Header and Footer.

   Note: The header area appears and the Header and Footer Toolbar displays (Figure 10.3).

2. Select the **Page Setup** button 🕮 on the Header and Footer Toolbar.

   *Note: The Layout tab should be selected. (If necessary, select the **Layout** tab.)*

3. In the Headers and Footers section, choose the desired option.

FIGURE 10.3

Header and Footer Toolbar

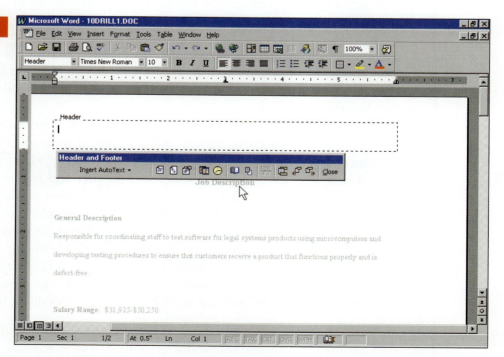

For example, select the **Different first page** option.

Note: To toggle the option on or off, click once on the box to display the check mark. (The option is selected when the check mark displays.)

4. Select **OK** to return to the Header area.

   Note: The header area is now labeled First Page Header.

5. Type the header information or leave the header blank to create a blank header on the first page.

   For example, to create a blank first page header, do not type anything.

Finish-Up Instructions

❖ Continue with the following Steps to Create a Second Page Header and Insert Page Numbers.

 ## Create a Second Page Header and Insert Page Numbers

1. Select the **Show Next** button ⬚ on the Header and Footer Toolbar.

2. Type and format the header information for the second and subsequent pages.

   For example, type **Assistant Software Testing Supervisor** and press **Tab** twice to move the insertion point to the right tab at the right margin. Type the word **Page**, then press the **Spacebar** once.

3. To insert a Page Number field, select the **Insert Page Number** button ⬚ on the Header and Footer Toolbar.

   *Note: The page number 2 appears in the Header area where the insertion point is located. This is a field and can be deleted only by selecting the number and then pressing the **Delete** key.*

4. Select the **Close** button on the Header and Footer Toolbar to return to the document window.

Finish-Up Instructions

❖ To view the header, select the down triangle next to the **Zoom** button and choose **Two Pages**. Notice the header displays on page 2 only. After viewing the document, select the down triangle next to the **Zoom** button again and select **100%**.

❖ Use the *new* filename **10header.doc** and save the file on your file disk.

❖ Print one copy.

Start-Up Instructions

❖ The file named **10header.doc** should be displayed in the document window.

Steps to Create a Footer and Insert a Date

1. With the insertion point located at any position on page 1, select **View, Header and Footer**.

   Note: The First Page Header area and the Header and Footer Toolbar display.

2. Select the **Switch Between Header and Footer** button .

   Note: A Footer area displays at the bottom of the document window. The footer area is labeled First Page Footer.

3. Type and format the text for the First Page Footer.

   For example, press the **Tab** key once to move the insertion point to the center tab, then type **Revision Date:** and press the **Spacebar** once.

4. To insert a date field into the footer, select the **Insert Date** button on the Header and Footer Toolbar.

   *Note: When using the **Insert Date** button, the date will appear in the same format as last selected when using the **Insert, Date and Time** option. This date is a field and will be updated to the current date whenever the document is printed or saved. If the date is not automatically updated, select the date field and then press **F9**.*

5. To use the same footer on the second and subsequent pages, select the footer text, then select the **Copy** button on the Standard Toolbar. Select the **Show Next** button on the Header and Footer Toolbar, then select the **Paste** button on the Standard Toolbar.

   For example, select the footer text, select **Copy, Show Next**, and select **Paste**.

   *Note: If necessary, select the **Center** alignment button on the Formatting Toolbar to center the footer information.*

6. Select the **Close** button on the Header and Footer Toolbar.

Finish-Up Instructions

❖ To view the footer, select the down triangle next to the **Zoom** button and choose **Two Pages**. After viewing, select the down triangle next to the **Zoom** button and select **100%**.

❖ Use the *new* filename **10footer.doc** and save the file on your file disk.

❖ Print one copy.

Start-Up Instructions

❖ The file named **10footer.doc** should be displayed on the screen.

Edit Headers and Footers

1. Select **View, Header and Footer**.

2. To view another header, select the **Show Next** button ⬚ repeatedly until the desired header displays.

> For example, select the **Show Next** button ⬚ to display the header for the second and subsequent pages. (The header area will be labeled Header.)

3. Make the desired changes to the header text using customary editing methods.

> For example, select the word **Page** and the **page number field**, then type **Job Description**.

> *Note: The text Job Description should be aligned flush right (see Figure 10.4).*

4. To edit a footer, select the **Switch Between Header and Footer** button ⬚ on the Header and Footer Toolbar, then select the **Show Next** button ⬚ repeatedly until the desired footer displays.

> For example, select the **Switch Between Header and Footer** button ⬚ to display the second page footer. (The footer area will be labeled Footer.)

5. Make the desired changes to the footer text using customary editing methods.

> For example, press **End** to go to the end of the current line. Press **Enter** once to start a new line. Type the word **Page** and press the **Spacebar** once. Select the **Insert Page Number** button ⬚ to insert the page number field. (If necessary, select the **Center** button.)

6. If desired, make revisions to the next or previous footer.

> For example, select the **Show Previous** button ⬚ on the Header and Footer Toolbar to display the First Page Footer area, then follow the directions in step 5 to insert the word **Page** and the page number field.

7. Select the **Close** button on the Header and Footer Toolbar

Shortcut to Select a Header or Footer:

1. In the Print Layout View, scroll through the document until the desired header or footer is displayed.

2. Move the mouse pointer into the header or footer area and double-click.

> *Note: The Header and Footer Toolbar will display, and the header or footer can be edited or deleted.*

3. When changes have been made, select the **Close** button on the Header and Footer Toolbar.

Finish-Up Instructions

❖ Select the down triangle next to the **Zoom** button and choose **Two Pages** to view the changed header and footer. Page 2 of your document should look similar to Figure 10.4. Select the down triangle next to the **Zoom** button again and select **100%**.

FIGURE 10.4

Partial document
with header and
footer

Assistant Software Testing Supervisor   Job Description

Duties and Responsibilities

1.   Coordinate and schedule functionality testing of all new software products
     and releases.

2.   Facilitate information flow between New York and San Francisco personnel
     to assist hotline representatives in resolving technical and/or unusual
     problems.

3.   Provide support, research, and record keeping for beta testing of all products.

4.   Assign, review, and monitor work of Software Testing Technicians and
     provide instruction and training to such staff.

5.   Oversee Market Support and Study Technicians to ensure requests for
     information received via the technical hotline or beta sites are responded to
     in an accurate and timely manner.

6.   Communicate results of testing to supervisor and director and recommend
     further testing if necessary.

7.   Organize and coordinate problem-solving reporting process. Verify reported
     problems and track resolution.

8.   Organize data files and test cases to be used for updating future releases.
     Assist in preparation of test script files to electronically test software.

9.   Maintain in-house master and vault copies of all software.

10. Assist Technical Systems Analyst, legal staff, and systems programmers in
     program development.

Duties and responsibilities may be added, deleted, or changed at any time at the
discretion of management, formally or informally, either verbally or in writing.

Revision: (current date)
Page 2

❖   Use the *new* filename **10edit footer.doc** and save the file on your file disk.

❖   Print one copy and close the document.

Delete Headers and Footers

Note: These steps are for your information.

1. Select **View, Header and Footer**.
2. Use the **Switch Between Header and Footer** 🔲 and the **Show Next** 🔲 buttons until the desired header or footer displays.
3. Select all text in the header or footer area, then press the **Delete** key.
4. Select **Close** on the Header and Footer Toolbar.

Print Page Numbers

Each page of a multi-page document should be numbered. Word provides a quick way to create a header or footer containing only the page number. If the pages are numbered at the bottom, the number 1 is printed at the bottom of the first page. If pages are numbered at the top, the first page of the document may or may not be numbered.

Page numbers can be set to print at the top or bottom of the page and at the left margin, centered, or at the right margin. The default position for page numbers is .5" from the top of the page or .5" from the bottom of the page. The **Position** option in the **Page Numbers** dialog box is used to specify whether the page numbers will be placed at the top or bottom of the pages, while the Alignment option determines whether the page numbers will be aligned at the left or right margin, centered, or aligned at the inside or outside margins of facing pages. The **Format** button in the Page Numbers dialog box can then be selected to display the Page Number Format dialog box. Page numbers can be set to print as lowercase letters (a, b, c, etc.) or uppercase letters (A, B, C, etc.), lowercase Roman numerals (i, ii, iii, etc.), uppercase Roman numerals (I, II, III, etc.), or Arabic numbers (1, 2, 3, etc.).

A different beginning page number can be set by selecting the **Start at** option in the Page Number Format dialog box. For example, to begin numbering pages with page 4, type 4 in the Start at box in the **Page Numbering** section (see Figure 10.6).

Once the page number has been inserted, it can be edited or deleted. See the Steps to Edit Headers and Footers beginning on page 274.

Start-Up Instructions

❖   Open the file named **10drill1.doc** located on the data disk.

Steps to ▶ **Number Pages**

1. With the insertion point located at any position on page 1, select Insert, Page Numbers.

   Note: The Page Numbers dialog box displays.

2. Click in the **Position** box and choose the desired page number position option.

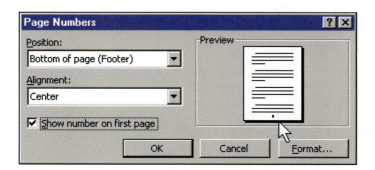

FIGURE 10.5

Page Numbers dialog box

FIGURE 10.6

Page Number
Format dialog
box

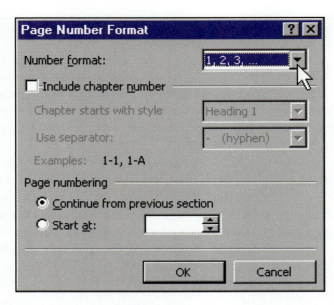

For example, check that the **Bottom of page (Footer)** option displays. If necessary, click in the Position box and choose the **Bottom of page (Footer)** option.

3. Click in the **Alignment** box and select the desired page number alignment option.

   For example, click in the **Alignment** box and select **Center**.

   Note: A sample of the page number location displays in the Preview box (see Figure 10.5).

4. If the page number is to be in a footer, a check mark should display in the Show number on first page box.

   For example, check that **Show number on first page** is selected. If necessary, select the **Show number on first page** option.

   Note: A check mark must display in the Show number on first page option box for the number to print on the first page.

5. Select **OK**.

   *Note: Select **Print Preview** to display the page number. If necessary, select the **Next Page** button (located at the bottom of the vertical scroll bar) to observe the page number on the second page. Select **Close** to return to the document window.*

Finish-Up Instructions

❖ Use the *new* filename **10page number.doc** and save the file on your file disk.

   Note: One line of a paragraph may display by itself on the bottom of page 1 and on the top of page 2. This will be changed in Steps to Control Text Flow.

❖ Continue with the Steps to Change the Page Numbering Format.

Start-Up Instructions

❖ The file named **10page number.doc** should be displayed in the document window.

Steps to **Change the Page Numbering Format**

1. With the insertion point located at any position on page 1, select **Insert, Page Numbers**.

2. Select **Format**.

   Note: The Page Number Format dialog box displays (see Figure 10.6).

3. Click in the Number format box, select the desired number type.

   For example, select **I, II, III, . . .**

4. Select **OK** to return to the Page Numbers dialog box.

5. Select **OK** to return to the document window.

Finish-Up Instructions

❖ Select the **Print Preview** button to display the Roman numeral page number(s). Click on the page number to enlarge the preview. Select **Close**.

❖ Use the *new* filename **10change numbering format.doc** and save the file on your file disk.

   Note: One line of a paragraph may display by itself on the bottom of page 1 and on the top of page 2. This will be changed in Steps to Control Text Flow.

❖ Continue with the Steps to Control Text Flow.

Control Text Flow

To enhance a document's appearance and provide easy reading of the information, standard typography rules are used to control the minimum number of paragraph lines displayed on a page and the lines of text that should be kept on the same page. Word's **Line and Page Breaks** options are used to designate where text is allowed to flow between pages so that text automatically breaks at the desired line even when text is added or deleted. (See Figure 10.7.)

There are four standard rules used to determine the flow of text. Word provides options that can be used to follow these rules and to control text flow.

Rule 1: There should be a minimum of two lines of a paragraph at the bottom and/or top of a page. In other words, the first two lines or last two lines of a paragraph will not be separated from one page to another. Separated lines are traditionally called *orphans* (one line displayed at the bottom of the previous page) and *widows* (one line displayed at the top of the next page). Word's default is to have the Widow/Orphan control option turned on. To check whether the Widow/Orphan control option is on, select the entire document, then select **Format, Paragraph**, and choose the **Line and Page Breaks** tab. The **Widow/Orphan control** option should be selected. Choose **OK**.

Rule 2: Headings and sideheads should not be separated from the first line of the next paragraph. In other words, the heading or sidehead should not be on one page and the first line of the following paragraph displayed on the next page. To control the heading or sidehead and first paragraph line, place the insertion point in the heading or sidehead, then select **Format**, **Paragraph**, choose the **Line and Page Breaks** tab, select **Keep with next**, select **OK**.

Rule 3: Whenever possible, a short paragraph should not be divided. To prevent the lines of a short paragraph from being divided, place the insertion point in the paragraph, then select **Format**, **Paragraph**, choose the **Line and Page Breaks** tab, select **Keep lines together**, select **OK**.

Rule 4: Chapter titles and sometimes section titles should start at the top of a page. Place the insertion point in the title or other element that is to begin a new page and select **Format**, **Paragraph**, choose the **Line and Page Breaks** tab, select **Page break before**, select **OK**.

Start-Up Instructions

❖ The file named **10change numbering format.doc** should be displayed in the document window.

❖ The nonprinting symbols should be turned on. (If necessary, select the **Show/Hide** button.)

Control Text Flow

1. Place the insertion point in the heading or sidehead that may be followed by a page break.

   For example, place the insertion point in the sidehead **Duties and Responsibilities.**

FIGURE 10.7

Paragraph dialog box with the Line and Page Breaks tab selected

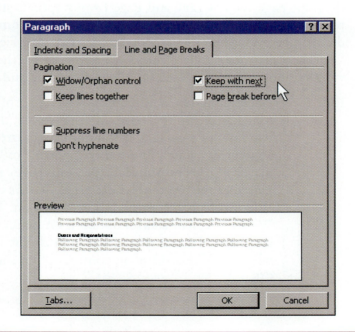

2. Select **Format, Paragraph**.

3. If the Line and Page Breaks tab is not displayed, click on the **Line and Page Breaks** tab.

4. In the Pagination section, select the desired option.

   For example, select the **Keep with next** option to keep the sidehead with the following paragraph.

   Note: A black check mark displays in the box next to the words Keep with next. (See Figure 10.7.)

5. Select **OK**.

   Note: If nonprinting symbols are turned on, a small dark square displays to the left of the sidehead (i.e., Duties and Responsibilities) to indicate that special paragraph formatting (e.g., Keep with next) has been applied to the text.

Finish-Up Instructions

❖ Check that the Widow/Orphan control is turned on (press **Ctrl** and **a** to select the entire document; select **Format**, **Paragraph**, choose the **Line and Page Breaks** tab; if necessary, select the **Widow/Orphan control** option; select **OK**).

   Note: Check that the check mark is black.

❖ With all text selected, change the font size to **12 point**.

❖ Use the *new* filename **10keep with next.doc** and save the file on your file disk.

❖ Print one copy and close the document.

   Note: The side heading Duties and Responsibilities has been kept on the same page with the text that follows the heading.

Create Footnotes and Endnotes

A multi-page document can include footnotes or endnotes. The footnote or endnote reference provides information such as the name, date, and page number of the source from which the information being discussed was obtained. Footnotes and endnotes are also referred to as reference notes or sources.

Once a footnote or endnote is created, Word automatically places the footnote or endnote reference number in the document text. The reference number is superscripted (i.e., raised slightly above the text line).

The footnote and endnote reference information can be displayed in the document window by selecting **Print Preview** or **View, Print Layout**.

Footnote reference information is printed at the bottom of the page on which the text reference number is located. A 2-inch separator line is placed above the footnote reference information. The first line of the footnote reference information is indented, the footnote reference number is superscripted, and the information is printed with vertical line spacing of one. A blank space is placed between footnotes (see Figure 10.8).

Endnotes are automatically placed at the end of the document. A hard page break (**Ctrl** and **Enter**) is inserted after the last line of text in the document so that endnotes will print on a separate page. A title, such as Notes, is usually placed at the top of the endnote page. Depending on the requested design/style, the first line of the endnote reference information may either begin at the left margin or be indented, and the information may be printed with vertical line spacing of one or two. A blank line is usually placed between endnotes. Word's default is to place a separator line before the endnotes, but this can be deleted when the endnotes are placed on a separate page.

To change the number format and view other options for footnotes or endnotes, choose the **Options** button in the **Footnote and Endnote** dialog box. In the Note Options dialog box, numbers, uppercase or lowercase Roman numerals, letters, or a symbol set can be designated in the Number format box (see Figure 10.9). The **Place at** options are used to specify whether footnotes should be printed at the bottom of the page or beneath the text (if the text stops before the end of the page) and whether endnotes should be printed at the end of the document or at the end of each section. A different starting number can be entered in the **Start at** box. For footnotes, the Numbering options include *Continuous* (throughout the document), *Restart each section*, and *Restart each page*. Endnote Numbering options include *Continuous* and *Restart each section*.

Start-Up Instructions

❖ Open the file named **10drill3.doc** located on the data disk.

❖ If necessary, select the Print Layout View (select **View**, **Print Layout**).

Steps to Create Footnotes

1. Place the insertion point to the right of the text being referenced.

   For example, place the insertion point after the period in the last sentence of the first paragraph, which ends with the word "annually."

2. Select **Insert, Footnote**.

   Note: The Footnote and Endnote dialog box displays. A solid dot in the circle next to the word Footnote indicates that the Footnote option is selected. (The setting from the last use displays.)

3. Select the desired Insert option.

   For example, check that **Footnote** is selected. (If necessary, select **Footnote**.)

4. Select the desired Numbering option.

   For example, check that **AutoNumber** is selected. (If necessary, select the **AutoNumber** option.)

5. Select **OK**.

   Note: In the Print Layout View, a divider line and footnote number display at the bottom of the current page.

FIGURE 10.8

Partial document
with footnote

four-year scholarships have been established for children of firefighters who
have died in the line of duty. Other Lieberman Enterprises programs have
been set up for graduates of West City Community College, city employees,
and Norfolk high school teachers. In response to the need for more
qualified science teachers, for example, Lieberman Enterprises offers training
in computer science to high school teachers. A Science Seminar Program
provides science teachers with updated teaching materials and methods.[2]

---

[1] J. Russell Mason, The President's Report to the Board of Directors,
Spring 1995, p. 2.

[2] Ibid., p. 3.

6. To indent the footnote, press the **Home** key to move the insertion point to
the left of the superscripted character in the footnote and press the **Tab** key
once.

> For example, press the **Home** key to place the insertion point
> to the left of the number 1; press the **Tab** key.

7. Type the footnote information.

> For example, press the **End** key to move the insertion point
> to the right of the superscripted reference number. Type
> **J. Russell Mason, The President's Report to the Board of
> Directors, Spring 1995, p. 2.** Press the **Enter** key once.

8. To return to the location of the footnote reference number in the document,
press **Shift** and **F5** repeatedly until the insertion point displays beside the
footnote reference number.

> For example, press **Shift** and **F5** twice (or more, if necessary)
> until the insertion point displays beside the footnote reference
> number located after the word annually.

Finish-Up Instructions

❖ Place the insertion point after the last period in the third paragraph, which
ends with the word "methods."

❖ Repeat steps 2–7 to create the following footnote:

> **Ibid., p. 3.** (Do not press **Enter**.)

❖ Scroll down and place the insertion point after the last period in the final
paragraph, which ends with the word "centers."

❖ Repeat steps 2–7 to create the following footnote:

> **Lois Hodges, "Contribution to Community Education,"** *The Times
> Crier*, **3 May 1996, p. 10.**

❖ To keep the sidehead Education Programs with the following paragraph, scroll up and locate the insertion point in the sidehead; select **Format, Paragraph**; choose the **Line and Page Breaks** tab; select **Keep with next**; select **OK**.

❖ Use the *new* filename **10footnote3.doc** and save the file on your file disk.

❖ Print one copy.

Start-Up Instructions

❖ The file named **10footnote3.doc** should be displayed in the document window.

❖ The Print Layout View should be selected. (If necessary, select the **Print Layout** button.)

Edit a Footnote or Endnote

Note: The same method is used to edit footnotes and endnotes. For information on creating endnotes, see the Steps to Create Endnotes on page 275.

1. In Print Layout View, scroll to the location of the footnote(s).
   For example, scroll to the bottom of page 2 where footnote 3 is displayed.

2. Make corrections using customary editing methods.
   For example, in footnote 3 change p. 10 to **p. 24**.

Finish-Up Instructions

❖ Save the file again using the same filename, **10footnote3.doc**.

Start-Up Instructions

❖ The file named **10footnote3.do**c should be displayed in the document window.

❖ The Print Layout View should be chosen when using the Steps to Delete a Footnote or Endnote.

Delete a Footnote or Endnote

Note: The same method is used to delete footnotes and endnotes. For information on creating endnotes, see the Steps to Create Endnotes on page 275.

1. Select the footnote or endnote reference number in the document.
   For example, select the footnote reference number 2 that displays after the third paragraph.

2. Press the **Delete** key once. The footnote/endnote number and the footnote/endnote information are both deleted.

*Note: If other footnotes or endnotes follow the deleted footnote or endnote, the remaining footnotes/endnotes are automatically renumbered. Select the **Next Page** button on the vertical scroll bar to display the last footnote, which is now footnote 2.*

Finish-Up Instructions

❖ Use the *new* filename **10footnote final.doc** and save the file.

❖ Print one copy and close the document.

Start-Up Instructions

❖ Open the file named **10drill3.doc** located on the data disk.

❖ Place a hard page break at the end of the document (**Ctrl** and **End**, **Ctrl** and **Enter**).

❖ The Print Layout View should be selected. (If necessary, select the **Print Layout** button.)

Steps to ➤ ## Create Endnotes

1. Place the insertion point to the right of the text being referenced.

   For example, scroll up and place the insertion point to the right of the period in the last sentence in the first paragraph, which ends with the word "annually."

2. Select **Insert, Footnote**.

   Note: The Footnote and Endnote dialog box displays.

3. Select the **Endnote** option.

4. If necessary, select the **AutoNumber** option.

5. Select the **Options** button.

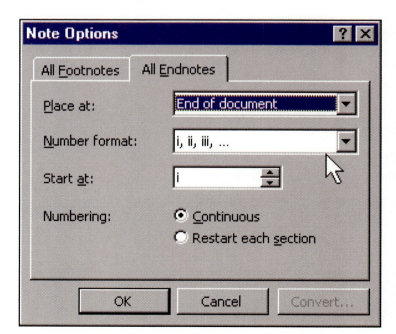

FIGURE 10.9

Note Options dialog box

*Note: The Note Options dialog box displays (see Figure 10.9). The **All Endnotes** tab should be selected.*

6. Click once in the Number format box.

7. Select the desired number format.

> For example, select the **1, 2, 3, . . .** format.

Note: Word's default Number format for endnotes is lowercase Roman numerals; however, it is more common to use Arabic numerals.

8. Select **OK** twice.

Note: In the Print Layout View, a divider line and endnote number display at the end of the document. The insertion point is located to the right of the endnote number.

9. To indent the endnote, press the **Home** key to place the insertion point to the left of the superscripted character in the endnote and press the **Tab** key once.

> For example, press the **Home** key to place the insertion point to the left of the number 1 and press the **Tab** key once.

10. Type the endnote information.

> For example, press the **End** key to place the insertion point to the right of the superscripted number, and type **J. Russell Mason, The President's Report to the Board of Directors, Spring 1995, p. 2.** Press **Enter** once.

11. To return to the endnote reference number in the document, press **Shift** and **F5** repeatedly until the insertion point displays beside the footnote reference number.

> For example, press **Shift** and **F5** twice (or more, if necessary) until the insertion point displays beside the endnote reference number located to the right of the word "annually".

Note: The insertion point returns to the referenced text, and the number 1 displays at the end of the paragraph. A separate page for the endnotes will be created later.

Finish-Up Instructions

❖ Place the insertion point after the last period in the third paragraph, which ends with the word "methods."

❖ Repeat steps 2–11 to create the following endnote:

> **Ibid., p. 3.** (Press **Enter** once.)

❖ Place the insertion point after the last period in the final paragraph, which ends with the word "centers."

❖ Repeat steps 2–11 to create the following endnote:

> **Lois Hodges, "Contribution to Community Education,"** *The Times Crier,* **3 May 1996, p. 24.**

❖ Use the *new* filename **10endnotes.doc** and save the file on your file disk.

❖ Continue with the Steps to Remove the Default Separator Line.

 Remove the Default Separator Line

1. Select View, Normal.

2. Select View, Footnotes.

   Note: A note pane displays at the bottom of the document window.

3. Click on the words All Endnotes in the left corner of the note pane. Select the item to be changed.

   For example, select Endnote Separator.

   Note: The separator line will appear in the note pane; the endnote text is no longer displayed.

4. Select the separator line and press Delete to remove it.

5. Select the Close button in the note pane.

Finish-Up Instructions

❖ To view all endnotes, select the **Print Layout View** button. If necessary, scroll down the page to view the endnotes.

❖ With the insertion point in the blank line above the first endnote, type **Notes** and press **Enter** once. Center and bold the word "Notes."

   *Note: A page break should be placed above the first endnote. (If necessary, place the insertion point at the end of the document text and press **Ctrl** and **End**.)*

❖ Use the same filename, **10endnotes.doc**, and save the file again.

Print Specific Pages

After printing a multi-page document, one or more of the pages may need to be edited and reprinted. To specify the exact pages to print, the **Pages** option is selected in the Print dialog box, and the desired pages are entered as follows:

➤ Place a comma between nonconsecutive pages, e.g., 1,3 or 2,4,6.

➤ Place a hyphen between the beginning and ending page numbers to print a consecutive range of pages, e.g., 5-9.

➤ A combination of these methods can be used, e.g., 4,5, 8-11 or 2-4, 6. Page numbers must be typed in numerical order. If, for example, you specified pages 8, 2-5, only page 8 will print. If your document contains more than one section, the page number and section number are entered. For example to print from page 5 in section 2 through page 8 in section 3, enter p5s2-p8s3.

Also, a single page can be printed by typing the page number in the **Pages** box or by placing the insertion point anywhere on the page, selecting **File**, **Print**, choosing the **Current page** option, and selecting **OK**. When the **Current page** option is selected, only the page where the insertion point is located will print.

FIGURE 10.10

Print dialog box specifying pages to be printed

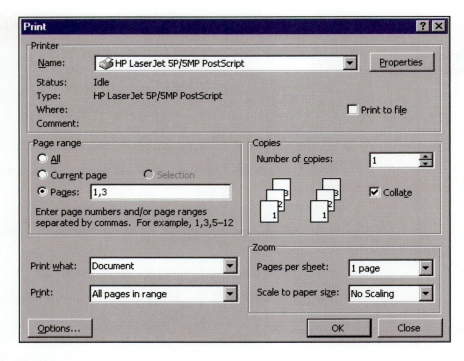

Start-Up Instructions

❖ The document containing the pages to print should be displayed in the document window. For example, the file named **10endnotes.doc** should be displayed in the document window.

Print Specific Pages

1. Select **File, Print**.

2. Select the **Pages** option in the Page range area of the Print dialog box (see Figure 10.10).

3. In the Pages box, type the page numbers to be printed.

   For example, type **1,3** to print pages 1 and 3 only.

4. Select **OK**.

Finish-Up Instructions

❖ Close but do not save the document.

The Next Step

Chapter Review and Activities

Self-Check Quiz

T F 1. A multi-page report is printed with vertical line spacing of one or two.

T F 2. A footer can be typed once but printed on all pages of a multi-page document.

T F 3. A header is normally printed on all pages of a document.

T F 4. Footnotes are consecutively numbered and printed on the page where the information is referenced.

5. Press _____ and **Enter** to place a hard page break in a document.
   a. **Ctrl**
   b. **Alt**
   c. **Shift**
   d. **Home**

6. When page numbers are inserted, the options available in the Page Number Format dialog box are _____.
   a. lowercase or uppercase letters
   b. lowercase or uppercase Roman numerals
   c. numbers (1, 2, 3, etc.)
   d. all of these

7. The _____ option on the Line and Page Breaks tab can be used to prevent a heading and the following paragraph from being printed on two separate pages.
   a. **Widow/Orphan control**
   b. **Keep lines together**
   c. **Keep with next**
   d. none of the above

8. What option must be selected on the Layout tab after selecting the **Page Setup** button to create a blank header on the first page and a regular header on the second and subsequent pages?
   a. **Different odd and even**
   b. **Different first page**
   c. **Blank first page**
   d. **Show number on first page**

9. State the difference between a footnote and a footer.

10. Explain how to remove the endnote separator line.

Enriching Language Arts Skills

Spelling/Vocabulary Words

contagious—transmitted by contact; spread from one to another.
knowledge—the state of knowing; understanding gained through study or experience.
magic—the art that claims to control or forecast natural events or forces.
talisman—an object believed to have magical or protective powers; charm.
technological—affected by or resulting from scientific and industrial progress.
velvet—a smooth, dense pile fabric usually made from silk or rayon.

Quotation Marks with Punctuation

Always place a comma or period inside a closing quotation mark.

Example:

"I wonder," said Joan to herself, "how I got myself into this situation."

Place a question mark or exclamation point inside closing quotation marks if the question or exclamation pertains only to the quoted information. Place a question mark or exclamation point outside the closing quotation marks if the question or exclamation pertains to the entire sentence.

Examples:

Jan said, "Help me!" (The exclamation pertains only to the quoted information.)

Was the returned check marked "Insufficient Funds"? (The question pertains to the entire sentence.)

Semicolons and colons are placed outside closing quotation marks.

Example:

The following items were in a package marked "Fragile": an antique bowl, four glasses, and a pitcher.

Activities

Activity 10.1—Create a Multi-Page Document with Page Numbers and Text Flow Control

1. Type the following report with the spacing and bolding as shown.

Diamond Family of Funds

The Funds are two of the funds in the Diamond Family of Funds. The Company was organized as an Illinois corporation on January 10, 1994, and currently offers shares of three other series: the Illinois Tax-Free Bond Fund, the Ginnie Mae Fund, and the Variable Rate Government Fund. The Board of Directors of the Company supervises the Funds' activities and monitors their contractual arrangements with various service providers.

Lomond Bank Contract

Lomond Bank is the Funds' investment adviser, transfer and dividend disbursing agent, and custodian. In addition, Lomond Bank is a shareholder servicing agent of the Funds and a selling agent under a selling agreement with the Funds' distributor. Lomond Bank, one of the fifteen largest banks in the United States, was founded in 1865 and is the third oldest bank in the western United States.

As of December 31, 1993, various divisions and affiliates of Lomond Bank provided investment advisory services for approximately $195 billion of assets of individuals, trusts, estates, and institutions. Lomond Bank also serves as the investment adviser to the other separately managed series of the Company and to eight other registered, open-end management investment companies, which consist of several separately managed investment portfolios. Lomond Bank is located at 455 Sansome Street, San Francisco, California 94163.

Gregor Contract

Gregor is the Funds' sponsor and administrator and distributes the Funds' shares. Gregor is a full-service broker/dealer and investment advisory firm located at 1422 Locust Street, St. Louis, Missouri 63101. Gregor and its predecessor have been securities and investment services for more than 55 years. Additionally, they have been providing discretionary portfolio management services since 1982. Gregor currently manages investment portfolios for pension and profit-sharing plans, individual investors, foundations, insurance companies, and university endowments.

Shareholder Meetings

Although the Company is not required to hold annual shareholder meetings, special meetings may be required for purposes such as electing or removing Directors, approving advisory contracts and distribution plans, and changing the Funds' investment objectives or fundamental investment policies.

Voting Rights

All shares of the Company have equal voting rights and will be voted in the aggregate, rather than by series, unless otherwise required by law (such as when the voting matter affects only one series). As a shareholder of the Funds, you are entitled to one vote for each share you own and fractional votes for fractional shares owned.

---

2. Use the filename **10Diamond family.doc** and save the file on your file disk.

3. Select the body text including the sideheads and set a vertical line spacing of two (**Ctrl** and **2**).

---

4. Bold the first sidehead, **Lomond Bank Contract**.

5. With the insertion point in the first sidehead, turn on the Keep with next option (select **Format**, **Paragraph**, **Line and Page Breaks** tab, **Keep with next**, **OK**).

6. Use the Format Painter feature to copy the first sidehead format to the remaining sideheads (select the first sidehead, double-click on the **Format Painter** button; select each of the remaining sideheads; select the **Format Painter** button again to turn off the Format Painter feature).

7. Check that Widow/Orphan control is turned on (select the entire document; select **Format**, **Paragraph**, **Line and Page Breaks** tab; if necessary, click on the **Widow/Orphan control** box to place a check mark in the box; select **OK**).

8. Use page numbering to print numbers at the bottom center of each page (select **Insert**, **Page Numbers**; select the **Position** box; select **Bottom of Page (Footer)**, choose the **Alignment** box; select **Center**, **OK**).

9. In Print Layout View, scroll down to display the page numbers.

10. Use the *new* filename **10Diamond funds.doc** and save the file on your file disk.

11. Print one copy and close the document.

Activity 10.2—Create a Header for a Two-Page Memorandum

1. Open the memorandum with the filename **10act2.doc** located on the data disk.

2. Create a blank first page header (select **View**, **Header and Footer**; select the **Page Setup** button; select **Different first page** on the Layout tab, **OK**).

   Note: If necessary, move the Header and Footer Toolbar (point to the Header and Footer Title bar, click and hold the mouse button while dragging the Toolbar down away from the Header area).

3. Create a three-line header for the second and subsequent pages (select the **Show Next** button); then type the following information at the left margin:

   Rapid River Relocation (Press **Enter**.)
   Date: (Select the **Insert Date** button and press **Enter**.)
   Page (select the **Insert Page Numbers** button and press **Enter** once.)

4. Select the **Close** button on the Header and Footer Toolbar.

5. In Print Layout View, scroll down to display the second page header.

6. Place reference initials at the end of the memo (press **Ctrl** and **End**, type **JM** followed by a forward slash (/) and your initials in lowercase letters).

7. Use the *new* filename **10rapid river.doc** and save the file on your file disk. Print one copy.

8. Optional: Fax this memorandum to your instructor via a local fax, or write an e-mail message to your instructor that you are sending this assignment. Attach this file to your e-mail message.

9. Close the document.

Activity 10.3—Create a Header and Footer for a Multi-Page Document

1. Open the report with the filename **10act3.doc** located on the data disk.

2. Select the body text and set the vertical line spacing to two (**Ctrl** and **2**).

3. Create a blank first page header (select **View**, **Header and Footer**; select the **Page Setup** button; select **Different first page** on the Layout tab, **OK**).

4. Create the header for the second and subsequent pages by selecting the **Show Next** button and type the following information with the format shown:

   Book Review (Press **Tab** twice.)   **The Overview Effect**

5. With the Header and Footer Toolbar still displayed in the document window, create a footer to place page numbers at the bottom center of each page (select the **Switch Between Header and Footer** button, press the **Tab** key once; select the **Insert Page Number** button, highlight the tab symbol and page number; choose the **Copy** button on the Toolbar; select the **Show Previous** button, choose the **Paste** button; **Close**).

   Note: If necessary, move the Header and Footer Toolbar (point to the Header and Footer Title bar, click and hold the mouse button while dragging the Toolbar down away from the Header area).

6. In the Print Layout View, scroll down to display the page number and header.

7. Use the *new* filename **10book review.doc** and save the file on your file disk.

8. Print one copy and close the document.

Activity 10.4—Create a Footer and Footnote for a Multi-Page Document

1. Open the report with the filename **10act4.doc** located on the data disk.

2. Set the **Keep with next** option for the sideheads (with the insertion point located in the first sidehead, **Graphic Design Factors**, select **Format**, **Paragraph**, **Line and Page Breaks** tab, **Keep with next**, **OK**; select the sidehead, click once on the **Format Painter** button, scroll down and select the sidehead **Summary**).

3. Create a footer (select **View**, **Header and Footer**; select the **Switch Between Header and Footer** button) then type the following information:

   Desktop Publishing and Graphic Design (Press **Tab** twice.)   **Page** (Select the **Insert Page Number** button.)

4. Select the **Close** button on the Header and Footer Toolbar.

5. Create a footnote using the following information:

   a. Place the insertion point after the last character in the document and select **Insert**, **Footnote**. If necessary, select the **Footnote** option and the **AutoNumber** option; then select **OK**.

  b. Press **Home** to place the insertion point in front of the footnote number 1 and press the **Tab** key once. Press the **End** key to move the insertion point to the right of the footnote number.

  c. Type the following footnote:

   LaVaughn Hart and Katie Layman, "Desktop Publishing and Graphic Design," *The California Business Teacher*, Spring 1990, pp. 22–23.

  d. Press **Shift** and **F5** repeatedly until the insertion point displays beside the footnote reference number in the document window.

   Note: If you used Normal View, select **Close** *on the note pane.*

6. To view the multi-page document with footers and a footnote, select the **Print Preview** button, choose the **Multiple Pages** button, and select the third button on the first row to view three pages.

7. Select **Close** to exit Print Preview.

8. Use the *new* filename **10desktop publishing.doc** and save the file. Print one copy.

9. Optional: Fax this memorandum to your instructor via a local fax, or write an e-mail message to your instructor that you are sending this assignment. Attach this file to your e-mail message.

10. Close the document.

Challenge Your Skills

Skill 10.1—Create a Header and Footnotes; Format a Multi-Page Document; Download a Table from the Internet

1. Open the multi-page document named **10skill1.doc** located on the data disk.

2. Download the file named **10Table.doc** from the Internet using the following instructions:

  a. Your file disk must be in the disk drive. Activate your Internet program.

  b. After http:www., type prenhall.com/cgi-bin/ftpset.cgi?ect/business_education.q-002/layman.

  c. Select the file named **10Table.doc**.

   Note: If using Netscape, 10table.doc automatically opens in Word. Use **File, Save As** *and save the file on your disk. Close the file and skip to step e.*

  d. If necessary, select the location for your disk and check that the filename**10table.doc** displays; select **OK**.

  e. When the file is downloaded, exit your Internet program.

3. After the file is downloaded, insert the table, **10Table.doc**, above the sidehead Duties of Stock Exchange Staff.

Hint: Place the insertion point at the desired location in the document; select Insert, File and choose the file named 10Table.doc.

4. Make decisions regarding:

> Margins and line spacing
> Alignment and fonts
> Table format
> Text flow (line and page breaks)
> Header format and placement
> Spacing before and after, capitalization, and bold for title and sideheads

5. Create the following footnotes in the document.

 a. Place the first footnote reference at the end of the first body text paragraph. Footnote text: **The Southwest Stock Exchange Bulletin, p. 6.**

 b. Place the second footnote reference at the end of the third body text paragraph. Footnote text: **EITAK Commodities Annual Report, p. 2.**

 c. Place the third footnote reference at the end of item number 2, . . . eliminating the order match problem. Footnote text: **Ibid.**

6. Create an appropriate header including the page number.

7. Use the *new* filename **10stock exchange.doc** and save the file.

8. Print one copy. Close the document.

Skill 10.2—Create a Footnote and Page Numbering for a Multi-Page Document; Language Arts

1. Open the multi-page document with the filename **10skill2.doc** located on the data disk.

2. Make decisions regarding:

> Margins
> Fonts and font sizes
> Alignment
> Headers and footers
>
> Line spacing
> Formatting of title and subtitle
> Hyphenation
> Text flow

3. Correct three spelling errors, three punctuation errors, and two misused words.

4. Create the following footnote in the document.

 a. Place a footnote reference after the exclamation point in the last sentence of the document. Footnote text: **Bill Pearce, "Everyday Magic,"** *Modern Living Journal*, **August 1992, p. 10.**

5. Number the document pages at the bottom right corner.

6. Use the *new* filename **10everyday magic.doc** and save the file.

7. Print one copy.

8. Optional: Fax this letter to your instructor via a local fax, or write an e-mail message to your instructor that you are sending this assignment. Attach this file to your e-mail message.

9. Close the document.

→ Skill 10.3—Integrate Microsoft Office and Use the Memo Wizard to Create a Two-Page Memorandum

1. Select the **Start a New Document** button on the Microsoft Office Shortcut Bar, or select **File**, **New**.

2. In the New dialog box, select the **Memos** tab. Double-click on **Memo Wizard**.

3. Use the following information to complete the memo wizard:

   a. Use the **Professional** style

   b. Use the title **Interoffice Memo**.

   c. Use the current date. The memo is from Anita Sheldon, Regional Vice President, and the subject is Health-Wise Foods.

   d. The memo is being sent to Jake P. Scagliotti, Business Development Manager. Copies of the memo should be sent to K. R. Harper, Constance Wong, Clark Zavala, and Regional Staff. A separate page for a distribution list is not needed.

   e. Make a decision regarding the closing items needed, i.e., writer's and typist's initials, enclosures, and attachments.

   f. Choose the date, topic, and page number for the header information. The topic is the same as the memo subject. See step 3c.

4. The memorandum body text follows:

As you know, we have recently acquired Health-Wise Foods, a leading maker of healthy cookies, crackers, and snacks. Before purchasing Health-Wise Foods, our research identified 8-Midnight outlets as potential customers for healthy snack products. We solicit your support in directing your sales organization to aggressively pursue all 8-Midnight outlets to sell the advantages of Health-Wise products.

The following concerns have been expressed by several 8-Midnight franchises:

1. maintaining balanced inventories
2. improving turnover
3. introducing new items
4. meeting customer demands

We are currently preparing a response to each of these concerns and will be communicating our responses via our Direct Sales Representative. If you have any suggestions regarding our response to these concerns, please e-mail your comments to me. We anticipate finalizing our reply by the first of next week.

Our Direct Store Delivery organization has the ability and the opportunity to simplify their cookie and cracker needs. We must sell each and every franchise operator on our ability to take care of their needs as the dominant category leader. We possess the products and the market share to maximize their sales and profits. It is up to us to SELL this story and to develop those local in-store partnerships that move their/our business forward and upward.

Both the Marketing Support Division and the Direct Account Promotions Division have developed additional incentive plans to be offered to franchise operators. These promotions are based on the overall sales potential of the franchise and the types of promotions that have been successful in the past.

Each Direct Sales Representative should create a list of any franchises that seem hesitant. This list should be discussed with the Marketing Support or Direct Account Promotions team leaders for the sector to develop an individual plan for the franchise.

Keep us posted on your successes!

5. Use the filename **10Scagliotti.doc** and save the file on your file disk.

6. Print one copy.

7. Optional: Fax this memo to your instructor via a local fax, or write an e-mail message to your instructor that you are sending this assignment. Attach this file to your e-mail message.

8. Close the document.

Create a Form Letter and Mailing List

Features Covered

- Create a data source file
- Create a main document
- Merge a main document with a data source file
- Edit a data source file and a main document
- Output merged letters directly to a printer
- Select data records to be merged

Objectives and Introduction

After successfully completing this chapter, you will be able to create a data source file and merge it with a main document. You will understand fields and records and learn how to use the Mail Merge Helper. In addition, you will be able to edit a data source file and main documents and select specific data records to be merged.

A form letter, one type of main document, is a standard letter that is sent to many individuals or companies. The same letter can be typed once, merged with a list of names and addresses, and printed. It can be used for collecting overdue accounts, requesting donations, presenting product information, etc. The list of names and addresses is referred to as the data source file.

Create a Data Source File

The *data source* is a group of variables and field names. A *variable* is information that changes in each form letter and can include names, addresses, dollar amounts, dates, special comments, etc. The variable information is referred to as *data*. The data source can also be used to print envelope addresses or to create a mailing list (see Chapter 12).

Each set of variable information is referred to as a *record*. In other words, a record refers to all of the data for one entity, e.g., one company's name, address, city, state, and zip code.

A *field name* is a descriptive name used to identify a variable such as an address or dollar amount. Word suggests field names for variables that are commonly used when creating documents for merging. The field names can be accepted or deleted, or a new field name(s) can be added.

Word provides a Mail Merge Helper dialog box to help create the main document and data source and to merge the data with the main document. First a choice is made to determine the location where the main document is to be created, i.e., in the active window or in a new main document. Once you have designated the location for the main document, the data source is created. The field names for the variables are suggested by Word in the Create Data Source dialog box. The unneeded field names are selected and removed from the list of available field names. The data source is given a filename and the choice is made to either add new records to the data source (choose **Edit Data Source**) or to add merge fields to the main document (choose **Edit Main Document**).

When the **Edit Data Source** button is selected, a Data Form dialog box displays with the field names listed beside blank boxes where the variable information can be typed. After typing the information for all records, select **View Source** to display the typed data. The data displays in a table. The first table row is called a header row and contains the bolded field names. The second and following table rows contain records. The data can be edited and columns and/or rows added or deleted. The data source file should be checked and saved. After completing, checking, and saving the data source records, the main document (form letter) is created. See the section Create a Main Document later in this chapter.

Start-Up Instructions

❖ A new document window should be displayed. If necessary, select the **New** button on the Standard Toolbar.

 Create a Data Source File

1. Select **Tools, Mail Merge**.

   Note: The Mail Merge Helper dialog box displays (see Figure 11.1).

FIGURE 11.1

Mail Merge Helper dialog box

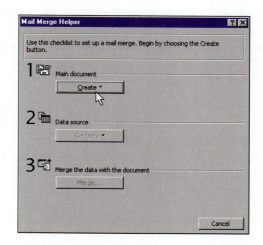

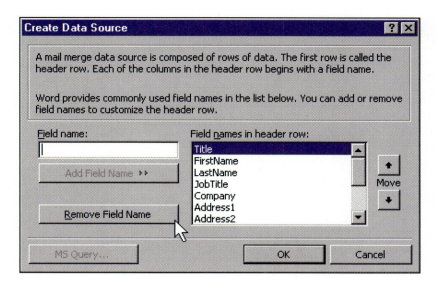

FIGURE 11.2

Create Data
Source dialog
box

2. Select the **Create** button in the Main document area.

3. Select **Form Letters**.

   Note: A Microsoft Word message box displays.

4. Select the **New Main Document** button.

   Note: The Mail Merge Helper dialog box displays again.

5. Select **Get Data, Create Data Source**.

   Note: The Create Data Source dialog box displays (see Figure 11.2).

6. Remove each unneeded field name by selecting the field name and then selecting the **Remove Field Name** button.

   For example, select **Job Title**, then select the **Remove Field Name** button. Repeat to remove the field names **Address2**, **Country**, **HomePhone**, and **WorkPhone**.

   Note: If necessary, scroll down the list of field names to view additional field names.

7. If desired, add new field names by typing the desired field name in the Field name box and selecting the **Add Field Name** button.

   For example, no new field names are needed at this time. Continue to step 8.

8. Select **OK**.

9. In the Save As dialog box, type the filename for the data source file. If necessary, change to the drive and/or directory where the data source file is to be stored. Select **Save**.

   For example, type the filename **11data1.doc**. (If necessary, change to the drive where your file disk is located. Select **Save**.)

   Note: A Microsoft Word message box displays.

10. Select **Edit Data Source**.

   Note: The Data Form dialog box displays (see Figure 11.3).

FIGURE 11.3

Data Form
dialog box

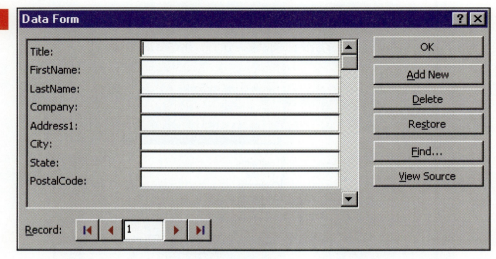

11. Enter the information for each field. Press the **Tab** key to move from field to field. After you have entered the information for the last field of a record, select the **Add New** button to obtain a new data form.

For example, enter the following information into the Data Form:

Mr.	Tab
Herbert	Tab
Lyle	Tab
Lyle Hardware	Tab
346 Jocelyn	Tab
San Jose	Tab
CA	Tab
95123	Select **Add New**.
Ms.	Tab
Kressy	Tab
Gueraz	Tab
Kressy's Supplies	Tab
5524 Baker Avenue	Tab
Dallas	Tab
TX	Tab
75206	Select **Add New**.
Mr.	Tab
Yat-Sun	Tab
Lo	Tab
New Moon Paints	Tab
286 NW 59th Avenue	Tab
Portland	Tab
OR	Tab
97210	Do *not* select **Add New**.

12. When all the records have been completed, select the **View Source** button.

Note: The Database Toolbar and a table with all records display.

13. Turn on table gridlines.

    For example, select **Table, Show Gridlines.**

14. Check the accuracy of the data in each table cell. Make any necessary changes to the data in the table.

15. Save the data source file (select the **Save** button).

    Note: The data source file has already been given a name in step 9 (i.e., 11data1.doc).

Finish-Up Instructions

❖ Continue with the Steps to Create a Main Document.

Create a Main Document

A *main document* is the information that remains the same in each letter (see Figure 11.4). The main document also includes the field names that correspond to the variable information that will print in each letter. Field names are placed in the main document to indicate the exact location for each field. The main document may be referred to as a form letter because many main documents are used to create form letters. However, a main document may also be used to create other types of merged documents such as reports and mailing labels.

Because field information in a data source file can vary, Word has provided special instructions to give the user more control over the varied information. Some fields in the data source can be empty, e.g., a company field may not be needed in all records. Blank cells in the data source indicate fields that contain no data. When the data source and main document are prepared for merging, the **Merge** button can be selected to obtain the Merge dialog box. When the default option **Don't print blank lines when data fields are empty** is chosen, the **Enter(s)** that ordinarily result from a blank field will not be placed in the merged document.

A form letter can be used over and over again with the date set up to change with each use. The date field is inserted in the form letter at the location at which the current date is to print. To insert a date field, the **Update automatically** option is selected in the Date and Time dialog box. To check that the date is inserted as a field in the form letter, click on the date; a gray shading will display on the date field.

When a field name is inserted in a document, the field name is displayed between chevrons, e.g., «Title». *Field codes* can also be displayed with the field name. When the field codes display, the word MERGEFIELD is inserted before each field name, e.g., { MERGEFIELD Title }. To display (or hide) field codes, select **Tools, Options, View** tab, then select the **Field codes** option. For easier viewing of the field codes, turn off the nonprinting symbols (select the **Show/Hide** button) and choose a **150% Zoom** view (select the **Zoom** button and choose **150%**).

❖ The data source file named **11data1.doc** should be displayed in the document window.

 Create a Main Document

1. With the data source file displayed in the document window, select the **Mail Merge Main Document** button 🖹 on the Database Toolbar.

   Note: A new document window and the Mail Merge Toolbar display.

2. If desired, insert the date as a field code.

   For example, select **Insert, Date and Time**. If necessary, select the **Update automatically** option. Select the third date format and choose **OK**. Press **Enter** five times.

3. Select the **Insert Merge Field** button in the Mail Merge Toolbar.

   Note: A list of the field names in the data source file displays.

4. Select the desired field name.

   For example, select **Title** and press the **Spacebar** once.

5. Repeat steps 3 and 4 to insert the desired field names. Also, remember to include punctuation and spacing as needed with the field names.

   For example, insert the following field names with the indicated spacing and punctuation:

   a. Insert the **FirstName** field name and press the **Spacebar**.

   b. Insert the **LastName** field name and press **Enter**.

   c. Insert the **Company** field name and press **Enter**.

   d. Insert the **Address1** field name and press **Enter**.

   e. Insert the **City** field name, type a **comma**, and press the **Spacebar**.

   f. Insert the **State** field name and press the **Spacebar**.

   g. Insert the **PostalCode** field name and press **Enter** twice.

   h. Type **Dear** and press the **Spacebar** once.

   i. Insert the **Title** field name and press the **Spacebar** once.

   j. Insert the **LastName** field name, type a **colon**, and press **Enter** twice.

   *Note: If the Office Assistant displays, select the **Cancel** button in the Office Assistant message box.*

   k. Type the remainder of the letter in Figure 11.4. Notice that the **Company** field is also inserted in the first sentence of the first paragraph.

   Note: Your main document should look similar to Figure 11.4.

6. Save the main document.

   For example, click on the **Save** button, type the filename **11Main Doc1.doc,** and select **Save**.

FIGURE 11.4

Main document
containing field
names

Date

«Title» «FirstName» «LastName»
«Company»
«Address1»
«City», «State» «PostalCode»

Dear «Title» «LastName»:

We are pleased to announce a very special discount offer to all our friends at
«Company». All orders placed during the next 30 days also receive an
additional 25 percent discount in addition to our already low prices.

Our new catalog is enclosed. Please note the new electrical supplies and
materials that we have recently added to our excellent line of products.

Sincerely,

Deidre Anderson, Sales Manager
LLB Lighting Fixtures

DA/xx
11Main Doc1.doc

Enc.

Finish-Up Instructions

❖   Continue with the Steps to Merge a Main Document with a Data Source
     File.

Merge a Main Document with a Data Source File

Once the main document and data source file are created and saved, the files
are combined by selecting the **Merge to New Document** button ▣, **Merge to
Printer** button ▣, or the **Merge...** button [Merge...] on the Mail Merge Toolbar. If
the **Merge to Printer** button ▣ is selected, the merged letters are sent directly to
the printer. To select specific records to be merged, the **Merge...** button [Merge...] is
chosen (see the section Select Data Records to Be Merged later in this chapter).
When the **Merge to New Document** button ▣ is selected, all the merged letters
display in a new document window with each letter in a separate section. If non-

printing symbols are turned on, a **Section Break (Next Page)** bar displays between each merged letter.

Once the main document and data source file have been merged, check the merged letters for accuracy. If any errors exist, close (but do not save) the merged file and access the main document or data source file to make corrections. Once the necessary corrections have been made, the main document or data source file is saved, and the main document and data source file are merged again. If desired, the merged letters can be saved; however, saving the merged letters is not recommended because the same information has been saved previously in the main document and data source file.

A copy of each letter is printed using the normal Print feature. Because a section break is placed between each letter, each letter will print on a separate page. If only one or two of the merged letters are to be printed, see Steps to Select Data Records to Be Merged on page 301.

After the main document is merged with the data source file, printed copies of both the main document and the data source file can be very useful for filing or reference purposes. If desired, the data source information and table structure can be changed to display the information in a more attractive and readable manner. For example, widening the columns, selecting a smaller font, and/or changing the table position to center will help make the table easier to read.

If desired, envelopes and mailing labels can also be created using the merge process (see Chapter 12, page 320).

Start-Up Instructions

❖ To continue, the files named **11data1.doc** and **11Main Doc1.doc** must have been previously created.

Merge a Main Document with a Data Source File

1. The main document to be merged and the Mail Merge Toolbar should be displayed in the document window. If necessary, open the main document file.

   For example, the file named **11Main Doc1.doc** and the Mail Merge Toolbar should be displayed.

2. Select the **Merge to New Document** button 🖹 on the Mail Merge Toolbar.

   Note: In a moment the merged letters display in the document window. "Form Letters# . . ." displays in the Title bar. Scroll through the letters and check that each letter and address have merged properly.

Finish-Up Instructions

❖ Optional: Use the filename **11Merge1.doc** and save the merged letters.

❖ Print one copy of the merged letters. Close the merged letters.

❖ Continue with the Steps to Edit a Data Source File and Steps to Edit a Main Document.

Edit a Data Source File and a Main Document

Often the information in a data source file or main document must be updated or altered. The data source file is changed by adding and/or deleting a record(s) or field(s). The data in any field can be changed also. A main document is changed by deleting or inserting fields and/or by changing the text of the document. The record information in the data source file and the text in the main document can be altered using normal editing procedures.

Records can be added, deleted, or edited by selecting options in the Data Form dialog box, by displaying the data source file and using the **Add Record** or **Delete Record** buttons on the Database Toolbar, or by selecting data in the table and inserting new information. To insert or delete a field(s), display the data source file and select the **Manage Fields** button. Also, if desired, records and fields can be added or deleted using the same procedures as used to edit a table (see Chapters 5 and 6).

An edited main document and/or data source file should be saved again before merging. After a main document or data source file is changed, all or specific data source records can be merged with the main document.

Start-Up Instructions

❖ The file named **11Main Doc1.doc** should be displayed in the document window.

Edit a Data Source File

1. With the main document displayed in the document window, select the **Edit Data Source** button on the Mail Merge Toolbar.

   Note: The Data Form dialog box displays.

Insert a New Record

2. Select the Add New button.

3. Type the information for the new record into the appropriate field boxes.

   For example, insert the following information into each field and press the **Tab** key (except do not press the **Tab** key after the last field):

   Ms.
   Juanita
   Alvarado
   Alvarado Electrical
   347 Tiyunga Blvd.
   North Hollywood
   CA
   91600

Edit an Existing Record

4. Locate the desired record by clicking on the left triangle ◄ or right triangle ► button located beside the Record box.

    For example, click on the left triangle button ◄ until record 2, **Ms. Kressy Gueraz**, displays.

    Note: The ◄ button displays the first record and the ► button displays the last record.

5. Make the desired changes to the record information.

    For example, change the Address1 field to **4140 Mercury Drive.**

6. When all changes to the existing records have been made and all new records have been added, select the **View Source** button.

    *Note: When **View Source** is selected, the data source, **11data1.doc**, displays in the document window. The new record has been added and the address of Ms. Kressy Gueraz has been changed.*

Add a New Field

7. Select the **Manage Fields** button 🖼 on the Database Toolbar.

    Note: The Manage Fields dialog box displays.

8. Type the name of the new field in the Field Name box.

    For example, type **Percent.**

9. Select the **Add** button.

10. Select **OK** to exit the Manage Fields dialog box.

    Note: A new column with the heading Percent has been added to the data source table.

11. Type the desired information into the cells in the new field (column).

    For example, type the following information into the cells of the Percent field (column):

    10 percent
    12 percent
    20 percent
    15 percent

12. When all changes have been made, select the **Save** button to save the edited data source file.

13. Select the **Mail Merge Main Document** button 🖼 to return to the main document.

Finish-Up Instructions

❖ Continue with the Steps to Edit a Main Document.

❖ The file named **11Main Doc1.doc** should be displayed in the document window. If necessary, open the file named **11Main Doc1.doc**, or, if the data source file named **11data1.doc** is displayed in the document window, select the **Mail Merge Main Document** button 🗐.

Steps to

Edit a Main Document

1. With the main document displayed in the document window, make the necessary corrections.

   For example, delete **25 percent** in the last sentence of the first paragraph and insert the merge field **Percent** (select the **Insert Merge Field** button on the Mail Merge Toolbar, click on **Percent**).

   Note: Be sure to check that one space precedes and one space follows the field name.

2. Change the filename in the document identification notation.

   For example, scroll to the end of the document and change the filename from **11Main Doc1.doc** to **11Main Doc2.doc**.

3. Save the edited main document.

   For example, click on **File, Save As,** type the *new* filename **11Main Doc2.doc** and select **Save**.

Finish-Up Instructions

❖ Continue with the Steps to Output Merged Letters Directly to a Printer on page 300.

Output Merged Letters Directly to a Printer

One problem that can occur with large data files is that the computer may not have enough memory to store all the merged letters at one time. This can cause the merge process to stop before it has merged all the letters. Using the **Records to be merged** option in the Merge dialog box to limit the number of records to be merged may be helpful (covered in the next section), or it may be more efficient to use the **Merge to Printer** option and output the information directly to the printer to avoid an out-of-memory error.

The **Merge to Printer** option can be used to reduce the memory needed during the merge operation. Sending merged letters directly to the printer can avoid some memory problems, but should be used only with a data source file and main document that have been merged and checked previously for errors. Otherwise, a lot of paper can be wasted!

Start-Up Instructions

❖ The file named **11Main Doc2.doc** should be displayed in the document window. (If necessary, open the file named **11Main Doc2.doc**.)

 ## Output Merged Letters Directly to a Printer

1. With the main document containing the merge field codes in the document window, select the **Merge to Printer** button located on the Mail Merge Toolbar.

   Note: The Print dialog box displays.

2. Select **OK**.

   Note: The Printing message box displays briefly in the document window with the message, "Now printing Page 1 . . ." The printing message disappears when the merge is complete and the letters are sent to the printer.

Finish-Up Instructions

❖ Check the printed letters for accuracy.

❖ Continue with the Steps to Select Data Records to Be Merged.

Select Data Records to Be Merged

If data records to be merged are not sequentially arranged in the data source file, the **Query Options** button can be selected from the Merge dialog box and the options on the Filter Records tab used to specify criteria (rules) to be met when selecting records to be merged. (See Figure 11.5.) For example, you could choose to merge only records for people who live in a certain state. The criteria consist of three parts: (1) the field name, (2) the comparison phrase, and (3) the text or numbers with which to compare the contents of the data field. Six criteria can be specified. When more than one criteria are created, the criteria are connected by AND or OR. When AND is used, Word selects only records that match all criteria. When OR is used, Word selects records that satisfy at least one criterion.

Once the Filter Records tab has been used to select specific records, Word remembers the criteria specified and will continue to select only records that meet the criteria. Select the **Clear All** button on the **Filter Records** tab to clear the specified criteria. You can then create new criteria or merge all records in the data source file.

If the desired data records to be merged are in sequential order, the range of records can be specified in the **Records to be merged** area of the Merge dialog box. For example, to merge records 2–5, type **2** in the From box, type **5** in the To box of the Merge dialog box, and select **Merge**.

Start-Up Instructions

❖ The main document **11Main Doc2.doc** should be displayed in the document window. Select the **Edit Data Source** button to display the data source file **11data1.doc**.

❖ Select the **Add New** button and type the following information in the appropriate field boxes in the Data Form dialog box:

> **Mr.**
> **Brian**
> **DeGeorgio**
> **DeGeorgio Lighting**
> **7822 Western Street**
> **Seattle**
> **WA**
> **98121**
> **15 percent**

❖ Edit the record of Mr. Yat-Sun Lo using the following information:

> Click on the left triangle button ◄ in the Record area to display record 3. Change the Address1 field to **2600 NW 97th Street**.

❖ Select the **View Source** button.

❖ Select the **Save** button to save the updated data source file.

❖ Select the Mail Merge Main Document button 📑.

Steps to

Select Data Records to Be Merged

1. Select the **Merge...** button Merge... on the Mail Merge Toolbar.

   Note: The Merge dialog box displays.

2. Select the **Query Options** button.

   Note: The Query Options dialog box displays.

3. With the **Filter Records** tab selected, click on the down arrow in the top Field box and select the desired field name.

   For example, select **LastName**.

4. Click on the down arrow in the top **Comparison** box and select the desired option.

   For example, check that **Equal to** displays.

5. Select the Compare to box and type the desired criteria.

   For example, type **DeGeorgio**.

6. Click in the first column (on the left side) **And/Or** option box and choose the desired option.

   For example, select **Or**.

7. Repeat steps 3 through 5 to create additional criteria.

FIGURE 11.5

Query Options
dialog box with
criteria

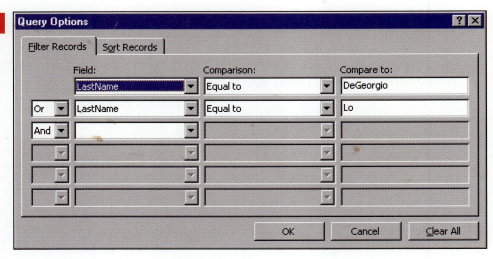

For example, create a second criterion using the following information:

Field: **LastName**
Comparison: **Equal to**
Compare to: **Lo**

Note: Your Query Options dialog box should look similar to Figure 11.5.

8. When all needed criteria have been created, select **OK**.

Note: The Merge dialog box displays again.

9. Select the **Merge** button.

Note: In a moment, the specified letters display in the document window.

Finish-Up Instructions

❖ Print the two letters.

❖ Close the merged letters. Do not save the file.

❖ Clear the Query Options (select the **Merge...** button, choose **Query Options**, select **Clear All**, **OK**, **Close**).

❖ Close the **11Main Doc2.doc** and **11data1.doc** files, and if necessary save the changes to the file(s).

The Next Step

Chapter Review and Activities

Self-Check Quiz

T F 1. A form letter may be referred to as the data source file.

T F 2. An example of a variable is a company name.

T F 3. A form letter is sent to many individuals or companies.

T F 4. Word provides suggested field names in the Create Data Source dialog box.

T F 5. Criteria can be specified as a basis for merging nonsequential records.

6. Mail Merge is selected from the _____ menu.
  a. **Tools**
  b. **Insert**
  c. **Edit**
  d. **Format**

7. The _____ is referred to as data.
  a. form letter
  b. field name
  c. variable information
  d. main document

8. The main document contains the letter text, _____, spacing, and any other information that remains the same in each letter.
  a. filenames
  b. data source
  c. field names
  d. none of these

9. State the difference between a record and a field.

10. Give one reason why the date would be inserted as a field in the main document.

Enriching Language Arts Skills

Spelling/Vocabulary Words

investigate—to observe or study; to examine; to conduct an official inquiry.
quality—degree of excellence; superior.
thoroughly—completely; carefully; fully.

Nonrestrictive Clause

A nonrestrictive clause is a clause that is not essential to the meaning of the sentence and, therefore, is set off by a comma or commas.

Example:

We will meet next Thursday for our planning meeting, which was postponed last week.

Activities

Activity 11.1—Create a Data Source File and Main Document; Use Mail Merge

1. Create a data source file using the following information:

    a. In a document window, access the Create Data Source dialog box (select **Tools**, **Mail Merge**, **Create**; select **Form Letters**, **New Main Document**; select **Get Data**, **Create Data Source**).

    b. In the Create Data Source dialog box, highlight and *remove* the following field names: **JobTitle**, **Company**, **Address2**, **Country**, **HomePhone**, and **WorkPhone** (select the desired field names in the **Field names in header row** list; select the **Remove Field Name** button).

    c. Add the field name **Amount** (if necessary, double-click in the **Field name** box, type the desired field name, select **Add Field Name**).

    d. Exit the Create Data Source dialog box. Use the filename **11Club Data.doc** and save the file (select **OK**; if necessary, select or type the drive where your file disk is located followed by a colon and the filename; select **OK**).

    e. Select the **Edit Data Source** button to display the Data Form dialog box.

    f. In the Data Form dialog box, fill in the field name boxes with the following information. Press the **Tab** key to move to the next field. Select **Add New** to begin a new record.

Mr.	Ms.	Mr.
William	Pearl	Dayton
Barstow	Diamante	Darlington
145 Newton Road	RR 10 Box 25	455 Aspen Avenue
Chicago	Lancaster	Denver
IL	PA	CO
60656	17603	80239
$5,500	$3,200	$6,000

*Note: Do **not** select **Add New** after the last record.*

g. View and save the data source records (select the **View Source** button, make any needed changes, select the **Save** button).

h. Go to the main document window (select the **Mail Merge Main Document** button).

2. Create the main document using the following information:

a. Create the date field (select **Insert**, **Date and Time**; check that the **Update automatically** option is selected; choose an appropriate date format; select **OK**; press **Enter** five times).

b. Type the following letter and insert the merge fields as shown. (Use the **Insert Merge Field** button to select the field names for the form letter). Remember to press the **Spacebar** or **Enter** key and type a punctuation mark as needed after each field name.

Date

«Title» «FirstName» «LastName»
«Address1»
«City», «State» «PostalCode»

Dear «Title» «LastName»:

Because of your outstanding credit record, you have been selected to receive our new Samson's Warehouse credit card.

Your credit limit will be «Amount». You may use your new Samson's Warehouse credit card at all of the Outlet Club stores.

If you take advantage of this special offer within the next 30 days, you will also receive 15 percent off your first Samson's Warehouse credit card purchase. Call our toll free number today, 1-800-555-6520, to activate your Samson's Warehouse credit card.

Sincerely,

Warren T. Harding
Vice President, Sales

WTH/xx
11Club Main.doc/disk6

3. Use the filename **11Club Main.doc** and save the file on your file disk.

4. Merge the main document **11Club Main.doc** with the data source file **11Club Data.doc** (select the **Merge to New Document** button).

5. Optional: Print one copy of each letter.

6. Close all documents. Do not save the merged letters.

Activity 11.2—Create a Data Source File and Main Document; Edit the Data Source File; Select Data Records

1. Create a data source file using the following information:

   a. In a document window, access the Create Data Source dialog box (select **Tools**, **Mail Merge**, **Create**; select **Form Letters**, **New Main Document**; select **Get Data**, **Create Data Source**).

   b. In the Create Data Source dialog box, highlight and remove all field names with the exception of FirstName and LastName (select the desired field names in the **Field names in header row** list; select the **Remove Field Name** button).

   c. Add the field names **Department**, **MailStop**, **Rank**, **Step**, and **Amount** (if necessary, double-click in the **Field name** box, type the desired field name, select **Add Field Name**).

   d. Exit the Create Data Source dialog box. Use the filename **11Salary data.doc** and save the file (select **OK**; if necessary, select or type the drive where your file disk is located followed by a colon and the filename; select **OK**).

   e. Select the **Edit Data Source** button to display the Data Form dialog box.

   f. In the Data Form dialog box, fill in the field name boxes with the following information. Press the **Tab** key to move to the next field. Select **Add New** to begin a new record.

Martin A.	Mai	Wanda L.
Bonifacio	Ling	Mallard
Marketing Department	Finance Department	Shipping Department
Mail Stop 390	Mail Stop 195H	Mail Stop 251B
Rank B	Rank C	Rank D
Step 5	Step 8	Step 5
$32,000	$65,000	$28,000

*Note: Do **not** select **Add New** after the last record.*

g. View and save the data source file (select the **View Source** button, make any needed changes, select the **Save** button).

h. Go to the main document window (select the **Mail Merge Main Document** button).

2. Create the main document using the following information:

a. Change the top margin to **1.75"**.

b. Create the date field (select **Insert**, **Date and Time**; check that the **Update automatically** option is selected; choose an appropriate date format; select **OK**; press **Enter** five times).

c. Type the following letter and insert the merge fields as shown. (Use the **Insert Merge Field** button to select the field names for the form letter.) Remember to press the **Spacebar** or **Enter** key and type a punctuation mark as needed after each field name.

Date

Private and Confidential
«FirstName» «LastName»
«Department»
«Mailstop»

CONFIRMATION OF SALARY LEVEL

I am pleased to confirm your salary level for the new fiscal year.

On the salary schedule, you are in «Rank» on «Step» with a new annual adjusted salary of «Amount».

If you have any questions, please telephone Jean Leandro at Ext. 2966.

SEYMOUR CANDARA, HUMAN RESOURCES DIRECTOR

SC/xx
11Salary Main.doc/diskS

---

3. Use the filename, **11Salary Main.doc**, and save the file.

4. Merge the main document **11Salary Main.doc** with the data source file **11Salary data.doc** (select the **Merge to New Document** button).

5. Optional: Print one copy of each letter.

6. Close but do not save the merged letters.

7. Edit the data record for Wanda Mallard to change her salary to **$29,300** (select the **Edit Data Source** button; click on the right triangle button in the **Record** box until **3** displays; make desired changes).

8. Add two new data records (select **Add New** and type in the information).

Victoria	**Harrison T.**
Larsen	**Chevalier**
Research and Development	**Shipping Department**
Mail Stop 198D	**Mail Stop 281C**
Rank A	**Rank D**
Step 8	**Step 2**
$95,000	**$13,500**

   *Note: Do **not** select **Add New** after the last record.*

9. View the data source file and make any needed changes (select **View Source**; make any needed changes).

10. Save the edited data source file (select the **Save** button).

11. Select data records and merge only the added and corrected data records with the salary form letter (select the **Mail Merge Main Document** button; select the **Merge...** button; click in the From box, type **3**; click in the To box, type **5**, select **Merge**).

12. Optional: Print one copy of each letter.

13. Close all documents. Do not save the merged letters.

Challenge Your Skills

Skill 11.1—Create a Data Source File and Main Document; Edit and Select Specific Data Records

1. Use the following information to create a data source file:

   a. In the Create Data Source dialog box, remove the field names that will not be needed, i.e., **Title**, **JobTitle**, **Company**, **Address2**, **Country**, and **WorkPhone**.

   b. Add the Field Names: **BranchName**, **AcctNumber**, and **BranchNumber**.

   c. Use the filename **11Bank Data.doc**.

   d. Type the information for each data record as follows:

Red Castile	Willard Ritchy	Lela Perez
4251 W. Plains Road	697 S. Bayfair Street	834 San Antonio Road
Texas City, TX 77591	Baytown, TX 77520	San Antonio, TX 78212
713-555-4923	713-555-8321	210-555-2535
Houston Branch	Houston Branch	San Antonio Branch
HO 23959007	HO 23956008	SA 46289002
713-555-6003	713-555-6003	210-555-9200
Barbara Deacon	Luiz Ortega	Lawrence Delby
5233 Blevins Avenue	P.O. Box 2695	2469 Lincoln Drive
Dallas, TX 75206	Kerrville, TX 78028	Dallas, TX 75243
214-555-2133	210-555-1824	214-555-9243
Dallas Branch	San Antonio Branch	Dallas Branch
DA 54328801	SA 46288001	DA 54326803
214-555-1010	210-555-9200	214-555-1010

   Note: The first phone number is the HomePhone. The second phone number is the BranchNumber.

2. Create the main document that follows. Make decisions regarding:

   Bold
   Margins
   Alignment
   Fonts
   Spacing

Date

«FirstName» «LastName»
«Address1»
«City», «State» «PostalCode»

ACCOUNT NUMBER: «AcctNumber»

Thank you for submitting your change of address. In order to protect the security of your accounts, we need you to verify the information shown below by calling the «BranchName», «BranchNumber».

> «FirstName» «LastName»
> «Address1»
> «City», «State» «PostalCode»
> «HomePhone»

Thank you for allowing Union Financial Group to serve your investment needs. If you have any questions, please contact our «BranchName» between 9 a.m. and 4 p.m., Monday through Friday.

UNION FINANCIAL GROUP

UFG/xx
11Bank Main.doc/diskA

---

3. Use the filename **11Bank Main.doc** and save the main document file on your file disk.

4. Merge the data source file **11Bank Data.doc** with the main document file **11Bank Main.doc**.

5. Print one copy of each letter.

6. Edit the data source records and change the phone number of the Houston Branch to **713-555-8900**.

7. Use the **Query Options** to select only the Houston branch records for merging.

   *Hint: In the Filter Records tab, select the field name **BranchName**. Check that **Equal to** displays in the Comparison box; type **Houston Branch** in the Compare to box.*

8. Merge the specified records (i.e., the Houston branch) and print one copy of the merged letters.

9. Close all documents. Do not save the merged letters.

◆ Skill 11.2—Create a Data Source File and Main Document; Language Arts

1. Create a data source file using the following information:

   a. Determine the field names to delete and create any field names needed (see the main document that follows).

   b. Use the filename **11Hotel Data.doc**.

   c. Type the information for each data record as follows:

Mr. Mark Sitkowski	Ms. Rahimi Kahir	Mr. Brandon Cardenas
Financial Officer	Budget Director	Chief Accountant
Devon Communications	Discount Software	Western Trucking
3823 Parkside Blvd.	1370 Dartmoor Avenue	342 Mason Blvd.
Los Angeles, CA 90010	Miami, FL 33139	Arlington, VA 22203
15 percent	20 percent	10 percent

2. Create the main document that follows. Make decisions regarding:

   Bold
   Margins
   Alignment
   Fonts
   Enclosure notation

3. Correct three spelling errors, two misused words, and two punctuation errors.

Date

«Title» «FirstName» «LastName»
«JobTitle»
«Company»
«Address1»
«City», «State» «PostalCode»

Dear «Title» «LastName»:

On March 19, seven people were delayed in an elevator that became stuck between floors off our Western Business Hotel in Tucson. It is my understanding that you were one of those seven people. Therefore, I want to convey my apologies and assure you the situation is being throughly envestigated.

The Western Business Hotel is proud to provide the highest standard in service and guality which has been our hallmark since opening in 1981. We hope on your next visit that your will experience the high standards of Western Business Hotels.

Enclosed is a «percent» discount coupon for your use when visiting the Western Business Hotel.

We are looking forward to your next visit and I extend my sincere apologies for any inconvenience that occurred during your stay.

Respectfully,

Belinda Jampour
General Manager

BJ/xx
11Hotel Main.doc/disk03

Enc.

4. Use the filename **11Hotel Main.doc** and save the main document on your file disk.

5. Merge the data source file **11Hotel Data.doc** with the main document file **11Hotel Main.doc**.

6. Print one copy of each letter.

7. Close all documents. Do not save the merged letters.

Create Envelope Addresses and Mailing Labels

Features Covered

- Create envelope addresses
- Create mailing labels
- Create a full page of the same mailing label
- Create and sort mailing labels using a new main document and an existing data source file
- Create and print a single label

Objectives and Introduction

After successfully completing this chapter, you will be able to create envelope addresses, create a full page of the same label, and create and print a single label. In addition, you will be able to create and sort mailing labels using a new main document and an existing data source file.

Once a main document is merged with a data source file, envelope addresses or mailing labels can be created for each letter or document. Using existing data source addresses or letter addresses to create envelope addresses or mailing labels can expedite the process of setting up and printing addresses on envelopes or labels.

Create Envelope Addresses

Envelope addresses are easily created using the **Tools**, **Envelopes and Labels** feature. Word reviews the file in the current document window and automatically identifies the address information, or an address can be typed in the address area of the Envelopes and Labels dialog box.

Once Word has identified the address information and the Envelopes and Labels dialog box is displayed, the **Envelopes** tab should be selected (see Figure 12.1). The address information displays in the Delivery address box. If Word has incorrectly identified the address information, the correct address can be typed.

If no address information is found in the document displayed in the window, the Delivery address box will be empty and an address can be typed.

A previously typed return address may display in the Return address box. If the return address is not to be printed on the envelope, select the **Omit** option. If the **Omit** option is selected (a check mark displays in the Omit option box), no return address displays in the Preview box and no return address will be printed on the envelope.

The Envelope Options dialog box (See Figure 12.2) is used to change fonts and to select an envelope size and/or mailing options. The font for the return or mailing addresses can be changed easily by selecting the **Font** button located in the Delivery or Return address areas.

The U.S. Postal Service requests that mailing addresses be typed with vertical line spacing of one and no italic text or indented lines. For a standard large No. 10 envelope, the address is placed approximately 2 to 2½ inches from the top edge and 4 to 4½ inches from the left edge of the envelope. Word automatically places the address on an envelope at the location suggested by the U.S. Postal Service.

For many years, the Postal Service preferred addresses to be typed in all uppercase letters with no punctuation; however, the main concern of the Postal Service is that the typed address be placed in an area easily read by OCR (optical character recognition) equipment. OCR equipment scans addresses electronically and sorts mail quickly, thus expediting the mail service.

Using uppercase letters and no punctuation or using lowercase letters with initial capitals and punctuation are now both considered acceptable forms for mailing addresses. Typing envelopes or mailing label addresses in uppercase letters with no punctuation is recommended, however, because it is more efficient to type characters in one case and keystrokes are saved when punctuation is omitted. The U.S. Postal Service also accepts abbreviations, such as RD, AVE, ST, DR, and BLVD, in the street addresses on envelopes and mailing labels.

The position of the return or mailing addresses can be changed by selecting the **Options** button on the Envelopes tab. If desired, the From left and From top positions can be changed in the Delivery address and/or the Return address area. Word can also create the POSTNET (POSTal Numeric Encoding Techniques) bar code for any zip code. Select the **Delivery point barcode** option to print a bar code above the delivery address. (The POSTNET bar code is used by the U.S. Postal Service to expedite the routing of mail.) Also, the FIM (Facing Identification Mark) option can be selected to print a code that identifies the face of a courtesy reply envelope. The FIM is used by the Postal Service during presorting.

Start-Up Instructions

❖ Open the file named **12torres.doc** located on the data disk.

Create an Envelope Address

1. With the insertion point located at any position in the letter, select **Tools, Envelopes and Labels.**

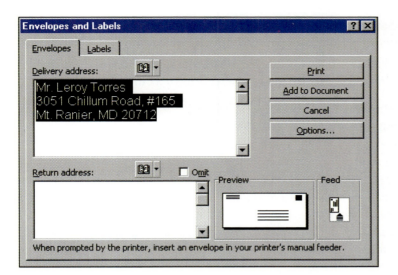

FIGURE 12.1

Envelopes and
Labels dialog
box

*Note: The Envelopes and Labels dialog box displays (see Figure 12.1). Check that the Envelopes tab is selected. If necessary, select the **Envelopes** tab. The address for the letter displays in the Delivery address box. If a return address was previously typed, the return address displays in the Return address box. If a delivery address is not displayed, you can click in the Delivery address box and type an address.*

2. If a return address is desired, click in the **Return address** box, or if a return address is displayed, select all lines of the return address. Type the desired return address.

    For example, click in the **Return address** box, or if a return address is displayed, select all lines of the return address. Type your name and return address information.

3. Select the **Options** button.

    Note: The Envelope Options dialog box displays (see Figure 12.2).

4. Select the desired envelope options.

    For example, check that the **Delivery point barcode** is selected. (If necessary, select the **Delivery point barcode** option.)

    Note: The bar code displays above the address lines in the Preview box.

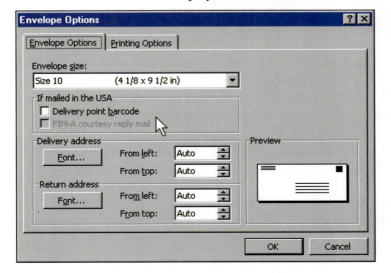

FIGURE 12.2

Envelope
Options dialog
box

5. Check that an envelope size displays. If necessary, click on the down arrow at the right of the **Envelope size** box and click once on the desired envelope size.

For example, check that **Size 10 (4⅛ x 9½ in)** displays in the **Envelope size** box or **make a selection of your own.**

6. Select the **Font** button in the Delivery address area and choose a font and size.

For example, select **Times New Roman, 14 point.**

7. Select **OK** twice.

8. Select the **Add to Document** button.

*Note: A message displays, "Do you want to save the new return address . . .?" Select No. The envelope information is placed (added) at the beginning of the letter followed by a section break. To view the letter and/or envelope, select the **Print Preview** button. Choose the **Multiple Pages** button; choose any button on the first row. Select **Close**.*

To Print an Envelope from the Document Window

9. The insertion point should be located on the page (section) containing the envelope address and bar code.

10. Select **File, Print.**

11. Select **Current Page.**

12. Select **OK.**

Note: The printer pauses, allowing an envelope to be inserted in the printer or paper tray. Use of plain paper is OK for this practice activity. Activate your printer by pressing the appropriate button. The address prints on the paper in the appropriate area.

Finish-Up Instructions

❖ Use the *new* filename **12envelope.doc** and save the file. Close the document.

Create Mailing Labels Using Predefined Labels

Mailing labels are short forms on which names and addresses are printed. Mailing labels come in various sizes. Two commonly used sizes are 2⅝ x 1" and 1⅓ x 4". Generally, the labels are attached to backing paper that is 11 inches in length. The self-adhesive mailing label is removed from this paper and placed on an envelope.

Mailing labels are usually designed with one, two, or three columns per page. Preferably the address is printed two to three spaces from the left edge of the form and on the second or third line down from the top edge of the page.

Word provides predefined label formats for both dot matrix and laser/ink jet printers. Various Avery-brand label product numbers and sizes are available in the Label Options dialog box. (Avery-brand labels are sold in most office supply stores or stationery departments.)

The label information, i.e., height, width, page size, and type, is listed in the Label information area of the Label Options dialog box (see Figure 12.3). Select the **Details** button to view the exact location of the label on the backing paper. The details of the top and side margins, label height and width, and number of labels across and down the page are shown. (The details displayed will depend on the printer that is selected.) The vertical and horizontal pitch, which is the space between label rows and label columns, displays. The details can be changed if the selected labels do not exactly match the dimensions and layout of your labels. If desired, the **New Label** button in the Label Options dialog box can be used to custom-design a label size.

Mailing labels can also be created by using the Merge feature (see Chapter 11). The same data source file used with the form letter main document can be merged with a new main document that has been formatted to create mailing labels. (See Steps to Create and Sort Mailing Labels Using a New Main Document and an Existing Data Source File on page 320.)

Start-Up Instructions

❖ An empty document window should be displayed. If necessary, select the **New** button on the Standard Toolbar.

Create a Full Page of the Same Mailing Label

1. Select **Tools, Envelopes and Labels**.

   Note: The Envelopes and Labels dialog box displays.

2. If necessary, select the **Labels** tab.

3. In the Address box, type the desired mailing label address.

   For example, type the following address:

   Mackenzie Plumbing
   5673 Sandpiper Street
   Helena, MT 59601

4. Choose the desired print option.

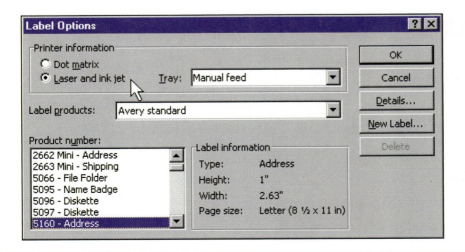

FIGURE 12.3

Label Options dialog box

For example, check that the **Full page of the same label** option is selected. (If necessary, select the **Full page of the same label** option.)

5. To select the desired label size, select **Options**.

   Note: The Label Options dialog box displays (see Figure 12.3).

6. In the Printer information area, choose the desired option.

   For example, select your printer type, i.e., **Dot matrix** or **Laser and ink jet**.

7. In the Product number box, select the desired product number.

   For example, *if using a dot matrix printer,* select 4144 - **Address**; *if using a laser or ink jet printer,* select 5160 - **Address**.

   Note: Label information including type, height, width, and page size displays in the Label information area.

8. Select **OK**.

9. Select the **Print** or **New Document** button.

   For example, select **New Document**.

   *Note: The document window displays the labels as they will appear on a page when printed. If desired, select the down arrow next to the **Zoom** button and **50%** to view more of the labels on the screen.*

Finish-Up Instructions

❖ Use the filename **12labels.doc** and save the labels on your file disk.

❖ Print one copy of the labels. (Plain paper is OK.)

   *Note: If the printer pauses, select the **Form Feed**, **Online**, or **Start button** on the printer.*

❖ Close the document.

Start-Up Instructions

❖ A new document window should be displayed. If necessary, select the **New** button.

❖ Select the down arrow next to the **Zoom** button and choose 75%.

❖ The nonprinting symbols should be displayed. If necessary, select the **Show/Hide** button.

Create Mailing Labels for Different Addresses

1. Select **Tools, Envelopes and Labels**.

   Note: The Envelopes and Labels dialog box displays.

2. If necessary, select the **Labels** tab.

3. Select the **Options** button.

4. In the Printer information area, select the desired option.

   For example, select your printer type, i.e., **Dot matrix** or **Laser and ink jet**.

5. Select the desired Product number.

   For example, *if using a dot matrix printer,* select **4611 - Address**; *if using a laser or ink jet printer,* select **5662 - Address**.

6. Select **OK** to return to the Labels card in the Envelopes and Labels dialog box.

7. Choose the **New Document** button.

   Note: The label outlines display in the document window. (If necessary, select Table, Show Gridlines to see the label outlines.)

8. If desired, select all labels and change the paragraph indent and line spacing.

   For example, press **Ctrl** and **a** to select all labels, choose **Format, Paragraph**; on the Indents and Spacing tab, click on the up arrow in the **Left** indentation box until **0.3"** displays; repeat for the **Right** indentation; select **OK**.

9. Click beside the first end-of-cell symbol in the first label.

10. Type the label information; press **Shift** and **Enter** after each line and press the **Tab** key once or twice to move to the next label.

    For example, type the following labels:

    MICHELLE BRADFORD (Shift and Enter)
    75 CEDARWOOD STREET (Shift and Enter)
    ROCKVILLE MD 20850 (Tab once or twice)

    ELENORA L LASSEN (Shift and Enter)
    106 CABRILLO STREET (Shift and Enter)
    TEANECK NJ 07666 (Tab once)

    A F SALAS (Shift and Enter)
    1200 LAURELWOOD STREET (Shift and Enter)
    PHILADELPHIA PA 19130 (Tab once or twice)

    GORDON WHIPPLE (Shift and Enter)
    INDUSTRIAL TRAINING (Shift and Enter)
    400 ROUND HILL DRIVE (Shift and Enter)
    NEWARK DE 19713

    *Note: It is not necessary to press the **Tab** key after the last zip code.*

Finish-Up Instructions

❖ Use the filename **12Individual Labels.doc** and save the file on your file disk.

❖ If desired, select **Print Preview, One Page** to display the labels on a full page. Select **Close**.

❖ Print one copy. (Plain paper is OK.)

   Note: The printer may pause waiting for mailing labels to be manually placed in the tray. If necessary, press the online button to activate the printer.

❖ Close the document.

Create and Sort Mailing Labels Using a Main Document and an Existing Data Source File

Mailing labels can be easily created using a new main document and an existing data source file. The Mail Merge Helper is used to create or access the mailing labels for an existing data source file. With the assistance of the Mail Merge Helper, a new main document is created, the data source file is opened, the new main document is set up with the desired label product number and merge field names, and the data are merged with the new main document.

If desired, the data for the mailing labels can be arranged in an assigned order by specifying the field name(s) to be used for sorting. For example, the data source records can be presorted by zip code to receive discounts on mail rates.

The new main document file that contains the chosen labels and merge fields can be saved and used again at a later time. If the data source records are changed, the new main document file can be used to merge the changed records. Open the new main document and merge the changed records by selecting the **Mail Merge** button, choosing **Query Options**, specifying the number of the records to be merged, and selecting **Merge**.

If an envelope is desired for each merged letter, use the Mail Merge Helper. After selecting **Create** in the Main Document area, select **Envelopes**. An envelope size and the desired fields can be selected by following the same steps used to create mailing labels.

Start-Up Instructions

❖ The file named **11data1.doc** created in Chapter 11 must be available.

❖ A new document window should be displayed. If necessary, select the **New** button.

 Steps to Create and Sort Mailing Labels Using a New Main Document and an Existing Data Source File

1. Select Tools, Mail Merge.

2. Select Create, Mailing Labels.

3. Select the New Main Document button.

4. Select Get Data, Open Data Source.

5. Double-click on the desired filename.

     For example, double-click on **11data1.doc**.

6. Select the Set Up Main Document button.

   Note: The Label Options dialog box displays.

7. In the Printer information area, select the desired option.

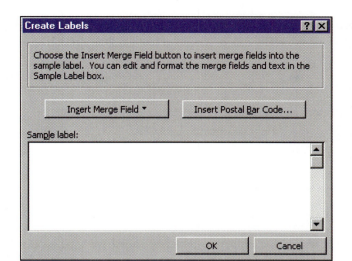

FIGURE 12.4

Create Labels
dialog box

For example, select your printer type, i.e., **Dot matrix** or **Laser and ink jet.**

8. Select the desired Product number.

   For example, *if using a dot matrix printer,* select **4605 - Address**; *if using a laser or ink jet printer,* select **5262 - Address.**

9. Select **OK.**

   Note: The Create Labels dialog box displays (see Figure 12.4).

10. To display the list of field names, select the **Insert Merge Field** button, choose the desired field names and use spacing, **Enters**, and punctuation as desired.

    For example, set up the labels with the field codes and format as follows:

    «Title» «FirstName» «LastName»
    «Company»
    «Address1»
    «City», «State» «PostalCode»

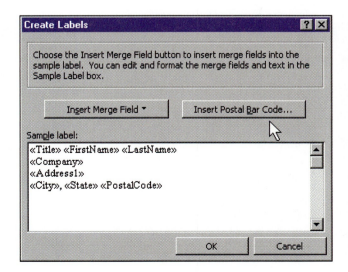

FIGURE 12.5

Create Labels
dialog box with
field names

Note: The field names displayed in the Sample label box should be arranged in the order that the information is to print on the mailing label (see Figure 12.5).

11. Select the **Insert Postal Bar Code** button.

12. Click in the **Merge field with ZIP code** box.

13. Select the field name that contains the zip code information.

    For example, select **PostalCode**. Select **OK**.

Note: The message "Delivery point barcode will print here!" displays at the top of the Sample label box.

14. Select **OK** once.

    Note: The Mail Merge Helper dialog box displays.

15. To save the new main document containing the chosen labels and field names, select the **Edit** button in the Main document area and choose **Mailing Label: ...**

    Note: The "Zip Code not valid!" message that displays in each label will be replaced by a bar code when the main (label) document is merged with the data source file.

16. Save the label main document.

    For example, click on the **Save** button, use the filename **12label main.doc**, and save the label main document on your file disk.

17. Select the **Merge...** button Merge... on the Mail Merge Toolbar.

Sort Records to Be Merged

18. Select the **Query Options** button.

    Note: The Query Options dialog box displays.

19. If necessary, select the **Sort Records** tab.

    Note: The Sort Records tab displays (see Figure 12.6).

20. Click in the **Sort by** box.

    Note: The list of field names displays.

FIGURE 12.6

Sort Records tab in the Query Options dialog box

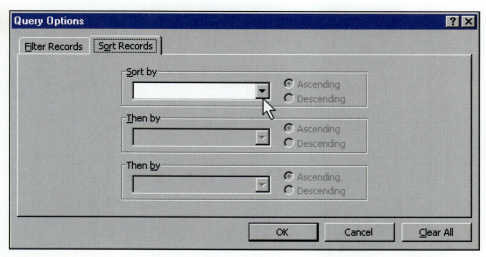

21. Select the field name to be used for sorting.

    For example, scroll down the list and select **PostalCode**.

22. Select the desired sort order, i.e., **Ascending** or **Descending**.

    For example, check that **Ascending** is selected. (If necessary, select **Ascending**.)

23. Select **OK**.

    Note: The hourglass may display briefly while the data records are being sorted.

24. Select **Merge**.

    Note: In a few moments the merged and sorted mailing labels display. Notice that the labels (reading from left to right) are arranged in ascending zip code order, i.e., 75206, 91600, 95123, 97210, 98121. Also notice that a bar code has been inserted at the top of each label.

Finish-Up Instructions

❖ Use the filename **12sorted labels1.doc** and save the label file on your file disk.

❖ Print one copy. If the printer pauses to allow you to insert labels, press the necessary button(s) on the printer to begin printing. (Plain paper is OK.)

❖ Close all documents. Select **Yes** to save changes.

Create and Print a Single Label

Word provides the capability of printing a single label. Printing a single label is useful when a mailing label is needed for a large envelope, such as a 5" x 7" or 9" x 12" size envelope. The single label feature also enables you to create a label at an exact location on the label sheet.

The **Single Label** option is chosen in the Envelopes and Labels dialog box on the Labels tab. After an address is typed and the **Single Label** option is selected, a choice can be made about row and column location on the label sheet. For example, if the labels in the first two rows and the first column of the third row were previously used on a 3-column, 10-row label sheet, specify row 3, column 2, for the location at which the next label is to print.

Start-Up Instructions

❖ An empty document window should be displayed. If necessary, select the **New** button to obtain an empty document window.

 ## Print a Single Label

1. Select **Tools, Envelopes and Labels**.

   *Note: The Labels tab should be displayed. (If necessary, select the **Labels** tab.)*

2. In the Address box, type the desired mailing address.

For example, type:

Mr. Whitaker Jones
TCX Entertainment Company
7001 West Jefferson Blvd.
Los Angeles, CA 90016

3. Select the **Options** button.

4. Select the Printer information and Product number.

   For example, *if using a dot matrix printer,* select **Dot matrix** and choose the **4144 - Address** product number. *If using a laser or ink jet printer,* select **Laser and ink jet** and choose the **5160 - Address** product number.

5. Select **OK**.

6. In the Print area at the bottom of the dialog box, select **Single Label**.

7. In the Print area, select the desired row location where the label is to be printed on the form.

   For example, click on the up arrow beside Row until **3** displays.

8. In the Print area, select the desired column location where the label is to be printed on the form.

   For example, check that **2** displays in the Column box. (If necessary, click on the up or down arrow until the **2** displays.)

9. Select the **Print** button.

   Note: Using plain paper is OK. If necessary, activate your printer by pressing the appropriate button. The address prints on the label form in the row and column specified.

Finish-Up Instructions

❖ If necessary, close the document window. Do not save the document

The Next Step

Chapter Review and Activities

Self-Check Quiz

T F 1. Self-adhesive mailing labels are removed from their backing paper and placed on envelopes.

T F 2. When using Envelope Options, fonts can be changed for the delivery address but not for the return address.

T F 3. When typing information in a mailing label using a predefined label format, the **Tab** key is pressed to move to the next label.

T F 4. The letter address must be selected *before* **Tools, Envelopes and Labels** is chosen.

T F 5. The records of a data source file can only be sorted by the city name.

6. U.S. Postal Service regulations request that mailing addresses be printed with _____.
   a. line spacing of one
   b. line spacing of two
   c. indented lines
   d. italic characters

7. The _____ button in the Envelopes tab of the Envelopes and Labels dialog box is selected to change the position of the return or delivery address.
   a. **Add to Document**
   b. **Options**
   c. **Print**
   d. none of the above

8. A standard large business envelope is referred to as a No. _____ envelope.
   a. 6
   b. 8
   c. 10
   d. 12

9. List two occasions when only a single label would need to be printed.

10. List one reason for printing the Delivery point barcode with envelopes or mailing label addresses.

Enriching Language Arts Skills

Spelling/Vocabulary Words

acknowledgment—confirmation; acceptance.
construe—understood; comprehended; explained.
contingent—dependent on or conditioned by something else.
physician—a doctor of medicine.

Subject-Verb Agreement

Verbs must agree in number with their subjects. If a subject is singular (one), use a singular verb; if a subject is plural (more than one), use a plural verb.
Examples:

Laurel and Sharee are co-owners of the condominium.

Our president, as well as all staff members, is looking forward to developing good relationships with new clients.

To determine if a subject and verb are in agreement, omit the words between the subject and verb.

Examples:

*The **legs** of the chair **were** damaged.*
    *(The **legs were** damaged.)*

***Gerald**, together with his two daughters, **is** to arrive on an evening flight.*
    *(**Gerald is** to arrive on an evening flight.)*

Activities

Activity 12.1—Create Mailing Labels for Different Addresses

1. Select **Tools, Envelopes and Labels**. The **Labels** tab should be selected.

2. Use the following information to select the desired label.

    a. On the Labels card, select **Options**.

        If using a dot matrix printer, select the **4144 - Address** Product number.

        If using a laser or ink jet printer, select the **5160 - Address** Product number.

    b. Select **OK, New Document**.

    c. Select all labels and set the spacing before the paragraphs to **6 pt**. (**Ctrl** and **a**; select **Format, Paragraph**; click in the **Left** indentation box and type **.25**; and select **OK**).

3. Click in the first label. Type the following names and addresses in uppercase letters with no punctuation. Press **Shift** and **Enter** after each line as shown and press the **Tab** key once or twice after each zip code.

MR DUANE AMOON (**Shift** and **Enter**)
580 PASE ROAD (**Shift** and **Enter**)
BOSTON MA 02154 (**Tab** once or twice)

MS SYLVIA QUARK (**Shift** and **Enter**)
2115 DOLORES STREET #9 (**Shift** and **Enter**)
GARDEN CITY KS 67846 (**Tab** once or twice)

MR IRVIN BOTELHO (**Shift** and **Enter**)
68 NORRIS PLACE (**Shift** and **Enter**)
DETROIT MI 48220 (**Tab** once or twice)

MRS CINDY YEN (**Shift** and **Enter**)
400 VIA ARRIBA DRIVE (**Shift** and **Enter**)
MOREHEAD KY 40351 (**Tab** once or twice)

MS HEATHER JEUNG (**Shift** and **Enter**)
302 SKYLARK ROAD (**Shift** and **Enter**)
ROCKVILLE IL 61111

---

*Note: It is not necessary to press the **Tab** key after the last zip code.*

4. Use the filename **12addresses.doc** and save the address labels on your file disk.

5. Print the address labels.

6. Optional: Fax these labels to your instructor via a local fax, or write an e-mail message to your instructor that you are sending this assignment. Attach this file to your e-mail message.

7. Close the document.

Activity 12.2—Create and Sort Mailing Labels Using a New Main Document and an Existing Data Source File

*Note: The file named **11Club Data.doc** created in Chapter 11, Activity 11.1, must be completed and available on your file disk.*

1. Use the following information to create and sort mailing labels:

   a. An empty document window should be displayed. If necessary, select the **New** button to obtain an empty document window.

   b. Select **Tools**, **Mail Merge**, choose **Create**, **Mailing Labels**.

   c. Select **New Main Document**, **Get Data**, **Open Data Source**.

   d. Double-click on the file named **11Club Data.doc**.

   e. Select **Set Up Main Document**, choose your printer type, i.e., dot matrix or laser/ink jet.

   f. Select the Product number. *If using a dot matrix printer,* choose **4605 - Address**. *If using a laser or ink jet printer,* choose **5261 - Address**.

   g. Select **OK** and choose the **Insert Merge Field** button; select the desired field names using the following format:

   «Title» «FirstName» «LastName»
   «Address1»
   «City», «State» «PostalCode»

   h. Select **OK**, choose **Edit** in the Main document area, select **Mailing Label: . . .** , click on the **Save** button and type the filename **12Club Label Main.doc**.

   i. Select the **Merge...** button; select **Query Options**.

   j. Select the **Sort Records** tab, select the down triangle beside the **Sort by** box, choose **LastName**, **Ascending** order, select **OK**.

     k.   Merge the main document **12Club Label Main.doc** and the data source file **11Club Data.doc** (select **Merge**).

2. Use the filename **12Finished Labels.doc** and save the labels on your file disk.

3. Print one copy. Close all documents. Select **Yes** to save changes.

Activity 12.3—Create an Envelope Address from a Letter

1. Type the following letter:

(Use current date)

Mr. Bolivar C. Vasquez
832 Wright Road
Ashland, OR 97520

Dear Mr. Vasquez:

The probate procedure is now complete in the case of Mrs. Francisca Vasquez. We enclose copies of the final documents for your records.

A check in the amount of $3,565 is enclosed for your fees as the personal representative of this estate.

It has been a pleasure to assist you with this matter. If I can be of additional assistance in the future, please contact me.

Sincerely,

Lorelei T. Snelling
Attorney at Law

LTS/xx
12vasquez.doc/diskp

Enc.

---

2. Use the filename **12vasquez.doc** and save the file.

3. Create an envelope address (select the **Tools, Envelopes and Labels**; if necessary, select the **Envelopes** tab).

4. Check that the delivery address is correct.

5. Click or select all lines in the **Return Address** box; type your name and address.

6. Select the **Options** button; select the **Delivery point barcode** option.

7. Check that **Size 10 (4⅛ x 9½ in)** displays in the Envelope size box.

8. Change the font size for the delivery address (select the Delivery address **Font** button; double-click in the **Size** box, type **13**, select **OK** twice).

9. Place the envelope information at the beginning of the letter (select **Add to Document**). Do not save the new return address as the default return address (select **No**).

10. View the envelope (select the **Print Preview** button, select **Close**).

11. With the insertion point in the page (section) where the envelope appears, print the envelope (select **File**, **Print**, **Current Page**, **OK**).

12. Use the *new* filename **12vasquez with env.doc** and save the file on your file disk.

13. Close the document.

Challenge Your Skills

Skill 12.1—Create a Full Page of the Same Mailing Label; Create a Single Mailing Label

Part I

1. Create a full page of the same mailing label. Make decisions regarding:

   Printer information
   Product number for a 2- or 3-column label form

2. Type the following address:

   Nanette Kiane DePasquale
   United Fiber, Inc.
   5555 Thunderwood Avenue
   Hollywood, CA 90038-3197

3. Use the filename **12nanette.doc** and save the file on your file disk.

4. Print the page of labels.

5. Close any open document window(s).

Part II

1. Create a single label and make decisions regarding:

   Printer information
   Product number for a 2- or 3-column label form
   Print the label in column 2, row 3

2. Type the following address:

   Mr. Joel M. Agyekum
   Courtyard Appraisal Company
   1023 Commerce Blvd.
   Marietta, GA 30060

3. Print the single label.

4. Close any open document window(s).

Skill 12.2—Create Mailing Labels for Different Addresses

1. Use the Product number **4605** (dot matrix) or Product number **5662** (laser or ink jet) and create a label file. Set the spacing before paragraphs to **6 pt**. Type the following information.

JOHN R CREVELING
HUMAN RESOURCES
MANAGER
1330 PICKERING PLACE
LAKEWOOD CO 80226

ANA EKSTER
VICE PRESIDENT
COMPUDATA
460 MATTOS AVENUE
WESTERBURY NY 11590

THELMA MADANSKI
SKYWEST PUBLIC GOLF
COURSE
P O BOX 668
LAKE CITY FL 32056

D L HAZARI
ENVIRONMENTAL AUTO BODY
6534 WARM SPRINGS AVENUE
FT COLLINS CO 80525

RICARDO LARCHE
123 CHAPEL TERRACE
NEW CITY NY 10956

PAULA KURTZ
P O BOX 6995
NASHVILLE TN 37221

KUN S HAO
BUDGET DIRECTOR
AGORRA RENTAL AGENCY
445 S SKYWEST AVENUE
LOS ANGELES CA 90071

KENT DUDLEY
HUMAN RESOURCES
DIRECTOR
160-20 91ST STREET
HOWARD BEACH NY 11414

SABRA PESSANO
55 WYCOMBE STREET
ST PAUL MN 55102

2. Select all labels, choose a font of your choice, and use a 12-point size.

3. Use the filename **12skill2 Labels.doc** and save the file.

4. Print the mailing labels.

5. Optional: Fax these labels to your instructor via a local fax, or write an e-mail message to your instructor that you are sending this assignment. Attach this file to your e-mail message.

6. Close the document.

❖ Skill 12.3—Create a Main Document, Data Source File, and Mailing Labels; Language Arts

1. Use the Mail Merge Helper to create the data source file and main document. Use an appropriate filename for the data source file.

2. In the Create Data Source dialog box, determine the field names needed and remove the field names that are not needed.

3. Use the following variable information to create the data source file:

Mr. Avelino Ray
82 Greenhaven Road
Lee Summit, MO 64063
Grade 8
$12.50

Ms. Arlene Phelan
408 Mohr Lane
St. Louis, MO 63113
Grade 7
$11.60

Mr. Yoshi Takayanagi
1401 La Mesa Place, #210
Cape Girardeau, MO 63701
Grade 5
$9.45

Mrs. Rebecca Sylvester
One Langhorn, Apt. 7
Sedalia, MO 65301
Grade 7
$15.80

4. Use the traditional block style letter to create the main document. Make decisions regarding:

    Margins
    Alignment
    Fonts
    Reference initials
    Filename for main document
    Document identification
    Enclosure notation

5. Correct four spelling errors, two misused words, one punctuation error, and one grammar error.

Date

{Inside
address
fields}

Dear {salutation fields}:

I am pleased to confirm our offer too you to join Mark Twain Regional Investment Company.

You will be working in the Telecommunications Department. Your position will be a Customer Service Representative, {gradenumber field}, with an hourly salary of {payrate field}.

Your employment is contingant upon your passing a physical examination conducted by a phycisian designated by Mark Twain. The Human Resources Department will make arrangements for the physical and will notify you and your supervisor of the scheduled appointment time. Failure to take this physical exam will be consrued as resignation from your position.

Two documents, *Working at Mark Twain Regional Investment Company* and the *Employment Agreement*, is enclosed with this letter. These provide a summary of provisions regarding your employment with Mark Twain. Please read both of these documents carefully. On your first day of work, you will be asked to sign the aknowledgment form contained in the *Working at Mark Twain Regional Investment Company* document, as well as the *Employment Agreement*, ensuring that you have received copies and agree to adhere to there terms.

I look forward to your joining our team at Mark Twain Regional Investment Company. If you have questions concerning your employment please call me at 804-555-8020.

Sincerely,

T. Paul Thanos
Human Resources Director

6. Merge the main document and data source file to create a personalized letter for each new employee.

7. Optional: Print the merged letters.

8. Create mailing labels for each new employee (create a new main document—you determine an appropriate Product number to be used with your printer). Save the label main document using an appropriate filename.

9. Merge the data source file and new main document to create a mailing label for each new employee.

10. Print the mailing labels.

11. Close all documents.

Part 3
Checking Your Step

Production Project 3.1—Copy Text Between Document Windows to Create Personalized Letters and Envelopes

1. Create a document that contains the following standard paragraphs:

Invest WorldWide Fund

The Invest WorldWide Fund provides stability by spreading your investment across international markets. This fund is well structured to respond to changing market conditions. Investors with a long-term investment outlook will benefit from the fund's high degree of stability and current income. This fund provides monthly distribution of dividends.

Tax-Free Bond Fund

This fund provides a tax-free shelter for long-term investments. Although the return is lower, the capital risk is minimal. All investments are made in municipal bonds.

Current Stock Fund

The Current Stock Fund provides an avenue for the smaller investor to participate in the stock market. Funds can be transferred into and out of this fund without penalty or fee, making this a great short-term investment instrument with high potential return.

Environment Series

The Environment Series provides for investment in the securities of companies that meet specific environmental protection criteria. This fund enables investors to support companies that promote environmentally safe products and services. Although earnings tend to be slightly lower than some other funds, the Environment Series has proven itself as a steady growth investment for environmentally conscious investors.

2. Use the filename **3Standard funds.doc** and save the standard paragraphs document.

3. Use the following information and the standard paragraphs document to create personalized letters for the following individuals:

    a. Ms. Sabrina Epperson
       5881 Munras Avenue
       Tucson, AZ 85715-0118
       Ms. Epperson is interested in investments that provide high current income.

    b. Ms. Rosa Maria Felice
       98 Plumtree Drive
       Morgan Hill, CA 95037-7567
       Ms. Felice is interested in investing in environmentally conscious companies.

    c. Mr. and Mrs. James R. Falconi
       4848 McMahan Road
       Charleston, SC 29403-8005
       Mr. and Mrs. Falconi are interested in investing in a fund that provides a tax shelter for long-term investments.

    d. Mr. Kyle Abrego, Jr.
       6035 Good Hope Road, #8
       Milwaukee, WI 53223-0652
       Mr. Abrego is interested in a short-term investment with high potential earnings.

    e. The letters are from Gabriela Hale, Investment Planner.

    f. Make decisions regarding:

       Letter style
       Margins
       Alignment
       Fonts
       Which investment fund description to be copied into each letter
       Reference initials/document identification/enclosure notation
       Filename for saving each letter

    g. The body text of the letter follows:

       Thank you for contacting Hale Investment Planning regarding investment programs. Below is a brief description of a program I feel, based on our conversation, will meet your investment needs.

> Copy the investment fund description that addresses each individual's interest from the file named **3Standard funds.doc**.

Please call me after you have reviewed the enclosed brochure about the fund. I will be happy to answer any additional questions you may have and to assist you with your investment strategy.

4. Create an envelope for each letter.

5. Save each letter on your file disk. Use filenames of your choice.

6. Print one copy of each letter.

7. Close all documents.

Production Project 3.2—Format a Multi-Page Report with a Footnote and Page Numbering; Use the Thesaurus

1. Open the report with the filename **3pact2.doc** located on the data disk.

2. Make decisions regarding:

> Margins
> Justification
> Fonts
> Widow/Orphan control
> Spacing before and after sideheads
> Bold/underline/capitalization of title and sideheads
> Possible replacement words from the Thesaurus for double-underlined words
> Page numbering using the Page Number feature
> Page number position on the page

3. Use the following information to create a footnote:

   a. Place the footnote reference after the period in the last sentence of the document.

   b. Footnote text: **Plan of Cooperative Ownership, Book 1, 1992, pp. 95–96.**

4. Use the *new* filename **3Agreement.doc** and save the file.

5. Print one copy.

6. Optional: Fax this document to your instructor via a local fax, or write an e-mail message to your instructor that you are sending this assignment. Attach this file to your e-mail message.

7. Close the document.

Production Project 3.3—Create and Merge a Main Document and Data Source File; Create and Sort Mailing Labels

1. Use the Mail Merge Helper to create the data source file and main document. Use an appropriate name for the data source file.

2. In the Create Data Source dialog box, determine the field names needed, removing the field names that are not needed.

3. Use the following addresses to create the data source file:

Mrs. Darlene Marx
Oakwood Terrace
85 E. Hawkins Street, #10
Columbus, OH 43215-3008
Location:
    Robert Righetti, Inc.
    306 Arlington Blvd.
    Columbus, OH
Phone Inquiry: 614-555-5665

Mr. Buck Chilton
Busenbury Place
600 Blyon Court, Apt. 4
Tulsa, OK 74119-9101
Location:
    Bradley Archer
    3066 Fourth Street
    Tulsa, OK
Phone Inquiry: 918-555-6306

Mr. Howard J. Smith
505 Enterprise Street
Cincinnati, OH 45240-0150
Location:
    Theodore McKee, Inc.
    1010 Wright Blvd.
    Cincinnati, OH
Phone Inquiry: 513-555-5999

Ms. Susan F. Cling
4805 Williams Avenue
Tulsa, OK 74119-3036
Location:
    Bradley Archer
    3066 Fourth Street
    Tulsa, OK
Phone Inquiry: 918-555-6306

4. Use the traditional block style letter to create the main document. Make decisions regarding:

    Margins
    Justification
    Fonts
    Placement of merge field codes
    Reference initials/document identification/enclosure notation

---

(Insert the date as a field)

(Inside address fields)

Dear (salutation fields):

It is our pleasure to inform you that you have been selected to participate in a very special Market Test Sale to be held next month in (use field names for city and state). The purpose of this special event is to judge the public's acceptance of One Price Sales. Over 250 new Dodge, Ford, Cadillac, and Nissan models will be tagged with their suggested retail price and a Maximum Final Discount price.

Shopping for a new car or truck will never be easier. Sales personnel have been instructed to assist all shoppers in locating the right vehicle for their needs without negotiating price. There will be no surprises.

This One Price Sale will last until the end of next week at the following location:

Location: (use field names for location)

Phone Inquiries: (use field name)

In addition to the new models, a large selection of demonstrators, rental returns, and used cars and trucks will be drastically discounted for immediate sale. All vehicles will be specially marked for this sale.

This invitation is being made exclusively to you. Remember, there is absolutely no reason to wait for lower prices.

Sincerely,

Merle F. Rushing
Marketing Research Director

---

5. Use the filename **3Market Test.doc** and save the file.

6. Merge the letter main document and the data source file to create personalized letters.

7. Print one copy of each letter and close all documents.

8. Create a 2- or 3-column label main document. Select an appropriate label for your printer. The labels should include the postal bar code.

9. Use the filename **3Market Test Labels.doc** and save the label main document.

10. Merge the label main document and the data source file to create a mailing label for each recipient. Print one copy of the mailing labels.

11. Close all documents.

✦ ■ Production Project 3.4—Create a Document; Use Shrink to Fit; Language Arts

1. Open the file named **3Right.doc** located on the data disk.

2. Make decisions regarding:

    Margins
    Alignment
    Fonts
    Spacing above and below sideheads and body text paragraphs

3. Correct two spelling errors, two misused words, five punctuation/grammar errors, and two number errors.

4. Use Print Preview and determine whether it is appropriate to use the Shrink to Fit feature to place all the document text on one page.

---

5. If the document will be printed on two pages, create an appropriate header and footer.

6. Use a *new* filename of your choice and save the file on your file disk.

7. Print one copy.

8. Optional: Fax this document to your instructor via a local fax, or write an e-mail message to your instructor that you are sending this assignment. Attach this file to your e-mail message.

9. Close the document.

Part 4
A Step Ahead

Advanced Documents and Features

Chapters 13–16

- Create border lines
- Insert a picture (graphic image)
- Size and position graphic images
- Create page borders
- Use the AutoShapes feature
- Create WordArt
- Create a watermark
- Insert text into an AutoShape
- Kern text and change character spacing
- Set exact line spacing
- Use AutoText
- Use the Spike
- Create superscripts, subscripts, ordinals, and fractions
- Sort text alphabetically or by date
- Use AutoFormat

- Edit, create, and apply styles
- Use existing templates to create new templates
- Record and play macros
- Arrange, maximize, minimize, move, restore, and resize document windows
- Create, revise, and print summary information
- Use and Find Files feature
- Print multiple files, copy, move, rename, and delete files
- Use the Favorites feature
- Create folders and convert files
- Assign a password
- Use DOS without exiting Word
- Cancel the printing of documents

Create a Flier, Letterhead, and Newsletter

Features Covered

- Create border lines
- Insert a picture (graphic image)
- Size, position, and change text wrap for graphic images
- Create page borders
- Use the AutoShapes feature
- Format AutoShapes
- Position and size a graphic image using the mouse
- Create WordArt
- Create a watermark

Objectives and Introduction

After successfully completing this chapter, you will be able to place border lines in a letterhead; retrieve, position, and size graphic images (pictures); and place borders around an entire page. You will also learn how to use the AutoShapes feature to insert pre-drawn shapes into a document. In addition, you will be able to use the WordArt feature to create interesting text effects and watermarks that repeat on each page of a document.

Word's graphic features are used to illustrate an idea by means of a picture (graphic image) or to present text or data in an interesting and appealing manner. In addition, horizontal and vertical graphic lines can be used to separate text to create a more pleasing appearance and assist with easier reading.

Word provides many graphic images that can be retrieved into a document. In addition, the Microsoft Clip Gallery, provided with Microsoft Word 2000, contains collections of graphic objects that can be inserted into your Word document.

Graphic images created by other graphic programs can also be retrieved into Word documents. These images must be saved in a format that can be interpreted by Word, such as **.pcx** (PC Paintbrush) or **.jpg** (Joint Photographic Experts Group).

Create a Letterhead
with Border Lines

A letterhead can be created using different fonts, point sizes, and borders. First, type the text for the letterhead unformatted, then select the fonts, point sizes, graphic lines, and alignment.

Use different fonts and point sizes as well as text attributes such as bold and italic. The placement of letterhead text can be changed by using the alignment options. Border lines can be placed above, below, or around the letterhead text to further enhance appearance.

Start-Up Instructions

❖   Open the file named **13drill1.doc** located on the data disk.

Create Border Lines

1. Place the insertion point at the location at which the border line should be inserted.

   For example, check that the insertion point is located in the line that contains the company name.

2. Select the **Tables and Borders** button ⊞ on the Standard Toolbar.

   Note: The Tables and Borders Toolbar displays.

3. Move the mouse pointer into the **Line Style** box [_____ ▾] and click once. Click on the desired line style.

   For example, click on the double-line border that has a thick top line and a thin bottom line.

Change the Color of Border Lines

4. Select the **Border Color** button 🖉 on the Tables and Borders Toolbar

   Note: A palette of colors displays.

5. Select the desired color.

   For example, select **Teal** or make a choice of your own.

6. Click on the down triangle beside the **Border** button 🔲▾ on the Tables and Borders Toolbar and select the desired border option.

   For example, click on the down triangle beside the **Border** button and choose the **Top Border** option.

   *Note: The name of the **Border** button changes depending on the last selected border position, e.g., Outside Border, Top Border, Inside Border. A double-line border displays above the text containing the insertion point.*

Finish-Up Instructions

❖ Locate the insertion point in the line containing the city, state, and zip.

FIGURE 13.1

Sample
letterhead with
border lines

Bayview Chiropractic Center

42 Bayview Street, Suite 4   Voice: (919) 555-8030
Newport, North Carolina 28570-3002   Fax: (919) 555-2588

❖ Click in the **Line Style** box [⎯⎯⎯⎯⎯⎯] on the Tables and Borders Toolbar. Scroll down and select the double-line border that has a thin top line and thick bottom line.

❖ Select the **Border Color** button and choose the color that matches the top border line inserted in step 5.

❖ Click on the down triangle beside the **Border** button and choose the **Bottom Border** option.

❖ Close the Tables and Borders Toolbar.

Note: Your letterhead should look similar to Figure 13.1.

❖ Use the *new* filename **13Letterhead.doc** and save the file.

❖ Print one copy and close the document.

Create a Flier with a Graphic Image

A flier created in Word can include border lines, graphic images, and text printed in different font styles and point sizes. (See Figure 13.4 on page 347.)

Once the flier text is typed, the text is formatted with the desired fonts, point sizes, alignment, and appearance. Border lines can be placed above, below, or around selected text or the entire page.

When a graphic image is inserted, small handles (boxes), often referred to as sizing handles, display at the edges and corners of the graphic image. These handles can be used to increase or decrease the size of the graphic image. (See Steps to Change the Size and Position of a Graphic Image Using the Mouse on page 352.)

Start-Up Instructions

❖ Open the file named **13drill2.doc** located on the data disk.

❖ Select the **Zoom** button and choose the **Whole Page** option.

Insert a Picture (Graphic Image)

1. With the insertion point at any location on the page, select **Insert, Picture**.

2. Select the source of the graphic image.

   For example, select **Clip Art.**

   Note: The Insert ClipArt dialog box displays (see Figure 13.2).

3. With the **Picture tab** forward, click on the folder containing the desired graphic image.

    For example, scroll down and click on the **Sports & Leisure** folder.

    Note: Several rows of ClipArt samples display.

4. Scroll through the samples and point to the desired picture, and click once.

    For example, point to the tennis picture and click once.

    Note: A pop-up window displays.

5. Click once on the **Insert clip** option to retrieve the selected graphic image. Select the **Close** button on the Insert Clip Art dialog box.

    Note: The tennis graphic image is placed in the document window. The image is very large but will be sized and positioned using the Steps to Size, Position, and Change the Text Wrap for a Graphic Image.

Finish-Up Instructions

❖ Use the *new* filename **13 Tennis flier.doc** and save the file on your file disk.

❖ Continue with the Steps to Size, Position, and Change the Text Wrap for a Graphic Image

Start-Up Instructions

❖ The file named **13 Tennis flier.doc** should be displayed in the document window.

Size and Change the Text Wrap and Position for a Graphic Image

1. Select the graphic image by moving the mouse pointer onto the graphic image and clicking once.

2. If necessary, right click the mouse button on the selected picture and choose **Show Picture Toolbar**.

FIGURE 13.2

Insert ClipArt dialog box

3. Select the **Format Picture** button 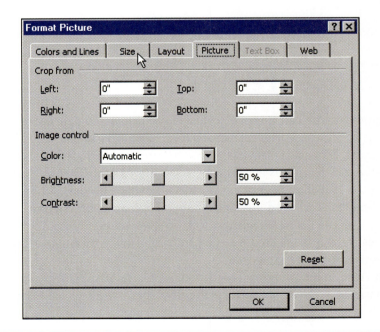 on the Picture Toolbar.

   Note: The Format Picture dialog box displays (see Figure 13.3).

Size the Graphic Image

4. Select the **Size** tab.

5. In the **Size and rotate** area, triple-click in the **Height** box and type the desired height.

   For example, type **2.5** in the **Height** box in the **Size and rotate** area.

   *Note: Because the **Lock aspect ratio** option is active (a check mark should be displayed beside this option), Word will automatically adjust the width of the graphic image when a new height is specified. The adjusted width will display if you click in the Width box. The Height and Width options in the Scale area will also be updated when a different height or width is specified.*

Change Text Wrap

6. Select the **Layout** tab.

7. In the **Wrapping** style area, select the desired wrapping style.

   For example, select **Tight**.

8. Select the desired Horizontal alignment option.

   For example, select **Left**.

9. Select **OK**.

Position the Graphic Image

10. With the graphic selected, point, click, and hold the mouse while dragging the graphic down to the right of the where, when, etc. lines.

FIGURE 13.3

Format Picture
dialog box

Finish-Up Instructions

❖ Click once outside of the graphic image.

❖ Use the same filename, **13 Tennis flier.doc**, and save the file.

❖ Continue with the Steps to Create a Page Border.

Start-Up Instructions

❖ The file named **13 Tennis flier.doc** should be displayed in the document window.

Create a Page Border

1. Place the insertion point at any location on the page.

2. Select **Format, Borders and Shading.**

   Note: The Borders and Shading dialog box displays.

3. Select the **Page Border** tab.

4. Select the desired Setting option.

   For example, select the **Box** setting option.

5. Select the desired **Style, Color, Width,** or **Art** for the border.

   For example, click in the **Art** box. Scroll down and select the border art.

6. Select **OK.**

Finish-Up Instructions

❖ Replace the year with the current year.

❖ Use the same filename, **13 Tennis flier.doc**, and save the file.

   Note: Your flier should look similar to the flier shown in Figure 13.4.

❖ Print one copy and close the document.

Use the AutoShapes Feature

The AutoShapes feature can be used to insert pre-drawn shapes into a document. There are seven categories of AutoShapes: Lines, Basic Shapes, Block Arrows, Flowchart, Stars and Banners, Callouts, and More Shapes.

The AutoShapes feature is accessed by selecting **Insert, Picture, AutoShapes** or by selecting the **AutoShapes** button on the Drawing Toolbar. When **Insert, Picture, AutoShapes** is selected, an AutoShapes Toolbar displays containing the buttons for each of the seven categories of AutoShapes (see Figure 13.5). When the **AutoShapes** button is selected on the Drawing Toolbar, a menu displays showing the seven different categories.

When an AutoShape category is selected, a palette of shapes displays. Select the desired shape and draw the shape in the document window. The format (size,

FIGURE 13.4

Flier with
graphic image

Fourth Annual Tennis Tournament

WHERE: Ridgemark Resort

WHEN: June 15, 1999
        8:00 a.m.

COST: $35 per person

SIGN-UP: In the Clubroom

Singles   ❋   Doubles   ❋   Mixed Doubles
Juniors   ❋   Seniors

Special Exhibition Match Starring Tennis Legends
Andrea McGee and Billie Jean Ashe

Awards Dinner to follow in the Elegant Tuscany Dining Room

Proceeds to Benefit West Valley High School Athletics Department

position, color, and text wrap) of the drawn shape can be modified. To modify the AutoShape format, move the mouse pointer into the Autoshape, click the *right* mouse button and choose **Format AutoShape.** To use the Menu bar, select **Format, AutoShape.**

If text is desired within the AutoShape, Word can automatically add a text box that fits the shape of the AutoShape. To add text, move the mouse pointer into the AutoShape, click the *right* mouse button and choose **Add Text.**

Start-Up Instructions

❖ A new document window should be displayed. (If necessary, select the **New** button.)

❖ The Print Layout View should be selected. (If necessary, select the **Print Layout View** button.)

❖ Select the **Zoom** button and choose the **Whole Page** option.

Use AutoShapes

1. Select **Insert, Picture, AutoShapes**.

   Note: The AutoShapes Toolbar displays in the document window, and the Drawing Toolbar displays at the top of the document window.

2. Select the desired AutoShapes category button on the AutoShapes Toolbar.

   For example, select the **Basic Shapes** button ▣.

   Note: A palette of shapes displays.

3. Click on the desired shape.

   For example, click on the **Heart** shape (sixth row, first column).

4. Move the mouse pointer onto the page.

   Note: The mouse pointer is a crosshair.

5. Press and hold the mouse button and drag down and to the right until the shape reaches the desired size. Release the mouse button.

   For example, with the mouse pointer located at the top left margin, press and hold the mouse button and drag down and to the right until the Heart shape almost fills the page. Release the mouse button.

   Note: The exact size is not important at this time. We will size the shape in the next several steps.

Size the AutoShape

6. With the AutoShape selected, move the mouse pointer into the AutoShape.

7. Click the *right* mouse button and select **Format AutoShape**.

   Note: The Format AutoShape dialog box displays.

8. Select the **Size** tab.

9. In the **Size and rotate** area, set the desired **Height** and **Width** for the AutoShape.

   For example, triple-click in the **Height** box and type **7.5**. (Do not type the final period.) Triple-click in the **Width** box and type **6**. (Do not type the final period.)

   Note: The Lock aspect ratio option is turned off so you can set the height and width of the AutoShape independently.

FIGURE 13.5

AutoShapes Toolbar

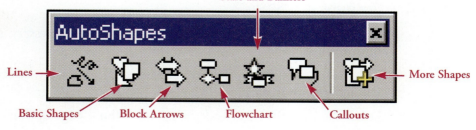

Lay Out the AutoShape

10. In the Format AutoShape dialog box, select the **Layout** tab.

11. Set the desired Wrapping style for the AutoShape.

    For example,

    a. Check that the **In Front of** text option is selected. (If necessary, click on the **In Front** of text option.)

    b. In the **Horizontal** alignment area, select **Center**.

Change the Color of the AutoShape

12. In the Format AutoShape dialog box, select the **Colors and Lines** tab.

13. To change the line color, click in the **Color** box in the **Line** area and select the desired color.

    For example, click in the **Color** box in the **Line** area and select the **Red** color button.

14. To change the style of the AutoShape line, click in the **Style** box in the **Line** area and select the desired style.

    For example, click in the **Style** box in the **Line** area and select the **6 pt** solid line style.

15. Select **OK** to select the Format AutoShape dialog box.

Add Text to the AutoShape

16. With the AutoShape selected and the mouse pointer on the AutoShape, click the *right* mouse button.

    *Note: A shortcut menu displays containing an **Add Text** option. If there is no Add Text option on the shortcut menu, click once to remove the menu, click once on the AutoShape, and then click the* right *mouse button again. The Add Text option is available only when the AutoShape is selected* before *clicking the* right *mouse button.*

17. Select the **Add Text** option.

    *Note: A gray border displays around the outside of the AutoShape. Select the **Zoom** button and choose **75%** so that you can see the text as you type.*

18. Type and format the desired text.

    For example, type and format the text similar to Figure 13.6.

Finish-Up Instructions

❖ Add a page border (select **Format, Borders and Shading**, click on the **Page Border** tab, select the Box setting, click in the **Art** box, scroll down and click on the red hearts border, select **OK**).

❖ Select the **Zoom** button and click on **Whole Page** option.

❖ If necessary, click on the heart and drag it to the approximate center of the page.

❖ Close the AutoShapes Toolbar.

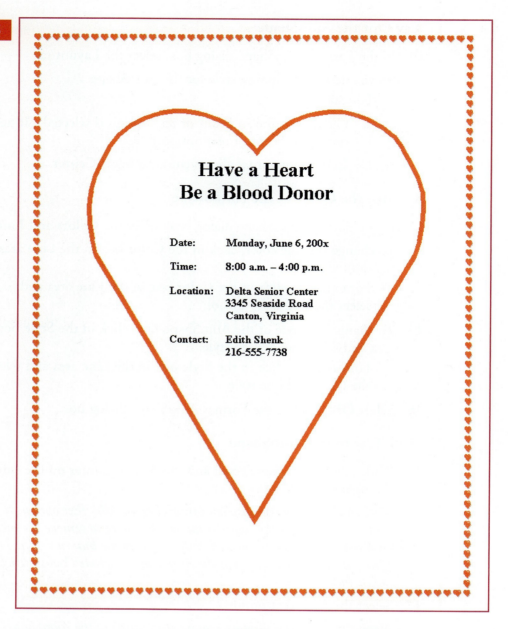

FIGURE 13.6

Flier created using an AutoShape

**Have a Heart
Be a Blood Donor**

Date: Monday, June 6, 200x

Time: 8:00 a.m. – 4:00 p.m.

Location: Delta Senior Center
             3345 Seaside Road
             Canton, Virginia

Contact: Edith Shenk
             216-555-7738

❖ If desired, select the **Drawing** button ▥ on the Standard Toolbar to remove the Drawing Toolbar.

❖ Use the filename **13Hearts.doc** and save the file on your file disk.

❖ Print one copy. Close the document.

Create a Newsletter

A typical newsletter includes text columns, graphics, and borders. Different fonts and point sizes can be used for the newsletter text (see Figure 13.9). A newsletter usually contains several sections with different formats. For example, a newsletter may have a section with a one-column format that contains the title, subtitle, and issue date and a second section with a multi-column format that contains the newsletter text and graphic images.

A border can be placed around the newsletter title, subtitle, and issue date to create a nameplate. Shading can be added to enhance the nameplate.

The **Columns** button on the Standard Toolbar can be used to specify the desired number of columns for the newsletter body text. (See Chapter 8, Steps to Create Newspaper-Style Columns on page 205.)

Graphic images (pictures) can be placed in the document to add visual appeal. When a graphic image is inserted, the image can be positioned relative to the edge of the page or the margins. When a graphic image is selected and non-printing symbols are turned on, an anchor displays to the left of the paragraph that is closest to the graphic image. If the graphic image is moved, the anchor will relocate to the left of the paragraph closest to the graphic image's new location.

A mouse can be used to change the position and/or size of a graphic image. To use the mouse to position or size a graphic image, the graphic image must be selected. To select a graphic image, move the mouse pointer into the graphic image and click once. When selected, a border with small handles (boxes) displays around the graphic image. A selected graphic image can be deleted by pressing the **Delete** key.

Start-Up Instructions

❖ Open the file named **13drill4.doc** located on the data disk.

Steps to Create a Newsletter Nameplate

1. Type or select the text to be the newsletter nameplate.

   For example, select the first three lines of text.

Add a Border

2. Select the **Tables and Borders** button ▦ on the Standard Toolbar.

   Note: The Tables and Borders Toolbar displays.

3. To select the desired line style, move the mouse pointer to the **Line Style** box ▭▾ and click once. Click on the desired line style.

   For example, click on the first double-line style.

4. To change the thickness of the line, click in the **Line Weight** box ½▾ on the Tables and Borders Toolbar and select the desired line thickness.

   For example, click in the **Line Weight** box ½▾ and select 1½ pt.

5. To select the desired border placement, click on the down triangle beside the **Border** button ▢▾. Select the desired border placement button.

   For example, click on the down triangle beside the **Border** ▢▾ button and select the **Outside Border** button.

   Note: The selected text displays inside a double-line border.

Shade the Nameplate

6. Move the mouse pointer to the down triangle beside the **Shading Color** button on the Tables and Borders Toolbar and click once. Select the desired shading color.

   For example, click on the **Gray 15%** shading color (first row, fifth column).

Finish-Up Instructions

❖ Close the Tables and Borders Toolbar.

❖ To format the body text of the newsletter in two columns, select the text beginning with the heading "When Showing Your Home" to the end of the document. Select the **Columns** button on the Standard Toolbar and click on the second column.

❖ Click once to deselect the text.

❖ Use the *new* filename **13Newsletter.doc** and save the file on your file disk.

Start-Up Instructions

❖ The file named **13Newsletter.doc** should be displayed in the document window.

❖ The Print Layout View should be selected. (If necessary, select the **Print Layout View** button.)

❖ Place the insertion point beside the first heading, "When Showing Your Home." Select the **Zoom** button and choose the **Whole Page** option.

❖ Select **Insert**, **Picture**, **Clip Art**. Click on **Buildings**, click on **Inspectors**, select **Insert Clip**. Click on the **Close** button ☒ in the Insert ClipArt dialog box.

❖ Click once on the **inspectors** graphic image. Select the **Format Picture** button 🖾 on the Picture Toolbar.

   Note: If the Picture Toolbar is not displayed, click on the graphic image once. If necessary, move the mouse pointer onto the graphic image, click the right *mouse button, and select* **Show Picture Toolbar***.*

❖ On the **Format Picture**, **Layout** tab, select the **Square** option in the **Wrapping** Style area. Select **OK**.

   Note: Don't worry about the size and position of the graphic image. We will be adjusting the size and position using the following steps.

> **Steps to**

Change the Size and Position of a Graphic Image Using the Mouse

1. If necessary, click once on the graphic image to select it.

   Note: Small handles (boxes) display at the corners and edges of a selected graphic image.

Size an Image

2. Move the mouse pointer onto a handle at the corner or edge of the graphic image until a double-headed arrow displays. Press and hold the mouse button and drag to enlarge or reduce the size of the graphic image. Release the mouse button.

> For example, move the mouse pointer to the handle (small box) at the upper left corner of the graphic image until a double-headed arrow displays. Press and hold the mouse button and drag down and to the right until the arrow touches the left shoulder of the inspector. Release the mouse button.

Position a Graphic Image Using the Mouse

3. Move the mouse pointer into the graphic image until a four-headed arrow displays. Press and hold the mouse button and drag to the desired location. Release the mouse button.

> For example, move the mouse pointer into the graphic image to display a four-headed arrow. Press and hold the mouse button and drag until the graphic image is centered in the middle of the page. Release the mouse button. (See Figure 13.9.)

Finish-Up Instructions

❖ To contour the flow of text around the shape of the graphic image, select the **Format Picture** button ▨ on the Picture Toolbar. Choose the **Layout** tab and select the **Tight** option. Select **OK**.

❖ Move the mouse pointer away from the graphic image and click once to deselect the graphic image. Close the Picture Toolbar.

❖ Use the same filename, **13Newsletter.doc**, and save the file.

❖ Continue with the Steps to Create WordArt.

Create WordArt

Word provides a graphic feature called WordArt that is used to create text in special shapes such as circles, curves, and waves. The WordArt Gallery provides a palette of styles. After selecting a style and typing the desired WordArt text, the desired font, alignment, and color are chosen. A different style can also be specified by selecting the **WordArt Shape** or **WordArt Gallery** button on the WordArt Toolbar.

After the WordArt text is typed and the font and size are chosen, select **OK** in the Edit WordArt Text dialog box. The WordArt is then placed in a box in the document window and a WordArt Toolbar displays enabling you to make further changes to the WordArt. The box is sized by moving the mouse pointer onto the black handles displayed along edges and corners of the selected box, pressing the mouse button, then dragging the box. When the box reaches the desired size, release the mouse button. WordArt is positioned by moving the mouse pointer anywhere inside the box containing the WordArt, pressing and holding the mouse button, and dragging the box to the desired location. When the box is in the desired location, release the mouse button. WordArt can also be sized and positioned using the options on the **Size** and **Layout** tabs in the **Format WordArt** dialog box.

WordArt can be edited by moving the mouse pointer to the WordArt and double-clicking to display the WordArt Toolbar. Make changes as desired to the text, such as font, shape, and color. When the changes are complete, move the mouse pointer away from the WordArt and click once.

Start-Up Instructions

❖ The file named **13Newsletter.doc** should be displayed in the document window.

❖ If necessary, turn on nonprinting characters (select the **Show/Hide** button).

❖ If desired, use a **75% Zoom** view.

❖ Create a section with a one-column format at the end of the document. Scroll down to view the end of the document. Select the two blank lines (paragraph symbols) located at the end of the document. Select the **Columns** button and click on the first column.

❖ If desired, turn off nonprinting characters.

Create WordArt

1. Place the insertion point on the page where the WordArt is to be inserted.

   For example, place the insertion point on the second blank line at the end of the document.

2. Select **Insert, Picture, WordArt**.

   Note: The WordArt Gallery dialog box displays (see Figure 13.7).

3. Select the desired WordArt style.

   For example, select the fourth style on the first row.

4. Select **OK**.

   Note: The Edit WordArt Text dialog box displays containing the words "Your Text Here" (see Figure 13.8).

5. Type the desired text in the WordArt Text box.

   For example, type the following:

   Stacie McCandless (Press **Enter**.)
   Creating Moving Experiences (Press **Enter**.)
   For Buyers and Sellers (Do **not** press **Enter**.)

6. Click in the **Font** box and scroll through the list of font names. Click on the desired font.

   For example, click on **Cosmic Sans MS** or **make a font choice of your own**.

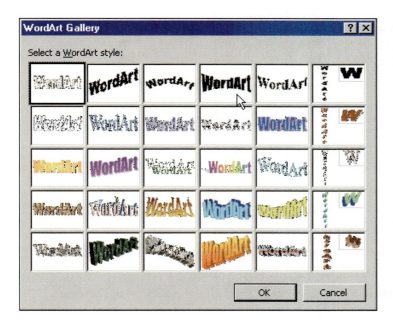

FIGURE 13.7

WordArt Gallery
dialog box

7. If desired, change the size of the WordArt text.

   For example, change the size of the WordArt text to **32**.

8. Select **OK** to exit the Edit WordArt Text dialog box.

   Note: The WordArt is placed in a box in the document window and a WordArt Toolbar displays. The buttons on the WordArt Toolbar are used to continue formatting the WordArt.

9. If necessary, move the WordArt Toolbar up above the WordArt. For example, click on the Title bar of the WordArt Toolbar and hold the mouse while dragging the Toolbar above the newly created WordArt.

10. To position the WordArt, move the mouse pointer onto the WordArt text until a four-headed arrow displays. Press and hold the mouse button and drag the WordArt to the desired location. Release the mouse button.

FIGURE 13.8

Edit WordArt
Text dialog box

For example, drag the WordArt down below the two columns of text on page 2 of the newsletter and release the mouse button.

Note: The WordArt must be selected to obtain the four-headed arrow. If the four-headed arrow does not display, click once on the WordArt.

11. To change the color of the WordArt text, select the **Format WordArt** button ⬜ on the WordArt Toolbar.

12. Select the **Colors and Lines** tab in the Format WordArt dialog box.

13. Click in the **Color** box in the **Fill** area and select the desired color.

    For example, click in the **Color** box in the **Fill** area and select a color of your choice.

14. Select **OK** to exit the Format WordArt dialog box.

15. To change the style or shape of the WordArt text, select the **WordArt Gallery** button ⬜ or the **Shapes** ⬜ button on the WordArt Toolbar.

    For example, if desired, use the **WordArt Gallery** ⬜ and **Shapes** ⬜ buttons to experiment with different styles and shapes.

Finish-Up Instructions

❖ Move the mouse pointer away from the WordArt text and click once to deselect the WordArt.

❖ Insert page numbers at the bottom center of both pages of the newsletter. (Select **Insert**, **Page Numbers**, click on the down arrow to the right of the **Alignment** box, and select **Center**. Select **OK**.)

Note: Your newsletter should look similar to the newsletter shown in Figure 13.9. The shape and style of your WordArt may be different depending on which style and shape you selected in step 15.

❖ If necessary, the graphic image on page 1 can be resized so the columns end on approximatly the same line.

❖ Use the *new* filename, **13Newsletter Final.doc**, and save the file.

❖ Print one copy.

Create a Watermark

A watermark is text or a graphic image that can be repeated on each page of a document. The watermark text or graphic image is printed in a light gray or light color on the page. Other text and/or images can be placed on top of the watermark image. In order for the watermark to display on more than one page of the document, the Header and Footer feature is used. The mouse can be used to size and position the watermark at any location on the page (see Steps to Change the Size and Position of a Graphic Image Using the Mouse on page 352).

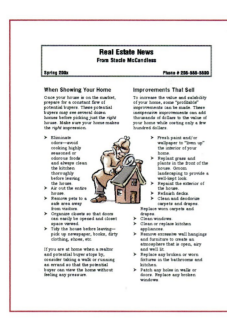

FIGURE 13.9

Final newsletter

To lighten the colors of a watermark graphic, select the **Image Control** button on the Picture Toolbar and choose the **Watermark** option. The Watermark Image Control option automatically changes the image to light colors or light gray. If the watermark includes text, select the text and change the font color to a light color or a light gray.

Start-Up Instructions

❖ Open the file named **13Letterhead.doc** created earlier in this chapter.

❖ The **Print Layout View** should be selected. (If necessary, select the **Print Layout View** button.)

❖ Move the mouse pointer to the down arrow located to the right of the **Zoom** button and click once. Select the **Whole Page** option.

Steps to Create a Watermark

1. Select **View, Header and Footer**.

    Note: The Header and Footer Toolbar displays, and the Header and Footer areas display at the top and bottom of the document window. If necessary, move the Header and Footer Toolbar so that center of the page is visible.

2. Type or insert the desired watermark text or graphic image.

    For example, select **Insert, Picture, Clip Art**. Click on the **Health and Medicine** category, click on **Chiropractors**, choose **Insert Clip**. Close the **Insert clip** dialog box.

    Note: The graphic image displays in the Header area.

Size the Watermark Graphic Image

3. Move the mouse pointer onto the graphic image and click once to select the image.

Note: If necessary, move the Picture Toolbar down and to the left. A thin black border with black boxes at the corners and edges displays around the graphic image.

4. Select the Format Picture button 🖼 on the Picture Toolbar.

   Note: If the Picture Toolbar is not displayed, move the mouse pointer onto the graphic image, click the right *mouse button, and select* **Show Picture Toolbar.**

5. Select the Size tab.

6. In the Size and rotate area, set the desired height and/or width.

   For example, triple-click in the **Height** box and type **2.5.**

7. Select the **Layout** tab. In the Wrapping style area, click on **Behind text**; click **OK.**

8. Close the Picture Toolbar.

Lighten the Watermark Graphic Image Color

9. On the Picture Toolbar, select the Image Control button ◳ and choose the Watermark option.

   Note: The image changes to a light-gray color.

Position the Watermark

10. To position the watermark, the graphic must be selected, i.e., small boxes display at the corners and edges of the border. If necessary, click on the graphic image.

11. With the four-headed arrow displayed, drag the watermark to the desired location on the page.

    For example, drag the watermark graphic image and visually center the image vertically and horizontally on the page.

12. Close the Header and Footer Toolbar.

    Note: The Picture Toolbar is removed from the screen when you close the Header and Footer Toolbar.

Finish-Up Instructions

❖ Use the *new* filename **13Watermark.doc** and save the file on your file disk.

❖ Print one copy.

❖ Close the document.

The Next Step

Chapter Review and Activities

Self-Check Quiz

T F 1. A graphic image can be inserted at the location of the insertion point in a document or in a box.

T F 2. Only a graphic image can be used as a watermark.

T F 3. Border lines can be placed above, below, or around a paragraph.

T F 4. A mouse can be used to size a graphic image, text box, or AutoShape.

T F 5. The vertical and horizontal positions of an AutoShape cannot be changed once the AutoShape has been drawn.

6. Which of the following is not an AutoShape category?
   a. Basic Shapes
   b. Circles
   c. Stars and Banners
   d. Block Arrows

7. The small handles (boxes) that display on the edges and corners of a graphic image _____.
   a. indicate that the graphic image is selected
   b. can be used to size the graphic image
   c. allow text to flow through a graphic box
   d. both a and b

8. WordArt is used to create text in special shapes such as _____.
   a. curves
   b. circles
   c. waves
   d. all of the above

9. Write down the name of the directory where Word's graphic files are stored on your system.

10. A text box or graphic image is selected when _____ display at the edges and corners of the frame or graphic image.

Enriching Language Arts Skills

Spelling/Vocabulary Words

anonymously—without a name.
appropriate—suitable for a certain occasion or use; fitting.
complaints—an expression of dissatisfaction or discontent.
coordinator—a person who manages and arranges tasks in the proper order.
detachable—being disconnected; removable.
prompt—punctual; arriving on time; immediate.

Initials Abbreviated

Periods or spaces are not placed after the letters of an acronym such as IRS (Internal Revenue Service) or TWA (TransWorld Airlines).

Examples:

Always remember to mail your tax return to the IRS by April 15.

St. Louis is a hub for TWA.

Activities

Activity 13.1—Create a Flier with a Graphic Image and Borders

1. Open the file named **13act1.doc** located on the data disk.

2. With the insertion point blinking at the top left of the first word, press the **Enter** key five times. Then press **Control** and **Home**. Select the **Zoom** button and choose the **Whole Page** option.

3. Insert the graphic image named **computers** at the top of the document. (With the insertion point located in the blank line at the top of the document, select **Insert, Picture, Clip Art**; click on **Science and Technology**; click on **computers**; select **Insert** clip: close the **Insert** ClipArt dialog box.)

4. Use the following information to size and position the graphic image:

   a. If necessary, move the mouse pointer into the graphic image and click once to select the image.

   b. If necessary, click the *right* mouse button and select the **Format Picture** option.

   c. Select the **Size** tab. In the **Size and rotate** area, triple-click in the **Height** box and type **1.75**.

   d. Select the **Layout** tab. Click on the **Tight** Wrapping style. Select the **Center** Horizontal alignment option.

   e. Select **OK**.

Recycle Your Computer—Swap It

Computer Swap Meet
Hardware, Software, & More!

Date: Saturday and Sunday, July 2 and 3

Time: 9:00 a.m. - 6:00 p.m.

Location: San Juan Center
                518 Main Street, Denver

Contact: Marlene Karrass at 303-555-3888

Buy, sell, and trade! There is something for everyone!

- Hard drives, keyboards, monitors, mice, and printers

- Trade all types of hardware including fiber optic cable

- Games, utilities, and all types of software

- New! Auction for used computer systems and selected software

Sponsored by the Denver Computer Users Group
For information call: 303-555-1100 or 1-800-555-SWAP

5. Use the following information to place a 1½ pt double-line border around the entire page.

    a.   Click outside the graphic image to locate the insertion point at any location on the page.

    b.   Select **Format, Borders and Shading**.

    c.   Select the **Page Border** tab.

    d.   Select the **Box** setting.

    e.   Click in the **Style** box. Scroll down and select the double-line border style.

f. Click in the **Color** box and **make a color choice of your own.**

g. Click in the **Width** box and select 1½ **pt.**

h. Select **OK.**

6. If necessary, delete the extra blank line at the bottom of the document so the document fits on one page.

7. Use the *new* filename **13Swap meet.doc** and save the file on your file disk.

8. Print one copy.

9. Optional: Fax the document to your instructor via a local fax machine, or write an e-mail message to your instructor that you are sending this assignment. Attach this file to your e-mail message.

10. Close the document

Activity 13.2—Create a Flier Using an AutoShape and a Page Border

1. In a new document window, change the left and right margins to 1". Select the **Zoom** button and select the **Whole Page** option.

2. Select **Insert, Picture, AutoShapes.**

3. Select the **Basic Shapes** button on the AutoShapes Toolbar. Select the **Octagon** button (second row, second column).

4. Move the mouse pointer onto the page and draw an octagon approximately **8"** high and **6.5"** wide.

5. Use the following information to format the octagon:

a. With the mouse pointer inside the octagon, click the *right* mouse button and choose the **Format AutoShape** option.

b. Select the **Colors and Lines** tab.

c. In the **Line** area, click in the **Color** box and select **Red.**

d. Click in the **Style** box and select the **6 pt** triple-line style.

e. Select the **Size** tab. In the **Size and rotate** area, set the **Height** to **8"** and the **Width** to **6.5".**

f. Select the **Layout** tab. Check that the **In front of text** option is selected. Click on **Center** in the **Horizontal** alignment area.

g. Select **OK.**

6. Use the following information to add text to the AutoShape:

a. With the mouse pointer inside the octagon, click the *right* mouse button and choose the **Add Text** option.

b. Type and format the text as shown in the flier on page 363.

7. Close the AutoShapes Toolbar.

8. Add the 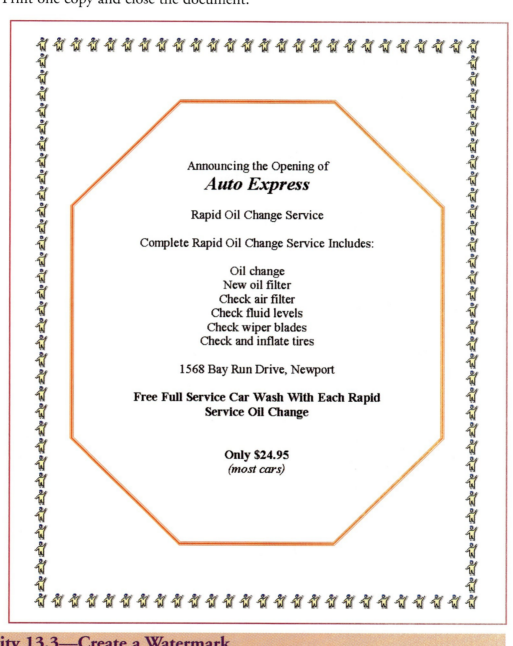 page border. (With the insertion point at any location on the page, select **Format**, **Borders and Shading**. Choose the **Page Border** tab. Select the **Box** setting. Click in the **Art** box. Scroll down and click on the border. Select **OK**.)

9. Use the filename **13Auto express.doc** and save the file on your file disk.

10. Print one copy and close the document.

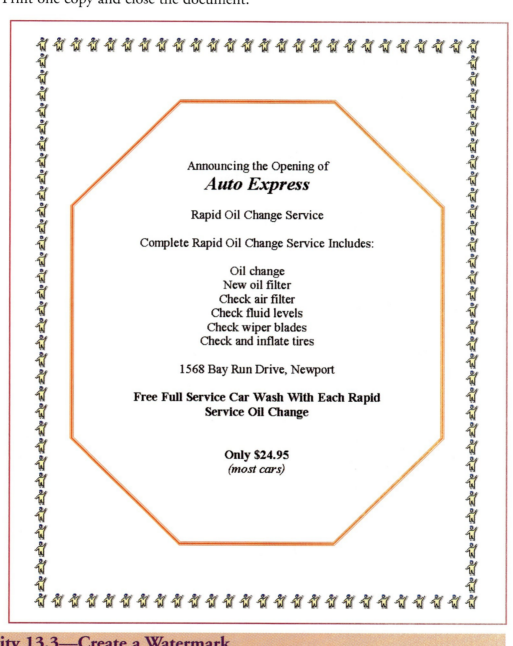

Announcing the Opening of
Auto Express

Rapid Oil Change Service

Complete Rapid Oil Change Service Includes:

Oil change
New oil filter
Check air filter
Check fluid levels
Check wiper blades
Check and inflate tires

1568 Bay Run Drive, Newport

**Free Full Service Car Wash With Each Rapid
Service Oil Change**

Only $24.95
(most cars)

🟪 Activity 13.3—Create a Watermark

1. Open the file named **13act3.doc** located on the data disk.

2. Create a watermark using the **Darts.wmf** graphic image.

    a. Select **View**, **Header and Footer**.

b. Select the **Zoom** button and choose the **Whole Page** option.

c. Select **Insert, Picture, Clip Art**. If necessary, click on the **Symbols, Ornaments, Insert Clip Art**. Close the Clip Art dialog box.

d. *Right*-mouse click on the graphic; select **Format Picture**. On the **Size** tab, triple-click in the **Height box**, and type **2.5**. Repeat for the width. Click on the **Layout** tab and select **Behind text, Center, Horizontal** alignment, **OK**.

e. Lighten the colors of the graphic image. (Click once on **Ornaments.wmf** graphic image. Select the **Image Control** button on the Picture Toolbar; select the **Watermark** option; **OK**.)

Note: If the Picture Toolbar is not displayed, click on the graphic image once, click the right *mouse button, and choose* **Show Picture Toolbar***.*

f. With the graphic selected, move the image to the middle of the page.

g. Select **Close** on the Header and Footer Toolbar.

3. Use the *new* filename **13Customer Service.doc** and save the file on your file disk.

4. Print one copy.

Note: Your document should look similar to the document shown below.

5. Optional: Fax the document to your instructor via a local fax machine, or write an e-mail message to your instructor that you are sending this assignment. Attach this file to your e-mail message.

6. Close the document.

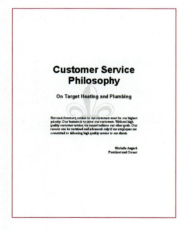

Challenge Your Skills

Skill 13.1—Create a Flier with Graphics

1. Use the following information and create a flier for the Summer Fishing Derby.

   a. The Fishing Derby will be held on July 12 in Vancouver, Washington.

   b. Prizes will be awarded for the largest fish caught. First Place Prize is $1,000; Second Place Prize is $500; and Third Place Prize is $250.

   c. The entry fee is $125.

   d. The contact person is Mabel Wyman (360) 555-6600. The Summer Fishing Derby is sponsored by the Vancouver Fishing Association.

   e. Create appropriate WordArt, or insert an appropriate ClipArt image of your choice.

   f. Make decisions regarding:

      Fonts and point sizes for flier text
      Position and size of graphic images/WordArt
      Page border

2. Use the filename **13Fishing derby.doc** and save the file on your file disk.

3. Print one copy.

4. Optional: Fax the document to your instructor via a local fax machine, or write an e-mail message to your instructor that you are sending this assignment. Attach this file to your e-mail message.

5. Close the document.

Skill 13.2—Create a Newsletter with Graphic Images and WordArt; Language Arts

1. Open the file named **13skill2.doc**. Use a two-column style similar to the one shown in Figure 13.9 to create the newsletter.

   a. Make decisions regarding:

      Fonts and point sizes (a 10- to 12-point size is recommended for the newsletter body text)
      Borders and shading for the newsletter nameplate
      Spacing between the border and nameplate text
      Alignment
      Hyphenation
      Widow/Orphan control

   b. Insert several ClipArt images to illustrate the information in the newsletter. (Suggested images are from the **Communications** or **People at Work** categories.)

c. If desired, create WordArt to enhance the newsletter.

2. Correct four spelling errors, three punctuation/grammatical errors, and two misused words.

3. Use the *new* filename **13Open Connect.doc** and save the file on your file disk.

4. Print one copy.

5. Close the document.

Create Documents Using Special Features

- Kern text and change character spacing
- Set exact line spacing
- Use AutoText
- Use the Spike
- Automatically create superscripts, subscripts, ordinals, and fractions

Objectives and Introduction

After successfully completing this chapter, you will be able to enhance the appearance of documents by using typesetting features such as kerning, character spacing, and setting an exact line spacing amount. You will also be able to use the AutoText and Spike features to eliminate repetitious typing. In addition, you will learn how to automatically create superscripts, subscripts, ordinals, and fractions.

Use Typesetting Features

Word provides advanced typesetting features to enhance the appearance of documents. These typesetting features include kerning, character spacing, and setting an exact amount of space between lines of text in a paragraph.

Kerning is used to improve the readability of text. After a document is typed, the manual kerning feature can be used to adjust the space between two characters. With manual kerning, for example, the space between the letters AV can be reduced to AV. In addition, the automatic kerning feature can be used to kern specific pairs of letters. The automatic kerning feature is turned on by selecting **Format, Font, Character Spacing, Kerning for fonts, OK**. This feature then automatically adjusts the spacing for all occurrences of predefined pairs of letters. The Word program defines which pairs of letters are to be kerned depending on the font in use. In other words, kerned pairs of letters will vary depending on the font.

The character spacing feature (also known as tracking) is used to increase or decrease the amount of space between letters in selected text or in an entire document. Condensing character spacing allows more text to be compressed into the same amount of space. By expanding the character spacing, words can be stretched out to create a special effect (see Figure 14.2).

Word automatically adjusts the line spacing to accommodate the largest point size in each line. At times, however, it is desirable to control the exact amount of spacing between lines of a paragraph, especially if different font sizes are used in the same paragraph. In order to make the line spacing uniform, an exact amount of line spacing can be specified.

Start-Up Instructions

❖ Open the file named **14drill1.doc** located on the data disk.

❖ The space between the lines of the indented paragraphs is not equal because two different point sizes have been set. For example, you may notice that in the document, there is more spacing between the first and second lines than between the second and third lines in the paragraph that begins "Look for the recycling . . ." The Steps to Set Exact Line Spacing will be used to correct this problem. *(Note: Because additional changes will be made to the text, do not be concerned about the spacing and alignment at this time.)*

Steps to ▶ **Manually Kern Text**

1. Select the two letters to be kerned.

   For example, select the **ur** in the word **Curbside** located in the title.

2. Select **Format, Font**.

3. Select the **Character Spacing** tab.

   Note: The Character Spacing tab displays (see Figure 14.1).

4. *To decrease (condense) the amount of space between the letters,* click on the down triangle located to the right of the **By** box in the Spacing area until the desired amount of kerning displays.

FIGURE 14.1

Character
Spacing tab

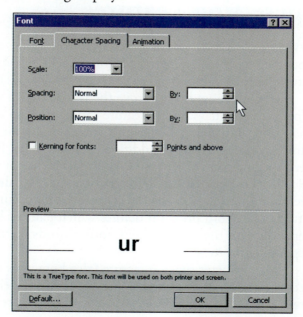

For example, click on the down triangle located to the right of the **By** box in the Spacing area until **0.5 pt** displays.

Note: While clicking on the down triangle, look in the Preview box. The two letters will have moved slightly closer to each other.

To increase (expand) the amount of space between the letters, click on the up triangle located to the right of the **By** box in the Spacing area until the desired amount of kerning displays.

5. When the characters are the desired distance apart, select **OK**.

Finish-Up Instructions

❖ Select the letters **id** in the word **Curbside** in the title.

❖ Repeat steps 2–5 and decrease the amount of space between the letters to **0.3 pt**.

❖ Select the letters **Re** in the word **Recycling** in the title.

❖ Repeat steps 2–5 and decrease the amount of space between the letters to **0.4 pt**.

❖ Select the letters **lin** in the word **Recycling** in the title.

❖ Repeat steps 2–5 and decrease the amount of space between the letters to **0.4 pt**.

❖ Use the *new* filename **14Curbside 1.doc** and save the file.

❖ Optional. Print one copy.

❖ Continue with the Steps to Change Character Spacing.

Start-Up Instructions

❖ The file named **14Curbside 1.doc** should be displayed in the document window.

 ## Change Character Spacing

1. Select the desired word(s) where character spacing is to be changed.

   For example, select the lead words **Plastic Containers**.

2. Select **Format, Font**.

3. If necessary, select the **Character Spacing** tab.

4. *To expand (increase) the space between each character,* click on the up triangle located to the right of the **By** box in the Spacing area.

   For example, click on the up triangle until **1.5 pt** displays.

   If the space between each character is to be condensed (decreased), click on the down triangle located to the right of the **By** box in the Spacing area.

5. Select **OK**.

   Note: Additional space has been placed between each letter in the selected words.

❖ Use the **Format Painter** button to copy the expanded character spacing to each lead word. (With the lead words Plastic Containers selected, double-click on the **Format Painter** button. Select the rest of the lead words, i.e., Glass Containers, Metal Containers, and Newspapers. When all lead words have been formatted, click on the **Format Painter** button once.)

❖ Check the alignment of the indented paragraphs. If necessary, increase or decrease indents in order to align all the paragraphs.

❖ Use the same filename, **14Curbside 1.doc**, and save the file again.

❖ Continue with the Steps to Set Exact Line Spacing.

Start-Up Instructions

❖ The file named **14Curbside 1.doc** should be displayed in the document window.

Steps to ➤ ## Set Exact Line Spacing

1. Select the text where the line spacing is to be set.

   For example, select all paragraphs except the title.

2. Select **Format, Paragraph**.

   *Note: The **Indents and Spacing** tab should be selected.*

3. Click in the **Line spacing** box and select the **Exactly** option.

   Note: 12 pt displays in the At box located to the right of the Line spacing box.

4. Click on the up triangle (to increase space) or down triangle (to decrease space) located to the right of the **At** box to display the desired line spacing amount.

   For example, click on the up triangle until **20 pt** displays.

5. Select **OK**.

   Note: Additional spacing has been placed between the paragraph lines. Also notice that the spacing between the lines of each paragraph is the same even though there are different font sizes within the paragraphs.

Finish-Up Instructions

❖ Click once to deselect the text.

❖ Use the *new* filename **14Curbside final.doc** and save the file on your file disk.

   Note: Your document should look similar to Figure 14.2.

❖ Print one copy. Close the document.

Curbside Recycling

On behalf of the men and women of Curbside Recycling, thank you for all your efforts to make the recycling program a success. Last year, over 10,000 tons of materials were recycled through the curbside program.

The following items can be placed curbside for recycling:

Plastic Containers Look for the recycling triangle on the bottom of plastic containers. All #1 PETE plastic containers and #2 HDPE plastic containers can be recycled.

Glass Containers Rinse glass containers and bottles before recycling. Labels do not have to be removed.

Metal Containers Rinse metal food and beverage containers before recycling. Some common recyclable containers include: aluminum, steel, bi-metal food and beverage cans (e.g., soup, pet food, coffee, fruit, and vegetable cans).

Newspapers Recycle newspapers and newspaper inserts only. Do not include magazines or junk mail.

Use AutoText

AutoText entries are shortcut abbreviations that can be typed in place of a longer word or group of words. AutoText entries can also include graphic images, borders, and special symbols. When the AutoText entry name is typed and the **F3** key is pressed, the expanded word or group of words displays in the document window. For example, an AutoText entry named "agreement closing" could contain a standard closing paragraph, signature line, and reference initials for a business letter. When the words "agreement closing" are typed and the **F3** key is pressed, the text of the closing paragraph, the signature line, and the reference initials are instantly placed in the document window.

When AutoText entries are created, Word also remembers text format, e.g., font and point size. To include paragraph formatting (e.g., alignment, indents, line spacing), be sure to include the paragraph mark (hard return) when selecting the text to be an AutoText entry.

AutoText entries are stored in the *Normal.dot* template. The *Normal.dot* template is usually active unless another template has been selected. (See Chapter 15 for information on templates.) Once an AutoText entry has been created, the entry is available to be used in any document. If an AutoText entry is no longer needed, the entry can be deleted.

Start-Up Instructions

❖ Open the file named **14drill2.doc** located on the data disk. The file contains a closing paragraph, signature line, reference initials, and an enclosure notation. These will be used to create an AutoText entry named "agreement closing."

❖ Select the typist's initials and insert your own initials.

Steps to ▶ Create an AutoText Entry

1. Select the text that will be an AutoText entry.

   For example, select all of the text.

2. Select **Insert, AutoText, New**.

   Note: The Create AutoText dialog box displays (see Figure 14.3). Word proposes the first couple of words of the selected text as the AutoText name. This name can be accepted or a different name can be typed.

3. If desired, type a different name for the AutoText entry.

   For example, type **agreement closing**.

4. Select **OK**.

   Note: The AutoText entry "agreement closing" is created, and the Create AutoText dialog box is exited automatically.

Finish-Up Instructions

❖ Close the document named **14drill2.doc**. Do not save any changes.

❖ Continue with the Steps to Insert an AutoText Entry.

FIGURE 14.3

Create AutoText
dialog box

Start-Up Instructions

❖ Open the file named **14Lunghi.doc** located on the data disk.

 ## Insert an AutoText Entry

1. Place the insertion point at the location in the document where the AutoText entry should be inserted.

   For example, place the insertion point in the second blank line below the last paragraph in the letter.

2. Type the AutoText name and press **F3**.

   For example, type **agreement closing** and press **F3**.

   *Note: If you forget an AutoText entry name, select **Insert**, **AutoText**, click on the **AutoText** option, choose the **AutoText** tab, and double-click on the desired AutoText entry name.*

Shortcut:

1. With the option **Show AutoComplete tip for AutoText and dates** turned on in the AutoCorrect dialog box (**Tools, AutoCorrect, AutoText** tab), type the first few characters in the AutoText entry's name. Word displays the first couple lines of the AutoText in a ScreenTip box.

2. If the displayed text is correct, press **Enter** or **F3** to place the contents of the AutoText in the document. To ignore the AutoText tip box suggestion, keep typing.

Finish-Up Instructions

❖ Use the *new* filename **14AutoText.doc** and save the file on your file disk.

❖ Print one copy and close the document.

❖ If necessary, select the **New** button to display a document window.

❖ Continue with the Steps to Delete an AutoText Entry.

 ## Delete an AutoText Entry

1. Select **Insert, AutoText,** click on the **AutoText** option.

2. Highlight the name of the AutoText entry to be deleted.

   For example, check that **agreement closing** is selected. (If necessary, click on **agreement closing**.)

3. Select the **Delete** button.

4. Select **Close**.

Edit an AutoText Entry

Note: The following steps are for your information.

1. Insert the AutoText entry into a document window.

2. Edit the text as desired.

3. Select the text.

4. Choose **Insert, AutoText,** and choose the **AutoText** option.

5. Select the original AutoText entry name in the **Enter AutoText entries here** list. Select **Add.**

6. Select **Yes** to the message "Do you want to redefine the AutoText entry?".

Use the Spike

The Spike is a special AutoText entry that allows you to cut items located in different areas of a document and insert them into another document as a group. Text or graphics can be accumulated in the Spike and then transferred to a new location. The Spike feature is useful when creating new documents so as not to have to rekey information. For example, the Spike feature can be used to accumulate the main points from a report document to make a new report file listing these main points.

Once all items are accumulated in the Spike, the information is transferred to an existing document or to a new document by typing the word **Spike** and pressing **F3**. The information placed in the Spike can be transferred to as many different locations as needed. This information remains in the Spike until the contents of the Spike are transferred. The Spike is emptied by pressing **Ctrl** and **Shift** and **F3**.

Text can also be accumulated (collected) and pasted (up to 12 items) by using the **Clipboard Toolbar**. See the Shortcut on page 375.

Start-Up Instructions

❖ 💾 Open the file named **14drill3.doc** located on the data disk.

 Use the Spike

1. Select the text to be accumulated in the Spike.

   For example, select the first two lines containing the title, date, and time of the first seminar (i.e., **Introduction to Publishing Hardware and Software, April 5, 200x, 8:30 a.m. -12:30 p.m.**) and the following blank line.

2. Press **Ctrl** and **F3**.

   Note: The selected text is removed from the document window and placed in the Spike.

3. Select the next text to be accumulated in the Spike.

   For example, select the second seminar title, date, and time (i.e., **Publishing with Interactive Media, April 5, 200x, 1:00 - 5:00 p.m.**) and the following blank line.

4. Press **Ctrl** and **F3**.

5. Repeat steps 3 and 4 and accumulate any other desired text in the Spike.

    For example, place the remaining seminar titles, dates, and times (including the blank line that follows each paragraph) in the Spike.

6. When all desired text has been selected and accumulated in the Spike, close the document but do not save the changes.

7. Open an existing file or select the **New** button to create a new file.

    For example, select the **New** button. Change the top margin to **2"** and the left and right margins to **.75"**. Press the **Enter** key three times.

8. *To insert the contents of the Spike,* type **Spike** and press the **F3** key.

    To insert the contents of the Spike and empty the Spike, press **Ctrl** and **Shift** and **F3**.

    For example, insert the contents of the Spike and empty the Spike by pressing **Ctrl** and **Shift** and **F3**.

    Note: The contents of the Spike are placed in the document window.

Shortcut:

1. Display the Clipboard Toolbar (right mouse click on a Toolbar and choose **Clipboard**).

2. Select the desired text and then click on the **Copy** button located on the Clipboard Toolbar.

3. Repeat for up to 12 copied items.

4. Locate the insertion point where desired and click on the **Paste All** option to insert the copied and collected text.

Finish-Up Instructions

❖ Place the insertion point at the top of the document and type the title **Upcoming Seminars**. Select the title and change the font to **Garamond, 18 point**. Center the title.

❖ Use the filename **14Seminars.doc** and save the file on your file disk.

❖ Print one copy and close the document.

Create Superscripts, Subscripts, Ordinals, and Fractions

Superscripts are characters that are printed a fraction above the text line, and subscripts are characters that are printed a fraction below the text line (see Figure 14.4). Superscripts and subscripts are used, for example, when printing names of chemicals, algebraic equations, or degrees of temperature.

Word can automatically superscript ordinals such as 1st, 2nd, 3rd, etc., and create typographically correct fractions for ¼, ½, and ¾. To verify that Word will automatically create ordinals and fractions, select **Tools**, **AutoCorrect**, choose the **AutoFormat As You Type** tab, and check that the **Ordinals (1st) with superscript** and **Fractions (1/2) with fraction character** (½) options are selected. Choose **OK**.

Start-Up Instructions

❖ An empty document window should be displayed. (If necessary, select the **New** button.)

❖ Use a **150%** view (select the down arrow next to the **Zoom** button; choose **150%**).

❖ The nonprinting symbols should be displayed. (If necessary, select the **Show/Hide** button.)

 ## Create a Superscript

1. Type the desired text.

   For example, type (y - 3b)4 and press the **Tab** key twice.

   *Note: Pressing the **Tab**, **Spacebar**, or **Enter** key after the character to be a superscript makes it easier to insert additional text later.*

2. Select the character to be a superscript.

   For example, select the 4.

3. Select **Format, Font**. If necessary, select the **Font** tab. Select the **Superscript** option in the Effects area. Select **OK**.

   Note: The selected character displays as a superscript in the document window.

4. Before continuing to type, locate the insertion point where you will continue typing.

   For example, click to the right of the second tab symbol.

 ## Create a Subscript

1. Type the desired text.

   For example, type HCO3 and press the **Tab** key twice

2. Select the character to be a subscript.

   For example, select the 3.

3. Select **Format, Font**. If necessary, select the **Font** tab. Select the **Subscript** option in the Effects area. Select **OK**.

   Note: The selected character displays as a subscript in the document window.

4. Before continuing to type, locate the insertion point where you will continue typing.

   For example, click to the right of the second tab symbol.

$(y - 3b)^4$	HCO_3	$\frac{1}{4}$	1st
$x^2 - y^3 + z^2$	H_3PO_4	$\frac{3}{4}$	3rd

Examples of superscripts, subscripts, fractions and ordinals

Create Automatic Fractions

1. Type the desired fraction.

   For example, type **1/4**.

2. Press the **Spacebar, Tab** key or **Enter** key.

   For example, press the **Tab** key once.

Create Ordinals

1. Type the desired ordinal.

   For example, type **1st**.

2. Press the **Spacebar, Tab** key, or **Enter** key.

   For example, press the **Enter** key twice.

Finish-Up Instructions

❖ Using the Steps to Create a Superscript, Steps to Create a Subscript, Steps to Create Automatic Fractions, and Steps to Create Ordinals, type the equation, formula, fraction, and ordinal in the second line of Figure 14.4.

*Note: After creating the first superscript or subscript and before performing any other operation, select the next number to be superscripted or subscripted and choose **Edit, Repeat Font Formatting**.*

❖ Use the filename **14Superscripts.doc** and save the file on your file disk.

❖ Print one copy and close the document.

The Next Step

Chapter Review and Activities

Self-Check Quiz

T F 1. To set an exact amount of line spacing, select the text to be affected, select **Format**, **Paragraph**, click in the **Line spacing** box, choose **Exactly**, change the amount of spacing in the **At** box, and select **OK**.

T F 2. Information can be accumulated in the Spike then inserted into a new or existing document.

T F 3. Word can create typographically correct fractions for ¼, ½, and ¾.

T F 4. Character spacing (tracking) is used to expand or condense the amount of space between letters in selected text.

T F 5. An AutoText entry is inserted into a document by typing the AutoText entry name and pressing the **F3** key.

6. A superscript is a character that prints a fraction _____ the text line.
   a. above
   b. below
   c. on
   d. none of these

7. To manually kern two characters, use the _____ option in the **Format** menu.
   a. **Font**
   b. **Character**
   c. **Paragraph**
   d. **Tab**

8. A subscript is a character that prints a fraction _____ the text line.
   a. above
   b. below
   c. on
   d. either a or c

9. List two examples of ordinals.

10. Write one example in which you personally might use the AutoText or Spike features.

Enriching Language Arts Skills

Spelling/Vocabulary Words

average—being midway between extremes; in the middle.

convenient—easy to use; readily available; handy.

flexibility—the ability to respond or conform to changing or new situations; the ability to adapt.

valuable—worth a good price; of great service, worth, or benefit.

Independent Adjectives

Two consecutive adjectives that modify the same noun are separated by a comma.

Example:

Orlando performs his job duties in an effective, diligent manner.

Activities

■ Activity 14.1—Change Character Spacing and Set Exact Line Spacing

1. Open the file named **14act1.doc** located on the data disk.

2. Select the title and increase the character spacing by 2 points (select **Format**, **Font**, **Character Spacing** tab; click in the **By** box located in the Spacing area and type **2**; select **OK**).

3. Select the first lead word, **Professionalism**, and increase the character spacing by 1.5 points (select **Format**, **Font**, **Character Spacing** tab; click in the **By** box located in the Spacing area and type **1.5**; select **OK**).

4. Use the **Format Painter** to copy the character spacing of the lead word **Professionalism** to the other lead words, **Flexibility**, **Attendance**, **Cooperation**, and **Deadlines**. (If necessary, select the word **Professionalism**; double-click on the **Format Painter** button; select each lead word; when all lead words have been formatted, click on the **Format Painter** button again.)

5. Select all paragraphs except the title and set exact line spacing of 18 points (select **Format**, **Paragraph**; click in the **Line spacing** box on the Indents and Spacing card, select **Exactly**; click on the up triangle located to the right of the **At** box until **18 pt** displays; select **OK**).

6. Use the *new* filename **14Office tips.doc** and save the file on your file disk.

7. Print one copy

8. Optional: Fax this document to your instructor via a local fax, or write an e-mail message to your instructor that you are sending this assignment. Attach this document file to your e-mail message.

9. Close the document.

Activity 14.2—Use the Spike to Create an Overhead Transparency

1. Open the file named **14act2.doc** located on the data disk.

2. Select the title, **Accounting Terms**, and the following two blank lines.

3. Press **Ctrl** and **F3** to place the selected text in the Spike.

4. Select the first heading, **Accrued Expenses**, and the following blank line.

5. Press **Ctrl** and **F3** to place the selected text in the Spike.

6. Select the next heading and the following blank line.

7. Press **Ctrl** and **F3**.

8. Repeat steps 6 and 7 to accumulate the remaining headings in the Spike.

9. When all of the remaining headings have been accumulated in the Spike, close the file named **14act2.doc** but **do not** save the changes.

10. Select the **New** button.

11. Press **Ctrl** and **Shift** and **F3** to retrieve the contents of the Spike and empty the Spike.

12. Format the text for use as an overhead transparency (e.g., use a large font size; use a bulleted or numbered list). Check that the same amount of space displays between items. If necessary, delete or insert spacing as needed.

13. Use the filename **14Accounting terms.doc** and save the file on your file disk.

14. Print one copy and close the document.

Activity 14.3—Create Subscripts

1. In a new document window, type and center all the following text. In a 150% Zoom view, create subscripts as shown. (Select the **Zoom** button, choose **150%**, select the character to be a subscript; choose **Format**, **Font**; select **Subscript** on the Font tab; select **OK**. Select the next number to be a subscript; choose **Edit**, **Repeat Font Formatting**. Repeat for all numbers to be subscripts.

CHEMICAL COMPOUNDS—Nitrogen and Potassium

Nitrobenzene: $C_6H_5NO_2$
Nitroglycerin: $C_3H_5(NO_3)_3$
Potassium Oxalate: $K_2C_2O_4H_2O$
Potassium Sulfate: K_2SO_4

2. Use the filename **14subscript activity.doc** and save the file on your file disk.

3. Print one copy and close the document.

Activity 14.4—Create Superscripts

1. In a new document window, type and center all the following text. Using a 150% Zoom, create superscripts as shown. A lowercase letter "o" is used to represent the degree symbol. (Select the **Zoom** button, select the first lowercase **o** to be superscripted; choose **Format, Font**; select **Superscript** on the Font tab; select **OK**. Select the next letter **o** to be a superscript and choose **Edit, Repeat Font Formatting**. Repeat for all the o's.)

DEGREES OF TEMPERATURE

Celsius vs. Fahrenheit

$0^oC = 32^oF$
$15^oC = 60^oF$
$22^oC = 72^oF$
$37^oC = 100^oF$
$100^oC = 212^oF$

2. Use the filename **14Superscript activity.doc** and save the file.

3. Print one copy and close the document.

Challenge Your Skills

Skill 14.1—Create and Use AutoText

1. Create an AutoText entry using the following information.

    a. Type the following text:

If the foregoing meets with your approval, please indicate your agreement by signing the original copy hereof and returning it to the undersigned.

Sincerely,

WIZARD PRODUCTIONS

Estrellita Aguinaldo

ACCEPTED and AGREED TO:

By: _____

Date: _____

EA/xx

Cc: Standards and Practices Department

---

    b. Select all the text and create an AutoText entry named letter closing.

    c. Close the document. **Do not** save the file.

2. Type the following letter. Insert the **letter closing** AutoText entry at the end of the letter where shown.

382   Chapter 14—Create Documents Using Special Features

(Use current date)

Ms. Monique Prospero
Prospero Fashions
24363 NW 17th Avenue
Miami, FL 33169

Dear Ms. Prospero:

This will serve to confirm our agreement regarding the merchandise to be supplied by you for use on the Future Visions program.

1. You will provide, without charge or expense, the following merchandise for such performers as may be designated by Wizard Productions for use by such performers solely on the above-mentioned program: Tiffany Sandborn's Wardrobe.

2. You understand and agree that Wizard Productions shall have the right to disclose the receipt of this consideration in the form of an announcement similar to the following: Tiffany Sandborn's Wardrobe Furnished by Prospero Fashions.

3. Said announcement shall be made at each broadcast or rebroadcast of the specific program on which the merchandise furnished by you is used, but you shall not make any claim or be entitled to any damages in the event such announcement is inadvertently omitted.

4. This letter when signed by both parties shall constitute the entire agreement between the parties, supersede any prior oral or written understanding, and may not be modified or amended except in writing.

(Insert the AutoText entry named **letter closing**.)

---

3. Change the left and right margins to 1". Select the entire document and change the font to **Times New Roman, 10 point**.

4. Use the filename **14Prospero letter.doc** and save the file on your file disk.

5. Print one copy and close the document.

6. Optional: Open the file named **14Lunghi.doc** located on the data disk. Insert the AutoText entry named **letter closing** after the last paragraph. Use the *new* filename **14Lunghi final.doc** and save the file on your file disk. Print one copy and close the file.

7. Delete the AutoText entry named **letter closing** (in a document window, select **Insert, AutoText, AutoText** option; select **letter closing, Delete, Close**).

1. Open the file named **14skill2.doc** located on the data disk. Make decisions regarding:

   > Margins
   > Fonts and sizes for title, sideheads, and body text
   > Alignment
   > Widow/Orphan control
   > Text attributes for the title and sideheads
   > Character spacing for title and sideheads
   > Use of the Format Painter
   > Superscripts or subscripts for service names (e.g., 55 Checking$^+$ or
   >   Easy Checking$_+$)
   > Alignment of paragraphs
   > Header or footer text and placement

2. Correct four spelling errors, five punctuation/grammatical errors, and two mis-used words.

3. Use the *new* filename **14Bank Services.doc** and save the file.

4. Print one copy.

5. Once the document is formatted and saved, use the Spike to create a new document that contains the title and sideheads.

6. Format the new document as a flier announcing Savanna National Bank's services. Make decisions regarding:

   > Font and point sizes
   > Margins
   > Alignment
   > Borders
   > Graphic images

7. Use the *new* filename **14Bank Services Flier.doc** and save the file.

8. Print one copy.

9. Optional: Fax the flier to your instructor via a local fax machine, or write an e-mail message to your instructor that you are sending this flier. Attach the flier file to your e-mail message.

10. Close the document.

Create Documents Using Special Functions

Features Covered

- Sort text alphabetically or by date
- Use AutoFormat
- Edit, create, and apply styles
- Use existing templates to create new templates
- Record and play macros

Objectives and Introduction

After successfully completing this chapter, you will know how to use the Sort function to sort text numerically, alphabetically, and by date. You will also learn how to use the AutoFormat feature to instantly format documents. You will be able to edit, create, and apply styles to quickly format documents and use a template to format a document. In addition, you will learn to record and play macros to expedite your work.

Word provides many special functions to expedite document production and eliminate repetitious tasks. The Sort function makes alphabetical and numerical sorting easy and quick. Macros can be created to perform quickly and efficiently those tasks that must be repeated on a regular basis. Styles, templates, and the AutoFormat functions make it easy to develop and apply a custom look to your document(s).

Create Alphabetically and Numerically Sorted Text

The Sort function is used to arrange paragraphs, table rows, and words in alphabetical, numerical, or date order. In this chapter we will be sorting by only words and dates. Sorting table rows was covered in Chapter 6. A list of names can be sorted alphabetically, and a list of numbers can be sorted numerically. Text can be selected to sort in alphabetical (Text), numerical (Number), or date (Date) order. Text can also be sorted either in descending or ascending order. Ascending order begins with letter A through Z or the lowest number to the highest number; descending order begins with letter Z through A or the highest number to the lowest number.

For the purpose of sorting, a paragraph is defined as any text that ends with a single hard return (**Enter**). When sorting words that begin with the same character, Word uses the character(s) that follows to determine the correct order. For example, if there are two last names that begin with the same letter, the second (then the third, fourth, etc.) character in the names is used to determine the alphabetical order.

Before sorting a document, all text to be sorted is selected. The Sort dialog box is used to choose the Sort by option (Column, Field, Word, or Paragraph) and to define criteria. A sort criteria identifies the type of sort (Text, Number, or Date), the order of the sort (ascending or descending), and the portion of text to sort (column, field, word, or paragraph).

When a sort is performed, Word reorders the text in accordance with the information specified in the Sort by box and then uses any additional information in the Then by box to refine the sort. For example, if a list of names is to be sorted by last name and several individuals have the same last name, the last name is selected in the **Sort by** box and the first name is selected in the **Then by** box.

Start-Up Instructions

❖ Open the file named **15drill1.doc** located on the data disk.

❖ To sort text by words, the field separator must be set as a space. Select **Table, Sort, Options**; select **Other**; press the **Spacebar** once, **OK, Cancel**.

Steps to ▶ Sort by Word or Paragraph

1. Select the text to be sorted.

   For example, scroll to the bottom of the document, or press **Ctrl** and **End**, and select all the names in the distribution list.

2. Select **Table, Sort**.

3. To change the Sort by option, click on the down triangle located to the right of the Sort by box and click on the desired option.

   For example, to sort the distribution list by last name, select **Word 2**.

4. To select a different type of sort, i.e., **Text, Number,** or **Date**, click on the down triangle located to the right of the Type box and select the desired type.

   For example, if necessary, select **Text**.

5. Select the sort order, i.e., **Ascending** or **Descending**.

   For example, if necessary, select **Ascending**.

Create a Secondary Sort Criteria

6. Select the down triangle located to the right of the **Then by** box and click on the desired option.

    For example, click on **Word 1**.

7. Select the desired sort type and sort order.

    For example, check that **Text** is selected in the Type box and that **Ascending** is selected as the sort order.

8. Select **OK**.

    Note: The distribution list is sorted by last name (Word 2). When the last names were identical, the first initial (Word 1) was used to sort the list.

Finish-Up Instructions

❖ Select the xx's above the Distribution List and type your initials in lowercase letters

❖ Use the *new* filename **15sorted by word.doc** and save the file on your file disk.

❖ Print one copy and close the document.

Start-Up Instructions

❖ Open the file named **15drill2.doc** located on the data disk.

Steps to ▶ Sort by Date

1. Select the lines of text to be sorted.

    For example, select the entire list of products, including the column headings Product Name, Version No., and Release Date.

2. Select **Table, Sort**.

    Note: Word proposes a sort criteria. This criteria can be accepted or changed.

3. If necessary, select the **Header Row** option in the **My list has** area to prevent Word from sorting the column headings with the rest of the list.

    For example, select the **Header Row** option so that the column headings, Product Name, Version No., and Release Date, will not be sorted with the rest of the text.

4. To change the Sort by option, click on the down triangle located to the right of the **Sort by** box and click on the desired option.

    For example, select **Release Date**.

    Note: Word automatically changes the sort type to Date.

5. Select the sort order, i.e., **Ascending** or **Descending**.

    For example, select **Descending**.

6. Select **OK**.

Finish-Up Instructions

❖ Select the xx's above the Distribution List and type your initials in lowercase letters.

❖ Use the *new* filename **15sorted by date.doc** and save the file on your file disk.

❖ Print one copy and close the document.

Use AutoFormat

The AutoFormat feature quickly formats a document using Word's built-in styles. (For more information on the built-in styles, see the following section, Use Styles to Format Documents.) The AutoFormat feature is accessed by selecting **Format**, **AutoFormat**. When the AutoFormat feature is accessed, the formatting can be reviewed and accepted or rejected.

Start-Up Instructions

❖ Open the file named **15drill3.doc** located on the data disk.

Steps to Use AutoFormat

1. With the insertion point located at any position in the document or with the desired text selected, select **Format, AutoFormat**.

   For example, place the insertion point at any location in the document and select **Format, AutoFormat**.

   Note: The AutoFormat dialog box displays.

2. Choose the desired options.

   For example, check that the **AutoFormat now** option is chosen and that **General document** displays in the **Please select a document type to help improve the formatting process** box.

3. Select **OK**.

   Note: The document is formatted using Word's built-in styles.

Finish-Up Instructions

❖ Select the **Print Preview** button to view the formatted document. If necessary, select the **Zoom** button and choose **100%**. Select **Close** to return to the document window.

❖ Insert page numbers at the bottom center [select **Insert**, **Page Numbers**, **Bottom of pag**e (footer), **Center** alignment, **OK**].

❖ Use the *new* filename **15AutoFormat.doc** and save the file on your file disk.

❖ Print one copy.

❖ Continue with the Steps to Edit a Style.

Use Styles to Format Documents

A style is a group of formatting instructions that can be applied to related sections of text and saved and used in other documents. For example, a style can be used to format all sideheads of a report to print in 16-point Bookman Old Style. Use of styles saves time and ensures consistency throughout a document. Applying the same style repeatedly to related sections saves time because many formatting changes can be made instantly. Also, if a style is changed, the new format is automatically assigned to all text in the current document in which the style has been previously applied.

There are two types of styles: *Paragraph* and *Character*. A *Paragraph* style is used to affect the appearance of an entire paragraph. For example, a Paragraph style could change the font and point size, set center justification, and bold the title of a report. A *Character* style is used to apply font and text attributes to selected text. For example, a Character style might apply bold and italic text attributes to specified text. To apply a Paragraph style, locate the insertion point anywhere in the paragraph to be affected. To apply a Character style, select the text to be affected.

Word has several built-in styles that can be used to format body text, headings, headers/footers, footnotes/endnotes, list bullet, etc. When the down triangle beside the **Style** box is selected, a list showing several built-in styles displays. If no new styles have been created, the Style box will contain only built-in styles, such as *Normal*, *Heading 1*, and *Heading 2*.

Normal is the default style that is automatically applied to all paragraphs of a document unless another style is chosen. The Normal style is also the style that is used as the basis for many other styles. By making a change to the Normal style, all the styles that are based on the Normal style will also be changed. For example, if Normal style has the font 10 point, Times New Roman, the styles that are based on the Normal style, such as Body Text and List Bullet, will also have the font 10 point, Times New Roman. If the font for the Normal style is changed to 12 point, Times New Roman, the font for the styles that are based on the Normal style will also change.

New styles can be created "by example" or by choosing formatting options in the New Style dialog box. The "by example" method is used to create styles based on previously formatted text. To create a style from scratch, the options in the New Style dialog box are used.

Styles are edited by selecting **Format**, **Style**, highlighting the desired style name, and selecting **Modify**. The options in the Modify Style dialog box are then used to change the existing style format. When a style is edited, any text in the current document that was previously formatted with the edited style will be changed to reflect the new format specifications.

When a document containing styles is saved, the edited, or new styles, are also saved. These styles can then be used to format other documents by copying the style information from the existing document into another document.

Start-Up Instructions

❖ The file named **15AutoFormat.doc** should be displayed in the document window.

FIGURE 15.1

Style dialog box

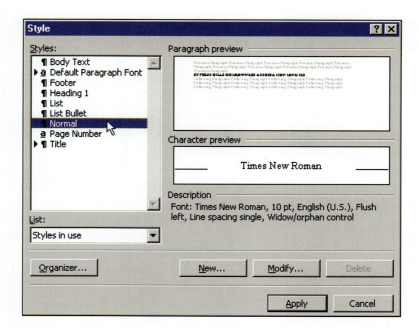

Steps to   Edit a Style

1. Select **Format, Style**.

   *Note: The Style dialog box displays containing a list of existing styles (see Figure 15.1). The styles listed are the built-in styles currently being used to format this document that are available for formatting all documents. More styles can be listed by selecting the down triangle beside the List box and selecting **All styles**.*

2. Click on the style to be edited.

   For example, click on the style name **Normal**.

3. Select **Modify**.

   Note: The Modify Style dialog box displays. A description of the format of the style displays in the Description area (see Figure 15.2).

FIGURE 15.2

Modify Style
dialog box

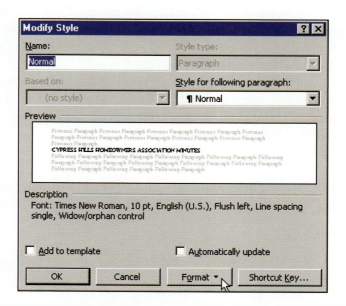

4. Use the options in the Modify Style dialog box to make the desired changes to the style.

> For example, select the **Format** button and click on **Font**. Select the **Font** tab and change the font to **Garamond, 11 point**, or **make a font choice of your own**. Select **OK**.

Note: As formatting options are selected, the description of the style changes in the Description area.

5. Select **OK** to exit the Modify Style dialog box.

6. Select **Close** to exit the Style dialog box.

Note: The font for the document body text will have been changed.

Finish-Up Instructions

❖ Select **Format, Style**, click on the style name **Title**, and select **Modify**. Select **Format, Font**, and change the font size to **14 point**. Select **OK** twice; select **Close**.

❖ Use the *new* filename **15Styles.doc** and save the file on your file disk.

Start-Up Instructions

❖ The file named **15Styles.doc** should be displayed in the document window.

Create a New Style

1. Place the insertion point in the paragraph that will be formatted with the new style.

> For example, place the insertion point in the text "Board of Directors Meeting."

2. Select **Format, Style**.

3. Select **New** in the Style dialog box.

Note: The New Style dialog box displays. Word proposes the name Style1 in the Name box.

4. Type the desired style name in the Name box.

> For example, type **Centered Subtitle**.

5. Click in the **Based on** box and select a style that most closely matches the new style.

> For example, scroll down the list and select **Subtitle**.

Note: A sample of the style format displays in the Preview box, and the description, Subtitle +, displays in the Description box.

6. If necessary, click in the **Style type** box and select the desired style type, i.e., **Character** or **Paragraph**.

> For example, check that **Paragraph** displays in the Style type box.

---

7. Use the options in the New Style dialog box to create the desired format for the new style.

   For example, select the **Format** button and click on **Font**, and change the font to **Garamond, Bold Italic, 11 point**, or **make a font choice of your own**. Select **OK**.

8. Select **OK** and choose **Apply**.

   Note: The words "Board of Directors Meeting" are centered and display bold and italic.

Finish-Up Instructions

❖ Use the same filename, **15Styles.doc**, and save the file. (The newly created style will also be saved.)

❖ Continue with the Steps to Create a Paragraph Style By Example.

Start-Up Instructions

❖ The file named **15Styles.doc** should be displayed in the document window.

 Steps to

Create a Paragraph Style By Example

1. Select and format a paragraph as desired.

   For example, scroll down and select the first bulleted item "Own a home . . ." Select the **Numbering** button to change the bullet characters to a number. Select the **Increase Indent** button twice. Select **Format, Paragraph,** in the **Spacing** area; click on the up triangle beside the **After** box to display **6 pt**; select **OK**.

2. Move the mouse pointer to the **Style** box in the Formatting Toolbar (first box on the left of the Formatting Toolbar) and click once in the **Style** box to highlight the current style name. (Do **not** click on the down triangle beside the Style box.)

   For example, click once in the **Style** box to highlight the **List Bullet** style name.

3. Type the new style name and press **Enter**.

   For example, type **Numbered List** and press **Enter**.

Finish-Up Instructions

❖ Use the same filename, **15Styles.doc**, and save the document. (The newly created style will also be saved.)

❖ Continue with the Steps to Apply Styles.

Start-Up Instructions

❖ The file named **15Styles.doc** should be displayed in the document window.

Steps to **Apply Styles**

1. *To apply a Paragraph style,* place the insertion point between any two characters in the paragraph, or select the paragraphs to be affected. Click on the down triangle located to the right of the Style box on the Formatting Toolbar. Click on the desired Paragraph style name.

   For example, select the two remaining bulleted items. Click on the down triangle located to the right of the **Style** box, scroll down, and click on the **1. Numbered List** style name.

2. *To apply a Character style,* select the text to be affected. Click on the down triangle located to the right of the Style box on the Formatting Toolbar. Click on the desired Character style name.

   For example, no character styles need to be applied at this time.

Finish-Up Instructions

❖ Scroll to the top of the document and place the insertion point between any two characters in the date, September 4, 200x, and change the style to **Centered Subtitle** (click on the down triangle located to the right of the Style box, click on **Centered Subtitle**).

❖ Use the same filename, **15Styles.doc**, and save the file on your file disk.

❖ Print one copy and close the document.

Start-Up Instructions

❖ Open the file named **15Minutes.doc** located on the data disk.

❖ Use the *new* filename **15Minutes Formatted.doc** and save the file on your file disk.

Steps to **Copy Styles to Format Another Document**

1. Select Format, Style.

2. Select the Organizer button.

   *Note: The Organizer dialog box displays; the **Styles** tab should be selected.*

3. Select the Close File button located below the left column.

   *Note: The name of the button changes to **Open File**.*

4. Select the Close File button located below the right column.

   *Note: The name of the button changes to **Open File**.*

5. Select the Open File button located below the left column

   Note: Word automatically looks in the Templates folder and displays template files (*.dot*).*

6. Click in the **Look in** box and select the drive and/or folder where the file containing the styles to be copied is stored. If necessary, select a different option in the **Files of type** box. Double-click on the name of the file that contains the desired styles.

> For example, click in the **Look in** box and select the drive where your file disk is located. Click in the **Files of type** box and select **Word Documents (*.doc)**. Double-click on **15Styles.doc** located on your file disk.

Note: The words "15Styles.doc" display in the Styles available in box in the left column, and the left column contains a list of the styles in the document.

7. Select the **Open File** button located below the right column.

Note: Word automatically looks in the Templates folder and displays template files (.dot).*

8. Click in the **Look in** box and select the drive and/or folder where the file to which the styles should be copied is stored. If necessary, select a different option in the **Files of type** box. Double-click on the name of the file that contains the styles to be changed.

> For example, click in the **Look in** box and select the drive where your file disk is located. Click in the **Files of type** box and select **Word Documents (*.doc)**. Double-click on **15Minutes Formatted.doc** located on your file disk.

Note: The words "To 15Minutes Formatted.doc" display above the second column. Your Organizer dialog box should look similar to Figure 15.3.

9. Select the style(s) to be copied.

> For example, scroll down to the bottom of the list of styles in the left column. Press and hold the **Shift** key and click once on the last style name to select all the styles.

10. Select the **Copy** button located between the columns.

Note: A message box displays asking, "Do you wish to overwrite . . . ?".

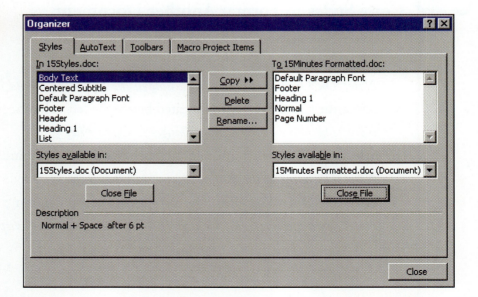

FIGURE 15.3

Organizer dialog box

11. Select **Yes to All** to overwrite all existing built-in styles with the edited styles.

    *Note: The selected styles are copied to the **15Minutes Formatted.doc** document.*

12. Select **Close**.

Finish-Up Instructions

❖ Select **Format**, **AutoFormat** and choose **OK**.

❖ Select the title at the top of page 1 and modify the title style to apply a **16 point** font (select **Format**, **Style**, select **Title**, click on **Modify**, select **Format**, **Font**, click on **16**, select **OK twice**, **Apply**).

❖ Select the two subtitle paragraphs (Board of Directors Meeting and the date). Apply the **Centered Subtitle** style. (If necessary, see step 1 of the Steps to Apply Styles.)

❖ Use the same filename, **15Minutes Formatted.doc**, and save the file.

❖ Print one copy and close the document.

Use Templates

A template is a model for a document. A template stores information on how a document is to be formatted, e.g., margins and styles. Templates can also contain elements such as border lines, graphics, AutoText entries, and macros. Unless another template is selected, the *Normal.dot* template is attached when a new document is created. Word provides other templates for many common types of documents such as memos and letters (see Appendix C for examples of supplied templates).

Using templates to format documents can save time and create a consistent look. Templates can be used over and over to format documents. For example, a memo template can be used to format all the memos created in a company. By using the same template, all the memos will have a similar appearance.

A template can be attached to a new document by selecting **File**, **New** and double-clicking on the desired template name. Once a template is attached to a document, the styles associated with the template can be applied to the document text by selecting **Format**, **AutoFormat** or by using the **Style** box on the Formatting Toolbar. Existing styles can be edited and new styles created using the Steps to Edit a Style on page 390 and Steps to Create a New Style on page 391.

An existing template can also be used as the basis for creating a new template. For example, after reviewing the elements (styles, fonts, borders, graphics, etc.) in the Contemporary Memo template, you decide that, although you like the majority of the elements, there are several elements that need to be slightly altered. After changing the desired elements, the template is saved under a new name. Using an existing template as the basis for a new template saves time because many of the existing elements can be used and only a few elements will need to be changed. The new template can be saved and used over and over again to create documents.

Normally, the user templates are stored in the Templates folder created by Word when Word was installed (e.g., **C:\Microsoft Office\Templates**). The

Templates folder contains several subfolders named for the different types of documents that the templates can be used to create. For example, the Templates folder contains a subfolder named Letters & Faxes, which contains the template and Wizard files that can be used to create letters and faxes.

If template files will be stored in locations other than the Templates folder created by Word, select **Tools**, **Options**, choose the **File Locations** tab, select the **User templates** option, choose **Modify**, and then select the name of the drive and/or folder where Word should look for the template files. Select **OK**, **Close**.

When Templates are to be saved by Workgroups, the default for Workgroup templates should be set. Set the templates for Workgroups by choosing **Tools**, **Options, File Locations** tab, select **Workgroup templates**.

 Steps to ## Create a New Template Based on an Existing Template

1. Select **File, New**.

    *Note: Do **not** select the New button.*

2. In the New dialog box, select the tab that contains the icon for the template to be used as the basis of the new template.

    For example, select the **Memos** tab.

3. Click once on the desired template name.

    For example, click once on the file named **Professional Memo**.

4. In the Create new area, select the **Template** option.

5. Select **OK**.

    Note: In a moment, the words Template1 - Memo... display in the Title bar, and the template containing sample text displays in the document window (see Figure 15.4). If desired, print the template and determine the elements, such as fonts, font sizes, and borders, to be changed. The sample text in the template contains information on how to use the template.

FIGURE 15.4

Document window containing Professional Memo template

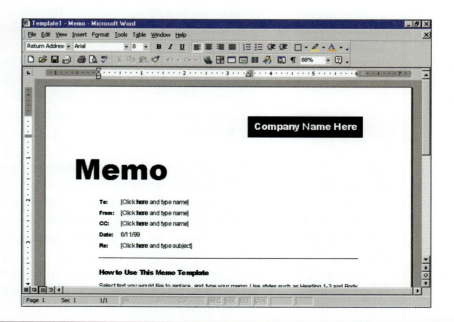

Chapter 15—Create Documents Using Special Functions

6. Edit the template elements as necessary.

   For example, use the following information to edit the template elements:

   a. Select the text "**Company Name Here**" in the frame at the top of the document. Type **RHP and Associates**. Select the **Center** alignment button.

   b. Insert your name beside the lead word **From**. (Move the mouse pointer to the words "**Click here and type name**" located beside the lead word **From** and click once; type your name.)

   c. Change the font for the Normal style to **11 point** and the font for the Message Header Label style to **10 point**. (Select **Format**, **Style**, select the **Normal** style in the Styles list, and select **Modify**. Select the **Format** button and choose **Font**. Select **11** in the Size box. Select **OK** twice. Select the **Message Header Label** style in the Styles list and select **Modify**. Select the **Format** button and choose **Font**. Select **10** in the Size box. Select **OK** twice. Select **Close**.)

   d. Select and delete the "How to Use This Memo Template" subheading and the text that displays below the horizontal border line.

   e. Scroll down to view the bottom of the page. Double-click on the footer text (**1**). Delete the footer text. Select **Close** on the Header/Footer Toolbar.

7. When all the changes have been made to the template elements, select the **Save** button, choose the drive and folder where the template should be saved, and type the template name. Select **Save**.

   For example, if necessary, select the drive where your file disk is located. Create a folder on your file disk by selecting the **Create New Folder** button , typing **My Templates** in the Name box, and selecting **OK**. Double-click on the **My Templates** folder. Delete the name in the File name box and type your initials and the word **Memo.dot** (e.g., **LH Memo.dot**). Select **Save**.

   Note: The new template is saved and the name displays in the Title bar.

8. Print a copy of the template.

9. Close the template file but *do not* save the changes.

Finish-Up Instructions

❖ Select **File**, **New**.

❖ Select the **General** tab.

   *Note: An icon with the name of your memo template (e.g., **LH Memo.dot**) should be displayed. If no icon displays for your template, select **Cancel**. Select the **New** button, select **Tools**, **Options**, and choose the **File Location** tab. Select the **User template** option, choose **Modify**, select the drive where your file disk is located, select the **My Templates** folder, choose **OK**, and select **Close**. Repeat the first two Finish-Up Instructions.*

❖ Double-click on the icon for your memo template.

Note: In a moment, the top portion of a memo displays.

❖ Use the following information to complete the memorandum.

   a. The memorandum is to your instructor.

   b. A copy should be sent to a fellow student.

   c. The topic of the memorandum is **Advantages of Using Templates to Create Documents.** Press **Enter.**

   d. You create the body text for the memorandum (three or four sentences).

❖ Use the filename **15Template Advantages.doc** and save the file on your file disk.

Note: The new filename displays in the Title bar. The new template name does not display in the Title bar, but is listed and saved in the directory with the new name.

❖ Print one copy and close the document.

Use Macros

Macros are shortcuts that eliminate repetitive action. Macros are especially useful when your actions involve selecting several menus or making changes in dialog boxes. Macros are created by recording keystrokes and mouse selections. Because Word remembers each keystroke and mouse selection when a macro is being recorded, the macro should be planned before the recording process is started. Write down each step needed to create the macro.

To begin recording a macro, select **Tools, Macro, Record New Macro** and give the macro a name. If desired, a description of the purpose of the macro can be typed. The macro can be made available to all documents by placing the macro in the *Normal.dot* (global template), or the macro can be made available only to documents created using a specific template. To make a macro available only to documents created using a specific template, select the desired template before selecting **Tools, Macro, Record New Macro.** When the Record Macro dialog box displays, choose the desired template listed in the **Store macro in** box. At this point, if desired, the macro can be assigned a toolbar or keyboard shortcut.

Once the macro has been named and a decision has been made about assigning the macro to a toolbar or keyboard shortcut, the Record mode becomes active. A Macro Record Toolbar containing **Stop Recording** ■ and **Pause Recording** ▐▶ buttons will display in the document widow, and the mouse pointer will change to a pointer arrow with a cassette tape icon to indicate that the Record mode is on.

Word remembers each keystroke and mouse selection made while the Record mode is on. When recording a macro, the mouse can be used to select buttons, commands, and options. However, the mouse cannot be used to select text or to move the insertion point in the document window. Selecting text and moving the insertion point must be accomplished using keystrokes. When all the desired keystrokes and mouse selections have been completed, the **Stop**

Recording button ■ is selected on the Macro Record Toolbar. The macro is automatically saved when the **Stop Recording** button ■ is selected.

The **Pause Recording** button ❚❙● on the Macro Record Toolbar can be selected while the Record mode is on to allow you to perform steps that should not be recorded. To resume recording, select the **Pause Recording** button ❚❙● again.

Once a macro is recorded, the macro can be played as often as needed by selecting **Tools**, **Macro**, and choosing **Macros**. Double-click on the desired macro name, or press the assigned shortcut keys. The macro performs each recorded step. When all the recorded steps have been completed, you can edit, save, print, or close the file by using normal procedures. Changes to a document created by a macro do not alter the macro; the macro can be used again and again.

Start-Up Instructions

❖ A new document window should be displayed. (If necessary, select the **New** button.)

 ## Record a Macro

1. In a clear document window, select **Tools, Macro, Record New Macro**.

   Note: The Record Macro dialog box displays (see Figure 15.5). The suggested name, Macro1, is highlighted in the Macro name box.

2. In the Macro name box, type the name of the macro.

   For example, type **mylabels**. (Do not type the period.)

3. Click in the **Description** box at the end of the sentence that states "Macro recorded . . ." and press **Enter**. Type a description of the purpose of the macro.

   For example, place the insertion point at the end of the text in the Description box and press **Enter**. Type **Creates a sheet of labels with my address**. (Do not type the period.)

   Note: If desired, a macro can be assigned a toolbar or a keystroke shortcut (keyboard).

4. To assign the macro either a toolbar or keyboard shortcut, select the **Toolbars** or **Keyboard** button in the **Assign macro to** area.

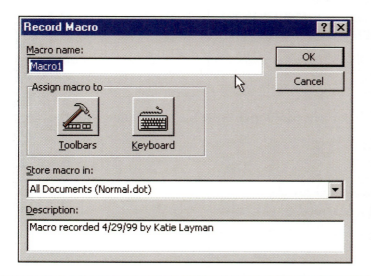

FIGURE 15.5

Record Macro dialog box

For example, to assign a keyboard shortcut for the **mylabels** macro, select the **Keyboard** button. The insertion point is now located in the Press new shortcut key box. Press **Ctrl** and **F1**. Select **Assign**. Select **Close**.

*Note: The Stop Recording Toolbar displays with Stop Recording and Pause Recording buttons. From now on, every keystroke or mouse selection you make will be remembered by Word until you select the **Stop Recording** button on the Stop Recording Toolbar. A small cassette icon is attached to the mouse pointer.*

5. Perform the actions to be recorded.

   For example, perform the following steps:

   a. Select **Tools, Envelopes and Labels**.

   b. Select the **Labels** tab.

   c. Click in the Address box and type:

      Your name (Press **Enter**)
      Your address (Press **Enter**)
      Your City, State Zip (Do *not* press **Enter**)

   d. Select **Options**.

   e. In the Product number box, select **5260 - Address** (if using a laser or ink jet printer) or **4144 - Address** (if using a dot matrix printer).

   f. Select **OK**.

   g. Check that the **Full page of the same label** option is selected in the Print area.

   h. Select **New Document**.

   i. When the page of labels displays, select all the labels by pressing **Ctrl** and **a**.

   j. Change the font to **Bookman Old Style, 11 point** or **make a font choice of your own**.

   k. To deselect the text, press the up arrow key once.

6. When all actions to be recorded have been performed, select the **Stop Recording** button ▪ on the Macro Record Toolbar.

   For example, the **mylabels** macro is complete. Select the **Stop Recording** button ▪.

*Note: The macro is automatically saved when the **Stop Recording** button is selected.*

Finish-Up Instructions

❖ Close the document (do *not* save the file). Continue with the Steps to Play (Run) a Macro.

Start-Up Instructions

❖ The macro named **mylabels** must have been created using the previous Steps to Record a Macro.

Play (Run) a Macro

1. Press the keyboard shortcut keys assigned to the macro or select **Tools, Macro,** choose **Macros**; double-click on the desired macro name.

   For example, press **Ctrl** and **F1** to play the mylabels macro

   Note: In a few moments, the labels containing your name and address display in the document window. The document can now be edited, saved, printed, etc., in the same manner as any other document.

Finish-Up Instructions

❖ Use the *new* filename **15address labels.doc** and save the file.

❖ Print one copy and close the document.

❖ Continue with the Steps to Delete a Macro.

 Delete a Macro

1. Select **Tools, Macro** and choose **Macros**.
2. Click on the macro name to be deleted.

   For example, click on **mylabels**.
3. Select **Delete**.
4. Select **Yes** to the message "Do you want to delete macro . . . ?".
5. Select **Close** to exit the Macro dialog box.

The Next Step

Chapter Review and Activities

Self-Check Quiz

T F 1. Before a character style is applied, the desired text must be selected.

T F 2. Text can be sorted in alphabetical or numerical order.

T F 3. Descending sort order is A through Z, or lowest to highest.

T F 4. The Record Macros dialog box can be used to run a macro.

T F 5. A template is a model for a document and stores information on how a document is to be formatted.

6. A template can contain _____.
   a. styles
   b. borders and graphics
   c. AutoText
   d. all of the above

7. When the **Format**, **AutoFormat** option is chosen, _____.
   a. the document is formatted using built-in styles
   b. the document is spell checked
   c. you can review and accept or reject format changes

8. Two types of styles are _____ and Character.
   a. Document
   b. Paragraph
   c. Page
   d. Column

9. Define a style and state two advantages of using styles.

10. Explain why a macro should be planned before you begin to record it.

Enriching Language Arts Skills

Spelling/Vocabulary Words

amend—to change or modify for the better; to make right.

authority—the power to control, influence, or administer.

exclusive—not shared with others; limiting possession, control, or use to a single individual or group.

fiscal—of or relating to financial matters; of or relating to taxation, public revenue, or public debt.

Apostrophe Used to Show Possession

If a noun is singular and used to show possession, add an apostrophe (') and an s. If the noun is plural or the final letter in the noun is an s, add only an apostrophe after the s.

Examples:

The secretary's table was misplaced.

The brothers' houses and the Lexis' garage are on the corner of Piedmont and High Streets.

Activities

■ Activity 15.1—Use AutoFormat

1. Open the file named **15act1.doc** located on the data disk.

2. Apply the built-in styles by selecting the **Format, AutoFormat** option, and choosing **OK**.

3. Insert page numbers at the bottom center of all pages (select **Insert, Page Numbers, Bottom of page (Footer), Center, OK**).

4. Use the *new* filename **15Bank Services.doc** and save the formatted report on your file disk.

5. Print one copy

6. Optional: Fax this document to your instructor via a local fax, or write an e-mail message to your instructor that you are sending this assignment. Attach this file to your e-mail message.

7. Close the document.

■ Activity 15.2—Sort Information by Number and by Date

Part I

1. Open the file named **15act2.doc** located on the data disk and use the following instructions to sort the list of employees by salary.

2. Select the entire document (**Ctrl** and **a**).

3. Select **Table, Sort**.

4. Select the **Options** button and select **Tabs** in the Separate fields at area. Select **OK**.

5. Make the following selections in the Sort by area:

Sort by:	**Salary** or **Field 3**
Type:	**Number**
Sort order:	**Ascending**

6. Select **OK**.

7. Click once to deselect the text.

8. Select all text and select **Center** alignment (**Ctrl** and **a**, select the **Center** button).

9. Use the filename **15Salaries.doc** and save the file on your file disk.

10. Print one copy.

Part II

> *Note:* *Use the following instructions to sort the list of employees by date of hire in descending order.*

1. Select the entire document.

2. Select **Table, Sort**. Select the **My list has Header row** option.

3. Select the **Options** button and select **Tabs** in the Separate fields at area. Select **OK**.

4. Make the following selections in the Sort by area:

Sort by:	**Date Hired**
Type:	**Date**
Sort order:	**Descending**

5. Select **OK**.

6. Click once to deselect the text.

7. Use the *new* filename **15Date of Hire.doc** and save the file on your file disk.

8. Print one copy and close the document.

Activity 15.3—Sort Lines

1. Create the memorandum shown below:

Memorandum

To: See Distribution Below

From: Kai Won

Date: (Use current date)

Subject: Reprint Procedures Meeting

A meeting has been scheduled for Monday in the West Conference Room on the fourth floor to discuss the proposed changes in the reprint procedures for all documents. Your input would be greatly appreciated.

Please call me at Ext. 4253 to confirm your attendance.

KW/xx

Distribution:

Robert Killa
Drandis Johnson
Susan Colombo

Jad Riccetti
Nadereh Dib
Kristi Paulsen
Janelle Johnson

2. Use the filename **15Reprint memo.doc** and save the file on your file disk. Print one copy.

3. Use the following information to sort the distribution list in ascending order by last name (Word 2). Use **Then by** to sort the distribution list by first names when last names are the same.

   a. Select the names in the distribution list.

   b. Select **Table**, **Sort**.

   c. To change the field separator or a space, select the **Options** button, choose **Other**, and press the **Spacebar** once. Select **OK**.

   d. In the **Sort by** box, select **Word 2**. If necessary, select **Ascending**.

   e. In the **Then by** box, select **Word 1**. If necessary, select **Ascending**.

   f. Select **OK**.

4. Save the file again using the same filename, **15Reprint memo.doc**.

5. Print one copy.

6. Optional: Fax this memo to your instructor via a local fax, or write an e-mail message to your instructor that you are sending this assignment. Attach this file to your e-mail message.

7. Close the document.

Activity 15.4—Create a New Fax Cover Sheet Template

1. Create a new fax cover sheet template using the following information:

   a. Select **File**, **New**.

   b. Select the **Letters & Faxes** tab. Click on the **Professional Fax** icon. Select **Template** in the Create new area, and select **OK**.

   c. Select the text **Company Name Here**, located in a frame at the top right of the document, and type **Applied Plastics, Inc.**

      Note: If desired, choose a 100% Zoom view.

   d. Insert the return address, phone number, and fax number by clicking once on "Click here and type return address and phone and fax numbers" located at the top left of the document. Type the following:

   2429 Rolling Hill Way
   Martinez, CA 94553
   925-555-2434
   925-555-2469 (FAX)

e. Click on the words "Click here and type name" located to the right of the lead word **From**. Type your name.

f. Delete the text that follows the word **Comments**.

2. Save the new fax cover sheet template using the following information:

   a. Select the **Save** button.

   b. Select the drive where your file disk is located and double-click on the **My Templates** folder.

      Note: If necessary, create a new folder named My Templates (see step 7, Steps to Create a New Template Based on an Existing Template, on page 396).

   c. In the File name box, type **your initials** and the words **Fax template.dot**.

   d. Select **Save**.

3. Print one copy of the new fax cover sheet template and close the template.

Challenge Your Skills

Skill 15.1—Create and Apply Styles

1. Open the file named **15skill1.doc** located on the data disk.

2. Edit the Normal style as follows:

   Font: **Garamond, 14 point**, or **make a choice of your own**.

3. Create the following new styles.

Name:	P-Title
Type:	Paragraph
Based on:	Title
Font:	Arial, Bold, 24 point
Paragraph:	Spacing After—18 pt
Name:	P-Subtitle
Type:	Paragraph
Based on:	P-Title
Font:	Arial, Bold, 20 point
Name:	P-Level 1
Type:	Paragraph
Based on:	Normal
Font:	Garamond, 18 point, or make your own choice
Paragraph:	Spacing After—12 pt
Name:	P-Level 2
Type:	Paragraph
Based on:	P-Level 1

| Font: | Garamond, 14 point, or make your own choice |
| Paragraph: | Left indent of .5"; Spacing After—6 pt |

4. Apply the new styles to the document paragraphs.

   Hint: Apply the P-Level 1 style to items numbered 1 and 2. Apply the P-Level 2 style to the items listed with lowercase letters. A style can be applied to multiple paragraphs by selecting the desired paragraphs before *choosing the down triangle beside the Style box.*

5. Use the *new* filename **15Presentation.doc** and save the formatted presentation on your file disk.

6. Print one copy.

7. Optional: Fax the presentation to your instructor via a local fax, or write an e-mail message to your instructor that you are sending this assignment. Attach this file to your e-mail message.

8. Close the document.

Skill 15.2—Create a Macro to Select, Copy, Paste, and Sort a Table

1. Open the file named **15skill2.doc** located on the data disk.

2. Use the following information to create a macro that selects, copies, pastes the copy, and sorts the table by salesperson and sales volume.

   a. Place the insertion point to the left of the "C" in the word "Client" in the first cell of the table.

   b. The macro name is to be **Revenue**. If desired, the macro can be assigned the keystrokes **Alt** and **1**.

   c. Select and copy the table.

      *Hint: To select an entire table, place the insertion point in a table cell and choose **Table, Select, Table**.*

   d. Paste a copy of the table below the heading Monthly Revenue Report by Salesperson.

      Hint: Use the arrow keys to relocate the insertion point. The mouse cannot be used to select text or to move the insertion point when a macro is being recorded.

   e. Select the copied table and sort the table by salesperson in ascending order.

   f. Copy the table. Paste the copy of the table below the heading Monthly Revenue Report by Sales Volume.

   g. Select the copied table and sort the table by sales volume in descending order.

   h. Deselect the table.

   i. Stop recording.

3. Close the document. Do not save the changes.

4. Open the file named **15Revenue.doc** located on the data disk.

5. Place the insertion point in the first table cell and run the revenue macro.

6. Use the *new* filename **15Final Revenue Report.doc** and save the file on your file disk.

7. Print one copy and close the document.

8. Delete the **Revenue** macro.

Skill 15.3—Sort Paragraphs; Language Arts

1. Open the file named **15skill3.doc** located on the data disk.

2. Make decisions regarding bolding and fonts for the title, ballot measure numbers, and names.

3. Correct one number format error, four spelling errors, three punctuation/ grammatical errors, and five misused words.

4. Select all paragraphs except the title.

5. Sort the paragraphs numerically in descending order by the ballot measure number.

6. Use the *new* filename **15ballot sorted 1.doc** and save the sorted file on your file disk.

7. Print one copy.

8. Select all paragraphs except the title.

9. Sort the paragraphs alphabetically in ascending order by the first word in each ballot measure name.

    Hint: Use Word 2 as the Sort by criteria.

10. Use the *new* filename **15ballot sorted 2.doc** and save the sorted file on your file disk.

11. Print one copy and close the document.

Manage Document Windows and Files

16

Features Covered

- Arrange, maximize, minimize, move, restore, and resize document windows
- Create, revise, and print the document summary information
- Use the Find feature
- Print multiple files
- Copy, move, rename, and delete files
- Create folders and subfolders
- Use the Favorites feature
- Convert files to and from other word processing formats
- Assign a password
- Use DOS without exiting Word
- Cancel the printing of a document

Objectives and Introduction

After successfully completing this chapter, you will be able to arrange, maximize, minimize, move, restore, and resize document windows as well as create, revise, and print document summary information. You will also learn how to open and print multiple files; delete, rename, move, and locate files; create and delete folders and subfolders; and use the Favorites feature to quickly access files or folders. In addition, you will learn how to use Word's file conversion and password features. You will also learn how to access DOS without exiting Word and cancel the printing of a document.

The Windows in Word

A Word document window displays after the Word program is launched. Word keeps track of the most recent documents you have worked on and lists them at the bottom of the **File** menu. To open one of these files, simply click on the filename. Up to nine documents can be listed at the bottom of the **File** menu. To change the number of files listed at the bottom of the **File** menu, select **Tools**, **Options**, **General**, increase or decrease the number in the **Recently used file list** box, select **OK**.

As each new file is created, Word sequentially numbers each document window, for example, Document1, Document2, etc. The document number displays in the Title bar. After a file is saved, the filename displays in the Title bar. Any document window can be arranged, maximized, minimized, moved, restored, resized, or closed.

Start-Up Instructions

❖ Create five files as follows:

    a.   In a new document window, type **This is file 1.**; press **Enter** twice.

    b.   Use the filename **16 File 1.doc** and save the file on your file disk.

           Note: Do not close the file.

    c.   Select the **New** button on the Standard Toolbar; type **This is file 2.**; press **Enter** twice.

    d.   Use the filename **16 File 2.doc** and save the file on your file disk.

           Note: Do not close the file.

    e.   Select the **New** button on the Standard Toolbar; type **This is file 3.**; press **Enter** twice.

    f.   Use the filename **16 File 3.doc** and save the file on your file disk.

           Note: Do not close the file.

    g.   Select the **New** button on the Standard Toolbar; type **This is file 4.**; press **Enter** twice.

    h.   Use the filename **16 File 4.doc** and save the file on your file disk.

           Note: Do not close the file.

    i.   Select the **New** button on the Standard Toolbar; type **This is file 5.**; press **Enter** twice.

    j.   Use the filename **16 File 5.doc** and save the file on your file disk.

           Note: Do not close the file.

 Arrange All Document Windows

1. Select **Window, Arrange All**.

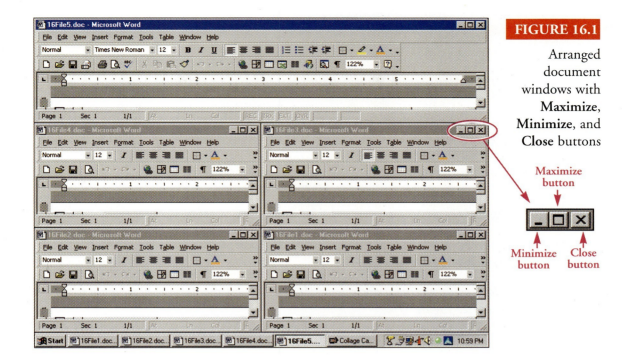

FIGURE 16.1

Arranged document windows with **Maximize**, **Minimize**, and **Close** buttons

Maximize button

Minimize button   Close button

*Note: When **Arrange All** is selected, all open document windows are visible. The active window displays at the top or top left of the screen with the Title bar highlighted (see Figure 16.1).*

Activate/Change the Active Window

1. Place the mouse pointer in the desired window and click once to activate the window.

   For example, move the mouse pointer to the various open windows and click.

   Note: Remember, a window is active when its Title bar is highlighted or displayed in a different color.

Maximize a Window

1. If more than one window is displayed on the screen, activate the desired window and select the **Maximize** button □ to view the window in full size.

   For example, activate and maximize the window containing the file named **16 File 4.doc**.

   *Note: The document window containing the file named **16 File 4.doc** displays in full size on the screen.*

Restore a Maximized Window

Note: Restoring a document window is the process of returning the document window to its previous size.

1. With the document window maximized on the screen, return the window to its previous size by selecting the **Restore** button ⬜ located at the right end of the Menu bar.

   For example, select the **Restore** button ⬜ in the window containing the file named **16 File 4.doc**.

   Note: The file is returned to its previous size (i.e., before it was maximized).

Minimize a Window

Note: Minimizing a document window reduces the document window to a small icon (see Figure 16.2).

1. Activate the desired window and then select the **Minimize** button ⬜ located in the Title bar of the document window.

   For example, activate and minimize the window containing the file named **16 File 3.doc**.

   Note: In the Taskbar, the Title bar of the minimized document window displays (see Figure 16.2).

Restore a Minimized Window

1. On the Taskbar, touch the mouse pointer on the Title bar of the document window to display the full document name.

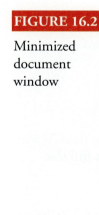

FIGURE 16.2

Minimized document window

Minimized document window

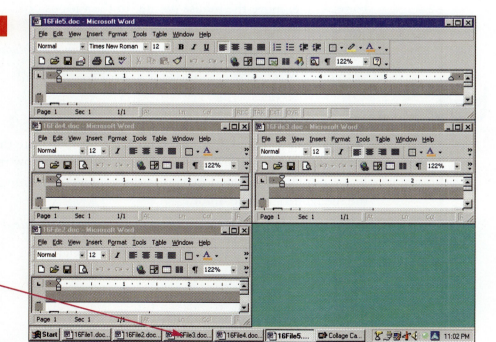

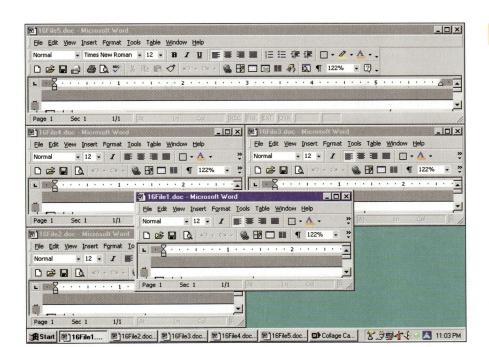

FIGURE 16.3

Moved
document
window

For example, touch the mouse pointer on the Title bar of the
window containing the file named **16 File 3**.

2. Click once on the Title bar of the minimized document window.

 ## Move a Window

Note: The window to be moved must be smaller than the maximum size.

1. Locate the mouse pointer in the Title bar of the desired document window;
press and hold the mouse button.

For example, move the mouse pointer to the Title bar of the
document window containing the file named **16 File 3.doc**;
press and hold the mouse button.

2. Drag the window to the desired position and release the mouse button.

For example, drag the window containing the file named
16 File 3.doc to approximately the center of the screen (see
Figure 16.3).

 ## Resize a Window

Note: The window must be smaller than the maximum size.

1. Locate the mouse pointer on the document window's left, right, or bottom
edge until a double-headed arrow displays. Press and hold the mouse button,
drag the window outline to the desired size, then release the mouse button.

For example, activate the window that contains the file
named **16 File 2.doc**. Move the mouse pointer to the top
edge of the document window and increase the window
height.

Close a Window

1. Click on the **Close** button ☒ located on the far right side of the Title bar.

   For example, click on the **Close** button ☒ on the Title bar of the window containing filename **16 File 2.doc**.

Start-Up Instructions

❖ Maximize the file named **16 File 4.doc**.

Close All Windows

1. Press and hold the **Shift** key while selecting the **File** menu.

2. Select **Close All**.

   *Note: When all document windows are closed, an empty screen, with the words "Microsoft Word" in the Title bar, and the Menu bar display. The Standard and Formatting Toolbars also display, but most of the buttons are shaded gray, indicating that the options are not currently available. If a file has been changed and the changes have not been saved, a message box displays asking whether you want to save the changes to the document. Select **Yes** to save the changes, or select **No** to close the document without saving the changes.*

3. Maximize the Microsoft Word Window.

   For example, click on the **Maximize** button ◻ on the Microsoft Word Title bar.

Create Summary Information

Summary information can be created for a document to provide specific information about a file, such as the title of the document, subject, and the name of the author. Also, keywords can be included that can be used later to search for a document. In addition, in the Comments box you can type information you may want to refer to later. The summary information is created by selecting **File**, **Properties**, choosing the **Summary** tab, and typing the desired information in the option boxes (see Figure 16.4). If desired, Word can prompt you for summary information when you first save a document.

Once the summary information is typed, the information can be changed (updated) and saved. If desired, you can print a document's summary information along with the document, or the summary information can be printed separately.

Start-Up Instructions

❖ Open the file named **16 File 5.doc** located on your file disk.

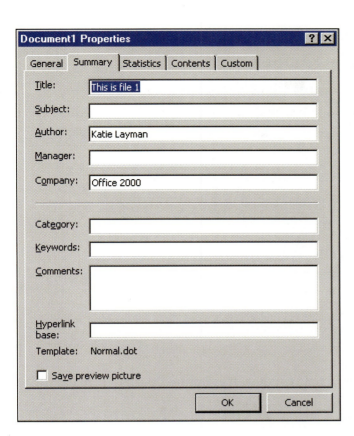

FIGURE 16.4

Summary tab in
the Properties
dialog box

 Steps to **Create Summary Information After a Document Is Saved**

1. Select **File, Properties**. If necessary, select the **Summary** tab.

   Note: A proposed title displays. Also, the author's name and company name may display (see Figure 16.4).

2. Select the **Statistics** tab.

   Note: The Created, Modified, and Accessed dates are displayed. These dates are saved and updated by Word and cannot be changed by the user.

3. Select the **Summary** tab.

4. Check that the **Title** information is highlighted and type the title of the file.

   For example, type **This is a sample file.**

5. Click in the **Subject** box and type the words that identify the document's subject.

   For example, type **Sample.**

6. To change the name of the author, click in the **Author** box or select the name in the Author box and type the name of the author.

   For example, click in the **Author** box and type your name.

   Note: If desired, type any additional information in the Keywords and Comments boxes.

7. Select **OK**.

Revise Summary Information

1. Select **File, Properties**. If necessary, select the **Summary** tab.

2. Select the option(s) to be changed and type the updated information.

   For example, in the Author box, select your name and type the name of a friend.

3. Select **OK** to save the updated summary information.

Print Document Properties

1. Select **File, Print**.

2. Click in the **Print what** box and select **Document properties**.

3. Select **OK**.

   Note: The Document properties print; the document does not print.

Finish-Up Instructions

❖ Close the document window. It is not necessary to save the file.

Create Summary Information Every Time a New Document Is Saved

Note: The following steps are for your information. If these steps are followed, the Summary Info dialog box will display every time a new document is saved or exited.

1. With a document window displayed, select **Tools, Options**.

2. Click on the **Save** tab.

3. Click in the **Prompt for document properties** box.

4. Select **OK**.

Manage Files

The options in the Save As and Open dialog boxes are used to perform the usual disk maintenance tasks of copying, moving, renaming, and deleting files. Additional options include printing multiple files, creating folders/subfolders, removing folders, and searching for a specific filename or text contained in a file.

The Find feature is used to quickly locate a file by finding a filename or partial filename, searching for text that is contained in the file, searching for the last modified date, or searching for a property, such as company or comments. For example, if there is a file named *j fox letter1.doc* on your disk but you cannot remember the entire filename, the file can be located by typing *j fox*.doc* in the File name box of the Open dialog box and selecting the drive letter where the file is located. Word will search for any filename that begins *j fox* and ends with the extension.*doc*.

A document can be located by searching for specific criteria. Choose the drive or folder in the **Look in** box. Select **Tools**, **Find**, and choose the Property and/or Condition desired. Word will locate any files on the selected drive and/or folder that contain the specified condition.

The Favorites feature provides a fast method to access frequently used files, folders, and subfolders without having to remember where the files, folders, or subfolders are located. Files, folders, and subfolders can be added to your list of Favorites by selecting **Tools**, **Add to Favorites** option in the Save As dialog box. When a file, folder, or subfolder is added to your Favorites, it can be accessed quickly by choosing the **Favorites** button located in the left-side bar of the Save As or Open dialog box.

When a file is deleted, the file is placed in the Recycle Bin. If necessary, the file can be retrieved from the Recycle Bin. For example, if a file is accidentally deleted, the file can be retrieved by accessing the Recycle Bin folder and selecting the deleted file. The file remains in the Recycle Bin until the Recycle Bin is emptied. If desired, a file can be deleted but not placed in the Recycle Bin. To delete a file without placing the file in the Recycle Bin, press the **Shift** key while selecting the **Delete** option or pressing the **Delete** key.

Start-Up Instructions

❖ The files named **16 File 1.doc**, **16 File 2.doc**, **16 File 3.doc**, **16 File 4.doc**, and **16 File 5.doc** created earlier in this chapter should be available on your file disk.

Steps to

Find Files by Filename

1. Select the **Open** button.

   Note: The Open dialog box displays. The insertion point is blinking in the File name box.

2. In the File name box of the Open dialog box, type the name or partial name of the file(s) to be found.

   For example, type **16 Fi*.doc**. (Do not type the final period.)

   *Note: The asterisk is a "wildcard" character and is a substitute for multiple characters. In this example, **16 Fi*.doc** instructs the search to find all filenames that begin with **16 Fi** and have the extension **.doc**.*

3. If necessary, click on the down arrow located to the right of the **Look in** box and select the desired drive letter.

   For example, if necessary, click on the down arrow located to the right of the **Look in** box and select the drive letter where your file disk is located.

   *Note: If the search is to include looking for a file(s) in subfolders, select the **Tools** button, click on **Find** and choose the **Search subfolders** option.*

4. Select the **Tools** button or press **Enter**.

Note: A list of files that match the specified filename or partial filename displays in the Open dialog box. If desired, the name of a file(s) can be selected and the **Open** *button chosen to open the document(s).*

5. Select **Cancel** to exit the Open dialog box.

Start-Up Instructions

❖ The files **16 File 1.doc**, **16 File 2.doc**, **16 File 3.doc**, **16 File 4.doc**, and **16 File 5.doc** must be available on your file disk.

Print Multiple Files

1. Select the **Open** button.

2. In the **Look in** box, select the location of the files to be printed.

   For example, select the drive letter where your file disk is located.

3. Click on the first file that you wish to print.

   For example, click on the filename **16 File 1.doc**.

4. *To select a list of nonconsecutive files,* press and hold the **Ctrl** key while you click on each desired filename you wish to print.

   For example, press and hold the **Ctrl** key and click on the filename **16 File 5.doc**.

   To select a list of consecutive files, press and hold the **Shift** key while you click on the last file you wish to print.

5. Move the mouse pointer onto one of the selected filenames. Click the *right* mouse button.

   Note: A popup menu displays.

6. Select **Print**.

   Note: Each document is printed.

Start-Up Instructions

❖ Open the file named **16 File 1.doc**.

Create a Folder

1. Select **File, Save As**.

2. Click in the **Save in** box in the Save As dialog box and select the desired drive letter and/or folder name.

   For example, select the drive letter where your file disk is located.

3. Select the **Create New Folder** button 📁.

   Note: Check that a:\ or b:\ displays below Current Folder in the New Folder dialog box.

4. Type the new folder name in the Name box.

> For example, type your last name.

5. Select **OK** to create the new folder and to exit the New Folder dialog box.

   Note: The new folder name displays in the Save in box. Notice the file folder icon displaying next to the folder name.

Create a Subfolder

6. With your last name folder displayed in the **Save** in box, select the **Create New Folder** button .

7. Type the new subfolder name.

> For example, type your first name.

8. Select **OK**.

   Note: The new folder icon and the subfolder name display below the Save in box.

9. Select **Cancel** to exit the Save As dialog box.

Finish-Up Instructions

❖ Close the file **16 File 1.doc** and continue with the Steps to Copy a File(s).

Steps to Copy a File(s)

1. Select the **Open** button.

   Note: The Open dialog box displays.

2. Select the **Up One Level** button until the drive letter where your file disk is located displays in the **Look** in box.

3. In the list of filenames/folder area, select the file(s) to be copied.

> For example, to select the files named **16 File 1.doc, 16 File 2.doc, 16 File 3.doc, 16 File 4.doc,** and **16 File 5.doc,** click once on the file named **16 File 1.doc,** move the mouse pointer to the file named **16 File 5.doc,** press and hold the **Shift** key and click once. Release the **Shift** key.

   *Note: All files between **16 File 1.doc** and **16 File 5.doc** are selected. To select nonconsecutive files, select the first filename, move the mouse pointer to the next filename, press the **Ctrl** key, and click once.*

4. Move the mouse pointer onto one of the selected filenames. Click the *right* mouse button.

   Note: A pop-up menu displays.

5. Select **Copy**.

6. In the list of filenames/folders area, move the mouse pointer onto the folder and click the *right* mouse button.

> For example, move the mouse pointer onto your last name folder and click the *right* mouse button.

Note: A pop-up menu displays.

7. Select **Paste**.

Finish-Up Instructions

❖ When the copy process is completed, double-click on your last name folder.

Note: Your last name folder displays in the Look in box, and your first name subfolder and copied files display.

❖ Use steps 3–7 of the Steps to Copy a File(s) and copy the files named **16 File 2.doc** and **16 File 4.doc** from your last name folder to your first name subfolder.

❖ To view the copied files, double-click on your first name folder. Word lists the copied files below the Look in box.

❖ Select **Cancel** to exit the Open dialog box.

Add Files/Folders to Favorites

1. Select the **Open** button.

2. If necessary, click in the **Look in** box and select the desired drive.

   For example, click in the **Look in** box and select the drive where your file disk is located.

3. Select the file, folder, or subfolder to be added to your Favorites.

   For example, click once on your last name folder.

4. Select the **Tools** button and choose the **Add to Favorites** option.

   Note: No change displays on your screen.

5. Select **Cancel** to exit the Open dialog box.

Finish-Up Instructions

❖ Continue with the Steps to Use the Look in Favorites Feature.

Use the Look in Favorites Feature

1. Select the **Open** button.

2. Choose the **Favorites** button [image].

   Note: The Favorites folder displays in the Look in box, and a list of the items that have been added to the Favorites displays.

3. Select the desired filename, folder name, or subfolder name.

   For example, double-click on your last name folder.

   Note: The list of folder(s) and filenames in your last name folder displays.

Finish-Up Instructions

❖ To exit the Open dialog box, select the **Cancel** button.

Delete Items from the Favorites Folder

1. Select the **Open** button.
2. Select the **Favorites** button .
3. Move the mouse pointer to the filename, folder, or subfolder to be deleted from the Favorites folder and click the *right* mouse button.

   For example, move the mouse pointer to your last name folder and click the *right* mouse button.

   Note: Deleting the file, folder, or subfolder name from the Favorites folder does not delete the file, folder, or subfolder from the disk drive.

4. Select **Delete**.
5. Select **Yes** to the message, "Are you sure you want to send . . . to the Recycle Bin?".
6. Select **Cancel** to exit the Open dialog box.

Finish-Up Instructions

❖ Continue with the Steps to Delete a File(s).

Delete a File(s)

Note: All files to be deleted must be closed.

1. Select the **Open** button.
2. Select the drive and/or folder in which the file(s) to be deleted is (are) located.

   For example, if necessary, select the drive in which your file disk is located. Double-click on your last name folder; then double-click on your first name subfolder.

3. Select the filename(s) to be deleted.

   For example, select the files named **16 File 2.doc** and **16 File 4.doc** located in your first name folder.

4. Move the mouse pointer onto one of the selected files and click the *right* mouse button.
5. *To delete the file(s) to the Recycle Bin,* select the **Delete** option.

   To delete the file(s) but not place the file(s) in the Recycle Bin, press the **Shift** key while selecting the **Delete** option.

   For example, press the **Shift** key while selecting the **Delete** option to delete the selected file(s) from the disk without placing the file(s) in the Recycle Bin.

   Note: The Confirm Multiple File Delete dialog box displays.

6. Select **Yes** to delete the selected file(s).

   Note: The files are deleted.

---

7. Select Cancel to exit the Open dialog box.

 ## Open Multiple Files

1. Select the Open button. Select the drive and/or folder that contains the files to be opened.

   For example, if necessary, select the drive where your file disk is located. Double-click on your last name folder.

2. Click on the first file to be opened.

   For example, click on the file named **16 File 1.doc**.

3. *To select a list of nonconsecutive files,* press and hold the Ctrl key while you click on each desired filename you wish to open.

   For example, select the files named **16 File 2.doc** and **16 File 4.doc**.

   To select a list of consecutive files, press and hold the Shift key while you click on the last file you wish to open.

4. Select Open.

   Note: Word opens each file in a separate document window. The last file opened displays in the document window. Multiple files can be open at the same time. The number of files that can be opened depends on the amount of memory available.

Finish-Up Instructions

❖ Select **Window**, **Arrange All** to display all open document windows.

❖ Press **Shift** and select **File**, **Close All**.

❖ Clic on the **Maximize** button in the Microsoft Word Title bar.

Convert File Formats

Word for Windows provides a method to change the file format of a document. A document can be saved to another file format or converted from a different file format. For example, a document originally saved in WordPerfect for Windows can be converted to a Word file format. In addition, a Word document can be saved in another format, such as MS-DOS text.

Start-Up Instructions

❖ Open the file named **16 File 1.doc** located on your file disk.

 ## Save a File in a Different Format

1. Select File, Save As.

2. Type the desired filename in the **File name** box.

For example, type **16 different format**. (Do not type the final period.)

3. Click in the **Save as type** box.

   For example, scroll down the list of file types and select **WordPerfect 5.1 for DOS (*.doc)**.

4. Select **Save**.

   *Note: If a message displays stating that the document contains formatting that will be lost upon conversion, select **Yes** to continue the save process or select **No** to cancel. The file named **16 different format.doc** is now saved in the WordPerfect 5.1 for DOS file format. The file named **16 File 1.doc** is still available on your file disk and is saved in the Word file format.*

Finish-Up Instructions

❖ Close the document.

 Open a File Created in a Different Program Format and Save as a Word File

1. Select the **Open** button and double-click on the desired file.

   For example, double-click on **16 different format.doc**.

   *Note: The message "Word is converting . . ." displays briefly at the bottom left of the screen. When the document displays, you may see the field {PRIVATE} in the document. Word inserts a "Private" field when converting text created using a different format. The field contains data needed to convert a document back to its original file format. To hide the field, select **Tools**, **Options**, **View** and deselect **All** in the **Formatting marks** area. To show the other formatting marks on the screen, click on **Tab characters**, **Spaces**, **Paragraph marks**, **Hidden text**, and **Optional hyphens** in the **Formatting marks** area.*

2. Select **File, Save As**.

3. Select the down triangle next to the **Save as type** box.

   For example, select **Word Document [*.doc]**.

4. Select **Save**.

5. Click on **Yes** to save the file in the Word format.

   *Note: The file named **16 different format.doc** is now saved in the Word file format.*

Finish-Up Instructions

❖ Close the document.

Provide File Security

Once a file is created, the file can be saved and given a password. Each time the saved file is opened, the password is requested. The password must be remembered by the user because there is no method available for finding a forgotten password. A password can be removed or changed at any time (but only if you remember the current password).

Passwords are case-sensitive (an uppercase "W" and a lowercase "w" are considered two different characters) and can contain as many as 15 characters made up of numbers, letters, symbols, and spaces.

There are two password options: **Password to open** and **Password to modify**. The **Password to open** option restricts access to the file to only users who know the password. With the **Password to modify** option, any user can open the file, with or without the password, as a read-only document. To edit and save the file using the existing filename, the password must be entered. If the file is opened as a read-only file, the user can edit the file, but the file must be saved using a different name. If the **Read only recommended** option is selected and a password is inserted in the **Password to open** box, a file can be opened either as a regular document or as a read-only document.

Start-Up Instructions

❖ Select the **New** button on the Standard Toolbar.

❖ Type the following sentence:

> **This is a very secret file that no one but me should ever see.**

 ## Create or Change a Password

1. Select **File, Save As**.

2. Type the desired filename.

   > For example, type **16Secret.doc**. (Do not type the final period.)

3. Select **Tools**, **General Options**.

   Note: The Save dialog box appears with the Save tab selected.

4. Click in the **Password to open** box located in the lower left corner of the dialog box.

5. Type the desired password in the **Password to open** box.

   > For example, type **007**. (Do not type the final period.)

   Note: To ensure privacy, the typed characters are displayed as asterisks on the screen. Remember, passwords are case-sensitive and can contain as many as 15 characters made up of numbers, letters, symbols, and spaces.

6. Select **OK**.

   Note: The Confirm Password dialog box appears.

7. Type the password again in the **Confirm Password** dialog box.

8. Select OK.

9. If necessary, select the disk drive where your disk is located. Select Save in the Save As dialog box.

   Note: You will be returned to the document window.

Finish-Up Instructions

❖ Close the document.

 ## Open a File That Has Been Protected with a Password

1. Select the Open button.

2. Double-click on the desired filename.

   For example, double-click on **16Secret.doc**.

   Note: The Password dialog box displays.

3. Type the password exactly as typed when the password was created.

   For example, type **007**. (Do not type the final period.)

   Note: As the password is typed, asterisks display on the screen.

4. Select OK.

   Note: The password-protected file displays.

 ## Remove a Password

1. With the password-required document open, select File, Save As.

2. Select Tools, General Options.

   Note: The Save dialog box displays.

3. Double-click in the Password to open box.

4. Press the Delete key.

5. Select OK.

6. Select Save to save the file without the password.

Finish-Up Instructions

❖ Close the document window.

Use DOS Without Exiting Word

Dos commands such as *format*, *chkdsk* (check disk), *dir* (directory), *date*, *erase*, and *diskcopy* can be accessed without exiting the Word program. Windows allows multiple programs to run at the same time.

Use DOS Without Exiting Word

1. Select the Start button.

2. Select Programs.

3. Select the MS-DOS Prompt option.

   Note: After a few moments, the MS-DOS window displays in black and white.

4. Type and execute the desired DOS command.

   For example, type **ver** and press **Enter**.

   Note: The number of the Windows version in use displays in brackets, e.g., [Version 4.00.1111].

5. If desired, type another DOS command or type **exit** to close the MS-DOS window.

   For example, type **exit** and press **Enter**.

Cancel the Printing of a Document

Once a document has been sent to print, the printing may be stopped or canceled. Word gives you the option in **Tools**, **Options**, **Print** tab to set the print feature to allow background printing. This feature allows you to print one document while working in another document. If background printing is turned on in **Tools**, **Options**, **Print** tab, a print command can be canceled by double-clicking on the printer icon in the Taskbar (the printer icon only displays when a file is printing), selecting the document, and pressing **Delete**. If background printing is not turned on, a Printing dialog box briefly displays; select **Cancel** to stop a print command. Windows Print Queue can also be used to cancel the printing of a document.

   If you are having trouble printing a document, check that the printer is turned on and that the printer cables are securely connected. Also, if a printer is shared, check the switch box or local area network (LAN) connection (see your instructor). Before resending a print job, check Windows Print Queue for any filenames of documents waiting to print. If necessary, delete the filenames of the documents that should not be printed.

 ## Access Print Queue

   Note: The following steps are for your information.

1. After a document has been sent to print, select the Start button.

 2. Select Settings, Printers.

   Note: The Printers window displays.

3. Double-click on the desired printer icon.

4. To delete a file from the print queue, move the mouse pointer to the name of the document to be deleted from the print queue and click the *right* mouse button. Select **Cancel Printing**.

5. *To close the window for your printer,* click on the **Close** button in your Printers window Title bar.

   To return to Word without closing the Printers window, select the **Microsoft Word** button in the Taskbar.

The Next Step

Chapter Review and Activities

Self-Check Quiz

T F 1. When multiple document windows are open, select **Window**, **Arrange All** to display all the documents on the screen.

T F 2. The **Maximize** button can be selected to reduce the size of a document window.

T F 3. All open document windows can be closed at once by holding down the **Shift** key and selecting **File**, **Close All**.

T F 4. You can print a document's summary information without printing the document.

T F 5. The number of files that can be open at one time depends on the amount of available memory.

T F 6. Word can change the file format for a document, i.e., save a file as a WordPerfect 5.1 DOS file.

7. The maximum number of characters that can be used as a password is _____.
   a. 9
   b. 16
   c. 23
   d. 15

8. The Favorites feature provides a fast method to access frequently used _____.
   a. folders
   b. files
   c. subfolders
   d. all of these

9. List five file management tasks that can be accomplished using the Save As or Open dialog boxes.

10. List the steps to open multiple files.

Enriching Language Arts Skills

Proofreading Hints

When proofreading a document, read the document twice: once for content and meaning and once to check grammar, spelling, and punctuation. When proofreading your own work, place the original document/draft beside the screen and read across, comparing line by line. Read aloud with a second person to compare the printed copy with the original document/draft.

Examples of errors to look for when proofreading:

Repeated words	The wedding reception will be held *on on* Sunday at the Palmer Country Club.
Misused or missing words	The transaction is *not* legal. The transaction is *now* legal.
Missing punctuation	The cost was *$2516.* (should be $25.16)
Misspelled names	Kathryn or Catherine
Transposed letters/numbers	The *item* is 10:00 a.m. (should be time) The report is due October *21.* (should be October 12)

Activities

Activity 16.1—Arrange and Maximize Document Windows

1. Open four files of your choice from your file disk.

2. Arrange all windows (select **Window**, **Arrange All**).

3. Maximize one of the document windows (double-click on the **Maximize** button in the desired document's Title bar).

4. Close all document windows (press and hold the **Shift** key and select **File**, **Close All**).

Activity 16.2—Print Multiple Files

1. Select the **Open** button.

2. If necessary, click in the **Look in** box and choose the drive letter where your file disk is located.

3. Select two or three consecutive files located on your file disk.

4. Move the mouse pointer onto one of the selected files and click the *right* mouse button.

5. Print the selected files (select the **Print** option).

Activity 16.3—Create and Print Document Properties Information

1. Open one of the files from your file disk and review the document to determine the subject of the document.

2. Create a summary information for your chosen file. Fill in the title, subject, author, and keywords boxes with the appropriate information (select **File**, **Properties**; on the **Summary** tab, type the desired information in the appropriate boxes; select **OK**).

3. Print the summary information (select **File**, **Print**; click in the **Print what** box; choose **Document properties**; select **OK**).

4. Save and close the document.

Challenge Your Skills

Skill 16.1—Create Folders and Copy and Delete Files

1. Create two folders on your file disk using the folder names **Folder 1** and **Folder 2**.

2. Select the six files for Chapter 13 from the data disk and copy to **Folder 1**. (Copy the files named **13act1.doc**, **13act3.doc**, **13drill1.doc**, **13drill2.doc**, **13 drill3.doc**, and **13skill2.doc**.)

3. Copy the files named **13drill1** and **13drill2** from **Folder 1** to **Folder 2**.

4. In **Folder 1**, delete the Chapter 13 file named **13drill3.doc**.

Part 4
Checking Your Step

Production Skill Builder Projects
Chapters 13–16

Production Project 4.1—Create a Flier with Graphic Image(s); Use Character Spacing

1. Use the following information to create a flier:

   a. A safari to Africa is scheduled for May 15–30, 200x. The safari is being coordinated by Francene Engdahl of Safaris Unlimited. Francene can be contacted at 319-555-2550.

   b. The safari package includes airfare, accommodations, sightseeing tours, and daily breakfast.

   c. The cost of the safari package is $4,495 per person.

   d. Use one or two images (**Insert, Picture, Clip Art**) to enhance the appearance of the flier. Suggested pictures are: Animals—lions, Transportation—air travel or airplanes, Maps—world, or make a choice of your own.

   e. Use WordArt, borders, and spacing as desired.

   f. Make decisions on appropriate fonts and sizes for the text.

   g. Use character spacing to adjust the spacing between words and letters as desired.

2. Use the filename **4Safari flier 1.doc** and save the file.

3. Print one copy.

4. Optional: Fax this flier to your instructor via a local fax, or write an e-mail message to your instructor that you are sending this assignment. Attach this file to your e-mail message.

5. Close the document.

Production Project 4.2—Use Superscripts, Subscripts, and Ordinals

1. Create the following document using superscripts, subscripts, and ordinals:

SUPERSCRIPTS, SUBSCRIPTS, AND ORDINALS

COMPLEMENTARY ANGLES

$20°$ $70°$ $30°$ $60°$

SUPPLEMENTARY ANGLES

$75°$ $105°$ $60°$ $120°$

CHEMICAL FORMULAS

Barium Stearate = $Ba(C_{18}H_{35}O_2)_2$

Magnesium Hydroxide = $Mg(OH)_2$

Sulfapyridine = $NH_2C_6H_4SO_2NHC_5H_4N$

Thiopental = $C_{11}H_{18}N_2O_2S$

ORDINALS

Attend our 10th anniversary sale!

Judy lives at 632 NW 8th Street.

---

2. Use the filename **4Project 2.doc** and save the file.

3. Print one copy and close the document.

Production Project 4.3—Use the Spike to Create an Overhead Transparency

1. Open the file named **4pact3.doc** located on the data disk.

2. Use the Spike feature to create an overhead transparency consisting of the document title and the sideheads contained in the file named **4pact3.doc**.

3. After the title and sideheads have been accumulated in the Spike, create a new document, insert the text from the Spike, and empty the Spike.

4. Format the new document as an overhead transparency. Make decisions regarding:

   Fonts and point sizes
   Alignment
   Spacing between paragraphs

5. If desired, insert a graphic image (picture) of your choice.

6. Use the *new* filename **4mail overheads.doc** and save the overhead transparency file.

7. Print one copy and close all documents.

1. Open the file named **4pact4.doc** located on the data disk.

2. Use AutoFormat to apply the built-in styles to the document.

3. Edit the built-in styles as follows:

Style name:	Normal
Font:	Arial, Regular, 11 point, or make a choice of your own

Style name:	Title
Font:	Britannic Bold, 16 point, or make a choice of your own
Paragraph:	Spacing After—18 pt

Style name:	Heading 1
Font:	Britannic Bold, 14 point, or make a choice of your own
Paragraph:	Spacing Before—12 pt; Spacing After—6 pt

4. Create the following new Character style:

Style name:	TV Prog Name
Style type:	Character
Font:	Arial, Bold Italic, 11 point, or make a choice of your own

5. Review the document and apply styles as necessary. For example, find each occurrence of the program name *Unresolved Investigations* and apply the TV Prog Name character style. Check that all the sideheads have been formatted with the Heading 1 style.

6. Correct one spelling error, three punctuation errors, one dollar amount format error, one misused word, and one repeated word error.

7. Use the *new* filename **4Sr Attorney Job Description.doc** and save the formatted document.

Part 5
A Giant Step

Use Desktop Publishing

Chapters 17–19

- Use landscape orientation
- Insert previously created text into a document or text box
- Create a shadow border
- Insert a PCX file into a document
- Create a caption
- Rotate and reverse text
- Insert an image from the Microsoft Clip Gallery
- Create a text box for pull quote text
- Create unequal column widths
- Create different headers/footers for odd and even pages
- Create a drop cap
- Automatically indent the first line of paragraphs
- Create a sidebar text box and insert text
- Create a fill-in form template
- Edit a form template
- Create a calculation field

Create a Tri-Fold Mailer Brochure

17

Features Covered

- Use landscape orientation
- Insert previously created text into a document or text box
- Create a shadow border
- Insert a PCX file into a document
- Create a caption
- Rotate and reverse text
- Insert an image from the Microsoft Clip Gallery

Objectives and Introduction

After successfully completing this chapter, you will be able to use landscape orientation and multiple columns to create a two-sided, tri-fold mailer brochure. You will also learn how to create special effects using shadow borders, rotated text, reversed text, and pictures from the Microsoft Clip Gallery.

Brochures come in all shapes and sizes. One of the most common brochures is the tri-fold mailer. Information is printed on both sides of the page. Generally, a three-column format is used, and the pages are printed in landscape orientation (i.e., 11" x 8.5") as shown in Figures 17.1 and 17.2. Often a tri-fold mailer will include graphic images, border lines, and special effects such as shadow boxes, rotated text, and reversed text. The features presented in this chapter will be used to develop the tri-fold mailer brochure shown on page 449.

Format a Brochure

Before you create a brochure in Word 2000, it is a good idea to create a mock-up—a hand-drawn representation of how the final brochure will look. From the mock-up, you can decide on the page orientation (landscape or portrait), num-

FIGURE 17.1

Mock-up of a
tri-fold mailer
brochure

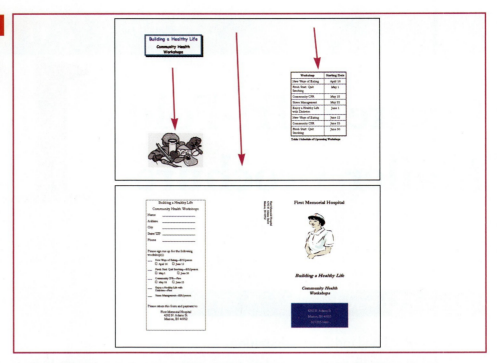

ber of columns, margins, types of borders to be used, where graphic images will be placed, and what special effects will be used. The mock-up can also show where text will be placed in each column (see Figure 17.1).

One of the first decisions that must be made is what page orientation will be used—portrait or landscape. Until now, all of the documents that have been created in this book have used portrait orientation (i.e., 8.5" x 11"). Word can also be used to create documents using landscape orientation (see Figure 17.2). When landscape orientation is selected, Word automatically rotates text when the document is printed so that the text prints horizontally in relation to the long (11-inch) side of the page.

Once page orientation has been decided, the number of columns can be set. For example, if a tri-fold mailer is to be created, three columns usually are set. Margins are also set. Small margins generally are used so that as much information as possible can be placed on the page. If a laser printer will be used to print the brochure, margins greater than .25 inch are used because the printer cannot place text closer than about .25 inch from the edges of the page. (Note: Although the area that cannot be printed varies from printer to printer, a .25-inch margin generally can be used.)

To enhance the appearance of a brochure, the color of borders and text can be changed. If a color printer is available, Word can print text, graphic images, and borders in the specified colors. Any Windows-supported color printer can be used (e.g., HP Deskjet 500C Series, IBM Color Printer, and HP Paintjet XL).

Start-Up Instructions

❖ An empty document window should be displayed. (If necessary, select the **New Blank Document** button.)

❖ The Print Layout View should be used. (If necessary, select the **Print Layout View** button or choose **View, Print Layout**.)

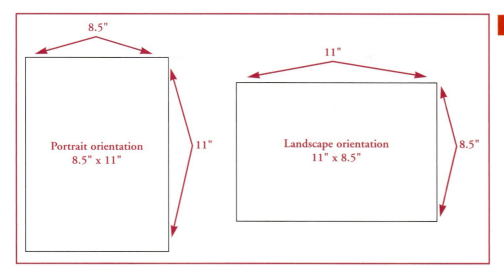

FIGURE 17.2

Portrait and
landscape
orientation

 Use Landscape Orientation

1. Select File, Page Setup.
2. Select the Paper Size tab.
3. Select Landscape in the Orientation area.
4. Select OK.

Finish-Up Instructions

❖ Set the top and bottom margins to .75". Set the left and right margins to .4".

❖ Select **Format, Columns.** Create three equal-width columns with **.8"** spacing between columns.

❖ Use the filename **17landscape brochure.doc** and save the file on your file disk.

Insert Previously Created Text into a Document or Text Box

Text that has been previously created and saved can be inserted into a document or text box. When a previously saved file is inserted into a document or text box, the original text file remains untouched; only a copy of the text is placed into the document or text box. The copy of the text can then be formatted and changed as desired. This way, any formatting or editing of the text that has been inserted into a document or frame does not affect the original text file.

Text is inserted into a document or text box by using the **Insert, File** command and choosing the desired file. The **Insert, File** command is very useful if several people are creating text files that will be combined to create a final document. For example, each person might create a different portion of a brochure. When all sections are completed, the **Insert, File** command can be used to place each text file into the brochure document.

❖ The file named **17landscape brochure.doc** should be displayed in the document window.

Insert Previously Created Text into a Document or Text Box

1. Select **Insert, File**.

2. Type or select the location and name of the desired file.

   For example, select the file named **17brochr.doc** located on the data disk 🖫 .

3. Select **OK**.

   *Note: The text contained in the file named **17brochr.doc** displays in the document window. Scroll up to view the text on page 1 of the brochure.*

Finish-Up Instructions

❖ Use the same filename, **17landscape brochure.doc**, and save the file.

Create a Shadow Border

The shadow border (box) special effect is created by choosing the **Shadow** option on the Borders tab in the Borders and Shading dialog box. The color of the border can be changed if desired; however, the color of the shadow will remain black.

Start-Up Instructions

❖ The file named **17landscape brochure.doc** should be displayed in the document window.

Create a Shadow Border

1. Type or select the text to be enclosed in the shadow border.

   For example, select the first two lines of text, **Building a Healthy Life** and **Community Health Workshops**, located at the top of the first column on page 1.

2. Select **Format, Borders and Shading**.

3. On the Borders tab, select the **Shadow** option in the Settings area.

4. Click in the **Width** box and select the desired line width.

   For example, select the 4 ½ **pt** line width.

Change the Color of the Border

5. Click in the **Color** box.

6. Click on the desired color.

For example, select **Dark Blue** (top row, third from the right).

Note: Although the color of the border line changes, the shadow remains black.

7. Select **OK**.

Finish-Up Instructions

❖ Select the title, **Building a Healthy Life**, and change the font to **Comic Sans MS, 16 point, Bold** or **make a font choice of your own**. Select the subtitle, **Community Health Workshops**, and change the font to **Comic Sans MS, 14 point, Bold** or **make a font choice of your own**.

❖ Move the mouse pointer away from the selected text and click once to deselect the text.

❖ Use the *new* filename **17Brochure shadow.doc** and save the file on your file disk.

Insert a PCX File into a Document

Graphic images created in different programs can be retrieved into a Word document. For example, a drawing created in PC Paintbrush (filename extension *.pcx*) can be retrieved into a Word document. Below is a list of some of the popular graphic file formats that can be inserted into a Word document.

Computer Graphics Metafile *(.cgm)*   Tagged Image File Format *(.tif)*
Encapsulated PostScript files *(.eps)*   WordPerfect graphics files *(.wpg)*
Graphics Interchange Format *(.gif)*   PC Paintbrush files *(.pcx)*
JPEG File Interchange Format *(.jpg)*   Photo CD *(.pcd)*
Portable Network Graphics *(.png)*   Macintosh PICT files *(.pct)*
Windows Bitmap *(.bmp)*   Windows Metafile *(.wmf)*
Windows Enhanced MetaFile *(.emf)*

Start-Up Instructions

❖ The file named **17Brochure shadow.doc** should be displayed in the document window.

❖ Click the **Zoom** button and select **75%**.

❖ Scroll down so that the bottom of the first column on page 1 is displayed.

❖ Place the insertion point to the left of the first character in the sidehead "New Ways of Eating."

❖ The Print Layout View should be used. (If necessary, select the **Print Layout View** button or choose **View, Print Layout**.)

 Insert a PCX File into a Document

1. Select **Insert, Picture, From File**.

Note: The Files of type box displays All Pictures (.emf; *.wmf; *.jpg...). If necessary, click on the **Files of type** box and choose **All Pictures...***

2. If necessary, click in the **Look in** box and click on the drive letter and/or folder where the desired file is located.

    For example, if necessary, click in the **Look in** box and click on the drive letter and/or folder where your data disk is located.

3. Double-click on the desired filename.

    For example, double-click on the file named **Food.pcx**.

Finish-Up Instructions

❖ Click once to select the graphic image (picture). (Move the mouse pointer onto the graphic image and click once.)

*Note: The Picture Toolbar should display. If the Picture Toolbar does not display, move the mouse pointer onto the graphic image, click the right mouse button, and select **Show Picture Toolbar**.*

❖ Select the **Format Picture** button 🖼 on the Picture Toolbar.

❖ Use the following information to size and lay out the graphic image.

    a. Select the **Size** tab.

    b. Triple-click in the **Height** box in the **Size and rotate** area and type **1.9**.

    c. Triple-click in the **Width** box of the **Size and rotate** area and type **2.8**.

    d. Select the **Layout** tab, click on the **Square** option in the **Wrapping style** area.

    e. Select **OK**.

❖ Scroll down the page so you can see the end of column 1. Click and hold the mouse pointer on the food graphic and move it below the last paragraph in column 1.

❖ Move the mouse pointer away from the graphic image and click once to deselect the image and remove the Picture Toolbar.

❖ Use the same filename, **17Brochure shadow.doc**, and save the file.

Create a Caption

Captions can be created for pictures, text boxes, tables, equations, etc. A caption usually contains a label, such as the word Figure or Table, and a number. If desired, additional text can be added to the caption, for example, *Table 1 Upcoming Workshops*. The **Position** option in the Caption dialog box is used to place a caption above or below a selected item.

Word automatically numbers each caption. For example, when a caption is created for the first table in a document, the label "Table 1" is inserted. When a caption is added to another table in the document, the label "Table 2" is automatically inserted. Each type of label (Figure, Table, Equation, etc.) will have its own numbering sequence. For example, if your document already contains captions *Table 1* and *Table 2* and you then insert a picture and create a caption using the *Figure* label, the new caption label will be *Figure 1*. Caption numbers are also automatically updated as additional captions are inserted. If captioned items are moved or deleted, the remaining caption numbers will be automatically updated.

If desired, a new label can be created by selecting the **New Label** button in the Caption dialog box (see Figure 17.3) and typing the desired label name. The numbering format for captions can be changed by selecting the **Numbering** button and choosing the desired numbering format, e.g., 1, 2, 3, or a, b, c.

The **AutoCaption** option in the Caption dialog box is used to tell Word to automatically create a caption for a specific type of object. For example, you can tell Word to insert a caption as each table is created in a document. When the **AutoCaption** option is selected, the AutoCaption dialog box displays. Select the type of object for which captions are to be automatically created and specify the label and numbering format.

Each time a caption is inserted, Word automatically applies the Caption style to the label, number, and any additional text that you insert. If desired, the caption style can be modified (see Chapter 15, for information on modifying styles).

Start-Up Instructions

❖ The file named **17Brochure shadow.doc** should be displayed in the document window.

Create a Caption

1. Select the item for which a caption is to be made.

   For example, select the table in column 3 on page 1 (place the insertion point in any table cell, select **Table, Select, Table**).

2. Select **Insert, Caption**.

   Note: The Caption dialog box displays. The label Table 1 displays in the Caption box (see Figure 17.3).

3. Type the desired caption that will display with the label.

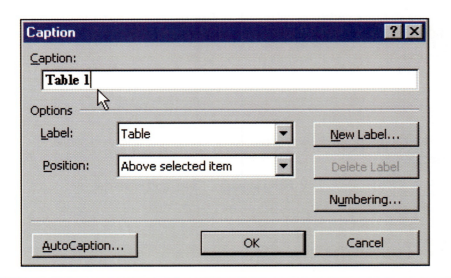

For example, press the **Spacebar** once and type **Schedule of Upcoming Workshops**.

4. Click in the **Position** box and select the desired position for the caption.
   For example, select **Below selected item**.

5. Select **OK**.

Finish-Up Instructions

❖ Select the label (i.e., Table 1) and the caption text. Change the font to Garamond, or make a font choice of your own.

❖ Use the *new* filename **17Brochure page 1.doc** and save the file on your file disk.

❖ If desired, print a copy of page 1 (select **File**, **Print**; in the Page range area, select **Current page**; select **OK**).

Start-Up Instructions

❖ The file named **17Brochure page 1.doc** should be displayed in the document window.

❖ If necessary, turn on nonprinting characters (select the **Show/Hide** button).

 ## Create a Dashed Border for a Tear Sheet

1. Select the text to be enclosed in the dashed box.
   For example, select all the text in column 1 on page 2 (including any blank lines at the top and/or bottom of the column).

2. Select **Format, Borders and Shading**.

3. Select the **Box** option in the Settings area of the **Borders** tab.

4. Click on the desired style in the **Style** box.
   For example, select the second dashed line style.

5. To change the line width, click in the **Width** box and select the desired width.
   For example, select the ¾ **pt** width.

6. Select **OK**.

Finish-Up Instructions

❖ Move the mouse pointer away from the selected text and click once to deselect the text.

❖ Use the same filename, **17Brochure page 1.doc**, and save the file.

Rotate Text and Reverse Text

Two special effects that can be created using Word are rotated text and reversed text. In order to rotate text, the text is placed in a text box. The **Format, Text Direction** command can then be selected. Text in a text box can be rotated 90 degrees or 270 degrees. After the rotated text has been created, the text box can be positioned at the desired location on the page. To rotate text in 1-degree increments, create the text using WordArt. Select **Format, WordArt,** and type the desired amount of rotation in the **Rotation** box on the Size tab.

Reversed text (white or light text on a dark background) is accomplished by choosing a dark shading for a paragraph(s), text box(es), table(s), or cell(s), then changing the color of the text to white. If black is chosen as the shading color, Word automatically changes the color of the text in the selected paragraph(s), text box(es), table(s), or cell(s) to white. If another shading color is selected for the shading, the color of the text must be manually changed to white.

Start-Up Instructions

❖ The file named **17brochure page 1.doc** should be displayed in the document window.

❖ Nonprinting characters should be displayed. (If necessary, select the **Show/Hide** button.)

❖ Place the insertion point to the left of the "F" in "First" (column 2, page 2).

❖ Insert a column break by selecting **Insert, Break, Column break, OK.**

❖ Place the insertion point on the second blank line in column 2 on page 2.

 ## Create Rotated Text in a Text Box

1. Select Insert, Text Box.

2. Move the mouse pointer to the location where the text box should be placed. Press and hold the mouse button and drag down and to the right to draw a rectangle.

   For example, move the mouse pointer to the top of the second column on page 2. Press and hold the mouse button while dragging down and to the right to draw a rectangle approximately 1.5" wide and .75" deep.

   Note: Do not worry about the exact size or position of the text box. We will size and position the text box in a few moments.

3. Type the desired text in the text box.

   For example, type:

   **First Memorial Hospital
   4292 N. Adams Street
   Marion, IN 46952**

4. If desired, change the font and/or size of the text.

FIGURE 17.4

Text Direction -
Text Box dialog
box

For example, change the font to **Garamond, 10 point** or
make a font choice of your own.

5. To rotate the text, select **Format, Text Direction.**

    Note: The Text Direction - Text Box dialog box displays (see Figure 17.4).

6. Select the desired Orientation button.

    For example, select the [Text] Orientation button.

7. Select **OK.**

Size, Position, and Format the Text Box

8. Select **Format, Text Box.**

9. Select the **Size** tab and set the height and width for the text box.

    For example, triple-click in the Height box and type **1.5.**
    Triple-click in the Width box and type **.7.**

10. Select the **Layout** tab and choose the desired layout.

    For example, click on **Square** in the Wrapping style area

11. Select the **Colors and Lines** tab and set the fill color, line color, etc., for the text box.

    For example, click in the **Color** box in the Line area and select **No Line.**

12. Select **OK.**

Finish-Up Instructions

❖ Select the graphic box and move it over to the top left of column 2 (see exanple on page 447).

❖ Use the *new* filename **17Brochure page 2.doc** and save the file on your file disk.

Start-Up Instructions

❖ The file named **17Brochure page 2.doc** should be displayed in the document window.

1. Select the text to be reversed.

   For example, in the third column on page 2, select one blank line above the address, the address, phone number, and one blank line below the phone number.

2. Select the **Tables and Borders** button ⊞ to display the Tables and Borders Toolbar.

3. Select the down triangle beside the **Shading Color** box ⬚ and click on the desired shading color.

   For example, select **Dark Blue**.

Change the Color of the Text

4. Select the down triangle beside the **Font Color** button 🅰 on the Formatting Toolbar and click on the desired color.

   For example, click on **White**.

5. Click once to deselect the text.

6. Close the Tables and Borders Toolbar.

Finish-Up Instructions

❖ Change the color of the brochure title and sideheads to **Dark Blue** (select the desired text; select the down triangle beside the **Font Color** button, and choose the desired color). Change the font for each sidehead to **Comic Sans MS** or **make a font choice of your own**.

❖ Use the same filename, **17Brochure page 2.doc**, and save the file.

Insert an Image from the Microsoft Clip Gallery

The Microsoft Clip Gallery, provided with Microsoft Office 2000, contains a collection of clip art that can be inserted into your Word documents. The Microsoft Clip Gallery can also be used to access pictures, sounds, and motion clips that have been imported into the Clip Gallery or downloaded from the Web. For more information about downloading additional clips from the Web, see the Steps to Download Additional Clips from the Web on page 450.

The collection of clip art is divided into categories, such as Animals, Buildings, Business, Cartoons, Entertainment, and Symbols. Each category contains several clip art images. Additional clip art images can also be downloaded from the Web.

Start-Up Instructions

❖ The file named **17Brochure page 2.doc** should be displayed in the document window.

❖ Nonprinting characters should be displayed. (If necessary, select the **Show/Hide** button.)

Insert an Image from the Microsoft Clip Gallery

1. Place the insertion point at the location where the clip art image is to be inserted.

   For example, place the insertion point on the second blank line below the words "First Memorial Hospital" located in the third column of page 2.

2. Select **Insert, Picture, Clip Art**.

   *Note: The **Insert ClipArt** window displays (see Figure 17.5). The **Pictures** tab should be selected. (If necessary, click on the **Pictures** tab.)*

3. Select the desired category.

   For example, scroll down and click on **Healthcare & Me...**

4. Click on the desired clip art image.

   For example, click on **Nursing** (second row, first column), or select an image of your choice.

5. Select **Insert Clip**.

6. Size and position the graphic image as needed.

   For example, use the mouse to size and position the clip art image in the third column of page 2. The image should be approximately 2" tall and centered horizontally in the column.

FIGURE 17.5

Microsoft Insert ClipArt window

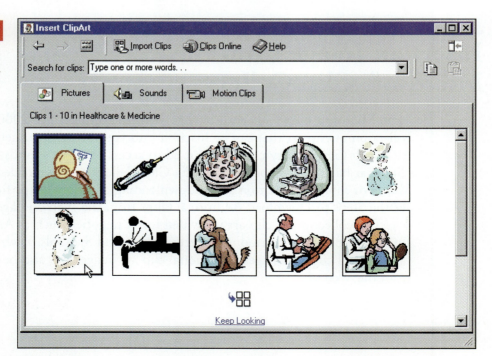

Finish-Up Instructions

❖ Move the mouse pointer away from the clip art image and click once to deselect the image and remove the Picture Toolbar.

❖ Review the brochure. Check for any spacing or formatting problems. Check the placement of the reversed text at the bottom of the third column on page 2. If necessary, add or delete blank lines to position the reversed text appropriately.

❖ Use the *new* filename **17Brochure final.doc** and save the file on your file disk.

❖ Print one copy of the tri-fold mailer brochure. Your final brochure should look similar to the tri-fold mailer brochure shown below.

Building a Healthy Life
Community Health Workshops

First Memorial Hospital is proud to present our "Building a Healthy Life" series of health workshops. Our goal is to provide timely, convenient workshops that address the health concerns faced by everyone.

We look forward to seeing you at our upcoming workshops.

New Ways of Eating

This six-session program meets once a week to help you learn how to improve your health through a low-fat, low-cholesterol diet while still enjoying your food. Discussions will include tips on maintaining a healthy diet when dining

out or traveling, spotting hidden fat and cholesterol on product labels, and healthy, good-tasting recipes. World-renown chef Phyllis Swallow will provide healthy recipes and food preparation techniques. The cost of the workshop is $25.

Stress Management

This three-session program meets once a week to discuss how stress influences your health and techniques for coping with stress. The cost of the workshop is $20.

Community CPR

Learn how you can save a life. This two-day workshop covers adult, child, and infant CPR. Also covered is the Hemlich maneuver for clearing airway obstructions for both adults and children. This workshop is free.

Enjoy a Healthy Life with Diabetes

This eight-session program meets twice a week to provide an overview of diabetes and strategies for controlling diabetes including diet, blood glucose monitoring, insulin, and medications. A personal diabetes management plan is developed for each participant. This workshop is free.

Fresh Start: Quit Smoking

Learn how to stop smoking and remain smoke-free. This eight-session program meets once a week to assist you to stop smoking and to resist the urge to begin again. Also covered are strategies for handling relapses. The cost of the workshop is $25.

Workshop	Starting Date
New Ways of Eating	April 16
Fresh Start: Quit Smoking	May 1
Community CPR	May 18
Stress Management	May 22
Enjoy a Healthy Life with Diabetes	June 1
New Ways of Eating	June 12
Community CPR	June 23
Fresh Start: Quit Smoking	June 30

Table 1 Schedule of Upcoming Workshops

Building a Healthy Life

Community Health Workshops

Name _____

Address _____

City _____

State/ZIP _____

Phone _____

Please sign me up for the following workshop(s):

____ New Ways of Eating—$25/person
☐ April 16   ☐ June 12

____ Fresh Start: Quit Smoking—$25/person
☐ May 1   ☐ June 30

____ Community CPR—Free
☐ May 18   ☐ June 23

____ Enjoy a Healthy Life with Diabetes—Free

____ Stress Management—$20/person

Please return this form and payment to:

First Memorial Hospital
4292 N. Adams St.
Marion, IN 46952

First Memorial Hospital
4292 N. Adams Street
Marion, IN 46952

First Memorial Hospital

Building a Healthy Life

Community Health Workshops

4292 N. Adams St.
Marion, IN 46952
317-555-9400

Steps to Download Additional Clips from the Web

Note: The following steps are for your information only.

1. Select **Insert, Picture, Clip**.
2. If necessary, select the **Pictures** tab.
3. Select the **Clips Online** button.

   Note: If a "Connect to Web for More Clip Art,. . ." message box displays, select OK.

4. Your Internet service will dial to access the Internet (if you are not already online).
5. Click on the message that displays, "Please click here to jump to Clip Gallery Live."

   Note: In a few moments, the Microsoft Clip Gallery Live page displays.

6. If necessary, Read the End-User License Agreement and select the **Accept** button to accept the agreement.
7. Select the type of clip to be downloaded, e.g., Pictures, Sounds, or Motion, by choosing one of the four icons displayed on the left side of the page.

   For example, select the **Pictures** icon (first button on the left).

8. Select a picture.
9. Select Download this clip now! (Click on the down arrow below the picture.)
10. Continue to respond to any prompts for downloading the picture.

    For example, click on the **Save File** option and choose the location for the file.

11. Click **OK** or **Open** to download the file.
12. To disconnect, select the **Close** button on the right side of the Title bar.
13. If necessary, close the Insert ClipArt dialog box.

    Note: Check with your instructor or instructional aide for additional instructions.

The Next Step

Chapter Review and Activities

Self-Check Quiz

T F 1. Information is printed on both sides of a tri-fold mailer brochure.

T F 2. When text is printed in landscape orientation, the top of the page is the 11-inch side.

T F 3. Previously created text cannot be inserted into a document.

T F 4. Text in a text box can be rotated in 1 degree increments.

T F 5. Graphic images created using PC Paintbrush cannot be inserted into a Word document.

T F 6. Word automatically updates caption numbers when captioned items are moved or deleted.

7. To insert existing text into a document, select _____, **File**, type or select the location and the name of the desired file, choose **OK**.
   a. **Open**
   b. **Insert**
   c. **Window**
   d. **File**

8. Using WordArt, text can be rotated in _____.
   a. 15-degree increments
   b. 90-degree increments
   c. 1-degree increments
   d. 45-degree increments

9. List the steps to create a caption for a table.

10. List two ways you might use rotated and reversed text in your documents.

Enriching Language Arts Skills

Spelling/Vocabulary Words

effective—producing the desired result.

demonstrate—to prove; to display or operate.

freelance—one who acts independently; one who pursues a profession without long-term contractual commitment to a single employer.

techniques—procedures by which a task is accomplished.

tuition—a fee for instruction.

Parentheses

Parentheses can be used to set off nonessential expressions that might otherwise confuse the reader. The information within the parentheses provides supplemental information that has no direct bearing on the main idea of the sentence or paragraph. Words, phrases, or clauses can be enclosed within parentheses. Unless a comma, colon, or semicolon is necessary to the text within parentheses, place the punctuation outside the closing parenthesis. If the text within the parentheses is a complete sentence, the final punctuation is placed within the parentheses.

Examples:

The actual gross sales for the quarter were $1,050,000 (compared with projected sales of $795,000).

If you are planning to attend the next sales conference (March 5), please contact the travel department immediately.

Several staff members will attend the sales conference next month. (The conference will be held in Hawaii.)

Activities

Activity 17.1—Create a Tri-Fold Mailer Brochure

1. Use the skills learned in this chapter and the following information to create the tri-fold mailer brochure shown on page 454.

   a. Use landscape orientation (select **File**, **Page Setup**, **Paper Size** tab, **Landscape**).

   b. Change the top and bottom margins to .5" and the left and right margins to .4".

   c. Create three equal-width columns with .8" spacing between columns (select **Format**, **Columns**; set the number of columns to **3**; check that the **Equal column width** option is selected; increase the spacing between columns to .8").

   d. Insert the brochure text that is saved on the data disk under the file-name **17act1.doc** (select **Insert**, **File**; if necessary, click in the **Look in** box and select the drive letter where the file disk is located; double-click on **17act1.doc**).

   e. Select the blank line at the top of the document, the words "Safety Guidelines," and the blank line below the title. Create a shadow box with a 4 ½ **pt** line. Change the color of the lines to **Red**. (Select the text; select **Format**, **Borders and Shading**; on the Borders tab, select the **Shadow** option; select 4 ½ **pt** line width; click in the **Colors** box, select **Red**. Select **OK**.)

   f. Insert a column break before the title Hampton Homes in the second column of page 2 (place the insertion point in the blank line above the title, Hampton Homes; select **Insert**, **Break**, **Column Break**, **OK**). If necessary, change the font size for the text in column 1 to fit in one column.

   g. Use text box to create rotated text that contains the following text:

      Hampton Homes
      1424 Forest Way
      Athens, GA 30602

Click on the second blank line in the second column on page 2; select **Insert**, **Text Box**.

At the top of the second column on page 2 draw a rectangle approximately **2"** wide and **1"** deep.

Type the address information.

Change the font to **10 point**. Select **OK**.

Select **Format**, **Text Direction** and choose the [Text] Orientation button. Select **OK**.

Select **Format**, **Text Box**.

Select the **Size** tab and set the height to **1.5"** and the width to **.7"**.

Select the **Layout** tab and click on **Square** wrapping style. Choose **Horizontal** alignment, **Right**.

Select the **Color and Lines** tab and set the line color to **No Line**. Select **OK**.

h. Insert the inspectors image or an appropriate clip art image from the Picture tab of the **Insert ClipArt** dialog box. (Place the insertion point on the third blank line below the title in column 3 on page 2. Select **Insert**, **Picture**, **Clip Art**. Select Buildings, inspectors picture. Select **Insert Clip**. Close the Insert ClipArt dialog box.)

i. Size and position the residential house image. (Click on the image. Select the **Format Picture** button on the Picture Toolbar. On the Size tab, set the height to **1.3"** and width to **2.8"**; click on the **Relative to original picture size** option to turn it off. On the Layout tab, choose the **Square** wrapping style then click on **Center**. Select **OK**.)

j. Select the blank line above the address, and select the address, phone number, and the blank line below the phone number in the third column on page 2. Create reversed text with a shaded background. (Select the text. Select the **Tables and Borders** button, select the down triangle beside the **Shading Color** box and choose **Red**. Select the down triangle beside the **Font Color** button on the Formatting Toolbar and select **White**.)

k. Insert border lines above and below the title, Hampton Homes, located in the third column on page 2. Use the Tables and Borders Toolbar to specify color, line style, line width, and position for the border lines. Adjust font size or spacing as needed.

l. Close the Tables and Borders Toolbar.

m. Optional. Change the font color for the title and sideheads, selecting a color of your choice.

2. Use the filename **17Hampton Brochure.doc** and save the file on your file disk.

Note: Your brochure should look similar to the brochure shown on page 454.

3. Print one copy.

4. Close the document.

Safety Guidelines

Introduction

Hampton Homes is committed to the safety of our employees. Each year many employees are injured while on the job. Most on-the-job injuries can be prevented or minimized by observing the safety practices outlined in this brochure. Two of the most common safety hazards are falls, trips, and slips and back injuries.

If you find a safety hazard, inform your supervisor immediately. A safe work area benefits everyone.

Review these safety guidelines and apply them to your everyday activities, both on and off the job.

Falls, Trips, and Slips

Falls, trips, and slips are the most common types of accidents. Be aware of your surroundings and remember the following:

➔ Wipe up spills immediately.

➔ Pick up debris around your work area.

➔ Keep boxes, low-level cards, etc., out of doorways and away from traffic areas.

➔ Make sure that telephone and electrical cords are under desks or along walls.

➔ Open doors slowly. Watch for oncoming traffic.

➔ Report torn carpets, cracked tiles, etc.

Back Injuries

Back sprains usually result from improper lifting, bending, standing, or sitting. Your back is a complex mechanism that needs respectful handling.

➔ Practice good posture.

➔ Don't turn, twist, or bend to pick up objects even if they are light.

➔ Avoid slouching or slumping. Sit firmly against the back of chairs.

➔ Lift with your legs, not your back.

➔ Don't carry anything heavier than you can manage with ease.

Be Prepared

Not all accidents and emergencies can be eliminated. Therefore, it is important to be prepared for any accidents or emergencies.

➔ Keep emergency telephone numbers in a convenient location near your telephone.

➔ Know the location of the nearest emergency exit.

➔ Know where fire extinguishers are located and how to use them.

➔ Learn CPR, the Heimlich maneuver, and other first aid procedures.

What to do if

There is a FIRE

➔ Report the fire to the fire department immediately.

➔ If possible, extinguish small fires using a fire extinguisher.

➔ Calmly evacuate the building. Make your way quickly and safely to the nearest emergency exit.

➔ If the room fills with smoke, get as close as possible to the floor.

There is an EARTHQUAKE

➔ Move away from windows and loose objects.

➔ Stand in a doorway or seek shelter under sturdy furniture.

➔ Do not use elevators or escalators.

There is an INJURY

➔ Do not move the injured person unless there is danger of further injury.

➔ Call 911 for professional help immediately.

➔ If you are trained, administer CPR or other first aid.

Using a Fire Extinguisher

Most of the fire extinguishers at Hampton Homes are ABC all-purpose and can be operated using these instructions. Only fight fires if it is safe to do so and after alerting the fire department of the situation. To operate a fire extinguisher, remember the following simple steps:

➔ Pull the pin or plastic loop.

➔ Aim the extinguisher so that it discharges at the base of the fire. Grip the handle and neck area for better control. Some units have a hose or horn.

➔ Squeeze the handles together.

➔ Sweep the base of the fire using a side-to-side motion. The sweeping motion pushes the flames away from you.

Hampton Homes
1424 Forest Way
Athens, GA 30602

Hampton Homes

Serving the Athens Area for 50 Years

1424 Forest Way
Athens, GA 30602
706-555-1242

Challenge Your Skills

Skill 17.1—Create a Tri-Fold Mailer Brochure; Language Arts

1. Use the following information to create a tri-fold mailer brochure similar to the one shown on page 456.

   a. The text for the brochure is saved on the data disk under the file-name **17skill1.doc**.

   b. Make decisions regarding:

   Margins
   Spacing between columns
   Colors for borders, shading, and text
   Shadow and dashed boxes
   Font for title, headings, and brochure text
   Rotated and reversed text

   c. Insert appropriate clip art.

   d. Create the following caption for the table located in the third column on page 1.

   Table 1 Upcoming Seminars

2. Correct four spelling errors, one parenthesis error, two punctuation/grammatical errors, and three misused words.

3. Use the filename **17Newsletter brochure.doc** and save the file on your file disk.

4. Print one copy.

   Note: An example of the final tri-fold brochure is shown on page 456. Your brochure does not need to match this example.

5. Close the document.

Creating the Ultimate Newsletter

This two -day seminar for marketing professionals, salespeople, fund-raisers, and writers will introduce you to techniques for designing and producing newsletters with impact.

Imagine going back to the office with powerful techniques to assist you to quickly and effortlessly create your next newsletter. You will have all the skills you need to produce a visually attractive newsletter that will grab the attention of all your readers (without breaking your budget).

Learn to Write Like a Pro

Learn proven copywriting tips that will assist you in writing informative and interesting articles. The seminar will also cover how to create effective attention-grabbing headlines that draw readers to your newsletter. You will also learn how to stretch (or shrink) copy to fit and to overcome writer's block in order to meet the deadline.

The seminar will also introduce you to resources for filler articles and art and provide specific guidelines on how to hire freelance writers to assist you with articles.

Once the Articles Are Written

Anyone that produces a newsletter knows that having the articles is only half the battle. On day two of this seminar, we will discuss editing techniques, design concerns, and obtaining the necessary approvals before publication. We will also explore the

computer equipment and software needed to produce a professional-looking newsletter.

We will also demonstrate the effective use of photographs, graphs, and charts in newsletters and discuss affordable sources of artwork and clip art.

Design Associates Guarantee

If you are not happy with the information you receive at the seminar, your money will be refunded No questions asked.

Seminar City	Date
Atlanta, GA	June 4-5
Baltimore, MD	June 15-16
Pittsburgh, PA	August 1-2
St. Louis, MO	September 3-4
Reno, NV	October 1-2
Oakland, CA	October 14-15
Sacramento, CA	October 23-24
Los Angeles, CA	November 1-2

Table 1 Upcoming Seminars

Register Today
Seminar Tuition
$225 per person

Name: _____

Address: _____

City: _____

State/ZIP: _____

Phone: _____

Please sign me up for the following seminar:

___	Atlanta, GA	June 4-5
___	Baltimore, MD	June 15-16
___	Pittsburgh, PA	August 1-2
___	St. Louis, MO	September 3-4
___	Reno, NV	October 1-2
___	Oakland, CA	October 14-15
___	Sacramento, CA	October 23-24
___	Los Angeles, CA	November 1-2

Please return this form with payment to:

Design Associates
4692 Lafayette St.
Salem, MA 01970

Design Associates
4692 Lafayette Street
Salem, MA 01970

Design Associates

Creating the Ultimate Newsletter

Learn Proven Ways to Make Your Newsletter Better

4692 Lafayette Street
Salem, MA 01970
508-555-1399

Create a Magazine Article

Features Covered

- Insert a pull quote into a text box
- Create unequal column widths
- Create different headers/footers for odd and even pages
- Create a drop cap
- Automatically indent the first line of paragraphs
- Insert text in a sidebar text box

Objectives and Introduction

After successfully completing this chapter, you will be able to create columns of unequal widths, different footers for odd and even pages, and drop caps. In addition, you will learn how to automatically indent each paragraph in a document and how to create pull quotes and sidebar text.

Word 2000 has continued to incorporate and enhance many of the functions that have traditionally been accomplished through the use of typesetting or desktop publishing programs. In this chapter, you will perform many desktop publishing functions to enhance publications such as magazine articles.

Create a Magazine Article

Before beginning to create a magazine article, decisions need to be made about the graphic images to be included, the number of columns, and the widths of columns. Also, decisions need to be made on the use of special fonts and other effects such as borders and shading.

Many magazine articles include pull quotes and sidebars. A *pull quote* is a small portion of article text that is excerpted from the article and placed in a separate frame. The purpose of a pull quote is to attract attention to the article. Therefore, the font of the pull quote text is often changed and/or enlarged. In addition, borders are usually placed above, below, or around the text to set the quote off from the article text.

A *sidebar* is a box or area that contains information that is related to the article text. The purpose of a sidebar is to further explain a subject covered in the article or to provide additional statistics or information that may interest the reader.

One of the main purposes of a magazine article's format is to entice people to read the article. Therefore, special text effects, such as shadow, embossed, or engraved text, rotated text, and drop caps, are used to add visual interest. If desired, WordArt can also be used to create unusual text effects for titles. Graphic images or pictures are also often included in a magazine article to enhance page appearance or to illustrate the article's key points.

Start-Up Instructions

- ❖ Open the file named **18drill1.doc** located on the data disk.

- ❖ The Print Layout View should be used. (If necessary, select the **Print Layout View** button or choose **View, Print Layout**.)

 Steps to

Use the Shadow Text Effect

1. Select the desired text.

   For example, select the word "Multimedia" in the article title.

2. Select **Format, Font**.

3. Select the **Shadow** option in the Effects area.

4. Select **OK**.

5. Click once to deselect the text.

Finish-Up Instructions

- ❖ Select the down arrow beside the **Zoom** box and choose **Whole Page**.

- ❖ Continue with the Steps to Create a Text Box for Pull Quote Text.

Steps to

Create a Text Box for Pull Quote Text

1. Select **Insert, Text Box**.

2. Move the mouse pointer to the location where the text box containing the pull quote text should be placed. Press and hold the mouse button while dragging down and to the right to draw a rectangle. Release the mouse button when the rectangle is the desired size.

   For example, move the mouse pointer to approximately the center of the page, press and hold the mouse button, and drag down and to the right to draw a rectangle approximately 2¼" wide and 1" deep. Release the mouse button.

3. If necessary, click on an edge of the text box to select the text box.

   Note: Sizing handles (boxes) display at the corners and edges of the text box.

4. Select **Format, Text Box**.

5. Set the width and height for the frame.

   For example:

   a. Select the **Size** tab. Triple-click in the **Height** box and type **1.3**.

   b. Triple-click in the **Width** box and type **2.6**.

6. To wrap the text around the frame, select the **Layout** tab and choose the **Square** Wrapping style option. Also, select the **Center** option in the Horizontal alignment area.

7. To remove the line around the text box, select the **Colors and Lines** tab, click in the **Color** box in the Line area, and select **No Line**.

8. Select **OK**.

Place a Border Above and Below a Text Box

9. With the text box selected, click on the **Tables and Borders** button 🔲 to display the Tables and Borders Toolbar.

10. Click in the **Line Style** box 🔲 and select the desired line style.

    For example, select the single line style.

11. Select the **Line Weight** box 🔲 and choose the desired weight.

    For example, select the 2¼ **pt** weight.

12. Select the down triangle beside the **Border** button 🔲 and choose the desired border position.

    For example, select the **Top Border** button. Click on the down triangle again and select the **Bottom Border** button.

13. If desired, shade the frame by selecting the down triangle beside the **Shading Color** button 🔲 and choosing a shading color.

    For example, select the **Gray-10%** shading color.

14. Close the Tables and Borders Toolbar.

15. Type, copy, or insert the desired text for the pull quote.

    For example, select the down triangle beside the **Zoom** box and choose **100%**. Select and copy the first sentence (i.e., "How much . . .") below the heading "The Consumer's Challenge . . ." located on page 2. Click in the pull quote text box on page 1 and select the **Paste** button.

16. Format the pull quote text.

    For example, select the pull quote text and change the font to **Bold, 16 point**. Change the alignment to **Center**.

Finish-Up Instructions

❖ Use the *new* filename **18Pull quote.doc** and save the file on your file disk.

❖ Continue with the Steps to Create Unequal Column Widths.

Create Unequal Column Widths

Until now, only equal width newspaper columns have been created. However, it is also possible to create columns with different widths. When creating columns with different widths, it is important to remember that the total of the widths of all columns and the space between the columns should equal the width of the page minus the margins. For example, if the default 1.25-inch left and right margins are used, the total widths of all columns and the space between columns should equal 6 inches.

In the Columns dialog box, Word 2000 has two preset options for creating unequal column widths, i.e., **Left** and **Right**. When either the **Left** or **Right** preset option is selected, Word automatically creates a two-column layout with one wide column and one narrow column with .5 inches of space between the columns. If desired, the number of columns, widths of the columns, and the width of the space between the columns can be changed. When the number of columns, the width of a column(s), or the width of the space between columns is changed, Word automatically recalculates the width of the other column(s).

Also, after the number of columns has been selected, the width of each column can be changed using the horizontal ruler. To adjust the width of a column using the ruler, move the mouse pointer to the middle of the column marker between the columns, press and hold the mouse button, drag to the desired width, and release the mouse button. To change the space between two columns, place the mouse pointer on the left or right edge of the column marker, press and hold the mouse button, and drag left or right to increase or decrease the space between the two columns.

Start-Up Instructions

❖ The file named **18Pull quote.doc** should be displayed in the document window.

❖ The Print Layout View should be used. (If necessary, select the **Print Layout View** button or choose **View, Print Layout**.)

Create Unequal Column Widths

1. Select the text to be placed in columns

   For example, select all of the article text beginning with the first sentence, "Multimedia. Probably no . . ."

2. Select **Format, Columns**.

3. Select the desired number of columns in the Presets area.

   *For example, select the **Right** option in the Presets area to create two columns with the left column wider than the right column.*

   Note: *In the Preview area, Word displays a wide left column and a narrow right column (see Figure 18.1).*

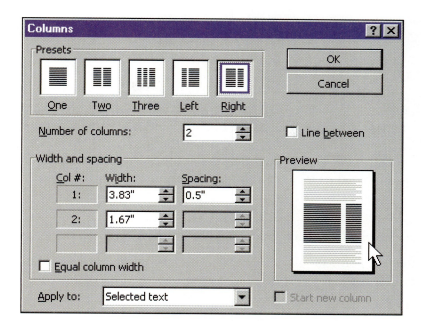

FIGURE 18.1

Columns dialog
box with the
Right option
selected in the
Presets area

Change the Preset Column Widths

4. Click on the up or down triangle beside the **Col # 1 Width** box, or triple-click in the **Col # 1 Width** box and type the desired width.

    For example, click twice on the down triangle located beside the Col # 1 Width box to display **3.7"**.

5. To change the amount of space between column 1 and column 2, click on the up or down triangle located to the right of the **Spacing** box until the desired spacing displays, or triple-click in the **Spacing** box and type the desired spacing.

    For example, click twice on the down triangle located beside the **Spacing** box to display **0.3"**.

    Note: As the space between columns is changed, Word automatically recalculates the width of column 2. Column 2 should have a width of 2".

6. When all column widths have been set, select **OK**.

    *Note: To view the columns, select the down triangle beside the **Zoom** box and choose **Whole Page**. Click on the **Previous Page** button, if desired. Select the down triangle beside the **Zoom** box again and choose **100%**.*

7. Click once to deselect the text.

Finish-Up Instructions

❖ Use the same filename, **18Pull quote.doc**, and save the file.

Create Different Headers/Footers for Odd and Even Pages

If desired, different headers/footers can be created for odd and even pages of a document. Different headers/footers are often created when the pages of a document will be printed on both sides of the paper (back to back). As you look at the footers of this book, notice that the page numbers are printed at the left margin on even-numbered pages and at the right margin on odd-numbered pages.

Start-Up Instructions

❖ The file named **18Pull quote.doc** should be displayed in the document window.

❖ The insertion point should be located at the beginning of the document (**Ctrl** and **Home**).

 ## Create Different Headers/Footers for Odd and Even Pages

1. Select **View, Header and Footer**.

2. Select the **Page Setup** button ⊞ on the Header and Footer Toolbar.
   Note: The Layout tab of the Page Setup dialog box displays.

3. Select **Different odd and even** in the Headers and Footers area.

4. Select **OK**.

5. If necessary, select the **Switch Between Header and Footer** button ⊞ on the Header and Footer Toolbar to switch to the footer pane.

   For example, select the **Switch Between Header and Footer** button ⊞ to display the Odd Page Footer - Section 1 pane.

6. Type and format the header/footer text.

   For example:

   a. Type **Applications of Information Technology**. (Do not type the period.)

   b. Press the **Tab** key twice to move the insertion point to the right margin.

   c. Select the **Insert Page Number** button ⊞ on the Header and Footer Toolbar.

   d. Select the footer text and change the font to **Arial, 9 point**.

7. Select the **Show Next** button ⊞ to move the insertion point to the Even Page Footer - Section 2 pane.

8. Type and format the desired header/footer text.

   For example:

   a. Select the **Insert Page Number** button ⊞.

   b. Press the **Tab** key twice.

    c. Type **Multimedia: Teaching the Computer to Sing and Dance.** (Do not type the period.)

        Note: The text may extend beyond the right margin. That's OK.

    d. Select the footer text and change the font to **Arial, 9 point.**

        Note: The footer text should now display within the footer pane.

9. Select **Close** on the Header and Footer Toolbar.

Finish-Up Instructions

❖ Use the *new* filename **18footer.doc** and save the file on your file disk.

❖ Continue with the Steps to Create a Drop Cap.

Create a Drop Cap

A drop cap is a special effect that is often used in the first paragraph of an article or at the beginning of key sections in a document. The first character of the first word in a paragraph is enlarged, and the remaining text is indented to allow space for the enlarged character. Word provides two positions for drop cap characters: **Dropped** and **In Margin**. The **Dropped** position option places the character within the text area, and the **In Margin** position option places the drop cap character in the left margin.

When a drop cap is created, the character is placed in a frame. The amount of space between the frame and the paragraph text can be set by typing the desired amount in the **Distance from text** box in the Drop Cap dialog box. Often the font for the drop cap character is changed to provide a contrast between the drop cap character and the rest of the text. The font of the drop cap character can be specified right in the Drop Cap dialog box. The size of the drop cap character is automatically determined by Word based on the number of corresponding lines of text the character is to be dropped. For example, if a larger drop cap character is desired, increase the number in the **Lines to drop** box.

Start-Up Instructions

❖ The file named **18footer.doc** should be displayed in the document window.

 Create a Drop Cap

1. Place the insertion point to the left of the character that will become a drop cap, or select the characters to be drop caps.

    For example, place the insertion point to the left of the **M** in the word "Multimedia" in the first sentence of the body text.

2. Select **Format, Drop Cap.**

    Note: The Drop Cap dialog box displays (see Figure 18.2).

3. Select the desired position for the drop cap letter, i.e., **Dropped** or **In Margin.**

FIGURE 18.2

Drop Cap dialog
box

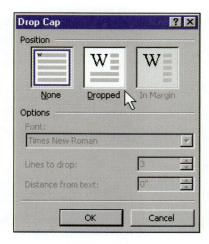

4. Select the desired font for the drop cap letter.

   For example, select **Century Schoolbook** or make a font choice of your own.

5. In the **Lines to drop** box, type or select the number of lines that the letter should be dropped.

   For example, select the down triangle next to the **Lines to drop** box once to display 2.

6. If desired, specify a distance between the drop cap letter and the other letters using the **Distance from text** option.

   For example, triple-click in the **Distance from text** box and type **.02**.

7. Select **OK**.

   *Note: The drop cap displays in the document window. The drop cap letter has been automatically placed in a frame. To edit the drop cap character, e.g., change the size or font, click on the drop cap character and choose **Format**, **Drop Cap**.*

Finish-Up Instructions

❖ Use the same filename, **18footer.doc**, and save the file on your file disk.

❖ Continue with the Steps to Automatically Indent the First Line of Paragraphs.

Automatically Indent the First Line of Paragraphs

To save space, the first line of each paragraph is indented so that an extra blank line is not needed between paragraphs. The first line of each paragraph can be indented manually by moving the insertion point to the beginning of each paragraph and pressing the **Tab** key. However, the first line of paragraphs can be automatically indented by changing the style that was used to format the paragraphs. For example, the Body Text style can be modified to indent the first line of each body text paragraph .25" and the space after the paragraphs can be deleted. Once the Body Text style has been modified, all the paragraphs that are formatted with the Body Text style will be indented automatically.

Start-Up Instructions

❖ The file named **18footer.doc** should be displayed in the document window.

 ## Automatically Indent the First Line of Paragraphs

1. Place the insertion point in any paragraph that is currently formatted with the desired style.

    For example, place the insertion point in the first paragraph in column 2 on page 1, which begins "The lure and range of . . ."

    Note: The Body Text style has been applied to this paragraph and other paragraphs in the article.

2. Select **Format, Style**.

3. If necessary, click on the name of the style to be modified.

    For example, the style named **Body Text** should be highlighted.

4. Select **Modify**.

5. In the Modify Style dialog box, select **Format, Paragraph**.

6. On the Indents and Spacing tab, click in the **Special** box and select **First line**.

7. Triple-click in the **By** box and type the desired indent amount.

    For example, triple-click in the **By** box and type **.25**.

8. If desired, make other changes to the paragraph format.

    For example, set the **Spacing After** to **0** (zero).

9. Select **OK** twice. Select **Close**.

    Note: The first line of all paragraphs in the article that had been formatted with the Body Text style are now indented.

Finish-Up Instructions

❖ Use the *new* filename **18First line indent.doc** and save the file on your file disk.

❖ Continue with the Steps to Create a Sidebar Text Box and Insert Text.

Start-Up Instructions

❖ The file named **18First line indent.doc** should be displayed in the document window.

❖ The Print Layout View should be used. (If necessary, select the **Print Layout View** button or choose **View**, **Print Layout**.)

Steps to Create a Sidebar Text Box and Insert Text

1. Display the page on which the text box will be placed and click once to place the insertion point anywhere on the page.

   For example, select the down triangle beside the **Zoom** box and choose **Whole Page**. Scroll down to display page 2. Click once to place the insertion point on page 2.

2. Select **Insert, Text Box**.

3. Draw a text box at the desired location on the page.

   For example, draw a text box at the bottom of the page that extends from the left margin to the right margin and is approximately 4" tall (see Figure 18.3).

4. If necessary, click on the edge of the text box to select the text box.

5. Select **Format, Text Box**. Select the **Size** tab and set the height and width of the text box.

   For example:

   a. Triple-click in the **Height** box and type 4.

   b. Triple-click in the **Width** box and type **6**.

6. Select the **Layout** tab and choose the **Square** Wrapping style option.

7. Select the **Colors and Lines** tab. In the Line area, click in the **Color** box and choose **No Line**.

8. Select **OK**.

9. Type or insert the desired information in the frame.

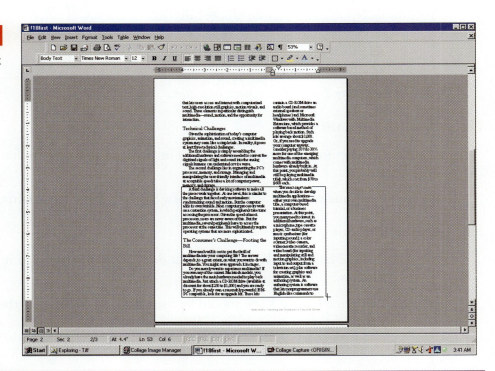

FIGURE 18.3

Sidebar text box

For example, insert the file named **18Side1.doc** located on the data disk by selecting **Insert, File**. If necessary, select the drive/folder where the data disk is located. Double-click on the file named **18Side1.doc**.

Note: If necessary, adjust the height of the text box to accommodate the text and position the box at th bottom of page 2.

10. If desired, place a border around the text box.

For example, select **Format, Borders and Shading**. On the **Borders** tab, select the **Box** option in the Setting area. Choose the 1½ **pt** line width in the Width box. Select **OK**.

Finish-Up Instructions

❖ Use the *new filename* **18Multimedia article.doc** and save the file on your file disk.

❖ Print one copy. Close the document

Note: Your final document should look similar to the magazine article shown on page 468

The Next Step

Chapter Review and Activities

Self-Check Quiz

T F 1. When the number of columns, the width of a column(s), or the space between columns is changed, Word automatically recalculates the width of the other column(s).

T F 2. Once the number of unequal width columns is selected, the width of each column can be changed by using the horizontal ruler.

T F 3. When a drop cap letter is created, the character is placed in a frame.

T F 4. The font of pull quote text cannot be changed.

5. The preset option(s) for creating unequal width columns is/are _____.
   a. **Left**
   b. **Right**
   c. **Top**
   d. both a and b

Multimedia

Teaching the Computer to Sing and Dance

Multimedia. Probably no other "buzzword" is causing as much excitement today. To understand the excitement, just consider the "show biz" appeal of these few examples.

- *Microsoft Bookshelf for Windows*, a single CD-ROM disk contains seven reference works, including a "talking" dictionary that demonstrates

> **How much will it cost to put the thrill of multimedia into your computing life?**

correct pronunciations and a book of quotations that includes digitized recordings of such luminaries as John F. Kennedy, an atlas that plays every country's national anthem, and a concise encyclopedia illustrated with high-resolution graphics and narrated animations showing how certain processes work. And, like any computer file, the CD-ROM can be searched by key word or phrase, taking a lot of the tedium out of research. *Bookshelf* is just one of a growing list of multimedia software titles that merge entertainment and education.

- A computerized information kiosk at the Montreux Jazz Festival allowed users to call up biographies, photos, and performance videos of all the performers.

- Thousands of workers are now learning Microsoft Word, Lotus 1-2-3, and other popular applications via interactive multimedia tutorials that are

enlivened with music, graphics, and motion. A 1990 Department of Defense study concluded that such tutorials take about a third less time, cost about a third less, and are more effective than traditional training methods.

The lure and range of such applications have sparked predictions that a multimedia revolution is just over the horizon. The revolution is still in the making, though, in part because multimedia generates almost as much confusion as excitement.

Multimedia—A Definition

One source of confusion is the misuse of the term multimedia itself. You may see it used to describe everything from an animated, talking, and singing children's book on CD-ROM to a high-resolution monitor. Although there's no official definition, most computer experts agree that multimedia refers to a computer system

that lets users access and interact with computerized text, high-resolution still graphics, motion visuals, and sound. Three elements in particular distinguish multimedia—sound, motion, and the opportunity for interaction.

Technical Challenges

Given the sophistication of today's computer graphics, animation, and sound, creating a multimedia system may seem like a simple task. In reality, it poses at least three technical challenges.

The first challenge is simply assembling the additional hardware and software needed to convert the digitized signals of light and sound into the analog signals humans can understand or vice versa.

The second challenge lies in augmenting the PC's processor, memory, and storage. Managing and manipulating the user-friendly interface of multimedia at acceptable speeds takes a lot of computer power, memory, and storage.

A third challenge is devising software to make all the pieces work together. At one level, this is similar to the challenge that faced early moviemakers: synchronizing sound and motion. But the computer adds its own wrinkle. Most computer processors work on a contention system, in which peripherals take turns accessing the processor. Given the speed of most processors, users are never aware of this. But for

multimedia, several peripherals have to access the processor at the same time. This will ultimately require operating systems that are more sophisticated.

The Consumer's Challenge—Footing the Bill

How much will it cost to put the thrill of multimedia into your computing life? The answer depends, to a great extent, on what you want to do with multimedia. You might even approach it in stages.

Do you merely want to experience multimedia? If you own any of the current Macintosh models, you already have the main hardware needed to play back multimedia. Just attach a CD-ROM drive (available at discount for about $250 to

A Confusion of Standards

Both consumers and software developers are confused by the lack of standards for multimedia. To a great extent, computer standards are forged in the marketplace: the companies that garner the largest market share set a de facto standard that others follow. The IBM PC and Microsoft MS-DOS are good examples. At this point, a number of players are set to battle it out.

Apple Computer maintains that its Macintosh models are multimedia-ready. With the bundled authoring system of HyperCard, many users are already developing their own multimedia applications. Macintosh multimedia applications have an especially strong presence in education. Another highly publicized standard has been proposed by Multimedia PC Marketing Council, a trade organization made up of Microsoft and a number of major hardware vendors. Like the VHS logo on videotape, the MPC logo is meant to reassure consumers and establish a multimedia platform.

IBM, the industry giant, is pursuing its own course. Its first multimedia PC uses both Windows and OS/2 in tandem, and the company is currently developing a number of multimedia configurations that will target a variety of business and educational customers.

$1,000) and you are ready to go. If you already own a reasonably powerful IBM-PC compatible, look for an upgrade kit. These kits contain a CD-ROM drive an audio board (and sometimes external speakers or headphones) and Microsoft Windows with Multimedia Extensions, which provides a software-based method of playing back motion. Such kits average about $1,000. Or, if you need to upgrade your computer anyway, consider paying 10% to 30% more for one of the emerging multimedia computers, which comes with multimedia hardware already built in. At this point, you probably will still be playing multimedia titles, which cost from $70 to $600 each.

The next stage comes when you decide to develop multimedia applications—either your own multimedia title, a computer-based tutorial, or a business presentation. At this point, you many need to invest in additional hardware, such as a microphone, tape cassette player, CD-audio player, or music synthesizer (for inputting sound); a color scanner, video camera, videocassette recorder, and video board (for inputting and manipulating still and motion graphics, including input to and output from a television set); plus software for creating graphics and animation, as well as an

authoring system. An authoring system is software that lets nonprogrammers use English-like commands to create interactive computer programs. One popular authoring system is HyperCard; it is bundled with all Macintosh computers. Similar, relatively inexpensive authoring and presentation software is available for IBM-PC compatibles. More sophisticated authoring software costs as much as $8,000. Some multimedia developers have invested more than $50,000 in their studios.

Reprinted with permission from Introduction to Computers and Information Systems by Larry Long. Prentice Hall, 1994.

6. Different headers and footers are often created when the pages of a document are printed on _____.
   a. both sides of the paper
   b. one side of the paper
   c. neither of these

7. Word provides two positions for drop cap characters. The two positions are _____.
   a. **Dropped** and **In Margin**
   b. **Dropped** and **Out of Margin**
   c. **Dropped** and **Above Margin**

8. The _____ command is used to automate the process of creating drop cap letters.
   a. **File**, **Drop Cap**
   b. **Format**, **Drop Cap**
   c. **Tools**, **Drop Cap**

9. List one purpose for indenting the first line of each paragraph.

10. A pull quote is a small portion of text excerpted from an article and placed in a separate _____.

Enriching Language Arts Skills

Spelling/Vocabulary Words

essential—necessary; indispensable.
repetitive—repeated action; redundant; continual; unending.
static—showing little change or movement.
symptoms—an indication of change in bodily sensation or function that indicates a disorder or abnormality.
trauma—a bodily injury that has a lasting mental or physical effect; breakdown; wound.

Em and En Dashes

The em dash (—), a typographic symbol about the width of the character m, is often used in place of a comma. Press the hyphen key twice (--) to create a dash on a typewriter or computer keyboard. The en dash (–), a typographic symbol about the width of the character n, is used as a hyphen or as a substitute for the word "to" e.g., July–September. The correct typographic symbols for em and en dashes have traditionally been used in books, newspapers, and advertisements, and are recommended for use when creating a professional-looking document. Word automatically centers en and em dashes

Examples:

Our notebook sales have increased 20 percent since last year—from $50,000 to $60,000.

The annual report for fiscal year 1996–97 will be available at the end of April.

Activities

■ Activity 18.1—Create a Magazine Article

1. Open the file named **18act1.doc** located on the data disk.

2. Create the article title using WordArt and the following information:

   a. Select a 75% Zoom view.

   b. Place the insertion point on the blank line below the graphic image.

   c. Select **Insert, Picture, WordArt**.

   d. Select the fourth style in the first row. Select **OK**.

   e. Type Weekend Astronauts. Change the font to **Century Gothic**, bold, **32 point**, or select a font of your own choice. Select **OK**.

      Note: If necessary, click on the WordArt and drag upward to align the title to the right of the graphic image.

   f. Select the **Format WordArt** button on the WordArt Toolbar.

   g. Select the **Size** tab. Set the **Height** to **1.25"** and the **Width** to **3.5"**.

   h. Select the **Layout** tab. Click on the **Square** Wrapping style. Select the **Right** Horizontal alignment option.

   i. Select **OK**.

   j. Close the WordArt Toolbar.

3. Select the article text beginning "Are you ready . . ." to the end of the document.

4. Select **Format, Columns** and create two columns using the **Left** option in the Presets area. Change the width of Col # 1 to **2.25"** and the spacing between columns to **.4"**. Select **OK**. Click once to deselect the text.

5. Create footers for odd and even pages using the following information:

   a. With the insertion point located on page 1, select **View, Header and Footer**.

   b. Select the **Page Setup** button and choose **Different odd and even**. Select **OK**.

   c. Select the **Switch Between Header and Footer** button to switch to the Odd Page Footer - Section 1 pane.

   d. In the Odd Page Footer pane, type **S**pacefarers Monthly. Press the **Tab** key twice and select the **Insert Page Number** button. Select the footer text and change the font to **Garamond, 11 point** or make a font choice of your own.

   e. Select the **Show Next** button.

   f. In the Even Page - Footer Section 2 pane, select the **Insert Page Number** button. Press the **Tab** key twice and type **Weekend**

Astronauts. Select the footer text and change the font to **Garamond, 11 point** or make a font choice of your own.

    g.   Select **Close** on the Header and Footer Toolbar.

6.   Create a text box for the pull quote text.

    a.   Select the **Whole Page** view. If necessary, scroll up to view page 1.

    b.   Select **Insert, Text Box.**

    c.   Move the mouse pointer to the center of page 1 and draw a rectangle approximately **2.75"** in width and **1"** in height. (See page 472)

    d.   Select **Format, Text Box.**

    e.   Select the **Size** tab. Set the **Height** to **1.25"** and the **Width** to **3"**.

    f.   Select the **Layout** tab and choose the **Square** Wrapping style option.

    g.   Select the **Colors and Lines** tab. In the Line area, click in the **Color** box and select **No Line.** Select **OK.**

    h.   Change to 75% Zoom view. Then select and copy the text, **Who is made of the "right stuff"? Everyone**, which is located in the first paragraph in column 2 on page 1.

    i.   Click in the pull quote text box and select the **Paste** button.

    j.   Change the font of the pull quote text to **Garamond, bold, 22 points** or make a font choice of your own. Change the alignment of the pull quote text to **Center.**

    k.   Select the **Tables and Borders** button to display the Tables and Borders Toolbar.

    l.   Click in the Line Style box and select the triple-line style. Click on the down triangle beside the **Border** button and choose the **Top Border** button. Click on the down triangle again and select the **Bottom Border** button.

    m.   Close the Tables and Borders Toolbar.

    Note: If necessary, locate the pull quote text box in the center of the columns (see page 472).

7.   Create a drop cap for the first character of the first paragraph. (Place the insertion point to the left of the first character in the first paragraph of the article text. Select **Format, Drop Cap.** Select the **Dropped** option. Change the font to **Garamond, bold** or make a font choice of your own. Check that **3** displays in the Lines to drop box. Triple-click in the **Distance from text** box and type **.05.** Select **OK.**)

8.   Modify the Body Text style so that the first line of each body text paragraph is indented **.35"** and there is no spacing after the paragraphs.

    a.   Place the insertion point in a paragraph that has been formatted with the Body Text style. For example, click in the second paragraph of column 1.

    b.   Select **Format, Style.** With the Body Text style highlighted in the Styles list, select **Modify.**

c. Select **Format**, **Paragraph**. Click in the **Special** box and select **First line**. Triple-click in the **By** box and type **.35**. Click on the down triangle beside the **Spacing After** box until **0** displays. Select **OK** twice. Select **Close**.

9. Create a text box that will contain the sidebar text. The sidebar text is located in the file named **18Side2.doc** located on the data disk.

   a. Select the **Whole Page** view and scroll down to view page 2.

   b. Select **Insert**, **Text Box**. Draw a rectangle that is approximately 6" in width and 5½" in length at the top of page 2.

   c. Select **Format**, **Text Box**.

   d. Select the **Size** tab. Set the **Height** to 5.4" and the **Width** to 6".

   e. Select the **Colors and Lines** tab. In the Line area, click in the **Color** box and select **No Line**.

   f. Select the **Layout** tab and choose the **Square** Wrapping style option.

   g. Select **OK**.

   h Click in the text box. Select **Insert, File** and insert the file named **18Side2.doc** located on the data disk.

   i. Change to **50%** view. Select all the text in the text box. Select **Format, Border, and Shading**. Choose the **Shadow** option. Scroll down the Style list and select the double-line style and choose a 1½ **pt** line width. Select **OK**.

10. Use the *new* filename **18Astronauts article.doc** and save the file on your file disk.

    Note: Your final document should look similar to the article shown below.

11. Print one copy. Close the document.

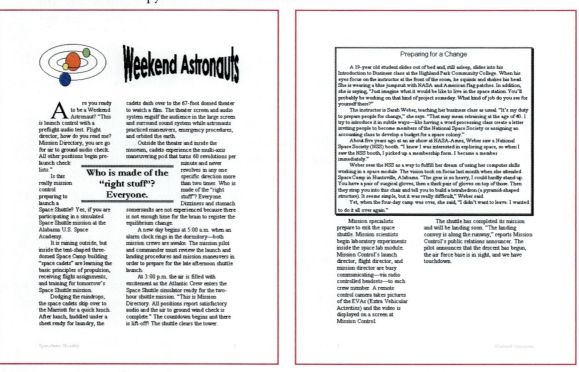

Challenge Your Skills

1. Open the file named **18skill1.doc** located on the data disk. Review the text and determine an appropriate pull quote.

2. Correct five spelling errors, two punctuation/grammatical errors, three misused words, and one parenthesis error.

3. Make decisions regarding the placement and size of a graphic image(s). Check for appropriate images in the Insert ClipArt dialog box.

4. The article title is **Smart Tips for the Workplace**. Make decisions regarding using WordArt or shadow text effects to format the article title.

5. Make decisions regarding:

   > Number and widths of columns and spacing between columns
   > Placement and text for pull quote
   > Use of a drop cap
   > Indentation for paragraphs
   > Placement and format of sidebar information
   > Footers for odd and even pages of the article

6. The sidebar text is contained in a file named **18Side3.doc** located on the data disk.

7. Use the *new* filename **18Smart Tips article.doc** and save the document on your file disk.

   Note: An example of the final article is shown on page 474. Your document does not need to match the example.

8. Print one copy and close the document.

smart Tips for the workplace

Computers are becoming an essential part of the workplace and increasingly popular at home. Workers who regularly use computers often complain of headaches, back and muscle aches, blurred vision, stress, and wrist pain. When designing a computer workstation, it is important to consider the individual(s) who will use the workstation and the type of work that will be performed at the station.

One of the most common problems for people working at computer workstations is physical strain. The most common symptoms include aches and pains of the neck, shoulder, back, arm, wrist, and hand, as well as headaches. These complaints stem from several problems. Constant upper body movement may result in various neck, wrist, and back discomforts. Constant sitting at a keyboard staring at the computer monitor without frequent breaks increases muscle tension. Inadequate workplace design and furnishings may aggravate the various muscle aches. Improper chair size and poor back support are the most common

Review the document and determine an appropriate pull quote.

causes of back pain. One of the most common problems is carpal tunnel syndrome.

What Is Carpal Tunnel Syndrome?

Carpal tunnel syndrome is a painful hand disorder caused by stressful and repetitive motions of the hand. Although the site of the injury is the wrist, pain is usually felt in the hand. Excessive movement of the wrists or holding the wrists in static positions for long periods of time can irritate the nerves, tendons, and arteries inside a narrow formation of ligament and bone at the wrist—the carpal tunnel. In the early stages of carpal tunnel syndrome, symptoms can include numbness and tingling in the hand, pain in your hands and wrists, and the dropping of objects. Initially, the symptoms occur at night; however, the symptoms soon appear during the day and intensify.

Carpal tunnel syndrome is preventable. Preventing carpal tunnel syndrome depends on many factors including good posture, work environment, and exercise.

Carpal Tunnel Exercises

Before typing and during breaks throughout the day, perform the following stretching exercises. None of these exercises should cause discomfort.

Wrist Bends

➤ With your forearm resting on the edge of a table, grasp the fingers of one hand with the other hand and gently bend back the wrist, stretching the hand and wrist. Hold for five seconds. Repeat for other wrist.
➤ Place your hand palm down with fingers spread on a table. Gently press the hand against the table, stretching the fingers and wrist. Hold for five seconds. Repeat for other hand.

Wrist and Finger Stretches

➤ Press both palms together at chest level. Slowly lift your elbows up and away from the sides of your body as far as they can comfortably go. Hold for five seconds. Repeat three or four times.
➤ Clench your hands into tight fists. Release and stretch the fingers as far as they will go.
➤ Flex each finger across the palm to touch the tip of the thumb.
➤ Raise your arms over your head and stretch out the fingers as if you were attempting to touch the ceiling.

Wrist Strengtheners

➤ With your arm resting on a table, make a loose fist with one hand palm up.
➤ Use the other hand to gently press down and against the clenched hand. Resist the force with the closed hand for five seconds. Keep wrists straight.
➤ Turn the clenched hand palm down and use the other hand to gently press down and against the clenched hand. Resist the force with the clenched hand for five seconds. Keep wrists straight.
➤ Turn the clenched hand sideways with your thumb facing up and use the other hand to gently press down and against the clenched hand. Resist the force with the clenched hand for five seconds. Keep wrists straight.
➤ Turn the clenched hand palm down. Place your other hand against the knuckles of the clenched hand and use the other hand to gently press against the clenched hand. Resist the force with the closed hand for five seconds. Keep wrists straight.
➤ Repeat the sequence five times.
➤ Repeat for other hand.

If your work includes using a computer or other keyboard machine, be sure to practice proper posture and good keyboarding techniques. When typing, move only the fingers and always maintain a straight-wrist position. If your keyboard has a pad, use it to rest your wrists during breaks. Stretching and strengthening exercises to build up the muscles in the wrists and forearms are very important. (See the Carpal Tunnel Exercises in the sidebar for further information.) However, if you have

advanced carpal tunnel syndrome, do not perform the listed exercises.

In the case of advanced carpal tunnel syndrome, wrist splints and injections of anti-inflammatory medications may reduce swelling and decrease the compression on the nerve. If these measures fail to provide relief, surgery may be necessary. After surgery, it is important to exercise as soon as possible in order to regain full function and mobility in your hands and wrists.

Carpal tunnel syndrome often occurs in people who do repetitive tasks— housewives, secretaries, meat cutters, assembly line workers, carpenters, musicians, etc. Women are five times more likely than men to develop carpal tunnel syndrome. Carpal tunnel syndrome is also referred to as repetitive truama disorder or overuse syndrome.

Minimizing Physical Strain

To minimize physical strain, a computer workstation should provide the worker with a comfortable sitting position, sufficiently flexible to reach, use, and see the computer monitor, keyboard, and documents. When designing a workstation, keep the following guidelines in mind.

1. The chair should have an easily adjustable seat height and backrest position. The chair height should be adjusted so that the worker's feet rest

firmly on the floor and his/her thighs are parallel to the floor.

2. Adjust the screen height so that the top of the screen is at or below eye level. Adjust the screen angle to reduce glare.

3. If the worker will be viewing a document and the screen, adjust the document to the same height, distance, and orientation as the screen.

4. Place the keyboard so that the wrists remain straight when typing. Provide a wrist rest.

5. Adjust lighting to reduce glare on the screen, but still provide adequate lighting for normal paperwork.

Physical stress can also be reduced by taking regular breaks, varying tasks, and performing simple exercises.

Create Fill-in Forms

- Create a fill-in form template
- Edit a form template
- Create a calculation field

Objectives and Introduction

After successfully completing this chapter, you will be able to create a form template that contains text fields, check box fields, and drop-down fields and use the form template to create a document. In addition, you will learn how to edit a form template and create a field that calculates the total of the values in other fields.

Word's form field features can be used to create online forms. These forms are stored as templates. The form templates contain form fields and the wording to appear in each document that is created using the template.

Create a Form Template

A form template is a model for a document. A form template can contain text fields, check box fields, and drop-down fields. When a new document is created using a form template, a copy of the structure, fields, and text displays in the document window. Data is then entered into text fields, check boxes are selected, and items are selected from drop-down lists to fill out (complete) the form document. The form document is then saved and printed.

To create a new form, a template must be created. A new template can be based on the *Normal.dot* template or on another template that more closely matches the structure of the new form. Form templates can contain three different types of form fields: text fields, check box fields, and drop-down fields. Each type of form field can be customized. For example, a text form field can be customized to accept only numbers and to display the numbers in a specific format.

Before beginning to create a form template, develop a mock-up or illustration of how the final form should look. Determine the types of form fields that will be used to enter data and the structure that best meets the needs of the people who will be using the form. Form fields can be placed in table cells or inserted into text. See Figure 19.1 for two examples of form templates.

FIGURE 19.1

Two examples of form templates

Printing Quote

Customer Name:	Contact:	Phone Number:	Date of Quote:
Quantity:	Finish Size:	Description:	
Paper Stock:	Ink: Black	Number of Pages:	☐ Camera Ready
Self-Cover: ☐	Separate Cover: ☐	Cover Stock:	Cover Ink: none
Typesetting Services:	☐ Desktop Publishing	☐ Lino Output	☐ Paste-up
	☐ Paper	☐ Film	
Binding:	☐ Saddle Stitch	☐ Perfect binding	☐ Spiral
	☐ Pad	☐ NCR Pad	☐ Stapled
☐ 3-hole Drill	☐ 2-hole Drill	☐ Folded	☐ Cut
Printing Quote:	Typesetting Quote:	Binding Quote:	Total Printing Quote: $0.00

GOLDEN HAVEN RESORT

Dear   :

Thank you for choosing Golden Haven Resort for your lodging accommodations. We are pleased to confirm your reservation for the following:

Arrival Date:
Departure Date:
Room Rate:
Number of Rooms:
Non-smoking Room: ☐ Yes   ☐ No
Guarantee Method: Visa

To avoid any charges to your account, cancellations must be made within 24 hours of your arrival date. Check in time is   and check out time is   .

If you have any questions or need further assistance, please contact the Lodging Department at (800) 555-9250.

Sincerely,

Lodging Department

A Forms Toolbar is available to assist you in developing a form template. The buttons on the Forms Toolbar to insert and customize fields are: the **Text Form Field** button, the **Check Box Form Field** button, the **Drop-Down Form Field** button, and the **Form Field Options** button. As form fields are inserted, Word automatically creates a bookmark name for each field, e.g., Text1, Check1, Dropdown1. These bookmark names can also be used when creating formulas and macros.

To assist users in filling out a form, Help messages can be created for the form fields. Help text is added by selecting the **Add Help Text** button in the Form Field Options dialog box. In the Form Field Help Text dialog box, either the **Status Bar** tab or **Help Key (F1)** tab is selected and the desired Help text is then typed in the **Type your own** box, or an AutoText entry name is selected. A Help message of up to 138 characters can be displayed in the Status Bar. If the **Help Key (F1)** tab is selected, Word creates a message box that will display when the **F1** key is pressed by the user. The message box can contain a Help message of up to 255 characters.

Once the form template is completed, the form is protected by selecting the **Protect Form** button. When the **Protect Form** button is selected, the form template cannot be edited. (For information on editing a form template, see the section Edit a Form Template and Create Calculation Fields later in this chapter.) The form template is then saved. By default, Word saves template files in the directory specified on the File Locations tab, User Templates setting of the Options dialog box. If desired, the template can be saved in a different location by selecting a drive and/or folder in the Save As dialog box. However, if a template file is saved in a file location other than the one specified on the File Locations tab in the Options dialog box, the template name will not display in the New dialog box.

Create a Fill-in Form Template

1. Select File, New.

    Note: The New dialog box displays.

2. Select a template that is similar to the one you wish to create, or select the Blank Document icon on the General tab to create a template from scratch.

    For example, select the General tab and click once on the Blank Document icon.

3. In the Create New area, select the Template option.

4. Select OK.

    Note: Template1 displays in the Title bar.

5. Format the template as needed.

    For example,

    a. Change all margins to .5".

    b. Type COUNTRYWIDE TRUCKING COMPANY. Press Enter and type Employee Evaluation Form. Press Enter twice.

    c. Select COUNTRYWIDE TRUCKING COMPANY and Employee Evaluation Form. Change the alignment to Center and the font to Arial, bold.

FIGURE 19.2

Forms Toolbar

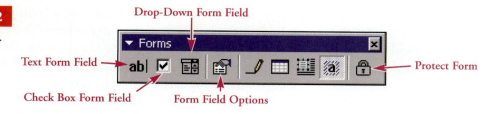

Drop-Down Form Field

Text Form Field → ab| ☑

Check Box Form Field

Form Field Options

Protect Form

d. Place the insertion point on the second blank line below the words Employee Evaluation Form and create a table with **3 rows** and **5 columns**.

6. To display the Forms Toolbar, move the mouse pointer into the Standard or Formatting Toolbar and click the *right* mouse button once. Move the mouse pointer to **Forms** and click the left mouse button.

    Note: The Forms Toolbar displays (see Figure 19.2). If the Forms Toolbar displays on top of the table, move the mouse pointer into the Forms Toolbar Title bar, press and hold the mouse button, and drag the Toolbar down and to the right.

7. Type text and select Forms Toolbar buttons to create the desired form.

    For example,

    a. In the first cell of the table, type **Social Security:** and press **Enter**.

    b. On the Forms Toolbar, select the **Text Form Field** button ab|.

        Note: A gray area indicating that a field has been inserted displays in the table.

    c. Select the **Form Field Options** button 🔳.

        Note: The Text Form Field Options dialog box displays (see Figure 19.3).

    d. Double-click in the **Maximum length** box and type **11**. Select **OK**.

    e. Press the **Tab** key to move the insertion point to the first cell in column 2. Type **Last:** and press **Enter**. Select the **Text Form Field** button ab|.

    f. Press the **Tab** key to move the insertion point to the first cell in column 3. Type **First:** and press **Enter**. Select the **Text Form Field** button ab|.

FIGURE 19.3

Text Form Field Options dialog box

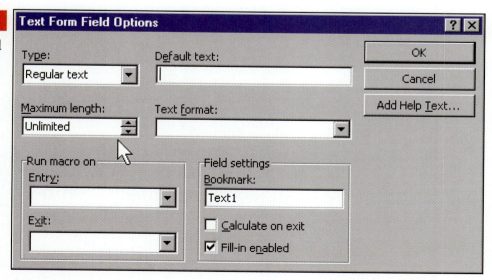

FIGURE 19.4

Form Field
Help Text dialog
box

g. Press the **Tab** key to move the insertion point to the first cell in column 4. Type **Middle:** and press **Enter**. Select the **Text Form Field** button `abl`.

h. Press the **Tab** key to move the insertion point to the first cell in column 5. Type **Employee No.:** and press **Enter**. Select the **Text Form Field** button `abl`.

i. Select the **Form Field Options** button.

j. Click in the **Type** box and select **Number**.

k. Double-click in the **Maximum length** box and type **5**.

l. Click on the down arrow located to the right of the **Number format** box and select **0** (whole numbers).

m. Select the **Add Help Text** button. On the Status Bar tab, select the **Type your own** option. Type **Enter the employee's five-digit identification number** (see Figure 19.4). Select **OK** to exit the Form Field Help Text dialog box.

n. Select **OK** to exit the Text Form Field Options dialog box.

o. Press the **Tab** key to move the insertion point to the first cell of row 2. Type **Department:** and press **Enter**.

p. Select the **Drop-Down Form Field** button.

q. Select the **Form Field Options** button.

Note: The Drop-Down Form Field Options dialog box displays (see Figure 19.5).

r. In the Drop-down item box, type **Accounting**. Select **Add** or press **Enter**. Type the following item names in the **Drop-down item** box. Select **Add** after each item.

> **Delivery**   (select **Add** or press **Enter**)
> **Human Resources**   (select **Add** or press **Enter**)

FIGURE 19.5

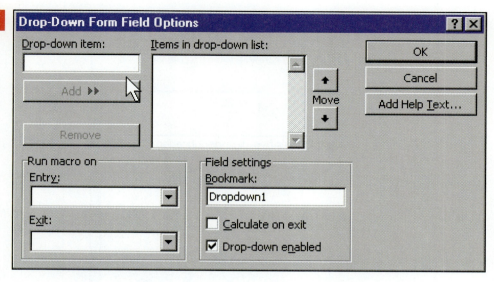

Sales	(select **Add** or press **Enter**)
Warehouse	(select **Add** or press **Enter**)

s.   Select **OK**.

*Note: The first item in the drop-down list (i.e., Accounting) displays in
the drop-down form field.*

t.   Press the **Tab** key to move the insertion point to row 2, column 2.
Type **Position:** and press **Enter**. Select the **Text Form Field** button ![abl]

u.   Press the **Tab** key to move the insertion point to row 2, column 3.
Type **Date of Evaluation:** and press **Enter**. Select the **Text Form Field**
button ![abl]. Select the **Form Field Options** button ![icon]. In the Type
box, select **Date**. In the Date Format box, select **M/d/yy**. Select **OK**.

v.   Press the **Tab** key to move the insertion point to row 2, column 4.
Type **Date in Position:** and press **Enter**. Select the **Text Form Field**
button ![abl]. Select the **Form Field Options** button ![icon]. In the Type
box, select **Date**. In the Date format box, select **M/d/yy**. Select **OK**.

w.   Press the **Tab** key to move the insertion point to row 2, column 5.
Type **Date of Last Review:** and press **Enter**. Select the **Text Form Field**
button ![abl]. Select the **Form Field Options** button ![icon]. In the Type box,
select **Date**. In the Date format box, select **M/d/yy**. Select **OK**.

x.   Press the **Tab** key to move the insertion point to row 3, column 1.
Type **Type of Evaluation:** and press the **Tab** key once to move the
insertion point to row 3, column 2.

y.   Select the **Check Box Form Field** button ![box]. Press the **Spacebar**
twice. Type **Probationary review**.

z.   Press the **Tab** key to move the insertion point to row 3, column 3.
Select the **Check Box Form Field** button ![box]. Press the **Spacebar**
twice. Type **6-month review**. Press the **Tab** key once to move the
insertion point to row 3, column 4. Select the **Check Box Form Field**
button ![box]. Press the **Spacebar** twice. Type **Annual review**. Press the
Tab key to move the insertion point to row 3, column 5. Select the

Check Box Form Field button ☑. Press the **Spacebar** twice. Type **Salary increase**.

8. Format the form as needed.

   For example,

   a. Select all the text in the table and change the font to **Arial, 9 point**.

   b. Select **Format, Paragraph**, type **3 pt** in the **Spacing before** and **Spacing after** boxes on the Indents and Spacing tab. Select **OK**.

   c. Place the insertion point below the table and press the **Enter** key once. Continue to create the form by inserting the file named **19evaltx.doc** located on the data disk (select **Insert, File**; if necessary, select the drive/folder where the data disk is located; double-click on **19evaltx.doc**).

   Note: The form should look similar to the form shown in Figure 19.6.

9. When the form is completed, select the **Protect Form** button 🔒 on the Forms Toolbar.

10. To remove the Forms Toolbar, click on the **Close** button located at the right of the Forms Toolbar Title bar.

FIGURE 19.6

Fill-in form template with text fields, drop-down fields, and check box fields

11. Save the form template.

> For example, select the **Save** button. In the Save in box, select the drive where your file disk is located. Double-click on the **My Templates** folder. Type the template name **evaluation** followed by a space and **your initials** (e.g., **evaluation LH**).

*Note: If you do not see a folder named My Templates on your file disk, create the folder by selecting the **Create New Folder** button , typing My Templates in the Name box, and selecting OK. Then double-click on the My Templates folder and continue with the process to name and save the form template.*

When the form template is saved, Word will automatically add the extension .dot to the template filename. Unless another drive/folder is selected, template files are saved to the directory specified for User templates on the File Locations tab in the Options dialog box.

12. Close the document.

Finish-Up Instructions

❖ Continue with the Steps to Use a Fill-in Form Template.

Steps to ▶ Use a Fill-in Form Template

1. Select **File, New**.

2. Select the desired tab.

> For example, select the **General** tab or the **My Templates** tab.

*Note: An icon with the name of your form template (e.g., evaluation LH.dot) should be displayed. If no icon displays for your template, select **Cancel**. Select the New button, select **Tools, Options**, and choose the **File Locations** tab. Select the User Templates option, choose **Modify**, select the drive where your file disk is located, select the **My Templates** folder, choose **OK**, and select **Close**. Repeat steps 1 and 2.*

3. Double-click on the desired form template icon.

> For example, double-click on the icon for your evaluation form template.

4. Enter the needed information into the form fields. Press the **Tab** key to move from field to field.

> For example, enter the information shown in Figure 19.7.

*Note: To insert an X in a check box, tab to the desired check box and press the **Spacebar**, or move the mouse pointer to the check box and click.*

5. When the information has been entered into the necessary fields, save and print the document using normal procedures.

> For example, use the filename **19Edmonds evaluation.doc** and save the file on your file disk. Print one copy.

Finish-Up Instructions

❖ Close the document.

COUNTRYWIDE TRUCKING COMPANY
Employee Evaluation Form

Social Security: 555-98-1357	Last: Edmonds	First: Marci	Middle: R.	Employee No.: 26425
Department: Delivery	Position: Driver (local)	Date of Evaluation: 4/5/00	Date in Position: 4/15/98	Date of Last Review: 4/15/99
Type of Evaluation:	☐ Probationary review	☐ 6-month review	☒ Annual review	☐ Salary increase

	Needs Improvement	Meets Requirement	Exceeds Requirement	Comments
Customer Service	☐	☐	☒	
Completeness of Paperwork	☐	☐	☐	
Driving Record (Safety)	☐	☒	☐	
Follows Company Policies	☐	☒	☐	
Dependability	☐	☐	☒	
Cooperation with Others	☐	☒	☐	
Job Responsibility	☐	☒	☐	
Job Attitude	☐	☐	☒	
Overall Rating	☐	☒	☐	

Strong Areas of Performance

Marci excels in customer service. She is always ready to meet the customer's needs.

Areas Needing Improvement

Check all forms for completeness and accuracy before leaving customer site and before turning in forms to accounting.

Action Plan

Supervisor will review procedures by completing forms. Supervisor will receive all paperwork for the next two weeks to ensure completeness and accuracy. Any problems will be discussed immediately with Marci.

Supervisor's Comments

Marci has proven to be a very dependable and hard-working employee. She has shown the ability to address customer needs effectively. She has a positive, "get the job done" attitude.

Employee Comments

I acknowledge that the above evaluation has been discussed with me.	**Employee Signature:**	**Date:**

FIGURE 19.7

Completed fill-in form created using the evaluation.dot template

Edit a Form Template and Create Calculation Fields

To edit a form template, open the template file and turn protection off. Once the form template is unprotected, changes can be made to existing fields, text can be edited, and new fields can be added. After the form template has been edited, protect and save the form template.

A calculation field is a special type of text field that contains a formula. When a calculation field is created, a formula is typed in the Expression box in the Text Form Field Options dialog box. The results of the formula display in the calculation field. When typing a formula, either the field's cell address or bookmark name can be used.

When creating a form that will contain a calculation field, determine which fields will be referenced in the calculation field formula. Turn on the **Calculate**

on exit option for each field that will be referenced in the calculation field formula. The **Calculate on exit** option tells Word to update the results of the calculation field when a number is typed in the referenced field and the field is exited by pressing the **Tab** or arrow keys.

Start-Up Instructions

❖ To complete the following drill, copy the file named **quote.dot** located on the data disk to the **My Templates** folder on your file disk. For information on copying files, see Chapter 16, page 419.

Steps to

Edit a Form Template and Create Calculation Fields

1. Select **File, Open**. Click in the **Files of type** box and select **Document Templates (*.dot)**.

2. In the **Look in** box, select the desired drive and/or folder where the template file is located.

   For example, select the drive where your file disk is located and choose the **My Templates** folder.

3. Double-click on the desired template name.

   For example, double-click on **quote.dot**.

4. To display the Forms Toolbar, move the mouse pointer into the Standard or Formatting Toolbar and click the *right* mouse button once. Move the mouse pointer to **Forms** and click the left mouse button.

5. Select the **Protect Form** button to turn off the protect feature so that the form can be edited.

6. Edit the form as desired.

   For example, add the following fields:

   a. Click below the words "Printing Quote" located in the last row of the table. Select the **Text Form Field** button ![abl]. Select the **Form Field Options** button ![icon]. Set the Type to **Number** and the Number format to **$#,##0.00;($#,##0.00)**. Select the **Calculate on exit** option. Select **OK**.

   b. Click below the words "Typesetting Quote." Select the **Text Form Field** button ![abl]. Select the **Form Field Options** button ![icon]. Set the Type to **Number** and the Number format to **$#,##0.00;($#,##0.00)**. Select the **Calculate on exit** option. Select **OK**.

   c. Click below the words "Binding Quote." Select the **Text Form Field** button ![abl]. Select the **Form Field Options** button ![icon]. Set the Type to **Number** and the Number format to **$#,##0.00;($#,##0.00)**. Select the **Calculate on exit** option. Select **OK**.

7. Place the insertion point at the location where the calculated value is to be displayed.

   For example, click below the words **Total Printing Quote**.

8. Select the **Text Form Field** button ![abl].

9. Select the **Form Field Options** button 🖼.

10. Click in the **Type** box and select **Calculation**.

 Note: An equals sign (=) displays in the Expression box.

11. In the Expression box, type the desired formula.

 For example, move the mouse pointer to the right of the equals sign and click. Type the formula **SUM(A10:C10)**. (Do not type the period.)

12. If desired, click on the down arrow beside the **Number format** box and select a number format.

 For example, select the **$#,##0.00;($#,##0.00)** number type. Select **OK**.

13. Select the **Protect Form** button 🔒 on the Forms Toolbar.

14. Close the Forms Toolbar.

15. Select **File, Save** to save the form template.

Finish-Up Instructions

❖ Close the template.

❖ Select **File**, **New**. On the **General** or **My Templates** tab, double-click on the icon for **quote.dot**.

❖ Enter the information shown in Figure 19.8 into the Printing Quote form.

 Note: When you tab over to the Total Printing Quote, the amount is automatically calculated.

❖ Use the filename **19Printing Quote.doc** and save the form on your file disk.

❖ Print one copy.

❖ Close the document.

Printing Quote			
Customer Name: Lusk & Synder	Contact: Irage	Phone Number: 615-555-9200	Date of Quote: (insert current date)
Quantity: 1000	Finish Size: 8.5 x 11	Description: Tri-fold brochure	
Paper Stock: 67 lb card stock–blue	Ink: Custom	Number of Pages: 2	☐ Camera Ready:
Self-Cover: ☐	Separate Cover: ☐	Cover Stock: ▨	Cover Ink: none
Typesetting Services:	☐ Desktop Publishing	☐ Lino Output	☐ Paste-up
	☐ Paper	☒ Film	
Binding:	☐ Saddle Stitch	☐ Perfect binding	☐ Spiral
	☐ Pad	☐ NCR Pad	☐ Stapled
☐ 3-hole Drill	☐ 2-hole Drill	☒ Folded	☐ Cut
Printing Quote: $745.75	Typesetting Quote: $25.00	Binding Quote: $40.00	Total Printing Quote: $810.75

FIGURE 19.8

Completed fill-in form created using the **quote.dot** template

Print and Save Form Data Only

If desired, the data entered into a form can be printed onto preprinted forms (without printing the form structure). Also, the data entered into a form can be saved without saving the structure of the form. When only data are saved, Word creates a Text Only file that can be imported into other programs such as a database program.

Print Data on a Preprinted Form

Note: The following steps are for your information only.

1. Insert the preprinted form into your printer.
2. With the completed form displayed in the document window, select File, Print.
3. Select the Options button.
4. Select the Print data only for forms option in the Options for current document only area.
5. Select OK.
6. Select OK to print the data.

Save Data Only

Note: The following steps are for your information only.

1. Select File, Save As.
2. Choose Tools.
3. Select General Options.
4. Select Save data only for forms option.
5. Select OK.
6. Type the desired filename in the File name box and select Save.

The Next Step

Chapter Review and Activities

Self-Check Quiz

T F 1. A form template can contain text fields, check box fields, and drop-down fields.

T F 2. When creating a calculation field, a formula is typed in the Expression box in the Text Form Field Options dialog box.

T F 3. A form template must be unprotected before the template can be edited.

T F 4. A drop-down form field can be customized; however, a text form field cannot be customized.

T F 5. Help text can be added to form fields to assist the user when the form is being filled out.

6. After a form template is completed, the _____ button is selected to protect the form.
   a. **Lock Form**
   b. **Protect Form**
   c. **Lock Document**
   d. **Save**

7. Which of the following is **not** a type of text form field?
   a. regular text
   b. current date
   c. column
   d. calculation

8. A Help message that will display in the Status Bar can contain up to _____ characters.
   a. 100
   b. 255
   c. 53
   d. 138

9. There are six types of text form fields available in the Text Form Field Options dialog box. List the six types.

10. List two actions that should be taken before creating a form template.

Enriching Language Arts Skills

Spelling/Vocabulary Words

arbitration—the hearing and determination of a dispute or grievance between parties by a person or persons appointed by mutual consent or statutory provision.

grievance—a complaint or the grounds for a complaint against a situation viewed as unjust.

interpretation—the act or process of explaining or clarifying.

Colons, Capitalization, and Punctuation for Bulleted and Enumerated Lists

Place a colon after an independent clause that introduces a bulleted or enumerated (numbered) list. An introductory clause frequently includes words such as *the following* and *as follows*. When creating a bulleted or enumerated list, capitalize the first word and insert a final punctuation mark (period, question mark, or exclamation point) after each item that is a complete sentence or phrase. Do not capitalize the first word or insert final punctuation when bulleted or enumerated list items are not complete thoughts.

Example:

The following qualifications are suggested for an air-conditioning mechanic applicant:

1. high school diploma or equivalent plus three years' experience

2. a valid drivers license

3. successful compliance with job-related medical standards

4. proof of U.S. citizenship or valid work permit

Activities

Activity 19.1—Create a Form Template

1. Use the following information to create the form template shown on page 491.
   a. Select **File, New, General** tab, **Blank Document** icon, **Template, OK**.
   b. Set the top margin to **2"**.
   c. Display the Forms Toolbar (move the mouse pointer into the Standard or Formatting Toolbar and click the *right* mouse button once; select **Forms**).

d. Create a text form field that automatically inserts the current date. (Select the **Text Form Field** button. Select the **Form Field Options** button. In the Type box, select **Current Date**. In the Date format box, select **MMMM d, yyyy**. Select **OK**.) Press the right arrow key to deselect the field. Press **Enter** four times.

e. Create a text form field for the guest's name. Create the Help message "Enter guest's name" to display in the Status Bar. (Select the **Text Form Field** button. Select the **Form Field Options** button. Select the **Add Help Text** button. On the Status Bar tab, select the **Type your own** option. Type **Enter guest's name**. Select **OK** twice.)

f. Press the right arrow key to deselect the field. Press **Enter** once.

g. Select the **Text Form Field** button to create a field for the guest's address. (If desired, create the Help message "Enter guest's street address" to be displayed in the Status Bar.)

h. Press the right arrow key to deselect the field. Press **Enter** once.

i. Select the **Text Form Field** button to create a field for the guest's city, state, and zip code. (If desired, create the Help message "Enter guest's city, state, and zip code" to be displayed in the Status Bar.)

j. Press the right arrow key to deselect the field. Press **Enter** twice. Type the word **Dear** and press the **Spacebar** once.

k. Select the **Text Form Field** button to create a field for the salutation. (If desired, create the Help message "Enter guest's name for the salutation" to be displayed in the Status Bar.) Press the right arrow key to deselect the field.

l. Type a colon (:) and press **Enter** twice. Type the following paragraph.

Thank you for choosing Golden Haven Resort for your lodging accommodations. We are pleased to confirm your reservation for the following:

m. Press **Enter** twice after the last character in the paragraph.

n. Press the **Tab** key once. Type **Arrival Date:** and press the **Tab** key twice. Select the **Text Form Field** button. Select the **Form Field Options** button. Change the Type to **Date** and the Date format to **MMMM d, yyyy**. Select **OK**.

o. Press the right arrow key to deselect the field. Press the **Enter** key once. Press the **Tab** key once. Type **Departure Date:** and press the **Tab** key once. Select the **Text Form Field** button. Select the **Form Field Options** button. Change the Type to **Date** and the Date format to **MMMM d, yyyy**. Select **OK**.

p. Press the right arrow key to deselect the field. Press the **Enter** key once. Press the **Tab** key once. Type **Room Rate:** and press the **Tab** key twice. Select the **Text Form Field** button. Select the **Form Field Options** button. Change the Type to **Number** and the Number format to **$#,##0.00;($#,##0.00)**. Select **OK**.

q. Press the right arrow key to deselect the field. Press the **Enter** key once. Press the **Tab** key once. Type **Number of Rooms:** and press the **Tab** key once. Select the **Text Form Field** button. Select the **Form Field Options** button. Change the Type to **Number** and the Number format to **0**. Select **OK**.

r. Press the right arrow key to deselect the field. Press the **Enter** key once. Press the **Tab** key once. Type **Non-smoking Room:** and press the **Tab** key once. Select the **Check Box Form Field** button. Press the **Spacebar** once and type **Yes**. Press the **Tab** key once. Select the **Check Box Form Field** button. Press the **Spacebar** once and type **No**.

s. Press the **Enter** key once. Press the **Tab** key once. Type **Guarantee Method:** and press the **Tab** key once. Select the **Drop-Down Form Field** button. Select the **Form Field Options** button. In the Drop-down item box, add the following items:

> **Visa**
> **MasterCard**
> **American Express**
> **Check**

t. Select **OK**.

u. Press the right arrow key to deselect the field. Press the **Enter** key twice and type the following text, inserting the text form fields as indicated:

> **To avoid any charges to your account, cancellations must be made at least one day before your arrival date. Check-in time is** (insert a **Text Form Field**; set the **Type** to **Date** and the **Date format** to **h:mm am/pm**) **and check-out time is** (insert a **Text Form Field**; set the **Type** to **Date** and the **Date format** to **h:mm am/pm**).

> **If you have any questions or need further assistance, please contact the Lodging Department at 800-555-9250.**

> **Sincerely,**

> **Lodging Department**

2. Proofread the form.

3. Protect the form template (select the **Protect Form** button).

4. Close the Forms Toolbar.

5. Use the name **reserve.dot** and save the form template to the **My Templates** folder on your file disk (select **File**, **Save**; in the Save in box, select the drive where your file disk is located; double-click on the **My Templates** folder; type the template name **reserve.dot**; select **Save**).

6. Print a copy of the form. Close the document.

7. Use the reserve form template to create the document shown below (select **File, New**; on the General tab, click on the **reserve.dot** icon; select **OK**). Press the **Tab** key to move from field to field.

Current date

Ms. Bernice Musante
2421 Smoketown Road
Woodbridge, VA 22191

Dear Ms. Musante:

Thank you for choosing Golden Haven Resort for your lodging accommodations. We are pleased to confirm your reservation for the following:

Arrival Date:	(Insert a date three week from the current date)
Departure Date:	(Insert a date two days after the arrival date)
Room Rate:	$149.95
Number of Rooms:	2
Non-smoking Room:	☒ Yes ☐ No
Guarantee Method:	American Express

To avoid any charges to your account, cancellations must be made at least one day before your arrival date. Check-in time is 2:00 PM and check-out time is 11:30 AM.

If you have any questions or need further assistance, please contact the Lodging Department at 800-555-9250.

Sincerely,

Lodging Department

---

8. Use the filename **19Musante reservation.doc** and save the completed form.

9. Print one copy. Close the document.

■ Activity 19.2—Edit a Form Template and Create Calculation Fields

1. Copy the file named **Invoice2.dot** located on the data disk to the **My Templates** folder on your file disk.

2. Open the form template named **Invoice2.dot** [select **File, Open**; in the Files of type box, select **Document Templates** (*.dot); select the drive where your file disk is located; double-click on the **My Templates** folder; double-click on **Invoice2.dot**].

3. Display the Forms Toolbar (move the mouse pointer into the Standard or Formatting Toolbar and click the *right* mouse button once; select **Forms**).

4. Unprotect the form (select the **Protect Form** button).

5. Edit the form text as follows:

> *Note: If necessary, point to the title bar of the Forms Toolbar, click and hold the mouse, and drag the Toolbar to the right.*

   a. Select the words "Company Name" and type **Wooten Consulting**.

   b. Select the words "Company address" and type **2956 Greene Street**.

   c. Select the words "Phone number" and type **509-555-3246**.

   d. Select the words "City, State, Zip" and type **Spokane, WA 99207**.

   e. Select **File, Save** to save the edited form template.

6. Click in the first cell below the column heading "Rate/Hour." Select the **Text Form Field** button. Select the **Form Field Options** button. Set the Type to **Number** and the Number format to **$#,##0.00;($#,##0.00)**. Select the **Calculate on exit** option. Select **OK**.

7. Click in the first cell below the column heading "Total." Select the **Text Form Field** button. Select the **Form Field Options** button. Set the Type to **Calculation**. In the Expression box, type **=(B2*D2)** to multiply the number of hours by the rate. Set the Number format to **$#,##0.00;($#,##0.00)**. Select the **Calculate on exit** option. Select **OK**.

8. Click in the second cell below the column heading "Rate/Hour." Create a **Text Form Field**. Set the Type to **Number** and the Number format to **#,##0.00**. Select the **Calculate on exit** option. Select **OK**.

9. Click in the second cell below the column heading "Total." Create a **Text Form Field**. Set the Type to **Calculation**. In the Expression box, type **=(B3*D3)**. Set the Number format to **#,##0.00**. Select the **Calculate on exit** option. Select **OK**.

10. Click in the third cell below the column heading "Rate/Hour." Create a **Text Form Field**. Set the Type to **Number** and the Number format to **#,##0.00**. Select the **Calculate on exit** option. Select **OK**.

11. Click in the third cell below the column heading "Total." Create a **Text Form Field**. Set the Type to **Calculation**. In the Expression box, type **=(B4*D4)**. Set the Number format to **#,##0.00**. Select the **Calculate on exit** option. Select **OK**.

12. Click in the fourth cell below the column heading "Rate/Hour." Create a **Text Form Field**. Set the Type to **Number** and the Number format to **#,##0.00**. Select the **Calculate on exit** option. Select **OK**.

13. Click in the fourth cell below the column heading "Total." Create a **Text Form Field**. Set the Type to **Calculation**. In the Expression box, type **=(B5*D5)**. Set the Number format to **#,##0.00**. Select the **Calculate on exit** option. Select **OK**.

14. Click in the fifth cell below the column heading "Rate/Hour." Create a **Text Form Field**. Set the Type to **Number** and the Number format to **#,##0.00**. Select the **Calculate on exit** option. Select **OK**.

15. Click in the fifth cell below the column heading "Total." Create a **Text Form Field**. Set the Type to **Calculation**. In the Expression box, type =(**B6*D6**). Set the Number format to **#,##0.00**. Select the **Calculate on exit** option. Select **OK**.

16. Click in the sixth cell below the column heading "Total." Create a **Text Form Field**. Set the Type to **Calculation**. In the Expression box, type =**SUM(ABOVE)**. Set the Number format to **$#,##0.00;($#,##0.00)**. Select **OK**.

17. Protect the form (select the **Protect Form** button).

18. Close the Forms Toolbar.

19. Use the *new* filename **invoice xx.dot** (substitute your initials for xx) and save the modified template to the My Templates folder on your file disk.

20. Close the template.

21. Select **File, New**. On the General tab, double-click on the **invoice xx.dot** icon.

22. Use the information shown on page 494 to complete the form. Press the **Tab** key to move from field to field.

23. Use the filename **19Hammons invoice.doc** and save the document.

24. Print one copy. Close the document.

Wooten Consulting
509-555-3246

2956 Greene Street
Spokane, WA 99207

Consulting Services Invoice

Invoice Date: 5/5/99

Client Name: Hammons Accountancy Corp.
Contact Person: Miguel Salazar
Address: P.O. Box 2254
City, State Zip: Spokane, WA 99210

Date	No. of Hours	Description of Services	Rate/Hour	Total
5/6/99	5	Consultation on implementation of Windows NT and Microsoft Office 2000 as company standard	$65.00	$325.00
5/11/99	2	Meeting to schedule staff training on Windows NT and Microsoft 2000 applications	45.00	90.00
5/14/99	3	Assessment of conversion of existing database to Microsoft Access	65.00	195.00
				0.00
				0.00
			Invoice Total	$610.00

Challenge Your Skills

Skill 19.1—Create and Use a Form Template

1. Create the form template shown on page 495.

2. Correct three spelling errors, two misused words, two punctuation/grammatical errors and one capitalization error.

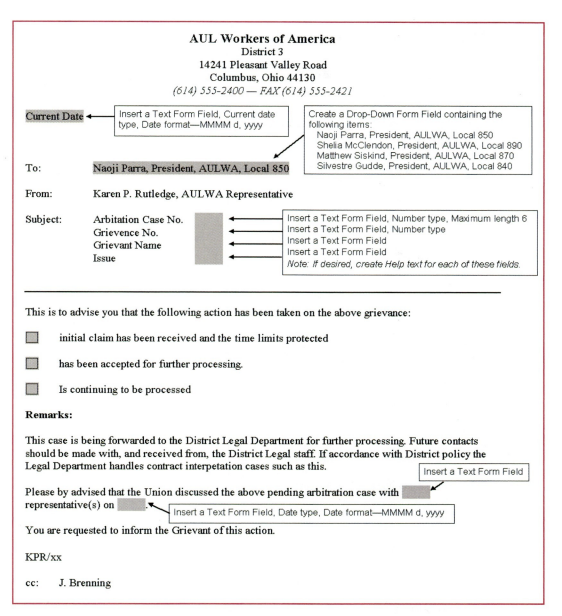

AUL Workers of America
District 3
14241 Pleasant Valley Road
Columbus, Ohio 44130
(614) 555-2400 — FAX (614) 555-2421

Current Date ◄— Insert a Text Form Field, Current date type, Date format—MMMM d, yyyy

Create a Drop-Down Form Field containing the following items:
 Naoji Parra, President, AULWA, Local 850
 Shelia McClendon, President, AULWA, Local 890
 Matthew Siskind, President, AULWA, Local 870
 Silvestre Gudde, President, AULWA, Local 840

To: Naoji Parra, President, AULWA, Local 850

From: Karen P. Rutledge, AULWA Representative

Subject: Arbitation Case No.   ◄— Insert a Text Form Field, Number type, Maximum length 6
            Grievence No.   ◄— Insert a Text Form Field, Number type
            Grievant Name   ◄— Insert a Text Form Field
            Issue   ◄— Insert a Text Form Field
                                        Note: If desired, create Help text for each of these fields.

This is to advise you that the following action has been taken on the above grievance:

☐   initial claim has been received and the time limits protected

☐   has been accepted for further processing.

☐   Is continuing to be processed

Remarks:

This case is being forwarded to the District Legal Department for further processing. Future contacts should be made with, and received from, the District Legal staff. If accordance with District policy the Legal Department handles contract interpetation cases such as this.

Please by advised that the Union discussed the above pending arbitration case with ▆▆▆ ◄— Insert a Text Form Field
representative(s) on ▆▆▆ .   ◄— Insert a Text Form Field, Date type, Date format—MMMM d, yyyy

You are requested to inform the Grievant of this action.

KPR/xx

cc: J. Brenning

3. When the form template is completed, protect and save the template to the My Templates folder on your file disk using the filename **19Grievance.dot**.

4. Print one copy of the template.

5. Close the document.

6. Use the **19Grievance.dot** template to create the document shown on page 496.

AUL Workers of America
District 5
39456 Pleasant Valley Road
Columbus, Ohio 44130
(614) 555-3333 — FAX (614) 555-3314

Current Date

To: Silvestre Gudde, President, AULWA, Local 840

From: Karen P. Rutledge, AULWA Representative

Subject: Arbitation Case No.   455665
                     Grievence No.   1245554
                     Grievant Name   Bibeau, Les
                     Issue   Employment Status

This is to advise you that the following action has been taken on the above grievance:

☒   initial claim has been received and the time limits protected

☐   has been accepted for further processing.

☐   Is continuing to be processed

Remarks:

This case is being forwarded to the District Legal Department for further processing. Future contact should be made with, and received from, the District Legal staff. If accordance with District policy the Legal Department handles contract interpretation cases such as this.

Please by advised that the Union discussed the above pending arbitration case with Assemtec Electronics representative(s) on (insert last Tuesday's date).

You are requested to inform the Grievant of this action.

ML/xx

cc: J. Brenning

7. Use the filename **19Bibeau case.doc** and save the file on your file disk.

8. Print one copy. Close the document.

Part 5
Checking Your Step

Production Project 5.1—Create a Tri-Fold Mailer Brochure

1. Create a tri-fold mailer brochure using the following information:

    a. The brochure describes the mini-vacation packages offered by Lakeview Mansion Resort and Golf.

    b. The brochure text is contained in the file named **5pact1.doc** located on the data disk.

    c. Make decisions regarding:

    > Margins, number of columns, spacing between columns
    > Font, point size, and alignment for text
    > Use of shadow borders
    > Colors for borders and text
    > Appropriate graphic image(s) from the Insert Clip Art dialog box
    > Rotated text for second column of page 2 (return address)
    > Use of graphic image(s)/clip art, reversed text, and borders for
    >   the third column of page 2 (the cover of the brochure)

2. Use the filename **5Lakeview brochure.doc** and save the file.

3. Print one copy.

4. Close the document.

Production Project 5.2—Create a Magazine Article (Group Project)

1. In groups of 3–5 people, write a magazine article that contains a pull quote(s), sidebar information, different left and right page footers, columns with different widths, and graphic images.

2. Suggested article topics:

    Favorite features of Word 2000
    Favorite features of Windows
    Incorporating sound and/or animation into documents
    Desktop publishing features in Word 2000

3. Make decisions regarding:

    Margins
    Use of WordArt for article title
    Font and point size for article text
    Use of drop cap
    Column widths
    Pull quote information, format, and placement
    Appropriate graphic image(s)
    Sidebar information, format, and placement
    Use of shadow borders, shadow text, reversed text, and/or rotated text
    Indentation for first line of paragraphs
    Footer text

4. Save the final magazine article using the filename **5magazine project.doc**.

5. Print one copy and close the document.

Production Project 5.3—Create and Use a Form Template

1. Create the form template shown on page 499. Make decisions regarding:

    Types of form fields to be created
    Adding Help text
    Alignment of text within the table
    Table borders
    Fonts and point sizes

    Hint: *To indent text within a table cell, press **Ctrl** and **Tab**.*

2. When the form template is completed, protect and save the template to the My Templates folder on your file disk using the filename **PC Rental Checklist.dot**.

3. Print one copy of the template.

4. Close the template.

PC RENTAL CHECKLIST

Customer Name:		Phone Number:	

*Text Form Field
Current Date type,
Date Format M/d/yy*

Date Out: **Current Date**

Date In:

*Text Form Field
Date type, Date
Format M/d/yy*

Model Number: **Pentium III**

Serial Number:

Drop-Down Form Field with the following items: Pentium III 586-233 586-200 Laptop Pentium

Accessories included:	Yes	No
Power Supply	☐	☐
A/C Cable	☐	☐
VGA Cable	☐	☐
Mac Cables	☐	☐
Mouse/Trackball	☐	☐
Portable CD-ROM	☐	☐
Speakers	☐	☐
Fax/Modem (PC Card)	☐	☐

Additional Supplies:

Received By:	Returned By:
Date:	Date:

5. Use the **PC Rental Checklist** template and create the form document shown on page 500.

   Note: If necessary, change the File Location for User Templates to the My Templates folder on your file disk.

6. Use the filename **5Bunkowski Rental.doc** and save the file.

7. Print one copy

8. Close the document.

   Note: Change the File Location for the User Templates to the default folder used on your system. If necessary, ask your instructor or instructional assistant for the correct file location for User Templates.

PC RENTAL CHECKLIST

Customer Name: Wanda Bunkowski			Phone Number: 504-555-3374	
Date Out: Current Date			Date In: Insert a date one week from the current date	
Model Number: Pentium III			Serial Number: S44311	
Accessories included:		Yes		No
Power Supply		☐		☒
A/C Cable		☒		☐
VGA Cable		☒		☐
Mac Cables		☐		☒
Mouse/Trackball		☒		☐
Portable CD-ROM		☒		☐
Speakers		☒		☐
Fax/Modem (PC Card)		☐		☒
Additional Supplies: Zip 100 external drive				
Received By:			Returned By:	
Date:			Date:	

Part 6
Step Right Up

Create Special Documents

Chapters 20–24

- Turn on line numbering
- Use the Track Changes feature
- Use the Compare Documents feature
- Mark hidden text
- Insert comments into a document
- Create a bookmark
- Create, number, and edit an outline
- Create a table of contents
- Create an index
- Create a table of authorities
- Create cross-references
- Create a paragraph style containing a border
- Create a style containing a special symbol
- Create cross-references within a document
- Create a master document by inserting subdocuments

- Create a formula to multiply two cells
- Split cells
- Name cells using a bookmark
- Create a formula by pasting a bookmark
- Create a chart using Microsoft Graph
- Import a spreadsheet file
- Create repeated table heading
- Convert, embed, and link information from other programs into Word
- Use an IF field
- Use Find Record
- Merge a data source file from another Microsoft application
- Create and edit a Fill-in field
- Use the Set Bookmark field

Use Advanced Editing Techniques

Objectives and Introduction

After successfully completing this chapter, you will be able to use the Line Numbering feature to print a line number beside each line of text in a document, use the Track Changes feature to mark inserted and deleted text, and use the Compare Documents feature to mark the differences between two documents. You will also be able to use the Comments and Hidden text features to insert notes into a document and the Bookmark feature to electronically mark a specific portion of text.

Turn On Line Numbering

A number can be placed beside each line of text in a document. Line numbering is often used for legal documents and other documents in which text needs to be referenced by line numbers.

The Line Numbers dialog box is used to turn on line numbering and to control how line numbers are printed (see Figure 20.1). The **Start at** option is used to change the number of the first line. For example, instead of beginning the line numbering at number 1, line numbers can be set to begin at number 100. The **Count by** option is used to specify the interval at which numbers will be printed. For example, Word 2000 can be instructed to print line numbers every fifth line.

Lines numbers are placed in the left margin. The default (Auto) position for line numbers is .25 inches to the left of text in a single-column layout and .13 inches to the left of text in a multi-column layout. If desired, the distance between the line numbers and text can be increased or decreased by specifying the desired amount of space in the **From text** box in the Line Numbers dialog box.

When the **Restart each page** option is selected in the Line Numbers dialog box, the line numbers on each page begin counting again from the number designated in the **Start at** box. If the **Restart each section** option is selected, the line numbers begin counting again at the beginning of each section from the number designated in the **Start at** box. If the **Continuous** option is selected, the lines on all pages of a document will be numbered consecutively.

The font, color, or text attributes (bold, italic, etc.) for the line numbers can be changed by modifying the Line Number style. Select **Format**, **Style**, choose the **Line Number** style name, choose **Modify**, **Format**, **Font**, and make the desired change(s) in the Modify Style dialog box.

After line numbers have been turned on, the numbers can be viewed in the document window; however, it may be necessary to use the horizontal scroll bar to view the left margin of the page. Also, the **Page Width** or **Whole Page Zoom** option can be selected to view the placement of the line numbers on the page. The line numbers can also be viewed by selecting the **Print Preview** button.

If desired, line numbers can be suppressed by selecting the paragraph(s) for which you want to suppress the line numbers and choosing **Format**, **Paragraph**. On the Line and Page Breaks tab, select **Suppress line numbers** and choose **OK**. Line numbers are turned off by choosing **File**, **Page Setup**. On the Layout tab, select the **Line Numbers** button. Click on **Add line numbering** to deselect the option and select **OK** twice.

Start-Up Instructions

❖ Open the file named **20drill1.doc** located on the data disk.

Steps to ➤ ## Turn On Line Numbering

1. Place the insertion point at the location at which the line numbering should begin.

   For example, place the insertion point at the beginning of the document.

2. Select **File, Page Setup**.

3. Select the **Layout** tab.

4. Select the **Line Numbers** button.

   Note: The Line Numbers dialog box displays (see Figure 20.1).

5. Select **Add line numbering**.

6. Select or change any desired option(s).

   For example, check that the option settings in the Line Numbers dialog box match the settings shown in Figure 20.1.

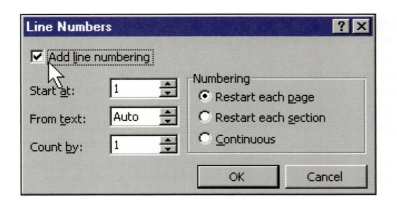

FIGURE 20.1

Line Numbers
dialog box

7. Select **OK** to exit the Line Numbers dialog box.

8. Select **OK** to exit the Page Setup dialog box.

Note: If necessary, use the horizontal scroll bar to scroll to the left to view the line numbers. Line numbers can also be viewed by selecting the down triangle beside the Zoom box and choosing the Page Width or Whole Page option.

Finish-Up Instructions

❖ Use the *new* filename **20Line Numbers.doc** and save the file on your file disk.

❖ Print one copy and close the document.

Use the Track Changes Feature

The Track Changes feature can be used to mark editing changes automatically in a document. When the **Track Changes** feature is turned on in the Highlight Changes dialog box, inserted text is underlined, the strikethrough text attribute is applied to deleted text, and a revision bar displays in the margin next to lines that contain inserted or deleted text. The editing changes display in a color.

If more than one person edits a document, different colors can be used to distinguish the revisions of each reviewer. Word has eighteen colors/shading available for marking changes. Word uses the information stored on the User Information tab of the Options dialog box to determine the name of the person editing a document. Each piece of inserted or deleted text is marked with the date, time, and the reviewer's name. This information can be viewed by placing the insertion point in the edited text and pausing for a moment. A ScreenTip displays, showing the name of the person who made the change, the date and time that the change was made, and whether the text was inserted or deleted. The revision can be accepted or rejected. Other revisions can be located by selecting the **Find** button.

After various reviewers revise copies of the document, the suggested revisions of each reviewer can be merged into the original document. To merge the revisions into the original document, open the file containing the revisions and then select **Tools, Merge Documents**. Type or select the name of the original document and select **Open**. Repeat this process until the revisions for all copies of the document have been merged into the original document.

The method and color used to mark revised text can be changed. By default, inserted text is underlined. If desired, the method of marking inserted text can be changed to bold by selecting **Tools, Options** and making the desired changes to the options on the Track Changes tab. (See the Steps to Change the Method of Marking Tracked Changes on page 507.)

After revisions have been made, the Accept or Reject Changes dialog box can be used to **Accept All** changes or to **Reject All** changes. If a change(s) is accepted, Word removes deleted text and removes the color and underline (or other selected attribute) from inserted text. If a change(s) is rejected, Word deletes inserted text and removes the strikethrough attribute. Formatting changes made by editors remain whether the **Accept** or **Reject** changes option is chosen. Changes can also be accepted or rejected one at a time.

A Reviewing Toolbar can be used to expedite many of the functions available for the Track Changes feature. To obtain the Reviewing Toolbar, *right* mouse-click on a displayed Toolbar and select **Reviewing**. After changes are made and the Track Changes feature is turned on, the **Previous change** and **Next change** buttons are used to locate changes. The changes can be accepted or rejected, one at a time, using the **Accept Change** or **Reject Change** button.

Start-Up Instructions

❖ Open the file named **20drill2.doc** located on the data disk.

Steps to ▶ Use the Track Changes Feature

1. Select **Tools, Track Changes, Highlight Changes**.

   Note: The Highlight Changes dialog box displays (see Figure 20.2).

2. Select the desired option(s).

   For example, select **Track changes while editing**. The **Highlight changes on screen** and **Highlight changes in printed document** options should also be selected.

3. Select **OK**.

   Note: TRK displays in the Status bar to indicate that the Track Changes feature is turned on.

4. Make the desired changes.

   For example, highlight the word "**completely**" in the second sentence of the first paragraph and type the word **fully**.

   Note: When the word "fully" is typed, the letters display in a color and are underlined, and the word "completely" is formatted as strikethrough text (e.g., ~~completely~~).

FIGURE 20.2

Highlight Changes dialog box

FIGURE 20.3

Membership and Voting Rights

Section 1

Every owner of a lot that is subject to assessment shall be a member of the Association. Each owner is obligated to promptly, ~~completely~~fully, and faithfully comply and conform to the Articles, Bylaws, Covenants, Conditions, and Restrictions.

<u>Membership in the Association shall not be transferred, pledged, or alienated in any way except upon the sale of the lot. Any attempt to make a prohibited transfer is void.</u>

Section 2

The Association will have ~~a single~~one class of voting membership that shall be all owners who are entitled to one vote for each lot owned. When more than one person owns an interest in any lot, all such persons shall be members. The vote for such lot will be exercised as they determine, but in no event shall more than one vote be cast with respect to any lot.

Section 3

Any provision calling for membership approval of action to be taken by the Association shall require the assent of the prescribed percentage of Association members existing at the time of such action. If the proposed action is favored by a majority of the votes cast at the membership meeting, but such vote is less than the required percentage of members, the approval of members who are not present in person must be given in writing ~~sixty~~forty-five (~~60~~45) days prior to such action being implemented.

Shortcut:

1. In the Reviewing Toolbar, select the **Track Changes** button.

   Note: *To obtain the Reviewing Toolbar, point to a displayed Toolbar and* **right mouse-click;** *choose* **Reviewing**.

Finish-Up Instructions

❖ Make the changes shown in Figure 20.3.

❖ Use the *new* filename **20revisions.doc** and save the file on your file disk.

❖ Print one copy.
   Note: *The marks shown on the left side of the screen may print on the right side of the paper.*

Start-Up Instructions

❖ The file named **20revisions.doc** should be displayed in the document window.

Change the Method of Marking Tracked Changes

1. With the insertion point located anywhere in the document, select **Tools, Options**.

2. Select the **Track Changes** tab.

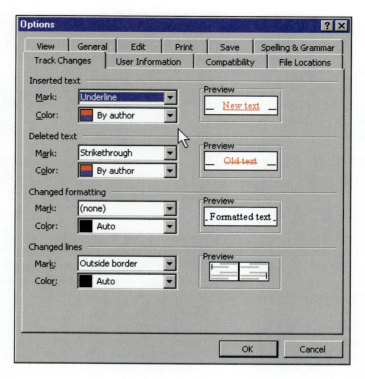

FIGURE 20.4

Track Changes
tab in the
Options dialog
box

Note: The Options dialog box with the Track Changes tab displays (see Figure 20.4).

3. Select the desired option(s) for the display of Inserted text, Deleted text, Changed formatting, and Changed lines.

   For example, in the Inserted text area, click in the **Mark** box and select **Bold**. Click in the **Color** box and select **Black**.

4. Select **OK**.

   Note: The inserted text in the document now displays in bold instead of underlined.

 Steps to Remove Marks for All Tracked Changes

1. Place the insertion point at the top of the document (**Ctrl** and **Home**).

2. Select **Tools, Track Changes, Accept or Reject Changes**.

3. Select the desired option.

   For example, to accept the revisions, select **Accept All**. Select **Yes** to the message, "Do you want to accept all remaining changes without viewing them?".

4. Select **Close** to exit the Accept or Reject Changes dialog box.

   Note: The color and bolding for the inserted text has been removed, and the deleted (strikethrough) text has been removed from the document.

Finish-Up Instructions

❖ Use the same filename, **20revisions.doc**, and save the file again.

❖ Print one copy.

- Turn off the Track Changes feature (select **Tools Track Changes**, **Highlight, Changes**, Track changes while editing, **OK**).

- To return to the default method for marking revisions, select **Tools, Options**. In the Inserted text area, click in the **Mark** box and select **Underline**. Choose **Color**, **By author**. Select **OK**.

- Close the document.

Use the Compare Documents Feature

The Compare Documents feature is used to identify the differences between the text in two files. When documents are compared, Word 2000 uses revision marks to identify inserted and deleted text. Inserted text is underlined; deleted text is formatted with the strikethrough attribute. All editing changes are marked in color. After the documents have been compared, revision marks can be removed using the Steps to Remove Marks for All Tracked Changes on page 508.

Start-Up Instructions

- Open the file named **20drill3.doc** located on the data disk.

Use Compare Documents Feature

1. Make desired revisions.

FIGURE 20.5

Revised text

Tuition Assistance Program

Steller Systems ~~recognizes~~ *acknowledges* that continuing education is important to the development of motivated and informed employees. Therefore, the company's Tuition Assistance Program reimburses hourly employees who work at least ~~20~~ *30* hours per week and salaried employees for expenses related to degree programs and/or courses at accredited colleges *and universities*. To be eligible for tuition assistance, employees must have been employed by Steller Systems for a period of one year.

The maximum reimbursement for covered expenses and tuition is $~~725~~ *1,125* per year.

For example, make the revisions shown in Figure 20.5. Select **File, Save As,** and the *new* filename **20Compare.doc** and save the file on your file disk.

2. Select **Tools, Track Changes**.

3. Select **Compare Documents**.

   Note: The Select File to Compare with Current Document dialog box displays.

4. Double-click on the desired filename to compare.

   For example, double-click on the file named **20drill3.doc** located on the data disk.

   Note: In a moment, the document displays with revision marks showing the inserted and deleted text.

Finish-Up Instructions

❖ Use the same filename, **20Compare.doc**, and save the file again.

❖ Print one copy and close the document.

Mark Hidden Text

The Hidden text feature is useful for creating notes, questions, messages, or confidential information that can be displayed (be visible on the screen) or hidden (not displayed on the screen). By using Hidden text, a single document can be used for more than one purpose. For example, a list of employee names, departments, business phone numbers, home phone numbers, and home addresses can be created, marking the home phone numbers and home addresses as hidden text. The complete document, including the hidden text, can then be printed for managers, while a second document containing only the employee names, departments, and business phone numbers can be printed for everyone else in the company.

Hidden text displays in the document window when nonprinting characters are turned on or if the **Hidden text** option is selected on the View tab of the Options dialog box. Text that has been formatted as hidden will print if the **Hidden text** option is selected on the Print tab of the Options dialog box.

Start-Up Instructions

❖ Open the file named **20drill4.doc** located on the data disk.

❖ Turn on **Show/Hide** feature. (If necessary, select **Tools**, **Options**, **View** tab and click on **ALL** in the formatting marks area; deselect all the other options in the formatting area; **OK**.)

❖ Turn on table gridlines. (If necessary, choose **Table**, **Show Gridline**).

Use the Hidden Text Feature

1. If necessary, select the **Show/Hide** button ¶ to display the nonprinting characters.

2. Select the text to be hidden.

   For example, highlight the Salary column (move the mouse pointer above the column heading "Salary" until a down arrow displays and click once to select the entire column).

3. Select **Format, Font**.

4. On the Font tab, select **Hidden** in the Effects area.

5. Select **OK**.

6. Click once to deselect the text.

   Note: A dotted underline displays below the text formatted as hidden.

7. Select the **Show/Hide** button to turn off the display of nonprinting characters.

   Note: When nonprinting characters are turned off, the hidden text will not display; however, the table gridlines for the hidden column will continue to display.

Finish-Up Instructions

❖ Use the *new* filename **20hide text.doc** and save the file on your file disk.

❖ Print one copy.

   Note: The hidden text should not print. If the hidden text does print, deselect the **Hidden text** *option on the Print tab in the Options dialog box (see Steps to Print Hidden Text).*

Start-Up Instructions

❖ The file named **20hide text.doc** should be displayed in the document window.

 ## Print Hidden Text

1. Once text has been marked as hidden, select **Tools, Options**.

2. Select the **Print** tab.

3. Select the **Hidden text** option in the Include with document area.

4. Select **OK**.

5. Choose the **Print** button.

Shortcut:

1. After text is marked as hidden, select **File, Print**.

2. Choose **Options**.

3. Select the **Hidden text** option in the Include with document area.

4. Select **OK** twice.

Finish-Up Instructions

❖ To turn off the printing of hidden text, select **File, Print, Options**; click on the **Hidden text** option in the Include with document area. Select **OK**. Select **Close**.

❖ Close but do not save the document.

Insert Comments

Comments (notes) can be placed within a document using the Comments feature. Comments can remind you of special formatting or printing requirements or other tasks that need to be accomplished. For example, a comment might remind you to load letterhead paper into the printer before printing the document or to call to verify the title of the addressee before sending a letter. The Comments feature can also be used to collect the responses of people who review a document. For example, a proposal can be sent via e-mail (electronic mail) to several people asking for their input. The reviewers can insert their comments into the document and return the document to the originator of the document.

When a comment is created, a comment reference mark is placed in the document at the location of the insertion point or following the selected text, which is highlighted in yellow. The comment mark is formatted as hidden text and displays only if nonprinting characters are turned on or if the **Hidden text** option is selected on the View tab of the Options dialog box.

The comment mark contains the initials of the reviewer (as stored in the User Info tab of the Options dialog box) and the comment number. Comments are numbered sequentially throughout a document. If a comment is added or deleted, Word automatically renumbers the comments.

When creating or viewing comments, the Comments From window displays at the bottom of the document window and includes the page where the text for the comment is being referenced, the comment reference mark(s), and the comment text. If desired, comments from a single reviewer or from all reviewers can be displayed by clicking in the **Reviewers** box in the Comments From window and selecting the desired reviewer's name or selecting **All Reviewers**. If sound equipment is installed on your system, the **Insert Sound Object** button can be used to record a voice comment.

Comments can be located in a document by selecting **Edit, Go To**, choosing **Comment** in the Go to what box, and selecting the **Next** or **Previous** button. To delete a comment, choose **View, Comments**, highlight the comment reference mark in the document window, and press the **Delete** key. If desired, comment text can be moved from the Comments From window into the document by selecting the desired comment text and dragging the text to the desired location in the document.

If copies of a document are distributed to several reviewers, the comments from each reviewer can be merged into the original document so that all the comments can be reviewed at one time. To merge the comments into the original document, open the document containing the comments; select **Tools**, **Merge Documents**; type or select the name of the original document; and select **OK**. Repeat this process until the comments in each copy of the document have been merged into the original document.

Printing comments can be accomplished by selecting the **Options** button in the Print dialog box, choosing the **Comments** option in the Include with document area, and selecting **OK** twice. When the **Comments** option is selected, Word automatically selects the **Hidden text** option. When the document is printed, the comment reference mark(s) is printed in the document, and the comment text is printed on a separate page. A page reference is included with the comment text. If you wish to print only the comment text (without the document), select **File**, **Print**, select **Comments** in the Print what box, and choose **OK**.

Start-Up Instructions

❖ 🖬 Open the file named **20drill5.doc** located on the data disk.

 Steps to **View Comment**

1. Select **Tools, Options, View** tab, and check that **All** is selected in the Formatting marks area. Select **OK** to exit the Options dialog box. If necessary, turn on nonprinting characters by selecting the **Show/Hide** button.

2. To display the comments, move the mouse pointer to the highlighted text (yellow background) and pause for a moment.

   For example, move the mouse pointer to the highlighted subject line and pause.

Note: The comment displays.

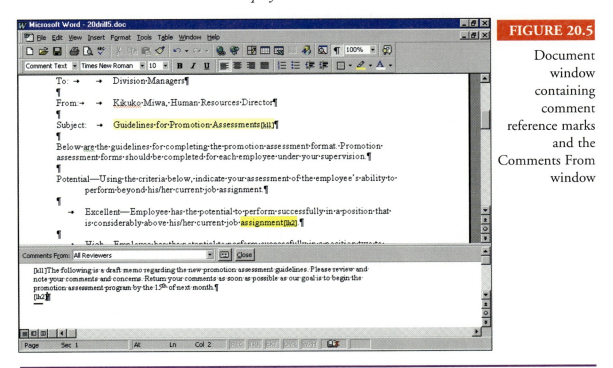

FIGURE 20.5

Document window containing comment reference marks and the Comments From window

3. To close the Comments ScreenTip box, move the mouse pointer away from the highlighted text.

 Insert Comments

1. Select the text where the comment is to be made, or place the insertion point at the location at which the comment should be inserted into the document.

   For example, place the insertion point after the final period in the paragraph that begins "Excellent— . . ."

2. Select **Insert, Comment**.

   Note: The last word of the sentence is highlighted in yellow and a comment reference mark is placed in the document. The comment mark is formatted as hidden text. The comment mark contains the initials stored in the User Information tab of the Options dialog box followed by a comment number (see Figure 20.5). The comment reference mark is also placed in the Comments From window displayed at the bottom of the document window.

3. Type the comment text in the Comments From window.

   For example, press the **Spacebar** once and type the following:

   I suggest that the following sentence be added to this paragraph: This designation should be reserved for employees who have the potential for top-level management. (Type your initials.)

4. Select the **Close** button on the Comments From window.

Shortcut:

1. With the Reviewing Toolbar displayed, select the **Insert Comment** button.

Finish-Up Instructions

❖ Place the insertion point in the blank line below the last paragraph in the document.

❖ Repeat steps 2–4 and create the following comment:
   I suggest the following scale:

   Now—Employee is ready for promotion.
   6-18—Employee will be ready for promotion in 6 to 18 months.
   18-36—Employee will be ready for promotion in 18 to 36 months.
   36-60—Employee will be ready for promotion in 36 to 60 months.
   (type your initials)

❖ Use the *new* filename **20comments.doc** and save the file.

❖ Continue with the Steps to Print Comments.

Start-Up Instructions

❖ The file named **20comments.doc** should be displayed in the document window.

Steps to ▶ **Print Comments**

1. Select **File, Print**.

2. Select the **Options** button.

3. Select **Comments** in the Include with document area.

   Note: The Hidden text option is automatically selected when the Comments option is chosen.

4. Select **OK** twice.

   Note: When the document is printed, the comment reference marks, which are formatted as hidden text, are printed in the document and a separate page(s) containing the comment text is printed.

Finish-Up Instructions

❖ Turn off the printing of comments (select **File**, **Print**, **Options**; deselect **Comments** and **Hidden text** in the Include with document area; select **OK**; select **Close**).

❖ Close but do not save the document.

Create Bookmarks

The Bookmark feature enables you to electronically mark a specific portion of text in a document in a manner similar to placing a paper bookmark in a book to mark a reference or page. Several bookmarks can be placed in a document. Each bookmark is given a unique name. A bookmark name can contain up to 40 characters, including letters, numbers, hyphens, and underscores but no spaces.

By default, the location of bookmarks does not display in a document. If desired, bookmark indicators can be displayed by selecting **Tools**, **Options**, choosing the **View** tab, selecting **Bookmarks** in the Show area, and choosing **OK**. The bookmark indicator displays as a very large I-beam.

Bookmarks can also be used when creating cross-references in a document (see Chapter 22), naming cells and performing calculations in a table or text, and inserting information in a mail merge document (see Chapter 24).

Start-Up Instructions

❖ Open the file named **20drill6.doc** located on the data disk.

Steps to ▶ **Create a Bookmark**

1. Place the insertion point at the location where the bookmark will be inserted.

   For example, place the insertion point at the beginning of the heading Shopping Malls on page 2 of the document.

2. Select **Insert, Bookmark**.

Note: The Bookmark dialog box displays.

3. Type the desired bookmark name.

   For example, type **shopping_malls**. (Do not type the period.)

   Note: A bookmark name can be up to 40 characters (letters, numbers, hyphens, and underscores) but no spaces.

4. Select **Add**.

   *Note: No change displays in the document window. To view the bookmark indicator, select **Tools**, **Options**. On the View tab, select the **Bookmarks** option in the Show area. Select **OK**. A large I-beam displays at the location where the bookmark was created.*

Finish-Up Instructions

❖ Place the insertion point at the beginning of the heading **Apartment Complexes** on page 3 of the document.

❖ Repeat steps 2–4 to create a bookmark named **apartment**.

❖ Place the insertion point at the beginning of the heading **Warehouse/ Distribution Properties** on page 4.

❖ Repeat steps 2–4 to create a bookmark named **warehouse**.

❖ Use the *new* filename **20bookmarks.doc** and save the file on your file disk.

Start-Up Instructions

❖ The file named **20bookmarks.doc** should be displayed in the document window.

❖ Place the insertion point at the beginning of the document (**Ctrl** and **Home**).

Go to a Bookmark

1. Select **Edit, Go To**.

   Note: The Find and Replace dialog box displays with the Go To tab selected.

2. In the Go to what box, select **Bookmark**.

3. Click on the down arrow beside the **Enter bookmark name** box and select the desired bookmark name.

   For example, click on the **shopping_malls** bookmark name.

4. Select **Go To**.

   Note: The insertion point moves to the heading Shopping Malls on the second page of the document. The Go To dialog box remains on the screen to allow you to select a different bookmark location if desired.

5. Select **Close** to exit the Find and Replace dialog box.

Finish-Up Instructions

❖ Repeat steps 1–5 to go to the **warehouse** bookmark.

❖ Close the document.

Steps to Delete a Bookmark

Note: The following steps are for your information only.

1. Select **Insert, Bookmark**.
2. Click on the bookmark name to be deleted.
3. Select **Delete**.
4. Select **Close**.

The Next Step

Chapter Review and Activities

Self-Check Quiz

T F 1. When using line numbering, the default position for printing the numbers is .5 inch to the left of text in a single-column layout.

T F 2. When the Track Changes feature is turned on, the editing changes display in color.

T F 3. Word uses the information stored on the User Information tab of the Options dialog box to determine the name of the person editing a document.

T F 4. The Bookmark feature is used to place an electronic bookmark in a document.

5. In the Line Numbers dialog box, the distance between the line numbers and text can be changed by specifying the desired amount of space in the _____ box.
   a. Start at
   b. From text
   c. Count by
   d. none of these

6. Line numbers can be suppressed by choosing _____, **Paragraph**, and selecting **Suppress line numbers** on the Line and Page Breaks tab.
    a. **Format**
    b. **Tools**
    c. **Insert**
    d. **File**

7. When the Track Changes feature is turned on, deleted text is formatted with the _____ text attribute.
    a. bold
    b. underline
    c. italic
    d. strikethrough

8. After revisions have been made using the Track Changes feature, the Track Changes dialog box can be used to _____.
    a. accept all changes
    b. reject all changes
    c. review each change one at a time
    d. all of these

9. Give two examples of when you might use Word's Hidden text feature.

10. Give one example of how you might use Word's Comment feature.

Enriching Language Arts Skills

Spelling/Vocabulary Words

deductible—in insurance, the amount an individual must pay for services before the insurance pays for covered expenses.

excluding—preventing or keeping from entering a place or group; disregarding.

flexible—responsive to change; capable of being bent; adaptable.

prosthesis—an artificial replacement for a limb, tooth, or other part of the body. (Prosthetics is the plural form.)

restorative—tending to renew; corrective.

routine—a customary or regular procedure; ordinary; standard.

Contractions

An apostrophe is used to indicate where a letter(s) has been omitted when two words are combined to form a verb contraction. Generally, contractions are not used in formal business writing. Contractions can be used in personal letters or informal business documents.

Examples:

it's (it is)   *you're (you are)*
I've (I have)   *don't (do not)*
we'll (we will)   *they're (they are)*

Activities

■ Activity 20.1—Turn on Line Numbering; Use the Track Changes Feature

1. Open the file named **20act1.doc** located on the data disk.

2. Turn on the Line Numbering feature at the beginning of the document (place the insertion point at the top of the document, select **File**, **Page Setup**, **Layout** tab, **Line Numbers**, **Add line numbering**, **OK** twice).

3. Turn on the Track Changes feature (**Tools**, **Track Changes**, **Highlight Changes**, **Track changes while editing**, **OK**) and make the changes shown below.

The People of the State of Pennsylvania, represented in Senate and Assembly, do enact as follows:

1.   Section AB22-6.2.1, as added by chapter two hundred sixty-six of the laws of nineteen hundred ninety-four, is amended to read as follows:

AB22-6.2.1 Application for adjustment of initial rent—The tenant or owner of a housing accommodation made subject to this law by the Emergency Tenant Protection Act of nineteen hundred ninety-four may, within ~~ninety~~forty-five (45) days of the local effective date of this act or the commencement of the first tenancy thereafter, file with the Commissioner an application for adjustment of the initial legal regulated rent for such housing accommodation. The Commissioner may adjust such initial legal regulated rent upon a finding that the presence of unique or peculiar circumstances materially affecting the initial legal regulated rent has resulted in a rent which is substantially different from the rents generally prevailing in the same area for substantially similar housing accommodations.

1.   The tenant of a housing accommodation that was regulated pursuant to The City Rent And Rehabilitation Law or this law prior to September first, nineteen hundred seventy-eight, and that became vacant on or after January first, nineteen hundred and ninety-four, may file with the Commissioner within ~~ninety~~sixty (60) days after notice has been received an application for adjustment of the initial legal regulated rent for such housing accommodation. Such tenant need only ~~allege~~state that such rent is in excess of the fair market rent and shall present such facts which, to the best of his information and belief, support such allegation. The Rent Guidelines Board shall ~~promulgate~~develop and disseminate as soon as practicable after the local effective date of the Emergency Tenant Protection Act of nineteen hundred ninety-four guidelines for the determination of fair market rents for housing accommodations as to which any application may be made pursuant to this subdivision. In rendering a determination on an application filed pursuant to this subdivision, the Commissioner shall be guided by such guidelines and by the rents generally prevailing in the same area for substantially similar housing accommodations. Where the Commissioner has determined that the rent charged is in excess of the fair market rent, he shall, in addition to any other penalties or

remedies permitted by law, order a refund of any excess paid since January first, nineteen hundred ninety-two or the date of the commencement of the tenancy, whichever is later. Such refund shall be made by the landlord in cash or as a credit against future rents over a period not in excess of four months...

4. Use the *new* filename **20AB22-6.2.1.doc** and save the file on your file disk.

5. Print one copy.

6. Accept all the revisions (select **Tools**, **Track Changes**, **Accept or Reject Changes**, **Accept All**, **Yes**, **Close**).

7. Use the same filename, **20AB22-6.2.1.doc**, and save the file.

8. Print one copy and close the document.

Activity 20.2—Insert Comments

1. Open the file named **20act2.doc** located on the data disk.

2. View the comment contained in the document. (If necessary, turn on nonprinting characters by selecting the **Show/Hide** button. Point to the highlighted comment reference mark at the end of the subject line to display the comment. After reading the comment, move the pointer away from the highlighted text.)

3. Create the following comments:

   a. Place the insertion point at the end of the Week 2 row. Select **Insert**, **Comment**.

   b. In the Comments From window, press the **Spacebar** once and type **Based on competitors' promotions, I suggest that the coupon discount be $.45.** Type your initials.

   c. Place the insertion point at the end of the Week 4 row. Select **Insert**, **Comment**.

   d. In the Comments From window, press the **Spacebar** once and type **I suggest that the discount coupons be increased to $.40.** Type your initials.

4. Use the *new* filename **20sales promotions.doc** and save the file on your file disk.

5. Print one copy of the document including the comments (select **File**, **Print**, **Options**, **Comments**, **OK** twice). After the document and comments have been printed, turn off the printing of comments (select **File**, **Print**, **Options**; deselect **Comments** and **Hidden text**; select **OK**, **Close**).

6. Close the document.

1. In a new document window, create the following table:

Product Name	Suggested Price	Minimum Price
Econo printer stand with storage cabinet	$125.95	$ 99.95
Econo mobile computer cart	175.99	135.95
High-Line executive swivel chair (leather)	275.49	233.25
High-Line executive swivel chair (cloth)	225.75	179.95
Contempo computer desk	395.95	325.95
Contempo 2-drawer lateral file cabinet with lock	149.95	120.95

2. Use the filename **20hidden text activity.doc** and save the file on your file disk.

3. Print the document.

4. Format the Minimum Price column using the Hidden text feature (select the **Minimum Price** column, choose **Format**, **Font**, **Font** tab, **Hidden**, **OK**).

5. Print the document again. The column formatted as Hidden text should not print.

6. Close the document.

Challenge Your Skills

Skill 20.1—Use the Track Changes Feature

1. Open the file named **20skill1.doc** located on the data disk.

2. Turn on the Track Changes feature.

3. Locate each comment reference mark in the document. View the comment text and make the necessary changes to the document.

4. Use the *new* filename **20Peterson agreement.doc** and save the file on your file disk.

5. Print one copy of the document with the tracked changes.

6. Accept all revisions and save the document using the same filename, **20Peterson agreement.doc**.

7. Turn off the Track Changes feature (select **Tools**, **Track Changes**, **Highlight Changes**, click on **Track changes while editing** to deselect, select **OK**).

8. Insert page numbers at the bottom right of each page.

9. Make decisions regarding text flow (page breaks and widow/orphan lines, etc.)

10. Print the final document.

11. Close the document.

Skill 20.2—Create Bookmarks; Language Arts

1. Open the file named **20skill2.doc** located on the data disk.

2. Create bookmarks for the headings Medical Plans, Dental Plans, Vision Care Plans, and Prescription Drug Plans. Make decisions regarding appropriate names for each bookmark.

3. Insert page numbers. Make a decision regarding the location of the page numbers.

4. Correct four spelling errors, five punctuation/grammatical errors, one duplicated word and one number format error.

5. Center the text vertically on the page.

6. Use the *new* filename **20health benefits.doc** and save the file on your file disk.

7. Optional. Fax the document to your instructor via a local fax, or write an e-mail message to your instructor that you are sending this assignment. Attach this file to your e-mail message.

8. Print one copy of the document.

9. Close the document.

Outlines, Table of Contents, Indexes, & Table of Authorities

21

Features Covered

- Display the Outlining Toolbar
- Create, number, and edit an outline
- Collapse/expand (hide/show) an outline family
- Show/hide outline headings
- Move an outline family
- Create, format, and compile a table of contents, index, and table of authorities

Objectives and Introduction

After successfully completing this chapter, you will be able to display the Outlining Toolbar and create, number, and edit an outline. In addition, you will learn to create, format, and compile a table of contents, index, and table of authorities.

Creating an outline is often very useful when writing reports, manuscripts, or other multiple-page documents. An outline assists a writer in organizing thoughts and grouping related information. Once a document is written, Word provides tools to assist the writer in creating a table of contents or an index. A table of authorities is used to list the citations (sources) of statements made in a legal document.

Create an Outline

An outline is a list of ideas expressed in phrases or sentences. The outline can provide a brief summary for writing a document such as a report. The ideas in an outline are usually enumerated in levels. Word automatically formats each heading level in an outline with one of nine default heading styles. For the highest level

FIGURE 21.1

Sample outline
in Normal View

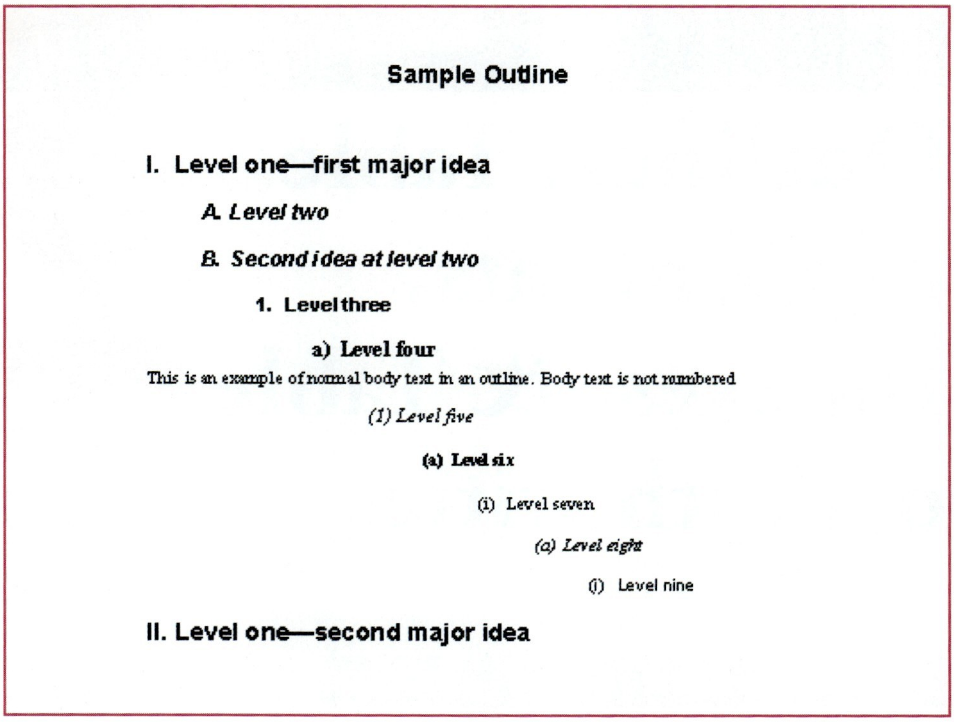

Sample Outline

I. **Level one—first major idea**

    A. *Level two*

    B. *Second idea at level two*

      1. **Level three**

        a) **Level four**

This is an example of normal body text in an outline. Body text is not numbered

          (1) Level five

            (a) Level six

              (i) Level seven

                (a) Level eight

                  (i) Level nine

II. **Level one—second major idea**

heading, Word uses the Heading 1 style; for the lowest level heading, Word uses the Heading 9 style. In addition, body text (text that is not numbered) can be included in an outline. An example of the nine heading styles and body text is illustrated in Figure 21.1. The heading styles can be changed by selecting **Format**, **Style**, choosing the style to be changed, and clicking on the **Modify** button.

The Outlining Toolbar appears at the top of the document window when **View**, **Outline** is selected or when the **Outline View** button, located next to the horizontal scroll bar, is chosen. The Outlining Toolbar provides buttons that can be used to quickly access the many outline features to format and edit an outline.

When typing or editing an outline, an outline item can be changed to the next lower level (demoted) by selecting the **Demote** button on the Outlining Toolbar. To change an outline item to the next higher level (promote), select the **Promote** button on the Outlining Toolbar.

An idea and indented related ideas and body text below the idea are a *family*. A family can consist of one or more ideas (levels). An outline family can be hidden (collapsed) or shown (expanded) in the document window or moved. When an outline family is moved, any outline ideas below the moved family will automatically be renumbered.

Outline families can be hidden so that only the first item in a family is visible. Hiding the related ideas assists a writer in organizing main ideas. If a main idea is moved, the hidden family(ies) is (are) also moved. Families can be hidden on an individual level or hidden by level for the entire outline. For example, to hide all families below Level three, select the **Show Heading 3** button on the Outlining Toolbar. Individual families are collapsed (hidden) by positioning the insertion point in the desired heading and then clicking on the **Collapse** button. The ability to collapse (hide) and expand (show) outline families is often referred to as collapsible outlining.

Outline heading definitions can be modified by selecting **Format**, **Bullets and Numbering**. Choose the **Outline Numbered** tab and **Customize**. The level

FIGURE 21.2

Outlining Toolbar

to be changed is selected by clicking on the up or down arrow in the Level option box. The desired Number format option is selected and the desired Number style is chosen. For example, the Level one heading can be modified to display with a bulleted character such as a diamond.

Start-Up Instructions

- An empty document window should be displayed. If necessary, select the **New** button.

Steps to Display the Outlining Toolbar

1. Select the **Outline View** button located to the left of the horizontal scroll bar, or select **View, Outline**.

   Note: *The Outlining Toolbar (see Figure 21.2) replaces the ruler. A minus icon displays to the left of the insertion point. Also, Heading 1 displays in the Style box in the Formatting Toolbar to indicate the first outline level.*

Steps to Create an Outline in the Outline View

1. Type the desired information.

   For example, type **Level one—first major idea**. (Do not type the period.) Press **Enter** once.

   Note: *Do not type the level numbers now. You will choose an outline numbering style later.*

2. Select the **Demote** button to position the insertion point for the next level.

   For example, to position the insertion point for the next lower level, select the **Demote** button once.

   Note: *Each time the* ***Demote*** *button is selected, the text is demoted one level and Word automatically indents the text to the next preset tab. A plus icon now displays to the left of the first heading level, indicating that a family (other levels) belongs to it. A minus icon displays to the left of the insertion point because no other levels exist after it. Heading 2 displays in the Style box because the Heading 2 style will be used to format the second outline level.*

3. Type the desired information for Level two.

   For example, type **Level two**. (Do not type the period.) Press **Enter** once.

   Note: *The minus icon displays and the insertion point remains at Level two.*

4. Type additional information at Level two.

   For example, type **Second idea at level two**. (Do not type the period.) Press **Enter** once.

   Note: *The minus icon displays.*

5. Select the **Demote** button ▶ on the Outlining Toolbar to position the insertion point for the next lower level.

    For example, select the **Demote** button ▶ to lower the level to Level three.

    Note: Heading 3 displays in the Style box.

6. Type the desired information.

    For example, type **Level three**. (Do not type the period.) Press **Enter** once.

7. Select the **Demote** button ▶ on the Outlining Toolbar to position the insertion point for the next lower level.

    For example, select the **Demote** button ▶ to lower the level to Level four.

8. Type the desired information.

    For example, type **Level four**. Press **Enter** once.

Create Outline Body Text

9. Select the **Demote to Body Text** button ▶ to position the insertion point for body text and to change the style to Normal.

    Note: A small open square icon displays beside the body text to indicate that the text is body text.

10. Type the body text.

    For example, type **This is an example of normal body text in an outline. Body text is not numbered**. (Press **Enter** once.)

11. Repeat steps 7 and 8 until all levels are typed.

    Note: The body text indents both lines of text in the Outline View.

    For example, create levels 5 to 9 as shown in Figure 21.1. Remember, your outline will be numbered and titled later in this chapter.

    Note: Do not change the spacing between lines of text.

12. Select the **Promote** button ◀ on the Outlining Toolbar to position the insertion point at the next higher level.

    For example, select the **Promote** button ◀ eight times to return to Level one.

    *Note: Heading 1 displays in the Style box. Each time the **Promote** button is selected, the text is raised to the next higher level.*

13. Type the desired information.

    For example, type **Level one—second major idea**. (Do not type the period and do **not** press **Enter**.)

Finish-Up Instructions

❖ Use the filename **21practice outline 1.doc** and save the file.

❖ Continue with the Steps to Number an Outline.

❖ The file named **21practice outline 1.doc** should be displayed in the document window.

Number an Outline

1. To number an outline, select the lines to be numbered.

   For example, select all lines of the outline.

2. Select **Format, Bullets and Numbering**; choose the **Outline Numbered** tab.

3. Select the desired numbering style.

   For example, select the bottom row, second from right outline number style.

   Note: The selected Outline numbering sample displays within a colored border.

4. Select **OK**.

Finish-Up Instructions

❖ Click on the **Show/Hide** button, if necessary, to display the nonprinting symbols

❖ Change to Normal View (select the **Normal View** button).

❖ Place the insertion point at the beginning of the document (**Ctrl** and **Home**).

❖ Add extra space and use the **Normal** style (press **Enter** three times; highlight beside the three new paragraph symbols and choose the **Style** button. Select **Normal**).

❖ Locate the insertion point beside the first paragraph symbol and type the outline title **Sample Outline**.

❖ Apply the title style (with the insertion point located anywhere in the title, choose **Format, Style**. Click in the **List** box and select **All Styles**. In the Styles list, scroll down and select **Title, Apply**).

❖ Use the same filename, **21practice outline 1.doc**, and save the file.

   Note: Your outline should look similar to the outline shown in Figure 21.1.

❖ Optional. Print one copy from the Normal View.

Start-Up Instructions

❖ The file named **21practice outline 1.doc** should be displayed in the document window.

Insert a New Item in an Outline

*Note: The Outline View should be displayed. (If necessary, select the **Outline View** button.)*

1. Place the insertion point to the right of the final character in the item that will precede the new item.

For example, place the insertion point to the right of the "r" in four (i.e., Level four).

2. Press **Enter** once to obtain the next outline number.

   Note: The level letter b) and the Heading 4 style display.

3. Type the desired outline item.

   For example, type **Second idea at level four**. (Do not type the period.)

Finish-Up Instructions

❖ Use the new filename **21practice outline 2.doc** and save the file.

❖ Continue with the Steps to Collapse (Hide) or Expand (Show) an Outline Family.

Start-Up Instructions

❖ The file named **21practice outline 2.doc** should be displayed in the document window.

 ## Collapse (Hide) or Expand (Show) an Outline Family

*Note: The Outline View should be displayed. (If necessary, select the **Outline View** button.)*

1. Place the insertion point in the first item of the family to be collapsed (hidden).

   For example, place the insertion point in Level five.

2. Select the **Collapse** button ▬ on the Outlining Toolbar repeatedly until the desired outline family is hidden.

   For example, click on the **Collapse** button ▬ four times.

   Note: The indented items below Level five are hidden and no longer display in the document window. A gray line displays below Level five to indicate that there are hidden levels.

3. To expand a collapsed family, place the insertion point in the level item above the item to be expanded; select the **Expand** button ➕ on the Outlining Toolbar repeatedly until the desired outline family is expanded.

   For example, place the insertion point in Level five; select the **Expand** button ➕ four times.

   Note: The indented outline family displays in the document window.

Finish-Up Instructions

❖ Continue with the Steps to Show Outline Headings.

Start-Up Instructions

❖ The file named **21practice outline 2.doc** should be displayed in the document window.

Show Outline Headings

> *Note: The Outline View should be displayed. (If necessary, select the **Outline View** button.)*

1. Place the insertion point anywhere in the outline.

2. Select the desired **Show Heading** number button on the Outlining Toolbar.

    For example, select the **Show Heading 2** button 2 .

    Note: Only Level one and two items display. Levels three through nine are temporarily removed (hidden) from the document window.

3. Show all hidden levels.

    For example, select the **Show All Headings** button All on the Outlining Toolbar.

Finish-Up Instructions

❖ Continue with the Steps to Move an Outline Family.

Start-Up Instructions

❖ The file named **21practice outline 2.doc** should be displayed in the document window.

❖ The Outline View should be displayed. (If necessary, select the **Outline View** button.)

❖ Hide outline items below Level seven. (Place the insertion point in the Level seven item and select the **Collapse** button twice.)

 Move an Outline Family

1. Move the mouse pointer to the plus icon ✛ beside the desired level item until a four-headed arrow displays; press and hold the mouse button and drag the thin horizontal line to the desired location.

    For example, move the mouse pointer to the plus icon ✛ beside the Level seven item until a four-headed arrow displays; press and hold the mouse button and drag the thin horizontal line straight up until the line displays between the Second idea at Level two and the Level three item. Release the mouse button.

    Note: Level seven displays highlighted between the second idea at Level two and Level three. The item is not aligned correctly and the family is still collapsed. That's OK.

2. To renumber and align the moved family, select the **Demote** ➡ or **Promote** ⬅ button until the desired level displays.

    For example, click on the **Promote** button ⬅ four times until the Level seven item is displayed with the number 1 level number.

Note: Click once in the Level seven item to deselect and notice that Heading 3 displays in the Style box.

3. To display the moved family, select the **Expand** button ⊞ on the Outlining Toolbar.

   For example, select the **Expand** button ⊞ twice.

Finish-Up Instructions

❖ Use the *new* filename **21practice outline 3.doc** and save the file.

❖ Optional. Print one copy. (Remember to change to **Normal View** before printing.) Close the document.

Create a Table of Contents

A table of contents lists the main topics in a report, newspaper, book, etc. Creating a table of contents is a three-part process:

1. The document is typed.
2. The table of contents entries are marked or the heading styles are applied.
3. The table of contents is formatted and compiled.

Many different formats can be used when creating a table of contents. For example, a border line can be placed below the main topics and the page numbers where the topics are located can be placed at the right margin (see Figure 21.3). The simplest method for creating a table of contents is to use Word's default heading styles, Heading 1 through Heading 9, to format the headings that will appear in the table of contents. The Heading 1 style is used to format the text that will be a level 1 entry in the table of contents; the Heading 2 style is used to format the text that will be a level 2 entry in the table of contents, and so on.

Once the desired heading styles have been applied, the table of contents is formatted and compiled. Before the table of contents is compiled, a predefined format can be selected in the **Formats** area of the **Table of Contents** tab (**Index and Tables** dialog box). Other formatting options can also be chosen, such as right-aligned page numbers, tab leaders, etc.

When the table of contents is compiled, the entries are placed at the location of the insertion point. The table of contents is usually placed on a separate page at the beginning of the document after the title page, if there is one. Lowercase Roman numeral page numbers are used for numbering the table of contents pages. The heading "Contents" is placed at the beginning of the table of contents and is often centered and bolded. A section break is placed after the table of contents entries, and the page number on page 2 is changed to begin numbering the text of the document as page 1.

Start-Up Instructions

❖ ■ Open the file named **21drill2.doc** located on the data disk.

Contents

PRESIDENT'S ANNOUNCEMENT	1
OPERATION CHANGES	1
A JOINT VENTURE	1
MARKET CONDITIONS	1
RAW LAND	2
RAW LAND/JOINT VENTURES	2

FIGURE 21.3

Sample table of contents

Steps to Create a Table of Contents Using Built-in Heading Styles

1. Place the insertion point at any position in the heading that is to be listed as a first-level entry in the table of contents.

   For example, place the insertion point in the heading "President's Announcement."

2. Select the desired style in the **Style** box on the Formatting Toolbar.

   For example, select the down arrow next to the **Style** box. Select **Heading 1**.

   Note: *The heading displays with the Heading 1 style.*

3. Place the insertion point at any position in the heading that is to be listed as a second-level entry in the table of contents.

   For example, scroll down and place the insertion point in the heading "Operation Changes."

4. Select the desired style.

   For example, select the down arrow next to the **Style** box. Select **Heading 2**.

5. Repeat steps 1 and 2 and apply the Heading 1 style to the desired headings.

   For example, apply the Heading 1 style to the following table of contents entries:

   A Joint Venture (located on page 1)
   Raw Land (located on page 2)

6. Repeat steps 3 and 4 and apply the Heading 2 style to the desired headings.

   For example, apply the **Heading 2** style to the following table of contents entries:

   Market Conditions (located on page 1)
   Raw Land/Joint Ventures (located on page 2)

7. After the styles have been applied to the headings, place the insertion point at the location in the document where the table of contents is to be displayed.

For example, place the insertion point to the left of the first character in the document (**Ctrl** and **Home**).

Format and Compile a Table of Contents

8. Select **Insert, Index and Tables**.

Note: The Index and Tables dialog box displays (see Figure 21.4).

9. Select the **Table of Contents** tab.

10. Select the desired format in the Formats box.

For example, select **Fancy**.

*Note: The options **Show page numbers** and **Right align page numbers** should be selected. Also, the **Show levels** option should be set for 2 or greater.*

11. Select **OK** to compile the table of contents.

Note: The table of contents displays above the report title, Land Management Investment.

12. Insert a section break after the table of contents.

For example, with the insertion point to the left of the "L" in "Land," select **Insert, Break, Next page, OK**.

13. Place a heading above the table of contents.

For example, press **Ctrl** and **Home**. Press **Enter** once, press the up arrow key once, and type the heading "**Contents.**" Select **Normal** in the Style box. Select the title **Contents**. Choose **Times New Roman, bold, 16 point** and select the **Center** alignment button.

14. Change the page numbers to lowercase Roman numerals for the table of contents pages.

For example, with the insertion point located on the page containing the contents, select **Insert, Page Numbers**. Select **Center** alignment, **Format**, and the **Number format** box.

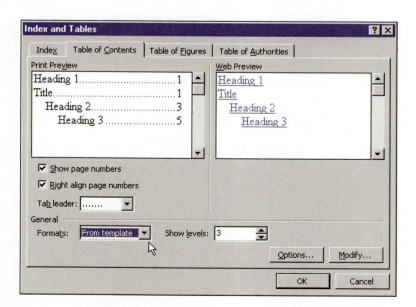

FIGURE 21.4

Index and Tables dialog box with Table of Contents tab selected

Choose lowercase Roman numerals, i.e., i, ii, iii. Select **OK** twice.

15. Change the page number on page 2 to begin numbering starting with 1.

For example, locate the insertion point on page 2 of the report. Select **Insert, Page Numbers**. Choose **Format,** select the **Start at** option in the Page numbering area; check that **1** displays in the Start at box. If necessary, select the **Number format** box. Choose **1, 2, 3 . . .** Choose **OK** twice.

*Note: If desired, select the **Print Preview** button and select **50%** to see the page numbers.*

Finish-Up Instructions

❖ Use the *new* filename **21toc2.doc** and save the file on your file disk.

❖ Move the mouse pointer to any of the Table of Contents headings and pause until a hand displays. Click once and the insertion point will be moved to the page where the topic information displays.

❖ Print one copy and close the document.

Update or Replace a Table of Contents

Note: The following steps are for your information only.

1. Place the insertion point at any location in the document containing the Table of Contents to be updated/replaced.

2. Select **Insert, Index and Tables**. If necessary, select the **Tables of Contents** tab.

3. Select **OK**.

Note: The message displays, "Do you want to replace the selected table of contents?" The highlighted table of contents displays behind the message box. (It is highlighted in a dark gray because it is a field code.)

4. Select **Yes**.

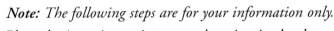

Create an Index

An index is an alphabetical listing of topics contained in a document. Entries in the index usually include a page number to indicate the location of the topic. Once a document is typed, main index entries and subentries can be marked, the index type and form chosen, and the index compiled.

Index entries can be marked automatically by using a concordance file. (A concordance is an index of subjects or topics.) The concordance file is an ordinary file that contains a two-column table. In the first column, the words to be indexed are typed exactly (matching the upper/lowercase letters) as displayed in the document to be indexed. The second column contains the main entry words (topics) that are to be listed in the index. The second column can also contain the subentry word(s). A colon separates the main entry and subentry. One row is used for each index entry (see Figure 21.5).

Also, index entries can be marked individually by selecting the word(s) to be indexed. Select **Insert**, **Index and Tables** and choose the **Index** tab. Select the **Mark Entry** button. In the Mark Index Entry dialog box, choose the **Mark** button. Index subentries and cross-reference entries can also be marked in the Mark Index Entry dialog box. An index can have up to seven levels of subentries.

After all entries have been marked, the Index format is chosen in the **Formats** area of the Index tab (in the Index and Tables dialog box). Once the index format has been chosen, the index is compiled. The compiled index organizes all topics alphabetically and lists the page numbers where the entries are located in the document.

An index is usually placed on a separate page at the end of the document. To provide a separate page for the index, insert a hard page break at the end of the document.

If a document is modified after the index has been compiled, the index can be updated to show new page numbers. In addition, new main index entries and subentries can be marked. When all changes to the document have been made, the index is updated by selecting **Insert**, **Index and Tables**, **Index** tab. Select **OK** and choose **Yes** in response to the question, "Do you want to update the selected index?".

Start-Up Instructions

❖ An empty document window should be displayed. If necessary, select the **New** button.

❖ Turn off capitalization for the first letter of a sentence (select **Tools**, **AutoCorrect**, **AutoCorrect** tab, deselect the option **Capitalize first letter of sentences**, select **OK**).

Create a Concordance File

Create a Main Entry

1. In a new document, create a table with one row and two columns.

   For example, select the **Insert Table** button and choose one row and two columns.

2. In the first column, type the text to be indexed exactly (upper/lowercase) as it displays in the document.

   For example, type **limited partnership**; press **Tab** to move the insertion point to column 2.

3. In the second column, type the main entry as it will display in the index.

FIGURE 21.5

Concordance file

limited partnership	Limited partnership
raw land	Joint venture:raw land
joint venture	Joint venture
Market Conditions	Market conditions
form of partnership	Joint venture:form of partnership

For example, type **Limited partnership**. (Do not type the period.) Press the tab key to obtain a new row.

Create a Subentry

4. In column 1, type the text to be indexed exactly (upper/lowercase) as it displays in the document.

   For example, type **raw land**; press **Tab** to move the insertion point to column 2.

5. Type the main entry followed by a colon and the subentry.

   For example, type **Joint venture:raw land** (do not press the **Spacebar** before or after the colon).

Finish-Up Instructions

❖ Repeat steps 2 and 3 to create the following main entries:

   joint venture   Joint venture
   Market Conditions   Market conditions

❖ Repeat steps 4 and 5 to create the following subentry:

   form of partnership   Joint venture:form of partnership

❖ Use the filename **21index.doc** and save the index concordance file.

   Note: If desired, the index concordance file can be closed.

❖ Continue with the Steps to Mark Index Entries Using AutoMark.

Start-Up Instructions

❖ Open the file named **21drill2.doc** located on the data disk.

Steps to ## Mark Index Entries Using AutoMark

1. With the document to be indexed displayed in the document window, select **Insert, Index and Tables**.

   Note: The Index and Tables dialog box displays.

2. Select the **Index** tab.

3. Select the **AutoMark** button.

   Note: The Open Index AutoMark File dialog box displays.

4. Select the desired index concordance filename.

   For example, double-click on the file named **21index.doc**.

   Note: Each index entry is marked. The entries display between braces, e.g., {XE "Limited partnership"}.

Finish-Up Instructions

❖ Continue with the Steps to Format and Compile an Index.

Steps to Format and Compile an Index

1. Place the insertion point at the location in the document where the index is to be compiled.

   For example, press **Ctrl** and **End** to locate the insertion point at the end of the document.

2. Type, center, and bold the index title.

   For example, type, center, and bold the word **Index**. Press **Enter** twice.

   *Note: If necessary, select the **Align Left** button to locate the insertion point at the left margin.*

3. With the insertion point two blank lines below the index title, select **Insert, Index and Tables**.

4. The Index tab should be displayed.

   For example, if necessary, select the **Index** tab.

5. Select the desired Type.

   For example, check that **Indented** is selected. (If necessary, select **Indented** in the Type area.)

6. Select the desired format.

   For example, scroll down in the Formats box and select **Bulleted**.

   Note: A sample of the selected format displays in the Print Preview box.

7. If necessary, deselect the **Right align page numbers** option.

8. Select the desired number of columns for the index in the Columns box.

   For example, select the up or down triangle in the **Columns** box until **1** displays.

9. Select **OK** to compile the index.

   *Note: The index's main entries and subentries along with page number locations display. A Section Break (Continuous) mark displays beside the last index entry. If desired, select the **Show/Hide** button to remove the nonprinting symbols from the document window.*

10. To place the Index on a separate page, locate the insertion point to the left of the "I" in the title "**Index**." Press **Ctrl** and **Enter**.

Finish-Up Instructions

❖ Use the *new* filename **21drill2 indexed.doc** and save the file on your file disk.

❖ Turn on the AutoCorrect option to capitalize the first letter of a sentence (select **Tools, AutoCorrect**, select the **Capitalize first letter of sentences** option, **OK**).

❖ Print one copy of the index page. Printing all pages of the document is optional.

*Note: If desired, check the pages for widow/orphan lines. If necessary, click on the RAW LAND heading and turn on **Keep with next**. (Select **Format**, **Paragraph**, choose **Keep with next** on the Line and Page Breaks tab.)*

❖ Close all document windows.

Create a Table of Authorities

A table of authorities is a list of the specific sources that are used to substantiate a statement or statements in a legal document. A source can include information such as a case name, volume, reporter, page, court and jurisdiction, and date. The source information is referred to as a citation. The most common sources cited are statutes and cases. Headings are used to group the listed sources, e.g., Statutes, Cases, Other Authorities (see Figure 21.6). A table of authorities is predominately used for cases being heard at an upper level court.

Creating a table of authorities is similar to creating a table of contents: the document is typed, the table of authorities entries are designated (marked), the citation format is chosen, and the table of authorities is compiled.

When a table of authorities entry is marked, the Mark Citation dialog box is used. In the Mark Citation dialog box, the selected text appears in both the **Selected text** and **Short citation** boxes. The selected text can be edited, if necessary, in the Selected text box. In the Short citation box, the complete information is usually deleted and the short form of the citation is typed. The short citation is used by Word to search the document for other occurrences of the same citation and to mark each occurrence automatically. The text in the Short citation field must be text that is always used in that citation and is unique to that citation. For example, the short form "Sandler v. Casale" is typed to represent the long citation that begins "Sandler v. Casale (1981) 125 . . ."

The **Category** box is used to indicate the category in the table of authorities where the source information (citation) will be listed. For example, "Sandler v. Casale . . ." is a case source and is listed under the heading "Cases" (see Figure 21.6).

Once the selected text and short citation text are prepared and the category is chosen, the **Mark** or **Mark All** button is selected. The **Mark** button inserts the table of authorities (TA) code only for the currently selected citation. When the **Mark All** button is selected, all citations that match those listed in the Selected text or Short citation boxes in the Mark Citation dialog box are marked with a TA field code. The field code displays between braces and follows the citation in the document, e.g., {TA \l "Sandler v. Casale (1981) 125 CA 3d 707, 178 CR265"\s "Sandler" \c1}. If TA field codes are not displayed, select the **Show/Hide** button.

Once table of authorities entries are marked, an entry can be edited by placing the insertion point in the field and making the desired changes. If necessary, select the **Show/Hide** button on the Standard Toolbar to display the table of authorities (TA) field code.

Before the table of authorities is compiled, the insertion point is placed at the location in the document where the citations are to be listed, which is usually the beginning of the document after the cover page, if any. On the Table of

FIGURE 21.6

Sample table of
authorities

TABLE OF AUTHORITIES
CASES
FDIC v. Air Florida System, Inc. 822 F 2d 833, 843 2
Jannis v. Ellis (1957) 308 P 2d 750, 149 CA 2d 751 CCP 1287 2
Sandler v. Casale (1981) 125 CA 3d 707,178 CR 265 2
OTHER AUTHORITIES
CP 86 (a) (10) 3

Authorities tab, the format for the table of authorities is chosen. For example, if the Classic format is chosen, the numbering format is text with dot leaders and a page number (see Figure 21.6).

The default table of authorities options displayed at the bottom and right side of the Table of Authorities tab are on and include: **Use passim**, **Keep original formatting**, **Tab leader** and **Category: All**. The Use passim option instructs Word to substitute the word Passim for the page numbers when the citation is noted on more than five pages in the document. (Passim means throughout or frequently.)

After the format is chosen, the defaults are checked and the table of authorities is compiled. A section heading is typed at the beginning of the compiled table of authorities, and a section break is placed after the listed citations. Lowercase Roman numeral page numbers are inserted on the table of authorities pages, and the page number is changed on page 2 to begin numbering the text as page 1.

Start-Up Instructions

❖ Open the file named **21legal4.doc** located on the data disk.

Steps to ➡ **Create Long and Short Citation Table of Authorities Entries**

1. Locate and select the desired citation.

    For example, select the citation **Sandler v. Casale . . . CR 265** on page 2 in the first paragraph under III, Law and Argument.

2. Select **Insert, Index and Tables**.

    Note: The Index and Tables dialog box displays.

3. If necessary, select the **Table of Authorities** tab.

4. Select the **Mark Citation** button.

    Note: The Mark Citation dialog box displays. The selected text displays in both the Selected text and Short citation boxes.

5. Click in the **Selected text** box and make any editing changes needed for the long citation.

    For example, if necessary, delete the comma at the end of the citation.

    *Note: If desired, the text can be selected, and character formatting such as bold (**Ctrl** and **b**) can be used.*

6. Select the desired category in the Category box.

> For example, check that **Cases** displays. (If necessary, select **Cases.**)

7. Edit the text in the Short citation box so Word can search for citations in the document.

> For example, check that the text in the Short Citation box is highlighted. (If necessary, select the text in the Short Citation box.) Type the short citation, i.e., **Sandler v. Casale.**

8. Select the **Mark All** button.

Note: The marked table of authorities entry code displays in the document window between braces, e.g., {TA\l Sandler v. Casale . . .}. The Mark Citation dialog box remains open in the document window.

9. Select the **Next Citation** button.

*Note: The next citation containing a "v." is located. After the **Next Citation** button is selected, Word searches through the document for the next occurrence of text commonly found in citations such as "in re" or "v.". If necessary, move the Make Citation window.*

10. Click once above the Mark Citation dialog box to locate the insertion point in the document window; select the desired citation.

> For example, click once on the document and then select the citation **FDIC v. Air Florida System . . . 843.**

11. Click once in the Selected text area of the Mark Citation dialog box.

Note: The selected text now displays in the Selected text and Short citation boxes of the Mark Citation dialog box.

12. Repeat steps 5–8.

> For example, use the Cases category and type **FDIC** in the Short Citation box. Select **Mark All.**

13. Select the **Next Citation** button.

Note: The short citation "FDIC" is highlighted. Since this abbreviation is contained in the same paragraph as the previously marked long citation, it is unnecessary to mark this citation. Continue with the next step.

14. Select the **Next Citation** button and repeat steps 10–12.

> For example, click once on the document and then select the citation **Jannis v. Ellis . . . CCP 1287.** Use the **Cases** category and type **Jannis v. Ellis** in the Short citation box. Select **Mark All.**

15. Select the **Next Citation** button.

Note: The message displays, "Word has reached the end of the document. Do you want to continue searching at the beginning?".

16. Select **No.**

Note: The previously marked Jannis v. Ellis citation displays highlighted and the Mark Citation dialog box remains on the screen. There is another citation that was not automatically found because it does not contain a "v." or "in re", etc. However, this citation should be marked and listed in the table of authorities.

17. Scroll to the desired location where the next citation is to be marked.

> For example, scroll to page 3 and select the citation **CP 86 (a) (10)** that is located at the end of the short paragraph that begins with the words "Jurisdiction remains . . ." The Category is **Other Authorities**. The short citation name is **CP 86**. Repeat steps 5–8.

18. Select **Close**.

Finish-Up Instructions

❖ Use the *new* filename **21TA marked 4.doc** and save the file on your file disk.

❖ Continue with the Steps to Format and Compile a Table of Authorities.

Start-Up Instructions

❖ The file named **21TA marked 4.doc** should be displayed in the document window with marked citations.

Format and Compile a Table of Authorities

1. Place the insertion point at the location in the document where the table of authorities is to be compiled.

> For example, press **Ctrl** and **Home** to place the insertion point to the left of the nonprinting paragraph symbol at the beginning of the document.

2. Select **Insert, Index and Tables**.

3. If necessary, select the **Table of Authorities** tab.

4. Select the desired format.

> For example, select the **Classic** format in the Formats area.

Note: A sample of the Classic format displays in the Print Preview box.

5. Select **OK** to compile the table of authorities.

Note: The Table of Authorities displays with the citations alphabetized in each category. Also, the page(s) for each citation displays.

6. With the insertion point located to the left of the Roman numeral I that displays below the table of authorities, create a section break by selecting **Insert, Break, Next page, OK**.

7. With the insertion point located on page 2, restart the page numbering to begin numbering at page 1 (select **Insert, Page Numbers**, choose **Format**, choose **Start at**, **1**, select **OK** twice).

8. Type a heading for the table of authorities.

> For example, locate the insertion point at the top of the table of authorities (press **Ctrl** and **Home**). Press **Enter** once, press

the up arrow key once, type **TABLE OF AUTHORITIES**, select the **Center** alignment button).

> *Note: The heading will appear in all uppercase because the TOA Heading style is in effect.*

9. Change the page numbering for the table of authorities page to lowercase Roman numerals (select **Insert, Page Numbers**, select **Format**, choose the down arrow beside the **Number format** box and highlight the lowercase Roman numerals **i, ii, iii, . . .**; select **OK** twice).

Finish-Up Instructions

❖ Optional. In the Print Layout View, scroll down the page to display the page numbers.

❖ Use the *new* filename **21TA final 4.do**c and save the file on your file disk.

❖ Print one copy of the table of authorities page. Printing all pages of the document is optional.

❖ Close the document.

Update or Replace a Table of Authorities

> *Note: The following instructions are for your information only.*

1. Select **Insert, Index and Tables**.
2. With the Table of Authorities tab selected, choose **OK**.

> *Note: A message displays, "Do you want to replace the selected category of the table of authorities?". The first category of the table of authorities is selected and displays behind the message box.*

3. Select **Yes** to update or replace the table of authorities.

> *Note: The table of authorities is updated or replaced.*

4. If the next category is also to be updated/replaced, repeat steps 1–3.

Shortcut:

1. Place the insertion point in a table of authorities field code; press **F9**.

Delete a Table of Authorities

> *Note: The following instructions are for your information only.*

1. Select all lines in the table of authorities.
2. Press the **Delete** key.

Self-Check Quiz

T F 1. Word can number nine outline levels automatically.

T F 2. Select **Tools**, **Outline** to begin creating an outline.

T F 3. When using the Outlining Toolbar, select the **Demote** button to move to the next lower outline level.

T F 4. When a table of contents is compiled, the entries are placed where the insertion point is located.

T F 5. All items in a numbered outline, including body text, are numbered.

6. A compiled index is usually placed on a separate page at the _____ of a document.
   a. beginning
   b. end
   c. middle
   d. none of these

7. The _____ box is used to indicate the category in the table of authorities where the source information (citation) will be placed.
   a. Section
   b. Area
   c. Statute
   d. Category

8. An outline family can include _____.
   a. an idea
   b. indented related ideas
   c. body text
   d. all of these

9. Creating a table of contents in Word is a three-part process. List the three parts.

10. The most common sources cited in a table of authorities are _____ and _____.

Enriching Language Arts Skills

Spelling/Vocabulary Words

faculty—the teachers of a school or one of its departments.
leave—(noun) permission to be absent from duty.
mandatory—required.
sole—unique, only one.

Percentage Amounts

Use figures for numbers that are followed by the word percent. Spell out the word percent unless the percentage amount is used in a table that contains statistical information or in a headline/title.

Examples:

Salaries are 30 percent of the total budget. (Percent spelled out)

Percentage of Males and Females		
Age Group	Male	Female
20-29	68.0%	65.0%
30-39	18.5%	19.5%
40-49	13.5%	15.5%

PRICES ARE SLASHED 40% STOREWIDE!!! (Headline information)

Activities

Activity 21.1—Create an Outline

1. Use the following information to create an outline. (If necessary, see the Steps to Create an Outline in the Outline View on pages 525–526.) Change to the Outline View. Type the following unnumbered outline with the indents shown. (Use the **Demote** button on the Outlining Toolbar to move the insertion point to the right to indent (demote) the outline levels. Use the **Promote** button on the Outlining Toolbar to move the insertion point to the left to promote the outline levels.)

The Computer (Hardware)
    CPU
    Keyboard
        101 keyboard with trackball
        Ergonomic keyboard
    Monitor
        Full screen

```
                        VGA
                        Multiscan
            Disk Drives
                        Hard disk drive
                        Floppy disk drive
            Printers
                        Laser
                        Inkjet
                                    Full color
                                    Monochrome
                        Dot matrix
Application Programs (Software)
            Word processing
                        Microsoft Word
                        WordPerfect
            Spreadsheet
                        Microsoft Excel
                        Quattro Pro
```

2. Number the outline (select all the outline entries; choose **Format**, **Bullets and Numbering** and select the **Outline Numbered** tab; select the second numbering style from the right in the bottom row).

3. Change to **Normal** View. Place the insertion point at the top of the document and press the **Enter** key three times. Select the three blank lines and apply the **Normal** style.

4. Type the outline title **Computer Systems** and apply the **Title** style (select **Format**, **Style**, click in **List** box, choose **All Styles**, click on the **Title** style, and choose **Apply**).

5. Use the filename **21activity 1.doc** and save the file.

6. Print one copy.

7. Optional. Fax the outline to your instructor via a local fax, or write an e-mail message to your instructor that you are sending this assignment. Attach this file to your e-mail message.

8. Close the document.

■ Activity 21.2—Create a Table of Contents and Index

1. Open the file named **21act2.doc** located on the data disk.

2. Apply the Heading 1 style to the sideheads with all uppercase letters, e.g., MEMBER MEETINGS on page 1 and MEMBER BINDER on page 2 (place the insertion point in the sidehead, select the down arrow beside the Style box, click on **Heading 1**).

3. Apply the Heading 2 style to the following sideheads, which display with upper- and lowercase letters (place the insertion point in the sidehead, select the down arrow beside the Style box, select **Heading 2**).

> Annual Meetings
> Special Meetings
> Notice of Meetings
> Place of Meetings
> Proxies
> Quorum

4. Format and compile the table of contents.

    a. Place the insertion point at the top of the document (**Ctrl** and **Home**).

    b. Select **Insert, Index and Tables**; choose the **Table of Contents** tab.

    c. Choose the desired format (select **Fancy** in the Formats box).

    d. Check that the following options are chosen, or change the following options if needed:

> Show page numbers
> Right align page numbers
> Show levels: 2
> Tab leader: None

    e. Select **OK**.

    f. Place a section break between the table of contents and the document (with the insertion point located to the left of the "B" in "BYLAWS," select **Insert, Break, Next page, OK**).

    g. Place a heading above the table of contents (press **Ctrl** and **Home**, press **Enter** once, press the up arrow key once, and type the heading **Contents**; choose the **Normal** style; select the heading, choose **Times New Roman, Bold** and **16 point**; select the **Center** alignment button).

    h. Change the table of contents page number to lowercase Roman numerals (select **Insert, Page Numbers**, select **Center** alignment, select **Format**; in the Number format box, select lowercase Roman numerals, i.e., **i, ii, iii**, . . .; select **OK** twice).

    i. Change the page number on page 2 to begin numbering starting with 1. (Locate the insertion point on page 2, select **Insert, Page Numbers, Format**; select the **Start at, 1**. Choose **1, 2, 3** . . . Choose **OK** twice.)

5. Use the *new* filename **21Activity toc.doc** and save the file on your file disk.

6. To develop an index, create a concordance file using the following information:

    a. In a new document window, create a table with one row and two columns.

    b. Turn off the capitalization for the first letter of a sentence (select **Tools, AutoCorrect**, deselect the option **Capitalize first letter of sentence**, select **OK**).

c. Type the following index entries using the exact upper/lowercase letters as shown. Remember to press **Tab** to move to the next column and to obtain a new row.

member meetings	Member meetings
annual meeting	Member meetings:annual meeting
Special meetings	Member meetings:special meetings
Executive Committee	Executive committee
proxies	Proxies
quorum	Quorum

7. Use the filename **21concordance.doc** and save the index concordance file on your file disk.

8. With the file named **21Activity toc.doc** on the screen, mark the index entries using the concordance file named **21concordance.doc** that was created in step 6 above (select **Insert, Index and Tables, Index** tab, **AutoMark**; type the drive letter where your file disk is located followed by a colon and filename **21concordance.doc**; select **OK**).

9. Format and compile the index (press **Ctrl** and **End**; type **Index**; press **Enter** twice; center and bold the index heading; place the insertion point below the index heading; select **Insert, Index and Tables, Index** tab; select **Formal** in the Formats box; deselect the **Right align page numbers** option; select **1** in the Columns box; select **OK**).

10. Place the index on a separate page (locate the insertion point to the left of the "I" in "Index"; press **Ctrl** and **Enter**).

11. Use the *new* filename **21act 2 final.doc** and save the file on your file disk.

12. Print one copy.

13. Optional. Fax this document to your instructor via a local fax, or write an e-mail message to your instructor that you are sending this assignment. Attach this file to your e-mail message.

14. Turn on the **Capitalize first letter of sentence** option (select **Tools, AutoCorrect**, choose **Capitalize first letter of sentence, OK**).

15. Close all document windows.

■ Activity 21.3—Create a Table of Authorities

1. Open the file named **21act3.doc** located on the data disk.

2. Create long and short table of authorities entries using the information in steps 2a–g. (Select the desired citation, select **Insert, Index and Tables**, choose **Table of Authorities** tab, choose **Mark Citation**; make any editing changes desired in the **Selected text** box; select the desired category in the Category box; type the short citation in the Short citation box; select **Mark All**; scroll through the document to locate the next citation to be marked. Repeat the process until all citations are created; select **Close** when finished.)

Note: The following descriptions of location of text are based on the Times New Roman font, 12 pt. If your font differs in type or size, you may need to look in the next paragraph or on the next page.

*Hint: It may be useful to print out a copy of the document, **21act3.doc**, to assist in locating the citations to be marked.*

a. Select the citation **Civil Code Section 1354** located on page 1, the second paragraph, first sentence. The category is **Statutes**. The short citation name is **1354**.

b. Select the citation **Civil Code Section 1355** located on page 2, the last paragraph, first sentence. The category is **Statutes**. The short citation name is **1355**.

c. Select the citation **Civil Code Section 1351, et seq** located on page 2, the last paragraph, third sentence. The category is **Statutes**. The short citation name is **1351**.

d. Select the citation that begins **B. Emerson, Condominium and Homeowner . . .(1988 2d ed)** on page 3 at the end of the first partial paragraph. The category is **Statutes**. The short citation name is **B. Emerson**.

e. Select the citation that begins **Marina Imperial Owners . . . 681-682 (1981)** located on page 3 in the second sentence of paragraph 2. The category is **Cases**. The short citation name is **Marina Imperial**.

f. Select the citation that begins **Carmel Cove Estates . . . App 1975** located on page 3 at the end of the second paragraph. The category is **Cases**. The short citation name is **Carmel Cove**.

g. Select the citation that begins **Cypress v. Thorsen . . . (1989)** located on page 4 in the first complete paragraph. The category is **Cases**. The short citation name is **Cypress**.

3. Create a table of authorities using the following information:

a. Format and compile the table of authorities (press **Ctrl** and **Home**, select **Insert, Index and Tables**, choose the **Table of Authorities** tab, choose **Classic** in the Formats box; if necessary, select **All** in the Category box, select **OK**).

b. Create the table of authorities page (with the insertion point to the left of the "S" in the title "Statement," select **Insert, Break, Next page, OK**).

c. Check on page 2 that the page numbering is set to begin numbering as page 1 (if necessary, place the insertion point on page 2, select **Insert, Page Numbers**, choose **Format, Start at, 1**, select **OK** twice).

d. Type a heading for the table of authorities (press **Ctrl** and **Home**, press **Enter** once, press the up arrow key once, type **TABLE OF AUTHORITIES**, select the **Center** alignment button, select the heading, and choose **Bold**). Remember, the Caps Lock key does not need to be pressed—the heading automatically displays in uppercase letters.

e. Change the page number on the table of authorities page to lower-case Roman numerals (select **Insert**, **Page Numbers**, **Format**, select **Number format**, choose **i, ii, iii, . . .**, select **OK** twice).

4. Use the *new* filename **21TA activity 3.doc** and save the file on your file disk.

5. Print one copy and close the document.

Challenge Your Skills

Skill 21.1—Create and Edit an Outline

1. Use the Outlining Toolbar to create the following outline. The paragraphs have been indented to show the levels for outline numbering. *(Hint: If the Outline feature places letters or numbers where you want a blank line, select the unwanted number or letter and select **Normal** in the Style box.)*

2. Make decisions regarding:

   > Margins
   > Alignment
   > Fonts
   > Outline numbering style and spacing
   > Page numbering

Purpose
Operator training
   On-the-floor training
   Monitor during trainee's first shift
Safety
Housekeeping
Handling procedure
   Loading trays
      Handle one caddie per hand
      Use the radial grasp
   Loading the plating fixture
      Hold end tightly
      Use only designated caddie
Load/unload substrates
   Loading procedure
      Place caddie on workbench
      Remove discs
      Transfer to plating line
   Unloading the fixture
      Wear latex gloves
         Visually inspect discs placed in new baths
         Label each caddie

Place full caddie on transfer cart
Wrap transfer cart in plastic foil

3. Use the filename **21skill1.doc** and save the file. (Optional. Print one copy.)

4. Insert the following title at the top of the outline. Format the style using the **Title** style.

Nickel Plating
Procedure to Load/Unload Substrates in Plating

5. Edit the outline as follows:

   a. Insert the following items under item III (i.e., Safety)

      A.   Carefully remove mandrels

      B.   Set mandrel correctly in place

   b. Insert the following second- and third-level items between items A and B under Handling procedure

      Unloading the mandrel
         Set disc straight in correct slot
         Avoid damaging the inside diameter of the discs
         Remove discs from tray

   c. Choose your numbering style.

6. Once changes are made, use the *new* filename **21skill outline.doc** and save the file again.

7. Print one copy.

8. Optional. Fax this document to your instructor via a local fax, or write an e-mail message to your instructor that you are sending this assignment. Attach this file to your e-mail message.

9. Close the document.

■ Skill 21.2—Create an Index and a Table of Contents; Language Arts

1. Open the file named **21skill2.doc** located on the data disk. Make decisions regarding:

      Margins
      Alignment
      Fonts
      Text flow, e.g., Keep text together, Widow/Orphan
      Bold/capitalization of titles, headings, and subheads
      Format of table of contents
      Format of index
      Page numbering
      Section break(s)

   *Hint: Print a copy of **21skill2.doc** to use as a guide when creating the index and table of contents.*

2. Correct three spelling errors, two misused words, one percentage error, and two punctuation errors.

3. Apply the **Title** style to the title **Black Hawk College Agreement**.

4. Apply the **Heading 1** and **Heading 2** styles to the appropriate headings in the document.

5. Create an index using a concordance file and mark all occurrences of the following main index entries and subentries. Remember, the entries in the first column of the concordance file must exactly match the case (upper and lower) of the words in the document. The following are the main entries and subentries:

> Preamble
> Recognition
> Leaves
> > Sick leave
> > Industrial accident or illness leave
> > Jury duty
> Transfers and Reassignments
> Professional Education Program
> > Multicultural Program
> > Learning Styles Program
> Layoffs
> Performance Evaluation Procedures
> > Contract employees
> > Regular employees

Hint: Remember to turn off the Capitalize first letter of the sentence option in the AutoCorrect dialog box.

Hint: When creating the concordance file, type the text to be indexed in the first column exactly as the text appears in the document. In the second column, type the entry as it should appear in the index. For example:

> Preamble   Preamble

When creating a subentry in the concordance file, type the subentry text in the first column, then type the main entry, a colon, and the subentry text in the second column. For example:

> Sick Leave   Leaves:sick leave

6. Use the filename **21Skill 2 concordance.doc** and save the concordance file on your file disk.

7. Format and compile the index. Create a separate page for the index at the end of the document.

8. Format and compile the table of contents and create a separate page for the table of contents at the beginning of the document.

Hint: Remember to reset the page number for the first page of the document (after the table of contents page) to 1.

9. Use the *new* filename **21Skill 2 final.doc** and save the file on your file disk.

10. Print one copy and close the document.

Use Advanced Features and Create Master Documents

22

Features Covered

- Create a paragraph style containing a border
- Create a style containing a special symbol
- Designate one style to follow another
- Create cross-references within a document
- Create a master document by inserting subdocuments
- Create cross-references to other documents

Objectives and Introduction

After successfully completing this chapter, you will be able to create a paragraph style containing a border and a special symbol. You will also be able to specify one style to follow another and learn to create cross-references and master documents. In addition, you will use cross-references in a master document.

Text and special symbols can be included in styles as well as formatting codes (see Chapter 15). Using styles can help you create documents with a consistent and professional appearance.

Use Advanced Styles

In Chapter 15, basic formatting styles such as margins, font changes, and justification, were created. In addition, many other formatting elements, such as borders and special symbols, can also be incorporated into a style. Also, if desired, text that is used often can be designated as part of a style. For example, a letter-head style can be created that contains text, different fonts, and borders, which can then be saved and used each time a letter is created.

551

A style can be automatically followed by another style. When one style is specified to follow another, the first style is in effect until the **Enter** key is pressed. When the **Enter** key is pressed, the first style is turned off and the next style is turned on.

Start-Up Instructions

- Open the file named **22drill1.doc** located on the data disk.

Steps to

Create a Paragraph Style Containing a Border

1. Place the insertion point in the paragraph in which the new style will be applied.

   For example, place the insertion point in the first sidehead, "Always Ask Questions."

2. Select **Format, Style**.

   Note: The Style dialog box displays.

3. Select the **New** button

   Note: The New Style dialog box displays.

4. In the Name box, type a name for the new style.

   For example, type **Sidehead**.

5. In the Style type box, choose the desired style type.

   For example, check that the **Paragraph** style displays in the Style type box. (If necessary, select the **Style type** box and choose **Paragraph**.)

6. To change the font, font style, or size, select the **Format** button, **Font**, make the desired changes, and select **OK**.

   For example, change the font to **Century Gothic, Bold, 14 point**, and select **OK**.

   Note: The format information, i.e., Normal + Font: Century Gothic, 14 pt, Bold, Don't hyphenate, displays in the Description area of the New Style dialog box. An example of the style also displays in the Preview box.

Place a Border Below the Paragraph

7. Select the **Format** button, **Border**.

   Note: The Borders and Shading dialog box displays.

8. With the Borders tab selected, choose the desired line style width in the **Width** box.

   For example, click on the down arrow located in the **Width** box and select **3 pt**.

9. Choose the desired border position and select **OK**.

   For example, click on the **bottom border** button in the Preview area to display the border line between the left and right brackets (see Figure 22.1). Select **OK**.

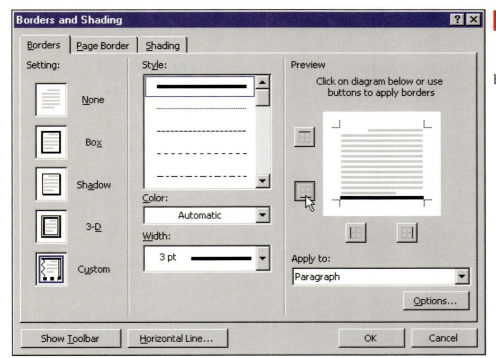

FIGURE 22.1

Borders and Shading dialog box with bottom border selected

Note: The New Style dialog box with the additional format information displays in the Description box, i.e., Border: Bottom (Single solid line, 3 pt Line width), Border Spacing: 1 pt. Also, the Preview box displays with the Border line below the sidehead.

10. When all the style formats have been specified, select **OK**.

    For example, select **OK**.

11. Select the **Apply** button to apply the new style to the paragraph containing the insertion point.

    Note: The sidehead displays with the new style applied, i.e., a bottom 3 pt width border and Century Gothic Bold font, 14 pt. The new style, Sidehead, also displays in the Style box in the Formatting Toolbar.

Finish-Up Instructions

❖ Apply the style to the next two sideheads, which begin "Listen to Advice . . ." and "There are No . . ." (place the insertion point in the desired sidehead, select the down arrow next to the Style box, choose the style named **Sidehead**).

❖ Use the *new* filename **22paragraph style.doc** and save the file.

Start-Up Instructions

❖ The file named **22paragraph style.doc** should be displayed in the document window.

Create a Style Containing a Special Symbol

1. Place the insertion point in the paragraph in which the new style is to be applied.

    For example, place the insertion point in the first body text paragraph which begins "To succeed as an entrepreneur . . ."

2. Select **Format, Style**.

3. Select the **New** button.

4. In the Name box, type a name for the new style.

    For example, type **paragraph symbol**.

5. Select the down arrow in the **Based on** box and select a style that is similar to the style being created.

    For example, scroll up and select **List Bullet**.

6. Select the **Format** button, **Numbering**.

7. With the **Bulleted** tab selected, select **Customize, Bullet**.

8. Click on the down arrow beside the **Font** box and select the desired symbol font.

    For example, select **Wingdings**.

9. Choose the desired symbol from the selected font.

    For example, double-click on the ➢ symbol in row 7, column 17, OK.

10. Make additional selections to modify the new style.

    For example, in the Text position area, **Indent at** box, select the down triangle until zero (**0**) displays; select the **Font** button, choose the Font **Color** box and select **Blue**; in the **Size** box, choose **14**; select **OK** three times.

11. Select **Apply**.

    Note: The symbol displays blue on your screen and will print in blue if you have a color printer.

Finish-Up Instructions

❖ Apply the paragraph symbol style to the other body text paragraphs (place the insertion point in the desired paragraph, click on the down arrow beside the **Style** box, choose the **paragraph symbol** style).

❖ Use the *new* filename **22symbol style.doc** and save the file.

❖ Continue with the Steps to Designate One Style to Follow Another.

 Designate One Style to Follow Another

1. Select **Format, Style**.

2. In the Styles box, select the style you want to specify as the following style.

For example, click once on the style name **Title**.

3. Select **Modify**.

    Note: The Modify Style dialog box displays.

4. In the **Style for following paragraph** box, select the style you want to specify as the following style.

    For example, click in the **Style for following paragraph** box and select the style named **Subtitle**.

5. Select **OK**.

6. Select **Close** to close the Style dialog box.

Finish-Up Instructions

❖ Press **Ctrl** and **Home** to locate the insertion point at the top of the document. Type the following text:

    Becoming a Successful Entrepreneur (do not press **Enter**).

❖ Click on the down triangle located beside the **Style** box. Click on the style named **Title**.

❖ Press **Enter** to activate the style specified to follow the Title style.

❖ Type the following text:

    Key Points to Remember

❖ Use the *new* filename **22style to follow another.doc** and save the file.

❖ Print one copy and close the document.

Create Cross-references Within a Document

The Cross-reference feature is used to direct readers from one area of a document to another area of a document. For example, in this textbook, cross-references are often used to direct readers from the text to a related figure. Cross-references can be linked to headings, figures, tables, bookmarks, etc.

An easy method for creating cross-references is to identify the item to be cross-referenced by creating a bookmark (see the section Create Bookmarks in Chapter 20). Once the item to be cross-referenced is bookmarked, use the Cross-reference dialog box to identify the Reference type (e.g., Bookmark), select the **Insert reference to** item (e.g., Page Number), and choose the **For which . . .** item (e.g., Figure1_1).

A cross-reference can contain more than one type of reference information. For example, both the bookmark name and page number can be inserted as the cross-reference. If the document containing the cross-reference is changed, the cross-reference is updated automatically in order to reflect new page numbers. To cross-reference items in different documents, the documents must be part of a master document. See Steps to Create a Cross-reference in a Master Document on page 561.

Start-Up Instructions

❖ To complete the drills, activities, and skills in this chapter, copy the following files located on the data disk to your file disk. For information on copying files, see Chapter 16, page 419.

22sbact1.doc	22sbsk4.doc
22sbact2.doc	22skill1.doc
22sbact3.doc	22subch1.doc
22sbact4.doc	22subch2.doc
22sbsk1.doc	22subch3.doc
22sbsk2.doc	22subch4.doc
22sbsk3.doc	22subch5.doc

❖ Open the file named **22subch1.doc** located on your file disk.

❖ Use Normal View. (If necessary, select the **Normal View** button.)

Steps to ➤ ## Create a Cross-reference Using Bookmarks

1. Place the insertion point where the reference is to be located in the document.

   For example, place the insertion point in the second body text paragraph between the words "page "and "for."

2. Select **Insert, Cross-reference**.

   Note: The Cross-reference dialog box displays.

3. Select the desired reference in the Reference type box.

   For example, select **Bookmark**.

   Note: The Bookmark had been previously created in the file.

4. Choose the desired Insert reference to item.

   For example, click on the down arrow in the **Insert reference to** box and click on **Page number**.

5. In the **For which bookmark** box, select the desired item.

   For example, check that **Figure1_1** is highlighted.

   Note: The Cross-reference dialog box should look similar to Figure 22.2.

FIGURE 22.2

Cross-reference
dialog box

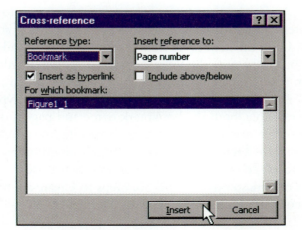

6. Choose the Insert button.

   Note: The page number is placed in the document at the location of the insertion point.

7. Select Close.

   Note: If you touch the mouse pointer on the cross-reference page number, a hand displays along with a ScreenTip that indicates the name of the bookmark. Click once on the page number (cross-reference) and the insertion point will "jump" to the cross-referenced item.

Finish-Up Instructions

❖ Save the file using the same filename, **22subch1.doc**.

❖ ▮ Open the file named **22subch2.doc** located on your file disk.

❖ Create a cross-reference using the following information:

   a. Place the insertion point in the second body text paragraph between the words "page" and "for."

   b. Repeat steps 2–7 in the Steps to Create a Cross-reference Using Bookmarks. In step 5, check that **Figure2_1** is highlighted.

❖ Save the file using the same filename, **22subch2.doc**.

❖ Close all document windows.

Create a Master Document

The Master Document feature in Word 2000 is useful for managing large documents such as a book with chapters. The master document is a file containing information that links other files (called subdocuments) to the master document file. The master document file also includes any formatting choices that will apply to the entire document. Subdocuments are files that are saved separately and when desired are assembled together into one master file (document). Any Word document can be a master document or a subdocument. One of the major advantages of creating a master document is that many individuals can then work on different sections of a project at the same time. The Master Document feature is then used to combine all the sections into one document.

To create a master document, use the Outline View. The Outline View contains the Outlining and Master Document buttons (see Figure 22.3). Use the **Insert Subdocument** button 🗗 to access the Word files that will be placed in the master document. Once the subdocuments are inserted in the master document, the formatting that is to be applied to the entire document is then set up.

After the master document containing subdocuments has been created and saved, information in a subdocument can be edited either in the master document or by opening the subdocument and making the desired changes.

To make it easier for several users to work simultaneously on the subdocuments in a master document, Word provides a file-locking feature. Word "locks" a subdocument when another user is currently working on the subdocument or when the subdocument's author has created a password for the document. A passworded document can be opened with the password or opened as a read-only document. When a subdocument is opened with a password, the subdocument is available as a read-write file, which means the subdocument can be viewed, edited, and saved. The subdocuments that are opened as read-only files can only be viewed and edited and then must be saved with a new filename.

When documents are shared, it may be helpful to know the owner (the person who created) the file. To determine who created a file, select **File**, **Properties** and choose the **Summary** tab. The name of the document owner is listed in the Author box. The name stored on the User Information tab of the Options dialog box (**Tools**, **Options**) is used to place the owner's name on a document when it is created and saved.

When a subdocument is inserted when the Outline View is on, the heading/outline symbols (◻ ⊕ ⊟) display beside the subdocument information. Note that when Word's heading styles are used to format the subdocuments, the plus and minus symbols display. When Word's heading styles are not used, a small square box displays (see Figure 22.3). The heading/outline symbols are used to move the headings and subordinate text to another location in the master document. Also, by clicking on the subdocument icon, all of the subdocument text is highlighted and can be deleted or relocated. If a lock icon 🔒 displays below the subdocument icon 🗔, expand the subdocuments. At the time of this writing, if the **Lock** button is used, the Toolbar features are turned off.

In the Outline View, each subdocument is placed in a separate section. A Continuous Section Break displays above and below each subdocument. To display the subdocuments' contents, select the **Expand Subdocuments** button 🗗 on the Outline Toolbar. Click on the **Collapse Subdocuments** button 🗗 to condense the expanded subdocuments. (***Note:*** *When the subdocuments are expanded, the* ***Collapse Subdocuments*** *button displays. When the subdocuments are condensed, the* ***Expand Subdocuments*** *button displays.)*

Formatting that applies to the entire document, such as page numbering, margins, and font type and size, is placed in the master document. If a subdocument contains formatting applied in the original subdocument, this formatting has precedence over the formatting applied in the master document. If a title page is desired, the title information is typed. Since each subdocument is a section of the master document, you can change section formatting, such as headers, footers, page numbers, and margins, at the beginning of each subdocument if you wish.

Start-Up Instructions

❖ Open a new document window.

Create a New Master Document by Inserting Subdocuments

1. Select **View, Outline**.

   Note: The Outlining/Master Document/Web Toolbar displays. If necessary, click on the up arrow located on the right side of the ***Go*** *button to exand the Outlining Toolbar. If the* ***Go*** *button is not displayed, right-mouse click on the Toolbar and select* ***Web***.

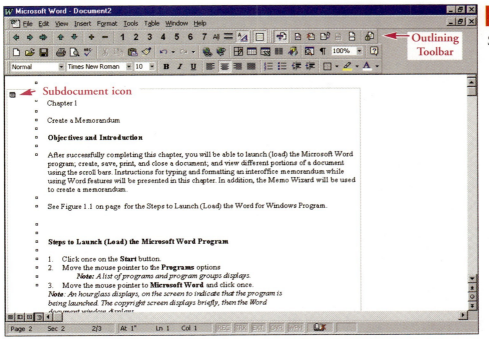

FIGURE 22.3

Subdocument in
Outline View

2. Select the **Insert Subdocument** button on the Outlining/Master Document Toolbar.

   Note: The Insert Subdocument dialog box displays.

3. Select the desired drive/folder where the subdocuments are located and double-click on the desired filename.

   For example, select the drive where your file disk is located; double-click on the file named **22subch1.doc**. Press **Ctrl** and **Home** to locate the insertion point at the beginning of the subdocument.

   Note: The subdocument displays with the heading/outline symbols shown in front of each document level. Also, a light-gray line displays around the subdocument (see Figure 22.3).

4. Locate the insertion point at the end of the subdocument.

   For example, press **Ctrl** and **End**.

5. Repeat steps 2–4 and insert the desired subdocuments.

   For example, insert the following subdocuments located on your file disk:

   22subch2.doc
   22subch3.doc
   22subch4.doc
   22subch5.doc

   Note: Scroll through the master document. Each subdocument is contained within a box; no formatting displays in the Master Document View.

Finish-Up Instructions

❖ Use the *new* filename **22master document.doc** and save the file on your file disk.

❖ Continue with the Steps to Show First Line Only.

Start-Up Instructions

❖ The file named **22master document.doc** should be displayed in the document window.

❖ The Outlining Toolbar should be displayed. (If necessary, select **View**, **Outline**.)

*Note: If necessary, click on the **Move buttons** arrow located to the right of the **Insert Subdocument** button.*

Show First Line Only

1. Select the **Show First Line Only** button ▤ on the Outlining Toolbar.

   Note: Scroll through the subdocuments, noting that only the first line of each paragraph is displayed. This feature does not affect the actual text in the documents.

2. To display all lines in the document window, select the **Show First Line Only** button ▤ again.

   For example, select the **Show First Line Only** button ▤ again.

Finish-Up Instructions

❖ Continue with the Steps to Create a Cross-reference in a Master Document.

Create Cross-references to Other Documents

Using a master document is the only way in Word to create cross-references to items in different documents. To create a cross-reference to information in different documents, simply open the master document in Normal View and create the cross-references just as if you were working in a single document. (Refer back to Steps to Create a Cross-reference Using Bookmarks on page 556 if necessary.)

To update cross-references to items in different documents, the master document must also be used. Select the master document and press **F9**.

Start-Up Instructions

❖ The master document named **22master document.doc** should be displayed in the document window.

❖ Use the Normal View. (If necessary, select the **Normal View** button.)

Create a Cross-reference in a Master Document

*Note: The Normal View or the Print Layout View can be used when creating cross-references in the master document. If the Outline View is used, all lines should be displayed. (If necessary, select the **Show First Line Only** button or the **Expand Subdocuments** button on the Outlining/Master Document Toolbar.)*

1. Place the insertion point at the desired location where the reference is to be inserted in the master document.

   For example, in Chapter 3 place the insertion point to the left of the last period in the final paragraph.

2. Select **Insert, Cross-reference**.

3. Choose the desired **Reference type, Insert reference to,** and **For which . . .** options.

   For example, check that the following options are highlighted, or select the following options: **Bookmark** in Reference type, **Page number** in Insert reference to, and **Chapter4** in the For which bookmark box.

4. Select the **Insert** button.

   Note: The page number is automatically inserted in the document, and the Cross-reference dialog box remains open in the document window.

5. Select **Close** to exit the Cross-reference dialog box.

Finish-Up Instructions

❖ Use the Normal View. (If necessary, select the **Normal View** button.)

❖ Type and format a title (press **Ctrl** and **Home**, type **Word 2000**, press **Enter** twice, type **Compiled by** followed by your name; select the title lines, change the font size to **20 point**, and choose **Center** alignment; select **File, Page Setup, Layout** tab, **Vertical** alignment, **Center, OK**).

❖ If necessary, click to deselect text. With the insertion point located in the title page, create a blank (different) first page footer and create a second page footer (select **View, Header and Footer**, select the **Switch Between Header and Footer** button, select the **Page Setup** button, select **Different first page, OK**; choose the **Show Next** button, type **Word 2000**, press **Tab** twice, select the **Insert Page Number** button, choose **Close**).

❖ Change the page number on page 2 to begin numbering at page 1 (locate the insertion point in page 2, select **Insert, Page Numbers, Format**; select the up triangle next to the **Start at** box until **1** displays; select **OK** twice).

❖ To update the cross-reference page numbers, select the entire document and press **F9**.

❖ Use the same filename, **22master document.doc**, and save the file on your file disk.

❖ If desired, select **Print Preview** and scroll through the master document.

❖ Optional. Print the master document.

❖ Close the document.

The Next Step

Chapter Review and Activities

Self-Check Quiz

T F 1. When one style is specified to follow another, the second style is in effect after the **Enter** key is pressed.

T F 2. Using a master document is the only way to create cross-references that point to items in different documents.

T F 3. Cross-references can be linked to figures, headings, tables, and bookmarks.

T F 4. To update cross-references, select the entire master document and press **F9**.

T F 5. In a master document, each subdocument is placed in a separate section.

6. The _____ is used to set up a master document.
   a. Cross-reference feature
   b. Outlining/Master Document Toolbar
   c. Borders Toolbar
   d. Bookmark feature

7. A style can contain _____.
   a. borders
   b. special symbols
   c. formatting changes
   d. all of the above

8. List one major advantage of creating a master document.

9. Define a subdocument.

10. State the main purpose of using a cross-reference.

Enriching Language Arts Skills

Spelling/Vocabulary Words

cuisine—a style of cooking or preparing food.
exception—the act of leaving out, excluding; a case not conforming to the general rule.
clients—customers, buyers; persons who seek the professional services of another.
minimal—least possible, smallest.
savor—taste or smell of something; to taste with enjoyment.

Basic Rules for Numbers

Generally, in written text numbers one through ten are spelled out. Also, numbers used in approximation and numbers at the beginning of a sentence are usually spelled out. Use figures when a number is followed by the word percent. Omit the colon and zeros when writing an even clock time.

Examples:

Thirty-one people are enrolled in the television course on Real Estate Appraisals. (Spell out a number at the beginning of a sentence.)

We will pick up eight additional passengers at the next bus stop. (Spell out numbers one through ten.)

Donald reported that around sixty people attended the luncheon. (Spell out a number used in approximation.)

We decreased our use of electricity by 12 percent this month. (Use a figure when the number is followed by the word percent.)

We will arrive in Houston at 3 p.m. (Colons and zeros are omitted when the clock time is even.)

Activities

Activity 22.1—Create a Master Document and Cross-references

1. Open a new document window.

2. Select the Outline View (select **View**, **Outline**).

   *Note: If the InsertSubdocument button is not displayed, click on the up arrow located to the right of the **Go** button.*

3. Create a master document by inserting the following subdocuments that are located on your disk. (Select the **Insert Subdocument** button; double-click on the desired subdocument filename. Repeat for each subdocument.)

   22sbact1.doc
   22sbact2.doc
   22sbact3.doc
   22sbact4.doc

   Note: These files must be located on your file disk. If the files are not on your file disk, see page 556 for the list of files that need to be copied.

4. Select the subdocuments (**Ctrl** and **a**) and change the font for all the text to **Charter BT**, **11 point**, or make a font choice of your own.

5. With the master document open, use the following information to create cross-references:

    a. In the last paragraph of Chapter 1, place the insertion point one space to the right of the word "pages."

    b. Select **Insert, Cross-reference**. Choose the desired **Reference type**, **Insert reference to**, and **For which bookmark** options (check that the following options are highlighted or select the following options: **Bookmark**, **Page number**, and **Chapter_3**).

    c. Select **Insert**. With the insertion point showing as an I-beam, click in the document window to the right of the cross-reference number. Press the **Spacebar** once and type the word **and**. Press the **Spacebar** once.

    d. With the Cross-reference dialog box displayed in the document window, place the insertion point to the left of the period in the last paragraph of Chapter 1 and repeat the instructions in step 5b. Select **Chapter_4** in the For which bookmark box.

    e. With the Cross-reference dialog box displayed, scroll down and locate the insertion point in the last paragraph of Chapter 4 (first page) to the left of the period. Repeat the instructions in step 5b and choose **Figure4_1** in the For which bookmark box.

    f. Exit the Cross-reference dialog box (select **Cancel**).

6. Change to Normal View (select the **Normal View** button).

7. Type and format a title (press **Ctrl** and **Home**, type **Free the Environment**, press **Enter** twice, type **Compiled by** followed by your name; select the title lines, choose **20 point**, **Bold**, **Center** alignment; select **File**, **Page Setup**, **Layout** tab, **Vertical alignment**, **Center**, **OK**).

8. Click to deselect. With the insertion point located in the title page, create a blank (different) first page footer and create a second page footer. (Select **View**, **Header and Footer**, select the **Switch Between Header and Footer** button, select the **Page Setup** button, select **Different first page**, **OK**; choose the **Show Next** button, type **Free the Environment**, press **Tab** twice—the page number 2 displays. If necessary, select the **Insert Page Number** button, select the footer text, and change to **11 point**; choose **Close**.)

9. Change the page number on page 2 to begin numbering at page 1 (locate the insertion point in page 2; select **Insert**, **Page Numbers**, **Format**; select the up triangle next to the **Start at** box until **1** displays; select **OK** twice).

10. To update the cross-reference page numbers, change to Outline View, select the entire document (**Ctrl** and **A**) and then press **F9**.

11. Change to Normal View.

12. Use the *new* filename **22activity 1 master.doc** and save the file on your file disk. If desired, select **Print Preview** and scroll through the document to check the page numbers.

13. Print one copy.

14. Optional. Fax this document to your instructor via a local fax, or write an e-mail message to your instructor that you are sending this assignment. Attach this file to your e-mail message.

15. Continue with Activity 22.2 or close the document.

Activity 22.2—Create Advanced Styles in a Master Document

1. Open the file named **22activity 1 master.doc** that was created in Activity 22.1.

   *Note: The Outline View should be displayed and the document expanded. If necessary, select **View, Outline**; select the **Expand Subdocuments** button ⊞.*

2. Create a chapter heading style using the following instructions:

   a. Place the insertion point at any position in the title, "Chapter 1— Save Power."

   b. Select **Format, Style, New**.

   c. In the Name box, type **Chapter title**.

   d. Check that **Paragraph** displays in the Style type box. (If necessary, choose **Paragraph** in the Style type box.)

   e. Change the font to **Century Schoolbook, 14 point, Bold** (select **Format, Font**; choose the desired font, font style, and size; select **OK**).

   f. Select **Format, Paragraph, Indents and Spacing** tab, **Alignment, Centered, OK**.

   g. Create a paragraph border (select **Format, Border**, select **Width 1½ pt**, click the **bottom border** button in the Preview box to display the border line between the left and right brackets, select **OK**).

   h. Select **OK** and choose **Apply**.

   Note: The bottom border will not display in Outline View.

3. Create a paragraph style that contains a symbol.

   a. Place the insertion point at any location in the first body text paragraph of Chapter 1.

   b. Select **Format, Style, New** and type the name for the new style, **graphic paragraph**.

   c. Select **Based on** and scroll down and select **List Bullet**.

   d. Select **Format, Numbering**.

   e. On the Bulleted tab, choose **Customize**, select the **Bullet** button, choose **Wingdings** in the Font box.

   f. Choose the ✳ symbol (row 6, column 2).

   g. Select **OK** three times; choose **Apply**.

   Note: The formatting displays in Print Layout or Normal View.

4. Apply the graphic paragraph and chapter title styles to all chapter titles and paragraphs in Chapters 1, 2, 3, and 4 (place the insertion point in the desired title or paragraph, select the **Style** button, choose the desired style name).

5. Use the *new* filename **22advanced styles.doc** and save the edited master document on your file disk.

6. Change to Normal View and print one copy of the master document.

7. Close the document.

Challenge Your Skills

◆ ▪ Skill 22.1—Create a Master Document, Cross-references, and Advanced Styles; Language Arts

1. Open the file named **22skill1.doc** located on your file disk.

2. With the insertion point located on page 2, use the Outline View and create a master document. Insert the following subdocuments located on your file disk. (If necessary, see page 556 for information on files to be copied.)

    22sbsk1.doc
    22sbsk2.doc
    22sbsk3.doc
    22sbsk4.doc

3. Correct four spelling errors, three punctuation errors, three number rule errors, and one misused word.

4. Use the filename **22skill master.doc** and save the file on your file disk.

5. Create cross-references for the four sentences on the title page and for the cross-reference in Section 3.

6. In Normal View, create a section title style. Make decisions for the style name, font type, size, alignment, and paragraph border. Apply the title style to each of the four section titles.

7. Create a style that contains a symbol of your choice. Make decisions for the style name, font type, size, alignment, and paragraph border. Apply this style to each of the four section paragraphs.

8. Make decisions regarding page numbering.

9. Use the same filename, **22skill master.doc**, and save the file on your file disk.

10. Optional. Fax this master document to your instructor via a local fax, or write an e-mail message to your instructor that you are sending this assignment. Attach the master document file to your e-mail message.

11. Print one copy.

12. Close the document.

Advanced Tables and Microsoft Graph

Features Covered

- Number cells automatically
- Split cells
- Create a formula to multiply two cells
- Name cells using a bookmark
- Create a formula by pasting a bookmark
- Create a chart using Microsoft Graph
- Insert a spreadsheet file
- Create repeated table headings

Objectives and Introduction

After successfully completing this chapter, you will be able to create a form using the Tables feature. While creating the table form, you will learn to number cells, split cells, create a formula to multiply two cells, name cells using a bookmark, and create a formula by pasting a bookmark. You will also learn to insert and link a spreadsheet, as well create repeated table headings for a multi-page table. Finally, using data from a Word table, you will learn to create a chart using Microsoft Graph.

Create a Form Using the Tables Feature

Business forms, such as expense reports and invoices, can be easily created using the Tables feature. When creating a form using a table, first determine the number of columns needed for the majority of rows, then create the table. Once the basic structure is created, table cells can be split for those rows that need additional columns. A single table cell can be split up into 63 columns if space is available.

Often a cell address is used to create formulas. To assist in identifying a table row, the rows can be quickly numbered using the **Numbering** button on the Formatting Toolbar. After the table formulas have been created and the row numbers are no longer needed, they can be removed by selecting the **Numbering** button again.

Formulas are placed in each cell that will contain a calculation. The formulas created in Word include symbols that indicate various math functions, known as *arithmetic operators*. The arithmetic operator symbols used in formulas are as follows:

+ (addition)   - (subtraction or negative number)
* (multiplication)   / (division)

When a contiguous group of cells is used in a formula, a colon is placed between the first cell address and the last cell address to avoid typing each cell address to be calculated. For example, if cells B1 through B8 are to be added, the formula =Sum(b1:b8) would be used; the cells shown within the parentheses will be added and the result placed in the cell in which the formula is located. The equals sign indicates the beginning of a formula, the word Sum is used to signify addition, the colon is used to indicate a range of cells, and the parentheses are used to enclose the cell addresses. If a formula contains cell addresses that are not consecutive, either a comma or an arithmetic operator can be used to separate the individual cell references. For example, =Sum(c6,c9,d11) and =Sum(c6+c9+d11) would both add the contents of cells c6, c9, and d11.

Often a bookmark name is created to identify a cell. The bookmark name becomes an easy way to refer to the cell address when creating a formula. For example, if cell b6 is named quantity and cell b8 is named amount, the formula =quantity*amount would multiply the two cells.

After a formula is placed in a cell, the formula result is usually displayed instead of the formula. A light-gray shading is applied to the background of the formula result. To view the formula components, select **Tools**, **Options** and choose the **Field codes** option in the View tab. The formula displays between braces as a field code, e.g., {=SUM(b3:b4)}. (If the formula is selected, it displays with a dark-gray shading.) If changes are made to any cell amounts and/or formulas, the results must be updated by clicking on the field code or the formula result and pressing **F9**. The results of a formula can also be updated by placing the mouse pointer on the field code or formula result, pressing the *right* mouse button, and selecting the **Update Field** option.

By default, the cell text (or numbers) are placed at the top of the cell. If the table row height is increased, click on the **Align...** button and select the **Center Align** button on the Tables and Borders Toolbar to center the cell contents vertically in the cell. The alignment buttons on the Formatting Toolbar are used to display numbers at the top left, top center, top right, center left, center, center right, bottom left, bottom center, and bottom right of the cell.

Start-Up Instructions

❖   ▢   Open the file named **23Trip.doc** located on the data disk.

Number Cells Automatically

> *Note: To assist in creating table formulas, number the table rows; the numbers will be removed after the formulas are created.*

1. Select the cells to be numbered.

   For example, select the first column starting on row 3 at the item "Hotel." (Obtain the right pointing arrow to the left of the word Hotel (inside the table border). Press and hold the mouse button while dragging down the left column.)

   Note: Only column 1 should be highlighted.

2. Select the **Numbering** button  in the Formatting Toolbar.

   Note: All items in column 1 are now numbered.

Finish-Up Instructions

❖ Use the *new* filename **23Trip1.doc** and save the file on your file disk.

❖ Continue with the Steps to Split a Cell.

Start-Up Instructions

❖ The file named **23Trip1.doc** should be displayed in the document window.

 Split a Cell

1. Place the insertion point in the cell to be split.

   For example, place the insertion point in row 7, column 1 (Mileage).

2. Select **Table, Split Cells**.

   Note: The Split Cells dialog box displays (see Figure 23.1).

3. Click on the up or down triangle beside the **Number of columns** or **Number of rows** box to increase or decrease the number displayed.

   For example, select the up triangle beside the **Number of columns** box until **3** displays.

4. Select **OK**.

   Note: The cell is divided into 3 columns and each cell is numbered.

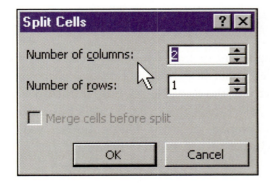

Finish-Up Instructions

❖ Type the mileage rate, **.32**, in the cell numbered 8.

❖ Type the number of miles, **826**, in the cell numbered 9.

❖ Click on the cell containing the word mileage and widen the cell if desired.

❖ Use figures and the m/d/yy format and type the current date in row 2, column 3, e.g., **5/17/00**.

❖ Use the same filename, **23Trip1.doc**, and save the file on your file disk.

Start-Up Instructions

❖ The file named **23Trip1.doc** should be displayed in the document window.

Create a Formula to Multiply Two Cells

1. Locate the insertion point in the cell where the results of the formula are to be displayed.

    For example, locate the insertion point in the numbered row 7, column 4 (the word "Mileage" displays in the first column).

2. Select **Table, Formula**.

    Note: The Formula dialog box displays.

3. Select the formula displayed in the Formula box and type the desired formula.

    For example, select the formula in the Formula box and type **=b9*c9** to multiply the mileage rate (.32) by the number of miles (826).

    Note: The number 9 is used because the row is actually the ninth row when the title and column heading rows are counted.

4. Select **OK**.

    *Note: The formula result, 264.32, displays. If a field code displays, select **Tools**, **Options**, **View** tab, deselect **Field codes** in the Show area, select **OK**.*

Finish-Up Instructions

❖ Create a formula to add the transportation costs (place the insertion point in numbered row 10, column 3; select **Table**, **Formula**; delete the word **ABOVE** and type **b6:b8,d9** within the parentheses; choose **OK**).

    Note: The total transportation cost is 1195.87. If necessary, check that the formula reads: =SUM(b6:b8,d9).

❖ Change the cell height and vertically center the text in row 2. (Select row 2, choose **Table**, **Table Properties**; with the **Row** tab selected, choose **Specify Height**, select **Exactly** in the Row Height box; in the **Specify Height** box, type **.3**; select **OK**. Select the **Tables and Borders** button to display the Tables and Borders Toolbar. Select the **Align...** button and choose **Center** on the Tables and Borders Toolbar. Close the Tables and Borders Toolbar.)

❖ Use the *new* filename **23Trip2.doc** and save the file on your file disk.

❖ Continue with the Steps to Name Cells Using a Bookmark.

Start-Up Instructions

❖ The file named **23Trip2.doc** should be displayed in the document window.

 ## Name Cells Using a Bookmark

1. Double-click on the cell amount in the desired cell.

   For example, move the mouse pointer to the first character in the cell amount in the numbered row 3 (actual row 5), column 3 (643.25) and double-click.

   Note: The entire cell amount should be highlighted with a dark-gray background.

2. Select **Insert, Bookmark**.

   Note: The Bookmark dialog box displays.

3. Type the desired name in the Bookmark name box.

   For example, with the insertion point blinking in the Bookmark name box, type **hotel**.

4. Select **Add**.

   *Note: To see the Bookmark indicator, click once to deselect the cell amount. (Nonprinting symbols should be displayed.) The figure is enclosed in braces. If the Bookmark indicator does not display, select **Tools, Options, View** tab, **Bookmarks, OK**. A beginning brace displays to the left of the cell amount, and a closing brace is located at the right of the cell amount. The bookmark braces do not print.*

Finish-Up Instructions

❖ Create a cell name using a bookmark for the following cells:

   Numbered row 10 (actual row 12), column 3   **transport**
   Numbered row 17 (actual row 19), column 3   **misc**

   Note: Be sure to highlight the entire cell amount when creating bookmarks.

❖ Continue with the Steps to Create a Formula by Pasting a Bookmark.

Start-Up Instructions

❖ The file named **23Trip2.doc** should be displayed in the document window.

 ## Create a Formula by Pasting a Bookmark

1. Locate the insertion point in the cell where the bookmark is to be placed.

   For example, to create a formula for the Grand Total, locate the insertion point in numbered row 18, column 3.

2. Select **Table, Formula**.

3. Select and delete the word **ABOVE** in the Formula box.

4. Choose the desired bookmark name from the Paste bookmark box.

   For example, click in the **Paste bookmark** box; choose **hotel**, type a **comma**.

5. Repeat step 4 and select the desired bookmark name(s).

   For example, select the **misc** bookmark; type a **comma**. Select the **transport** bookmark.

   Note: The formula in the Formula box should display as follows: =SUM(hotel, transport, misc).

6. Select **OK**.

   Note: The formula result, 1913.27, displays in the cell where the insertion point is located.

Finish-Up Instructions

❖ Remove the numbers by selecting the numbered rows in column 1, then clicking once on the **Numbering** button on the Formatting Toolbar.

❖ Create a formula in column 3 of the row containing the Total Payment/Reimbursement, and subtract the Advance Received amount from the Grand Total amount (place the insertion point in the desired cell, select **Table**, **Formula**, delete the formula in the Formula box and type **=c18-c19**). (Do not type the period.)

   Note: Since the Advance Received was greater than the Grand Total amount, the result is a minus amount (i.e., -186.73).

❖ Select row 2 and change the shading to 10% (use the **Shading Color** box on the Tables and Borders Toolbar and choose **Gray-10%**).

❖ Select the cell that contains the Total Payment/Reimbursement figure and use **Gray-10%** shading.

❖ Use the *new* filename **23Final Trip Report.doc** and save the file on your file disk.

   Note: Your form should look similar to Figure 23.2.

❖ Print one copy. Close the document.

Toggle Field Codes and/or Update a Field

*Note: The **Toggle Field Codes** option is used to display a formula in a cell. The **Update Field** option is used to recalculate a formula after a number(s) or a formula(s) has been changed. The following steps are for your information only.*

1. Place the mouse pointer (I-beam) on the desired cell amount, or select the entire table.

   For example, place the mouse pointer (I-beam) in row 20, column 3 (where the Total Payment/Reimbursement figure is located).

FIGURE 23.2

Final expenses
report form

Images Clip Art, Paper, and Printing Supplies Sales Representative Travel Report			
Item		**Week Ending:**	**5/17/00**
Hotel		495.90	
Meals		147.35	
Total Hotel and Meals			643.25
Taxi		44.00	
Airfare		855.00	
Parking and Tolls		32.55	
Mileage	.32	826	264.32
Total Transportation			1195.87
Miscellaneous		14.90	
Shipping (FedEx)		25.50	
Mailing		3.85	
Telephone		15.00	
Copying		6.90	
Faxing		8.00	
Total Miscellaneous			74.15
Grand Total			1913.27
Advance Received			2100.00
Total Payment/Reimbursement			-186.73
Printed Name:		Signature:	Date:
Note: Receipts are required for every expense			

2. Press the *right* mouse button.

3. Choose the desired option.

> For example, to display a field code, select the **Toggle Field Codes** option. To recalculate a formula, select the **Update Field** option.

Shortcut:

1. Place the mouse pointer (I-beam) on the desired cell amount, or select the entire table.

2. Press **F9** to update a field(s).

Create a Chart Using Microsoft Graph

The Microsoft Graph program is used to create charts within a Word document. A chart can be created using data from a Word table or new data. Data from spreadsheet programs, such as Microsoft Excel and Works, Lotus 1-2-3, and Quattro Pro, can be imported and used to create charts. Various chart types are available, such as bar, pie, line, and column, and each chart type can be formatted in various ways to make the data easier to understand.

Line, bar, and column charts show information along the x-axis and y-axis. The *x-axis* is the bottom horizontal line of a Graph chart. The *y-axis* is the left vertical line of a Graph chart. Information from the first column of a table or datasheet is placed in the chart legend. The **Data series in column** option can be used, however, to reverse this display and place the first column data in the x-axis and the row 1 data in the legend. The numbers in the table/datasheet cells are used to determine the values displayed on the *y* axis. The bars in the sample chart visually represent the value of each item in relation to the numbers shown on the y-axis.

To create a chart using the data from a Word table, first select the table cells that contain the necessary data. Then select **Insert, Picture, Chart**, or select **Insert, Object, Microsoft Graph 2000 Chart** to display a datasheet and sample chart. The menus and Toolbars display options and buttons to use to set up a chart.

If new data are desired in a table, place the insertion point at the place in the document where the chart is to be inserted before selecting **Insert, Picture, Chart**. Select the table rows and columns containing data. Click on the *right* mouse button, select **Clear Contents**, and type in the new data.

To format the legend, move the mouse pointer inside the chart legend and double-click to select it. The **Format Legend** dialog box displays with options to change the placement, font, or patterns of the legend. To change any other element of the chart, select the item, then click the *right* mouse button and select the appropriate format option from the shortcut menu.

After formatting the graph, click on any area of the document window that is outside the graph. The graph will appear in the document window. It can be easily moved to another position on the page and sized using the sizing handles.

Although the datasheet within the Graph program can be used to enter simple data, formulas cannot be used. Its primary purpose is to provide a quick way to change data from a table without returning to the document window or to enter data when only the chart is needed in the document.

The Graph program does not automatically update the chart if the data in the Word table are changed. To update the chart, select the cells containing the data, copy them, double-click on the chart to enter the Microsoft Graph program, and paste the new cells over the old ones in the datasheet.

Start-Up Instructions

❖ Open the file named **23Salary.doc** located on the data disk.

Steps to ➤ ## Create a Chart Using Microsoft Graph

1. Select the cells that contain the data from which the chart will be created.

   For example, select all cells in rows 4 through 9 (columns 1, 2, 3, 4, and 5).

2. Select **Insert, Picture, Chart**.

   *Note: The datasheet displays in the foreground with the **23Salary.doc** and sample chart underneath it similar to Figure 23.3.*

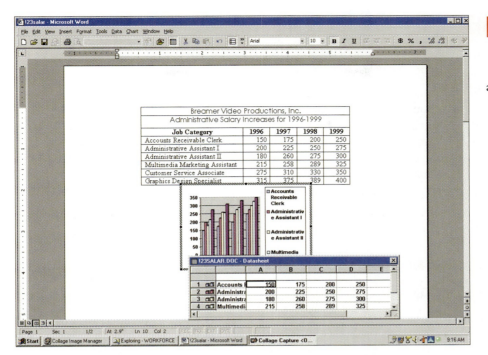

FIGURE 23.3

23Salary.doc
with datasheet
and sample chart

*Note: The datasheet and sample chart can also be displayed by selecting **Insert**, **Object** and double-clicking on **Microsoft Graph 2000 Chart** in the **Create New** tab.*

3. Type the data for the x-axis.

   For example, click in the blank cell above row 1 in column A and type **1996**; press the Tab key to move to column B and type **1997**. Repeat and type **1998** and **1999** in the top row of columns c and d.

4. Select the **Chart** menu on the Toolbar and choose **Chart Options** on the Menu bar.

   Note: The Chart Options dialog box displays.

5. With the **Titles** tab selected, fill in the desired information.

   For example,

   a. Click in the **Chart title** box and type **Salary Increases**.

   b. Click in the **Category (X) axis** box and type the title for the bottom (x-axis) of the chart. Type **Years**.

   c. Click in the **Value (Z) axis** box and type **Dollars**.

6. Select **OK** to exit the Chart/Options dialog box.

7. Enlarge the chart window.

   For example, place the mouse pointer on the sizing handle located at the bottom right corner until a double-headed diagonal arrow displays; press and hold the mouse button and drag right to approximately 3" deep and the same width as the table.

8. Select the chart title and change the font size.

FIGURE 23.4

Word document
with chart
created using
Microsoft Graph

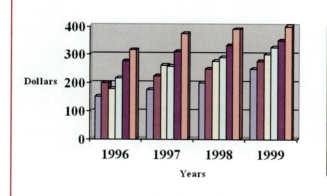

Breamer Video Productions, Inc.				
Administrative Salary Increases for 1996-1999				
Job Category	**1996**	**1997**	**1998**	**1999**
Accounts Receivable Clerk	150	175	200	250
Administrative Assistant I	200	225	250	275
Administrative Assistant II	180	260	275	300
Multimedia Marketing Assistant	215	258	289	325
Customer Service Associate	275	310	330	350
Graphics Design Specialist	315	375	389	400

Salary Increases

For example, click on the chart title until a box surrounds the title; select the **Font Size** button and choose **14**.

9. Select the legend and change the font size.

For example, click once on the legend to select the legend; select the **Font Size** button and choose **8**.

10. Return to the Word document window.

For example, click outside the chart anywhere in the Word document window.

Note: To return to the datasheet window and chart options, double-click on the chart.

Finish-Up Instructions

❖ Center the chart below the table. (Click on the chart and then select the **Center** alignment button.)

❖ Click once in an empty area of the window to deselect the chart.

❖ Select **Print Preview** to view the full page. Select **Close** to return to the document window.

❖ Use the *new* filename **23Salary chart.doc** and save the file on your file disk.

Note: Your file should look similar to Figure 23.4.

❖ Print one copy. Close the document.

Insert a Spreadsheet File

A spreadsheet file can be inserted easily into a Word document window. Word can open spreadsheet files from programs such as Microsoft Excel and Works, Lotus 1-2-3, and Quattro Pro. Inserting a spreadsheet into Word from a different program is often referred to as *importing*.

When a spreadsheet file is inserted, all of the file information is copied into a new or existing Word file. However, if only a portion of a spreadsheet file is to be inserted, a range (block of cells) is typed to indicate the exact rows and columns to be imported.

To insert a file from another application, select **Insert, File**. Select **All Files** (*.*) in the Files of type box. All files on the disk in the selected drive are displayed. If desired, a range of cells can be typed in the Range box. Double-click on the document to be opened. Once a spreadsheet file is inserted, any formatting features available for Word tables can be used. For example, the column widths can be increased or decreased or cells can be merged or split.

Also, a file can be inserted as an object and linked to its original source. If changes are made to the source file, they are automatically updated in the linked file.

Start-Up Instructions

❖ Open the file named **23Jaram.doc** located on the data disk.

Steps to Insert and Link a Spreadsheet File

1. Place the insertion point at the location where the spreadsheet file is to be inserted.

   For example, place the insertion point between the two body text paragraphs,

2. Select **Insert, Object**.

3. Click on the **Create from File** tab and choose the **Link to File** option. Then choose **Browse**.

4. If necessary, click in the **Files of type** box and select **All Files** (*.*).

5. Double-click on the desired filename.

   For example, double-click on the file named **23expens.xls** located on the data disk.

6. Select **OK**.

Finish-Up Instructions

❖ Scroll up to display the top of the worksheet.

❖ Use the following information to format the inserted spreadsheet:

   a. Change the left margin to 1.0 inches (choose **File, Page Setup**, change the Left margin to 1" and select **OK**).

b. Add or delete any spaces between paragraphs as needed.

c. Choose **10%** shading for each column that contains the Cost column head, including the column head itself (select the column cells, select the **Shading Color** button on the Tables and Borders Toolbar, select **Gray-10%**).

d. Replace the reference initials (xx) with your initials.

❖ Use the *new* filename **23Jaramillo Final.doc** and save the file on your file disk.

❖ Print one copy and close the document.

Repeat Table Headings in a Multi-Page Table

The second and subsequent pages of a multi-page table or spreadsheet should contain the header information that identifies the table columns. A row or consecutive rows from the first page of a multi-page table can be selected and repeated on the following page(s) by using the **Heading Rows Repeat** option in the **Table** menu. Once the **Heading Rows Repeat** option is selected, a check mark displays beside the option in the **Table** menu. To turn off the Headings option, select **Table, Heading Rows Repeat** again.

If the **Heading Rows Repeat** option is selected, Word automatically repeats the table headings when a table extends beyond one page. When changes are made to the heading on the first page of the table, the changes will automatically be updated on succeeding pages. However, Word will not repeat headings if a hard page break is inserted in the table.

Start-Up Instructions

❖ Open the file named **23tennis.doc** located on the data disk.

Steps to Create Repeated Table Headings

1. Select the row or rows to be used as a table heading.
   For example, select rows 1 and 2.

2. Select **Table, Heading Rows Repeat**.

   *Note: Select the **Print Preview** button and **Next Page** button to display the first two table rows that are repeated on the second page of the table. Select **Close** to exit Print Preview.*

Finish-Up Instructions

❖ Click once to deselect text.

❖ Insert page numbers (select **Insert**, **Page Numbers**, **Bottom of page (Footer)** position, **Center** alignment, **Center**, **OK**).

❖ Use the *new* filename **23tennis with heading row repeated.doc** and save the file on your file disk.

❖ Print one copy and close the document.

Use Information Created in Another Program

Information from other computer programs can be integrated into a Word document in one of three ways:

1. *Convert the information into Word's format.* This occurs automatically when information is copied from another program, such as an Excel spreadsheet, and pasted into a Word document using the **Edit, Copy/Edit, Paste** commands or the **Copy** and **Paste** buttons. It also occurs when the **Insert, File** command is used.

    Once information has been converted to Word's format, it has no connection with the former program or with the file from which it was copied. This method is best when the source information will not be updated or the original program will not be needed to edit the information.

2. *Embed the information in a Word document in its original format.* Use the **Insert, Object** or **Insert, Picture** commands. To edit an embedded object, the original program is activated by moving the mouse pointer to the object and double-clicking. The object cannot be edited in Word because it is not in Word's format. For example, the Steps to Create a Chart Using Microsoft Graph on page 574 embedded a Microsoft Graph object into a Word document. When the mouse pointer is moved to the chart and double-clicked, the Microsoft Graph program is activated.

    If the embedded object is edited, the changes are saved in the Word document. An embedded object maintains a connection to the original program but not to any specific file even if it was originally taken from a separate file. Embedded files greatly increase the size of the Word document, but are necessary when the information must be edited in the original program or if the source file will not always be available.

3. *Link the information to the original file and to the original program.* A link can be created by choosing the **Insert, Object** command. Select the **Create from File** tab and choose the **Link to file** option. Click on the **Browse** button and double-click on the filename desired. Select **OK**. When information is linked, a reference, or pointer to the file where the information is stored becomes part of the Word document. The information itself does not need to be stored in the Word document.

    To edit the linked file, *right* mouse-click on the object in Word and choose the linked worksheet object option. Select **Edit Link**. Make the desired changes. Click on the Word window (in the

Taskbar). The updated information displays. Use a linked file when the file size must be kept to a minimum and it is important to have current information. With a linked file, the source file must always be available. For example, a monthly sales report might contain a linked Excel spreadsheet showing the current sales figures. The source file in Excel would need to be available on a local or network drive.

The Next Step

Chapter Review and Activities

Self-Check Quiz

T F 1. A table cell can be split into columns but not rows.

T F 2. The asterisk (*) in the cell formula =D8*E8 indicates multiplication.

T F 3. Microsoft Graph can be used to create a chart based on data from a Word table.

T F 4. After the table row height is increased, text or numbers can be repositioned vertically in the cell using the **Format**, **Columns** option.

T F 5. When a spreadsheet is inserted into a Word document window, all or a portion of the spreadsheet can be inserted.

6. One way to create a chart from a Word table is to select the table data, choose **Insert**, **Object**, and double-click on _____ .
   a. **Microsoft Graph 2000 Chart**
   b. **Create from File, Link to File**
   c. **Manual Update**

7. To make the first two rows of a table repeat on each page, select the rows then select _____.
   a. **Edit, Headings**
   b. **View, Headings**
   c. **Table, Heading Rows Repeat**

8. To view the components of a formula, select **Tools**, **Options**, the **View** tab, and _____.
   a. field codes
   b. bookmarks
   c. picture placeholders
   d. hidden text

9. Write a formula to multiply the following cells in a Word table: c9, c11, and c15.

10. List one reason for naming a cell using a bookmark.

Enriching Language Arts Skills

Spelling/Vocabulary Words

annual—occurring once a year.
exceed—to go beyond the limit; surpass; excel.
quarterly—occurring at three-month intervals.
quota—share or goal assigned to a person or team.
reflect—to form an image of; to mirror.

Abbreviations in Table Column Headings

When creating tables and forms, abbreviations are often used in subtitles and column headings because of limited space. However, abbreviations should be used sparingly. If you are unsure of an abbreviation, consult a dictionary.

Common abbreviations:

account	acct.	incorporated	inc.
amount	amt.	miscellaneous	misc.
attention	attn.	number	No.
department	dept.	quarter	qtr.
dozen	dz. or doz.	received	recd.

Activities

Activity 23.1—Create an Invoice Using the Tables Feature; Create Formulas

1. Create a table with 5 columns and 10 rows.

2. Use the following information to format a table similar to the invoice table shown below.
   a. Merge the cells in row 1 (select row 1, choose **Table**, **Merge Cells**).

b. Increase the cell height of row 1 to **At Least 1.2 pt** (with the desired cell selected, select **Table**, **Table Properties**, click on **Specify Height** in the **Row** tab, click up to **1.2**, **At least**; and select **OK**).

c. Select and merge columns 1 through 4 in row 2 (select the desired cells, select **Table**, **Merge Cells**).

d. Increase the cell height for the merged cells in row 2 to **Exactly 1 inch**.

e. Type the unformatted information (text and numbers) as shown.

INVOICE				
A-1 Trophies and Awards 3668 Merritt Avenue Charleston, SC 29407				
To: Buckley County School District 1789 Revolution Avenue Moncks Corner, SC 29461			Date: (current date)	
Quantity	Stock No.	Description	Unit Price	Total Price
3	1295	Trophy/Football Player	12.00	
5	1366	Trophy/Hockey Player	15.50	
8	877	Trophy Stand	5.00	
		Subtotal		
		Sales Tax (8.5%)		
		Total		

3. Use the following information to format the table.

a. Select and center the word **INVOICE** in row 1; change to **18 point**.

b. Select row 3 (the column headings); choose **Center** alignment.

c. Select rows 4 through 10 and columns 1 through 5. Choose **Right** alignment.

d. Adjust the column widths so that each item fits on one line.

4. Create formulas for column 5, rows 4, 5, and 6 to multiply the Quantity by the Unit Price (with the insertion point in the desired cell, select **Table**, **Formula**; delete the displayed formula and use the following information).

Column 5, row 4: type **=a4*d4**, select the **$#,##0.00** number format

Column 5, row 5: type **=a5*d5**, select the **#,##0.00** number format

Column 5, row 6: type **=a6*d6**, select the **#,##0.00** number format

*Note: If an error message displays in the cell after selecting **OK** in the Formula dialog box, redo the formula, making sure to type an equals sign (=) before the formula. If the field codes display instead of a result, place the insertion point in a cell containing a formula, press the right mouse button, and select **Toggle Field Codes**.*

5. Create a formula in row 8, column 5 to add rows 4, 5, and 6 in column 5 (select **Table**, **Formula**, **=SUM[ABOVE]**, select the **#,##0.00** number format, **OK**).

6. Create a formula in row 9 to multiply row 8 in column 5 by the Sales Tax (select **Table**, **Formula**, delete the formula and type =e8*.085, select the #,#00.00 number format, **OK**).

7. Create a formula in row 10 to add rows 8 and 9, column 5 (select **Table**, **Formula**, delete the formula and type =e8+e9, select the $#,#00.00 number format, **OK**).

8. Select the entire table and place ¾ **pt** single line border around the form and the cells (choose **Table**, **Select Table**; on the Tables and Borders Toolbar, select the **Line Weight** button and choose ¾ **pt**; choose the **Borders** button and select **All Borders**).

9. Apply 10% shading to rows 3 and 10 (select the row, select the **Shading Color** button on the Tables and Borders Toolbar, select **Gray - 10%**).

Note: Your form should look similar to the form shown below.

INVOICE

A-1 Trophies and Awards
3668 Merritt Avenue
Charleston, SC 29407

To: Buckley County School District 1789 Revolution Avenue Moncks Corner, SC 29461	Date: (current date)

Quantity	Stock No.	Description	Unit Price	Total Price
3	1295	Trophy/Football Player	12.00	$ 36.00
5	1366	Trophy/Hockey Player	15.50	77.50
8	877	Trophy Stand	5.00	40.00
		Subtotal		153.50
		Sales Tax (8.5%)		13.05
		Total		$ 166.55

10. Use the filename **23Invoice.doc** and save the file.

11. Print one copy of the form.

12. Close the document.

Activity 23.2—Revise a Table Form; Name a Cell; Split a Cell; Update Formulas

1. Open the file named **23Invoice.doc** that was created in Activity 23.1.

2. Split the cell that contains the date into two columns (with the insertion point located in the date cell, select **Table**, **Split Cells**, Number of columns **2**, **OK**).

3. Enlarge the split cells by selecting row 2 and moving the mouse pointer to the border between column 1 and column 2 in row 2 until a double-headed arrow displays. Press and hold the mouse button and drag to the left approximately ½".

4. Delete the date in row 2, column 2. Move the word "Date:" in row 2, column 2 to row 2, column 3. Click after the colon in the word "Date:" and press **Enter** twice. Type the current date.

5. In row 2, column 2, type the words **Invoice No.** and press the **Enter** key once. Type **59422**.

6. Change the quantity of Trophy/Hockey Player to 7.

7. Update all table formulas (choose **Table**, **Select Table**, press **F9**).

8. Use a bookmark to name the cell containing the total amount. (Move the mouse pointer to the left of the first character in the total amount cell and double-click to highlight the entire cell amount with a dark-gray background. Select **Insert**, **Bookmark**. In the Bookmark name box, type **total**; select **Add**.)

9. Use the following information to type a note below the table and to insert a formula using the **total** bookmark.

   a. Press **Ctrl** and **End**. Press **Enter** once.

   b. Type the following: **Please send your check in the amount of**

   c. Press the **Spacebar** once and select **Table**, **Formula**, click in the **Paste bookmark** box, select **total**, and select **OK**.

   d. Press the **Spacebar** once and type the following: **to the attention of Alvin at the following address: Accounts Receivable, P.O. Box 49660, Charleston, SC 29407-9660.**

10. Enhance the table by using bold for the words Invoice, To:, Invoice No., and Date:. Also, bold the column headings.

11. Use the *new* filename **23Revised Invoice.doc** and save the file on your file disk.

Note: Your form should look similar to the form shown on page 585.

Chapter 23—Advanced Tables and Microsoft Graph

INVOICE

A-1 Trophies and Awards
3668 Merritt Avenue
Charleston, SC 29407

To: Buckley County School District 1789 Revolution Avenue Moncks Corner, SC 29461		Invoice No. 59422	Date: (current date)

Quantity	Stock No.	Description	Unit Price	Total Price
3	1295	Trophy/Football Player	12.00	$ 36.00
7	1366	Trophy/Hockey Player	15.50	108.50
8	877	Trophy Stand	5.00	40.00
		Subtotal		184.50
		Sales Tax (8.5%)		15.68
		Total		$ 200.18

Please send your check in the amount of $200.18 to the attention of Alvin at the following address: Accounts Receivable, P.O. Box 49660, Charleston, SC 29407-9660.

12. Print one copy.

13. Optional. Fax the printed copy of the invoice to your instructor via a local fax, or write an e-mail message to your instructor that you are sending this assignment. Attach this file to your e-mail message.

14. Close the document.

◼ Activity 23.3—Import an Excel Spreadsheet; Create a Chart

1. In a new document window, type, bold, and center the title 2xxx Cash Projection. Press the **Enter** key twice.

2. Insert the spreadsheet file **23Cash.xls**, cells **A1:E6** located on the data disk. (Place the insertion point in the second blank line after the title. Select **Insert**, **File**. If necessary, select the drive/folder containing the data disk. Click in the **Files of type** box and select **All Files** (*.*). Click in the Range box and type **A1:E6**. Click **OK**. Double-click on the filename **23Cash.xls**.)

3. Format the table using the following instructions:

   a. Change the alignment for the cells in row 1 to Center (select row **1**, select **Center** alignment button).

   b. Adjust the column widths so that column 1 displays the words in each row on one line. Adjust columns 2–5 to approximately ¾" wide.

   c. Place a border line of ¾ **pt** line weight around the table and cells.

   d. Select the entire document and change the font to **Arial**, **12 point**.

   e. Adjust columns, if necessary. Center the table horizontally.

4. Use the filename **23Cash Projections.doc** and save the file on your file disk.

5. Insert a chart below the table (place the insertion point in any cell of the table, select **Table**, **Select**, **Table**; select **Insert**, **Object**, **Create New** tab; select **Microsoft Graph 2000 Chart**; select **OK**).

6. Use the following information to format the chart.

   *Note: Close the datasheet window by clicking on the **Close** button.*

   a. Select **Chart**, **Chart type** on the Menu bar.

   b. On the **Standard Types** tab, choose the **Bar** chart type.

   c. Choose the Chart subtype—top row, first sample—**OK**.

   d. Choose **Chart**, **Chart Options** on the Menu bar..

   e. In the Titles tab, click in the Chart title box and type **Cash Projections**.

   f. Click in the **Category (X) axis** box and type **Quarters**.

   g. Click in the **Value (Y) axis** and type **Dollars**; select **OK**.

   h. Click outside the chart to return to the Word window.

   i. Move the mouse pointer onto the chart; select the Chart and click on the **Center** alignment button.

7. Click on the chart and enlarge it to approximately 3½" to 4" in height and the width by the width of the table.

   Note: Adjust the legend so no text overlaps in the chart. Double-click on the chart if necessary.

8. Use the same filename, **23Cash Projections.doc**, and save the file again.

9. Print one copy and close the document.

10. Optional. Fax the printed table and chart to your instructor via a local fax, or write an e-mail message to your instructor that you are sending this assignment. Attach this file to your e-mail message.

Challenge Your Skills

💾 Skill 23.1—Create Formulas; Use a Bookmark

1. Open the file named **23payrol.doc** located on the data disk.

2. Make decisions regarding the following:

   a. Formulas to calculate the results for column totals (row 6) and the Net Pay column. Choose an appropriate number format.

   Hint: Net pay is calculated by subtracting all deductions from the gross pay. The formula in column 6, row 3 may be written =b3-(c3+d3+e3).

   b. Create a bookmark for the cell amount in column 6, row 6.

Hint: Move the mouse pointer to the left of the first character in the cell amount and double-click to highlight the entire cell amount.

    c.   Place the insertion point in the first paragraph, second sentence, between the words "of" and "are." Insert the Total Net Pay amount using the bookmark name created in step 2b.

3.   Make decisions regarding the fonts and placement of the memorandum text.

4.   Use the *new* filename **23Final Payroll.doc** and save the file on your file disk.

5.   Print one copy and close the document.

6.   Optional. Fax the printed table and chart to your instructor via a local fax, or write an e-mail message to your instructor that you are sending this assignment. Attach this file to your e-mail message.

Skill 23.2—Create a Chart; Language Arts

1.   Open the file named **23sales.doc** located on the data disk.

2.   Correct three spelling errors, two punctuation/grammatical errors, and one abbreviation error.

3.   Format the table, making decisions about fonts, alignment, cell height, and borders.

4.   Create a chart for the table using Microsoft Graph. Make decisions about:

    a.   An appropriate bar or column chart.

    b.   Position of the legend.

    c.   An appropriate title for the chart. (If desired, select a different font and/or size for the title.)

    d.   Placement of the chart in the document.

5.   Use the *new* filename **23Final Report.doc** and save the file on your file disk.

6.   Print one copy of the document.

7.   Optional. Fax the printed table and chart to your instructor via a local fax, or write an e-mail message to your instructor that you are sending this assignment. Attach this file to your e-mail message.

Advanced Merging

Objectives and Introduction

After successfully completing this chapter, you will be able to use the IF field when merging a main document and a data source file. You will also be able to use the **Find Record** button to quickly locate records for updating information and will merge data from another Microsoft application. In addition, you will learn how to place a Fill-in field (a special command) in a form letter to allow users to input text from the keyboard as letters are merged.

The basics of Word's Merge feature, which combines main documents and data source files to produce individualized letters and mailing labels, were introduced in Chapters 11 and 12. In addition to the basics, the Merge feature has other options and commands, such as the Set Bookmark field, which can make the merge process more flexible and efficient, and allow Word to use data from other Microsoft applications.

Use an IF Field

An IF field allows you to define criteria that data must meet and to specify a different course of action depending on whether or not the condition is met. For example, Figure 24.1 shows the Insert Word Field: IF dialog box for a letter to be sent to customers informing them of a new time for refuse pickup. Customers

FIGURE 24.1

Insert Word
Field: IF dialog
box with criteria
defined

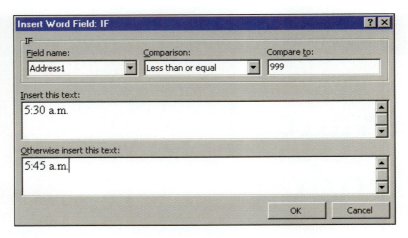

with street addresses that are 999 or less must have their refuse at the curb by 5:30 a.m.; all other customers must have their refuse at the curb by 5:45 a.m.

Sometimes a data source record will contain fields that are empty. For example, the Title field may be empty. The inside address in the form letter places the Title field on the same line as the FirstName and LastName fields; therefore, some letters will print with a blank space before the first name as shown in Figure 24.2. Since the Title field leaves a blank horizontal space, the IF field can be used to eliminate that blank horizontal space when a field is empty.

To insert an IF field, position the insertion point at the desired location, select the **Insert Word Field** button, then select **If...Then...Else** to display the Insert Word Field: IF dialog box. In the Insert Word Field: IF dialog box are three main sections: IF, Insert this text, and Otherwise insert this text. The IF section defines the criteria for evaluating data in a specific field. It contains three elements: Field name, Comparison, and Compare to.

The Comparison box is used to specify how the data is to be evaluated, such as equal to, not equal to, less than, or greater than. The Compare to box is used to specify the text or value that the data should meet (or not meet, depending on the comparison phrase selected in the Comparison box).

The Insert this text section (Then) of the Insert Word Field: IF dialog box contains the information to print if the criteria specified in the IF section *is* met. The Otherwise insert this text (Else) section of the Insert Word Field: IF dialog

FIGURE 24.2

Main document
without IF field
for Title

<<Title>> <<FirstName>> <<LastName>>
<<Company>>
<<Address1>>
<<City>>, <<State>> <<PostalCode>>

Dear <<Title>> <<LastName>>:

George Santana
2544 Morris Road
Cambridge, MA 92142

Merged letter address and
salutation with extra space
that resulted from an
empty Title field

Dear Santana:

FIGURE 24.3

Checking and
Reporting Errors
dialog box

box contains the information to print if the criteria specified in the IF section *is
not* met (see Figure 24.1).

Checking for errors before merging can save time. Before a main document
and data source file are merged, Word can assist in identifying various merge
errors. For example, if a field name in the main document does not match a field
name in the data source file, Word displays an Invalid Merge Field dialog box so
you can remove or replace the mismatched field.

After the **Check for Errors** button is selected in the Mail Merge Toolbar, the
Checking and Reporting Errors dialog box displays with three options: **Simulate
the merge and report errors in a new document; Complete the merge, pausing
to report each error as it occurs;** and **Complete the merge without pausing.
Report errors in a new document**. (See Figure 24.3.)

Start-Up Instructions

❖ Open the file named **24telecom.doc** located on your file disk.

❖ Select the **Mail Merge Helper** button in the Mail Merge Toolbar.

❖ Choose the **Get Data** button. Select the **Open Data Source** option.

❖ Choose the drive/folder and filename desired.

> For example, choose the drive/folder where the data disk is located
> and double-click on the file named **24data1.doc**.

❖ Choose **Edit Main Document**.

❖ Locate the insertion point in front of the third paragraph symbol after the
date, where the inside address is to be added. If necessary, turn on the nonprinting symbols (select the **Show/Hide** button).

Steps to ▶ Use an IF Field

1. Select the **Insert Word Field** button in the Mail Merge Toolbar.

2. Select the **If...Then...Else** option.

3. To begin the IF field, select the desired field name.

> For example, check that **Title** displays in the Field name box.
> (If necessary, select the down arrow next to the Field name
> box and choose **Title**.)

4. Select the desired comparison in the Comparison box.

> For example, select the down arrow next to the **Comparison**
> box, scroll down, and choose **is not blank**.

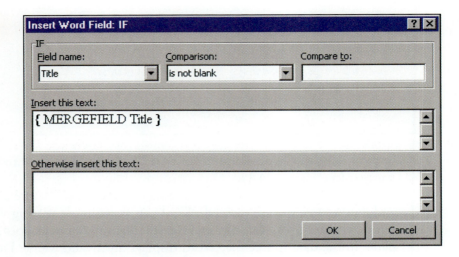

FIGURE 24.4

Insert Word
Field: IF dialog
box with If field
for Title

5. Type the desired information in the Compare to box.

   For example, the Compare to box will be left empty because the **is not blank** comparison was selected.

   *Note: The Compare to box is used whenever a Comparison box option is selected except for when the **is blank** and **is not blank** options are used.*

6. Type the desired text or merge field code(s) in the **Insert this text** box.

   For example, click in the **Insert this text** box; press **Ctrl** and **F9**; type **MERGEFIELD Title**; press the **right** arrow key twice, and press the **Spacebar** once.

   Note: The Insert Word Field: IF dialog box should match Figure 24.4.

7. Select **OK**.

   *Note: To display the IF field code, select **Tools**, **Options**, **View** tab, **Field codes**, **OK**. The IF field code containing the field information displays in the document window, i.e., { IF { MERGEFIELD Title }<> "" "{ MERGEFIELD Title } " "" }. If a sample of the merge data displays within the IF field code, e.g., "Ms.," turn off the field codes (select **Tools**, **Options**, **View** tab, **Field codes**, **OK**). Then turn the field codes back on (select **Tools**, **Options**, **View** tab, **Field codes**, **OK**).*

Finish-Up Instructions

❖ Locate the insertion point at the end of the IF field code.

   *Note: Do **not** press the **Spacebar**.*

❖ Continue to insert the desired merge fields, spaces, and punctuation using the following information:

   a. With the insertion point at the end of the IF field code, select the **Insert Merge Field** button; choose **FirstName**; press the **Spacebar** once.

   b. Select the **Insert Merge Field** button; choose **LastName**; press **Enter** once.

   c. Select the **Insert Merge Field** button; choose **Address1**; press **Enter** once.

d. Select the **Insert Merge Field** button; choose **City**, type a comma; press the **Spacebar** once.

e. Select the **Insert Merge Field** button; choose **State**; press the **Spacebar** once.

f. Select the **Insert Merge Field** button; choose **PostalCode**; press **Enter** once.

g. Select the **Insert Merge Field** button; choose **Country**; press **Enter** twice.

❖ Type **Dear** followed by a space; select the **Insert Word Field** button; choose the **If...Then...Else...** option.

❖ Use the following instructions to enter information into the Insert Word Field: IF dialog box:

a. Check that **Title** displays in the Field name box.

b. In the Comparison box, scroll down and select **is not blank**.

c. Click in the **Insert this text** box and press **Ctrl** and **F9**; type **MERGEFIELD Title**; press the **right** arrow key twice; press the **Spacebar** once; press **Ctrl** and **F9**; type **MERGEFIELD LastName**.

d. Click in the **Otherwise insert this text** box, press **Ctrl** and **F9**; type **MERGEFIELD FirstName**, select **OK**.

*Note: The main document containing the address and salutation with the IF fields should look similar to Figure 24.5. If a sample of the merge data displays within the IF field code, e.g., "Ms. Almanza," turn off the field codes (select **Tools**, **Options**, **View** tab, **Field codes**, **OK**). Then turn the field codes back on (select **Tools**, **Options**, **View** tab, **Field codes**, **OK**).*

e. With the insertion point located at the end of the IF field code, type a colon.

f. Scroll down the file and replace the x's in the reference notation with your initials. Use **File**, **Save As** and type the *new* filename **24IF Main.doc**.

*Note: Turn off field codes (select **Tools**, **Options**; select **Field codes** in the View tab, **OK**).*

{ TIME \@ "MMMM d, yyyy" }

{ IF { MERGEFIELD Title }<> "" "{ MERGEFIELD Title } " "" }{ MERGEFIELD FirstName } { MERGEFIELD LastName }
{ MERGEFIELD Address1 }
{ MERGEFIELD City }, { MERGEFIELD State } { MERGEFIELD PostalCode }
{ MERGEFIELD Country }

Dear { IF { MERGEFIELD Title }<> "" "{ MERGEFIELD Title } { MERGEFIELD LastName }" "{ MERGEFIELD FirstName }" }:

FIGURE 24.5

Main document address and salutation with IF fields

---

g. Select the **Check for Errors** button on the Mail Merge Toolbar. Choose **Complete the merge, pausing to report each error as it occurs**. Select **OK**.

Note: If merging mistakes are found, compare the merge fields to the information shown in Figure 24.5. Make any necessary corrections in the main document. If a field code displays at the location of the date, that's OK.

❖ Scroll through the letters by clicking on the **Next Page** and **Previous Page** buttons.

❖ Use the filename **24merge.doc** and save the merged letters on your file disk.

❖ Close the merged letter file but do not close the file named **24IF Main.doc**.

❖ Continue with the Steps to Use Find Record to Locate a Data Record.

Use Find Record

Modifying information in a data source file is necessary when a record is to be added, changed, or deleted. A record is easily viewed and changed using the **Edit Data Source** button in the Mail Merge Toolbar (see Chapter 11).

If a data source file is large, however, quickly accessing an individual record to be changed can save time. A record can be quickly located using the **Find Record** button in the Mail Merge Toolbar or the **Find** button in the Data Form dialog box. Type the desired text in the Find what box, then select the desired field in the In field box. When the **Find First** button is chosen, the record containing the typed text in the specified field name is found. After the record is found, close the Find in Field dialog box. If the Data Form dialog box is displayed, the found record appears immediately. If the main document window is open, select the **Edit Data Source** button to display the found record.

Steps to ➤ **Use Find Record to Locate a Data Record**

For Your Information

Note: The following instructions are for your information only.

1. Select the **Find Record** button in the Mail Merge Toolbar.

    Note: The Find in Field dialog box displays.

2. Type the desired text in the Find what box.

    For example, type **Wilshire**. (Do not type the period.)

3. In the In field box, choose the desired field.

    For example, click in the **In field** box, and choose **Address1**.

4. Select the **Find First** button.

    Note: After the record is found, the Find in Field dialog box remains in the document window. The number of the found records displays in the Mail Merge Toolbar in the Go to Record box (located in the middle of the Mail Merge Toolbar).

5. Select **Close**.

Finish-Up Instructions

Note: The following instructions are for your information only.

❖ Select the **Edit Data Source** button in the Mail Merge Toolbar.

Note: The first record that contains the text typed in the Find what box displays in the Data Form dialog box.

❖ To edit the record, click in the **Address1** box and change the Suite number to **184**.

❖ Select **OK**.

Note: At this writing, merging the document cannot be accomplished after the Find Record feature is used. If a record needs to be found and edited, use the Steps to Edit a Data Source File in Chapter 11

❖ Close the document named **24IF Main.doc**. Do not save the changes to **24data1.doc** or **24IF Main.doc**.

Note: If the Steps to Use Find Records to Locate a Data Record instructions were performed, it will be necessary to Exit Word and then launch the Word program again in order to perform a merge.

Merge a Data Source File from Another Microsoft Application

A data source file from another Microsoft application, such as Microsoft Access or Microsoft Excel, can be merged with a Word main document. The data source file is opened as usual by using the **Open Data Source** option from the **Get Data** button in the Mail Merge Helper dialog box.

To view all filenames, the **All Files** option in the **Files of type** box can be chosen. Also, the **Select method** option is chosen. After the data source document name to be opened is selected, the Confirm Data Source dialog box displays.

The Confirm Data Source dialog box contains the conversion options available for converting files from different data sources. Select the **Show All** option to display a complete list of converter options provided by Word.

When an Excel worksheet file is opened, either the entire spreadsheet or a range of cells can be specified. In order to know which range of cells to open from a spreadsheet, you would need to have access to a spreadsheet program where the data could be displayed. In this book, the range information is provided for you when needed.

Start-Up Instructions

❖ Open the file named **24GeoSea.doc** located on the data disk.

❖ If necessary, turn off the display of field codes (select **Tools**, **Options**, deselect the **Field codes** option on the View tab, select **OK**).

Merge a Data Source File from Another Microsoft Application

1. Select **Tools, Mail Merge,** or select the **Mail Merge Helper** button on the Mail Merge Toolbar.

2. Select the **Create** button and choose the desired type of main document.

   For example, select **Form Letters.**

3. Select the **Active Window** button or the **New Main Document** button.

   For example, select the **Active Window** button to use **24GeoSea.doc** as the main document.

4. Select the **Get Data** button. Choose **Open Data Source.**

5. Click in the **Files of type** box and select the appropriate file type.

   For example, click in the **Files of type** box and select **MS Excel Worksheets (*.xls).**

6. Choose the **Select method** option located at the right of the dialog box.

7. If necessary, choose the drive/folder and double-click on the desired filename.

   For example, double-click on the filename **24Mail.xls.**

   Note: The Confirm Data Source dialog box displays.

8. Choose the desired Open Data Source option.

   For example, choose **Microsoft Excel Worksheet via Converter.**

9. Select **OK.**

   Note: The Open Worksheet dialog box displays.

10. In the **Name or Cell Range** box, type the desired range or choose the **Entire Worksheet** option.

    For example, in the **Name or Cell Range** box, check that the words "Entire Worksheet" displays.

11. Select the **Format for Mail Merge** option.

12. Select **OK.**

    *Note: The path and filename for the data source are displayed below the **Get Data** button, e.g., **a:24Mail.xls.***

13. Close the Mail Merge Helper dialog box.

Finish-Up Instructions

❖ Choose the **Check for Errors** button on the Mail Merge Toolbar and select **Complete the merge, pausing to report each error as it occurs.** Select **OK.**

❖ Scroll through the merged letters, observing the names and addresses that were obtained from the Excel spreadsheet file, e.g., Kelly Ybarra, Yohannes

Wohlenberg. Close but do not save the merged letters. If necessary, make corrections to the main document.

❖ Use the *new* filename **24GeoSearch Main.doc** and save the file on your file disk.

❖ To complete the mail merge fields in the body of the main document, continue with the Steps to Create and Edit a Fill-in Field on page 598.

Request User Input in a Merged Letter

Special data that may be used only once in a document is often not saved in a data source file. A special field, (Fill-in Field) can be inserted in the main document to instruct the program to pause and request the user to type the needed information. The Fill-in field is placed in the main document at the position where the specific information will be entered.

When the main document containing the Fill-in field is merged with a data source file, the program will pause during the merging of each letter to allow the user to type the specific information. If the **Ask once** option was selected when the Fill-in field was created, Word will stop at the Fill-in field for the first record only. The information typed at that time will be used for all merged letters. When the special information has been entered and all letters have been merged, the insertion point displays at the bottom of the final merged letter.

Start-Up Instructions

❖ The file named **24GeoSearch Main.doc** should be displayed. (If necessary, open the file named **24GeoSearch Main.doc**.)

❖ Display the field codes (select **Tools**, **Options**, select **Field codes** in the View tab, **OK**).

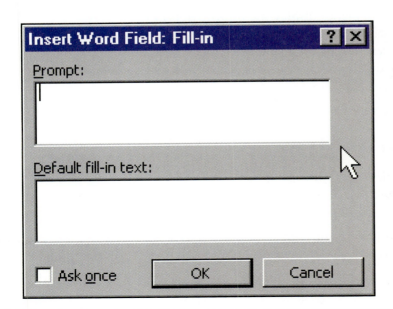

FIGURE 24.6

Insert Word Field: Fill-in dialog box

Create and Edit a Fill-in Field

1. Place the insertion point at the position where the Fill-in field is to be located.

   For example, place the insertion point between the words "is" and "and" in the last sentence of the second body text paragraph.

2. Select the **Insert Word Field** button in the Mail Merge Toolbar.

3. Choose the **Fill-in** option.

   Note: The Insert Word Field: Fill-in dialog box displays (see Figure 24.6).

4. In the Prompt box, type the desired information.

   For example, type **Enter User ID for:**. (Do not type the period.)

5. Click in the **Default fill-in text** box and type the desired information.

   For example, type **GUEST**. (Do not type the period.)

6. To instruct Word to only ask for the information once, select the **Ask once** option.

   For example, select the **Ask once** option so that you will only be asked to enter the user ID one time when the letters are merged.

7. Select **OK**.

   Note: A Microsoft Word message box displays with the prompt and default text. If a typographical error is noticed, complete step 8 and then make the correction(s) in the document window.

8. Select **OK**.

   Note: The FILLIN field code displays in the document, i.e., { FILLIN "Enter User ID for:" \d "GUEST" \o }.

9. To edit the fill-in field, place the insertion point at the desired location and choose the **Insert Merge Field** button.

   For example, to display the information in the **LastName** field in the Fill-in Prompt box, place the insertion point between the word **for** and the colon (:) in the FILLIN code; press the **Spacebar** once; select the **Insert Merge Field** button; click on **LastName**.

   Note: The LastName merge field is displayed in the FILLIN field code.

Finish-Up Instructions

❖ Use steps 1–7 and the following information to create another Fill-in field.

   a. In the last sentence of the second body text paragraph, place the insertion point to the left of the period.

   b. In the Prompt box, type **Enter Password for:**. (Do not type the period.)

   c. In the Default fill-in text box, type **PASS**. (Do not type the period.)

d. The Ask once option should not be selected. (Check that no check mark displays next to the Ask once option.)

e. Edit the Fill-in field. Place the insertion point between the word **for** and the colon (**:**) and press the **Spacebar** once; insert the **LastName** merge field.

f. Change the x's in the reference initials to your initials.

g. Change the filename below the reference initials to **24GeoSearch Main.doc**.

h. Use the same filename, **24GeoSearch Main.doc**, and save the file on your file disk.

i. Continue with the Steps to Merge a Document with User Input.

Start-Up Instructions

❖ The main document **24GeoSearch Main.doc** should be displayed in the document window.

 ## Merge a Document with User Input

1. Select the **Merge to New Document** button ▣.

    Note: The Microsoft Word message box displays with the prompt to Enter User ID for: Ybarra. (Ybarra is the last name of the first person listed in the data source file.)

2. Accept the default text or type new text; choose **OK**.

    For example, choose **OK** to accept the default User ID GUEST.

    Note: The Microsoft Word message box displays with the prompt to Enter Password for: Ybarra and the default password of PASS.

3. Accept the default text or type new text; choose **OK**.

    For example, type the password for Ybarra, which is **FERANGO**; choose **OK**.

    Note: Continue with the Finish-Up Instructions.

Finish-Up Instructions

❖ Repeat step 3 and enter the following passwords for the remaining records:

Wohlenberg	MODEM
Carvalho	LOCHNESS
Dunhill	HARTFORD
Leddy	JEANS

Note: When the user input is complete, the merged documents with the date field codes display. The codes do not print; if desired, turn off the field codes.

❖ Print one copy of each merged letter.

❖ Optional. Use the filename **24GeoSearch Merge.doc** and save the merged letter file. Close all document windows.

*Note: It is not necessary to save changes to **24GeoSearch Main.doc**.*

Use the Set Bookmark Field in a Mail Merge

Similar to a Fill-in field, the Set Bookmark field is used to insert information into a merged document that is not saved in the data source file. The Set Bookmark field inserts the same information in all the resulting merged documents, while the Fill-in field inserts information that is different in each merged document.

The Insert Word Field: Set dialog box is used to create the bookmark name and assign a value (or text). Since it does not print, this is usually placed at the beginning of the document where it will be easy to find. The bookmark field can be used over and over in the main document. Once the bookmark name and value are created, the bookmark field is inserted into the main document using the Cross-reference feature (see Chapter 22).

Start-Up Instructions

❖ Open the file named **24Job Main.doc** located on the data disk.

❖ If necessary, turn on nonprinting characters (select the **Show/Hide** button).

❖ If necessary, turn on field codes and bookmarks (select **Tools**, **Options**, **Field codes** and **Bookmarks** in the View tab, **OK**).

Steps to Use the Set Bookmark Field

1. Place the insertion point at the location where the Set Bookmark field is to be inserted.

   For example, place the insertion point on the third blank line after the letterhead.

2. Select the **Insert Word Field** button on the Mail Merge Toolbar.

FIGURE 24.7

Insert Word Field: Set dialog box

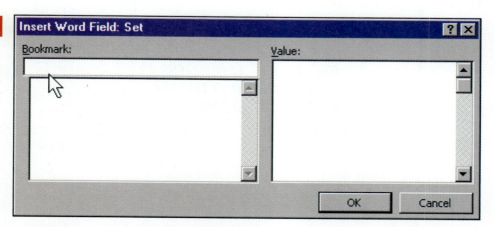

3. Choose the **Set Bookmark** option.

   Note: The Insert Word Field: Set dialog box displays (see Figure 24.7).

4. Type the desired information in the Bookmark box.

   For example, type **department** in the Bookmark box.

5. Click in the **Value** box and type the desired information.

   For example, type **Foreign Investment**. (Do not type the period.)

6. Select **OK**.

   Note: The Set Bookmark field displays in the document, i.e., { SET department "Foreign Investment" I} displays. Notice the I-beam (bookmark indicator) that displays before the final brace.

Insert the Bookmark Using the Cross-reference Feature

7. Place the insertion point where the bookmark is to be located.

   For example, place the insertion point in the first body text paragraph between the words "the" and "Department."

8. Select **Insert, Cross-reference**.

9. Choose the desired **Reference type**, **Insert reference to**, and **For which bookmark** options.

   For example, select **Bookmark** in the Reference type box, check that **Bookmark text** is highlighted in the Insert reference to box, and that **department** displays in the For which bookmark box.

10. Select **Insert**.

    Note: The Cross-reference field code displays, i.e., { REF department \h }, and the Cross-reference dialog box remains in the document window.

Finish-Up Instructions

❖ Use steps 7–10 and the following information to place another bookmark in the document.

   a. If necessary, scroll down or move the Cross-reference dialog box to display the first line of the second body text paragraph.

   b. Place the insertion point between the first two words, i.e., "The" and "Department."

   c. Click anywhere in the **Cross-reference** dialog box.

   d. Check that **Bookmark** is highlighted in the Reference type box, that **Bookmark text** is highlighted in the Insert reference to box, and that **department** is highlighted in the For which bookmark box.

   e. Select **Insert**.

❖ Select **Close** to exit the Cross-reference dialog box.

❖ Turn off field codes (select **Tools**, **Options**, choose **Field Codes** on the **View** tab, **OK**).

- Use the *new* filename **24Job Main bookmark.doc** and save the file.

- Select the **Check for Errors** button  on the Mail Merge Toolbar; select **Complete the merge, pausing to report each error as it occurs**; select **OK**.

  Note: Scroll through the letters and notice the results of the Set Bookmark fields. Also, check for any possible errors.

- Close the merged letters but do not save. Correct any errors in the main document.

- Optional. Select the **Merge to New Document** button; print one copy of each letter.

- Optional. Save the merged letters; use the filename **24Job Merge.doc**.

- Close all document windows.

The Next Step

Chapter Review and Activities

Self-Check Quiz
Language Arts
Activities
Challenge Your Skills

Self-Check Quiz

T F 1. The IF field can be used in the main document to control extra horizontal spacing when fields are empty.

T F 2. The **Check for Errors** button on the Mail Merge Toolbar can be used to identify a field name in the main document that does not match a field name in the data source file.

T F 3. Data from a different Microsoft application can be merged with a main document.

T F 4. One reason for using a Set Bookmark field is to insert information that has not been saved in the data source file.

T F 5. The Find Record feature is used to reduce the memory needed during the merge operation.

6. A data source file from a different Microsoft application, such as _____, can be merged with a Word document.
    a. Microsoft Access
    b. Microsoft Excel
    c. both a and b
    d. none of these

7. The three main sections in the Insert Word Field: IF dialog box are: IF, Insert this text, and _____.
    a. Otherwise insert this text
    b. Never insert this text
    c. Constantly insert this text
    d. none of the above

8. The _____ button is used to identify a mistake(s) when the main document and data source files are merged.
    a. **Merge to New Document**
    b. **Merge to Printer**
    c. **Find Record**
    d. **Check for Errors**

9. Give one example of why you would use the Fill-in field in a main document.

10. What is the difference between using a Fill-in field and using the Set Bookmark field?

Enriching Language Arts Skills

Spelling/Vocabulary Words

collect—to gather; to pick up.
cooperation—the act of working together.
initiation—beginning, start.
profitability—to make more money than an item costs.
separate—to sort into groups; to set or keep apart.

Abbreviations for Time

Type a.m. and p.m. with lowercase letters and no space between. Only one period is used if the abbreviation is the last element in a sentence.

Example: The planning meeting will begin at 9:30 a.m. and adjourn at 3:15 p.m.

Note: If Word's Insert, Date and Time command or a date-type Text Form Field are used, the time will be formatted AM or PM regardless of how the abbreviations are typed.

Activities

▣ Activity 24.1—Create a Main Document; Use IF and Fill-in Fields

1. Open the file named **24act1.doc** located on the data disk.

2. Use the following guidelines to link a graphic image to the main document and insert If...Then...Else... and Fill-in fields:

   a. Attach the data source file **24FirstBank Data.doc**. (Select the **Mail Merge Helper** button, **Get Data**, **Open Data Source**. Select the drive/folder where the data disk is located and double-click on **24FirstBank Data.doc**. Select **Close**.)

   b. If necessary, turn on field codes (select **Tools**, **Option**s, choose **Field codes** in the View tab, select **OK**).

   c. Insert an IF field in the inside address to avoid a blank horizontal space in records without a title (locate the insertion point to the left of the {MERGEFIELD FirstName} field code, select the **Insert Word Field** button, select **If...Then...Else...**, make sure **Title** appears in the Field name box, click in the **Comparison** box, scroll down and select **is not blank**, click in the **Insert this text** box, press **Ctrl** and **F9**, type MERGEFIELD Title, press the **right** arrow key twice, press the **Spacebar** once, select **OK**).

   d. Locate the insertion point to the left of the colon in the salutation and insert an IF field (select the **Insert Word Field** button, select **If...Then...Else...**, make sure **Title** appears in the Field name box, click in the **Comparison** box, scroll down, select **is not blank**, click in the **Insert this text** box, press **Ctrl** and **F9**, type MERGEFIELD Title, press the **right** arrow key twice, press the **Spacebar** once, press **Ctrl** and **F9**, type MERGEFIELD LastName, click in the **Otherwise insert this text** box, press **Ctrl** and **F9**, type MERGEFIELD FirstName, select **OK**).

   e. Change the font size to **12** for the **New If Merge** fields. (Select the **If Merge** field code after the salutation and click on the **Font Size** button and choose **12**. Select the **If Merge** field code at the beginning of the salutation and change the font size to **12**.

Note: Be sure to select the entire code so it is dark gray.

   f. Insert a Fill-in field that will request the new line of credit amount for each letter (locate the insertion point in the second body text paragraph to the left of the period in the first sentence; select the **Insert Word Field** button, choose **Fill-in**; in the Prompt box, type **Enter new credit line amount for:**, choose **OK** twice).

   g. Edit the Fill-in field so that the last name will appear in the Fill-in message box as each letter is merged (locate the insertion point between the word "for" and the colon in the FILLIN code, press the

Spacebar once, select the **Insert Merge Field** button, select **LastName**).

3. Change the x's in the reference initials to your initials.

4. Change the filename below the reference initials to **24FirstBank Main.doc**.

5. Use the *new* filename **24FirstBank Main.doc** and save the file on your file disk.

6. Merge the document with user input and use the following information (select the **Merge to New Document** button, type the desired amount, choose **OK**).

Marcus	$8,500
Dalzell	$7,800
Eckles	$10,000
Honea	$9,000

7. Turn off the display of field codes (select **Tools**, **Options**, select the **Field codes** option on the View tab, select **OK**).

8. Scroll through the letters and check for accuracy.

9. Print one copy of the merged letters.

10. Optional. Use the filename **24FirstBank Merge.doc** and save the merged letters.

11. Optional. Write an e-mail message to your instructor that you are sending this document. Attach this file to your e-mail message.

12. Close all documents.

*Note: It is not necessary to save changes to **24FirstBank Main.doc**.*

Challenge Your Skills

Skill 24.1—Set Bookmark and IF fields; Language Arts

1. Open the file named **24Skill Main.doc** located on the data disk. If necessary, turn on the display of field codes.

2. Select the **Mail Merge Helper** button to check that the **24Skill data** document is attached. If necessary, attach the data source file named **24Skill data.doc** located on the data disk. Use the **Get Data** button, **Open Data Source** option in the Mail Merge Helper dialog box.

3. Create a Set Bookmark field using the following information:

   a. Place the Set Bookmark field one line space above the date code.

   b. Use the bookmark name **area_name**.

   c. In the Value box, type **East Hartford**.

   d. Use the Cross-reference feature to insert the bookmark between the words "the" and "area" in the first sentence of the body text.

4. Insert the following paragraph between the two body text paragraphs. Place an IF...Then...Else field in the last sentence between the words "than" and "on" [create a field that will print 5:30 a.m. if the street address (Address1) is less than or equal to 999; otherwise, print 5:45 a.m.].

Note: Correct four spelling errors, four punctuation/grammatical errors, and one misused word.

Two recycling containers will be issued to each household and delivered during regular collections during the last week in December. Newspapers must be kept seperate from other recycled materials and placed in the container marked "Newspapers Only." The recycling containers must be placed on the curb no later than (place IF...Then...Else field here) on the day when your trash is normally colected. In addition trash collection will occur approximately one-half hour after collection of the recycling containers, but no later than 8A.M.

5. Make decisions regarding reference initials and the document identification notation.

6. Use the *new* filename **24Recycle Main.doc** and save the main document.

7. Merge the main document **24Recycle Main.doc** with the data source file **24Skill data.doc**.

8. Optional. Use the filename **24Recycle Merge.doc** and save the merged letters.

9. Print one copy of each merged letter.

10. Close all documents.

Part 6
Checking Your Step

Production Project 6.1—Create a Multi-Page Outline

1. Create the following outline. The paragraphs have been indented to show levels for outline numbering. Make decisions regarding:

    Margins
    Header/footer text and placement
    Outline numbering and spacing

Health care benefits
    Eligibility and coverage
        Who is eligible
        When coverage begins
            Employee coverage
            Dependent coverage
        When to enroll
            Upon employment
            Annual open enrollment
            Dependents
            At retirement
        Changing coverage
            Adding dependents
            Deleting dependents
        Contributions
            Employer's contribution
            Employee's contribution
            Retiree's contribution
            During a personal leave
        When coverage ends
        Other rules

Medical plan
    Overview
    Definitions
        Doctor
        Medically necessary treatment
        Deductible and copayment
        Allowable fee
    How to file claims
        Claims administrator
        How and when to file
        Appeal process for denied claims
    Inpatient hospital and surgery benefits
    Extended medical care
        Hospice
        Home health
        Skilled nursing facility care
    Outpatient facility and surgery benefits
    Other medical benefits
        Limited surgical procedures
        Maternity and family planning
        Psychiatric benefits
        Chiropractic treatment
    Exclusions from coverage
    Payment of benefits
Dental plan
    Diagnostic and preventative care
    Deductible
    Basic dental services
    Dental maximum
Time off benefits
Vacation
    Eligibility
    Accrual
Holidays
Personal choice days
    Eligibility
    Accrual
Sick leave
    Eligibility
    Accrual
Retirement benefits
Employee Retirement Income Security Act
ERISA-covered plans
    401(k) plans
    Defined contribution plans
    Defined benefit plans
Claiming benefits

2. Use the filename **6pBenefits outline.doc** and save the outline.

3. Print one copy.

4. Optional. Fax this document to your instructor via a local fax, or write an e-mail message to your instructor that you are sending this assignment. Attach this file to your e-mail message.

5. Close the document.

■ Production Project 6.2—Use the Revisions–Track Changes and Compare Documents Features

1. Open the file named **6pact2.doc** located on the data disk.

2. Turn on the Track Changes feature.

3. Locate each comment in the document and make the necessary changes to the document.

4. Use the *new* filename **6pminutes.doc** and save the file on your file disk.

5. Print one copy of the document with the marked changes.

6. Accept all the revisions and save the document using the same filename.

7. Turn off the Track Changes feature.

8. Make decisions regarding:

> Margins
> Fonts
> Header text
> Page number

9. Print the final document.

10. Close the document.

Production Project 6.3—Create a Form Using the Tables Feature

1. Use the Tables feature to create a form similar to the form shown on page 610. Make decisions regarding:

> Margins
> Number of rows and columns
> Font and size of text
> Formulas
> Merging and splitting cells
> Alignment and number format for cells
> Table borders and shading for cells
> Centering the table vertically and/or horizontally on the page

Snipes Roofing Company
46574 Parker Avenue

206-555-ROOF
Seattle, WA 98122

JOB WORK ORDER			
Job Name:		Bill To:	
Address:		Address:	
City/State/Zip		City/State/Zip	
Phone:		Phone:	

Description of Work	Estimated Cost

Order Date:		Actual Labor	
Order Taken By:		Actual Materials	
Start Date:		Total Labor & Materials	0.00
Contractor:		Tax (6.25%)	0.00
Date Completed:		Total Price	$ 0.00
I hereby acknowledge the satisfactory completion of the above described work:		Customer's Signature	Date:

Create a formula to add actual labor and actual materials

Create a formula to multiply total labor and materials by .0625

Create a formula to add total labor and materials and tax

2. Use the filename **6pWork order.doc** and save the form.

3. Print one copy.

4. Use the following information to fill in the form.

   a. Use your name and address for the Job Name, Address, City/State/Zip, Phone number, and Bill To information.

   b. In the Description of Work section, type **Repair leaks caused by storm.**

   c. In the Estimated Cost section, type **$975**.

d. Enter last Monday's date as the Order Date. The order was taken by **Janine**. Enter last Tuesday's date as the Start Date. The Contractor is **E. Niven**. Enter yesterday's date as the Date Completed.

e. The actual cost of labor was **$585.00**. The actual cost of materials was **$401.90**.

5. To update a formula, select the cell containing the formula and press **F9**.

6. Use the *new* filename **6pWork order 1.doc** and save the file on your file disk.

7. Print one copy of the completed form.

8. Optional. Fax this document to your instructor via a local fax, or write an e-mail message to your instructor that you are sending this assignment. Attach this file to your e-mail message.

9. Close the document.

❖❖ ▪ Production Project 6.4—Create Cross-references and an Index; Language Arts

1. Open the file named **6pact4.doc** located on the data disk.

2. Make decisions regarding:

> Margins
> Header/footer text
> Page numbering

3. Correct two spelling errors, two misused words, one number error, one percentage error, and two punctuation errors.

4. Create bookmarks for the two figures (tables) and for each of the four funds described on pages 3–6 of the document.

5. Review the document and create the needed cross-references. The cross-reference locations have been marked in the text with an asterisk (*). Delete the asterisk and insert the appropriate cross-references created in step 4.

6. Use the filename **6pAlden CAP.doc** and save the file on your file disk.

7. Develop a concordance file to use for indexing the document. Remember, the entries in the first column of the concordance file must match exactly the case (upper and lower) of the words in the document. The following are the main index heading entries:

> Capital Accumulation Program
> Risk
> Return
> Growth Stock Fund
> General Stock Fund
> Real Estate Fund
> Principal Fund

8. Use the filename **6pConcordance.doc** and save the concordance file.

9. Use the concordance file and mark all occurrences of the main index headings in the file named **6pAlden CAP.doc**. Format and compile the index on a separate page at the end of the document.

10. Save the file and print one copy.

11. Close the document.

Special Supplement

Integrating Microsoft Office

- Microsoft Excel

- Microsoft Access

- Microsoft PowerPoint

Integrating Microsoft Office

Features Covered

- Create a workbook in Excel
- Enter data in Excel
- Use formulas in Excel
- Format an Excel worksheet
- Create an Excel chart
- Link an Excel worksheet to a Word document
- Update linked documents
- Create a presentation using PowerPoint
- Link an Excel chart to a PowerPoint presentation
- Add a build animation and transition effect to a slide
- Create a database in Access
- Import a table into an Access database
- Use the Table Wizard
- Create and use a data entry form
- Create queries and reports

The Microsoft Office Suite

The Microsoft Office Suite is a group of software programs, often called applications or application programs, that provides many of the software functions necessary in the business office. The programs included in Microsoft Office Professional Edition are Word (word processing), Excel (electronic spreadsheet), Access (database), PowerPoint (presentations), Outlook (personal information manager), and Front Page (Web site creation and management tool). (See Microsoft Office program icons in Figure I.1.) Microsoft Office is designed to work well in the Windows environment and to increase productivity and accuracy. Some of the ways in which it does this are:

FIGURE I.1

Microsoft Office
program icons:
Word, Excel,
PowerPoint,
Access, and
FrontPage

**Microsoft
Word**

**Microsoft
Excel**

**Microsoft
PowerPoint**

**Microsoft
Access**

**Microsoft
FrontPage**

a. Microsoft programs use as many standard keystrokes and screen displays as possible. For example:

➤ Opening a file, saving a file, and closing a file are the same in Excel and PowerPoint as they are in Word 2000.

➤ The Online Help function for each of the programs can be activated using the instructions on pages 36–38 for using the Help feature.

b. Information can be easily transferred between all programs in Microsoft Office and can often be linked between applications. This reduces rekeying and allows up-to-date information to be available immediately.

c. The Microsoft programs retain some custom information across applications. For example, in any Open dialog box, you can designate folders to be placed in your "My Favorites" group. The same "My Favorites" group of folders is available in all Office applications, making it easier to find frequently used folders and to share information between applications.

d. Documents can be easily shared with co-workers across a network by sending the files directly to the co-worker via e-mail, by faxing documents directly from within the application, or by posting the files to a shared network folder. Co-workers can add notes to files suggesting changes or adding information, and documents can be reviewed and changed easily.

The example we will use throughout this chapter is the creation of an annual report by the LJK companies: LJK Holding Corp. (LJKH) and LJK Enterprises, Inc. (LJKE). Producing the combined annual report for these two intertwined companies involves many people working in all the Microsoft Office applications.

Create a Workbook in Excel

Microsoft Excel is an electronic spreadsheet program, most commonly used to perform numerical calculations rapidly and accurately. Within Excel, each individual spreadsheet is called a worksheet. Several worksheets can be combined in one file, referred to as a workbook.

In some ways, an Excel worksheet is similar to a Word table. For example, the **Tab** key is pressed to move from one column to the next, and a worksheet can be formatted by adding borders to the cells, changing fonts and font sizes, adding shading, or changing alignment. Also, columns are designated by letters, starting with A at the left and ascending through the alphabet to the right. Rows are numbered, starting with 1. The cell address consists of the column letter and the row number. For example, the first cell in the worksheet is always cell A1, and the address of the cell in the second column, third row, is always B3.

The information you need to complete the Excel spreadsheets in this chapter is summarized in Figure I.2. More information is available by selecting **Help** and using either the **Microsoft Excel Help or Show the Office Assistant** to research a particular topic.

In Excel, a cell must be selected before you start typing the data or formula. To select a cell, move the mouse pointer to the desired cell and click once. A dark border, called a *cell pointer*, will appear around the selected cell. When information is typed, the information will appear in the cell and in the Formula bar. After entering the data or formula, click once on the check mark button ✓ (called the **Enter** button) in the Formula bar to confirm the entry and to remain in the same cell, or press **Enter** to confirm the entry and to move to the next

Movement	Keystroke or Mouse Action
Left one cell	Press the ← key.
Right one cell	Press the → key.
Up one row	Press the ↑ key.
Down one row	Press the ↓ key.
First cell in next row	Press the ↓ key, then press **Home**.
First cell in worksheet	Press **Ctrl** and **Home**.
First cell in current row	Press **Home**.
Last cell in current row	Press **End**.
Move to any cell in worksheet	Move mouse pointer to cell and click.
Confirm entry, then stay in current cell	Click the ✓ button.
Confirm entry, then move one row down	Press **Enter**.
Confirm entry, then move one row up	Press **Shift** and **Enter**.
Confirm entry, then move one column to the right	Press **Tab**.
Confirm entry, then move one column to the left	Press **Shift** and **Tab**.
Change worksheet	Move the mouse pointer to the tab for the desired worksheet and click the left mouse button.
Name worksheet	Move the mouse pointer to the tab for the worksheet and click the *right* mouse button. Select **Rename**. Type the new worksheet name. Select **OK**.

FIGURE I.2

Excel keystrokes and mouse actions

row, in the same column. To move to the right, press **Tab**. Data in a spreadsheet are often entered from top to bottom instead of across rows. This is why pressing **Enter** moves the cell pointer to the next row, in the same column instead of going to the same row in the next column.

To edit a cell after data has been entered, select the cell, then press **F2** or move the mouse pointer to the Formula bar and click once in the Formula box where the cell contents are displayed. Use the **Backspace** or **Delete** keys to erase the error, then type the correct information and click on the **Enter** button or press **Enter**.

To select a group of cells, move the mouse pointer to the first cell and click once. Hold down the left mouse button and drag the mouse to select all of the desired cells. Release the mouse button. The first cell will appear with the cell pointer around it, while the other cells will appear with a dark background. The LJK companies have three financial reports in their annual report. We will create the first one here and the other two later.

 Steps to ## Open Excel and Start a New Workbook

Method 1: From the Windows Desktop

1. Select **Start, Programs, Microsoft Excel**.

    Note: Excel will open, displaying a blank workbook with the cell pointer in cell A1 of the first worksheet (see Figure I.3).

Method 2: From the Microsoft Office Shortcut Bar

1. Select the **Microsoft Excel** button from the Microsoft Office Shortcut Bar.

    Note: Excel will open, displaying a blank workbook with the cell pointer in cell A1 of the first worksheet (see Figure 1.3).

FIGURE I.3

Microsoft Excel worksheet

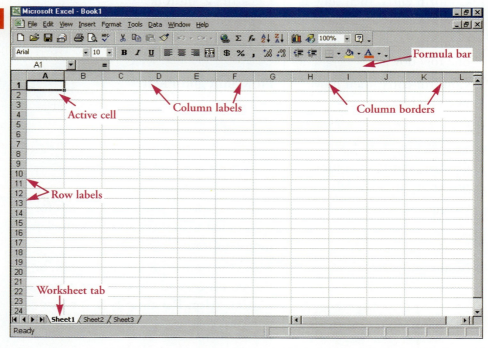

Finish-Up Instructions

❖ Practice navigating in the worksheet using the vertical and horizontal scroll bars and the mouse actions and/or keystrokes shown in Figure I.2.

❖ Continue with the Steps to Enter Data in Excel.

Start-Up Instructions

❖ The Excel program should be open with a blank worksheet displayed. (If necessary, open the Excel program using the Steps to Open Excel and Start a New Workbook from the previous section.)

❖ The cell pointer should be in cell A1. (If necessary, press **Ctrl** and **Home** to move the cell pointer to cell A1.)

 Steps to Enter Data in Excel

1. Type the title, subtitle, and column labels shown in the first three rows in Figure I.4. Refer to Figure I.2 for assistance in moving from cell to cell and row to row.

   Note: Type an apostrophe before typing the year in the column labels. This will let Excel know this is a text number, not a value. The column widths will be adjusted later. Don't worry if some of your text does not fit into column A.

Change Column Width in Excel

2. To increase the size of a column to fit the longest text in it, move the mouse pointer to the column line between the column labels until a double-headed arrow appears, then double-click.

   For example, after typing the first three rows of data, move the mouse pointer to the column label row between columns A and B until the double-headed arrow appears, and double-click.

3. Type the remainder of the information in Figure I.4 into the Excel worksheet. Adjust the column widths if necessary so that each item appears on one line. If you notice a mistake while still in the cell, correct it using the **Backspace** or **Delete** keys. For now, ignore mistakes after you leave the cell.

	A	B	C	D	E
1	Consolidated Financial Statement				
2	(Dollars in Millions)				
3		1999	1998	1997	
4	Net Sales (1)	13,724	12,244	11,244	
5	Cost of Goods Sold	5,624	5,243	4,233	
6	Advertising	822	277	433	
7	General Expenses (2)	4,600	4,550	3,422	
8	Operating Income (3)				

FIGURE I.4

Worksheet data

Name a Worksheet

4. Move the mouse pointer to the tab of the worksheet to be renamed and click the *right* mouse button.

   For example, move the mouse pointer to the tab labeled **Sheet1** and click the *right* mouse button.

5. Select **Rename**.

6. Type the new worksheet name. Press **Enter** or select **OK**.

   For example, type **Consolidated**, then press **Enter**.

Save the Workbook

7. Select the **Save** button on the Formatting Toolbar.

   *Note: The Save As dialog box will appear when the file is saved for the first time. After the file has been named, selecting the **Save** button will automatically save the current version of the file to the same filename.*

8. In the Save in box, select the drive/folder where the file is to be saved.

   For example, select the drive/folder containing your file disk.

9. Type the filename in the File name box.

   For example, if necessary, highlight the name Book1 by double-clicking on book1. Then type **Workbook for Annual Report** in the File name box.

10. Select **Save**.

11. To close the file, click on the inner **Close** button. To close **Excel**, click on the **Close** button on the top line of the screen.

    For example, click on the **Close** button on the top line of the screen to close Excel.

Use Formulas in Excel

Formulas are used in Excel to perform calculations such as adding and multiplying. Using a cell address in a formula is called *cell referencing*. When a value in a cell changes, any formula using that cell reference will automatically be recalculated. Formulas must start with an equals sign (=) and contain operators that determine what calculation will be performed. Four common operators are:

+ Addition
- Subtraction
* Multiplication
/ Division

When more than one operation is performed in a calculation, each operation is placed within parentheses. Excel always performs calculations starting with the innermost set of parentheses and working outward. For instance, in the Formula =(B3+C3)/C4, Excel would first add the values in B3 and C3 and then divide that number by the value in C4.

Formulas can be typed directly into cells or inserted into cells using the **Insert**, **Function** command. After selecting **Insert**, **Function** then selecting the Function category and Function name, the Function Wizard will guide you through the steps necessary to create the formula. While creating a formula, cell addresses can be added either by typing the cell address or by moving the mouse pointer to the cell address and clicking once.

When Excel copies formulas from one cell to another, it normally changes the cell references to match the relationship of the cell references in the original cell. For example, the formula =A1+A2+A3 is placed in cell A4, then copied to cell B4. In cell B4, the copied formula will read B1+B2+B3 because Excel noted that the relationship of the cells in the formula to the cell containing the formula was that they were all in the same column. This is known as *relative cell referencing*.

Sometimes, however, you will not want the cell address to change. For example, you may want to multiply each column by the value in cell D5. When the same cell is to be used, it is called *absolute cell referencing*, and must be designated by placing a dollar sign ($) in front of the cell column and cell number in the formula. For example, the formula =$D$5*(A1+A2) would add the contents of cells A1 and A2, then multiply the sum by the contents of cell D5. When the formula is copied from column A to column B, the formula would read =$D$5*(B1+B2).

 ## Open an Existing Workbook in Excel

1. Select the **Open Office Document** button on the Microsoft Office Shortcut Bar.
2. In the Look in box, select the drive/folder containing the workbook.
   For example, select the drive/folder containing your file disk.
3. Double-click on the workbook name.
   For example, double-click on the filename **Workbook for Annual Report.xls**.

Finish-Up Instructions

❖ Continue with the Steps to Add a Formula.

 ## Add a Formula

1. Click in the cell where the formula is to be located.
   For example, move the mouse pointer to cell B8 and click once.
2. Select **Insert, Function**.

   Note: The Paste Function dialog box displays.
3. Select the desired options in the Function category and Function name lists.
   For example, select **Math & Trig** in the Function category list. In the Function name list, scroll down and select **SUM**.
4. Select **OK**.

Note: The Formula Palette (SUM box) with the range B4:B7 in the Number 1 box displays. The message "Add all the numbers in a range of cells" also displays.

5. In the Number 1 box, type the address of the first cell to be used in the calculation, or move the **SUM** box so the first cell is visible. Click once on the cell to automatically insert the address in the Number 1 box.

    For example, move the Formula Palette SUM box to the upper right corner of the screen (move the mouse pointer to the top of the SUM box, hold down the left mouse button, and drag the box to the desired location; release the mouse button) and click once in the cell containing 1999 net sales (cell **B4**).

    Note: A marquee (a dashed border) flashes around cell B4.

6. Click once in the **Number 2** box and type the next cell address or the remainder of the formula.

    For example, click in the **Number 2** box and type -(**B5+B6+B7**).

    Note: Make sure the minus sign is placed in front of the first parenthesis. This formula will add the expenses together then subtract their sum from the Net Sales.

7. Select **OK** to insert the formula results into the cell.

    Note: The formula displays in the Formula bar, e.g., =SUM(B4,-(B5+B6+B7)). The formula will be displayed in the Formula bar until another cell is selected. The results of the calculation will appear in the cell.

Finish-Up Instructions

❖   Continue with the Steps to Copy a Formula to Another Cell.

 ## Copy a Formula to Another Cell

1. Select the cell to be copied by moving the mouse pointer to the desired cell and clicking once.

    For example, make sure cell B8 is selected.

2. Select the **Copy** button.

    Note: The border around cell B8 will change to a dashed border (called a marquee) *and will flash.*

3. Move the mouse pointer to the cell in which the formula is to be copied and click once to select it.

    For example, move the mouse pointer to cell **C8** and click once.

    Note: The dark border will move to C8 indicating it is selected. The flashing dashed border remains around cell B8.

4. Select the **Paste** button.

    Note: The formula has been copied, and the cell addresses in the formula have been changed from "B" to "C."

Shortcut:

1. Point to the bottom right corner of the outlined cell until a crosshair displays (+). Point, click, and hold while dragging the mouse to the desired cell(s).

Finish-Up Instructions

❖ Copy the formula to cell D8 then exit the Copy mode (move the cell pointer to D8, select **Paste**, press **Esc**).

*Note: After the last copy, press **Esc** to exit the Copy mode. To copy the formula to only one location, press **Enter**, which copies the formula and exits the Copy mode automatically.*

❖ Save the workbook using the same name (select the **Save** button).

Format an Excel Worksheet

In order to make data more readable, Excel offers many formatting options. To apply formatting, select the desired cells then the formatting options. Many of the options are similar to those in Word. For instance, to apply the text attribute of bold to the data in a cell, select the cell then the **Bold** button on the Formatting Toolbar. By default, text in cells is aligned at the left of the cell and values are aligned to the right. However, these defaults can be changed using the alignment buttons in the Formatting Toolbar. For more complex formatting options, select the cell or cells, click the *right* mouse button, and select **Format, Cells, Bold** on the Font tab. The width, number type, borders, and other formatting options are available in this menu. After setting the items as desired, select **OK** to exit the Formatting pane. When all desired formatting options have been applied, click once on any cell in the worksheet to deselect the cells.

One common formatting trick is to center the title of a worksheet across all the columns that contain data. This is done by selecting the columns over which the title is to be spread then clicking on the **Merge and Center** button ⊞. The Formatting Toolbar also contains buttons for adding borders to the cells, changing the cell's background color, and changing the color of the data in the cell. See Figure I.3 or move the mouse pointer to any button and wait a few seconds for the ToolTip to display.

To increase the row size to allow more white space, move the mouse pointer to the border line between rows until a double-headed arrow displays. Drag the mouse up or down until the row is the desired height.

While working in spreadsheets, you will often see a group of cells (a range) referred to as cell address 1:cell address 2, i.e., A1:B2. This is a shorthand method for referring to the range of cells that begins with cell address 1 and ends with cell address 2. For example, A1:B2 refers to all the cells in the range A1 through B2, which would be cells A1, A2, B1, and B2. This method of identifying a range of cells can be used whenever the cells are in a contiguous group. It is particularly useful in formulas in which it might be difficult to list all the individual cells.

Start-Up Instructions

❖ Excel should be open and the workbook **Workbook for Annual Report.xls** displayed on the screen.

 Format a Worksheet

1. Click on the first cell to be formatted, hold the left mouse button down, and drag to select all the desired cells. Release the mouse button.

   For example, select cells **A1:D1.** (Click on cell A1. Hold the left mouse button down and drag to select cells B1, C1, and D1. Release the mouse button.)

2. Select the desired formatting options.

   For example, click on the **Merge and Center** button. Click on the down triangle next to the **Fill Color** button. Select the aqua color in the third row. Click on the down triangle next to the **Font Color** button and select the **Dark Blue** color in the first row. Click on the down triangle next to the **Font Size** box and select **16.** Click on the **Bold** button. Select A2:D2 and choose the **Merge and Center** button.

3. Increase the height of any row in which additional white space is needed.

   For example, touch the mouse pointer on the row border between rows 2 and 3 along the left side of the worksheet until a double-headed arrow displays. Hold the left mouse button down and drag the line down approximately $^1/_8$". Release the mouse button.

4. Add borders to cells to provide separations, which make data easier to read, by selecting the cells, clicking on the down triangle next to the **Borders** button, and selecting the desired border.

   For example, select cells **A2:D2** (cells A2, B2, C2, and D2), then select the down arrow next to the **Borders** button. Click on the thick bottom border (second button in second row).

5. Change the alignment of column headings, if necessary, by selecting the cells then selecting the desired alignment button.

   For example, select cells **B3:D3** then click on the **Center** alignment button in the Formatting Toolbar. Click once to deselect the cells.

Finish-Up Instructions

❖ Add bottom borders to rows 4 and 8.

❖ Save the workbook using the same filename, **Workbook for Annual Report**.xls.

FIGURE I.5

LJK Holding
Worksheet

	A	B	C
1	1999	1998	1997
2	5,302	5,996	6,257
3	3,161	3,130	1,281
4	329	299	220
5	2,300	2,117	2,308

 Steps to   ## Create a Second Worksheet in a Workbook

1. Click on the tab for the next worksheet.

   For example, click on the **Sheet2** tab.

   Note: The next worksheet will display.

2. Name the worksheet if desired. Move the mouse pointer to the worksheet tab, and click the *right* mouse button. Select **Rename**, type the new name, then press **Enter**.

   For example, name the worksheet **LJK Holding 1999**.

Finish-Up Instructions

❖ Enter the data shown in Figure I.5. Remember to type an apostrophe before the dates (1999, 1998, and 1997).

❖ Format the worksheet to make it easier to read and more attractive.

❖ Save the workbook using the same filename.

Create an Excel Chart

The Excel Chart program is used to create graphs that illustrate worksheet data. First, select the cells to be included in the chart; then select the **ChartWizard** button. The ChartWizard displays and will walk you through the selection of a chart type and format. Use the Chart Toolbar to make any later formatting changes to add to the attractiveness and readability of the chart.

Both the data and the chart can be printed. If a color printer is available, the chart will print in color. To print the entire workbook, select the **Print** button, and choose the **Entire Workbook** option in the Print What section. To print only a portion of the worksheet, select the range of cells to be printed, **File**, **Print Area**, **Set Print Area**. Then select the **Print** button.

Start-Up Instructions

❖ Excel should be open and the workbook named **Workbook for Annual Report.xls** displayed on the screen.

❖ Select the **Consolidated** worksheet tab.

Create an Excel Chart

1. Select the cells to be included in the chart.

   For example, select cells **A3:D8** on the Consolidated worksheet.

2. Select the **ChartWizard** button on the Standard Toolbar.

   Note: The ChartWizard - Step 1 of 4 - Chart Type dialog box will appear.

3. Select the desired Chart type and Chart subtype, and then select **Next**.

   For example, if necessary, select the **Column** chart type. Select **Clustered column with a 3-D visual effect** (second row, first sample), then select **Next**.

   Note: The Chart Wizard - Step 2 of 4 displays.

4. Select the desired Data Range and Series in options.

   For example, check that the Data range **=Consolidated!$A$3:$D:$8** displays. Choose **Series in Rows**.

5. Select **Next**.

   Note: The Chart Wizard - Step 3 of 4 displays.

6. Fill in the desired options.

   For example, type the following:

Chart title	**Consolidated Statement 1997-1999**
Axis titles	Leave blank

7. Select **Next**.

   Note: The Chart Wizard - Step 4 of 4 displays.

8. Choose the desired option.

   For example, click on **As New Sheet**.

9. Choose **Finish**.

   Note: The chart will appear on the screen, with a tab labeled Chart1. Move and resize the legend as needed.

Finish-Up Instructions

❖ Click in any cell outside the chart to deselect it.

   Note: Your chart should look similar to the chart shown in Figure I.6.

❖ Save the workbook using the same filename.

Set a Print Area to Print a Portion of a Worksheet

1. Select the area of the worksheet to be printed.

   For example, on the Consolidated worksheet, select cells **A1:D8**.

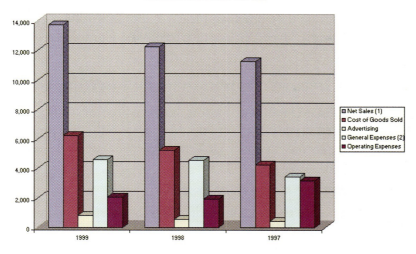

Consolidated Statement 1997-1999

FIGURE I.6

Excel chart

2. Select File, Print Area, Set Print Area.

3. Select the Print Preview button.

4. Select the Print button.

   Note: The Print dialog box displays.

5. Select OK.

Finish-Up Instructions

❖ Clear the print area (select **File**, **Print Area**, **Clear Print Area**).

❖ Save the workbook using the same filename.

Link an Excel Worksheet to a Word Document

After a worksheet has been created in Excel, it can be linked to a Word document, to a PowerPoint presentation, or even converted into an Access database. One advantage of linking the worksheet to a Word document is that any changes made to the worksheet in Excel will be reflected in the Word document because the Word document is using the original Excel file. The information can be linked by opening the Word document, and using the **Insert**, **Object**, **Create from File**, **Link to file** command to insert the worksheet as a Microsoft Excel object. This method can be used even if the person inserting the file does not know Excel or does not have direct access to the Excel program.

After linking the worksheet to the Word document, updates can be made automatically or manually. The default is for the updates to occur automatically whenever the document is opened. To update an Excel-linked spreadsheet, select Edit, Links in the Word program. Click on Open Source; the Excel program with the linked file will open. Make the changes to the spreadsheet. Click on the MS Word icon in the Taskbar. The changes will display in the Word document.

❖ The Excel program should be open, and the workbook **Workbook for Annual Report.xls** should be displayed. If necessary, select the **Consolidated** tab.

Link a Document Between Applications by Inserting an Object

1. Select the **Open Office Document** button on the Microsoft Office Shortcut Bar, select the desired drive/folder, and double-click on the filename.

   For example, open the file form **10-K Sample.doc** that is located on the data disk.

   Note: Word will start and display the selected file.

2. Scroll to the place where the worksheet data is to be inserted and click once.

   For example, scroll to page 5 and place the insertion point in the line above the words "[Insert Consolidated Worksheet from Workbook for Annual Report.xls here]" and click once.

3. Select **Insert, Object**.

   Note: The Object dialog box will appear.

4. Select the **Create from File** tab and click on the **Link to File** option.

5. Click on the **Browse** button. Double-click on the desired file. For example, double-click on **Workbook for Annual Report.xls**.

6. Select **OK**.

   Note: The copied worksheet data will appear in the document with sizing handles around it to indicate that it is the currently selected object.

Finish-Up Instructions

❖ If desired, choose a **75%** view (select **View, Zoom, 75%, OK**).

❖ Delete the line that states "[Insert Consolidated Worksheet from . . .]."

❖ Use the *new* filename **Report2.doc** and save the document on your file disk.

❖ Continue with the Steps to Update the Linked Document.

Start-Up Instructions

❖ The Word document **Report2.doc** should be displayed on the screen. The Excel program should be open and displayed as an icon on the Taskbar. If necessary, open the Excel program, and click on the **Minimize** button.

Update the Linked Document

1. In the Word screen, click on the **Spreadsheet Object**, select **Edit, Links**. Check that **Update Automatic** is selected. Click on the **Open Source** button.

2. Make the desired changes.

   For example, make the following changes to the information in the worksheet:

Delete the (3) after Operating Expenses.
Change the number in cell B5 to **6,243**.
Change the number in cell C6 to **543**.
Press **Enter** or **Tab** to move out of cell C6.

*Note: The calculations in row 8 should be automatically updated. If they do not change, press the update key, **F9**. The chart on the Chart1 tab will automatically reflect the new figures.*

3. Save the Excel workbook using the same filename.

4. Return to the Word program by clicking on the Microsoft Word icon (**Report2.doc**) in the Taskbar.

5. The numbers in the worksheet object should reflect the changes made to the linked worksheet. If they do not, select the worksheet object by clicking on it, and selecting Edit, Links. In the Links dialog box, make sure the Update Automatic option is selected or select the Update Now button.

Finish-Up Instructions

❖ Save the Word document using the same filename.

❖ Optional. Print page 5 of the **Report2.doc**. (Place the insertion point in page 5, choose **File**, **Print**; select **Current Page**, **OK**.)

❖ Close Word by selecting the **Close** button in the top row of the screen.

❖ Return to the Excel program. (If necessary, maximize the Excel worksheet window.)

❖ Optional. Print the consolidated worksheet.

❖ Close Excel by selecting the **Close** button in the top row of the screen.

Create a Presentation Using PowerPoint

PowerPoint belongs to a group of software known as presentation software or presentation graphics software. While its functions are not as well defined as word processing or spreadsheet programs, in general, presentation software makes it easier to organize and present information. PowerPoint can create slides, overhead transparencies, on-screen slide shows, speaker notes, and audience handouts.

Many attractive templates are shipped with PowerPoint. Using one of these as a starting point allows creation of an attractive presentation, even for beginners. In addition, some simple animation functions can be added to make the presentation more interesting.

If a Word document has been created using the built-in styles or outline format, it can be imported directly into PowerPoint using the Insert Slides from Outline feature. The headings will be formatted using the heading styles for the presentation template. In addition, outline text from many other word processing programs, including ASCII text files, can be imported and formatted quickly and easily.

When developing a presentation from scratch, PowerPoint's AutoContent Wizard is helpful. The AutoContent Wizard is available after selecting **File**, **New** and choosing the General tab. After going through the AutoContent Wizard dialog boxes, the template displays with a guide for writing presentations. As you delete the default text and add your own, you are also learning the basics of preparing a good presentation.

For practice, we will create a presentation for the annual shareholders meeting of the LJK companies. The slide show will be run on the computer and projected onto a large screen so everyone can view it easily.

Open PowerPoint and Begin a New Presentation

Method 1: From the Windows Desktop

1. Select Start, Programs, Microsoft PowerPoint.

    Note: PowerPoint will open, displaying the PowerPoint dialog box.

2. Select AutoContent wizard, Design Template, or Blank presentation to start a new presentation.

    For example, select Design Template.

3. Select OK.

    Note: The New Presentation dialog box displays.

4. Select the Presentation Designs tab.

Method 2: From the Microsoft Office Shortcut Bar

1. Select the Microsoft PowerPoint button on the Microsoft Office Shortcut Bar.

2. Select the desired option. For example, select **Design, Template, OK**.

❖ Continue with the Steps to Use a Design Template.

Start-Up Instructions

❖ PowerPoint should be open and the New Presentation dialog box with the **Design Templates** tab displayed.

Use a Design Template

1. Click on a template and review the design in the Preview section. Select each design until you find one that will work well with the presentation material. Select OK.

    For example, click on the template **Blends** and notice the Preview. Click on the template **Soaring** and select OK.

    Note: Microsoft PowerPoint opens with the New Slide dialog box displayed.

2. Double-click on the desired AutoLayout format for the first slide.

For example, double-click on the **Title** slide (first row, first column).

Note: The slide (Slide 1 of 1) will appear with placeholder text showing where to place the presentation title and subtitle (see Figure I.7). The outline view displays on the left side of the screen

3. Follow the instructions in the layout to replace the placeholder text with the presentation material.

For example, click in the box containing the placeholder text "Click to add title." Type the new title **LJK Enterprises**. (Do not type the period.) Click in the box containing the placeholder text "Click to add subtitle." Type the subtitle **Annual Report**.

4. Add a new slide by selecting the **New Slide** button 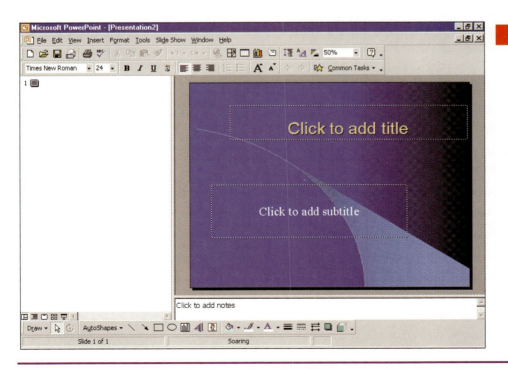 and double-clicking on the desired autolayout.

For example, select the **New Slide** button in the Standard Toolbar. Double-click on the **Bulleted List** slide (first row, second slide).

5. Follow the instructions in the layout to replace the placeholder text with the presentation material.

For example, click in the box containing the placeholder text "Click to add title." Type the title **International Holdings**. Click in the box containing the placeholder text "Click to add text." Type the following text, pressing **Enter** after each line (except the last line):

United Kingdom
New Zealand
South America
Middle East

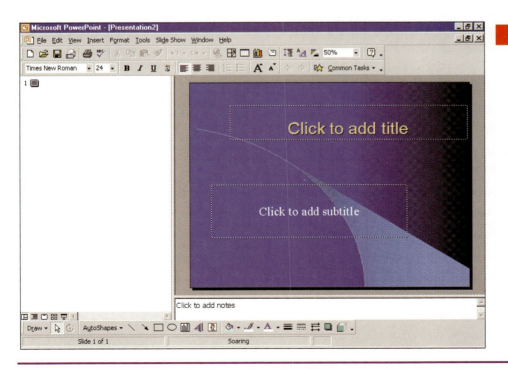

FIGURE I.7

Microsoft PowerPoint screen

6. Save the presentation by selecting the **Save** button, selecting a drive/folder, then typing a filename and selecting **Save**.

> For example, select the **Save** button. Select the drive/folder containing your file disk. Select the name in the **File Name** box and type the filename **Annual Presentation**. Select **Save**.

Finish-Up Instructions

❖ Optional. Print one copy of the presentation (select the **Print** button).

❖ Continue with the Steps to Link an Excel Chart to a PowerPoint Presentation.

Start-Up Instructions

❖ PowerPoint should be open, and the file **Annual Presentation.ppt** should be displayed.

 Steps to

Link an Excel Chart to a PowerPoint Presentation

1. Add a new slide and select a layout appropriate for a chart.

> For example, select the **New Slide** button and double-click on the the **Title Only** slide (third slide in the third row).

2. Select **Insert, Object** and click on the **Create from file** option.

3. Choose **Link** and select the **Browse...** button.

4. Select the location of your files. Double-click on **Workbook for Annual Report.xls**.

5 Select **OK**.

> *Note: The copied chart will appear in the slide with sizing handles around it to show that it is the currently selected object. Use the sizing handles and enlarge the chart so it is easier to read. (The black text of the title does not display well against the blue background. This will be changed in the following steps.)*

Change Colors in an Excel Chart Object

6. With the mouse pointer in the chart area, click the *right* mouse button once to display the Shortcut menu.

7. Move the mouse pointer to the **Linked Worksheet Object** option; click on **Edit**.

> *Note: The Excel program opens and the linked sheet for the **Workbook for Annual Report** displays.*

8. Select the range A1 through D8.

9. Click on the down triangle beside the **Fill Color** button. Click on the desired color.

> For example, click on the aqua color in the third row, fifth column.

> *Note: The chart with the new color will display.*

10. Select the **Microsoft PowerPoint** icon on the Taskbar.

    Note: The new color displays in the chart.

Finish-Up Instructions

❖ Click in the box containing the placeholder text "Click here to add title" and type **Consolidated Statement**.

❖ Save the presentation using the same filename.

❖ Close the Excel program. Select "Yes" to save changes.

Start-Up Instructions

❖ PowerPoint should be open, and the file **Annual Presentation.ppt** should be displayed.

 ### Add a Pre-drawn Shape

1. Display the slide in which the pre-drawn shape is to be added by clicking the **Next Slide** ⯆ or **Previous Slide** ⯅ buttons until the desired slide displays.

   For example, if necessary, select the **Previous Slide** button ⯅ to display slide 2.

2. Display the AutoShapes menu by clicking once on the **AutoShapes** button on the Drawing Toolbar.

3. Move the mouse pointer to the desired AutoShape category and click on the desired AutoShape.

   For example, select **Block Arrows** and click on the left-pointing arrow in the first row, second column (Left Arrow) .

   Note: The mouse pointer will change to a crosshair.

4. Move the mouse pointer to the position where the shape is to start. Hold down the left mouse button and drag until the desired shape and size are reached. Release the mouse button.

   For example, move the mouse pointer to the right of the bulleted list. Hold down the left mouse button and drag until the arrow is approximately 2" long and 1" wide. Release the mouse button.

   Note: The thick arrow will appear with sizing handles around it to indicate it is the currently selected object.

5. Change the color, pattern, or texture of the AutoShape by selecting the **Fill Color** button 🎨▾ and clicking on the desired color, or select one of the **Fill Color** options and double-click on the texture or pattern.

   For example, make sure the arrow is selected. (If necessary, select the arrow by clicking once on it.) Select the **Fill Color** button 🎨▾. Select **Fill Effects** and choose the **Texture** tab. Double-click on the **White marble** button (second row, second column).

Finish-Up Instructions

❖ Save the presentation using the same filename, **Annual Presentation.ppt**.

Start-Up Instructions

❖ PowerPoint should be open, and the file **Annual Presentation.ppt** should be displayed.

❖ Add a new slide at the end of the presentation (slide 4). (Display slide 3. Select the **New Slide** button. Select the AutoLayout **Blank** slide—third row, fourth column.)

Add Pictures or Clip Art to a Slide

1. Display the slide in which the picture is to be added.

   For example, if necessary, select the **Next Slide** 🔽 or **Previous Slide** 🔼 button to display slide 4.

2. Select **Insert, Picture, Clip Art** to display the graphics files available on your computer.

   For example, if the Microsoft Clip Gallery is installed, select **Insert, Picture, Clip Art**.

3. Double-click on the filename or the clip art desired.

   For example, in the Insert ClipArt dialog box, select **Animals** in the Category section. Click on the **lion** or click on an image of your own choice. Choose **Insert Clip** and close the **Insert ClipArt** dialog box.

4. Size and position the picture as desired.

   For example, enlarge the picture to approximately 2 ½ x 2 ½" and position the picture so that it is visually centered on the screen.

Finish-Up Instructions

❖ Save the presentation using the same filename, **Annual Presentation.ppt**.

Create an On-Screen Presentation

The slides created in PowerPoint can be used in many ways. One of the most impressive methods is to use the computer to run the slide show while projecting the computer display onto a movie screen. This allows many special effects, such as transitions from slide to slide and animation, to be easily incorporated into the presentation.

After creating each slide individually, the Slide Sorter View is used to set the animation and transition effects. Transitions are special visual effects that display as you move from one slide to the next. Many transition effects are available in PowerPoint. The transition effects can be set individually for each slide, or several slides can be set at once by holding down the **Shift** key while clicking on each slide. To move through the slide show automatically, select the **Slide Transition** button. Select the **Automatically after** in the Advance area and type the number of seconds to wait before displaying the next slide.

One animation available in PowerPoint is a "build" effect, which displays one paragraph or one word at a time. In addition, clip art or shapes can be animated to move from left to right or to "fly" across the screen. The animation can be set to occur automatically or when the mouse button is clicked.

After creating the slides and setting the transition and animation effects, select **Slide Show**, **View Show** to see how the show will look when it is played. If the slides are to advance automatically, select **Slide Show, Set Up Show**, choose **Using timings, if present** in the Advance slides section of the Set Up Show dialog box. While the slide show is playing, the Toolbars and other editing tools will disappear. If the **Manually** option in the Advance slides area has been selected, clicking on the screen will cause the next slide or next effect on the same slide to appear. Move the mouse pointer to the pop-up button at the bottom left of the screen and click once to display a menu of options, including **End Show**, **Pen**, and **Pointer** options.

When the slides and the timing are adjusted to your satisfaction, the entire presentation can be bundled onto floppy disks for use on another computer. Select **File**, **Pack and Go** to activate the Pack and Go Wizard. This will walk you through the steps needed to create a version of the slide show that can be transported to another computer. A run-time version of PowerPoint can be included that will allow the slide show to play on a computer that does not have PowerPoint installed. However, the computer must have Windows 95, 98, or Windows NT installed.

Start-Up Instructions

❖ The PowerPoint program should be open, and the file **Annual Presentation.ppt** should be displayed in the Slide View.

Add a Build Animation to a Slide

1. Go to the slide where animation is to be applied.

   For example, press the **Next Slide** ⬇ or **Previous Slide** ⬆ buttons to display slide 2.

2. Click on the area of the slide where the animation is to be applied.

   For example, click on the title **International Holdings**.

3. Click on the **Animation Effects** button ⭐. (If necessary, click on the **More Buttons** arrows at the right side of the Toolbar to display the **Animation Effects** button.)

   Note: The Animation Effects Toolbar displays.

4. Select the **Animate Title** button 🔲.

   Note: The button will appear "pressed in" to indicate it has been applied to the slide.

5. Select the **Custom Animation** button 🖼.

   Note: The Custom Animation dialog box will appear.

6. Make the desired selections in the Custom Animation dialog box. Then select **OK**.

For example, click on the **Effects** tab. Select **Fly** in the top left box of the Entry animation and sound area. Click on the down arrow next to the Right box and choose **From Top-Left** option. Select or check that **Whoosh** is displayed in the second box in the Entry animation and sound area. Make sure the **Don't Dim** option is selected in the After animation box. Check that **All at once** is displayed in the Introduce text area. Select **OK**.

Finish-Up Instructions

❖ Click on the text area listing the countries.

❖ Select the **Animate Slide Text** button 🔲 in the Animation Effects Toolbar.

❖ Select the **Custom Animation** button 🔳. Make the following selections in the Custom Animation dialog box; select **OK**.

Entry animation	**Fly, From Top**
Introduce text	**All at once; Grouped by 1st level paragraphs**
After animation	**Don't Dim**

❖ Select the **Next Slide** button twice to display slide 4, and click on the picture.

❖ Click on the lion clip art. Select the **Flying Effect** button in the Animation Effects Toolbar. Select the **Custom Animation** button 🔳. Set the options as follows; select **OK**.

Entry animation and sound	**Fly From Top-Left**
	Whoosh
After animation	**Don't Dim**

❖ Click once to deselect the picture. Close the Animation Effects Toolbar.

❖ Save the presentation using the same filename.

❖ Press **Ctrl** and **Home** to return to slide 1. Then select the **Slide Show** button on the left side of the scroll bar. Click repeatedly to observe the slides and animation effects.

Start-Up Instructions

❖ The PowerPoint program should be open, and the file **Annual Presentation.ppt** should be displayed in the Slide View.

Add a Transition Effect to a Slide

1. Go to the Slide Sorter view by clicking on the **Slide Sorter View** button 🔲 located to the left of the horizontal scroll bar, or select **View, Slide Sorter**.

   Note: A thumbnail picture of each slide displays in the Slide Sorter View.

2. Select the slide in which the transition is to be added.

For example, select all the slides by selecting **Edit, Select All**.

3. Select **Slide Show, Slide Transition**.

Note: The Slide Transition dialog box displays

4. Select the Transition type desired and any other options desired. Select **OK** when finished.

For example, click on the down arrow in the **Effect** box. Scroll down and click on **Dissolve**. Select the **Medium** option. Click on the **Automatically after** option in the advance area. Type **5** in the Seconds box. If a sound board and speakers are available on your computer, click on the down triangle next to the Sound box and select **Whoosh**. Make sure the **Loop until next sound** option is deselected (no checkmark). Select **Apply to All**.

Note: Your Slide Sorter View should look similar to the Slide Sorter View shown in Figure I.8. Notice that a small transition icon and :05 display below each slide to indicate that a transition and automatic 5 second advance has been specified for each slide. Also, animation icons display below slides 2 and 4 to indicate that animation has been specified for each of these slides.

Finish-Up Instructions

❖ Save the file using the same filename, **Annual Presentation.ppt**.

Start-Up Instructions

❖ The PowerPoint program should be open, and the file **Annual Presentation.ppt** should be displayed in the Slide View.

❖ Press **Ctrl** and **Home** to locate and activate slide 1.

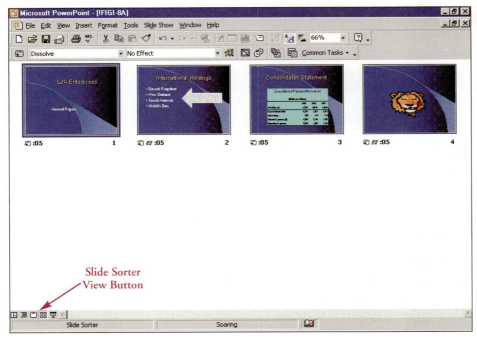

FIGURE I.8

PowerPoint Slide Sorter View

1. Select the **Slide Show** button 🖳 on the left of the horizontal scroll bar.

   *Note: The slides will display automatically one after the other then return to the view displayed when the **Slide Show** button was selected.*

Finish-Up Instructions

❖ Print the slides as handouts. (Select **File**, **Print**; click on the down arrow in the **Print What** box and choose **Handouts**. Check that 6 slides per page displays in the **Handouts** area. Select **OK**.)

❖ Save the file using the same filename, **Annual Presentation.ppt**.

❖ Close the PowerPoint program.

Create a Database in Microsoft Access

Microsoft Access is a database program that allows information to be stored, sorted, organized, displayed, and printed. In some ways, a database is similar to the data files created for a merge operation in Chapters 11 and 12. The information is divided into fields, such as LastName, FirstName, or Zip, and all the fields for one entity make up a record. However, a database allows much more information to be stored and has many more options for organizing, inputting, and outputting the information.

With Access, records can be grouped into tables, and multiple tables can be joined together to create the database. One advantage to this is that items in a linked table can be selected rather than keyed, thus reducing keystrokes and increasing accuracy. For example, a table of products and prices could be linked to an Order database. When customer orders are entered, the product items would be selected from the linked table, ensuring that the correct price information is used and that the product names are consistent.

Access offers many ways to customize a database entry so that clerical personnel can use the system even when they do not understand how the database operates. The Data Entry Form can be designed to be easy to use and attractive. Fields that must contain data can be formatted so that the user cannot leave the field without making an entry, and fields that must have numerical data can be formatted so that entering alpha characters produces an error message.

In each table, a primary key must be designated. The primary key cannot be duplicated within the table. For example, in a table containing customers, each customer would be assigned a Customer ID that would be unique. The primary key can be used to develop relationships between other tables. For example, in the Order database, each order would have both an Order ID and a Customer ID, because each order belongs to one and only one customer. Instead of typing in the Customer ID, the Customer ID field in the Order table can be linked to the Customer table and the Customer ID can be selected from those already entered in the Customer table. When a database system allows information to be shared between tables, it is called a *relational database*. A database system that does not have such connections is called a *flat database*.

An Access database can be used with merge letters in Word. The merge letter is created in Word, and then the Access database is opened. Select the table containing the data to be merged, then click on the down triangle next to the **OfficeLinks** button and click on the **Merge It with MS Word** option. *(Note: The OfficeLinks button will display as either ⬚▾ or ⬚▾ depending on which application was used last.)* Follow the steps in the Microsoft Word Mail Merge Wizard, which is very similar to the Word Merge feature described in Chapter 11, to complete the merge operation.

The database we will create is the mailing list of shareholders of the two companies, LJK Enterprises, Inc., and LJK Holding Corp. The basic structure of the database will be the creation of three tables, an entry form for clerical personnel to enter new stockholders, a query that lists only large shareholders in California, and a report that lists the large California shareholders in alphabetical order and shows the number of shares and type of stock they own. Because we will be creating a very simple database, we will use the Blank Database template. For more complex databases, Access provides templates that can be customized to fit different business and personal uses and a Database Wizard that gives guidance for customizing and using the templates.

Start-Up Instructions

❖ Copy the files **States.mdb** and **Meeting Notice.doc** to your file disk.

Steps to ➤ ## Open Access and Create a New Database

Method 1: From the Windows Desktop

1. Select Start, Programs, Microsoft Access.

   Note: The Microsoft Access dialog box will appear.

2. Select Blank Access database in the Create a new database using section; select OK.

   Note: The File New Database dialog box will appear. This dialog box functions in the same way as the Save dialog box discussed in Chapter 1.

❖ Continue with Step 3 under Create a New Database.

Method 2: From the Microsoft Office Shortcut Bar

1. Select the Microsoft Access button.

2. Select the Blank Access database option and choose OK.

   Note: The File New Database dialog box will appear. This dialog box functions in the same way as the Save dialog box discussed in Chapter 1.

Create a New Database

3. Select the drive/folder containing your file disk. Click in the **File name** box and delete the default filename. Type the filename for the new database and select **Create**. All Access databases should be named with the extension **.mdb**.

> For example, select the drive/folder containing your file disk. Click in the **File name** box, delete the default filename, then type **Shareholders.mdb**. Select **Create**.

Note: The Database window will appear (see Figure I.9). This window organizes the parts of the database. As each table, query, form, report, etc., is created for the database, it will be listed with the associated object.

Create a Table Using the Design View

4. Make sure the **Tables** object is selected. (If necessary, select **Tables** in the Objects list.)

5. Double-click on the method you want to use to create the table.

> For example, double-click on **Create Table in Design View** for the first table, which will contain a list of the types of stock a shareholder could own.

*Note: The Design view pane displays. This pane is used for setting up tables and formatting them. Click on the **Maximize** button, if necessary, to show the Design View pane in full view.*

6. In the first Field Name slot, type the name for the first field. Press **Tab**.

> For example, type **Stock type**. Then press **Tab**.

*Note: After **Tab** is pressed, the insertion point will move to the Data Type field, and the Field Properties pane will appear on the bottom third of the screen. The Data Type controls what types of data can be entered (e.g., Text, Number, Currency, Date, Lookup Wizard, etc.).*

FIGURE I.9

Access with Database window displaying

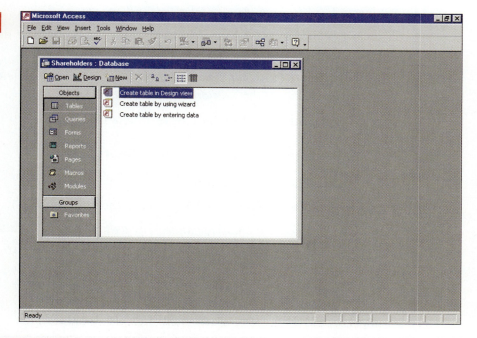

7. The default Data Type is Text. To select another Data Type, click on the down triangle that appears in the Data Type column and select the desired data type.

> For example, this field will be used to type the names of the stock types; therefore, the default of **Text** is correct.

8. Click on any of the formatting options in the General section of the Field Properties pane and make any additions or changes needed.

> For example, double-click in the **Field Size** box and type **25**. This will limit the field to 25 characters.

9. Set the primary key for the table. Move the insertion point to the field to be used as a primary key, click the *right* mouse button, and click on **Primary Key**.

> For example, move the insertion point to the **Stock Type** field, press the *right* mouse button, and click on **Primary Key**.

Note: A small key symbol will appear next to the field designated as the primary key. All tables must have one primary key. The field selected for the primary key must be one that will have a unique entry for each item in the table.

10. Click in the second Field Name slot, type the second field name, and press **Tab**.

> For example, click in the second Field Name slot, type the field name **Current Price**, and press **Tab**.

11. Set the data type for the second field.

> For example, click on the down triangle in the Data Type column, and click on **Currency**.

Note: Your table should look similar to the table in Figure I.10.

12. Close and save the table by selecting the **Close** button on the Design View pane.

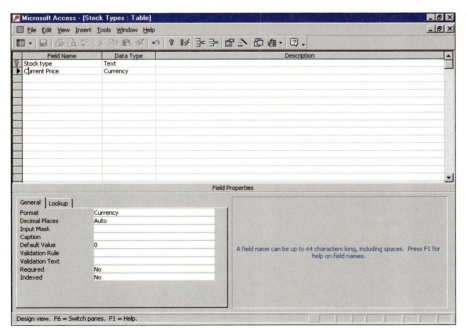

FIGURE I.10

Access Design View for Tables

Note: The message "Do you want to save changes to the design of table 'Table 1?'" will appear.

13. Select **Yes**.

   *Note: The Save As dialog box will appear because this table has not yet been assigned a name. After a name has been assigned to a table, selecting **Yes** will automatically resave the table to the same name.*

14. Type the name of the table, and select **OK**.

   For example, type **Stock Types**; select **OK**.

   Note: The Database window will reappear with the Stock Types table listed.

15. Close Access by selecting the **Close** button on the top line of the screen.

   *Note: It is not necessary to save the database because it was automatically saved when the table was closed. If you are unsure whether the database needs to be saved after an operation, check the **Save** button in the Standard Toolbar. It will be dimmed if the database has performed an automatic save during the operation.*

Start-Up Instructions

❖ The file **Shareholders.mdb** should be available on the file disk.

Open Access and an Existing Database

Method 1: From the Windows Desktop

1. Select **Start, Programs, Microsoft Access**.

   Note: The Microsoft Access dialog box will appear.

2. Check that the **Open an existing file** option is selected. (If necessary, click on this option.)

3. At the bottom of the dialog box, double-click on the database if it is listed, or double-click on the **More Files** option to display an Open dialog box.

   For example, double-click on the **More Files** option.

   Note: An Open dialog box will appear.

4. Select the drive/folder containing the database, and double-click on the desired filename.

   For example, select the drive/folder containing your file disk. Double-click on the file **Shareholders.mdb**.

   Note: The Database window will appear.

Method 2: From the Microsoft Office Shortcut Bar

1. Select the **Microsoft Access** button on the Microsoft Office Shortcut Bar.

2. Choose the **Open an existing file** option and select **OK**.

3. Select the drive/folder containing the database. Double-click on the desired filename.

For example, select the drive/folder containing your file disk and double-click on the file **Shareholders.mdb**.

Note: The Database window will appear.

 ## Enter Data into a Table

1. If necessary, click on the Tables button to display the tables in the database.

2. Click on the table in which data is to be entered. Select the Open button in the Tables window.

   For example, click on the **Stock Types** table and select the **Open** button.

   Note: The Stock Types table will appear in the Datasheet View with one row displayed. The Datasheet View will appear very similar to an Excel spreadsheet or a Word table.

3. Enter the following data, pressing Tab to move to the next column and to obtain the next row when you are in the last column. It is not necessary to type the dollar signs because the currency data type was set in the Design view.

Stock Type	Current Price
LJKH Common	$0.02
LJKE Preferred	$23.15
LJKE Common	$0.04
LJKH Preferred	$24.00

4. Click on the Close button in the Table window to return to the Database window.

Finish-Up Instructions

❖ Select the **Stock Types** table; select the **Open** button. Since the Stock Type field is the primary key for the table, Access has automatically sorted the table in alphabetical order based on this field. Close the Stock Types table (select the **Close** button in the Table window).

Import a Table into an Access Database

Sometimes the information you need will be available in other databases or in tables and databases supplied by vendors. For example, corporations can purchase mailing lists in many different formats, and lists of parts or customers may already exist in other databases created within the company. Access can use a wide variety of information. One common method of importing data is to place it in an ASCII delimited file. Another way to reuse data is to import a table from another database. For instance, a partial list of state abbreviations is available in the file **States.mdb**. We can import this table into the **Shareholders.mdb** database, and use it as a lookup table when we create the mailing list.

Start-Up Instructions

❖ The database **States.mdb** must be available on the file disk.

❖ Access should be open, and the **Shareholders** database should be displayed in the Database window.

Steps to ▸ Import a Table

1. If necessary, select Tables in the Objects list to display the tables in the current database.

2. Select the New button on the Database window.

3. Double-click on Import Table.

   Note: The Import dialog box will appear. This dialog box operates similarly to the Open dialog box discussed in Chapter 2.

4. Select the drive/folder containing the table file, and double-click on the filename.

   For example, select the drive/folder containing your file disk; double-click on the file named **States.mdb**.

   *Note: The Import Objects window will appear, listing all objects Access can import from the selected file. Since there is only one table in the **States.mdb** database, that table will be shown in the Tables section.*

5. Click on the object to be imported, and select OK.

   For example, click on the **STATES** table to select it; select **OK**.

   Note: When the import operation is complete, the Database window will appear with the imported object selected.

6. Select the imported table. Select the Design button. Set a primary key if necessary, and make any other changes to the table that are needed in the current database. Close the Design window and save the table.

   For example, select the **STATES** table, the **Design** button. *Right* mouse-click on the **STATE Field** name and choose **Pimary key**. Close the Design window. If necessary, select **Yes** at the prompt to save the table.

Finish-Up Instructions

❖ Continue with the Steps to Use the Table Wizard.

Tap into the Power of an Access Wizard

Access contains several types of Wizards to assist in creating tables, queries, reports, and even the entire database. The Wizards allow you to create complex objects without spending months learning Visual Basic and Access's programming features. For example, during the creation of a table using the Table Wizard, you can select a phone number field that is already set up to automatically format the numbers entered as a phone number. The one drawback to using the Wizards is that the Wizards may run slowly, especially on computers with less than 16M RAM.

Start-Up Instructions

❖ Access should be open, and the **Shareholders: Database** should be displayed in the Database window.

 Use the Table Wizard

1. If necessary, select Tables listed below Objects to display the current tables in the database.

2. Select the New button in the Database window.

3. Double-click on Table Wizard.

   Note: In a few moments, the Table Wizard dialog box displays (see Figure I.11). The Table Wizard dialog box contains a selection of sample tables on the left and a list of Sample fields for the currently highlighted table in the middle.

4. To see what fields a table contains, click on the table in the Sample Tables list on the left. Scroll through the fields in the middle list to review them.

   For example, click on several different tables in the Sample Tables list and review the fields contained in each. We are looking for a table that contains mailing information.

5. When you have decided on a table, click on it to highlight it.

   For example, click on the **Mailing List** table and check that the Business option is chosen.

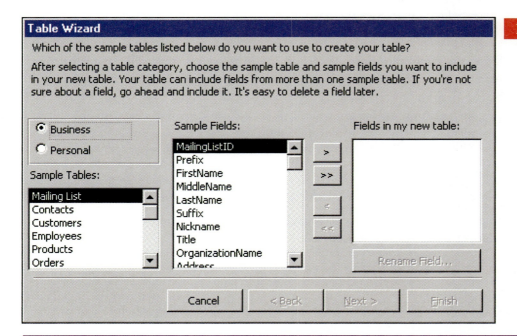

FIGURE I.11

Table Wizard dialog box

6. Select the fields from the Sample Fields list that you will need for your table. Click on the desired field, and then on the **right arrow** button [>] between the Sample Fields list and the Fields in my new table list to transfer the field to the new table.

> For example, the field **MailingListID** should be highlighted. (If necessary, click on the **MailingListID** field.) Click on the **right arrow** button [>] or double-click on **MailingListID**.

Note: The field MailingListID will now appear in the Fields in my new table list.

7. Continue selecting fields from the Sample Fields list and copying them to the Fields in my new table list until all the useful fields appear in the Fields in my new table list.

> For example, select each of the following fields, and then click the **right arrow** button [>] to copy it to the Fields in my new table list:
>
> **Prefix, FirstName, LastName, OrganizationName, Address, City, State, PostalCode, WorkPhone.**

*Note: If all or most of the fields in the Sample Fields list are needed, click on the **double-right** arrow [>>] button to move all of the fields into the Fields in my new table list. To move a field from the Fields in my new table list back to the Sample Fields list, click on it, and then click on the **left arrow** button.*

8. To rename a field, select the field and then click on the **Rename Field** button at the bottom of the Fields in my new table list. Type the new field name and select **OK**.

> For example, click on the **MailingListID** field; click on the **Rename Field** button. Type **ShareholderID** in the Rename Field box, and select **OK**.

9. Select **Next**.

10. Type a name for your table in the box after the question "What do you want to name your table?"

> For example, type **Shareholders** in the box for the table name.

11. Select the desired option for setting the primary key manually or for having Access set the primary key. When Access sets the primary key, it will usually be the first key in the table.

> For example, make sure the option **Yes, set a primary key for me** is selected. Access will designate the first field (ShareholderID) as the primary key.

12. Select **Finish**.

Note: In a few moments, the table will appear in the Tables window.

13. Select **View, Design View** to switch to the Design window, and make any changes or additions needed.

Link a Lookup Table to a Field

14. Click in the **Data Type** column for the field to which a lookup table is to be linked.

    For example, click in the **Data Type** column for the **State** field.

15. Click on the down arrow that appears in the Data Type column. Click on the **Lookup Wizard** option.

    Note: In a few moments, the Lookup Wizard dialog box displays.

16. Select the desired option for the Lookup Table, and select **Next**.

    For example, make sure the option **I want the lookup column to look up values in a table or query** is selected. If necessary, select this option. Select **Next**.

    Note: A list of the other tables and/or queries in the database will appear.

17. Select the desired view option(s).

    For example, make sure the **Tables** or **Both** option is selected in the View section. If necessary, click on the **Tables** option.

18. Click on the table that is to be used as the lookup table. Select **Next**.

    For example, check that **STATES** is selected, or if necessary, click on the **STATES** table, and select **Next**.

    Note: The field(s) available in the selected table will appear in the Available Fields list.

19. In the Available Fields list, click on the field or fields that are to appear as the lookup items when the column is entered. Click on the **right arrow** button ![>] to move the field into the Selected Fields list. When all necessary fields have been moved into the Selected Fields list, click on the **Next** button.

    For example, click on the **STATE** field in the Available Fields list. Click on the **right arrow** button ![>] to move the field into the Selected Fields list. Click on **Next**.

20. Increase or decrease the width of the column so that it will display attractively and be easy to read. *To change the column width to fit the widest text currently in the table,* move the mouse pointer to the top of the column on the right edge until a double-headed arrow appears, and double-click the left mouse button. *To increase or decrease the width,* move the mouse pointer to the right edge of the column until a double-headed arrow appears. Hold down the left mouse button and drag the line until the column is the desired width. Release the mouse button.

    For example, move the mouse pointer to the top of the column on the right edge until a double-headed arrow appears, and double-click the left mouse button.

21. Select **Next**.

22. Type the name to be assigned to the column and select **Finish**, or select **Finish** to accept the default column name and return to the Design window.

For example, the default name is State because the column had already been assigned that field name. Select **Finish** to accept the default name.

Finish-Up Instructions

❖ Select **Yes** to respond to the message, "Save now?"

❖ Scroll down and click in the blank Field Name slot below WorkPhone. Type the field name Stock Type, and press **Tab**. Click on the down triangle next to the Data Type column and select **Lookup Wizard**. Make the following selections in the Lookup Wizard dialog box.

  a. Select **I want the lookup column to look up the values in a table or query**. Select **Next**.

  b. Select **Stock Types**. Select **Next**.

  c. Move the Stock Type field into the Selected Fields list (click on **Stock Type** then on the right arrow button). Select **Next**.

  d. Adjust the width of the column if needed. Select **Next**.

  e. If necessary, type Stock Type as the label for the column. Select **Finish**. Select **Yes** to save now.

❖ Click in the next blank Field Name slot and type the field name **Number of Shares**. Press **Tab**. Click on the down triangle in the Data Type column and select **Number**.

❖ Select the **Save** button to save the table.

❖ Close the table (select the **Close** button on the Table window).

Create a Data Entry Form

Often it is necessary to have clerical personnel or temporary personnel assist in creating large databases. Access offers the ability to create forms of many different types. One of the most useful is a data entry form that can be designed to make data entry easier.

Start-Up Instructions

❖ Access should be open, and the **Shareholders: Database** should be displayed in the Database window.

Steps to **Create a Data Entry Form**

1. Select the Forms Object in the Database window, and select the New button.
    Note: The New Form dialog box will appear.

2. Click on the method to be used to create the new form.
    For example, click once on the **Form Wizard**.

3. Click on the down arrow in the bottom section of the New Form dialog box.

   Note: A list of the tables in the database will appear.

4. Click on the table to be used in the form.

   For example, click on the **Shareholders** table.

5. Select **OK**.

   Note: The Form Wizard begins.

6. Move the fields to appear on the form from the Available Fields list to the Selected Fields list. To move all the fields, click on the **double-right** arrow button ⟩⟩ . To move individual fields, click on a field, and then click on the **right arrow** button ⟩ .

   For example, click on the **double-right arrow** button ⟩⟩ to move all the fields from the Available Fields list to the Selected Fields list. Scroll up and click on the **ShareholderID** field in the Selected Fields list. Click on the **left arrow** button to move this field back into the Available Fields list. Because the ShareholderID will be created automatically by Access, we will not display it on the entry form. This is one way to prevent anyone accidentally typing a number in this column.

7. Select **Next**.

8. Select the layout to be used for the form, and select **Next**.

   For example, select **Columnar** and **Next**.

9. Select the style for the form, and select **Next**.

   For example, select **Blends**, **Next**.

10. Type the name for the form in the box at the top of the last page of the Form Wizard.

    For example, type **Shareholder Entry Form**.

11. Select the option desired to either view or modify the form.

    For example, select **Modify the form's design**.

12. Select **Finish**.

    Note: Wait momentarily. The form will appear in a Form window. Maximize the Form.

13. Make any desired modifications to the form using the tools shown in Figure I.12.

    For example, move and size the labels and data boxes to modify the form until it appears similar to the form shown in Figure I.12.

    Note: To move a label and its associated field, click on the label then on the field. Sizing handles will appear around both. Move the mouse pointer over the label/field until a hand with all fingers extended appears. Hold down the left mouse button and drag the label/field to the desired location. Release the mouse button. To change the size of a field, click on the field. Move the mouse pointer over the field until a double-headed arrow appears. Hold down the left mouse button and drag the edge of the field until the field is the desired size. Release the mouse button.

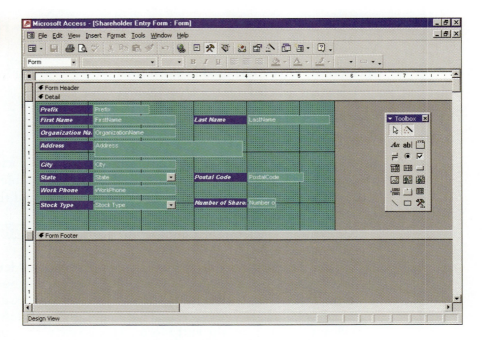

FIGURE I.12

Form in Design View

14. Select the Close button on the Design View window, then select Yes to save the form.

    Note: The Database window will appear.

Finish-Up Instructions

❖ Continue with the Steps to Enter Data Using a Form

Start-Up Instructions

❖ Access should be open and the **Shareholders: Database** should be displayed in the Database window.

Enter Data Using a Form

1. Select the Forms Object on the Database window and the form to be used. Select Open.

    For example, click on **Forms**. If necessary, click on the **Shareholder Entry Form**. Select **Open**.

2. Enter the data for each record, using the Tab or Enter keys to move from one field to the next.

3. To use the lookup tables in the State and Stock Type fields, click on the down triangle in to the field, and click on the appropriate item from the drop-down list.

4. When the data for the first record is complete, select the right arrow button in the Record section at the bottom left corner of the Form window, or press the Tab key to go to the next record.

5. Enter all the records and select the Close button on the Form window to return to the Database window.

I–36

Special Supplement—Integrating Microsoft Office

For example, enter all the records shown below using the Shareholder Entry Form. If you notice mistakes, correct them by moving the mouse pointer to the field, clicking once, then using the **Backspace** or **Delete** key to erase the current information. Type the correct information. When all the information has been entered, use the arrow buttons (◄ and ►) in the Record area to review all the records and proofread them. When the records are all correct, select the **Close** button.

Mr.
John
Wilson
Peterson, Jamison & Smith
4322 Janis Street
Ovid
CO
80744-2344
(303) 555-2433
LJKE Common
250

Mr.
Thomas
Amway
Nabor Brands
27842 DeLancy Street
Gadsden
AL
35901-2330
(205) 555-8923
LJKH Preferred
2500

Ms.
Jean
Devereau
Claremont Works
2443 Winton Avenue
Hayward
CA
94542-1511
(510) 555-2344
LJKE Preferred
2430

Mr.
T. Gordon
Breakwater
Nabor Biscuits, Inc.
12033 Michigan Street
Glenwood
AL
36034-2800
(205) 555-2994
LJKH Preferred
9820

Ms.
Lee
Rodriguez
Yarn Mills Clearing Company
9554 Dana Street
Atascadero
CA
93422-2400
(805) 555-9300
LJKE Common
7880

Ms.
Janice
Johnston
Lewis, March & Winters
552 B Street
Marysville
CA
95901-0990
(916) 555-4200
LJKE Preferred
3000

Mr.	Mr.
D.W.	Don
Zucker	Leone
Patterson Designs	Golf Tees
8994 Wilson Avenue	8945 Beatrice
Crescent Mills	Carmel Valley
CA	CA
95934-4333	93924-0996
(916) 555-2444	(408) 555-8924
LJKE Preferred	LJKE Common
5673	400

Note: *Select the previous record button* *to save the last record and to move to the previous record. It is not necessary to save the database after entering the records because each record is saved automatically when you move to the next or previous record.*

Start-Up Instructions

❖ Access should be open, and the database **Shareholders.mdb** should be displayed in the Database window.

Steps to **Merge Database Records with a Word Document**

1. Select the table with which the document is to be merged.

    For example, click on **Tables**. (If necessary, click on the **Shareholders** table.)

2. Click on the down triangle next to the **OfficeLinks** button in the Standard Toolbar, and click on the **Merge It with MS Word** option.

    Note: The Microsoft Word Mail Merge Wizard will begin.

3. Select the **Link your data to an existing Microsoft Word document** option and select **OK**.

    Note: The Select Microsoft Word Document dialog box will appear. This dialog box is similar to the Open dialog box discussed in Chapter 2.

4. Select the drive/folder containing the merge document, and double-click on the filename.

    For example, select the drive/folder containing your file disk; double-click on the file **Meeting Notice.doc**.

    Note: Word will open with the document Meeting Notice.doc displayed.

5. Add the Merge fields and any other items needed for the merge document. Follow the merge operation steps as explained in Chapter 11, page 296.

    For example, maximize the Word screen. Position the insertion point on the fourth line after the date. Select the **Insert Merge Field** button on the Mail Merge Toolbar. The field names from the Shareholders table will appear. Insert the fields as needed to create the merge document and save the merge document. Your document should look similar to the one shown in Figure I.13 on Page I–40.

Finish-Up Instructions

❖ Select the **Mail Merge Helper** button and check that the correct Shareholders database and Shareholders table is shown. Select **Merge** twice to complete the merge procedure. Check the letters. If necessary, make corrections to the database or the merge document and merge the document and database again.

❖ Optional. Use the filename **Meeting Notice Merge.doc** and save the merged letters to your file disk. Close the merged documents.

❖ Use the new filename **Meeting notice main doc** and save the document containing the field/merge codes.

❖ Close the main document and close Microsoft Word.

Create Queries and Reports in Access

Queries are used in a database to select records that meet certain criteria. A query can be very simple, such as finding all the records with CA in the State field, or more complex, involving the relationship between several fields or the calculating of values in several fields. Think of designing a query as figuring out how to ask a question in a way that the program will understand, while opening or running a query actually sends the program out to look at all the records in the database and come up with an answer.

To design a query, the table or tables on which the query will be built must be specified and the field names to appear in the query designated. If the query is only to be used on-screen or for a summary, you may only need to designate the field names that are the basis for the criteria. However, if a report is to be created from the query, you may want to have all or most of the field names placed in the query so they will be available for use in the report. When a report is based on a query, name the report and query so that it will be easy to remember that they belong together, i.e., Large Shareholders Query and Large Shareholders Report.

A report is a way to arrange the information in the database and present it in a readable and attractive manner. Generally, reports are printed and can be formatted in many different ways. A report can be based on the information in a table, or it can be based on the answer found by a query. The report is designed based on the field names in the table or query. The Report Wizard is useful for first-time report creation, but even a report created by the Wizard will probably need to be modified before it can be printed.

In the following steps, we will create a query to find all the shareholders who live in California and have more than 500 shares. We will then design a report to present this information in an attractive manner.

FIGURE I.13

Meeting
notice.doc with
merge fields
inserted

L J K Enterprises

12432 Avenue of the Americas   New York, New York 10019
Voice—(212) 555-2444 E-mail—ljkenter@aol.com

August 21, 2000

«Prefix» «FirstName» «LastName»
«OrganizationName»
«Address»
«City»,«State» «PostalCode»

Dear «Prefix» «LastName»:

The Annual Shareholders Meeting for LJK Enterprises, Inc., and LJK Holding
Corp. will be held on Saturday, September 9, 2000, at 1:30 p.m. in the Board
Room of the Headquarters Building. Your attendance is requested as required
in the Bylaws of the corporations.

For more information on designing queries and reports, use the Answer Wizard to search for information on the following topics: query, criteria, report.

Start-Up Instructions

❖ Access should be open, and the **Shareholders: Database** should be displayed in the Database window.

Create a Query

1. Select **Queries** in the Objects list in the Database window.

2. Select the **New** button in the Database window.

3. Select the method to be used to create the query. Select **OK**.

    For example, select **Design View** then **OK**.

    Note: The Show Table dialog box will appear.

4. Select the table on which the query is to be based, and then select **Add**. Repeat for each table needed for the query. Select **Close** to continue.

    For example, select the **Shareholders** table, **Add**, then **Close**.

    Note: The Design View for the query will appear. The table(s) added in the Show Table dialog box appears in the upper pane. The lower pane contains rows used to design the query.

5. Select the fields to be used in the query by clicking on the **Field** row in the bottom pane, clicking on the down triangle that displays in the field slot, and clicking on the desired field from the drop-down list.

    For example, move the mouse pointer to the **first slot** in the **Field** row in the bottom pane and click the left mouse button once. Click on the down triangle that appears on the right side of the slot. Click on the **Prefix** field. Continue selecting the slots in the Field row in order and add the following fields: **FirstName, LastName, City, State, Stock Type, Number of Shares.**

Note: The field names will appear in the Field row. Under them, in the Table row, is the table to which they belong (Shareholders).

6. To designate the order in which the items should appear when the query is run or opened, first click in the **Sort** row under the field to be used. Click on the down triangle that appears in the field slot, and click on the desired order (**Ascending** or **Descending**).

   For example, click on the **Sort** row under the **LastName** field. Click on the down triangle that appears in the slot, and click on **Ascending**.

7. If there are any fields that are needed for the query but that you do not want to appear when the query is run, click on the **Show** row under the field to deselect it. When a check mark appears in the **Show** row, the field will be displayed when the query is run or opened.

   For example, click on the **Show** row under the State field to deselect the option. Although we need the State field as part of our criteria, we will not need to display this field.

8. To designate the criteria to be used for the query, first click in the **Criteria** row under the field to be used to set the criteria. Type the criteria to be used. More than one field may be needed. If all the criteria must be met, place each one under its field in the Criteria row. This creates an "And" statement. If the record must meet one or the other of the criteria, place the second item in the "or" row. This creates an "Or" statement.

   For example, we need to specify that each record must have CA in the State field *and* more than 500 in the Number of Shares field. Click in the **Criteria** row under the State field. Type **CA**. (Do not type the period.) Click in the **Criteria** row under the Number of Shares field. Type **>500**.

Note: We have created an "And" statement, asking the program to show us only those records where CA appears in the State field and where a number greater than 500 appears in the Number of Shares field. Your query should match Figure I.14.

9. Check to make sure the query is functioning as you expect it to by selecting the Run button ▮ on the Toolbar.

Note: The records that match the criteria will appear in Datasheet View. Check that the records containing greater than 500 shares appear.

10. If the query does not produce the correct records, select **View, Design View** to return to the Design View window. Correct the query and repeat steps 8 and 9 until the query works correctly.

11. When the query works correctly, select the **Close** button on the Design or Datasheet window. Answer **Yes** when asked if you want to save changes.

Note: The Save As dialog box will appear.

FIGURE I.14

Access showing
Query Design
View window

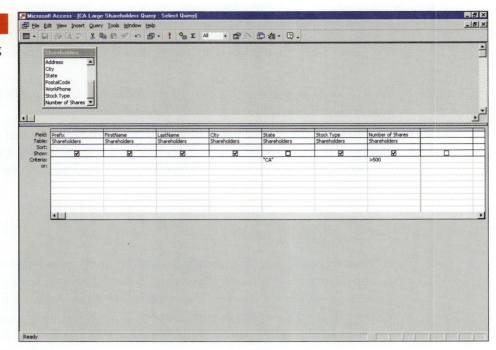

12. Type the name for the query, and select **OK**.

    For example, type **CA Large Shareholders Query**; select **OK**.

    Note: The Database window will appear with the new query displayed.

Finish-Up Instructions

❖ Display the query by selecting the name of the query, i.e. **CA Large Shareholders Query**, then selecting the **Open** button in the Database window.

❖ Close the Query window.

Start-Up Instructions

❖ Access should be open, and the **Shareholders: Database** should be displayed in the Database window.

❖ The query **CA Large Shareholders Query** created in the previous section must be available.

Create a Report Using a Query

1. Select **Reports** listed under the Objects list. Select the **New** button in the Database window.

    Note: The New Report dialog box will appear.

2. Click on the method to be used to create the report.

    For example, click on **AutoReport: Tabular**.

3. Click on the down triangle below the list of methods, then click on the table or query to be used as the basis for the report.

For example, click on the down triangle below the list of methods, and click on **CA Large Shareholders Query**.

4. Select **OK**.

    Note: The AutoReport Wizard will design the report and display it on the screen. This may take a few minutes on slower computers.

5. To modify the report design, select **View, Design View**.

    *Note: The report will appear in Design View. If desired, select the **Maximize** button.*

6. Make the desired modifications to the design.

    For example, make the following changes:

    a. The AutoReport automatically used the query name as the Report Header. To change the Report Header, click on the text **CA Large Shareholders Query**. Sizing handles will appear around the text showing that this item is selected. Move the mouse pointer to the left of the "C," hold down the left mouse button, and drag to select all the text in the Report Header box. Type the new Report Header, **Large Shareholders in California**.

    b. Use the horizontal scroll bar to display the far right side of the layout. Find the text "Number of Shares" in the Page Header area. Select **"Number of"** and type **Total**.

    Note: Your report in Design View should appear similar to that shown in Figure I.15.

7. To check the design, select **View, Print Preview**. Click on the report to reduce the size of the display and see the entire report.

8. Select the **Close Window** button on the Print Preview/Design window. Select **Yes** at the "Do you want to save changes?" prompt.

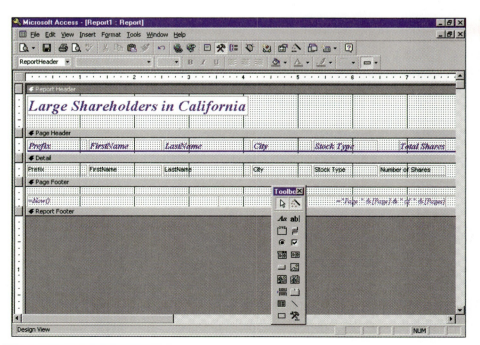

FIGURE I.15

Access with Report in Design View

Note: If this is the first time the report has been saved, the Save As dialog box will appear.

9. Type the report name and select **OK**.

   For example, type **CA Large Shareholders Report**; select **OK**.

   Note: The Database window will appear with the new report displayed.

Finish-Up Instructions

❖ Select the report name, then select the **Print** button to print the report.

❖ Close Access (click on the **Close** button at the top of the screen).

Start-Up Instructions

❖ Open a New Blank document in Word.

Use Paste Special

Note: In the following activity, an Excel spreadsheet will be copied and pasted to a Word document using the Paste Special feature.

1. With a blank Word document displayed on the screen, start Excel (click on **Start, Programs**, and choose **Microsoft Excel**).

2. Open the file named **Workbook for Annual Report.xls** that was created earlier in this Supplement. (You can open any available Excel workbook.)

3. Select and highlight the worksheet.

   Note: If the worksheet is large, select only a portion of the worksheet.

4. Select the **Copy** button.

5. On the Taskbar, click on the blank Microsoft Word document.

6. Select **Edit, Paste Special**.

7. In the As box, select **Microsoft Excel Worksheet Object**; choose **OK**.

   Note: The worksheet will display in the Word document as an object. The object can be moved or resized.

Finish-Up Instructions

❖ Use the filename **Word paste special** and save the file.

❖ Optional. Print one copy.

Finish-Up

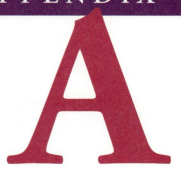

What Is a Microcomputer System?

A *microcomputer system* is a small computer system designed to provide methods for creating, processing, storing, and printing data. A small computer system normally includes the computer, keyboard, mouse, monitor, printer, and software programs. Most microcomputer systems today, however, include internal fax modems, sound boards, CD-ROM players, and stereo speakers and are referred to as *multimedia* systems.

The microcomputer system consists of two basic elements: hardware and software. The physical components of the microcomputer system are called *hardware;* the programs that instruct the computer to perform functions are called *software*.

Hardware

The microcomputer hardware includes the monitor (TV-like screen), keyboard, mouse, computer unit, disk drives, and printer. The hardware can be seen, felt, and touched. The IBM-PC and compatible computers enclose the disk drive(s) within the computer. The monitor, keyboard, mouse, and printer are attached to the computer via cables. The computer unit and the attached hardware make up a microcomputer system.

The computer unit holds the electronic circuitry where the main memory and central processing unit (CPU) reside. The CPU processes and controls information by storing data, performing operations, and transferring information from one location to another. The CPU is often referred to as the brains of the computer.

Software

Software programs are lists of instructions that tell the computer what to do. The master program is the operating system, e.g., Windows 95, 98, or Windows NT. The operating system directs the basic operation of the microcomputer system and carries out procedures within programs. Programs are more advanced software designed to perform specific tasks. Common applications (programs) include word processing, spreadsheet, database, communications, graphics, drawing, and desktop publishing programs.

Windows 95/98 (or other operating system) and other programs are stored on the computer's hard disk. A copy of Windows 95/98 is transferred to the computer's memory when the computer is turned on. Transferring a copy of a program to the computer's memory is called *launching (loading)* the program. The disk is *being read* when a copy of a program or other information is transferred from the disk into the computer's memory.

What Are Disks?

Disks are storage devices. Information that is processed and used by a computer must be stored on either a hard or floppy disk. Because the computer's memory is temporary, all programs and data are erased when the computer is turned off. Therefore, disks are used to store programs and data.

The rigid hard disk usually resides inside the computer and is not removed by the user. Programs are normally stored on a hard disk. However, removable hard disks, contained in plastic cartridges, are also available. A floppy disk, contained in a plastic cartridge or paper jacket, is flexible and can be handled by the user. Floppy disks are generally used to store data or files. The most commonly used floppy disk size is 3.5".

Information that has been created is saved on either a floppy disk or a hard disk. A floppy disk is referred to as a *file disk* or *data disk*. If information, such as a letter, memorandum, or statistical data, is not saved on a disk, the information will be lost from the computer's temporary memory when the computer is turned off. When a copy of the information is transferred from the computer's memory to a disk, the process is called *saving*. Saving information to a disk is also called "*writing*" to a disk.

Care for Floppy Disks

Floppy disks should be labeled using a felt-tip pen. Store disks in a dry, protected location. Avoid dust, smoke, bending, and extreme temperatures. (Keep disks out of the sun and away from beverage containers!) Any magnet or magnetized object can damage the data on a disk.

Formatting a Floppy Disk

Before information can be saved on a disk, the disk must be formatted (prepared) with electronic instructions to partition the disk into storage areas, to create a directory, to check for disk defects, etc.

The formatting process is usually performed only once. If a disk is formatted a second time, all information previously saved on the disk is erased. Floppy disks can be purchased preformatted. Much time can be saved by using preformatted disks.

 ## Format a File Disk Using Windows Explorer

1. If necessary, turn on the computer.
2. Select the **Start** button, choose the **Programs** option, and click on **Windows Explorer**.

3. In the All Folders box, move the mouse pointer to the drive letter where the file disk is located and click the *right* mouse button.

   Note: *A shortcut menu displays.*

4. Select Format.

   Note: *The Format dialog box displays.*

5. Generally, the Capacity option box displays the appropriate disk capacity. If necessary, however, select the down arrow button in the Capacity option box and select the correct disk capacity.

6. Select the desired format type. If the disk is being formatted for the first time, choose the Full option. If the disk has previously been formatted and you want to erase the data on the disk, select the Quick (erase) option.

7. If desired, type a name for the disk in the Label box.

8. Select Start.

9. When the Format Results dialog box displays, select Close.

10. Select Close to exit the Format dialog box.

What Is Windows 95/98?

Windows 95/98 is an operating system for IBM-PC and compatible micro-computers. Windows is a collection of related programs that control and manage the computer's operations. Windows handles the temporary storage and process-ing of information and directs the orderly transfer or sharing of information between the computer unit and the disk, monitor, keyboard, printer, etc. The Windows program allows the user to complete tasks such as launching (loading) programs, copying files, formatting disks, and deleting files. Windows provides a structure within which many programs can operate, and provides common ways of accomplishing tasks. For example, the procedure for saving a file is the same when working with most Windows programs. In addition, data can be easily transferred from one Windows program to another. For example, a graph created in a Windows spreadsheet program can be easily transferred to a Windows word processing program.

When Windows 95/98 is launched, the Desktop displays on the screen (see Figure 1.1 on page 12). The Windows program is often referred to as a graphical user interface (GUI) because icons (pictures) can be displayed on the screen to represent each program. The user can launch a program simply by placing the mouse pointer on the program icon and double-clicking the left mouse button. Programs can also be launched by selecting the **Start** button located on the Taskbar, choosing the **Programs** option, and clicking on the desired programs name.

Windows allows multiple programs to run at the same time. Each program is placed in a separate *window*. The windows for each application share common elements. For example, the Title bar, Menu bar, scroll bars, and **Close** button are elements common to each application. These common elements provide a stan-dard method for accomplishing tasks. For example, the **File**, **Print** option is used in any Windows application to print a document. As more and more programs are written for Windows, the common elements will simplify learning additional Windows programs.

Windows programs are also compatible with each other (i.e., the information in each program can be transferred and shared easily). For example, a spreadsheet file can be transferred to a Word document window. A *link* is established between the spreadsheet and Word files so that any changes made in the spreadsheet file are automatically changed in the linked file.

What Are Folders and Paths?

A *folder* is a named location on a disk where a group of files is stored. A folder is used to keep files organized in separate areas on the disk under different folder names. Programs such, as word processing, spreadsheet, and database programs, are usually stored on the computer's hard disk. The files for each application can be kept together in one folder location. For example, all Word program files are stored in a folder named Microsoft Office\Office.

Other folders can be created and grouped together in the Microsoft Office\Office folder. Any folders created under another folder are called *subfolders*. For example, if a subfolder named "Memos" was created under the folder My Documents, Memos would be a subfolder of the My Documents folder.

A *path* is a route from a disk drive letter (root folder) to the location of a file or subfolder. For example, the path for a file named **memo3.doc** that is located in the subfolder named Memos that is under the My Documents folder is: c:\My Documents\Memos\memo3.doc. When using Word 2000, the various folders and subfolders can be chosen in the Save As and Open dialog boxes (see Chapter 1, page 18, and Chapter 2, page 39).

What Is a Filename?

Every file to be saved is assigned a filename. In Windows 95/98, filenames can contain 1 to 255 characters and, if desired, a filename extension of one to three characters. The filename extension is separated from the first 1–255 characters by a period.

Any letter (a to z) or number (0–9) and most symbols can be used in a filename. A filename cannot contain backslashes, question marks, greater than symbols (>), lesser than symbols (<), or asterisks. For example, **morris letter.doc** or **martin ltr 3-5-96.doc** are valid filenames.

A filename should represent the information and/or person's name contained in the file. For example, a letter written to Gerry Anderson concerning tax assessment could be assigned the name **G. Anderson.doc** or **Anderson taxes.doc**.

Note: If files will be transferred to another computer that uses an earlier version of Windows or DOS, limit filenames to eight characters, a period, and a three-character extension. Also, some programs that run under Windows 95/ 98 may not accommodate long filenames. In this case, a short version of the filename will display.

Web Publishing

One of the many features of Microsoft Office 2000 is the ability to create Web pages without knowing HTML (HyperText Markup Language). Your Web site can be created for use on the intranet (Web pages available exclusively within a company's network) or Internet (Web pages available to the public).

Creating a Web page is quite easy, especially when using the **Web Page Wizard** accessed from the New dialog box. You can also create Web pages using the Web Page option in the General tab of the New dialog box or by using a normal Word document. If a normal Word document is used to create a Web page, use the **File, Save as Web Page** option to save the file.

HTML is the standard format used to create Web pages. In the past, you would need to learn HTML to create a Web page.

HTML tags are placed within the document as you type. For example, if you want text to be in bold, a bold tag would be placed before and after the text. Without tags, Web browsers would not be able to recognize this attribute. Fortunately, HTML has become the standard for the industry so Web browsers can interpret HTML tags. Now, you can create a Web page from a Word document or from a Web template. Your Web pages can also contain video clips, graphics, and other nifty features, but keep in mind the audience you want to attract. Not everyone has a modem fast enough or a graphics card capable of viewing the fancy features. If a page takes too long to load, your message may never get across.

The World Wide Web

The World Wide Web is one of a host of Internet services. The most popular, it uses hyperlinks to retrieve the various pages from individuals, communities, governments, universities, etc., that have been uploaded to the World Wide Web servers. Like the home computer that stores your text documents and programs, the Web server stores masses of documents and programs for the general public to access. In other words, it is a large network of connected computers. With a telephone line, modem, the right software, and a service provider, you are ready for the World Wide Web.

Page Layout

To get an idea of how Web pages appear, go online. View the various Web sites to see how hyperlinks and Web browsers work and to preview the layout and background color of various Web sites. You can incorporate some of these ideas into your own Web page. Ideas for Web page layouts can also be obtained by using Word's Web Page Wizard.

Steps to → **Explore the Web Page Wizard**

1. Click on New from the File menu.
2. Click on the tab entitled Web Pages.
3. Choose Web Page Wizard and click OK.
4. Click Next.
5. Click on Next again.
6. Select the Vertical Frame option.
7. Click on Next.
8. Click on Next twice.
9. Click on Browse themes. Once you choose a theme, click OK. Then click on Next and Finish.
10. The next screen will be a Web page document. You simply replace the text with your own.
    Note: A Frames Toolbar and Web Tools display.
11. Exit without saving the document.

Web Browsers

Web browsers are interfaces between you and the server. They make it easy for you to move from one Web site to another with the use of hyperlinks. Hyperlinks connect Web pages. Before you can view the results of your Web page, you will need to have a browser installed. Two of the most popular Web browsers are Internet Explorer, which is included with your Office 2000 CD, and Netscape Navigator, which can be downloaded from the Internet.

Web Addresses

To access a Web site you need to know its Uniform Resource Locator (URL) address. The URL identifies the type of Internet service that maintains the file. When you type in the complete address, the hyperlink is encoded with the URL address.

The first part of the address is called a *protocol*. A protocol with *http:/* stands for HyperText Transfer Protocol, which indicates that the file is on the World Wide Web server.

A sample address looks like this:

http://www.microsoft.com/folder name/filename

The location of the network is www.microsoft.com. If there is a path, it is included after the network location as shown in the sample address above.

Publishing Web Pages

Each service provider has rules on how you can upload your files to the Web. Most providers allow you one or two megabytes of free server space so you can publish your own Web page(s). Contact your service provider for uploading instructions.

Saving a Word Document as a Web Page

Type the document as normal. The Word document is saved as a Web page by selecting **File, Save as Web Page**. The document is saved in HTML format and the filename extension *.htm* is automatically added to the filename. An advantage of saving a Web Page document in HTML format is the capability of opening the document back into the Word program without loosing any of the Word file formats.

Viewing HTML Codes

Although it is not necessary, you can look behind your Web page to see the HTML source codes. Once your document has been saved as a Web document, you can check out the various HTML tags placed within your document. **HTML t**ags are marked with <> throughout the document. There will always be a beginning tag, i.e., <TITLE> with text between and an ending tag, i.e., </TITLE>. For example, <TITLE> My Home Page </TITLE>.

To view HTML codes, click **View** from the menu and choose **HTML Source**. You will be able to see the various tags and text embedded in the Web document. To exit, click the **Close** button on the Microsoft Development Environment [design] Title bar.

Steps to **Create a Web Page from Scratch**

1. Click on **File**.
2. Click on **New**.
3. Click on the **General** tab; select **Web Page**.

4. Click **OK**.

   Note: Notice that the button New Web Page has replaced the New Document button on the Standard Toolbar.

Choose Your Page Color and Design

   Note: Many Web pages have unique background color. At this point, the background is white. To change the background color, follow the steps below.

5. Click on **Format, Background**.

6. Choose a background color. For example, choose **Pale Blue**.

   Note: A light color background is recommended. Gray backgrounds are not the most dramatic, but the color is easy on the eyes and gets your message across with less eyestrain. Styles can be used to format the heading text. The heading should display the name of your business or the purpose of the Web page.

7. With the insertion point at the left margin, click on the **Style** drop-down arrow from the Style box on the Formatting Toolbar.

8. Choose **Heading 1**.

9. Click on the **Center** button on the Formatting Toolbar.

10. Type **(Your Name) Home Page**, i.e., Amy's Home Page.

11. Press **Enter** twice.

Insert a Horizontal Line

12. Select **Format, Borders and Shading**. On the **Borders** tab, choose the **Horizontal Line** button.

13. When the Horizontal Line dialog box displays, choose a line of your choice. Select **Insert Clip**.

Create Scrolling Text

   Note: Select View, Toolbars, Web Tools.

14. Click on the **Center** button on the Formatting Toolbar and press **Enter** once.

15. Select **Format, Font**. Change the font size to **18 point** and **Bold**. Select **OK**.

16. Select the **Scrolling Text** button on the Web Tools Toolbox.

   Note: The Scrolling Text dialog box displays. See Figure B.1.

17. Select the Scrolling Text in the Scrolling Text box and type **Favorite Choices**.

18. Change the speed by dragging the speed slider two notches from the Fast Speed.

19. Select a background color in the Background Color box, e.g., choose **Red** or **make a choice of your own**.

20. Click **OK**.

21. Click once outside the text box area.

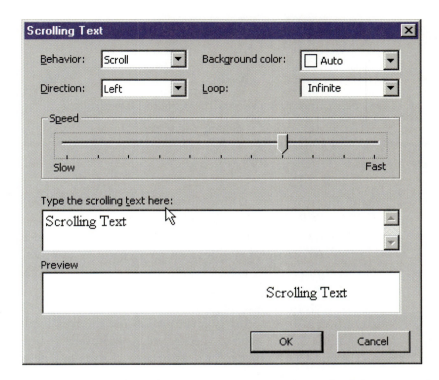

22. Press **Ctrl** and **End** to place the insertion point at the end of the text and press **Enter** twice.

23. Choose **Align Left** from the Formatting Toolbar.

24. Change the font back to **12 point**.

Create Bulleted and Numbered Lists

Note: Bulleted and numbered lists can be included in Web pages in much the same way as in a normal document. However, you can also add pizzazz by using images from the Bullets dialog box.

25. Click on **Format.**

26. Click on **Bullets and Numbering**.

27. Choose the **Bulleted** tab.

28. Select the **Picture** button to display a list of picture files that can be inserted as bullets. Click on a "Picture" bullet of your choice.

29. Click **Insert Clip** to insert the bullet at the location of the insertion point.

30. Type the following:
    Favorite Dishes
    Favorite Novels
    Favorite Web sites

Save as a Web Page

31. Click **File, Save as Web Page**. Use the filename **Your Home Page**. Select the desired drive/folder location.

32. Choose the **Save** button.

Note: On the Title bar, your web page name displays with the filename extension .htm.

Finish-Up Instructions

❖ Continue with the Steps to Create Hyperlinks.

Inserting Hyperlinks

After inserting a hyperlink, the text is enclosed in braces with the word HYPERLINK displaying at the beginning of the line containing the hyperlink. For example: {HYPERLINK [http://www.microsoft.com]}

Bulleted or numbered lists can be hyperlinks to other documents created on your computer, other areas of the same document, or other Web pages on the Internet. If you are inserting hyperlinks to someone else's Web page, you need to have the complete Web page address. You also need to connect to the Internet through your Internet provider to make sure the link works properly.

To link a Web page to specific areas of another document, you must first place a bookmark at each heading or area of the document you want linked. Hyperlinks on the Web page will link by bookmark names.

Type the text in step 1 below as a regular document. The document will contain three bookmarks and a direct link to the Microsoft and Prentice Hall Web pages. When we edit our Web page, we will link each bookmark.

 Create Hyperlinks

1. Open a new blank Word document and type the text shown below.

> Favorite Dishes
> Tacos a la Grande
> Silver Bell Potatoes
> Cookies with Milk
>
> Favorite Novels
> Charlie Ran Away with Sally
> Little Toy People
>
> Favorite Web Sites
> http://www.microsoft.com
> http://www.prenhall.com

> *Note: Use **Heading 3** from the **Styles** drop-down box for each category title. The URL addresses will automatically display as hyperlinks.*

2. Use the filename **Your Name Linking Page** and save the document on your data disk as a normal Word document.

Create Bookmarks

3. Place the insertion point in front of **Favorite Dishes**.

4. Select **Insert, Bookmark**.

5. Type **Favorite_dishes** (no spaces allowed) in the Bookmark Name box and click **Add**.

   *Note: If desired, display the Bookmark symbol by selecting **Tools**, **Options** and select the **Bookmarks** option on the View tab, **OK**.*

6. Move the insertion point in front of **Favorite Novels** and add the bookmark **Favorite_novels**.

7. Move the insertion point in front of **Favorite Web Sites** and add the book-mark **Favorite_Web_sites**.

8. Save the file using the same filename, **Your Name Linking Page**. Close the document.

Insert Hyperlinks

*Note: The file named **Your Name Home Page.htm** should be open.*

9. Select **Favorite Dishes**.

10. Click on the **Insert Hyperlink** button on the Standard Toolbar.

    Note: The Insert Hyperlink dialog box displays (see Figure B.2).

11. Select the Web page filename by clicking on the **File** button in the Browse for area. Double-click on **Your Name Linking Page.doc.**

12. Click on the **Bookmark** button. Double-click on the bookmark **Favorite_dishes**. Click **OK**.

    Note: The first bulleted paragraph on the Web page has been linked to the Favorite Dishes heading in the Linking Page document.

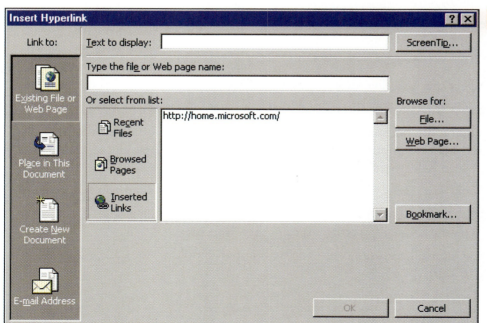

FIGURE B.2

Insert Hyperlink dialog box

13. Select the next bulleted item and repeat steps 9–12 to insert a link to the Favorite_novels bookmark in the Your Name Linking Page document.

14. Create a link to the Favorite_Web_sites bookmark in the Your Name Linking Page document.

15. Save your home page file.

16. To view your page from your default browser, click File, Web Page Preview. Click on Favorite Dishes. The Your Name Linking Page displays. Click the Back button on your Browser to return to your home page in the Word program. Print one copy of your home page and Linking Page. Continue with the Steps to Use the Drawing Toolbar.

Additional Frills

Web pages can contain clip art, video clips, pictures, and drawings. Click on Insert from the Menu bar to make your selection. In addition, the Webtools Toolbar can be displayed when working on a Web page.

Use the Drawing Toolbar

1. Your home Web page created earlier in this Appendix should be displayed.

2. Press Ctrl and End to locate the insertion point at the end of the home page document; press Enter twice.

3. Select 75% Zoom View.

View the Drawing Toolbar

4. Point to the Standard Toolbar and click with the *right* mouse button.

5. Choose Drawing.

Note: The Drawing Toolbar usually displays at the bottom of the screen.

Use the Autoshapes Callouts

1. Select the AutoShapes button on the Drawing Toolbar and choose Callouts.

2. Select the Cloud Callout, or make a choice of your own.

3. The mouse pointer is a crosshair. Touch on the left side below the text, click and hold the mouse button, and drag down and to the right approximately 3 inches. Release the mouse button.

Note: The Cloud Callout displays in a box with the insertion point blinking in the Callout.

4. Type the following text to visit another Web site.

www.anthill.com/sanjose/madeeasycomputerbooks

Use Drawing Toolbar Options

1. Widen the Callout box so the Web site displays on one line; click on the **Center** button.

2. With the Callout box selected, select the **Line Color** button on the Drawing Toolbar and choose **Red,** or make a choice of your own.

3. Select the www.anthill.com/sanjose/madeeasycomputerbooks line and click on the **Font Color** button. Choose **Indigo,** or make a choice of your own.

Insert a Bitmapped File

1. Press **Ctrl** and **End** to locate the insertion point at the bottom of the document.

2. If necessary, press **Enter** repeatedly until the insertion point is a couple lines below the Cloud Callout.

3. Press **Ctrl** and **Enter** to begin a new page.

4. Select **Insert, Picture, From file**. Choose the location for your data disk files; double-click on the filename **Bitmapped file for web page.bmp.**

   *Note: The bitmapped file displays. If desired, select **Print Layout** View and **Zoom, Whole Page.***

5. Use the same filename, **(Your Name) Home Page.**

6. Print one copy.

Creating Multiple Versions for a Document

Different versions of one document can be easily saved. This allows one or more people to work on the same document. All versions are saved under the same filename.

When the File, Version, Save Now option is used, a Save Version dialog box displays. Comments are typed by the user in the Comments on version area.

To open the various file versions, first open the file. Then select File, Versions, and the Versions in… dialog box displays. The Versions in… dialog box contains the Date and time, Saved by, and comments for the document. The various versions can be deleted, opened, or the comments viewed.

Steps to Create Multiple Document Versions

Note: Open the document named, Your name linking page.doc, created earlier in this Appendix.

1. Select **File, Versions.**

2. Click on Save Now.

3. In the Comments box type:

   This version contains 3 Favorites: dishes, novels, and web sites.

4. Select OK.

   Note: Press Ctrl and End, press Enter once, and type the following:

      Favorite Hobbies

      Dancing

      Hiking

      Racquet Ball

   (Select Favorite Hobbies and apply Heading Style 3.)

5. Select File, Versions, Save Now.

6. Type: This version contains 4 favorites including hobbies.

7. Select OK.

   Note: Press Ctrl and End, Press Enter and type the following:

      Favorite Music

      Rock and Roll

      Country and Western

   (Select Favorite Music and apply Heading Style 3.)

8. Select File, Versions, Save Now.

9. Type: This version contains 5 favorites to include hobbies and music.

10. Select OK.

11. Close the document.

Open a Different Version of a Document

1. Select the Open button and double-click on the filename desired. Double-click on Your name linking page.doc.

   Note: All added text is shown in the document.

2. To open a different version of the document, select File, Versions.

3. Double-click on the desired version. Double-click on the version that contains 3 favorites.

   Note: The version of the document containing 3 favorites displays with the Title bar highlighted. The version of the document containing all 5 favorites also displays. Notice the date and time appears in the Title bar beside the original filename.

4. Print both versions of the document.

5. Close both documents.

Microsoft FrontPage

Microsoft FrontPage is another Microsoft product that gives you added power for creating Web pages. FrontPage 2000 can help you upload your page to various servers, maintain your page with ease, and much more. Microsoft FrontPage can be obtained by clicking on the **FrontPage** button located on the Office Shortcut Toolbar.

Sample Graphic Images and Templates

air travel.wmf

anxiety.wmf

books.wmf

bread.wmf

busses.wmf

children.wmf

computers.wmf

crisis management.wmf

currency.wmf

dance.wmf

eye examinations.wmf

famous people.wmf

frustrated drivers.wmf

handshakes.wmf

inspectors.wmf

law enforcement.wmf

lions.wmf

light bulbs.wmf

lighthouses.wmf

magic.wmf

mechanics.wmf

mistakes.wmf

motion pictures.wmf

musical notes.wmf

telecommunications.wmf

question marks.wmf

research.wmf

religious facilities.wmf

skiing.wmf

summer.wmf

theatrical productions.wmf

traffic.wmf

trees.wmf

vaccinations.wmf

valentines.wmf

veterinary medicine.wmf

winter.wmf

women.wmf

workers.wmf

Sample Templates

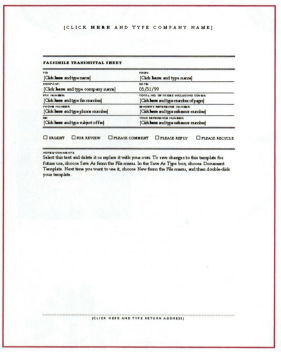

Elegant fax

Professional fax

Elegant memo

Professional memo

Contemporary letter

Contemporary résumé

Elegant résumé

Professional résumé

APPENDIX

Answers to Self-Check Quizzes

Chapter 1	Chapter 2	Chapter 3	Chapter 4	Chapter 5	Chapter 6
1. T	1. F	1. T	1. T	1. T	1. T
2. T	2. T	2. T	2. F	2. T	2. F
3. T	3. T	3. F	3. T	3. F	3. T
4. F	4. T	4. F	4. T	4. T	4. F
5. F	5. T	5. b	5. F	5. T	5. b
6. F	6. a	6. a	6. a	6. c	6. c
7. d	7. a	7. c	7. d	7. d	7. c
8. c	8. d		8. c	8. b	8. d

Chapter 7	Chapter 8	Chapter 9	Chapter 10	Chapter 11	Chapter 12
1. F	1. T	1. F	1. T	1. F	1. T
2. T	2. F	2. T	2. T	2. T	2. F
3. F	3. T	3. F	3. F	3. T	3. T
4. T	4. F	4. F	4. T	4. T	4. F
5. d	5. T	5. d	5. a	5. T	5. F
6. d	6. b	6. a	6. d	6. a	6. a
7. d	7. d	7. a	7. c	7. c	7. b
8. d		8. a	8. b	8. c	8. c

Chapter 13	Chapter 14	Chapter 15	Chapter 16	Chapter 17	Chapter 18
1. T	1. T	1. T	1. T	1. T	1. T
2. F	2. T	2. T	2. F	2. T	2. T
3. T	3. T	3. F	3. T	3. F	3. T
4. T	4. T	4. F	4. T	4. F	4. F
5. F	5. T	5. T	5. T	5. F	5. d
6. b	6. a	6. d	6. T	6. T	6. a
7. d	7. a	7. a	7. d	7. b	7. a
8. d	8. b	8. b	8. d	8. c	8. b

Chapter 19	Chapter 20	Chapter 21	Chapter 22	Chapter 23	Chapter 24
1. T	1. F	1. T	1. T	1. F	1. T
2. T	2. T	2. F	2. T	2. T	2. T
3. T	3. T	3. T	3. T	3. T	3. T
4. F	4. T	4. T	4. T	4. F	4. T
5. T	5. b	5. F	5. T	5. T	5. F
6. b	6. a	6. b	6. b	6. a	6. c
7. c	7. d	7. d	7. d	7. c	7. a
8. d	8. d	8. d		8. a	8. d

Sample Business Document Formats

Traditional Memorandum

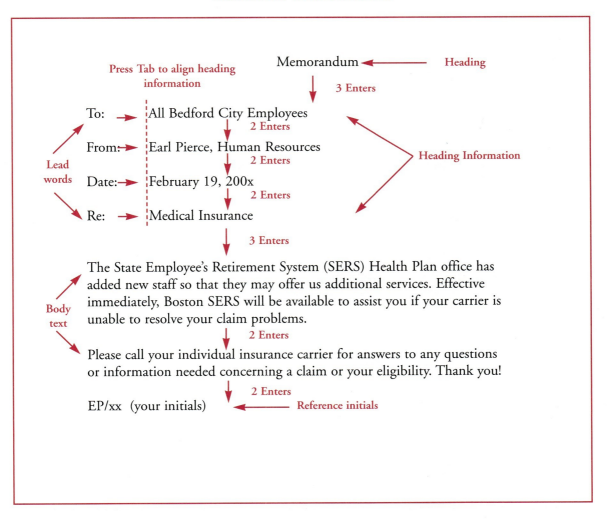

Traditional Block Style Letter

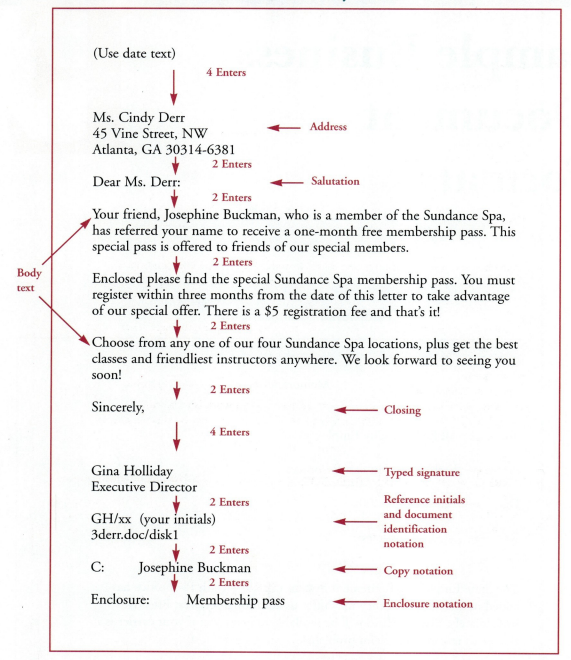

(Use date text)

4 Enters

Ms. Cindy Derr ← **Address**
45 Vine Street, NW
Atlanta, GA 30314-6381

2 Enters

Dear Ms. Derr: ← **Salutation**

2 Enters

Body text → Your friend, Josephine Buckman, who is a member of the Sundance Spa, has referred your name to receive a one-month free membership pass. This special pass is offered to friends of our special members.

2 Enters

Enclosed please find the special Sundance Spa membership pass. You must register within three months from the date of this letter to take advantage of our special offer. There is a $5 registration fee and that's it!

2 Enters

Choose from any one of our four Sundance Spa locations, plus get the best classes and friendliest instructors anywhere. We look forward to seeing you soon!

2 Enters

Sincerely, ← **Closing**

4 Enters

Gina Holliday ← **Typed signature**
Executive Director

2 Enters

GH/xx (your initials) ← **Reference initials and document identification notation**
3derr.doc/disk1

2 Enters

C: Josephine Buckman ← **Copy notation**

2 Enters

Enclosure: Membership pass ← **Enclosure notation**

AMS Simplified Style Letter

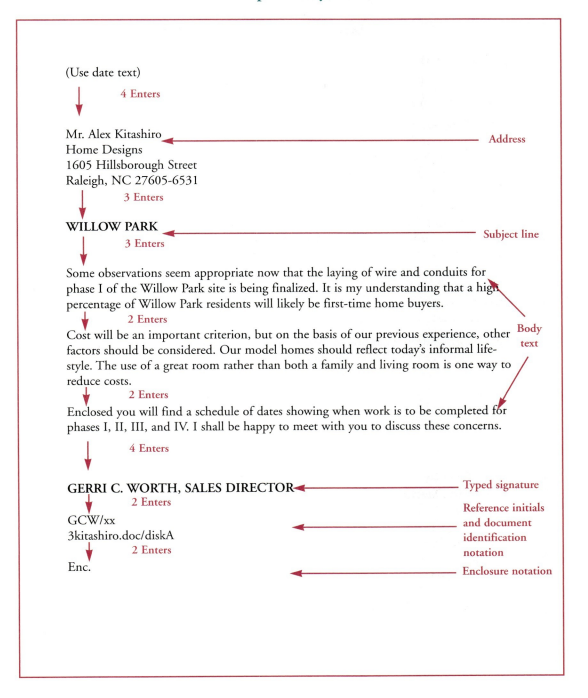

(Use date text)

4 Enters

Mr. Alex Kitashiro ← **Address**
Home Designs
1605 Hillsborough Street
Raleigh, NC 27605-6531

3 Enters

WILLOW PARK ← **Subject line**

3 Enters

Some observations seem appropriate now that the laying of wire and conduits for phase I of the Willow Park site is being finalized. It is my understanding that a high percentage of Willow Park residents will likely be first-time home buyers.

2 Enters

Cost will be an important criterion, but on the basis of our previous experience, other factors should be considered. Our model homes should reflect today's informal lifestyle. The use of a great room rather than both a family and living room is one way to reduce costs.

← **Body text**

2 Enters

Enclosed you will find a schedule of dates showing when work is to be completed for phases I, II, III, and IV. I shall be happy to meet with you to discuss these concerns.

4 Enters

GERRI C. WORTH, SALES DIRECTOR ← **Typed signature**

2 Enters

GCW/xx ← **Reference initials and document identification notation**
3kitashiro.doc/diskA

2 Enters

Enc. ← **Enclosure notation**

Résumé

Melba C. Aguas
410-555-0727

386 Foothill Road
Preston, MD 21655-0051

Educational Background

➜ Word Processing and Keyboarding, Adult Education Program, Union High School District 5/96
➜ Commerce College, Manila, Philippines. Received diploma in Business 5/93

Employment Experience

IBM Corporation, Cambridge, MA—2 years
    Inspector Operator for quality control of printed circuit boards. Performed end-of-line quality control for all boards in unit.

Conner Peripherals, Easton, MD—1 year
    Assembly Operator. Performed duties such as die plating, putting caps on parts, and die inspection.

National Nutrition Council, Philippines—1 year
    Clerk II. Assisted with budget preparation. Prepared vouchers for monetary appropriation and handled staff budget requests.

References

Available upon request.

Résumé
Tony Holmes
280 Olive Court, #10
San Jose, CA 95136-3505
(408) 555-5123

3 Enters

Employment Experience

Wells Fargo Bank, San Jose, California Enter
Business Loan Specialist. Responsible for providing quality customer service to the branches as well as to customers with business loans. September 1995 to the present. Enter and Tab twice

Bank of the West, San Jose, California Enter
Express Agent. Responsible for providing quality service to customers for their checking and savings accounts. June 1994 to August 1999. Enter and Tab

Educational Background

San Jose City College, San Jose, California Enter
Studied word processing, English, and business math. September 1995 to 1998. Enter and Tab twice

Fresno City College, Fresno, California Enter
Studied general office courses including microcomputer applications. September 1993 to June 1994. Enter and Tab twice

High School Diploma, Clovis High School, Clovis, California. Received 1992. Enter and Tab

Special Skills

Proficient with Microsoft Excel, Microsoft Word for Windows, and PageMaker. Enter and Tab

References

Available upon request.

One-Page Document Showing Standard Formatting
with Vertical Line Spacing of One and Left Justification

NOBRE News ← *Report title*

Leadership Appointments ← *Report subtitle*

It is with great pride that the New Orleans Board of Real Estate (NOBRE) announces Lonnie Nello's election as president-elect of the Louisiana Association of Realtors (LAR). Nello's leadership ability has been demonstrated extensively as current Treasurer for LAR, service for 15 years as a board member, and eight years as a National Realtor Association participant. He also served as the President of NOBRE.

12 points additional space

Who Is Lonnie Nello? ← *Sidehead*

12 points additional space

Mr. Nello is a high-performance leader with vision, experience, and commitment who is addressing the radical changes in the real estate industry. He is an expert in business who is successfully meeting the fiscal realities of a constantly changing business environment.

12 points additional space

He is a thoughtful and concerned leader who is personally motivated to seeking quality solutions for the future. Nello realizes that technology, consumer demands, and shrinking profits are mandating a dramatic reworking of traditional real estate practices.

Body text paragraphs

12 points additional space

In every buying decision, you ask, "How does this investment increase my profitability?" You must now make a decision whether to invest resources to remain Realtors. Nello is dedicated to enhancing the value of your membership.

12 points additional space

In discussing his immediate plans for the board, Nello comments:

12 points additional space

"My most immediate concern is to strengthen the Louisiana Association of Realtors by updating our use of technology and connecting our computer systems nationwide. In addition, I will be meeting with each member of the board to obtain ideas on ways to improve our service and profitability." ← *Paragraph indented from left and right margin*

12 points additional space

Lourdes Vargas, Past-President of NOBRE ← *Sidehead*

12 points additional space

Lourdes Vargas, who was the NOBRE President, was nominated to serve as a National Realtor Association (NRA) Director for a three-year term. She was instrumental in making local changes during a time when real estate prices were constantly changing.

12 points additional space

Miguel Soledad, Past-President of LAR ← *Sidehead*

12 points additional space

Miguel Soledad has been nominated to serve as IMPAC Trustee, subject to approval by the LAR Board of Directors. The appointment will be discussed at next month's meeting. The IMPAC Trustees hold the vital role of determining LAR support or opposition to statewide ballot initiatives and local property rights issues that could have statewide significance.

Summary of Enriching Language Arts

Chapter	Vocabulary Words	Grammar/Punctuation Rule
1	confirmation, guarantee, itinerary	Introductory Adverbs and Phrases—A comma often follows an introductory adverb or phrase, because the word or phrase provides a transition from the previous sentence.
2	novel, potential, significant	Introductory (Dependent) Clauses—A comma should follow a dependent clause. An introductory dependent clause often begins with *if*, *in*, *when*, *since*, or *as*.
3	deducted, promotion, standard	Appositives—Appositives are words that immediately follow a noun and further identify the noun but usually are not necessary to the meaning of the sentence. Appositives are set off by commas.
4	atrium, obstacle, punctuality, stressful	Compound Adjectives and Coordinating Conjunctions—Hyphenate two words that precede and describe a noun and function as a single adjective. A comma is placed before a coordinating conjunction (e.g., and, or, but) that joins two independent clauses.
5	development, preference, revision	Dollar Amount Formats—Use a comma to separate the number digits into groups of thousands. No space is placed between a number and the dollar sign. If even numbers are used in the body of a document or if a column of numbers has even dollar amounts, the zeros are omitted.

Chapter	Vocabulary Words	Grammar/Punctuation Rule
6	anticipated, budget, per diem	Single and Double Underlines for Dollar Amounts—Place a single underline between the last column amount and the total amount. In a table without borders, a total amount is usually emphasized by placing double underlines beneath the total amount.
7	ecology, post-secondary, wetlands	Commas Used in a Series—Commas separate words and/or ideas listed in a series.
8	mumbo jumbo, pitfalls, typography	Using the Abbreviations *e.g.* and *i.e.*—The abbreviation *e.g.* is used in place of "for example" and is often used when there are many possible examples and only a few are listed. The abbreviation *i.e.* is used in place of "that is" and is used when all potential conditions are listed. A period follows each initial with no space between the period and the initial. A comma follows the final period.
9	assessing, certified, comprehensive, forum, independent, productivity, technical	Spelling Hint—The Spell Checking feature approves words that are correctly spelled; however, a correctly spelled word can be incorrectly used in a sentence.
10	contagious, knowledge, magic, talisman, technological, velvet	Quotation Marks with Punctuation—Always place a comma or period inside a closing quotation mark. Place a question mark or exclamation point inside closing quotation marks if the question or exclamation pertains only to the quoted information. Place a question mark or exclamation point outside the closing quotation marks if the question or exclamation pertains to the entire sentence.
11	investigate, quality, thoroughly	Nonrestrictive Clause—A nonrestrictive clause is a clause that is not essential to the meaning of the sentence and is, therefore, set off by a comma or commas.
12	acknowledgment, construe, contingent, physician	Subject-Verb Agreement—Verbs must agree in number with their subjects. If a subject is singular (one), use a singular verb; if a subject is plural (more than one), use a plural verb.
13	anonymously, appropriate, complaints, coordinator, detachable, prompt	Initials Abbreviated—Periods or spaces are not placed after the letters of an acronym such as IRS (Internal Revenue Service) or TWA (TransWorld Airlines).

Chapter	Vocabulary Words	Grammar/Punctuation Rule
14	average, convenient, flexibility, valuable	Independent Adjectives—Two consecutive adjectives that modify the same noun are separated by a comma.
15	amend, authority, exclusive, fiscal	Apostrophe Used to Show Possession—If a noun is singular and used to show possession, add an apostrophe (') and an *s*. If the noun is plural or the final letter in the noun is an *s*, add only an apostrophe after the *s*.
16	(No vocabulary words)	Proofreading Hints—When proofreading a document, read the document twice: once for content and meaning and once to check grammar, spelling, and punctuation.
17	demonstrate, effective, freelance, techniques, tuition	Parentheses—Parentheses can be used to set off nonessential expressions that might otherwise confuse the reader. The information within the parentheses provides supplemental information that has no direct bearing on the main idea of the sentence or paragraph. Words, phrases, or clauses can be enclosed within parentheses. Unless a comma, colon, or semicolon is necessary to the text within parentheses, place the punctuation outside the closing parenthesis. If the text within the parentheses is a complete sentence, the final punctuation is placed within the parentheses.
18	essential, repetitive, static symptoms, trauma	Em and En Dashes—The em dash (—), a typographic symbol about the width of the character m, is often used in place of a comma. The en dash (–), a typographic symbol about the width of the character n, is used as a hyphen or as a substitute for the word "to," e.g., July–September. The correct typographic symbols for em and en dashes have traditionally been used in books, newspapers, and advertisements, and are recommended for use when creating a professional-looking document.
19	arbitration, grievance, interpretation	Colons, Capitalization, and Punctuation for Bulleted and Enumerated Lists—Place a colon after an independent clause that introduces a bulleted or enumerated (numbered) list. An introductory clause frequently includes words such as *the following* and *as follows*. When creating a bulleted or enumerated list, capitalize the first word and insert a final punctuation mark (period, question mark, or exclamation point) after each item that is a complete sentence or phrase. Do not capitalize the first word or insert final punctuation when bulleted or enumerated lists are not complete thoughts.

Chapter	Vocabulary Words	Grammar/Punctuation Rule
20	deductible, excluding, flexible, prosthesis, restorative, routine	Contractions—An apostrophe is used to indicate where a letter(s) has been omitted when two words are combined to form a verb contraction. Generally, contractions are not used in formal business writing. Contractions can be used in personal letters or informal business documents.
21	faculty, leave, mandatory, sole	Percentage Amounts—Use figures for numbers that are followed by the word percent. Spell out the word percent unless the percentage amount is used in a table that contains statistical information or in a headline/title.
22	cuisine, exception, clients, minimal, savor	Basic Rules for Numbers—Generally, in written text numbers one through ten are spelled out. Also, numbers used in approximation and numbers at the beginning of a sentence are usually spelled out. Use figures when a number is followed by the word percent. Omit the colon and zeros when writing an even clock time.
23	annual, exceed, quarterly, quota, reflect	Abbreviations in Table Column Headings—When creating tables and forms, abbreviations are often used in subtitles and/or column headings because of limited space. However, abbreviations should be used sparingly. If you are unsure of an abbreviation, consult a dictionary.
24	collect, cooperation, initiation, profitability, separate	Abbreviations for Time—Type a.m. and p.m. with lowercase letters and no space between. Only one period is used if the abbreviation is the last element in a sentence.